PAUL'S NEW PERSPECTIVE

CHARTING A SOTERIOLOGICAL JOURNEY

GARWOOD P. ANDERSON

IVP Academic

An imprint of InterVarsity Press
Downers Grove, Illinois

InterVarsity Press
P.O. Box 1400, Downers Grove, IL 60515-1426
ivpress.com
email@ivpress.com

*InterVarsity Press® is the book-publishing division of InterVarsity Christian Fellowship/USA®, a movement of
students and faculty active on campus at hundreds of universities, colleges and schools of nursing in the United
States of America, and a member movement of the International Fellowship of Evangelical Students. For
information about local and regional activities, visit intervarsity.org.*

All Scripture quotations, unless otherwise indicated, are the author's own translation.

Cover design: Cindy Kiple
Interior design: Beth McGill
Images: Saint Paul the Apostle by Marco Pino at Galleria Borghese, Rome, Italy / Bridgeman Images
    digital globe: © StudioM1/iStockphoto

ISBN 978-0-8308-5154-6 (print)
ISBN 978-0-8308-7315-9 (digital)

Printed in the United States of America ∞

Library of Congress Cataloging-in-Publication Data
A catalog record for this book is available from the Library of Congress.

P 23 22 21 20 19 18 17 16 15 14 13 12 11 10 9 8 7 6 5 4 3 2 1

Y 35 34 33 32 31 30 29 28 27 26 25 24 23 22 21 20 19 18 17 16

To my father, Kenneth Anderson, who passed into the nearer presence of God during my writing of this book, a gentle man who, following a Loving Shepherd, became what he loved.

CONTENTS

ACKNOWLEDGMENTS

Often one hears authors refer to the writing of a book on the analogy of giving birth. I have no idea about that. I've had kidney stones. My experience is akin to a different parental metaphor. This project feels rather more like sending off a five-year-old to second grade, having skipped kindergarten and first grade. Your friends tell you he will manage, but you worry that he might be embarrassed when he can't open a milk carton for himself or when he is caught counting on his fingers rather than having memorized his "math facts."

I am not a Pauline specialist, but perhaps like Luke, the amateur historiographer, I can say with just a touch of hyperbole that I have followed "all things from the top" (Lk 1:3) and suppose (*dokeō*, "presume"?) to add my narrative to the others. If I were granted but one desideratum of Pauline scholarship it would be that they all take a decade of Jubilee, cease publication, and let me catch up. But there is no catching up, and even with the help of very astute readers, I know that I am still not caught up. A seasoned and prolific NT scholar once advised me to write books quickly, since there will always be yet another thing to reckon with while you're trying to complete your project! From contract to completion this project has survived the publication of Wright's *Paul and the Faithfulness of God* and *Paul and His Recent Interpreters*; Sanders's *Paul: The Apostle's Life, Letters, and Thought*; Dunn's *Neither Jew nor Greek*; Campbell's *Reframing Paul* (while still forever digesting *The Deliverance of God*); and Barclay's *Paul and the Gift*, to name only the physically largest contributions to the field (and I write this perusing proofs of Peter Leithart's *Delivered from the Elements of the World* and not in time to make use of Richard Longenecker's new Romans commentary in the NIGTC series). It will be another decade until I will have reckoned with all of these, but new books continue apace.

My debts are many, beginning with these and many other scholars from whom I have learned so much about Paul, whom I thank with every footnote. I was aided immensely especially by three readers. Wes Hill and Mike Gorman exposed shortcomings with my argument in the kindest and most encouraging ways, and with keen analysis pointed me in more satisfactory directions. They are not responsible for my stubbornness. And Dan Reid's expert and encouraging guidance was especially helpful, both as my editor, but also as a Pauline scholar himself.

Multiple acknowledgments are in order. I am grateful to the Nashotah House Board of Directors for the granting of a sabbatical for the 2013–2014 academic year, during which time this project was launched and took its shape. It is a singular and rare pleasure that I enjoy teaching in a community saturated in Scripture and worship and among colleagues whose company I so enjoy. I am grateful to have had the opportunity to teach several courses directly and indirectly relevant. I was especially pleased to teach a seminar on the new perspective on Paul at Nashotah House and also to a class of InterVarsity Christian Fellowship staff at their National Institute of Staff Education and Training. Some of my keener seminary students—I recall especially John Milliken, Shane Gormley, Tyler Blanski, Ben Jefferies and Lars Skoglund—humored me by listening to early versions of the argument and, even when their grade did not depend on it, gave the impression that they found it interesting. The last two think they are responsible for the title; they might be.

My brother, Cameron, a mentor to his "little brother" for a half-century, was a special encouragement, sharing writing retreats with me in various cabins in Michigan's Upper Peninsula, our family's roots. And in an especially sweet coincidence, his book, *The Faithful Artist* (also with IVP), comes off the press almost simultaneously with this one.

Above all, I am most indebted to Dawn, my wife of thirty-two years, who thinks I "should write more," and who stands behind that urging with a keen eye for grammar and sense for style, having read the whole manuscript at least twice, loving red pen in hand, leaving marks of affection behind on every page.

Pentecost 2016

ABBREVIATIONS

AB   Anchor Bible

ABD   *Anchor Bible Dictionary*. Edited by David Noel Freedman.
            6 vols. New York: Doubleday, 1992.

ABRL   Anchor Bible Reference Library

ANRW   Aufstieg und Niedergang der römischen Welt

ANTC   Abingdon New Testament Commentaries

ASV   American Standard Version

BBR   *Bulletin for Biblical Research*

BDAG   Danker, Frederick W., Walter Bauer, William F. Arndt and
            F. Wilbur Gingrich. *A Greek-English Lexicon of the New
            Testament and Other Early Christian Literature*. 3rd ed.
            Chicago: University of Chicago Press, 2000.

BDF   Blass, Friedrich, and Albert Debrunner. Translated by Robert
            W. Funk. *A Greek Grammar of the New Testament and Other
            Early Christian Literature*. Chicago: University of Chicago
            Press, 1961.

BECNT   Baker Exegetical Commentary on the New Testament

Bib   *Biblica*

BJRL   *Bulletin of the John Rylands University Library of Manchester*

BNTC   Black's New Testament Commentaries

BTCB   Brazos Theological Commentary on the Bible

CBQ   *Catholic Biblical Quarterly*

CBQMS   Catholic Biblical Quarterly Monograph Series

CEB   Common English Bible

DLNT   *Dictionary of the Later New Testament and Its Developments.*
            Edited by Ralph P. Martin and Peter H. Davids. Downers
            Grove, IL: InterVarsity Press, 1997.

DPL   *Dictionary of Paul and His Letters.* Edited by Gerald F.
            Hawthorne, Ralph P. Martin and Daniel G. Reid. Downers
            Grove, IL: InterVarsity Press, 1993.

EBC   Expositor's Bible Commentary

EDNT   *Exegetical Dictionary of the New Testament.* Edited by Horst
            Balz and Gerhard Schneider. English translation. 3 vols.
            Grand Rapids: Eerdmans, 1990–1993.

ESV   English Standard Version

EvQ   *Evangelical Quarterly*

ExpTim   *Expository Times*

FJC   *The Faith of Jesus Christ: Exegetical, Biblical, and Theological
            Studies.* Edited by Michael F. Bird and Preston M. Sprinkle.
            Peabody, MA: Hendrickson, 2010.

GGBB   *Greek Grammar Beyond the Basics.* Daniel B. Wallace. Grand
            Rapids: Zondervan, 1996.

HBT   *Horizons in Biblical Theology*

HTR   *Harvard Theological Review*

ICC   International Critical Commentary

Int   *Interpretation*

IVPNTC   InterVarsity Press New Testament Commentary

JBL   *Journal of Biblical Literature*

JETS   *Journal of the Evangelical Theological Society*

JSNT   *Journal for the Study of the New Testament*

JSNTSup   Journal for the Study of the New Testament Supplement
            Series

JSPL	*Journal for the Study of Paul and His Letters*
JTS	*Journal of Theological Studies*
JVN:CSTJ	*Justification and Variegated Nomism: The Complexities of Second Temple Judaism*. Edited by D. A. Carson, Peter T. O'Brien and Mark A. Seifrid. Vol. 1. WUNT 2.140. Tübingen: Mohr Siebeck; Grand Rapids: Baker Academic, 2001.
JVN:PP	*Justification and Variegated Nomism: The Paradoxes of Paul*. Edited by D. A. Carson, Peter T. O'Brien and Mark A. Seifrid. Vol. 2. WUNT 2.181. Tübingen: Mohr Siebeck; Grand Rapids: Baker Academic, 2004.
KJV	King James Version
LEH	Lust, Johan, Erik Eynikel and Katrin Hauspie. *A Greek-English Lexicon of the Septuagint*. Rev. ed. Stuttgart: Deutsche Bibelgesellschaft, 2003.
Louw-Nida	Louw, J. P., and E. A. Nida. *Greek-English Lexicon of the New Testament: Based on Semantic Domains*. 2 vols. New York: United Bible Societies, 1989.
LSJ	Liddell, Henry George, Robert Scott and Henry Stuart Jones. *A Greek-English Lexicon*. 9th ed. with revised supplement. Oxford: Clarendon, 1996.
LW	*Luther's Works*. Edited by Jaroslav Pelikan et al. 55 vols. St. Louis: Concordia, 1955.
LXX	Septuagint (Rahlfs ed. unless otherwise indicated)
MHT	Moulton, James H., Wilbert Francis Howard and Nigel Turner. *A Grammar of New Testament Greek*. 4 vols. Edinburgh: T&T Clark, 1963.
MM	Moulton, James H., and George Milligan. *The Vocabulary of the Greek New Testament*. London: Hodder & Stoughton, 1930.
MT	*Masoretic Text*
NA[28]	*Novum Testamentum Graece*, Nestle-Aland, 28th ed.
NAB	New American Bible

NAC   New American Commentary

NASB   New American Standard Bible

NCB   New Century Bible

NET   New English Translation

NETS   *A New English Translation of the Septuagint.* Edited by Albert
           Pietersma and Benjamin G. Wright. New York: Oxford
           University Press, 2007.

NIB   *The New Interpreter's Bible.* Edited by Leander E. Keck. 12
           vols. Nashville: Abingdon, 1994–2004.

NICNT   New International Commentary on the New Testament

NIDB   *New Interpreter's Dictionary of the Bible.* Edited by Katharine
           Doob Sakenfeld. 5 vols. Nashville: Abingdon, 2006–2009.

NIDNTT   *New International Dictionary of New Testament Theology.*
           Edited by Colin Brown. 4 vols. Grand Rapids: Zondervan,
           1975.

NIDNTTE   *New International Dictionary of New Testament Theology and
           Exegesis.* Edited by Moisés Silva. 2nd ed. 5 vols. Grand
           Rapids: Zondervan, 2014.

NIGTC   New International Greek Testament Commentary

NIV   New International Version (2011 ed. unless otherwise indicated)

NIVAC   NIV Application Commentary

NJB   New Jerusalem Bible

NovT   *Novum Testamentum*

NovTSup   Supplements to Novum Testamentum

NPerP   *The New Perspective on Paul.* James D. G. Dunn. Grand
           Rapids: Eerdmans, 2008.

NPP   new perspective on Paul

NRSV   New Revised Standard Version

NSBT   New Studies in Biblical Theology

NT	New Testament
NTL	New Testament Library
NTPG	*The New Testament and the People of God*. N. T. Wright. Christian Origins and the Question of God. Minneapolis: Fortress, 1992.
NTS	*New Testament Studies*
OTP	*Old Testament Pseudepigrapha*. Edited by James H. Charlesworth. 2 vols. New York: Doubleday, 1983, 1985.
P&FG	*Paul and the Faithfulness of God*. N. T. Wright. 2 vols. Christian Origins and the Question of God 4. Minneapolis: Fortress, 2013.
P&PJ	*Paul and Palestinian Judaism*. E. P. Sanders. Philadelphia: Fortress, 1977.
PE	Pastoral Epistles (1 Timothy, 2 Timothy, Titus)
PG	Patrologia Graeca
PLJP	*Paul, the Law, and the Jewish People*. E. P. Sanders. Philadelphia: Fortress, 1983.
PNTC	Pillar New Testament Commentary
PRS	*Perspectives in Religious Studies*
RevExp	*Review and Expositor*
RSV	Revised Standard Version
SBLDS	Society of Biblical Literature Dissertation Series
SBLMS	Society of Biblical Literature Monograph Series
SJT	*Scottish Journal of Theology*
SNTSMS	Society for New Testament Studies Monograph Series
SP	Sacra Pagina
TCGNT	*A Textual Commentary on the Greek New Testament*. Bruce M. Metzger. 2nd ed. Stuttgart: Deutsche Bibelgesellschaft, 1994.

TDNT   *Theological Dictionary of the New Testament*. Edited by
              Gerhard Kittel and Gerhard Friedrich. Translated by
              Geoffrey W. Bromiley. 10 vols. Grand Rapids: Eerdmans,
              1964–1976.

THNTC   Two Horizons New Testament Commentary

TLNT   *Theological Lexicon of the New Testament*. Ceslas Spicq.
              Translated and edited by James D. Ernest. 3 vols. Peabody,
              MA: Hendrickson, 1994.

TNTC   Tyndale New Testament Commentaries

TPP   traditional Protestant perspective

TS   *Theological Studies*

UBCS   Understanding the Bible Commentary Series (Baker;
              formerly New International Bible Commentary; Hen-
              drickson)

UBS⁴   *Greek New Testament*, United Bible Societies, 4th ed.

WBC   Word Biblical Commentary

WDNTLR   *Westminster Dictionary of New Testament and Early Christian
              Literature and Rhetoric*. David E. Aune. Louisville, KY:
              Westminster John Knox, 2003.

WSPRS   *What Saint Paul Really Said: Was Paul of Tarsus the Real
              Founder of Christianity?* N. T. Wright. Grand Rapids:
              Eerdmans, 1997.

WUNT   Wissenschaftliche Untersuchungen zum Neuen Testament

ZECNT   Zondervan Exegetical Commentary on the New Testament

INTRODUCTION

Forecasting the Itinerary

I hadn't planned on reading these books. Though I had followed the debates around the so-called new perspective on Paul for some time,[1] I didn't think that this particular exchange would add much. I would sit it out. But, having been kindly invited to sit in on a discussion among pastors and learned lay leaders at a nearby burgeoning evangelical church, I conceded to read John Piper's critique of N. T. Wright and Bishop Wright's rebuttal, albeit quickly the first time.[2] For what it is worth, my original intuition was vindicated. Piper's critique was predictable on the whole, not to say without merit in certain respects. And, while adding some useful nuances to his previous arguments, Wright's reply was similarly unsurprising, at least to those familiar with the line of interpretation he had already offered.[3] What I found

---

[1]Subsequent references to the new perspective on Paul are by way of the abbreviation NPP. I concede that the NPP represents a diversity of views, but that does not render the designation meaningless. Sufficient for now is this concise description: the various revisions of a one-time consensus Protestant interpretation of Pauline theology that are rooted in, if not even required by, a broad sympathy with the reappraisal of Second Temple Judaism articulated by E. P. Sanders, *Paul and Palestinian Judaism: A Comparison of Patterns of Religion* (Philadelphia: Fortress, 1977).

[2]John Piper, *The Future of Justification: A Response to N. T. Wright* (Wheaton, IL: Crossway, 2008); and N. T. Wright, *Justification: God's Plan and Paul's Vision* (Downers Grove, IL: IVP Academic, 2009). I've had several (five) opportunities to interact with groups of clergy, parachurch workers and laypersons who had been assigned the two books to read, and, if my sampling was characteristic, it is fair to say that this exchange did not produce clarity.

[3]This, of course, preceded the publication of his Pauline magnum opus, N. T. Wright, *Paul and the Faithfulness of God*, 2 vols., Christian Origins and the Question of God 4 (Minneapolis: Fortress, 2013). But there was already available a small library of preliminary statements: N. T. Wright, *The Climax of the Covenant: Christ and the Law in Pauline Theology* (Edinburgh: T&T Clark, 1991);

more interesting than the books themselves was the discussion I observed. Among the dozen or so participants, nearly all held graduate degrees from seminaries, including some with PhDs in biblical studies, and the rest—this being a university town—PhDs in some other discipline. This group was high-powered. The discussion was not.

Although the deliberations were amiable, it turns out that we had a hard time finding our way into the actual arguments of the books, that is, beyond a discussion of the rhetoric, motives and social location of the authors. It would seem that we ourselves got caught up in each author's exasperation with the other, taking various sides for various reasons that were other than exegetical—perhaps most interestingly, with a strong impulse to extrapolate trajectories. By rights, Pastor Piper, our near neighbor a state to the west, should have been the favorite, given this church's theological heritage. But it turns out that Bishop Wright—on the other side of the Atlantic, and ecclesially on a different, if nearby, planet—garnered more sympathy, not necessarily, it seems, for having given a truer account of Galatians 2 or Romans 3 but for telling a story this gathering would find ultimately more compelling.

What I learned in the process—reinforced now several times in parallel settings—is that the NPP has won the day among many thoughtful Christians, though not always because they have found it the best account of Paul's texts—or should I say, not always because they can show it the best account. The same goes for the, sometimes more exegetically rigorous, resistance forces, who, while having no less instinct for story, find the NPP story unpersuasive, even if sometimes better told. Neither Tom Wright's compelling vision for the church and her mission rooted in his fresh account of the New Testament nor John Piper's passionate plea to appropriate once again the liberating power of the gospel makes either of them Paul's spokesperson, though we can be grateful for the faithful labors of both.

idem, *What Saint Paul Really Said: Was Paul of Tarsus the Real Founder of Christianity?* (Grand Rapids: Eerdmans, 1997); idem, *Paul: In Fresh Perspective* (Minneapolis: Fortress, 2005); and idem, "The Letter to the Romans: Introduction, Commentary and Reflections," in *NIB* (Nashville: Abingdon, 2002), 10:393-770. Regrettably, the most extensive engagement with *P&FG*, Christopher Heilig, J. Thomas Hewitt and Michael F. Bird, eds., *God and the Faithfulness of Paul: A Critical Examination of the Pauline Theology of N. T. Wright*, WUNT 2.413 (Tübingen: Mohr Siebeck, 2016), became available too late to be engaged in what follows.

Underneath the impasse—of which the Wright-Piper episode was but a fleeting sign—is a suspicion that the NPP offers an account that is more compelling for some texts than for others, and that the same might be said for its detractors. Behind the fog and sometimes fierce contention are accounts of Paul that succeed more than they fail, but that have polarized into alternatives that are doomed to fail at least some of the time. This book enters as a study of peacemaking—chiefly that peace which, according to the apostle Paul, Israel's God makes with alienated humanity and by which he restores his wounded creation, bringing both to their promised destinations. But more than a study, I might hope also that it is an exercise in peacemaking. The project originates in the sobering observation that Paul's students too frequently nourish contention, not least in the learned study of their mentor's accounts of how enmity and its causes have been overcome.[4] And although Pauline scholars vigorously debate numerous matters of theological significance, the disputes around the NPP are characterized by an especially acute acrimony.

The reasons are not elusive. More than grammatical fine points appear to be at stake and especially when the arguments trickle down from the lofty heights of the historical-descriptive philology of biblical scholarship to the lived and preached theology of Christians and churches that identify with certain ways of reading Paul. Indeed, even the very notion of *readings* of Paul will seem odious to some whose theology, at least as they would understand it, is shaped not by one of several possible understandings of Paul but by what the apostle most certainly declared—unambiguously, forcefully and with scriptural warrant. Some thus worry that the NPP subverts the sine qua non of the gospel—that we are graciously restored to God for eternal life by faith alone apart from any merit or deserving. Some worry that the entire basis of Protestantism's historic and principled distinction from Roman Catholicism is at risk. Some worry, while others hope that this is so.[5]

---

[4]Wright makes the same point: "The study of Paul has suffered because of these many divisions. It would be good if the process could be reversed, with the study of Paul becoming the instrument of their reconciliation" (*P&FG*, 2:1516). It remains a fair question to ask if Wright's own vigorous contribution is sufficiently tempered to achieve this end (see esp. John M. G. Barclay, "Paul and the Faithfulness of God," *SJT* 68, no. 2 [2015]: 235-43).

[5]Having taught this and related material in broadly Reformed evangelical, Wesleyan evangelical, parachurch evangelical and Anglo-Catholic settings, I can say anecdotally that the reaction to the NPP is strikingly different in each context. Not unexpectedly, the NPP arouses an admixture

That is not to say that objections to NPP scholarship are necessarily motivated by theological stubbornness, a desperate clutching to a theological tradition. The NPP program itself—if for now we can speak of this family of interpretive tendencies by way of generalization—for all of its prodigious scholarship still leaves lacunae in its wake and is beset with uncooperative evidence in the Pauline tradition. Or at least it seems so to not a few interpreters.[6] But as is so frequently the case, strenuous disagreement devolves into take-no-prisoners rhetoric, in which even the salutary contributions of the NPP must be rebutted or diminished, lest giving an inch of contested ground yields a mile.

That the interpretation of Paul's letters should issue forth in this sort of hardened intransigence, even sometimes bitterness, is unfortunate but perhaps not surprising. Yet it remains counterintuitive that persons of competence and good will who have given themselves to understanding Paul's rather small corpus of writings could be as frequently wrong and as egregiously so as their scholarly opponents seem to insist. In fact, that—I would like to think generous—intuition counts as something of a working premise in what follows. While it will be clear that I have serious misgivings with certain readings of Pauline texts, I still doubt that many are perverse. Or perhaps we could say, even those readings we find most dubious are almost surely right about something, and usually something rather important. Only as a last resort can I believe that well-intentioned readings of Paul— even those apparently at odds with one another—are grossly mistaken.

of anxiety and intrigue in the Reformed context, where it is clear that much is at stake. Wesleyans more characteristically relish the opportunity the NPP offers to restore a fuller, less strictly forensic, account of salvation, of course with much room for "sanctification." The more Catholically minded will not infrequently celebrate the dethroning of a Lutheran gospel—or at least its caricature—while finding the NPP generally unobjectionable, if not even salutary, inasmuch as it restores Paul to a Catholic theological vision.

[6]Scholarly critiques of the NPP are legion and will be taken up in more detail in chap. 1. The most useful full-scale treatment remains Stephen Westerholm, *Perspectives Old and New on Paul: The "Lutheran" Paul and His Critics* (Grand Rapids: Eerdmans, 2004). Much detailed interrogation is available via D. A. Carson, Peter T. O'Brien and Mark A. Seifrid, eds., *Justification and Variegated Nomism: The Complexities of Second Temple Judaism*, vol. 1, WUNT 2.140 (Grand Rapids: Baker Academic, 2001); and idem, *Justification and Variegated Nomism: The Paradoxes of Paul*, vol. 2, WUNT 2.181 (Grand Rapids: Baker Academic, 2004). A nearly comprehensive and frequently updated bibliography of "both sides" is available at Mark Mattison, "Bibliography" for "The New Perspective on Paul," *The Paul Page*, accessed March 23, 2016, www.thepaulpage.com/new-perspective/bibliography.

Whether this proves a facile or naive "beyondism" will be for others to judge. The project emerges nonetheless, frankly, from my inability to take sides on any number of recent skirmishes within Pauline studies. Yet that inability to take sides is not the same as an inability to take a position, or positions, as the case may be. To put it simply, the argument of this book insists that both "camps" are right, but not all the time. Thus a foundational working hypothesis in what follows is that there may be a variety of ways that apparently disparate readings might be found less incompatible and more happily complementary.

Perhaps the responsibility for these disparate reading lies not with the scholars but with Paul himself. After all, from the very beginning, Paul's line of thought was alleged obscure by some—many?—of his readers, and disputes over his *real* meaning have never subsided. Ambiguity and dispute seem to have attached to Paul's writings from the outset. Paul needs to tell the Corinthians what he *didn't mean* in his previous letter to them (1 Cor 5:9-11). He is charged with asserting views that he insists he didn't hold (e.g., Rom 3:8). The "James" responsible for the letter bearing his name seems to think Paul's views (or was it a misunderstanding of them?) require some significant nuancing, if not outright rebuttal (Jas 2:14-26). And notoriously 2 Peter concedes that Paul's letters are "hard to understand" and susceptible to grievous misappropriation (2 Pet 3:16). And if discrete texts prove difficult to unpack, how much more the attempt to account for the whole by way of theological synthesis. Pauline incoherence proves to be the easiest hypothesis to demonstrate and at the same time the unhappiest, a counsel of despair. One needn't even appeal to the theological presupposition of the inspiration of Scripture or a hermeneutical commitment to the coherence of Scripture to balk at the claim of Paul's confusion. All that is needed are the justifiable presumptions that Paul was intelligent, on the one hand, and of sufficient integrity and independence, on the other, that he would not baldly contradict himself for cynical or pragmatic advantage. This most scholars are willing to grant, though the incoherence of a changing and radically contingent Paul surely has had its advocates.[7]

---

[7]Most vigorously and notoriously, Heikki Räisänen, *Paul and the Law*, WUNT 1.29 (Tübingen: Mohr, 1983); see also (though more as a concession than as a thesis) E. P. Sanders, *Paul, the Law, and the Jewish People* (Philadelphia: Fortress, 1983).

d be instead that the problem is not so much with Paul but with scholars whose finely tuned instincts for detecting distinctions operate in overdrive in the reading of Paul. Close reading is, after all, the biblical scholar's calling card, and it is generally a more respectable practice in academic biblical studies to posit a disjunction than a harmonization, the latter always susceptible to the charge of special pleading. In fact, arguably this is the core impulse of critical biblical studies—the readiness to set especially confessional claims and expectations aside and follow the data where they lead. It is then a most efficient demonstration of guild membership to assert disjunction. It may be also that in an attempt at specificity and precision, the biblical scholar's theological description rests too many rungs down on the ladder of abstraction to offer accounts that are, in fact, complementary and only apparently disjunctive.[8] Moreover, in the rough and tumble of intramural argumentative rhetoric, hyperbole will sometimes issue forth that perhaps does not intend to be taken quite at face value.[9] Not infrequently, and I think especially recently, one observes a popular (and rhetorically effective) trope: "*x* is not about *y*," where *y* is a received, traditional or even populist reading or construct, providing a handy foil for a presumed more compelling alternative: "the atonement is not the gospel"; "Paul's soteriology is not forensic but rather participatory"; "God's righteousness is not a gift but rather his saving power"; "faith for Paul has nothing to do with mental assent but is rather personal trust"; and so on. While a powerful rhetorical tool, such claims often prove specious and, more importantly, frustrate mutual understanding.

Finally, we must contend with the possibility that Paul is not so much incoherent as his writings are contextually determined and that his expression of various matters developed over time. This, in fact, is the thesis

---

[8]It is an instructive exercise to compare, for example, the similar vintage works of Räisänen, *Paul and the Law*, and J. Christiaan Beker, *Paul the Apostle: The Triumph of God in Life and Thought* (Philadelphia: Fortress, 1980). Räisänen's contentment with the discovery of Pauline disjunctions produces little reflection beyond their cataloging, whereas Beker, no less aware of the same phenomena, forces himself to ask at a higher level of abstraction wherein coherence might be evident. For all of its extraordinary argumentative detail and nuance, a similar facile acquiescence to incommensurability repeatedly plagues Douglas A. Campbell, *The Deliverance of God: An Apocalyptic Rereading of Justification in Paul* (Grand Rapids: Eerdmans, 2009).
[9]I take this to be the point of Westerholm's somewhat mischievous chapter, "The Quotable Anti-'Lutheran' Paul," in *Perspectives Old and New*, 249-58.

of this book: as it regards his soteriology, Paul's letters show evidence of both a contextually determined diversity and also a coherent development through time. The argument of this book, then, contends with certain habits of Pauline interpretation that, while yielding important insights, have also frequently devolved into stalemates. In the first place, I attempt to hold together two sometimes contrary impulses: to give the occasional character of Paul's letters its due, a full recognition of the highly contingent quality of the letters, its also insisting that there remains nonetheless not only a coherence but also signs of soteriological development from Paul's (arguably) earliest to his (arguably) last extant letters.[10]

Second, and more controversially, I ask what becomes of the contours of Pauline soteriology when the deutero-Pauline (or as I will prefer, "disputed") letters are given voice at the table. It is clear from a survey of the seminal NPP literature that the primary contours of revised Pauline soteriology were forged in a seven-letter crucible of undisputed letters.[11] Honoring this distinction is standard practice in Pauline scholarship and, depending upon the circles in which one moves, entirely uncontroversial. Nonetheless, this would have, and continues to have, rather far-reaching consequences. As James Dunn himself concedes, "It is a fair comment that too little attention has been paid to the later writings of the Pauline corpus in the early days of the new perspective, presumably on the usual grounds that an attempt to grasp Paul's teachings should focus on the letters whose authorship by Paul is undisputed."[12] While the consequence of this restricted database has been

---

[10]Students of Pauline scholarship will recognize that, in arguing for both contextual determination *and* development, I am seeking to combine strategies that have sometimes been set over against each other: recognition of the contingent character of Paul's letters but also development in the trajectory of his thought.

[11]Romans, 1-2 Corinthians, Galatians, Philippians, 1 Thessalonians and Philemon are almost universally accepted as indisputably Pauline, with 2 Thessalonians, Colossians, Ephesians, 2 Timothy, 1 Timothy and Titus doubted by a substantial cadre of scholars (here listed in a roughly descending order of scholarly acceptance). It is not accidental that Dunn's seminal essay was an alternative account of Galatians 2:15-21; see James D. G. Dunn, "The New Perspective on Paul," *BJRL* 65 (1983): 95-122. Likewise, all of Dunn's following contributions to the NPP were focused on Galatians and Romans, with only the occasional reference to the other undisputed letters. E. P. Sanders also limits his investigation to undisputed letters in *Paul, the Law, and the Jewish People*.

[12]James D. G. Dunn, *The New Perspective on Paul* (Grand Rapids: Eerdmans, 2008), 55. For Dunn "later writings" also means deutero-Pauline; see, e.g., idem, *The Epistles to the Colossians and to Philemon: A Commentary on the Greek Text*, NIGTC (Grand Rapids: Eerdmans, 1996).

acknowledged in passing,[13] it does not appear that a wholesale reevaluation of the NPP has anywhere followed. Even notable conservative critics of the NPP who accept as authentic a thirteen-letter Pauline canon have seldom ventured beyond the seven undisputed letters to make their case, and those who have ventured into the disputed letters are understandably diffident.[14]

Reasons for focusing on the undisputed letters are several, and the instinct is perfectly natural if not even savvy. After all, in these letters, the authenticity of which almost no scholar has found the temerity to doubt, we find the greatest of Paul's discussion of the "law," "works [of the law]," "justification/righteousness," "faith," "grace" and even the vocabulary of atonement. Moreover, many would find the appeal to disputed letters, say, Colossians or Ephesians to say nothing of the Pastoral Epistles, in the pursuit of "Pauline theology" to be, at best, a distraction from the work at hand or, at worst, a stubborn choice to watch from the margins of the guild as an obscurantist. I don't suggest that the facile acceptance of the disputed letters is some sort of panacea or even to be preferred to their doctrinaire rejection. For here the opposite risk is no less in play—and not infrequently observed among conservative Pauline scholars: a text like Galatians 2:15-21 is assumed to say pretty much the same thing as Ephesians 2:1-10, or perhaps the latter provides the tacit frame for reading the former. In what follows, neither do I presume Pauline authorship of disputed letters, nor is it an ultimate goal to demonstrate authenticity. Rather, I explore the implications of a recovery of the once larger Pauline canon, though based on critical premises rather than theological presumption or professional necessity.

There might be at least two ways to do this, and in fact both will be explored: (1) to contend once again for the authenticity of some or all of the six disputed epistles (2 Thessalonians, Ephesians, Colossians, 1 Timothy, Titus and 2 Timothy)[15] or (2) to take more seriously the disputed Pauline

---

[13]See, e.g., Westerholm, *Perspectives Old and New*, 404-7; Dunn, *NPerP*, 55-58.

[14]Note, e.g., that six of Paul's "later" (= disputed) letters are consigned to a single chapter in Frank Thielman, *Paul and the Law: A Contextual Approach* (Downers Grove, IL: InterVarsity Press, 1994).

[15]For a similar impulse toward a more inclusive Pauline canon, see now also Wright, *P&FG*, 1:56-63. In addition to the seven undisputed letters, Wright affirms the authenticity of Colossians ("certainly"); 2 Thessalonians and Ephesians ("highly likely"); and possibly 2 Timothy ("may well be Paul")—though not, apparently, 1 Timothy and Titus ("a different category"). Wright's arguments are admittedly minimalist and consist primarily of his observation that earlier critical

letters as the witnesses to and legacy of Pauline theology, irrespective of our ability to establish actual authorship. That is to say that, even if the claim to Pauline authorship should prove unsustainable or unpersuasive, it remains the case that the primitive Christian movement received into an emerging canon texts that claim to speak the apostle's mind, quite possibly in certain cases even under the apostle's aegis, and the implications of this deserve more reflection than has heretofore been offered.[16] I will argue that the scholarly habit of dismissing these letters from the Pauline theology database is both consequential and regrettable and that, in fact, taking their witness into account does not yield an even more incorrigible incoherence but instead witnesses to certain Pauline trajectories. As a consequence, certain data that are frequently thought patent of pseudonymity hypotheses can with equal satisfaction be construed as the matured synthesis of previously witnessed strands of thought. And, far from subverting the NPP wholesale, the disputed letters frequently echo, if sometimes vestigially, with the same leitmotifs of the earlier, undisputed letters that spawned this recent re-appraisal of Pauline soteriology in the first place.

A parallel to this interest in the scope of the Pauline corpus is to take seriously the rhetorical and temporal location of Paul's letters, not merely as the routine business of New Testament introduction but as potentially consequential for theological exegesis. Although this concern will show itself relevant in various respects, I'm especially inclined to think that the frequent coupling of Galatians to Romans as texts that are mutually interpretive is a consequential misstep, too frequently taken.[17] The rhetorical occasions for these letters, upon which so much of the recent debates depend, are vastly different, a fact frequently and easily obscured by the substantial overlap of topics and language, including their shared appeals to certain Old Testament "proof texts." Nourishing that preemptive judgment is the predominance, at

scholarship functioned with various biases (e.g., against "early Catholicism," apocalypticism) that can now reasonably be shuttled. A similar openness to more than seven authentic letters (adding Colossians and "Ephesians" but not the Pastoral Epistles) is now pursued in Douglas A. Campbell, *Framing Paul: An Epistolary Biography* (Grand Rapids: Eerdmans, 2014).

[16]Besides most evangelical scholarship, where appeal to a thirteen-letter Pauline corpus is de rigeur, see Frank J. Matera, *God's Saving Grace: A Pauline Theology* (Grand Rapids: Eerdmans, 2012), as a notable recent attempt to account for the whole "Pauline" corpus.

[17]Contra, e.g., Francis Watson, *Paul, Judaism, and the Gentiles: Beyond the New Perspective*, 2nd ed. (Grand Rapids: Eerdmans, 2007); Campbell, *Deliverance of God*.

least in certain circles, of the so-called North Galatian hypothesis, which of necessity locates the letter in mid-50s, within a few years, if not even just months of Romans.[18] Persuaded instead by the evidence for a South Galatian hypothesis, I will argue that in fact Galatians predates Romans by some seven to nine years (preceding even the Thessalonian correspondence), a further historical reason to decouple the letters hermeneutically.[19] The chronological location of the Thessalonian and Corinthian correspondences (between Galatians and Romans) and Philippians (following Romans) among Paul's undisputed letters will factor into the larger argument, though admittedly with somewhat less consequence.

Finally, there is a deliberate effort in what follows to steer clear of an exclusive focus on Paul's supposed "doctrine of justification," preferring instead to explore the broader category of Pauline soteriology. This is not because "justification" is the eye of a scholarly storm from which even the intrepid never seem to escape alive. Nor is it that I want to join a chorus of diverse and sometimes unharmonious voices who wish to unseat justification as the center of Pauline theology, whether that be as Albert Schweitzer's "subsidiary crater," William Wrede's "polemical doctrine" or Douglas Campbell's "Justification theory." No, but there is in Schweitzer, Wrede and Campbell, and among this whole choir, a proper intuition that justification is not the be-all and end-all of Pauline "theology." My argument is slightly different, however. I do not claim that justification is not the center of Pauline theology, being highly suspicious of the whole notion of a center in the first place. I claim rather that Paul's notion of justification never ceases to be important while

---

[18]It should not be forgotten that, although the modern critical consensus has Galatians *preceding* Romans, the church's ancient presumption, assumed even during the Reformation era, was that Galations *followed* Romans chronologically and adumbrated its theological content. One could therefore appeal to Galatians' theological claims in the confidence that it was a mere abridgement of the larger argument of Romans. Gerald L. Bray, ed., *Galatians, Ephesians*, Reformation Commentary on Scripture, New Testament 10 (Downers Grove, IL: IVP Academic, 2011), xlii-xliii.

[19]It is noted, of course, that the southern destination of Galatians only allows for its earliest *possible* date, the *terminus ad quem*; it does not establish an early date. I will argue both for the South hypothesis and for the early date as the best account of the evidence. This is hardly a novel position, having been generally favored by conservative British scholarship (e.g., W. Ramsay, F. F. Bruce; albeit contra J. B. Lightfoot) and continuing to be the default position among a majority of North American evangelicals, many of whom were trained in the United Kingdom. Meanwhile, admitting exceptions of course, the North Galatian hypothesis characteristically holds sway among German scholars (sometimes as though self-evident) and within non-evangelical North American scholarship.

never becoming the telos of his soteriology. For this reason, *justification* has borne a soteriological burden it was never meant to bear, frequently breaking down under the imposition of definitions either too expansive, too narrow or frankly too tendentious. Indeed, the ruptured unity of the church catholic is owed in some measure to parties using the same terms differently and filing for a divorce on the ground of irreconcilable differences when a marriage counselor specializing in communication might have saved the relationship.[20] I argue instead that we best understand *Paul's* notion of justification not with regard to whether it belongs in the center or on the periphery, nor whether it is constitutive or polemical, nor even whether it is core or contingent—these distinctions being more heuristic than real. Rather, as I seek to demonstrate, justification for Paul is tributary to, and subsidiary within, a larger complex of salvation, in which justification is the thin edge of the Pauline soteriological wedge. To put it differently, the controlling metaphor here is not a puzzle with various ill-fitting pieces but an itinerary with a destination—called by various names—and, whatever it is and for all its seminal importance, justification is not that destination.

Having situated the argument in terms of methodological commitments, it remains to summarize the argument itself in brief. I maintain that the gains of the new perspective on Paul are indispensable, that we are permanently indebted and the better for the prodigious output of these scholars, surely for the questions raised and frequently also for the answers supplied. Nonetheless, as a comprehensive vision of Pauline soteriology, the NPP characteristically falls short in several important respects, some of which have been adumbrated above. Having problematized *justification* and its corollaries (e.g., "the law," "works [of the law]," "righteousness") especially over against a dominant Protestant tradition of reading Paul, the NPP characteristically falls captive to a limited data set, which its advocates have explored in impressive detail. But this central and originating concern, in combination with the limited data set of the seven undisputed epistles, results frequently in a synthetic vision that is smaller than the soteriology of the Pauline tradition. More to the point, I am persuaded that the NPP offers

---

[20]An important, and to me persuasive, leg of the argument in Alister E. McGrath, *Iustitia Dei: A History of the Christian Doctrine of Justification*, 3rd ed. (Cambridge: Cambridge University Press, 2005).

its most cogent readings as it concerns the earliest extant materials (i.e., especially Galatians) and that the account becomes progressively less persuasive beginning with the Corinthian correspondence, through Romans, up to and including Philippians. Not unexpectedly, the disputed Paulines are even less well accounted for by the substance of NPP axioms, and attempts to account for that material typically append awkwardly to the contours of the primary discussion. In short, I argue that the new perspective on Paul is a better account of Paul's older perspective.

Yet by the same token, if the argument that follows has merit, Luther might have done better to betroth himself to, say, Ephesians than to Galatians as his true "Katie von Bora."[21] If we find in the later Pauline letters texts that prove uncooperative for the NPP, no less suspect is the easy homogenization of the Pauline corpus, especially by those who count themselves as heirs of the Reformation and defenders of its soteriological tenets. If the crisis of the Gentile mission has inspired NPP sympathizers to find the Jew-Gentile motif everywhere, as we will see, an opposite, ahistorical error has characterized some of the rebuttals. In fact, I will argue that both perspectives are substantially correct in their appraisals of certain Pauline texts but that a failure to account adequately for the conditioning of the rhetorical occasion, on the one hand, and substantial development of Pauline soteriology throughout the whole Pauline tradition, on the other, subvert wholesale claims to have accounted for Paul's theology of salvation in its several dimensions.

To be more explicit, the case can be made that the NPP has nearly captured the earliest phase of the Pauline argument in Galatians, especially that Paul's discourse is conditioned by an urgent, on-the-ground crisis of how, against apparent scriptural testimony to the contrary and overcoming the skepticism of Jerusalem apostles, Gentiles can be admitted to covenantal membership apart from Torah observance, especially circumcision. I argue that, if not necessarily in every detail, yet substantially, the NPP has captured this Pauline moment and the Galatians argument with keen, even groundbreaking, insight. But it is a different story with Romans. Indeed, quite

---

[21]Luther's nun fiancée, who would become his wife: "The Epistle to the Galatians is my own epistle. I have betrothed myself to it. It is my Katie von Bora." Jaroslav Pelikan, "Introduction to Volume 26," *LW*, ix.

literally does Romans tell a different story and to a church that Paul had not evangelized or ever even visited and where there is no compelling evidence of a faction tempted to "Judaize," where to the contrary, Paul's sternest warning is reserved for a Gentile constituency, smugly independent of their Jewish roots.[22] I maintain that Romans evidences the theological budding of what retrospectively can be seen as the seeds planted in a different soil. If the crisis wrought by a backlash from the Gentile mission inflames an understandably defensive and impatient Paul in Galatians (as I will argue), the vista of the Spanish mission under the propelling aegis of the Roman church launches a more confident and measured Paul in the letter to the Romans. But in the process, not merely does the tone accommodate to the circumstance, but the substance of Paul's argument is morphing perceptibly. In particular, the question has become not how Gentiles gain a place in the covenant but how, the Gentiles' place in the covenant being assumed, the unity of Jew and Gentile can be preserved without subverting the salvation-historical priority of Israel. And that question, salient in its own right, is ultimately tributary to the even larger question of God's own rectitude in the outworking of the divine plan.

And, in what is perhaps the most important feature of Paul's developing soteriology, what begins as an ad hoc polemic against "works of the law" becomes a principled disavowal of meritorious works more generally. In this itinerary, Romans is treated less as Paul's crowning achievement or even less his "last will and testament"[23] than as the clearest evidence for a transition in Paul's soteriology: from (at risk of oversimplification) the largely horizontal crisis of Gentile covenant membership independent of the law to a more vertically oriented reconciliation to God gained by faith apart from works, works of any kind. Both letters traffic in the same concerns but with almost completely different aims and temperaments. What is emergent in

[22]Contra D. A. Campbell, *Deliverance of God*, esp. 495-518, who develops the thesis of Jacob Jervell, emphasizing the function of interloping teachers on the grounds of Romans 16:17-20. My reconstruction of the chronological relationship between Galatians and Romans—if not the majority view, hardly idiosyncratic—is not unlike the view disclaimed, albeit by means of broad caricature, by Campbell (ibid., 515-18). With regard to the factors that motivate the composition of Romans alone, I am in broad sympathy with the approach of A. Andrew Das, *Solving the Romans Debate* (Minneapolis: Fortress, 2007).
[23]Famously Günther Bornkamm, "The Letter to the Romans as Paul's Last Will and Testament," in *The Romans Debate*, ed. Karl P. Donfried, 3rd ed. (Peabody, MA: Hendrickson, 2005), 16-28.

Romans is then shown to be patent in the (arguably later) letter to the
Philippians. And what is patent in Philippians is established and further
confirmed in the disputed, and presumably later, letters. Paul's soteriology
becomes increasingly settled, principled and even abstract—while also expansive, not merely the drawing of Jew and Gentile into the family of
Abraham but the reconciliation of humanity to God and the cosmos to its
Creator—and not only the reconciliation of humanity to God but the transformation in Christ of the Adamic race into bearers once again of the divine
glory. While the Jew-Gentile conundrum, so prominent in Galatians and
then Romans, is never absent from Paul's soteriological discourse, it appears
not as a singular but as a multifaceted concern in the various letters. Likewise,
the works-faith antithesis, the sine qua non of Reformation interpretation,
has its roots in a rather different soil and is a response to questions rather
different from an anxious guilty party being excepted of divine judgment.[24]
Together, the expansion of the Pauline data set, giving full due to rhetorical
contingencies, and the exploration of a coherent development yield an account of Pauline soteriology that, while gratefully indebted to numerous
other accounts, is distinguishable from all of them. As reconstructed from
the whole corpus of the Pauline tradition, Paul's soteriology is best accounted for neither as heterogeneous incoherence nor as a homogenous
stasis but as a coherent itinerary comprehending new vistas. As it concerns
the current debates, I suggest that this is not an instance of one side getting
it right and the other getting it wrong but rather the simultaneous success
and failure of perspectives, which for their singularity cannot but fail to account for the whole.

---

[24]As NPP interpreters, beginning with Krister Stendahl, frequently insist. Krister Stendahl, *Paul Among Jews and Gentiles, and Other Essays* (Philadelphia: Fortress, 1976). This is a ubiquitous theme in N. T. Wright's early and popular work on Paul (e.g., *What Saint Paul Really Said*).

BREAKTHROUGHS, IMPASSES AND STALEMATES

Assessing the New Perspective

In what follows, I offer a summary account of this new perspective (NPP) in its various manifestations. There are now sufficient introductory surveys of the NPP so that it will not be necessary to add another full-scale introduction to the competent ones already available, yet perhaps at least a few readers will benefit from this close-at-hand reminder.[1] I trust it will be clear that I consider the NPP a necessary and salutary corrective that has advanced our understanding of Paul, his context, his aims and his theology. On the other hand, the NPP has achieved some of its widespread influence in a

---

[1]Two useful starting points are Michael B. Thompson, *The New Perspective on Paul* (Cambridge: Grove, 2002); and Kent L. Yinger, *The New Perspective on Paul: An Introduction* (Eugene, OR: Cascade, 2011). For a more detailed account, offering a broader context, albeit with a trenchant critique, see Stephen Westerholm, *Perspectives Old and New on Paul: The "Lutheran" Paul and His Critics* (Grand Rapids: Eerdmans, 2004), esp. 150-225. An article-length treatment of particular value is James A. Meek, "The New Perspective on Paul: An Introduction for the Uninitiated," *Concordia Journal* 27, no. 3 (2001): 208-33. In the end, however, one can hardly do better than the collection of essays from James Dunn, who gave the movement its name: *The New Perspective on Paul* (Grand Rapids: Eerdmans, 2008). Dunn's current views—a mature, or one might even say "chastened" account—are usefully summarized in "New Perspective View," in *Justification: Five Views*, ed. James K. Beilby and Paul R. Eddy (Downers Grove, IL: IVP Academic, 2011), 176-201. And for the most accessible, albeit not most recent or nuanced, account of N. T. Wright's distinctive approach, see *What Saint Paul Really Said: Was Paul of Tarsus the Real Founder of Christianity?* (Grand Rapids: Eerdmans, 1997), esp. 95-133. A useful and brief update that includes some autobiographical reflections is found in Wright's "New Perspectives on Paul," in *Justification in Perspective: Historical Developments and Contemporary Challenges*, ed. Bruce L. McCormack (Grand Rapids: Baker Academic, 2006), 243-77.

manner typical of major paradigm shifts, often by means of overcorrections sometimes compounded by sweeping rhetorical gestures. To the credit of architects and critics alike, there is evidence of an emerging more temperate and nuanced middle ground, and the present chapter intends to make a similar contribution, first by describing the gains of the NPP under four themes and then by assessing those same themes critically and offering certain qualifications.

1.1 WHAT WE (SHOULD HAVE) LEARNED
FROM THE NEW PERSPECTIVE

To speak of the new perspective on Paul is at its most basic to take account of two fundamental moves in recent biblical scholarship (if a half century can be considered "recent"). The first is a thoroughgoing reappraisal of the Judaism broadly contemporary with Jesus and his earliest followers, especially with respect to its implicit soteriology. The second is a more diverse set of reappraisals of Paul, albeit with certain family resemblances, in light of—perhaps, required by—the reappraisal of Judaism. These two "moves" can be differentiated and even theoretically separated, but in fact they form a compelling partnership in Pauline scholarship that would gain the label of convenience, "new perspective." In principle, earlier standard readings of Paul remain sustainable, though not without certain difficulties, even granting the new perspective on Judaism.[2] And for that matter, there is enough grist in the Pauline mill to drive fundamental reappraisals of Paul's motives and theology even apart from the new perspective on Judaism.[3] But it was the powerful synergy of the two perspectives in concert that fomented a revolution in Pauline studies, and it is for that reason that E. P. Sanders's opening gambit would prove so influential, combining in one place a devastating reappraisal of Judaism with a plausible, albeit less persuasive, account of Paul, the latter necessitated by the former.[4]

---

[2]As is more or less the case with, e.g., Frank Thielman, *Paul and the Law: A Contextual Approach* (Downers Grove, IL: InterVarsity Press, 1994); Westerholm, *Perspectives Old and New*; and even to some degree Carson, O'Brien and Seifrid, *JVN:CSTJ*.

[3]As was demonstrated already in Krister Stendahl, *Paul Among Jews and Gentiles, and Other Essays* (Philadelphia: Fortress, 1976). Less famously, but perhaps even more ahead of his time, Richard N. Longenecker wrote *Paul, Apostle of Liberty: The Origin and Nature of Paul's Christianity* (Grand Rapids: Baker, 1976), first published in 1964 by Harper & Row.

[4]I refer of course to E. P. Sanders, *Paul and Palestinian Judaism: A Comparison of Patterns of*

In what follows, I trace four themes that characterize the revision of Pauline biography and theology accomplished by the NPP. It is tempting—and it would be a fair bit easier—to move figure by figure and describe the work and unique contribution of each scholar. However, not only has this already been done quite adequately by others,[5] but my particular interest is less to divide and conquer and more to synthesize what is shared among the architects of the paradigm, noting of course that one or another is more responsible for this or that emphasis. I am at this point, however, specifically resisting an extensive engagement with the idiosyncrasies of a particular scholar. It goes without saying that, while sharing a broad set of convictions and tendencies, there will be countless matters of difference. But for our purposes it will prove more useful to note where the contributions of, for example, Krister Stendahl, E. P. Sanders, James Dunn and N. T. Wright, among others, stand in a continuity, with the cumulative building each upon the work of the other, sometimes by appropriation, sometimes by correction. Finally, what follows is first not only a description but also an affirmation of what I regard as fundamentally correct claims. I am arguing that each of these themes marks a genuine advance in our understanding of Paul, and I am commending these insights as ground gained from which there should be no retreat. I also take it as a given that such breakthroughs born of correcting zeal are frequently also attended by excess and hyperbole and that qualifications and refinements are often necessary and usually follow. But before we turn to a critique of the new perspective, we consider its several groundbreaking insights.

1.1.1 Reconsidering Paul's conversion. The conversion of the apostle Paul is arguably the most consequential historical event in the formative era of Christian history,[6] but its interpretation is a matter of dispute and even of theological consequence—both what happened and what it means.[7] In fact,

---

Religion (Philadelphia: Fortress, 1977); and idem, *Paul, the Law, and the Jewish People* (Philadelphia: Fortress, 1983). It should go without saying that even the most competent summaries of Sanders's work do not replace reading it, and engaging his arguments directly militates against the occasional mischaracterization one finds in unsympathetic accounts.

[5]See esp. Westerholm, *Perspectives Old and New*. It is true, however, that N. T. Wright's 2013 magnum opus, *Paul and the Faithfulness of God*, Christian Origins and the Question of God (Minneapolis: Fortress, 2013), has not yet figured into the various summary accounts.

[6]Assuming, of course, that the crucifixion and resurrection belong to a category of their own.

[7]See Bruce Corley, "Interpreting Paul's Conversion—Then and Now," in *The Road from Damascus:*

that it should be thought of as a "conversion" at all is now frequently disputed, never mind the church's ancient tradition of doing so.[8] In New Testament studies, that reevaluation of Paul's conversion was popularized especially in the 1963–1964 lectures of Krister Stendahl, who argued, plausibly enough, that it was a category mistake to regard the Christophany on the road to Damascus and its aftermath as a religious conversion.[9]

In the first place, neither Paul's allusions to (1 Cor 15:8; Gal 1:15-17) nor the Acts narrations of the event (Acts 9, 22, 26) describe it in terms of "conversion," "turning," "repentance" or even with respect to "salvation" or cognates. Rather, these texts repeatedly emphasize that Paul is being commissioned by the risen Lord to a Gentile mission: " . . . when he who had set me apart before I was born, and who called me by his grace, was pleased to reveal his Son to me, *in order that I might preach him among the Gentiles*" (Gal 1:15-16 ESV; cf. Acts 9:15; 13:47; 22:15, 21; 26:19-20). Here, "called" does not carry any particular soteriological overtones, as it well might in Pauline usage,[10] nor does "grace"; but instead "called by his grace" refers to Paul's vocation, the purpose of which (*hina*) was to "preach [Christ] among the Gentiles." As is often noted, there can be little doubt in this passage of at least two allusions to the prophetic corpus: (1) the language of being set apart before birth (lit. "from the womb of my mother") is reminiscent of other prophetic call accounts (Is 49:1; Jer 1:5); and (2) preaching among the Gentiles is arguably an allusion to and participation in the servant's vocation to be "a light to the Gentiles" (Is 42:6; 49:6; 51:4; cf. 60:3). Likewise, Paul's other reference to his encounter with the resurrected Christ in 1 Corinthians 15:8 refers specifically to his *apostolic* calling, as "one untimely born." All of this is confirmed in a variety of Acts narrations, featuring in certain cases a

---

The Impact of Paul's Conversion on His Life, Thought, and Ministry, ed. Richard N. Longenecker, McMaster New Testament Studies (Grand Rapids: Eerdmans, 1997), 1-17.

[8]Notably in the Feast of the Conversion of Saint Paul, commemorated on January 25 in Orthodox, Roman Catholic, Anglican and liturgical Protestant churches.

[9]Krister Stendahl, "The Apostle Paul and the Introspective Conscience of the West," *HTR* 56 (1963): 199-215. This and other essays were subsequently collected and published in Stendahl, *Paul Among Jews and Gentiles*, 7-23, 78-96. Although Stendahl is frequently credited for the paradigm shift, the point had been made, perhaps less memorably, by others before him.

[10]As it does, e.g., in Romans 4:17; 8:30; 9:7, 12, 24, 25, 26; 1 Corinthians 1:9, 26; 7:15, 17, 18, 20, 21, 22, 24; 10:27; 15:9; Galatians 1:6, 15; 5:8, 13; 1 Thessalonians 2:12; 4:7; 5:24; cf. Ephesians 4:1, 4; Colossians 3:15; 2 Thessalonians 2:14; 1 Timothy 6:12; 2 Timothy 1:9. Cf. Peter T. O'Brien, "Was Paul Converted?," in Carson, O'Brien and Seifrid, *JVN:PP*, 361-91.

commentary to the effect that the risen Christ had appointed Paul to preach to the Gentiles (Acts 9:15; 22:21; 26:16-18; cf. 13:47; 15:7).

But Stendahl and his followers are interested in more than simply aligning conceptions of the Damascus Road event with biblical language in a more disciplined way; the very language of "conversion" has misdirected subsequent Christian reflection, causing Paul to be read in artificial ways. It hardly needs saying that the observant Jew did not convert from irreligion to religious devotion, nor that his "conversion" could have been from one religion to another, given that a decisive separation of the Jesus movement from mainstream Judaism would be still decades in the future. But there is yet a more important reason for disclaiming Paul's conversion as such: we lack evidence in the New Testament that Paul underwent anything like a crisis in which anxiety of conscience and soteriological uncertainty were satiated by a sense of gracious divine acceptance.[11] As we will note below with respect to Philippians 3:2-6, the available evidence contradicts the picture of Paul as guilt-ridden and despairing of his ability to find God's approval. If Sanders's account of Judaism (on which, again, see below) is even remotely accurate, we should not have expected Paul's self-consciousness to match that of subsequent Christian conversion paradigms in which personal anxiety is frequently prerequisite for personal redemption. And when the autobiographical portions of Galatians (1:13-16) and Philippians (3:2-11) are given their due, we find that, far from anxiety, Paul exhibits what Stendahl called a "robust conscience," confident in his covenantal status.[12] Even were we to

---

[11]The tenacity of the view that Paul's conversion provided relief from prior—even if only recently recognized—guilt is evident in Piper's creative and psychologizing reading of the Acts narrative of Paul's encounter with Christ on the road to Damascus (John Piper, *The Future of Justification: A Response to N. T. Wright* [Wheaton, IL: Crossway, 2008], 87):

> I do not think it would be wild speculation to suggest that when Saul, who had hated Jesus and his followers, fell to the ground under the absolute, sovereign authority of the irresistible brightness of the living Jesus, his first thoughts would not be about his concepts, but about his survival. His first thoughts would not be about a new worldview and a new vocation [here Piper seeks to lampoon Wright], but whether he would at that moment be destroyed. What astonished Saul to the end of his days was first and foremost that a persecutor of the church should receive mercy instead of being cast into outer darkness.

The excerpt is a telling, if unwitting, verification of the "sociology of knowledge." Piper, a keen exegete and censorious biblicist, here goes quite "beyond what is written" so as to verify a familiar model of conversion by means of a "biblical" precedent. If Paul had the feelings that Piper suspects he had—who are we to say that he couldn't have?—neither he nor Luke has left any traces of that fact. Piper is, in essence, telling us what Paul *should* have felt.

[12]Moisés Silva is correct to protest that "conscience" is the wrong category to describe Paul's

regard Paul's former absence of anxiety as a contemptible hubris, we are left
still only with a culpable rather than a guilt-ridden Paul. This is especially
so if, with a growing majority of scholars, we take Romans 7:7-25 as other
than autobiographical of his pre-Christian struggle with the law.[13]

Thus, quite some time before the "Sanders revolution" with respect to
Judaism, we already have a quiet undoing of certain implicit tenets of a
Pauline model in which law provokes guilt and anxiety only to find relief in
a gospel free of works. That this was not Paul's *experience* must now be

---

blamelessness with respect to the law in Philippians 3:6. Paul is describing what must be regarded
as an empirical reality, not a subjective state of affairs (*Philippians*, 2nd ed., BECNT [Grand
Rapids: Baker Academic, 2005], 151-52). It does not follow, however, that Paul was therefore
stricken with a guilty conscience prior to (or even at the moment of) the revelation of Christ on
the road to Damascus. Of that the NT provides no evidence. Likewise, Silva protests that
blameless (ἄμεμπτος) does not mean "sinlessness" (cf. Thomas R. Schreiner, *Romans*, BECNT
[Grand Rapids: Baker Academic, 1998], 365). This is undoubtedly true, but strangely beside the
point. Paul's confidence as one "under the law . . . blameless" was dependent not on an imagined
sinlessness (one detects Christian anachronism in the Silva and Schreiner observation) but on
his having lived with a law-defined rectitude. There simply is no clear evidence to suggest that
behind Paul's apparent success in observing the law lurked a haunting sense of a more ultimate,
damning failure to please God. To find this in Paul's pre-Christian experience is to impose an
interiorizing and individualizing consciousness that is alien to Paul's thought in Philippians 3:6,
to say nothing of his larger argument. For a similar indifference to Paul's self-description in favor
of the interpreter's theological anthropology, see Paul F. M. Zahl, "Mistakes of the New
Perspective on Paul," *Themelios* 27, no. 1 (2001): 5-11.

[13]Some read this (or at least Rom 7:14-25) as autobiographical and descriptive of Paul's pre-
Christian (losing) battle with the law, depicting a crisis for the unconverted Paul, perhaps as
typical of Jewish experience more generally: e.g., W. D. Davies, *Paul and Rabbinic Judaism: Some
Rabbinic Elements in Pauline Theology* (London: SPCK, 1948), 23-26 (with respect to the Jewish
notion of the "evil impulse"); and Schreiner, *Romans*, 356-66 (as Paul understood his former
experience with the aid of Christian retrospection); cf. similarly, Stephen J. Chester, *Conversion
at Corinth: Perspectives on Conversion in Paul's Theology and the Corinthian Church*, Studies of
the New Testament and Its World (London: T&T Clark, 2003), 183-95. Others still regard it as
an autobiographical account of his *Christian* experience: e.g., C. E. B. Cranfield, *A Critical and
Exegetical Commentary on the Epistle to the Romans*, ICC (Edinburgh: T&T Clark, 1975), 1:340-
47 (Paul coming to understand the full ethical demand of the law as a Christian); and James D.
G. Dunn, *Romans*, WBC 38 (Dallas: Word, 1988), 1:382-84 (with a particular emphasis on Paul's
existential experience). But I concur with a growing number of NT scholars who regard Paul's
first-person account as a rhetorical device (*prosopopoeia*), some kind of speech-in-character
(albeit with no consensus as to which "character"!). So, e.g., Stanley K. Stowers, *A Rereading of
Romans: Justice, Jews, and Gentiles* (New Haven, CT: Yale University Press, 1994); Thomas H.
Tobin, *Paul's Rhetoric in Its Contexts: The Argument of Romans* (Peabody, MA: Hendrickson,
2004); Ben Witherington III and Darlene Hyatt, *Paul's Letter to the Romans: A Socio-Rhetorical
Commentary* (Grand Rapids: Eerdmans, 2004); Robert Jewett, *Romans: A Commentary*,
Hermeneia (Minneapolis: Fortress, 2007); and Christopher Bryan, *A Preface to Romans: Notes
on the Epistle in Its Literary and Cultural Setting* (New York: Oxford University Press, 2000). Not
surprisingly, there are permutations of the above positions in various combinations, especially
as it concerns the identity of the "I."

regarded as beyond serious dispute. But this does not mean that this could not be Paul's *gospel*, an assumption that seems mistakenly to trail the reconfiguration of Paul's conversion as if by necessity.[14] It does mean, however, that the burden of proof has shifted decidedly to the law → guilt → relief model. And it should be obvious—now at least in retrospect—that the revision of Paul's conversion experience would serve as a harbinger in miniature of the considerably more ambitious reappraisal of Second Temple Judaism, especially with regard to its "soteriology," to which we now turn.

1.1.2 Reappraising the "soteriology" of Judaism. By any account, E. P. Sanders's paradigm-shattering work on "Palestinian Judaism" must be regarded as among the most influential works of New Testament scholarship in the second half of the twentieth century, influencing not only Pauline research but the whole of New Testament studies.[15] The argument, anticipated by others but mainstreamed by Sanders, has now been so often recounted that a rehearsal of the highlights must suffice for our purposes.

Sanders begins with a sobering account of modern, mostly German Protestant, scholarship on Judaism that served generations of biblical scholars as the context for interpreting the New Testament. But, as Sanders sees it, this reconstructed background was in fact merely a foil, for it was obvious to these scholars that Jesus and early Christianity represent a decisive contrast, indeed a break, with contemporary Judaism. If Paul articulates a defect in his former religion (and that would be the right way to put it), it could be

---

[14]The assumption that the shape of Paul's conversion is somehow determinative of his own construal of the gospel afflicts not only those who intuitively conform Paul's experience to an evangelical, law → guilt → relief, *ordo salutis* (e.g., Zahl, "Mistakes") but curiously also some who reject that same *ordo*. It does not seem to occur to Stendahl, for example, that Paul's religious experience could have been one sort of thing while his kerygma might have been differently ordered. The same facile assumption seems to drive the otherwise impressively detailed and nuanced account of conversion in Douglas A. Campbell, *The Deliverance of God: An Apocalyptic Rereading of Justification in Paul* (Grand Rapids: Eerdmans, 2009), 125-66. But one can only wonder why Paul's conversion is assumed to be some kind of paradigm in the first place, given that he himself never appeals to it as such other than as a preparation for the apologia in Philippians 3:2-6. There is no reason to assume that Paul could not have evangelized Jews or God-fearers or "pagan" Gentiles with a rhetoric that bore little resemblance to his own experience and every reason to assume, in any case (not least from the evidence of Acts), that there was not a single pattern.

[15]On considerable influence of Sanders, see now William Baird, *The History of New Testament Research*, vol. 3, *From C. H. Dodd to Hans Dieter Betz* (Minneapolis: Fortress, 2013), 299-310; and more briefly, Stephen Neill and Tom Wright, *The Interpretation of the New Testament, 1861–1986* (New York: Oxford University Press, 1988), 372-75.

assumed that the defect existed, even if it would take the light of the Christian gospel to expose it. But once so exposed, it would not be hard to mine the literary detritus of Second Temple and especially rabbinic Judaism and so believe that one had discovered the failed Judaism of Paul's former life against which he now protested. This was a religion which, for all its noble, yea divine, beginnings, had degenerated into legalism and casuistry, where Torah observance was at once the Jew's burden and boast—a burden the rare honest Jew would have to confess he had not borne but which would none-theless not preclude the self-deluded a right to boast in their "righteousness." Indeed, such was Saul the Pharisee prior to the revelation on the road to Damascus. That whole picture—so effective as the dark background in which Christian light shines all the brighter—that whole picture, according to Sanders, was nothing but a pernicious caricature. And, as he would tell the cautionary tale, the scholars who had drawn the caricature and those who reproduced it were culpably negligent: for injecting historical schol-arship with a religious prejudice, for "cherry-picking" offending texts and deeming them characteristic apart from their larger contexts, but, above all, for promulgating an outsider's reading of Second Temple Judaism that was unsympathetic to its own story and internal logic.

Over against all of this, Sanders would offer his tour de force, a sympa-thetic description of the "pattern of religion" constitutive of Judaism of the Second Temple era. Sanders's basic claims are now well known. At the root of the whole project is a reestimation of the ideal of earnest Torah obser-vance, that is "nomism," which Sanders shows to be a datum easily miscon-strued by Christians who have a vested interest in the ultimacy of the Christian religion. As Sanders would stress repeatedly, it was not that Torah-observant Jews thought of themselves as amassing a treasury of merit, that their "salvation" would come from a verdict of good deeds outweighing bad. No, Torah observance was not a means by which individuals gained a fa-vored status with God; rather, Israel's God had already conferred that fa-vored *nation* status in making covenant with Abraham and his descendants, an initiative unmerited and preceding any obligation to keep command-ments. So it is that Sanders describes the Jewish "pattern of religion" as "covenantal nomism." Nomism (from the Greek *nomos*, "law"), the resolute commitment to law observance, is to be understood as a response to God's prior gracious initiative in calling and distinguishing a people, not as an anxious effort to gain by exertion what one already has by gratuity. Far from an oppressive adversary, the Torah is a gift of divine wisdom and its observance a joy. Moreover, it is manifestly not the case that the law expects perfect obedience such that a single lapse should abolish larger patterns of faithfulness. After all, this is patent in Torah itself, with its own cultic provisions for atonement and restitution, and repentance and restoration are manifestly the recourse of the righteous, not those abandoned to their wickedness. To be sure, Torah obedience is hardly incidental, but essential. But its function is, as Sanders would describe it, not "getting in" but "staying in" right covenant relations with God.[16] And even here, it is important to stress that Torah observance is not reducible to impersonal rule keeping but is rather human faithfulness to the covenant, which, if not precisely a mirror of divine faithfulness, is at least the natural relational, human counterpart.

Inevitably such a far-reaching revision, and one so potentially consequential, calls for an almost endless succession of qualifications (see below) or even full-on rebuttals.[17] Nonetheless, it is now fair to say that Sanders's hypothesis has succeeded, if by "success" we mean that it has replaced the once regnant paradigm as the default starting point for current and future conversations.[18] The extent of Sanders's success is that even those who find his account wanting find themselves nonetheless obliged to distance themselves from the caricatures of Judaism offered in earlier generations of scholarship.[19]

1.1.3 Reframing Torah observance. Beginning with his 1982 Manson Memorial Lecture delivered at the University of Manchester, James Dunn would

---

[16]Sanders, *P&PJ*, 17, 70, 212, 425, 548 and passim.

[17]To note just a few of the more prominent and substantial rebuttals: Mark Adam Elliott, *The Survivors of Israel: A Reconsideration of the Theology of Pre-Christian Judaism* (Grand Rapids: Eerdmans, 2000); A. Andrew Das, *Paul, the Law, and the Covenant* (Peabody, MA: Hendrickson, 2001); and Carson, O'Brien and Seifrid, *JVN:CSTJ*.

[18]As frequently noted, indeed by Sanders himself, not a few scholars had argued similarly, anticipating Sanders's conclusions, most notably George Foot Moore, *Judaism in the First Centuries of the Christian Era: The Age of the Tannaim*, 3 vols. (Cambridge, MA: Harvard University Press, 1927); and C. G. Montefiore, *Judaism and St. Paul: Two Essays* (London: Goschen, 1914).

[19]So, e.g., Westerholm, *Perspectives Old and New*, 408-39; and Carson, O'Brien, and Seifrid, *JVN:CSTJ*, passim.

build upon Sanders's foundation but would add a new frame of reference.[20] Dunn was eager to show that law observance could hardly be a discrete matter of religious piety, separable from other more worldly concerns, but rather that Torah observance was inherently a socially and politically freighted matter. Thus, Dunn would highlight the Jewish cultural crisis brought by the press of hellenization, especially as it was illustrated in the political history of the Maccabean resistance and for the duration of the subsequent Hasmonean dynasty. Since few scholars, Dunn included, were persuaded that Sanders had satisfactorily explained Paul's polemic against law and works of the law, the field was open for alternatives, and Dunn's proposal would become, and in some respects remains, the most characteristic account. Against the backdrop of Israel's political history, Dunn would show that a practice like circumcision occupied a function more profound and visceral in resistance to the pervasive threat of cultural assimilation to hellenization. Judaism's self-definition is at stake over against the threat of the aggressive imposition of hellenism. Indeed, even the coinage of the word *Judaism* itself is traceable to this crisis.[21] In such a context, to observe Torah was a political act, a protestation of faithfulness to Israel's one, true God in the face of ridicule, derision and even cultural genocide.[22] Although any sort of law observance could in principle carry this implication, Dunn initially would claim that the very phrase "works of the law," so familiar in Paul, functions as virtually a technical term for those particularly public and distinguishing practices—"boundary markers" or "identity badges" Dunn would call them—that marked Jews off from their neighbors in practices of observable fealty, chiefly kosher laws, purity concerns and, above all, circumcision.

Therefore, in Dunn's treatment, Paul's broadside aimed at "works of the law" takes on a rather different significance. Whereas Sanders had been

[20]"The New Perspective on Paul," delivered on November 4, 1982; first published as James D. G. Dunn, "The New Perspective on Paul," *BJRL* 65 (1983): 95-122; repr. as "The New Perspective on Paul," in *NPerP*, 99-120.

[21]2 Maccabees 2:21; 8:1; 14:38; 4 Maccabees 4:26; cf. Galatians 1:13-14. See, e.g., James D. G. Dunn, "Paul's Conversion—A Light to Twentieth Century Disputes," in *NPerP*, 347-62; repr. from *Evangelium—Schriftauslegung—Kirche*, ed. Jostein Ådna, Scott J. Hafemann and Otfried Hofius (Göttingen: Vandenhoeck & Ruprecht, 1997), 77-93.

[22]The sociopolitical dimension of Israel's Second Temple existence that Dunn works out via "works of the law" is ubiquitous in Wright's recent treatment of Jewish monotheism, understood especially as a political commitment, less a matter of abstract belief than an "agenda" for the real-world adversity that afflicted Israel (see esp. chap. 9, *P&FG*, 2:619-774).

content to say that Paul's critique of works of the law consisted merely in that they had become for Paul a beggarly and obsolete alternative to participation in Christ, who is the law's fulfillment, Dunn saw the matter differently. Dunn will agree with Sanders that the chief problem with "works of the law" is not that they are meritorious means of attaining favor with God but rather that they are the cultural peculiarities of a distinctive Jewish way of life.[23] To insist that Gentiles keep the works of the law is not to insist on a "works righteousness" but to assert a Jewish cultural particularity, with perhaps a nationalistic bent lurking in the shadows. And, if prosecuted with zeal as Paul once had, this cultural particularism with nationalistic hues would not only devastate Paul's divinely given vocation to preach Christ among the Gentiles; it would eventuate on practical grounds in two peoples of God, when Paul is everywhere insistent that there is to be but one family of Abraham.

One senses immediately that Dunn is on to something rather important, that, if not absent in earlier Pauline scholarship, was underdeveloped, and even critics of the NPP have acknowledged the importance of this dimension of Dunn's argument.[24] The Judaism of the Second Temple is everywhere afflicted by cultural and national hegemonies that threaten Jewish allegiance to the God of the covenant. In fact, in retrospect, it is even perhaps a bit surprising that Sanders had made so little of this dimension of Jewish Torah observance. One need only think, for example, of the decidedly political role that circumcision plays in 1–2 Maccabees to begin to appreciate how radical,

---

[23]To note but one particularly illustrative expression of the notion, perceptive of the social and pedagogical function of the law, see Letter of Aristeas 139-43:

> In his wisdom the legislator, in a comprehensive survey of each particular part, and being endowed by God for the knowledge of universal truths, surrounded us with unbroken palisades and iron walls to prevent our mixing with any of the other peoples in any matter, being thus kept pure in body and soul, preserved from false beliefs, and worshiping the only God omnipotent over all creation. Hence the leading priests among the Egyptians, conducting many close investigations and with practical experience of affairs, gave us the title "men of God," which is ascribed exclusively to those who worship the true God, and not to those who are concerned with meat and drink and clothes, their whole attitude (to life) being concentrated on these concerns. Such concerns are of no account among the people of our race, but throughout the whole of their lives their main objective is concerned with the sovereignty of God. So, to prevent our being perverted by contact with others or mixing with bad influences, he hedged us in on all sides with strict observances connected with meat and drink and touch and hearing and sight, after the manner of the Law. (James H. Charlesworth, ed., *The Old Testament Pseudepigrapha* [Garden City, NY: Doubleday, 1983], 2:22)

[24]See, e.g., Thielman, *Paul and the Law*, 48-68.

if not even traitorous, Paul's circumcision-free gospel must have seemed to the nomists of his day.[25] Or one need only reckon with the Jewish attraction to epispasm (a surgery designed to restore or lengthen the foreskin so as to overcome Jewish shame, e.g., in the gymnasium) to concur that inherited religious and soteriological categories of Jewish law keeping are much too thin a description to account for Jewish fidelity to the law.[26] The same might be noted with regard to Jewish dietary practices, strict avoidance of idolatry, revulsion over various profanations and sabbath keeping.[27]

This sociopolitical setting forms an all-important backdrop to Dunn's most innovative claims regarding the Pauline (and Jewish) phrase "works of the law." Although Dunn would modify the argument over time, his earliest position would treat it as essentially a technical term: Paul's "works of the law" would refer not to good behavior in some generalized way nor even to those works that the law enjoined in their entirety but in a focused manner to those distinguishing Jewish practices whose public expressions would mark out the practitioners as loyal to the covenant and as a peculiar people. By his famous and accessible redescriptions of "works of the law" law as "covenant boundary markers" and "identity markers," Dunn would effect a sea change and ignite a controversy not unlike that of Sanders's redescription of Judaism, though perhaps without the same staying power. Whereas few had found Sanders's account of Paul's polemic against Torah observance quite sufficient, now Dunn had closed the circuit, as it were, giving a plausible account of Paul's polemic against the law that honored the Sanders revolution while more adequately locating Paul's animus toward law observance in the practical exigencies of his Gentile mission.

---

[25]See, e.g., 1 Maccabees 1:15, 48, 60, 61; 2:46; 2 Maccabees 6:10; cf. 4 Maccabees 4:25.

[26]See Robert G. Hall, "Circumcision," *ABD* 1:1035-42; Ben Witherington III, *Grace in Galatia: A Commentary on St. Paul's Letter to the Galatians* (Grand Rapids: Eerdmans, 1998), 455-59. Note also, e.g., 1 Corinthians 7:18: μὴ ἐπισπάσθω, "do not remove the marks of circumcision"; cf. 1 Maccabees 1:15.

[27]On the eating of "common" or unclean food, see Tobit 1:10-11; 1 Maccabees 1:62; 2 Maccabees 6:18-20; 7:1-9; 4 Maccabees 5:3, 19, 25; 8:2, 12, 29; 11:16; 13:2; Letter of Aristeas 1:28-31. On the keeping and profanation of the sabbath, see, e.g., 1 Maccabees 1:43, 45; 2 Maccabees 6:6; 12:38; 15:2-4; 2 Baruch 84:8; Jubilees 1-2; 6:34-38; and passim, noting especially the notorious refusal of scrupulous Jews to engage battle on the sabbath and their resultant martyrdom (1 Macc 2:32-40; cf. 2 Macc 5:25-26; 8:26-27). On the issue of Jewish separatism and identity in the diaspora, see John M. G. Barclay, *Jews in the Mediterranean Diaspora: From Alexander to Trajan (323 BCE-117 CE)*, Hellenistic Culture and Society (Edinburgh: T&T Clark, 1996), 428-42.

If, in fact, the presumption of earlier scholarship—that Paul regarded the obedience to the law as doomed to failure given human incapacity—can no longer be taken for granted in the aftermath of the Sanders revolution, we find ourselves in need of a plausible account of his polemic against Torah observance. Clearly, the most theologically efficient and uncontroversial solution would have been for Paul to require proselytes to the Christian faith be circumcised and Torah observant, exploiting Jesus' messianic fulfillment as the ground and incentive for a massive Gentile mission project. That Paul did not do so on those grounds requires an explanation, and Dunn was not alone in regarding Sanders's answer as partial at best and unsatisfying. Dunn's proposal is thus a remediation of the shortcomings of Sanders's proposals, regarding both Judaism and Paul. From Dunn's perspective, Sanders's explanation was not so much mistaken as it was partial and, by comparison, excessively theoretical. In this regard, his claim that Paul's critique of law observance amounted to a salvation-historical obsolescence had been, if it is possible, too theological or, should we say, merely theological. In combating the dominant "Lutheran" view, Sanders had fought fire with fire, one theological account replacing another.

To be sure, Sanders had captured a central dimension of the Pauline vision. The argument of Galatians, for example, turns substantially on the rehearsal of a salvation history that puts the law in its place as a temporary provision subsequent in time and subordinate in force to covenantal promise—a mere codicil, an imprisonment, a custodian to minors who, having come of age, can dispense of its dispensation (Gal 3:15–4:9). Though less pronounced in Romans, still we find there the salvation-historical turning point, "but *now* apart from the law a righteousness of God is revealed" (Rom 3:21), and life in Christ is regarded as a kind of second marriage, the bonds of the law dissolved in death, the merry widow free to be the bride of Christ (Rom 7:1-6). Similar sentiments are rehearsed in Philippians 3, though from an autobiographical vantage, salvation history illustrated in Paul's personal history. It is, then, hard to fault Sanders's insight that for Paul the law's defects are not so much intrinsic as its function exhausted by means of its fulfillment. But in putting it this way, Sanders would treat a part of Paul's argument as nearly the whole, and, more consequentially, this would essentially cast Paul's ex post facto rationalization as though it were the generative insight.

It is not surprising then that Dunn's closer-to-the-ground account would strike a chord. It appeals to our intuition that theology might follow from certain pragmatic realities rather than the other way around, and by locating Paul's opposition to "works of the law" in the concrete experience of his mission to Gentiles, Dunn complements Sanders's account by filling in a more concretely plausible alternative. And Dunn's account would do further duty as an explanation of Paul's prohibition of boasting—not, as Dunn sees it, as a matter of pride of achievement but as national pride and smugness in covenantal privilege.[28] Whether or not one finds Dunn's account of Paul's Torah-free gospel entirely adequate for the whole of the Pauline corpus, there can be little question that he has restored a vital element of Paul's argument by recovering the social context in which Torah observance finds its meaning.

1.1.4 Renewing the covenant. It is one of the distinguishing features of the NPP to set Paul's theology—justification particularly—in a decidedly covenantal framework. This must be regarded as an important corrective for readings of Paul in which Christian theological interests had eclipsed Paul's matrix of Jewish categories. Over against a long tradition in Christian theology of understanding justification in a nearly exclusively "vertical" sense, the restoring of a right relationship of human beings to God, the NPP has argued that the more primary notion is membership in the covenant people, the seed of Abraham.[29] An emphasis on a covenantal soteriology is characteristic of almost all proponents of the NPP,[30] beginning of course with Sanders, for whom the establishment of covenant with an elect people is the chief evidence of divine grace toward Israel. As we have seen, this is fundamental to his account of Jewish

---

[28]This dimension of Dunn's argument, repeated in his Romans commentary, would be taken up but significantly amended by one of his students: Simon J. Gathercole, *Where Is Boasting? Early Jewish Soteriology and Paul's Response in Romans 1-5* (Grand Rapids: Eerdmans, 2002).

[29]It is granted that generalizations "vertical" and "horizontal" suggest a distinction too absolute, less nuanced than the positions of the scholars themselves. I use them sparingly here as a kind of shorthand for what is emphasized within the work of certain scholars.

[30]This is patent in Sanders's construal of Jewish soteriology as "*covenantal* nomism," and "covenant" forms the singular, ubiquitous backdrop for Wright's entire project. Dunn, for his part, carries the same torch, but more cautiously (see, e.g., James D. G. Dunn, "Did Paul Have a Covenant Theology? Reflections on Romans 9.4 and 11.27," in *The Concept of the Covenant in the Second Temple Period*, ed. Stanley E. Porter and Jacqueline C. R. de Roo, Supplements to the Journal for the Study of Judaism 71 [Leiden: Brill, 2003], 287-307; repr. in *NPerP*, 429-45).

soteriology.[31] But nowhere more so than in Wright's work do we find a repeated emphasis on covenant as basic to virtually all of Paul's thought, indeed as the unifying center to all Paul's theological reckoning. So emphatic is Wright's insistence on the covenantal matrix that his repetition of the theme approaches an almost polemical pitch.[32] Justification is not "getting right with God" nor the imputation from God of God's righteousness but rather membership in the covenant people, now redefined in the Messiah.

Of course, an emphasis on the covenant is not a novelty among Pauline theologies.[33] But for NPP scholars, this Josiah-like recovery of the covenant is not merely the recognition that Paul appealed to covenant in a handful of key passages—1 Corinthians 11, 2 Corinthians 3 and Galatians 3–4 chief among them.[34] It is rather the claim that the covenant is not Paul's occasional interest but the underlying category that his whole program presupposes. This is Wright's explicit claim, following Sanders's parallel argument with regard to the rabbis: that Paul didn't use the word "covenant" frequently "because it is everywhere presupposed."[35] This being so, it may be useful to

---

[31]E.g., in speaking of the basic character of justification, Sanders affirms that "righteousness in Judaism is a term which implies the *maintenance of status* among the group of the elect" (*P&PJ*, 554, emphasis original).

[32]See now Wright, *P&FG*, throughout, but esp. 2:774-1042. I don't recall Wright describing "covenant" as the "center" (a loaded term in Pauline scholarship) of Paul's thought, but if the term ever applied, it would seem to in this case.

[33]The emphasis is naturally important to a more confessional, Reformed work such as Herman N. Ridderbos, *Paul: An Outline of His Theology* (Grand Rapids: Eerdmans, 1975), esp. 333-41. More recently, note esp. Scott Hahn, *Kinship by Covenant: A Canonical Approach to the Fulfillment of God's Saving Promises* (New Haven, CT: Yale University Press, 2009).

[34]Paul's direct use of διαθήκη is limited to nine occurrences: Romans 9:4; 11:27; 1 Corinthians 11:25; 2 Corinthians 3:6, 14; Galatians 3:15, 17; 4:24; Ephesians 2:12. One should not confuse the relative paucity of direct references as though it were a certain indication of Paul's indifference to "covenant" as a substratum to his theological reckoning. On this point, see esp. the useful corrective of Stanley E. Porter, "The Concept of Covenant in Paul," in *The Concept of the Covenant in the Second Temple Period*, ed. Stanley E. Porter and Jacqueline C. R. de Roo, Supplements to the Journal for the Study of Judaism 71 (Leiden: Brill, 2003), 269-85; cf. Michael J. Gorman, *The Death of the Messiah and the Birth of the New Covenant: A (Not So) New Model of the Atonement* (Eugene, OR: Cascade, 2014), 51-53; and T. J. Deidun, *New Covenant Morality in Paul*, Analecta Biblica 89 (Rome: Biblical Institute Press, 1981), 45-50, who argues that the center of Pauline theology and ethics is none other than the "new covenant."

[35]Wright, *P&FG*, 2:781 and n. 21. He continues:

The point of invoking "covenant" as a controlling theme in Pauline soteriology is to highlight the way in which, in key passages in Galatians and Romans in particular, Paul stresses that what has happened in the gospel events has happened in fulfilment of the promises to Abraham, and has resulted in the formation (or the re-formation) of a people who are

sketch (quite literally) the NPP's covenantal soteriology, following in particular Wright's version, by offering some diagrammatic representations.[36]

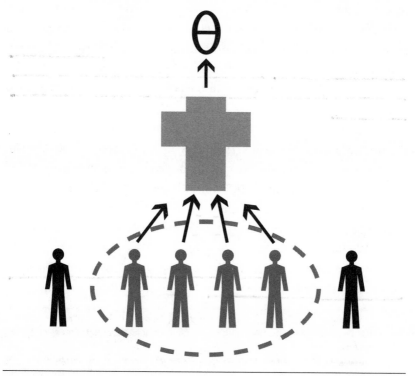

Figure 1.1. An individualist model of salvation via the "work of Christ"

It is evident that Wright's frequent foil is the popularization of Reformation construals of Pauline theology, the views most commonly held by evangelicals; thus, he writes as an evangelical but tweaking evangelical soteriology.[37] In particular, Wright finds fault with the heirs of the Reformation along three related lines: (1) as already discussed, they misconstrue first-century Judaism as tantamount to Pelagianism or pre-Tridentine

---

bound in a common life as a kind of extension or radical development of the covenantal life of Israel. (*P&FG*, 2:781-82)

[36]In what follows, I offer original and unauthorized diagrams, but I believe they do justice to the primary contours of Wright's views. I owe a special thanks to former student assistant Ben Jefferies for the design of the diagrams.

[37]Not only of Wright, but with respect to several NPP scholars, it could be said, to put it gently, that the generalizations about Reformation theology would not be the strongest leg of the argument. Dunn himself concedes that he knows little of Luther's oeuvre firsthand, but this does not prevent him and others from deriving a maximal rhetorical benefit from the cipher.

Catholicism;[38] (2) they tend overly to individualize Pauline soteriology so that the continuity of covenant and membership in the covenant family is all but missing from the picture; and (3) they conceive of justification in particular in strictly vertical terms, as though sinners "getting right with God" and enjoying a blessed afterlife were the questions driving Paul's formulation of his gospel, rather than, as it was, those questions arising from the Gentile mission. Drawn simply, the picture that Wright rejects might look something like figure 1.1, where the θ is, of course, God. The conception of salvation is that of individuals reconciled to God via the "work of Christ" (symbolized by the cross), and their collectivity, what would be their covenant membership—marked by a dotted line—is merely incidental to the more primary, individual reconciliation to God.

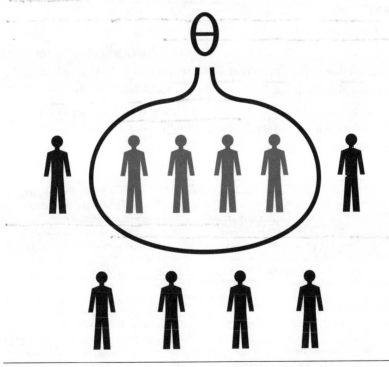

Figure 1.2. Jewish concept of covenant relationship with God

---

[38] A note famously sounded decades earlier by Krister Stendahl, *Paul Among Jews and Gentiles*, in essays dating back to the 1960s. Wright's use of "Pelagian" as a Christian mischaracterization of Judaism is a frequent rhetorical device.

But to appreciate what Wright finds deficient here, we must go backward and sketch a more properly Jewish, which is to say, covenantal, picture, as in figure 1.2. At its most basic, the initative is God's in choosing Abraham and his seed as his holy nation, bearers of the promise and ultimately the means by which God will remake the world. The law will be God's wise, gracious, enculturating gift for Israel to keep and to keep Israel.

If, however, ethnic Israel constitutes the default, though not ultimate, definition of God's covenant people, the Second Temple era is complicated by at least two factors: (1) On the one hand, with the crises of exile, diaspora and subsequent hellenization, Judaism will be a fractured entity in which Torah observance had been repristinated among the faithful while compromised among the accommodators. With Dunn, Wright understands Torah observance functioning as Jewish "covenant boundary markers," marking off Torah-observant Jews and proselytes as covenant members from the surrounding Hellenism.[39] There will thus be Jews who are regarded as only ethnically so (cf. Rom 2:25-29). (2) Meanwhile, in the context of the diaspora, Judaism engages (whether actively or passively remains a matter of debate) the surrounding world and draws to itself converts of various sorts, proselytes and God-fearers.[40] Figure 1.3 represents the covenant people as such, acknowledging that the proportions of

---

[39]While Wright has numerous differences with Dunn on a variety of issues, as it regards his construal of "works of the law," they are in full agreement: "[Dunn's] proposal about the meaning of 'works of the law' in Paul—that they are not the moral works through which one gains merit but the works through which the Jew is defined over against the pagan—I regard as exactly right" (Wright, "New Perspectives on Paul," 246). Wright's position is usefully summarized in his comments on Romans 3:20 in "The Letter to the Romans: Introduction, Commentary and Reflections," in NIB, 10:459-61. Both Wright and Dunn find extrabiblical support for this understanding in the Qumran scroll 4QMMT, on which see James D. G. Dunn, "4QMMT and Galatians," NTS 43, no. 1 (1997): 147-53 (repr. in NPerP, 339-46); and N. T. Wright, "4QMMT and Paul: Justification, 'Works,' and Eschatology," in History and Exegesis: New Testament Essays in Honor of Dr. E. Earle Ellis on His 80th Birthday, ed. Sang-Won (Aaron) Son (New York: T&T Clark, 2006), 104-32. On balance, I find Wright to show a clearer appreciation of the ways in which the sectarian text is distinguishable from what can be reconstructed of the Pauline context.
[40]See esp. Terence L. Donaldson, Paul and the Gentiles: Remapping the Apostle's Convictional World (Minneapolis: Fortress, 1997); and idem, Judaism and the Gentiles: Jewish Patterns of Universalism (to 135 CE) (Waco, TX: Baylor University Press, 2007). On the debated question of how active the Jewish "missionary" enterprise was, see Scot McKnight, A Light Among the Gentiles: Jewish Missionary Activity in the Second Temple Period (Minneapolis: Fortress, 1991); Martin Goodman, Mission and Conversion: Proselytizing in the Religious History of the Roman Empire (New York: Clarendon, 1994); and Michael F. Bird, Jesus and the Origins of the Gentile Mission (London: T&T Clark, 2006).

each group are unknowable and, for that matter, entirely in the eyes of the various beholders.

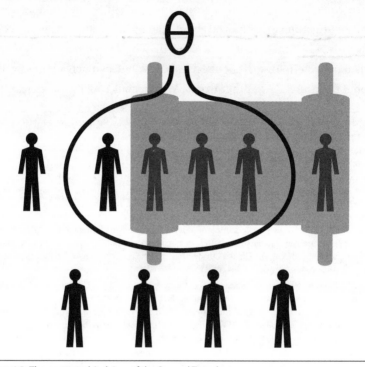

Figure 1.3. The contested Judaism of the Second Temple era

Thus, we have two consequences from this scenario. On the one hand, we can see that the constitution of "Israel" is a matter of contention and negotiation; on the other, the function of Torah observance comes to the fore as constitutive of Jewish identity. Almost certainly this accounts for the singular zeal of pre-Damascus Paul, the drive to align the circle of ethnic Israel with the circle of Torah-observant Israel, and we can have little doubt that prior to the Damascus Christophany and call, Paul's zeal for "works of the law" would have been unambiguous.

This background will help us then to understand Wright's description of the Pauline notion of justification. Repeatedly and insistently, Wright contends that justification is not the Pauline term for the restored relationship to God enjoyed by those in Christ but rather declaration of membership in covenant family: "'Justification' in the first century was not about how

someone might establish a relationship with God. It was about God's eschatological definition, both future and present, of who was, in fact, a member
of his people." Again, improving on Sanders, "[Justification] was not so
much about 'getting in,' or indeed about 'staying in,' as about 'how you could
tell who was in.' In standard Christian theological language, it wasn't so
much about soteriology as about ecclesiology; not so much about salvation
as about the church."[41] In other words, Wright could not be more clear than

---

[41]Both quotes from Wright, *What Saint Paul Really Said*, 119. The theme, however, is ubiquitous
in Wright's treatment of the term "justification," as illustrated here:

> If we come to Paul with these questions in mind—the questions about how human beings
> come into a living and saving relationship with the living and saving God—it is not jus-
> tification that springs to his lips or pen. The message about Jesus and his cross and resur-
> rection—"the gospel" . . . is announced to them; through this means, God works by his
> Spirit upon their hearts; as a result, they come to believe the message; they join the Chris-
> tian community through baptism, and begin to share in its common life and its common
> way of life. That is how people come into relationship with the living God. . . . Paul may
> or may not agree with Augustine, Luther or anyone else about how people come to per-
> sonal knowledge of God in Christ; but he does not use the language of "justification" to
> denote this event or process. (Wright, *WSPRS*, 116-17)

> Justification, to offer a fuller statement, is the recognition and declaration by God that
> those who are thus called and believing are in fact his people, the single family promised
> to Abraham, that as the new covenant people their sins are forgiven, and that since they
> have already died and been raised with the Messiah they are assured of final bodily resur-
> rection at the last. (N. T. Wright, "The Letter to the Galatians: Exegesis and Theology," in
> *Between Two Horizons: Spanning New Testament Studies and Systematic Theology*, ed. Joel
> B. Green and Max Turner [Grand Rapids: Eerdmans, 2000], 235)

> The word "justification," despite centuries of Christian misuse, is used by Paul to denote
> that which happens immediately after the "call": "those God called, he also justified"
> (Romans 8:30). In other words, those who hear the gospel and respond to it in faith are
> then declared by God to be his people, his elect, "the circumcision," "the Jews," "the Israel
> of God." They are given the status *dikaios*, "righteous," "within the covenant." (N. T.
> Wright, *Paul: In Fresh Perspective* [Minneapolis: Fortress, 2005], 121-22)

> At a stroke [referring to Gal 2:16], Paul has told us what it means to be "declared right-
> eous." It means to have God himself acknowledge that you are a member of "Israel," a
> "Jew," one of the "covenant family": the "righteous" in that sense. Yes, "righteous" means
> all sorts of other things as well. But unless it means at least that, and centrally, then verse
> 16 is a massive non sequitur. "We are Jews by birth, not 'gentile sinners'"; to say that, in
> the setting of a dispute about who you can eat with, and in the context of a statement about
> people "living as jews" and "living as gentiles" where what they have been doing is eating
> together (or not), leaves no elbow room for the phrase "declared righteous" to mean
> anything else at its primary level. *The whole sentence in its context, indicates that the ques-
> tion about two ways of "being declared righteous" must be a question about which com-
> munity, which table-fellowship, you belong to.* Do you, along with your allegiance to Jesus
> as Messiah, belong to a table-fellowship that is based on Jewish Torah? If you do, says Paul,
> you are forgetting your basic identity. What matters is not now Torah, but Messiah. *Justi-
> fication is all about being declared to be a member of God's people*; and this people is defined
> in relation to the Messiah himself. (Wright, *P&FG*, 2:856, emphasis original)

that he regards it a misuse of the term "justification" when it is used as a synonym for what are at best corollaries—reconciliation to God, forgiveness of sins or salvation—a category confusion which Wright considers the fallout from "centuries of Christian misuse."[42]

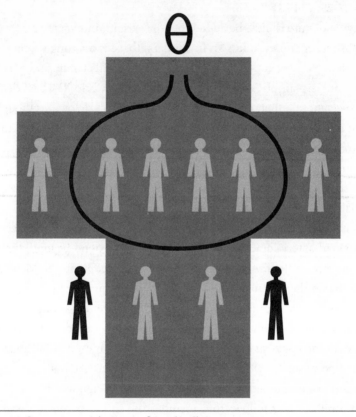

Figure 1.4. Covenant soteriology, reconfigured in Christ

Thus, structurally, Jewish eschatological justification and Christian justification are nearly identical, while materially they are radically different. Unlike the picture in which individuals are restored to God through Christ, forming only incidentally and not of necessity an elective fellowship of the redeemed, Wright understands that Christian justification, no less than its Jewish precursor, continues to consist in membership in the people of God, the children of Abraham. But now the children of Abraham are defined not

---

[42]Wright, *Paul: In Fresh Perspective*, 122.

by Torah-observance but by incorporation into Jesus the Messiah, the faithful Israelite, on the basis of faith that unites them to his faithfulness.[43] See figure 1.4. Moreover, for Paul that incorporation into the crucified, risen and exalted Christ is effected by the rite of baptism (Rom 6:3-6; 1 Cor 12:13; Gal 3:27-29; Col 2:11-12).

To this picture it must be added that for Wright, in a manner not paralleled in Dunn and even less so in Sanders, there is a strongly "missional" dimension to covenant. The election of Abraham, his family and posterity, is "the single-plan-of-God-through-Israel-for-the-world."[44] Thus, election and covenant find their ultimate meaning not in "soteriology" as though an end in itself, but in the pledge of the one and only God, Israel's king, to "set the world to rights," not apart from but through an elect people. The not infrequent failure of historic Israel to fulfill this vocation does not render the promise void, for the task laid down for Israel will be taken up by Jesus the Messiah and commuted to the covenant people reconstituted in him.[45]

Thus, Wright understands justification in decidedly corporate categories and toward soteriological ends that include, but extend beyond, the individuals who together will constitute God's elect people in the Messiah. It follows from the covenant status he describes as "justification" that a covenant member is—numbered with all of God's redeemed—forgiven, reconciled to God and ultimately, if not quite inevitably, saved. But what most Protestant theology has considered to be the inauguration of salvation or a past temporal subset within it Wright treats, in a sense, as but its context or even condition, granted of course with all the concomitant blessings and responsibilities that follow from membership in the covenant family. In

---

[43]Wright's description of justification, though more colorful and polemical, is, in this regard, quite similar to Sanders, who understands justification as transfer terminology for gaining membership in the saved body or covenant (Sanders, *P&PJ*, 470-72, 544-46).

[44]To use a favorite didactic explication of "covenant" from N. T. Wright, *Justification: God's Plan and Paul's Vision* (Downers Grove, IL: IVP Academic, 2009), first on p. 19 and then repeated frequently for emphasis, so as to grant his meaning to "covenant" and not some other.

[45]The last sentence raises the charge sometimes leveled at Wright of supersessionism, Messiah's people, the church, making off with Israel's promises if not even replacing Israel as God's covenant people. It is a charge to which Wright is clearly sensitive. For his defense, which distinguishes Paul's "supersessionism" as "Jewish supersessionism" (e.g., the Qumran community) over against the "hard" (e.g., Justin Martyr and Epistle of Barnabas) and "sweeping" (so, according to Wright, post-Barthian "apocalyptic" interpreters, e.g., J. L. Martyn), see Wright, *P&FG*, 2:805-11 and passim.

other words, as he often notes, this is a rather ecclesial account of Pauline soteriology, incorporation into Christ, under the condition of faith, effected by means of what the church would later call "sacraments," formed into an elect people for the sake of the world.[46]

1.2 Confessions of a New Perspective "God-Fearer"

As it concerns the NPP, I am but a "God-fearer," not a proselyte. For a few decades, I have wrestled with the attractiveness of the NPP, especially its capacity to set *certain* matters in a vivid, real-world relief. Nonetheless, neither taking anything back from the four gains just described nor damning by faint praise, I still consider each still in need of some nuance or qualification—as indeed one finds even among the NPP architects and advocates. In what follows, I do not so much find fault as I note that in certain cases the necessary setting aside of older wineskins was accompanied by a zealous tendency to overflow the new.

1.2.1 Not that kind of conversion, but still a conversion. The reappraisal of Paul's conversion described above is almost surely correct, and fifty years on the other side of Stendahl's article, the point seems almost obvious. Only with qualifications do we now refer to the Damascus Road event as a "conversion," and, as all our sources agree, that event certainly constituted the

---

[46]I suspect it is Wright's ecclesial intuition about union with Christ, effected in sacrament, that indirectly accounts for the acrimony that sometimes follows as he interfaces especially with evangelicals. Whereas for many of Wright's interlocutors Paul's notion of justification is absent any substantial role of covenant community or sacrament, to Wright these are intuitive. Although I cannot recall Wright appealing to it, it is not a stretch to see an echo—or should we say a foreshadowing?—of *extra ecclesiam nulla salus* ("outside the church there is no salvation") in his account of justification, which is strikingly continuous with Jewish soteriology. It can hardly be accidental that Wright's harshest critics tend to hail from Baptistic and "believers church" precincts, in which membership and good standing in the church catholic plays no particular role with respect to soteriology. Indeed, for some of Wright's more extreme naysayers, there is a habit of mind that associates sacraments by analogy with those very "works of the law" that are impotent to save, if not even an impediment should they be trusted to do so. While one can hardly consider Wright's interpretation of Paul to be uniquely or peculiarly Anglican, it is in this respect not incidentally Anglican, which is to say, in this respect, broadly catholic.

It is notable by way of contrast the extent to which Dunn is inclined to downplay baptism in his own account of Pauline soteriology: Paul "deemphasizes baptism"—not to say "devalues" (James D. G. Dunn, *The Theology of Paul the Apostle* [Grand Rapids: Eerdmans, 1998], 450 and n. 41). For Dunn, baptism is chiefly a "metaphor," which is "quite far removed from the actual performance of baptism in water" (Dunn, *Theology of Paul*, 452; cf. the discussion of Rom 6 in Dunn, *Romans*, esp. 1:311-13).

apostle's commission.[47] If the celebrated (and, not incidentally, thematized) conversions of, say, Augustine or Luther or John Wesley define conversion, then it is important to say that Paul's transition by which he became a follower of the resurrected Messiah is not a conversion—though it should be noted that neither in any of these cases, not even Augustine, do we witness a conversion from irreligion to religious devotion.

Nonetheless, in important respects we falsify Paul's experience on the Damascus Road to deny that it is a conversion, provided that we know what we mean and don't mean by the description. In the first place, at the very least, Paul's Damascus experience precipitated a realignment not from Judaism to Christianity but from one sect to another—from the Christ-opposing separatism of Pharisaic Judaism to a Christ-confessing Jesus sect that included Hellenists, "God-fearers" and proselytes, even embracing non-proselyte Gentiles.[48] And, as Alan Segal and others have noted, the event resulted in a wholesale change in community and in worldview for Paul.[49] From the company of zealous guardians of the tradition, Paul himself became a suffering member of the very community he had been persecuting. Even more tellingly, the Damascus event issued forth a radical reconfiguration of Paul's worldview, in which virtually every dimension of his covenantal monotheism was subject to revision, especially the story of Israel as he had understood it and his understanding of the Scriptures that told that story.[50] Second, according to Acts (and consistent with Paul's own theological emphases), Paul's transition to Christ allegiance was marked ritually

---

[47]See esp. James D. G. Dunn, "'A Light to the Gentiles': The Significance of the Damascus Road Christophany for Paul," in *The Glory of Christ in the New Testament*, ed. L. D. Hurst and N. T. Wright (Oxford: Clarendon, 1987), 251-66.

[48]I acknowledge the historical question begging of this sentence as it concerns the intractable questions of the ideological and ethnic identity of primitive Christian communties; the claim here is rather the significance of the change of Paul's communal affiliation as evidence of "conversion" (for a paradigmatic statement, see Peter L. Berger and Thomas Luckmann, *The Social Construction of Reality: A Treatise in the Sociology of Knowledge* [New York: Anchor Books, 1989], 144-50).

[49]Alan F. Segal, *Paul the Convert: The Apostolate and Apostasy of Saul the Pharisee* (New Haven, CT: Yale University Press, 1990); cf. Dunn, "Paul's Conversion—A Light to Twentieth Century Disputes."

[50]On the revision of Paul's worldview, see esp. the nuanced discussion of Donaldson, *Paul and the Gentiles*, 29-49; for a useful theoretical framework, see N. T. Wright, *The New Testament and the People of God*, Christian Origins and the Question of God (Minneapolis: Fortress, 1992), 31-80; and its further expansion in idem, *P&FG*, 1:351-537.

by baptism (Acts 9:18; 22:16) and experientially by the filling of the Spirit (Acts 9:17).[51] According to Acts 22:16, Paul's baptism was for the "washing away of sins," conditioned by "calling on [Jesus'] name" (cf. Acts 2:38).[52] If Paul was baptized in the near aftermath of the Christophany—and we have no reason to doubt the Acts narratives at this point (Acts 9:18; 22:16)—presumably he would have come to believe that, in baptismal union with Christ, he had gained all such benefits he elsewhere expounds in his letters (Rom 6:1-11; 1 Cor 12:13; Gal 3:26-29; Col 2:11-12).

Thus, Paul's ritually marked transition into a new community and consequent revision of convictions, though it is patently more, can scarcely be less than a conversion. This does not, of course, endorse the anachronistic refashioning of Paul's story after those who succeeded him as a presumed account of oppressing guilt and liberating grace. That Paul was "guilty" in the objective sense is beyond question; we only dispute that he was wracked with guilt subjectively. Nor can it be denied that the Christophany was an experience of "grace," but again it seems the grace assigned a vocation (Gal 1:15-16; cf. Acts 9:15). If it also yielded relief to a penitent heart, we don't know; neither Paul nor his Acts biographer describes the experience that way. Nor can Paul's story be paradigmatic for any and all subsequent Christian conversions: that it must be construed as sudden, whether or not it was; that the transition must be described as the imposition of monergistic will, never mind the convert's self-consciousness; that it be the intimate encounter of the solitary individual, without respect to the Body of the One calling; and so on. In certain respects, we can safely say that Paul's conversion, being unthematized by even his own later theology and unsocialized by a community of conforming conversion traditions, is the least paradigmatic of all.[53]

---

[51]Whatever is the presumed background and "meaning" of early Christian baptism for a Jew (for a recent survey, see Everett Ferguson, *Baptism in the Early Church: History, Theology, and Liturgy in the First Five Centuries* [Grand Rapids: Eerdmans, 2009], 60-82), it is hard to imagine that it is anything less than an expression of a decisive affiliation with the crucified Messiah and transition to the Christ-believing community.

[52]Assuming here that ἐπικαλεσάμενος τὸ ὄνομα αὐτοῦ ("calling on his name") is best understood as a participle of means: "be baptized and wash away your sins, *by* calling upon his name." In other words, the washing away of sins is linked irreducibly both to baptism and to an appeal to God.

[53]If there is a primary fault to be found in the numerous applications of social-science studies on conversion and religious adherence to the phenomenon of the apostle Paul and his communities, it is that, by working with paradigms at least indirectly or partially inherited *from* Paul and the New Testament, these studies do not sufficiently account for the unprecedented uniqueness, by

What remains of this conversion-or-call controversy—which in the end must be considered too much made of a keen observation—is the somewhat more interesting and vexing question of what Paul's conversion and call donated to his trajectories of thought and practice. In this regard, the scholarly debate has been carried out between those we might describe as "maximalists," who attribute a decisive generative influence to Paul's conversion experience, and "minimalists," who, without dismissing the importance of the conversion, make rather more room for the influence of Paul's prior beliefs, his cultural milieu and especially the exigencies of his several decades of mission.[54] The topic is too large and literature too vast to do any justice to the questions in short compass; a few observations must suffice.

The impulse to locate Paul's theological impulses in the Damascus Christophany is a useful hedge against historicist tendencies to account for Paul almost exclusively on the basis of his context and influences. While no one should deny that Paul is a product of his milieu, that context is not sufficient to account for his uniqueness nor for his self-attested volte-face from Christ's persecutor to his proclaimer. But as a correction, conversion maximalism tends to replace one sort of speculation with another, albeit more plausible, kind of speculation. To the extent that this front-end-loaded hypothesis inclines toward an early and relatively complete development of Pauline theology, it threatens to preempt accounts of Pauline development for which there is documentary evidence in favor of reconstructed extrapolations and inferences. Here again, I posit a middle ground. In one sense there is no peculiarly "Christian" Pauline conviction that cannot be traced back to the vision of the crucified Messiah vindicated as *Kyrios*. This event would be a

definition, of Paul's "Christian" experience. That is to say, it is hard to assess the probative value of sociological models that are drawn from communities that aspire to conformity to the progenitors of the model. It would, for example, be *at least* as useful to use the projected sectarianism of the New Testament to understand the modern phenomenon as vice versa.

[54]Pride of place among the conversion maximalists would be Seyoon Kim, *The Origin of Paul's Gospel*, WUNT 2.4 (Tübingen: Mohr, 1981); idem, *Paul and the New Perspective: Second Thoughts on the Origin of Paul's Gospel* (Grand Rapids: Eerdmans, 2001); cf. Mark A. Seifrid, *Justification by Faith: The Origin and Development of a Central Pauline Theme*, NovTSup 68 (Leiden: Brill, 1992). For a substantial engagement and critique of Kim's original thesis, see esp. Dunn, "'A Light to the Gentiles,'" although Dunn's Adam Christology is less convincing than the rest of the critique. Interestingly, Richard Longenecker's edited collection, *The Road from Damascus: The Impact of Paul's Conversion on His Life, Thought, and Ministry*, McMaster New Testament Studies (Grand Rapids: Eerdmans, 1997), is largely minimalist in its various contributions, save, naturally, for Seyoon Kim's essay.

paradox, oxymoron and sheer impossibility for Paul, requiring the replacement of one master story for another that could comprehend the incomprehensibility of a Messiah crucified, resurrected and exalted but without starting over.[55] The Damascus Road event is a deep reservoir from which Paul would draw for his whole missionary and letter-writing career, but there is no reason to assume that Paul drained the whole well in the immediate aftermath of his conversion.[56]

1.2.2 Covenantal nomism, but variegated. Sanders's achievement was not only scholarly but rhetorical, and his genius lay not merely in his deep acquaintance with the materials of the eras he surveys but also in his ability to project and sustain a large-scale thesis in the context of a rather detailed and otherwise arcane argument. Not only did Sanders sustain that argument, but also he attached it to memorable phrases and aphorisms—"covenantal nomism," "getting in" versus "staying in," "solution to plight" and his famously wry conclusion that "in short, *this is what Paul finds wrong in Judaism: it is not Christianity*."[57] These rhetorical moves are the handles fit to the hand of the nonspecialist, by means of which Sanders's account would become the dominant paradigm of New Testament scholarship, such that Sanders's adherents and (perhaps especially) his critics outnumber his readers several times over. But by this same token, the paradigm that would win the day would also prove vulnerable. The thesis of covenantal nomism is arguably too big, so sweeping that it risks dying the death of a thousand qualifications. Or, it might be asked, what if apparent exceptions don't prove the rule but merely weaken it? Whether one follows Sanders in every detail— or even should one, as I do, carry some large-scale objections—at the very

---

[55]Here, of course, I am echoing the infinitely more detailed account in Wright, *P&FG*; and, with the notion of a "master story," Michael J. Gorman, *Cruciformity: Paul's Narrative Spirituality of the Cross* (Grand Rapids: Eerdmans, 2001).

[56]If this also positions me somehow between so-called apocalyptic interpreters of Paul and their salvation-historical counterparts, that is all well and good, inasmuch as I confess to not understanding the need for a rigid bifurcation. Cf., e.g., Richard B. Hays, *The Faith of Jesus Christ: The Narrative Substructure of Galatians 3:1–4:11*, 2nd ed., Biblical Resource Series (Grand Rapids: Eerdmans, 2002); idem, *Echoes of Scripture in the Letters of Paul* (New Haven, CT: Yale University Press, 1989); and his enthusiastic review of Martyn's *Galatians*, idem, "Galatians: A New Translation with Introduction and Commentary," *JBL* 119, no. 2 (2000): 373-79; or, e.g., the peaceful coexistence of apocalyptic and *Heilsgeschichte* in J. Christiaan Beker, *Paul the Apostle: The Triumph of God in Life and Thought* (Philadelphia: Fortress, 1980).

[57]Sanders, *P&PJ*, 552 (emphasis original).

least we should say that he has succeeded in questioning a massive set of presumptions lacking historical rigor. And, once again, the burden of proof has been deposited at the feet of those who had mirror-read a Judaism that corroborated a certain reading of Paul.

If the criticisms of *P&PJ* are often predictable, they are not without basis. To begin with, the distinction made regarding Torah observance, that it is not a means of "getting in" but rather an obligation of "staying in," succeeds as a denial of a crasser form of legalism but is problematic as a refined description of the Jewish pattern of religion. In the first place, even in the form of a denial, "getting in" is a problematic description of Jewish religious phenomena in which "*getting* in" is, save for the proselyte and the sectarian (e.g., the Qumran community or Therapeutae), simply hereditary—at least once "in" is understood to refer to the people of God rather than a blessed afterlife. Thus to deny that Torah observance is the means of "getting in" is to push on an open door. From the perspective of covenantal nomism, the important, the *relevant* category, is merely "in"—that is, the covenant itself, that God has made such a thing with his people. And as far as I can tell, nearly everyone agrees, both Sanders's followers and his critics, that this is a matter of God's gracious initiative. It is, after all, the mainstream story line of the Old Testament texts, Abraham preceding Moses, Sinai following the exodus—the law being not the basis or means of Israel's relationship to YHWH but rather his gift to bless and distinguish his people.

That being so, sustaining that inheritance or, where in view, enjoying eschatological consolation as a faithful individual member of the covenant— what Sanders calls "staying in"—is clearly contingent on the faithfulness exercised in Torah observance. Thus, there is profound correlation between obedience to the law and eschatological salvation even in—*especially* in— Sanders's scheme. It is not, however, as Sanders would be quick to remind us, that such law observance stands in a causal relationship to eschatological salvation. Torah observance does not merit or earn salvation. Surely this is right, at least in some proper or technical sense. But by the same token, it is patent that non-observance constitutes a forfeiture of eschatological blessedness. It would be hard to fault a first-century Jew for drawing a false causal correlation between law observance and eschatological salvation, and it appears that at least some did exactly that.

This leads inevitably to a second point. What should be said of the apparent exceptions to Sanders's hypothesis? What is to be done, for example, with certain well-known texts of the Second Temple era that point in the direction, even if indirectly, of a merit theology? It would take us too far afield to engage in a close study of even a representative sampling of such texts.[58] Nonetheless, a few general comments are in order. First, we must not presume that a few apparent counterexamples to the pattern of covenantal nomism should be its undoing, as if Sanders and followers were unaware of such materials. One could certainly take to task Sanders's treatment of such texts on occasion, but his argument is too deeply rooted and the evidence explicable by means of covenantal nomism too ubiquitous to be undone by an apparent exception here or an infelicitous metaphor there.[59] Nonetheless, to the extent that Sanders finds the diverse branches of Judaism of the Second Temple united in a common root "pattern of religion," his thesis is vulnerable to the adducing of various counterexamples. At some point one is obliged to ask whether the exceptions are exceptional or simply signs of a more basic diversity untamed by a single paradigm. The counterthesis that Judaism was "variegated" strikes one as a matter of common sense rather than a discovery—not the undoing of Sanders's thesis but at least an important call for greater nuance.[60]

Meanwhile, if Sanders is right to deny that Torah observance is the means for "getting in" the covenant, the two most accessible and relevant historical

---

[58]The literature critical of the NPP is full of numerous examples; such catalogs and commentary can be found, e.g., in Das, *Paul, the Law, and the Covenant*; Gathercole, *Where Is Boasting?*; and Elliott, *Survivors of Israel.*

[59]One thinks, for example, of the weighing of merits in the balance. Although not a commonplace or formulaic account of eschatological judgment, the figure is common enough to be considered more than an anomaly: Wisdom of Solomon 6:18; 1 Enoch 38:1-2; 41:1; Testament of Levi 13:5-6; Sibylline Oracles 2:93-94; Psalms of Solomon 9:4-5; Pseudo-Philo 3:10; m. Avot 3.16. For Sanders's treatment, see *P&PJ*, 128-47, 212-38 and passim.

[60]I refer especially to Carson, O'Brien and Seifrid, *JVN:CSTJ*. For the most part, a series of treatments of various genres of Second Temple literature against Sanders's paradigm of "covenantal nomism," this remains the most important and detailed qualification of *P&PJ*. But its contribution is not easily summarized, a strength, in fact, of its nuance and detail. A majority of the authors finds covenantal nomism generally useful as a broad description of Second Temple Judaism (i.e., with respect to the corpus they assess), but almost all are agreed that it is not unfailingly apt for the phenomena they describe, though to lesser and greater degrees. On balance, the collection of essays constitutes a substantial refinement and qualification of the Sanders hypothesis but not quite its refutation. Indeed, some have criticized lead editor D. A. Carson for overstating the volume's opposition to Sanders in the volume's final summary essay (Carson, "Summaries and Conclusions," in *JVN:CSTJ*, 505-48).

Jewish examples of *actually* getting in—proselyte conversion, on the one hand, and Qumran sectarianism, on the other—actually prove too much. In both cases, the initiate's obligation is so bound up in taking on the obligations of the covenant (i.e., the law of Moses for the proselyte and nomism as appropriated by the Qumran sect) that it is hard to see that a getting-in-by-grace distinction is especially meaningful at the level of experience. So, ironically, if it is actually the "pattern of religion" that is being traced—that is, rather than the parsing of theological abstractions—one can only suppose that the initiate would naturally attach the blessings of covenant inclusion directly or indirectly to Torah-observance or to the particularized version of Torah-observance that prevailed in the community's standards. Again, with Sanders and the rest, this does not necessarily entail that covenant obedience therefore has become a *ground* or even *means* of eschatological salvation. But Sanders's success in demonstrating that fine distinction is a triumph of theological nuance rather than historical description. If, following Sanders, we find the psychological accounts of soteriologically anxious or sociologically inferior Jews not only anachronistic and speculative but crass, *P&PJ* remains a kind of overcorrection. While insisting that Judaism must be accounted for on its own terms, for failing to engage the experiential phenomena, Sanders's sympathetic account is nonetheless not sufficiently empathetic.

This raises a closely related observation, noted by several participants in this debate: it is hard to know what the balance and nuance that Sanders works so carefully to secure would have meant in the lived experience of Jews of various stripes in the Second Temple era. When Sanders commits to a descriptive and sympathetic account of Judaism, an interpretation of the dominant "pattern of religion," he chooses a noble but almost impossible task. Even the casual reader will notice that the salient analytic categories and the basic dualities that condition Sanders's account ("grace," "works," "mercy," "obedience," "merit," etc.) are decidedly Christian-theological, forged over two millennia of "our" internal wrangling. In certain respects, this is appropriate. It is, after all, *Christian* scholarship on Judaism that Sanders thinks has taken us down the wrong path, and those accounts are couched in Christian idiom to a much greater degree than even that of Sanders. Moreover, it is Sanders's purpose to explore Judaism as a prolegomenon to the study of the first Christian theologian. Nonetheless, vindicating Judaism on Christian terms is problematic and inevitably distorting.[61] And it is not hard to imagine that some Torah-observant Jews, whose documents Sanders synthesizes, would have had, if not less facility with, at least less practical use for these fine distinctions than a scholar with Sanders's modern interreligious concerns. There is good reason to believe that "lay" persons—possibly even frequently—mistakenly counted faithful obedience marking covenant identity as though it were a contribution of merit instead of *a matter of lived experience and intuition*, all the more so, when the Second Temple Jewish, albeit sectarian, documents that became the New Testament are included among the evidence.[62]

In short, to the extent that anyone can pass judgment on a hypothesis this ambitious, Sanders's account of Second Temple Jewish soteriology must be regarded as a needed and salutary remediation, substantially correct in its broad strokes and profoundly successful, owing to the rare combination of Sanders's workmanlike analysis and rhetorical skill. As subsequent research has demonstrated, however, the thesis admits of more exceptions than Sanders allowed. These do not accumulate to the overturning of the thesis but introduce a qualification considerable enough that Sanders's thesis ought to function more as a severe chastening than as an unassailable foundation for subsequent Pauline research.

1.2.3 "Works of the law": boundary markers and Israel's failure. There is no need to complain any more that Dunn's original claims regarding "works of the law" were overstated and cannot be sustained under cross-examination. Dunn already admits as much with admirable candor in a

---

[61]See now the incisive critique of John M. G. Barclay, *Paul and the Gift* (Grand Rapids: Eerdmans, 2015). Sanders's most persistent and trenchant critic along these lines is undoubtedly Jacob Neusner, *Judaic Law from Jesus to the Mishnah: A Systematic Reply to Professor E. P. Sanders*, South Florida Studies in the History of Judaism 84 (Atlanta: Scholars Press, 1993), esp. 49-78, 231-46 (cf. Martin Hengel and Roland Deines, "E P Sanders' 'Common Judaism,' Jesus, and the Pharisees," *JTS* 46, no. 1 [1995]: 1-70; and R. Barry Matlock, "Almost Cultural Studies: Reflections on the 'New Perspective' on Paul," in *Biblical Studies/Cultural Studies: The Third Sheffield Colloquium*, ed. J. Cheryl Exum and Stephen D. Moore [Sheffield: Sheffield University Press, 1998], 433-59).

[62]See especially Elliott, *Survivors of Israel*. Cf., e.g., Carson, "Summaries and Conclusions," 505-48, esp. 547-48; note also Hagner's comments to the same effect in his concluding essay in Peter Stuhlmacher and Donald A. Hagner, *Revisiting Paul's Doctrine of Justification: A Challenge to the New Perspective* (Downers Grove, IL: InterVarsity Press, 2001), 84-88.

series of articles on the topic: "It has been a matter of regret to me that my
initial formulation of the case I was making (regarding 'works of the law')
allowed it to be so readily dismissed."[63] It is unfortunate that critics of the
NPP will sometimes continue to use Dunn's 1983 version of the argument as
though it were the last thing he has to say about the topic.[64] Dunn has transparently changed his view that "works of the law" should be seen as a technical term for a limited subset of Jewish law that distinguished Jews from
their neighbors, covenant "boundary markers,"[65] now holding instead that
the expression properly denotes not just *some* but *all* that the law requires.
Although "'works of the law' is a more general phrase affirming the law in
all its requirements," Dunn avers that "when the phrase comes in the context
of Paul's mission to Gentiles, and particularly of Jewish believers trying to
compel Gentile believers to live like Jews, then its most obvious reference is
. . . particularly to the law in its role as a wall dividing Jews from Gentile, the
boundary markers that define who is 'inside' and who is 'outside.'"[66] This
fine-tuning of the earlier claim—shifting from an unlikely *meaning* for
"works of the law" and drawing attention to this social *function*—redeems
the previous unsustainable claim. At the very least, it seems impossible to
deny that "works of law" would have nothing to do with Jewish social
identity deeply embedded in resistance narratives yet facing profound pres-
sures toward cultural accommodation.

---

[63]James D. G. Dunn, "The New Perspective: Whence, What and Whither?," in *NPerP*, 1-97, esp.
23. See also chaps. 2, 3, 8, 17 and 19.

[64]E.g., Thomas R. Schreiner, *Galatians*, ZECNT (Grand Rapids: Zondervan, 2010), 160; Moisés
Silva, "Faith Versus Works of Law in Galatians," in Carson, O'Brien and Siefrid, *JVN:PP*, 218-19.
A frequent mischaracterization is that Dunn had identified the "works of the law" narrowly with
only three specific elements of Torah observance: circumcision, food laws and sabbath. Rather,
for Dunn, these were particularly illustrative of those public, and thus contended for, "identity
markers" that were essential to Jewish covenantal and cultural self-understanding. These three
categories were especially illustrative for Dunn not merely because he could trace a Jewish
emphasis on such matters but also because "pagan" observers themselves would highlight these,
often contemptuously, as distinctive to Jewish identity. And, not incidentally, these were the very
matters over which Paul contended in his letter to the Galatians (see, e.g., Gal 2:11-14; 4:10; 5:2;
6:12). Dunn's original statement is reprinted in *NPerP*, 99-120, see esp. 108-11; for a statement of
his subsequent clarification, see Dunn, *Theology of Paul*, 354-58, esp. n. 97.

[65]Dunn and followers have also used the language of "identity markers," "badges of covenant
membership" and "defining boundaries." See Dunn, "New Perspective: Whence, What and
Whither?"

[66]Dunn, "New Perspective View," 176-201, esp. 194. This, to my knowledge, is only the most recent
version of Dunn's modification of his earlier claim, but it is not unique, and he works the same
point out in much more detail elsewhere.

Table 1.1. Soteriological antitheses found in Paul's letters

Reference[a]	*not* by/from	*but* by/through
Gal 2:16a	*not* justified by works of law *ou dikaioutai ex ergōn nomou*	but[/except] through the faith[/fulness] in[/of] Jesus Christ *ean mē dia pisteōs Iēsou Christou*
Gal 2:16b ~	and *not* by the works of the law *kai ouk ex ergōn nomou*	even we believed on Christ Jesus, that we might be justified by faith in Christ *kai hēmeis eis Christon Iēsoun episteusamen, hina dikaiōthōmen ek pisteōs Christou*
Gal 3:2[b]	Did you receive the Spirit by works of the law *ex ergōn nomou to pneuma elabete*	or by the hearing of faith? *ē ex akoēs pisteōs*
Gal 3:24[c]	Thus the law had become our [mere] guardian until Christ *hōste ho nomos paidagōgos hēmōn gegonen eis Christon*	so that we might be justified by faith. *hina ek pisteōs dikaiōthōmen*
Rom 3:20-22	Therefore *by works of law* all flesh will *not* be justified before him *dioti ex ergōn nomou ou dikaiōthēsetai pasa sarx enōpion autou*	but now a righteousness apart from law is manifest . . . a righteousness of God through the faith[/fulnesss] in[/of] Jesus Christ for all who believe. *nyni de chōris nomou dikaiosynē theou pephanerōtai . . . dikaiosynē de theou dia pisteōs Iēsou Christou eis pantas tous pisteuontas*
Rom 3:28 ~	apart from works of the law. *chōris ergōn nomou*	For we hold that a person is justified by faith *logizometha gar dikaiousthai pistei anthrōpon*
Rom 4:4-5[d]	Now to one who *works*, the wage is *not* reckoned as a gift but as something owed *tō de ergazomenō ho misthos ou logizetai kata charin alla kata opheilēma*	but to the one who does not work but believes in him who justifies the ungodly, his faith is counted as righteousness. *tō de mē ergazomenō pisteuonti de epi ton dikaiounta ton asebē logizetai hē pistis autou eis dikaiosynēn*
Rom 4:13	For the promise to Abraham or to his seed that he would be heir of the world was *not* through the law *Ou gar dia nomou hē epangelia tō Abraam ē tō spermati autou*	but through the righteousness of[/ that comes by] faith. *alla dia dikaiosynēs pisteōs*
Rom 11:6[e]	But if it is by grace, it is no longer on the basis of works, otherwise grace would no longer be grace. *Ei de chariti, ouketi ex ergōn, epei hē charis ouketi ginetai charis*	
Phil 3:9	*not* having my own righteousness from law *mē echōn emēn dikaiosynēn tēn ek nomou*	but that [righteousness] which is through the faith[/fulnesss] in[/of] Christ, the righteousness from God based on faith. *alla tēn dia pisteōs Christou, tēn ek theou dikaiosynēn epi tē pistei*

Disputed Epistles		
Eph 2:8-9 ~	*not by works* (lest one should boast). *ouk ex ergōn, hina mē tis kauchēsētai*	For by grace are you saved through faith *tē gar chariti este sesōsmenoi dia pisteōs*
Titus 3:5	*not by works* which we have done in righteousness *ouk ex ergōn tōn en dikaiosynē ha epoiēsamen hēmeis*	*but* according to his mercy *alla kata to autou eleos*
2 Tim 1:9	*not according* to our works *ou kata ta erga hēmōn*	*but* according to his own purpose and grace. *alla kata idian prothesin kai charin*

[a]While the most common pattern is a denial ("not") followed by an adversative affirmation ("but rather"), Galatians 2:16, Romans 3:28 and Ephesians 2:8-9 are exceptions to the pattern, where the affirmation precedes the denial (thus marked ~).
[b]It is assumed that the answer to the first alternative ("by works of the law") is negative and to the second ("by hearing of faith") is affirmative; thus, the basic pattern of thought is present here as well.
[c]When it is understood that the παιδαγωγός (guardian) connotes a temporary, provisional (perhaps even harsh) custodianship, it is clear that the law's shortcomings are here contrasted by the fulfillment that comes with "faith."
[d]The contrast is reinforced in the following verse: "So also David pronounces a blessing upon the man to whom God reckons righteousness *apart from works*" (Rom 4:6).
[e]Romans 11:6 clearly departs from the "not ... but ..." pattern, while expressing the same fundamental antithesis, here between grace and works. Grace conditional on works would "no longer be grace." The emphatic character of the antithesis is highlighted all the more by the recognition that the rhetorical conditional (εἰ δὲ χάριτι) is assumed to be true for the sake of the argument ("but if [as we know it to be the case] it is by grace").

At the same time, one can wonder if "works of the law" as sociocultural impediment exhausts the whole of Paul's polemic. In the same way that Sanders's salvation-historical account of Paul's polemic against Torah observance proves inadequate, the same might be said of Dunn's supplementing correction. It can be doubted whether even Dunn's more modest claim regarding works of the law can be sustained with respect to its every occurrence, to say nothing of the various alternatives, "law" and "works." In fact, the revised, more modest claim invites more, not less, scrutiny—though of a different kind. Now that Dunn has rightly disavowed "works of the law" as a fixed, technical term focused explicitly on social demarcation, a burden shifts to the demonstration that any or all of its occurrences highlight that divisive social function. We should expect various contextual clues to indicate not only that separatist Jewish social existence is everywhere present as a corollary to Torah observance but that it is the particular, implicit critique of works of the law (and, where relevant, "law" and "works") when works of the law are judged inadequate. It would be necessary, then, to show that the permeating Pauline antithesis of works/law over against faith/grace can be accounted for primarily (if not solely) on the ground that the former creates or reinforces Jewish national privilege over against Gentile inclusion. But both the undisputed letters and the disputed are chock full of soteriological antitheses in which one putative vehicle of justification or salvation is denied and its alternative is affirmed: "not *x* but *y*." The pattern is important and ubiquitous enough to merit diagrammatic display and careful survey (see table 1.1, arranged in a chronological order to be defended later).

The object of this assemblage of data is not to presume that we can reason simplistically from it a Pauline soteriology. I don't claim that these examples speak for themselves; the meaning of each is contested, with context and nuance needing to be taken into account at every turn. But it remains the case that basic to Paul's "grammar" is a fundamental antithesis between "works," "law" and "works of law," on the one hand, and "faith," "grace" and "mercy," on the other. The point for now is that the import of this antithesis, which had appeared straightforward to most interpreters of Paul through the ages,[67] is no longer so obvious. It had been perfectly natural to intuit that if Paul was disclaiming that justification came by observance of the law, then he was refuting a mainstream tenet of Judaism, one tenaciously held even by certain Jewish Christians. The whole "old perspective" flows from this basic intuition, which, to be fair, is profoundly rooted in Paul's own grammar—or, as the NPP insists, comes from a certain way of reading that grammar. That there is a deeply embedded antithesis cannot be doubted; the NPP rightly asks that we not presume what is constituted in the contrast.

We engage these questions in greater detail in chapter six, so this is not yet the place for that argument. Suffice it for now to say that even supposing for the sake of the argument that the references to "works of the law" in Galatians

---

[67]Consider, e.g., Augustine on Romans 10:1-4:

These things [a censure of boasting] are said to the opponents of the city of God who belong to Babylon, who presume on their own strength and glory in themselves, not in the Lord. Included among them are the Israelites according to the flesh, earthborn citizens of the earthly Jerusalem, who, as the Apostle says, *being ignorant of the righteousness of God*—that is, the righteousness given to man by God, who is alone righteous and alone makes righteous—*and seeking to establish their own*—that is, as if it were their own achievement, not God's gift—*have not submitted to God's righteousness* (Rom 10:3). For in their pride they imagine that they can please God by their own righteousness rather than by the righteousness of God who is *a God of knowledge* and thus is also the judge of consciences, for he sees the thoughts that human beings have and knows that their thoughts are empty if they come from themselves and not from him. (*DCD* 17.4; *The City of God [De Civitate Dei]*, ed. Boniface Ramsey, trans. William S. Babcock, *The Works of Saint Augustine: A Translation for the 21st Century* [Hyde Park, NY: New City Press, 2012], 2:243)

can be shown to function as Dunn argues, I am not convinced that even Dunn's revised account of the phrase can carry the payload that he supposes: (1) As I will argue, the two occurrences in Romans (Rom 3:20, 28) are not entirely analogous to the uses in Galatians (Gal 2:16 [3x]; 3:2, 5, 10). (2) Once it is rightly acknowledged that "works of the law" refers to that which the law requires or deeds of obedience to the law in general, then it becomes clear that the expression cannot be isolated from various parallel expressions where the same cannot be demonstrated with respect to various verbal or conceptual synonyms (e.g., "work [sg.] of the law" [Rom 2:15]; *doing [poieō/poiētēs]* the law" [Rom 2:14; 10:5; Gal 3:10, 12; 5:3]; *"practicing [prassō]* the law" [Rom 2:25]; *"keeping [tēreō]* the righteous stipulations of the law [*ta dikaiōmata tou nomou*]" [Rom 2:26]; *"fulfilling [teleō, plēroō]* the law" [Rom 2:27; 8:4]). (3) Even more problematic is the claim that "works" used absolutely (i.e., not "of the law") functions as shorthand for the full expression, that when we read "works" it is patent that Paul means "works *of the law*." (4) Dunn's account, even in its moderated form, still does not reckon entirely with the logic internal to the Pauline antithesis, especially in such places where (a) the critique of Torah observance rests on Israel's failure to meet that standard consistently and (b) the polarity of the antithesis is not that of inclusion and exclusion but of effort contrasted with gratuity (e.g., Rom 9:11-12). (5) Finally, I will seek to show that Dunn's breakthrough, while an especially keen insight into Galatians, loses traction over the course of the Pauline canon, all the more so if certain disputed letters represent the natural trajectory of the undisputed letters rather than a departure from or a late imposition of a soteriology alien to Paul's own.[68]

1.2.4 Covenant membership, yes; but also reconciliation to God. Most Pauline scholars will now regard the recovery of covenant, an irrevocably

[68]It is not accidental that Dunn launched his "new perspective" account of "works of the law" with express reference to Galatians 2:15-21, esp. 2:16, and continued to make Galatians the touchstone of his treatment of the expression throughout the several iterations. Of course, this is naturally the case since of the eight uses of the phrase six are concentrated in Galatians (with the remaining two in Rom 3:20, 28). Thus, it is not surprising that the rhetorical context of Galatians would tend naturally to travel with the phrase and that the sort of crisis that Galatians represents would attach to the phrase. For this reason, Dunn's qualification of his earlier, and admittedly too restrictive, referent for "works of the law" does not prove fatal to his overall argument. On the other hand, the very fact that "works of the law" drops out of Pauline use but a works-grace antithesis perdures is itself reason to ask if the ethnological phenomenon of Galatians that Dunn captures so adroitly is rightly carried through as paradigmatic for the whole Pauline corpus.

Jewish category never abandoned, to be a secure forward step in our understanding of every dimension of Paul's thought.[69] And, to the extent that
Christian soteriology in certain contexts might skew individualistically and
be refracted through the Christian-theological prism, Sanders and Wright
especially offer a salutary corrective. But as a description of the Pauline
notion of *justification*, the emphatically covenantal construal of the NPP is
problematically absolute, sometimes muting corollary themes of reconciliation to God, peace with God, forgiveness and deliverance from wrath as
inseparable concomitants of the justification metaphor as Paul has appropriated it. Instead, from the NPP we find the frequent protestations that
justification is not about "getting right with God," or "getting saved" or "how
the sinner can find a gracious God." These common tropes, useful in distinguishing the NPP from its traditional Protestant perspective antecedent
(hereafter TPP),[70] date back at least to Stendahl, perhaps with Wright getting
the most use of the rhetoric more recently.[71]

More particularly, the general indifference to the theme of reconciliation
and corollaries within NPP quarters has proven consequential for the overall
shape of the NPP paradigm. To be sure, the NPP understands reconciliation
to have its place in Pauline theology as one soteriological metaphor among

---

[69]See n. 34 above. Nonetheless, dissent remains noteworthy. On the one hand, there is the worry
that Sanders and, especially, Wright have overemphasized the theme, filling silences (e.g., Dunn,
"Did Paul Have a Covenant Theology?"). But a more vociferous opposition comes from the
apocalyptic school (Martyn, Gaventa, de Boer, D. A. Campbell, etc.), which generally regards
the christological discontinuity as insufficiently accounted for in the preexisting categories. For
a characteristic dissent, see J. Louis Martyn, "Events in Galatia: Modified Covenantal Nomism
Versus God's Invasion of the Cosmos in the Singular Gospel; A Response to J. D. G. Dunn and
B. R. Gaventa," in *Pauline Theology*, vol. 1, *Thessalonians, Philippians, Galatians, Philemon*, ed.
Jouette M. Bassler (Minneapolis: Fortress, 1994), 168-74.

[70]One is faced with a conundrum to name the position efficiently, nonprejudicially and with
sufficient accuracy. Although it is common to call this the Lutheran view, clearly it extends far
beyond that tradition (Westerholm, *Perspectives Old and New*). Neither is it quite right to call it
the Reformed view since it is not uncommon, e.g., in Anglicanism, in the Wesleyan tradition
and in the non-Reformed Baptist tradition. And the "old perspective" is self-evidently regrettable
unless used (as I do in some cases) with a touch of irony. So I settle for "traditional Protestant
perspective" as the least worst alternative, conceding of course that elements of this exegesis are
found within contemporary Roman Catholic scholarship.

[71]See, e.g., Stendahl, *Paul Among Jews and Gentiles*, 3, 29, 131; James D. G. Dunn, ed., *Paul and
the Mosaic Law*, WUNT 89 (Tübingen: Mohr Siebeck, 1996), 232; Wright, *WSPRS*, 116, 120; idem,
Justification, 23, 116 (UK ed., 7, 96); idem, *P&FG*, 1:490, 2:968-69; and Bruce W. Longenecker,
The Triumph of Abraham's God: The Transformation of Identity in Galatians (Nashville:
Abingdon, 1998), 106. I am here aided by the useful collection of such materials in Westerholm,
Perspectives Old and New, 249-58.

others, but until quite recently, it has not held a prominent place in NPP accounts of Pauline soteriology. By "until quite recently" I am thinking especially of the renewed interest in reconciliation in Wright's recent magnum, about which I will have more to say later.[72] But even here, despite the renewed interest, it is not clear that reconciliation figures in a substantial way in the overall construal of Pauline soteriology. Instead, Wright locates the coordinates of justification in an unrelenting rehearsal of Israel's covenantal story—against such there is no law—but it can sometimes be wondered if he attends to the nearer context with nearly the same attentiveness. As it concerns Paul's soteriology, rather than mining the nearer lexicographical ore, Wright prefers to map the site of the mine by privileging his account of Israel's overarching covenantal narrative. While of course the background of Judaism antecedent to and contemporary with Paul forms the indispensable context, we should give no less attention to Paul's actual use of the language and the webs of verbal and metaphorical context that surround it. What we find—for example in Romans 4 and 5—are webs of collocated language that show "justification" to have especially to do with forgiveness (i.e., the nonreckoning) of sin (Rom 4:6-8), vindication and resurrection (Rom 4:25), peace with God (Rom 5:1; cf. 5:10), reconciliation to God (Rom 5:9-10) and rescue from wrath (Rom 5:9; cf. 1:18; 2:5, 8; 3:5; 4:15; 12:9), with justification as the first, proleptic installment of ultimate salvation (Rom 5:9; cf. 10:10; 13:11).[73] Yes, it is true that we do not want to make the error of

---

[72]See below, chap. 7, "Excursus: Reconciliation in Paul and the Faithfulness of God."

[73]One of several reasons for doubting the temporally bifurcated view of justification required by Wright's exegesis is that Paul characteristically uses δικαιόω in past-referring ways (Rom 3:4; 4:2; 5:1, 9; 6:7; 8:30; 1 Cor 4:4; 6:11; Gal 2:16, 17; 3:24; Tit 3:7), while future-tense uses are limited to four: Romans 2:13; 3:20, 30; Galatians 2:16. Of these four, Romans 3:20 and Galatians 2:16 are both quotations of Psalm 143:2 (142:2 LXX), where justification is clearly an inherited, default eschatological notion. Romans 3:30 is arguably a logical rather than temporal future, leaving only Romans 2:13 as the sole future-referring reference to justification in the Pauline corpus. If this text refers to the soteriological situation independent of Christ—that is, righteous Gentiles as a foil to faltering Jews—then it belongs to a category not unlike Psalm 142:2 LXX (Rom 3:20; Gal 2:16), a default reference to the Jewish eschatological assize rather than its Christian reinterpretation. Of course, Wright and numerous others are not at all persuaded by this account. The "righteous Gentile" of Romans 2 is not a pagan following general revelation and leading a successful moral life but rather a Spirit-endowed follower of Christ who by transformation comes to fulfill the law's righteous demands. I am not persuaded that this does justice to Paul's argument, his whole reason for appealing to the righteous Gentile in the first place, viz., that virtuous Gentiles who seek immortality and persist in well-doing only show Jewish failure to be all the more culpable.

collapsing all soteriological language into one amorphous, indistinct gener-
ality, but in prizing uniquely the covenantal category as he does, Wright
makes less of the textual cognates and corollaries to justification than he
might have. While we find in Wright's definition of justification nothing
ultimately missing, there is throughout a choice of accentuation, a prioriti-
zation of covenant as the *cantus firmus* that not infrequently imposes itself
into the foreground when it is perhaps a more fitting background.

Surely behind this emphasis on covenant membership is the proper attention the NPP gives to the integration of Gentiles into the covenant people.
Rightly, it is understood that this concrete question evolving in the vicissitudes of mission and community presses upon Paul an articulation of a
gospel in which Christ rather than Torah observance becomes the definition
of the new covenant community. I part company with NPP articulations
simply on this point: whereas I understand Paul's logic ultimately to move
from the vertical to the horizontal, Wright especially describes a movement
from horizontal to vertical. It cannot be said that the forgiveness of sins and
reconciliation to God are merely incidental to Wright or other NPP scholars,
but they are concomitants of covenant inclusion.[74] But, to the contrary, at

---

Meanwhile, as we will see in chap. 7, as it concerns the future vindication of those in Christ,
Paul's language moves decidedly toward σῴζω/σωτηρία. Clearly, in Romans 5:9-10, the future-
tense uses of σῴζω point to an eschatological completion of what is begun in justification (see
also Rom 13:11; 1 Cor 3:15; Phil 1:19, 28; 1 Thess 5:8-9; cf. 1 Tim 2:15; 2 Tim 2:10; 4:18). Paul has
actually no use for justification vocabulary to refer directly to the eschatological assize, save for
the above-mentioned inherited Jewish construct. For the Christian eschatological future, he
prefers and reserves the vocabulary of σῴζω/σωτηρία.

[74]Wright acknowledges that a corollary of justification as the declaration of covenant membership
is the forgiveness of sins, and over time he has become increasingly clear that for him these
belong together (cf. now Wright, *P&FG*, 2:943, 955, 1029-32 and passim). Even over against those
who have stressed justification as the inclusion of Jew and Gentile into a single family of God
over against forgiveness (e.g., Wright himself?), Wright now maintains that the two—covenant
membership and forgiveness—are indissoluble:

I freely grant that some of those who have highlighted the importance of the Jew-plus-
Gentile point in Paul have used it as a way of saying that Paul is therefore not, after all,
interested in God's dealing with sins and putting sinners in a right relation to himself. But
the fact that people draw false inferences one way is no reason we should draw them the
other way. (Wright, "New Perspectives on Paul," 259)

Justification, to offer a fuller statement, is the recognition and declaration by God that
those who are thus called and believing are in fact his people, the single family promised
to Abraham, that as the new covenant people *their sins are forgiven*. (Wright, "Letter to
the Galatians," 235, emphasis added)

What, then, is this vindication, this *dikaiōsis*? It is God's declaration that a person is in the
right—that is, (a) that *the person's sins have been forgiven* and (b) that he or she is part of

least by the writing of Romans, Paul's solution to the dilemma of Gentile inclusion into the covenant consists of starting fresh with *both* Jew and Gentile, as equally culpable before God and identically justified *by* God—and thus reconciled *to* God—on the basis of faith.

It is heartening in this regard to follow Wright's treatment of Ephesians 2 in *Justification: God's Plan and Paul's Vision*, where I take him to be saying nearly the same thing.[75] There Ephesians 2:1-10 describes the reconciliation of sinners to God by grace, through faith, apart from works (which Wright acknowledges as tantamount to the "old perspective"), and Ephesians 2:11-22 the reconciliation of Jew and Gentile into one body (not unlike the emphases of the "new perspective"), becoming one family by sharing the same ground of redemption and the same access to the God the Father through Christ: "We have come together: as Jew and Gentile were brought to the same point of helpless guilt, so together they have been raised to glorious heights in Christ."[76] This is Paul's logic as it concerns the full inclusion of Gentiles: equally culpable and helpless, both Jew and Gentile are restored to God in like manner (by faith apart from law) and are thus made into one new family. I maintain that this same logic, unmistakable in Ephesians, is already explicit in Romans, and then reiterated finally in 1 Timothy and Titus, the logic of Paul's theology of justification: the making of the two into one covenant family through a shared and singular reconciliation to one Father.[77]

1.3 CONCLUSIONS

I don't suggest that the preceding even begins to do justice to the whole landscape of the NPP nor especially to the scholars whose nuanced perspectives are only partially accounted for and then only briefly. Attentive readers

---

the single covenant family promised to Abraham. (Wright, "New Perspectives on Paul," 260, emphasis added; cf. 258-59, 264)

[75]Wright, *Justification*, 168-75 (UK ed., 144-51). I treat the same passage in the next chapter, where, though fundamentally in agreement with Wright, I argue that even the both/and (Eph 2:1-10 = TPP; Eph 2:11-22 = NPP) Wright advocates amounts to an oversimplification.

[76]Ibid., 169, there with respect to Ephesians 2:7 specifically.

[77]On this point, again Wright agrees: "Much of Paul's ministry is about 'reconciliation' between different people and groups. That was what he was doing with Philemon and Onesimus. But all of that is rooted in the ultimate 'reconciliation' which God himself has effected in the death of his son" (Wright, *P&FG*, 2:888). My difference with Wright concerns emphasis; to my reading, this theme of reconciliation of peoples by means of reconciliation to God is prominent in Paul's logic and comparatively muted in Wright.

will notice that each of the themes attaches not exclusively but particularly to certain architectural figures: Stendahl on Paul's conversion, Sanders on Second Temple soteriology, Dunn on the motivations for Torah observance and Wright on the centrality of covenant. Yet, with a bit of effort, it would be possible to show that each of these figures, among others, has reiterated all four themes, or nearly so. It is worth stressing again both the diversity of viewpoints, especially in matters of detail, and also the cumulative nature of what has become the NPP: how, for example, Stendahl anticipated several of the major themes while leaving a vacuum that Sanders filled in spades with historical detail, or how Dunn embraced Sanders's account in broad strokes but added to covenantal nomism the missing dimension of what we might call "resistance nomism,"[78] in the attempt to make better sense of Paul's polemic against "works of the law"; or how Wright embraces Sanders's covenantal nomism, vigorously expands Dunn's sociopolitical account of Judaism,[79] and, not uniquely but emphatically, insists that the variegated factions we call "Judaism" are best integrated less by a common theology or pattern of religion than by means of their shared covenantal story, a story that found its first-century participants still inhabiting the exile.[80] If we are to speak coherently of the NPP, it can only be of this diverse network of cumulative insight.

---

[78]Dunn's acceptance of Sanders's paradigm is noted from the beginning in Dunn, "New Perspective on Paul." "Resistance nomism" is my coinage, meant as (unauthorized) shorthand for Dunn's account of "works of the law."

[79]Broadly speaking, Wright follows Sanders's and Dunn's more seminal insights. Having summarized Sanders's account of Jewish soteriology, he concludes: "This is Sanders' thesis, and, despite some criticisms that have been launched, it seems to me thus far completely correct as a description of first-century Judaism" (Wright, *NTPG*, 334-35).

[80]Indeed, having announced and described the motif in some detail in *NTPG*, Wright reprises the argument at some length and with considerable vigor over against his detractors in *P&FG*. As Wright freely acknowledges, the pioneering work in this regard is Hays, *Faith of Jesus Christ*. Hays's paradigm launched a further, largely structuralist, reflection on the narrative dynamics of Paul's letters, including Bruce W. Longenecker, ed., *Narrative Dynamics in Paul: A Critical Assessment* (Louisville, KY: Westminster John Knox, 2002); and Ben Witherington III, *Paul's Narrative Thought World: The Tapestry of Tragedy and Triumph* (Louisville, KY: Westminster John Knox, 1994). Sharing Wright's commitment to the exile motif is James M. Scott, "Exile and the Self-Understanding of Diaspora Jews in the Greco-Roman Period," in *Exile: Old Testament, Jewish, and Christian Conceptions*, ed. James M. Scott, Supplements to the Journal for the Study of Judaism 56 (Leiden: Brill, 1997), 173-218. For a useful and ultimately supportive critique of Wright's earlier iterations, see Craig A. Evans, "Jesus and the Continuing Exile of Israel," in *Jesus and the Restoration of Israel: A Critical Assessment of N. T. Wright's "Jesus and the Victory of God,"* ed. Carey C. Newman (Downers Grove, IL: InterVarsity Press, 1999), 77-100.

The point of the above survey is to say that not only was the NPP's revolution justified on the ground of the evidence, but also its primary insights have a staying power as constructive correctives. At the same time, each of the leading tenets has elements of overcorrection or rhetorical overreach such that a wholesale or unqualified endorsement of the paradigm is not quite possible. With a growing number of Paul's students, I am inclined to say that the way forward is not in defending the more unyielding versions of the NPP but with Paul himself to say, as he did frequently, "Yes . . . but . . ." Yes, not that kind of conversion, but still a kind of conversion. Yes, the default interpretation of Jewish soteriology understood on its own terms cannot be an anxious merit theology, but the apologetic correction of that error must not valorize a diversity-flattening alternative. Yes, the sociopolitical, boundary-marking dynamic of Torah observance is fundamental to understanding Paul's polemic against "works of the law," but it is not the whole of Paul's critique. Yes, there can be little question that Paul is immersed in covenantal categories and that too many previous accounts of Paul's theology have erred by their exclusively "vertical" individualizing, but is the NPP itself not in danger of missing Paul's own definitions of terms?

As we will see, the "yes . . . but . . ."—or should we say, "almost . . . but not quite . . ."?—character of the NPP is further confirmed in close readings of certain Pauline texts, texts upon which the NPP shed considerable light but which, at the same time, exercise a certain resistance to the paradigm. To a set of such illustrative texts we turn next.

2

THE UNCOOPERATIVE PAUL

There could be several ways to account for the protracted, three-decade-long debate stirred by the NPP. The most ready explanation is stubbornness. Faced with this new paradigm, defenders of the traditional Protestant rendering of Pauline theology have just dug in to the foxhole, settling into comfortable acquired ways of reading Paul in which the theological superstructure now functions as buttress instead. Or perhaps the fault is with the purveyors of the NPP. Though confronted repeatedly with critiques and creditable rebuttals, inflamed with revisionist zeal, the allure of the novel or the shame of backtracking deter them from repentance. Even if there were some truth to either caricature, these accounts are unlikely, not to mention uncharitable. While it is tempting, and in some cases probably justified, to detect an aversion to the NPP with roots in a particular Christian confessional stance or to attribute advocacy to certain cultural trends,[1] such dismissals are too facile. Of course, Christian interpreters bring certain theological sensibilities to the text, and there is no completely escaping the reader's cultural context, but in the end it is the *texts* with which we must contend. And if this protracted debate sometimes frustrates for its partisan character, it remains a discussion about Pauline texts—or we can hope so, anyway. That is all to say that the problem actually lies with *Paul*. He is intractable. Paul inspires then resists both paradigms, refusing to cooperate exclusively with either.[2]

---

[1]E.g., the reevaluation of Judaism as necesssary Christian repentance for the horror of the Holocaust, or the NPP's recovery of a gospel of peace for a world wracked with enmity and ethnic violence.
[2]I don't pretend that this is a new insight, and in fact the claiming of some middle ground is now

The premise of this study is that, even as traditional readings of Paul leave too much unaccounted for, the NPP genuinely illumines numerous Pauline texts while others remain uncooperative. And, in fact, sometimes they are the very same texts! To a small, illustrative sampling we now turn, a handful of interpretive cruxes. These representative texts have been chosen as heuristics to illustrate the insufficiency of each paradigm, left to itself, to account for the whole of what Paul actually says. There is no attempt here to offer an exhaustive exegesis of any passage, and to some of these texts we will return in due course. Rather, I hope to demonstrate that texts that both paradigms have claimed for themselves actually need to be shared, and once shared, call into question the exclusive rights of both paradigms. It goes without saying that none of what follows is hidden from the advocates of either camp, and in every case an exegesis, or several, has been offered of the texts under discussion that is found satisfactory either to NPP proponents or its critics. Commendably, certain scholars have shown themselves deft at working the insights of the alternative paradigm into their exegesis. But in what follows, I'm suggesting that the paradigms themselves remain too deeply entrenched and that obedience toward one or the other may in fact result in a negligence of Paul.

2.1 PHILIPPIANS 3:1-11

Philippians might seem a strange place to begin, since for the most part the NPP has been erected and defended on the turf of Galatians and Romans. Yet the first half of Philippians 3 remains contested territory and a signal test case in competing accounts of the apostle's vision. This is so because in this impassioned autobiography, Paul's interpreters—both advocates and critics of the NPP—have found material on which to ground their cause. There is

---

something of a trend. Increasingly, Pauline scholars are arriving at this sort of moderating conclusion. We see it in the various adjustments made by Dunn along the way (disarmingly summarized in James D. G. Dunn, "The New Perspective: Whence, What and Whither?," in *NPerP*, 1-97). It is evident in the increasingly "both/and" rhetoric of N. T. Wright, *Paul and the Faithfulness of God*, Christian Origins and the Question of God (Minneapolis: Fortress, 2013). Similar moderation appears in Francis Watson's apparent volte-face from (or at least reframing of) earlier positions. (See Francis Watson, *Paul, Judaism, and the Gentiles: Beyond the New Perspective*, 2nd ed. [Grand Rapids: Eerdmans, 2007], 1-26; and idem, "Not the New Perspective," an unpublished paper presented to the British New Testament Conference, Manchester, September 2001 [no longer available online].)

something, as it were, for everyone here. And if we were scoring at home, we might say that Philippians 3:1-6 gives an edge to the NPP, while Philippians 3:7-11 is something of a bulwark for more traditional interpretations of Paul.[3] But even that proves too simplistic, as we will see.

We begin by noting features of the text that have proven amenable to the NPP. Although Paul uses neither the verb "to justify" nor the rarer cognate noun here, whatever else this is, it is at least a discourse on justification, which is not to say a narrowly forensic account of salvation. The argument climaxes in the announcement of a "righteousness" (*dikaiosynēn*) "from God" (*ek theou*) "on the basis of faith" (*epi tē pistei*) over against a "righteousness from the law" (*dikaiosynēn tēn ek nomou*) (Phil 3:9). As such, this is unmistakably an account of the substance of justification with all of its characteristic elements: righteousness apart from law on the ground of faith. Notably, as with Galatians, the larger context indicates that Paul's account of justification by faith serves a polemical interest as the theological ground of his warning against the threat of a "circumcision party"—those "dogs," "evil workers" and "mutilators" (Phil 3:2).[4] To note that Paul's recourse to justification by faith is here elicited by a concern parallel to that of Galatians is not necessarily to consign justification to the secondary status of an ad hoc polemical doctrine, but it remains significant that justification is appealed to so frequently, perhaps even exclusively, in the context of Jew-Gentile relationships in the church and disagreement over law observance.[5]

---

[3]Dunn is correct to note the relative lack of attention given Philippians 3 in the NPP debates and quite rightly regrets the missed opportunity for "rapprochement between old and new perspectives" (James D. G. Dunn, "Philippians 3.2-14 and the New Perspective on Paul," in *NPerP*, 469; cf. N. T. Wright, *P&FG*, 2:985). At the same time, Dunn himself is implicated in the neglect. It is a point of some interest that Dunn himself would write so prolifically from the vantage point of the NPP and only so late give Philippians 3:2-11 a thorough treatment. The essay is a model of balance, and one wonders how the NPP might have developed were Philippians 3 given more attention and earlier. The same can be said for the briefer treatment of this text now in *P&FG*, 2:984-92.

[4]Paul's strong language notwithstanding, it does not appear that a circumcision party is necessarily at hand or among the Philippian recipients. It seems unlikely (assuming the literary unity of the letter) that Paul would have delayed his warning to this point in the letter and without any anticipatory signals were he to regard the threat as present or imminent. More likely, the text bears witness to an enduring opposition to Paul encountered throughout his missionary career, a topic already raised with the Philippians ("to write *the same things* to you," Phil 3:1, emphasis added). So, e.g., Gordon D. Fee, *Paul's Letter to the Philippians*, NICNT (Grand Rapids: Eerdmans, 1995), 289-93.

[5]Noted also by Dunn, "Philippians 3.2-14," 473.

Second, in what constitutes a pillar of the NPP, Paul exudes only confidence and betrays no anxiety in his self-description of his preconverted life in Philippians 3:4-6. There is status and accomplishment both, but no striving of the sort one could have expected from an allegedly meritocratic Jew who had been driven to psychological crisis in his failed attempt to keep the Mosaic law. Instead, we find a swaggering confidence as Paul describes his impeccable heritable Jewish credentials ("circumcised the eighth day," "of the nation of Israel, of the tribe of Benjamin"), on the one hand, and his resolute fidelity to Torah ("a Hebrew of Hebrews; as to the law, a Pharisee; as to zeal, a persecutor of the church; as to righteousness under the law, blameless"), on the other.[6] With respect to a righteousness defined by Torah observance, Paul could describe himself as one who "had become blameless" (*genomenos amemptos*).[7] Scholars of the NPP—for that matter, the vast majority of Pauline scholars of all stripes—discern from this record that Paul's conversion, whatever we make of his subsequent theology, was not in the first instance catalyzed by a gospel of grace that liberated an anxious Paul from the oppressive demands of the law. Again, this does not mean that Paul could not have subsequently construed his account of the gospel so as to identify, or even elicit, and ameliorate that anxiety in others, but this text offers no autobiographical basis for such a rhetorical key change.

Although the "boast" of Philippians 3:4-6 could be, and *has* been, read as evidence for Jewish pride of achievement, NPP scholars are understandably inclined to refute that suggestion. Sanders is predictably eager to absolve Paul of the boast of self-righteousness, as though that had characterized his former Jewish experience. No, Paul's former righteousness by means of Torah observance was a genuine righteousness: not a faux self-righteousness, but rather "the righteousness which comes by law, which is therefore the peculiar result of being an observant Jew, which is *in and of itself a good thing*."[8] For Sanders, Paul had no choice but to deduce the superiority of Christ's offer of righteousness and thus to relegate his Jewish past and Torah observance to an inferior

---

[6]With many, I take "a Hebrew of Hebrews" to be essentially a cultural claim, Paul distinguishing his mode of Judaism as "pure," unsullied by Hellenistic cultural incursions.
[7]The aorist participle γενόμενος (from γίνομαι, "be," "become") is typically left untranslated, but it may be that Paul wishes to describe his "blameless" status with respect to the law as a learned obedience.
[8]E. P. Sanders, *Paul, the Law, and the Jewish People* (Philadelphia: Fortress, 1983), 44-45, emphasis original.

epoch, but Sanders insists Paul's rhetorical gesture must not be misread.[9] The fault of Paul's former righteousness is not that it was *self*-righteousness but that it was not a righteousness by faith *through Christ*—and this is the singular "fault" of nomistic righteousness, according to Sanders.

Likewise, Dunn is eager to soften Paul's polemics: "The sharpness of the contrast is not so much to denigrate what he had previously counted as gain, as to enhance to the highest degree the value he now attributes to Christ, to the knowledge of Christ, and to the prospect of gaining Christ."[10] Driving this, it seems, is an earnest desire to defend the boast of Philippians 3:4-6 from the charge of Paul's "former righteousness as something earned or achieved," "a moralistic or self-help righteousness," and to be relieved of the charge of supersessionism.[11] Instead, Dunn finds a fundamental continuity amidst Paul's largely contrastive argument, not least because Paul insists on using circumcision, albeit radically redefined ("who worship in the Spirit of God and boast in Christ Jesus and have no confidence in the flesh," Phil 3:3 NRSV), as the marker of true covenant belonging for his presumably majority Gentile audience. Thus, as Dunn sees it, the perdurance of that Jewish, covenantal category betrays its importance among Paul's core convictions.

As we would expect, Wright also stresses the covenantal dimensions of the self-description, understanding Paul's protestation that he was "blameless" in relationship to covenant membership:

> The listing of circumcision, race, tribe, descent, sect (i.e. Pharisee) and zeal
> are none of them about "moral achievement." Together they strongly suggest

---

[9]According to Sanders,

> Just as what is wrong with the law is that it is not Christ, so what is wrong with "righteousness based on the law" (Phil. 3:9) is that it is not *the* righteousness from God which depends on faith, which is received when one is "found in Christ," shares his suffering and is placed among those who will share his resurrection. That is, "righteousness" itself is a different righteousness. It is, in effect, the salvation which comes from belonging to Christ and that alone. Thus Paul does not differ only on the means. Means and end correspond. The *real* righteousness is being saved by Christ, and it comes only through faith. This implies, again, that it is not the activity of doing the law which is wrong as an activity. Rather, such a means leads to the wrong end (righteousness based on the law); and the end itself is wrong, since it is not salvation in Christ. (*P&PJ*, 551)

Sanders's famous sardonic summary of Paul and Judaism concludes this section: "In short, *this is what Paul finds wrong in Judaism: it is not Christianity*" (*P&PJ*, 552, emphasis original).

[10]Dunn, "Philippians 3.2-14," 481, emphasis original. The same concerns animate Wright's account of the passage (*P&FG*, 2:984-92).

[11]Dunn, "Philippians 3.2-14," 483.

that his claim to have been "blameless" in relation to "righteousness under the law" was not about "amassing merits and achievement," either. It was a matter of *demonstrating*, through Torah-practice, one's covenant membership as per the previous six categories.[12]

While the NPP does not find ground either for Jewish merit or for soteriological anxiety in Paul's Philippians boast, the text evinces a deep-seated sense of national privilege rooted in the exclusivity of the covenant. Paul's former confidence settles upon the election of a covenant people—circumcision, tribal lineage and cultural identity being signs of that favored status, marking Paul as a Jew literally par excellence. But for all that, the text bears witness to Paul as a Jew of standing, not of straining. Whatever pride or even attainment we might find here is not that of meritocratic self-righteousness but of zeal for the covenant.[13] Thus, Philippians 3:2-6 is sort of exhibit A of NPP axioms: the soteriologically confident Jewish Paul, secure in his covenantal standing, boasting (albeit retrospectively) in all its trappings, launching a discourse on righteousness by faith triggered by the threat of a Jewish-Christian particularism that in practice threatens the full inclusion of Gentiles as children of Abraham. It's all there.

Philippians 3, then, would seem to be a foothold in the Pauline corpus whence the NPP disabuses readers of certain convenient but dubious inferences: (1) That the Pauline biography forecasts certain versions of a later Christian kerygma—guilt and anxiety exacerbated by law and relieved by a gracious (i.e., works-free) gospel—has been in retreat for nearly a half century since the publication of Krister Stendahl's famous essay,[14] and, save for a stray counterpoint here or there, is now rejected by almost all Pauline scholars and of all stripes.[15] (2) Proving more durable, however, is the claim that Paul's pre-Damascus, Torah-confident boast points to a meritocratic soteriology, a burden under which not only Paul but all of devout Judaism

---

[12]Wright, *P&FG*, 2:988-89, emphasis original.

[13]A point Wright repeats with frequency (*P&FG*, 2:984-89). E.g., "Throughout this whole passage, the question at issue is not 'how might I earn God's favour?,' but 'what are the signs that I am a member of God's people?'" (ibid., 2:987; cf. 2:984).

[14]Krister Stendahl, "The Apostle Paul and the Introspective Conscience of the West," *HTR* 56 (1963): 199-215 (from a lecture given a year earlier); reprinted in Stendahl, *Paul Among Jews and Gentiles, and Other Essays* (Philadelphia: Fortress, 1976).

[15]Cf. Hawthorne's claim that the view is "now universally rejected" (Gerald F. Hawthorne and Ralph P. Martin, *Philippians*, rev. ed., WBC 43 [Nashville: Nelson, 2004], 187).

labored. Even otherwise careful Pauline scholars seem inclined to find in Philippians 3 what they expect to be there. Curiously, for example, Moisés Silva, after rightly insisting that "when the apostle speaks about the law [in Phil 3:5-6], he has in mind not the law in a historical vacuum but rather the law as it was understood and used in first-century Judaism," goes on to cite Calvin approvingly: "Paul uses the word 'law' loosely for the teaching of religion, *however much corrupted it was at that time, as Christianity is today in the Papacy.*"[16] To be sure, Silva offers a caveat, albeit faint ("Calvin goes *so far as to say* . . . without drawing the distinction *that sharply*"), but nonetheless the analogy of Second Temple Judaism to a presumably legalistic medieval Catholicism stands with implied approbation, to say nothing of Calvin's unlikely claim about Paul's use of "law," which is actually opposite of Silva's.[17] Although, as we will see, Paul does indirectly cast aspersions on his former nomistic righteousness, it is not because he regarded Judaism as a religion of merit. Markus Bockmuehl, whose comment on the soteriological import of the passage is more nuanced, is careful to negate a false inference with respect to Judaism more generally: "One must not of course extrapolate from Paul's high pre-Christian view of his achievements to clichés about the legalistic self-righteousness of Judaism in general." Instead, Bockmuehl follows a line of analysis consistent with the NPP. Paul had not been mistaken to "excel" in a righteousness in the law, but he "rejected the Jewish *nationalism* of his 'earlier life' (Gal. 1:13-14) precisely because in his encounter with Christ he discovered that the way of *narrow national exclusiveness* is not the one that God has chosen in Christ—and, perhaps, that the example of Abraham (Rom. 4; Gal. 3) shows this to have been God's intention all along." Yet this is not the whole of Paul's reason for dissent from his former righteousness, according to Bockmuehl. It is not just that Paul's former

---

[16]Moisés Silva, *Philippians*, 2nd ed., BECNT (Grand Rapids: Baker Academic, 2005), 152, emphasis added.

[17]More cautiously, Gordon Fee notes and affirms the sea change brought on by Sanders and Dunn, but nonetheless avers that the "ultimate theological consequences" of a capitulation to the circumcision party amounts to "adding a plus factor to grace, and thus of eliminating grace altogether by exchanging it for boasting in 'one's flesh'" (*Paul's Letter to the Philippians*, 297n50). Similarly Ralph Martin, in a friendly amendment to the first edition of Gerald Hawthorne's commentary, maintains that Paul's self-assessment of "blamelessness," precisely *because* it engenders such a boast, ultimately stands over against "God's gift . . . received in the pure gratitude of faith" (Hawthorne and Martin, *Philippians*, 187-88).

"righteousness" was "nationally appropriated," but also that it was "externally measured," and it is found wanting in comparison to a righteousness of a different "nature," a righteousness "granted and sustained by God."[18]

Rightly understood, Philippians 3:2-6 not only proves amenable to the NPP but even substantiates several of its cardinal insights. We should now judge it tendentious to so read Paul's boastful litany either as a smokescreen for a more primal pre-Christian anxiety or as a witness to a soteriology of merit, as though Paul (or Judaism, for that matter) had attempted to gain salvation on the merit of Torah observance. In this regard, we should say that while Philippians 3:2-6 gives ample evidence of Paul's former *nomism*, devotion to God expressed in fidelity to the stipulations of the law, taken on its own terms, this description does not substantiate the charge of *legalism*. Thus, certain attempts to cling to TPP premises with regard to Philippians 3:2-6, even in light of the NPP, are unconvincing.

Yet, if with respect to Philippians 3:2-6 we find the NPP largely vindicated or even confirmed, this is not the whole story. There are signs in the larger context that Paul's strong denunciation of his Jewish credentials is animated by more than what NPP scholars acknowledged, whose accounts of this passage, though true as far as they go, are ultimately more tepid than Paul's. As far as they go, it is hard to find fault with the NPP apologetic accounts of Paul's former righteousness that situate it sympathetically within Paul's Jewish worldview. But it remains the case that Paul himself ultimately disparaged (*zēmian, skybala*) the same righteousness that NPP scholars rehabilitate. The question remains: Why? And to what extent does that disclaiming of his former righteousness in the law count as a damning judgment against it?

It is not necessary to regard Paul's former righteousness as so much vaunted "self-righteousness" to appreciate the degree to which Paul would come to regard it as an insufficient righteousness. For example, by the time Paul claims in the sixth descriptor "as to zeal, a persecutor of the church," it is evident that there is something askew, even nefarious, in his former "righteousness," such that were Paul availed of modern typography, he might well have used the scare quotes I just have. To be sure, from the frame of reference

---

[18]Markus N. A. Bockmuehl, *The Epistle to the Philippians*, BNTC 11 (Peabody, MA: Hendrickson, 1998), 202.

in which zeal for the law counted as a *summum bonum*, Paul's persecution of the church can only be regarded with admiration, and this is precisely its contribution to Paul's argument.

Tied up as we are with *our* theological questions, it is easy to underplay Paul's rhetorical ends, the recognition of which breaks loose the TPP and NPP impasse. While the former is in search of the dilemma from which Paul was saved (and sure to have found it), the latter is highlighting Paul's continuity with Judaism. Nonetheless, in each case there is a subtle distortion of the intended contribution of Paul's self-description to the larger argument. All must acknowledge that this rhetorically charged account has no stake in questions that have preoccupied recent interpretation of Paul—his Jewish self-understanding, the nature of his conversion, his relationship to the law and so on. Rather, Paul's entire purpose is to flaunt his impeccable Jewish credentials and his supererogatory Torah zeal as a preemptive strike against opponents who would impose Torah on Gentile converts. After all, by such criteria Paul had everything in his favor; if it were about self-advantage, he above all should have been on the side of impelling Torah-observance—as indeed he once was, rather more as an enforcer than a missionary, for that matter. Thus, Paul's testimony is calculated to devastate at the root any such thought that he resists the claims of a circumcision party as if there were some deficiency in his own credentials. Of course, it is fair game to engage the text with the sorts of questions of which it is oblivious—that is, as long as we're quite aware of what we are doing and sensitive to the sorts of distortions that might be entailed.

In this case, all the evidence suggests that Paul now regards his former righteousness not merely as "former" but as intrinsically defective. This, of course, does not mean that he had viewed it so previously. And it certainly does not mean that the chief flaw of his "righteousness in the law" was that the law made impossible demands that drove Paul to despair. It does mean that if we are to identify the defect of Paul's former righteousness, it is necessary to do so in relationship to Philippians 3:7-11, where Paul turns from his Jewish heritage to his identity in Christ: "Yet whatever gains I had, these I have come to regard as loss because of Christ" (NRSV). It is recognized that the metaphor here is financial, "gains" (*kerdē*) as credits and "loss" (*zēmian*) as debit, and not only debit, but in language more raw, as so much "garbage" (*skybala*). This brash revaluation of Paul's impeccable Jewish credentials is well known and rhetorically powerful.[19]

If some have overread Paul's dramatic contrast in Philippians 3 by characterizing Paul's Jewish boast as so much vainglorious autosoterism, it appears that NPP scholars are in danger of underreading it. There is, after all, a deliberate contrast drawn between "a righteousness in the law" (Phil 3:6, *dikaiosynēn tēn en nomō*) or, as he later puts it, "my righteousness derived from the law" (Phil 3:9, *emēn dikaiosynēn tēn ek nomou*) and "that righteousness which is through the faith of/in Christ, the righteousness which is from God on the basis of faith" (Phil 3:9, *tēn dia pisteōs Christou, tēn ek theou dikaiosynēn epi tē pistei*).[20] In fact, although there is every reason to

[19]In light of this bold dismissal of Paul's former righteousness, Moisés Silva goes so far as to see Paul engaged in a "mock boast" calculated as an opportunity to expound his gospel as a matter of contrast (*Philippians*, 150-51). If by "mock boast" we mean insincere or untrue, then Silva cannot be followed. If "mock boast" means rhetorically preparatory, the point stands, but even here it can be wondered if Silva's Reformed gospel is not imposing itself. In other words, it is right to recognize the rhetorical force of the boast but mistaken to assume that the circumcision threat is but a convenient cipher for Paul's actual concern.
[20]The almost poetic passage invites and then frustrates efforts to conform it to a neat structural pattern. The indisputable element is that ἀλλά ("but") marks the contrast between the two kinds of righteousness. Beyond that, the parallels suggest different, equally plausible, possibilities.
The repetition of δικαιοσύνη invites a chiastic arrangement (see the first column in table 2.1) in which A and A′ are contrasting *sources* of righteousness ("my" over against a "from-God" righteousness). Then B and B′ follow suit, as opposing attributive (τήν) prepositional phrases, contrasting alternative *means* of righteousness.

Table 2.1. Analysis of Philippians 3:6-9

Chiastic Structure	Step Parallelism
μὴ ἔχων	μὴ ἔχων
A ἐμὴν δικαιοσύνην	A ἐμὴν δικαιοσύνην
B τὴν ἐκ νόμου	B τὴν ἐκ νόμου
ἀλλὰ	ἀλλὰ
B′ τὴν διὰ πίστεως Χριστοῦ,	A′ τὴν διὰ πίστεως Χριστοῦ,
A′ τὴν ἐκ θεοῦ δικαιοσύνην ἐπὶ τῇ πίστει	B′ τὴν ἐκ θεοῦ δικαιοσύνην ἐπὶ τῇ πίστει

These contrasts are impressively highlighted, but the arrangement obscures two seemingly significant features of the passage (see the second column in table 2.1): (1) the even more obvious contrast between τὴν ἐκ νόμου and τὴν ἐκ θεοῦ and (2) the third descriptor of τὴν ἐκ θεοῦ righteousness, that is, ἐπὶ τῇ πίστει. This suggests a different possibility: that the primary contrast is between A, "my righteousness," and A′, "the [righteousness] through faith in/of Christ," the former having its source in the law (B, τὴν ἐκ νόμου) and the latter "from God" (B′, τὴν ἐκ θεοῦ). In either case, it becomes clear is that there is a double contrast between AB ↔ B′A′ as wholes: "*my* righteousness derived from the law" as contrasted by "the through faith of [in] Christ/from-God righteousness." And also an inversely parallel relationship among the four elements, such that A and A′ contrast *source*: "*my* righteousness" ↔ "*from-God* righteousness"; and B and B′ contrast *means*: "by means of law" ↔ "by means of faith of [in] Christ."

think Paul's claim to have been "blameless" with respect to a righteousness as defined by the law was a true rather than deluded boast, it was also a decidedly qualified boast. Twice qualified, in fact. In the first place, Paul's Jewish credentials are all cast under the shadow of reasons to boast "*in the flesh*" (*en tē sarki*). Even apart from the counterpoint of Philippians 3:7-11, there is a muted character to this boast. Within a certain realm or with respect to certain measures, Paul possessed an unparalleled résumé. But it is clear not only from the surrounding context but also from Paul's characteristic use of "flesh" (*sarx*) that a boast "in the flesh" amounts to a damning by faint praise.[21] Furthermore, the claim of Philippians 3:6 that Paul was already "blameless" with respect to "righteousness [stipulated] in the law" must be taken as a true claim, but understood so only by giving full weight to the qualification "*in the law*."[22] Yet that "righteousness" can only be understood for what it was by way of contrast to the climactic description of his new-found righteousness—thrice modified: *from* (*ek*) God, *through* (*dia*) faith of/in Christ, *on the ground of* (*epi*) faith (Phil 3:9). Thus, Paul's blamelessness with respect to righteousness as measured by the law in Philippians 3:6 is depicted as true but nonultimate and later redescribed in similar terms as "*my* righteousness *that comes from the law*" (Phil 3:9).[23] By contrast, his new righteousness is an unqualified, ultimate righteousness, in comparison to which his "in the flesh," "in the law" righteousness is, to Paul, less than nothing, even odious.

To their credit, both Dunn and Wright show a sensitivity to these interior dynamics of Philippians 3:1-11. If an apologetic tendency is evident in crediting

---

[21]I don't suggest that Paul is invoking his characteristic anthropological meaning of σάρξ—human beings with regard to their compromised physical aspect characterized by weakness, corruption and rebellion—but rather with respect to the merely "outward side of life" (so BDAG, s.v. σάρξ [5], p. 916), in this case signs of covenantal privilege and fidelity.

[22]The 2011 NIV reads "righteousness . . . that comes from the law," which, while a considerable improvement over unnecessary and prejudicial "legalistic righteousness" of earlier editions, still leaves the impression that Paul is describing the law as the *basis* of his former righteousness rather than as its *measure* or *standard*. While it is true that, later, in Philippians 3:9 Paul will indeed describe the law as the basis or even source of his former righteousness (τὴν ἐκ νόμου), this is not the precise nuance of the claim here, that, as measured by the standard of the law, Paul's was beyond reproach.

[23]The expressions "a righteousness in the law" (Phil 3:6, δικαιοσύνην τὴν ἐν νόμῳ) and "my righteousness derived from the law" (Phil 3:9, ἐμὴν δικαιοσύνην τὴν ἐκ νόμου) are of course different, but they refer to the *same* law-based-and-measured righteousness by means of two different characterizations. So also Dunn, "Philippians 3.2-14," 483.

Paul with more tact than he intended toward his former rank in Judaism, at least it can be said that neither Dunn nor Wright is quite guilty of imposing a full-scale Galatians-like Judaizing controversy onto Paul's argument in Philippians 3:1-11.[24] An NPP scholar *might* have posited that behind the repudiation of Paul's former righteousness was the underlying concern (it would have to be underlying, since the text gives us no direct clue) that in its ethnocentrism or nationalistic pride, Paul's former boast exemplified a de facto, culturally enforced exclusion of Gentile believers in Christ. But, although Philippians 3:2-6 showcases certain salient features of the NPP, the passage as a whole does not lend itself to the sort of argument that animates the NPP with regard to Galatians. There is no suggestion in Philippians 3:7-11 that the deficiency of Paul's former righteousness lay in its practical impairment of Gentiles to enter the covenant, and, though it might have been tempting to argue so, Dunn and Wright are innocent of insinuating any such notion.

This leads to an important observation: all the evidence suggests that Paul is here taking to task the same, or at least very nearly the same, position that he confronted amidst the churches of Galatia; at the same time, his argument is noticeably different. We would get ahead of ourselves to detail those differences and to account for them here, but it must suffice for now to propose that the difference has to do with more than the admittedly different occasions of the two letters. The arguments differ because the substance of Paul's contention with the circumcision party, first captured in his letter to the Galatians, had developed from that early encounter to this later warning to the Philippians.[25]

Before we leave Philippians 3:1-11, there remains one more exegetical issue of considerable consequence, namely, the understanding of the "righteousness from God" (Phil 3:9). Wright is eager to note that the expression here, *tēn ek theou dikaiosynēn*, uniquely in the Pauline corpus, uses the preposition *ek*, indicating that this is "a righteous status *from God* . . . not

---

[24]Dunn comes close when he says, "The implication is fairly obvious that such reliance on ethnic identity carried with it the corollary that Gentiles, 'the uncircumcision' were debarred from the benefits of God's covenant with Israel" (ibid., 490). This is surely a correct observation, but the claim does not play a role in the argument of Philippians 3:1-11, nor does Dunn press the point.
[25]According to my chronology, this sets at least a decade between the writing of the two letters, on which see 4.3, "Chronology: Locating Paul's Letters," below.

God's own righteousness."[26] The observation is central to Wright's larger program of identifying the "righteousness of God" (*dikaiosynē tou theou*, i.e., not *ek [tou] theou*) as the covenant faithfulness of God, that is, not a status that God confers but the virtue of faithfulness proper to God's own character that motivates his powerful intervention on behalf of his people. But Wright's claim is subtle. Most assuredly, he does not deny that "righteousness" is a status that God confers; rather, he observes that the "righteousness of God" (*dikaiosynē tou theou*) is not the Pauline way to describe that reality. Thus, the "righteousnesss of God" (*dikaiosynē tou theou*) is not to be confused with—indeed, it seems to have nothing directly to do with—the "righteousness *from* God" (*ek theou dikaiosynē*). God can "give" righteousness, indeed a righteous status, but in doing so it is not *his* righteousness he gives.

It is, of course, technically correct and proper to distinguish the genitive construction from the prepositional phrase, and there is even a way to think of a righteousness that comes *from* God but that is not properly *God's* righteousness. Nonetheless, it is important to ask if there is more than grammar behind this finely parsed distinction, and it seems that there is. Wright's argument against the source genitive is substantiated in his appeal to the lawcourt metaphor:

> If we use the language of the law-court, it makes no sense whatever to say that the judge imputes, imparts, bequeaths, conveys or otherwise transfers his righteousness to either the plaintiff or the defendant. Righteousness is not an object, a substance or a gas which can be passed across the courtroom. . . . If and when God does act to vindicate his people, his people will then, metaphorically speaking, have the status of "righteousness." . . . But the righteousness they have will not be God's own righteousness. That makes no sense at all.[27]

It is not hard to see that Wright exercises a metaphorical maximalism here, by which the lawcourt serves not only as metaphorical source domain but also as target domain. The metaphor "walks on all fours," one might say. It is further clear that the distinction that Wright insists upon serves the larger interest in protecting his understanding of the *dikaiosynē theou* as

[26]Wright, *WSPRS*, 104. Cf. Wright, *P&FG*, 2:990-91.
[27]Wright, *WPRS*, 98-99. Cf. Wright, *P&FG*, 2:946-47.

"covenant faithfulness." Wright is correct to insist that we should not construe every reference to the "righteousness of God" as a neat subjective genitive: "the righteousness which God gives [unworthy sinners]," as if the phrase must always denote that singular notion. But one wonders if Wright's preventative medicine is too strong for the hypothetical ailment. If, taking a cue from Luther's tower epiphany,[28] confessional Protestantism was mistaken to make the "righteousness of God" always denote the status God imputes to the unrighteous, Wright's cure consists of a similarly rigid exegetical move, only now assigning a different referent—"covenant faithfulness"—to Paul's *dikaiosynē theou.*

In any case, one can at least derive from Philippians 3:9 the following: God does indeed confer or declare a righteousness of which he is the source (cf. Rom 5:17, *tēs dōreas tēs dikaiosynēs*). Furthermore, this righteousness that comes *from* God (*tēn ek theou*) is constrasted with, if not antithetical to, what Paul calls "my righteousness" (*emēn dikaiosynēn*), and the latter was sought by means of the law and the former gained by faith in Christ (or as it may be, the faithfulness of Christ).[29] In any case, the text clearly indicates that God is the source of a saving righteousness that comes into the possession of the one who has faith. While one is sympathetic with the concern that the "righteousness of God" not be taken preemptively in the Lutheran way in all of its occurrences, it is hard to avoid the impression that Wright is kicking against the goads in his resolute distinction between the righteousness *from* God and the righteousness *of* God.[30] The more important point, which all must concede, is that "righteousness" is something that, according to Paul, comes *from* God,

---

[28]The famous passage describing Luther's breakthrough regarding the "righteousness of God" reads as follows:

> I had greatly longed to understand Paul's letter to the Romans, and nothing stood in the way but that one expression "the righteousness of God," because I took it to mean that righteousness whereby God is righteous and acts righteously in punishing the unrighteous. . . . Night and day I pondered until . . . I grasped the truth that the righteousness of God is that righteousness whereby, through grace and sheer mercy he justifies us by faith. Thereupon I felt myself to be reborn and to have gone through open doors into paradise. The whole of Scripture took on a new meaning, and whereas before "the righteousness of God" had filled me with hate, now it became to me inexpressibly sweet in greater love. This passage of Paul became to me a gateway into heaven. (*LW*, 34:336-37)

[29]I introduce and discuss the *pistis Christou* debate in section 3.2.5 below.
[30]The clearer indication that Wright's understanding δικαιοσύνη τοῦ θεοῦ is preemptively rigid is found in his treatment of 2 Corinthians 5:21, on which see section 3.2.3, n. 92.

indeed, that it can elsewhere even be described as a *gift* of God (Rom 5:17, "the gift of righteousness").[31] This does not require that the prepositionless genitive elsewhere be taken as the equivalent of *ek tou theou*, but neither does it exclude the possibility that the genitive alone can elsewhere indicate source.

The point of the foregoing is singular: Philippians 3:2-11 underwrites both paradigms while failing to be fully cooperative with either. Certain facile TPP assumptions are exposed by Paul's actual testimony; the NPP apologia stumbles differently but over the same testimony; and, by privileging certain theological concerns, both accounts are in danger of eliding the actual rhetorical function of Paul's boast and relativizing of his former status.

2.2 ROMANS 3:21-4:8

In one sense the whole of Romans could be put to the test of the current exercise, that is, to see how perspectives old and new do justice to the texts themselves.[32] For the sake of illustration, we will consider only one crucial and instructive passage from Romans, chosen because of the way themes and emphases of both the NPP and TPP are found juxtaposed, one might even say entangled, in Romans 3:21-4:8.[33]

Here we are in the wheelhouse of the traditional Protestant (TPP) understanding of Paul, where a complex of the key tenets is held together in what

---

[31]Greek: τῆς δωρεᾶς τῆς δικαιοσύνης. There are a few lexical or grammatical fine points here: (1) the common translation of δωρεά as "free gift" is redundant in English, and the infelicity is not justified from the Greek (Paul is frequently guilty of pleonasm, but not here). (2) Rather than functioning as a second object (with "abundance of grace"), the genitive τῆς δωρεᾶς modifies τὴν περισσείαν ("the abundance")—"the abundance of the gift of righteousness," which is important to note, if difficult to convey in idiomatic English. (3) Almost surely τῆς δικαιοσύνης should be taken as an epexegetic genitive, i.e., "the gift *that consists* of righteousness."

[32]Another especially useful test case would be Romans 9:30-10:10 (or so), as it typically marks a strong divide between TPP and NPP scholars, each thinking that it speaks to their position with some clarity. It would be useful in this regard to compare the Romans commentaries of, say, James D. G. Dunn (*Romans*, 2 vols., WBC 38 [Dallas: Word, 1988]) and N. T. Wright ("Letter to the Romans: Introduction, Commentary and Reflections," in *NIB*, 10:393-770) with those of, say, Douglas J. Moo (*The Epistle to the Romans*, NICNT [Grand Rapids: Eerdmans, 1996]) and Thomas R. Schreiner (*Romans*, BECNT [Grand Rapids: Baker Academic, 1998]).

[33]I don't suggest that Romans 3:21-4:8 comprises in itself a natural unit; it is chosen here for heuristic convenience. With most scholars, I would understand this section to comprise three paragraphs (Rom 3:21-26, 27-31; 4:1-8) and to be part of the larger subsection of Romans 3:21-4:25. So, e.g., Moo, *Epistle to the Romans*, 245. Moo helpfully notes the anticipation of Romans 4:1-25 in 3:27-31 (see table 2.2).

seems to be a secure stronghold.[34] Not only so, the TPP view finds in this same text places where the NPP seems inevitably to stumble. The details being many and subtle, it will have to suffice to give a summary account of the passage, highlighting its apparently strong affirmation of the traditional Protestant interpretation while noting where that reading understates insights characteristic of the NPP.[35]

Having pronounced a universal dilemma on Jew and Gentile, both alike culpable and powerless to remediate, Romans 1:18–3:20 concludes with despair: "Now we know that whatever the law says it speaks to those who are under the law, so that every mouth may be stopped, and the whole world may be held accountable to God. For 'no human being will be justified in his sight' by works of the law, since through the law comes knowledge of sin" (Rom 3:19-20 RSV; quotation marks added to note the allusion to Ps 143:2). The indictment is not only comprehensive; at this stage of the argument, it leaves the reader hopeless, for the signal, abiding divine intervention in the human situation, the law of Moses, only renders humanity more culpable but no more righteous. The law reveals humanity's sorry estate but does not lift a finger to carry the burden it reveals. It can't; it turns out that's not its job.

For this reason, since the righteousness that human beings can accomplish of their own accord is paltry and insufficient, only a righteousness donated by God himself that does not depend on human accomplishment can be an adequate answer. And this is what Romans 3:21-26 describes in a

Table 2.2. Comparison of Romans 3:27-31 and Romans 4:1-25

Romans 3:27-31	Romans 4:1-25
Boasting is excluded (Rom 3:27a)	Abraham has no right to boast (Rom 4:1-2)
. . . because one is justified	. . . because Abraham was justified
by faith, not works of the law (Rom 3:27b-28)	by faith, not works (Rom 4:3-8)
Circumcised and uncircumcised	Circumcised and uncircumcised
are united under the one God	are united as children of Abraham
through faith (Rom 3:29-30)	through faith (Rom 4:9-17)

[34]Not surprisingly, these texts are explored in some detail by scholars associated with the critique of the NPP, e.g., D. A. Carson, "Atonement in Romans 3:21-26," in *The Glory of the Atonement: Biblical, Historical & Practical Perspectives: Essays in Honor of Roger Nicole*, ed. Charles E. Hill and Frank A. James III (Downers Grove, IL: InterVarsity Press, 2004), 121-39; and Simon J. Gathercole, "Justified by Faith, Justified by His Blood: The Evidence of Romans 3:21–4:25," in Carson, O'Brien and Seifrid, *JVN:PP.*

[35]For the sake of accountability, I choose to follow several classic and competent accounts in the vein of the TPP: John Murray, *The Epistle to the Romans*, NICNT (Grand Rapids: Eerdmans, 1968); C. E. B. Cranfield, *A Critical and Exegetical Commentary on the Epistle to the Romans*, ICC (Edinburgh: T&T Clark, 1975); Moo, *Epistle to the Romans*; and Schreiner, *Romans.*

compressed description not only of what God gives, righteousness, but how he is able to declare the unrighteous righteous, without gainsaying his own righteousness. God solves the human dilemma that Romans 1:18–3:20 described in its every dimension. The righteousness that God proffers is "apart from the law" (i.e., the Sinaiatic and Deuteronomic stipulations) while not unanticipated by the "law and prophets" (i.e., the Scriptures). Thus, it does not depend on either the law or human effort in any sense, both being impotent to save. Rather it comes as a divine gift[36] that is appropriated by all who believe, that is, those who have "faith in Jesus Christ."[37] All who so believe are "justified freely by his grace," that is, apart from any merit or work that they might contribute, but rather "through the redemption that is in Christ Jesus" (Rom 3:22-24). This change of status appropriated by faith is effected by atonement, but an atonement characteristically understood in a particular way, as spelled out (or, as the case may be, not *quite* spelled out) in Romans 3:25-26.

Of course, it is precarious to generalize with respect to the atonement—nuances and qualifications are plentiful even within a common interpretive tradition—but I think there is a sufficient family resemblance among TPP interpreters to justify proceeding, albeit with caution.[38] Whether the *hilastērion* (Rom 3:25) is understood as the gold lid of the ark (i.e., the *kappōret* or "mercy seat"; so NET) or as a reference to an atoning sacrifice more directly (KJV, NASB, ESV "propitiation"; RSV, NAB "expiation"; NRSV, NIV "sacrifice of atonement"), the difference may not be of great consequence, especially if, with respect to the former, *hilastērion* functions as metonymy for means of atonement.[39] Likewise, the famous debate between "expiation"

---

[36]In the TPP view, δικαιοσύνη θεοῦ is understood more or less as a subjective genitive—the righteousness God effects or gives. Even if various interpreters make use of other grammatical labels, effectively this is the contribution of the phrase in this context.

[37]Although there is variation within the NPP with regard to the interpretation of πίστις ['Ιησοῦ] Χριστοῦ (faith[fulness] in [of] [Jesus] Christ), the TPP is nearly uniform in regarding it as an objective genitive (i.e., "faith *in* Jesus Christ"). I address this much-debated question below in chap. 4.

[38]A characteristic and compelling summary can be found in Carson, "Atonement in Romans 3:21-26," which I use as a template for what follows. See now also Simon J. Gathercole, *Defending Substitution: An Essay on Atonement in Paul*, Acadia Studies in Bible and Theology (Grand Rapids: Baker Academic, 2015).

[39]That Paul means to refer to the "mercy seat" is increasingly recognized by interpreters (so, e.g., Robert Jewett, *Romans: A Commentary*, Hermeneia [Minneapolis: Fortress, 2007], 284-86; Moo, *Epistle to the Romans*, 232-37; Schreiner, *Romans*, 191-95; and Dunn, *Romans*, 1:171-72). This, of course, does not settle the question of what Paul intends by the reference.

(sin remediated) and "propitiation" (God's wrath appeased) has ultimately more to do with theological sensibility than lexical evidence, especially if one grants that the proximate referent of *hilastērion* is the "mercy seat." Nonetheless, all agree that, as *hilastērion*, Christ's death is an atonement for sin, not less than the means by which its alienating effects are overcome. Allowing for variations in detail, virtually all agree that, in God's putting forward Christ as the *hilastērion*, recompense for sin is meted out and its alienating consequences ameliorated.[40]

The syntax of the compressed expression is admittedly difficult, as indicated by the necessary freedom with which English translations reorder the prepositional phrases.[41] This does not mean that the train of thought is hopelessly ambiguous; there is an apparent logic, noted by almost all adherents to the TPP. Because the *hilastērion* bears and exhausts the recompense due human sin, God demonstrates that he is just. Justice, in this case, is demonstrated in the fact that God has not let humanity's formerly committed sins go unpunished (*tēn paresin tōn progegonotōn hamartēmatōn*); his patient

---

[40]Although it is a matter of some consequence, for the purpose of our survey, the question of whether ἱλαστήριον concerns only the expiation of sin or also the propitiation of divine wrath does not substantially affect the larger picture. The classic debate between C. H. Dodd ("Atonement," in *The Bible and the Greeks* [New York: Harper & Row, 1932]) and Leon Morris (*The Apostolic Preaching of the Cross* [London: Tyndale Press, 1955]) set the agenda for decades, although the discussion has now moved beyond it. Indeed, it is arguable that Dodd's position has enjoyed a substantial afterlife beyond its own merits with the assist of frequent refutations.
[41]In Greek the long sentence of Romans 3:25-26—actually a relative clause—contains nine consecutive prepositional phrases. I have broken them down accordingly in a wooden English translation to facilitate a comparison with the translations. See table 2.3.

Table 2.3. Prepositional phrases in Romans 3:25-26

ὃν προέθετο ὁ θεὸς ἱλαστήριον	whom God put forward as *hislastērion*
διὰ [τῆς] πίστεως	*through* faith
ἐν τῷ αὐτοῦ αἵματι	*in* his blood
εἰς ἔνδειξιν τῆς δικαιοσύνης αὐτοῦ	*for* the demonstration of his righteousness
διὰ τὴν πάρεσιν τῶν προγεγονότων ἁμαρτημάτων	*because of* the overlooking of formerly committed sins
ἐν τῇ ἀνοχῇ τοῦ θεοῦ,	*in* the forbearance of God
πρὸς τὴν ἔνδειξιν τῆς δικαιοσύνης αὐτοῦ	*for* the demonstration of his righteousness
ἐν τῷ νῦν καιρῷ,	*in* the present time
εἰς τὸ εἶναι αὐτὸν δίκαιον καὶ δικαιοῦντα	*so to be* he himself just and the one who justifies
τὸν ἐκ πίστεως Ἰησοῦ.	the one [who is] *from* faith of Jesus.

forbearance is not to be confused with moral indifference or injustice. That there is a retribution for sins is implied in the logic with which the paragraph concludes. The *hilastērion* bears the consequences of the formerly committed sins, showing that God, who makes (or counts) sinners just, is also, in doing so, himself just.

The outcome of this line of argument is that the universal, divine-human alienation is overcome in Christ's atoning sacrifice, a redemption offered apart from law keeping, to Jew and Gentile alike, received by faith in Christ. The human dilemma is universal—not so much *between* Jew and Gentile, but encompassing both—and ultimately with God, before whom humans stand guilty, condemned and helpless in themselves to remediate their circumstances. What humans cannot do for themselves by keeping the law, *achieving* righteousness, God does for them in Christ's atoning sacrifice that, expiating sin and (for most of the TPP) propitiating God, avails a righteousness appropriated by faith not secured by works.

It follows from this understanding of Romans 3:21-26 that Romans 3:27–4:8 offers a fuller unpacking of the key elements, especially of the antithesis between "works" and "faith." Because this redemption is accomplished by God alone and is received passively by human faith, it leaves no ground for boasting, a theme highlighted in Romans 3:27 and again in Romans 4:2.[42] The exclusion of boasting is expressly rooted in the works-faith antithesis, confirmed by two explanatory clauses: "For [*gar*] we hold that a man is justified by faith apart from works of law" (Rom 3:28). And again: "For [*gar*] if Abraham was justified by works, he has something to boast about, but not before God" (Rom

---

[42]Traditionally the problem of boasting is seen as a universal human disorder, though most more recent interpreters see it as a Pauline critique of Jewish covenantal confidence or even resilience. For the universal view, see the paradigmatic statement of Rudolf Bultmann, *Theology of the New Testament*, trans. Kendrick Grobel (New York: Scribner, 1951), 1:190-269 ("Man Prior to the Revelation Faith") and passim; on boasting in particular, see 1:42-44. For a more recent and more exegetical argument for the prohibition of boasting as a universal phenomenon, see C. E. B. Cranfield, "'The Works of the Law' in the Epistle to the Romans," *JSNT* 14, no. 43 (1991): 89-101. In general, this view has fallen out of favor, a majority of scholars preferring to see it as a Pauline critique of Judaism itself (so, e.g., Simon J. Gathercole, *Where Is Boasting? Early Jewish Soteriology and Paul's Response in Romans 1–5* [Grand Rapids: Eerdmans, 2001]). This being so, the debate has shifted to the nature or substance of Israel's "boasting." In general, the traditional Protestant interpreters understand it as a boast before God that appeals to Torah observance as worthy covenant faithfulness, whereas the NPP tends to see it less as a self-confidence and more as a national or covenantal confidence that glories in Israel's election and particularity, especially in the press of cultural pressure for conformity.

4:2 NRSV). Indeed, given that (1) Romans 3:19 summarizes the human plight by eliminating "works of the law" as a viable answer, (2) Romans 3:20 introduces a righteousness of God "apart from the law" as the answer to that plight, and (3) the entire passage forbids boasting twice on the ground of a works-faith antithesis, it cannot be surprising that the traditional Protestant interpretation finds grace, understood in a particular way, at the heart of this passage: "being justified *freely* [*dōrean*] by his *grace* [*tē autou chariti*]."

It would seem to TPP interpreters that this finds an indubitable confirmation in Paul's simple analogy in Romans 4:4, in which a "wage" (*misthos*), something "owed" (*opheilēma*), is contrasted to a "gift" (*charis*, the same word of course elsewhere translated as "grace"). This common-sense scenario is then applied in Romans 4:5 to the matter at hand, the justification of "the ungodly": "But to one who, not working but rather believing [*pisteuonti*] upon him who justifies the ungodly, such faith is reckoned as righteousness" (Rom 4:5). That works are not efficacious as a means of righteousness is further emphasized in the introduction to the quotation from Psalm 32: "So also [*kathaper*][43] David pronounces a blessing upon the man to whom God reckons righteousness [*logizetai dikaiosynēn*] apart from works [*chōris ergōn*]" (Rom 4:6). Finally, by means of the citation from Psalm 32:1-2, it becomes clear that Paul understands faith "reckoned as righteousness" as clearly entailing the forgiveness of sin apart from works of deserving.[44] From the perspective of the TPP it would be hard to know how the antithesis between works and faith, between qualifying effort and unmerited grace to the disqualified, could be made any clearer.

Indeed, from the vantage point of the TPP, Romans 4:4-8 is a sort of pay-dirt summarization of the whole complex. Here it is clear that Abraham's exercise of faith, which was "reckoned to him for [or, as] righteousness"

---

[43]While not infrequently there is a confusion in the textual tradition by which καθάπερ replaces καθώς (e.g., Rom 3:4; 9:13; 10:15; 11:8), here it appears that the reverse has happened, καθάπερ being found both in the earliest and the vast majority of manuscripts and καθώς only in D, F and G. The sense is similar, but καθώς γέγραπται ("just as it is written") is a characteristic introduction to a scriptural citation (thus probably explaining the change to καθώς here), whereas καθάπερ καί ("by the same token also . . .") indicates a relationship of continuity with the preceding argument.

[44]I discuss Paul's appropriation of Genesis 15:6 in greater detail below. For now it is sufficient to note that λογίζομαι εἰς δικαιοσύνην ("reckon/count/credit as righteousness") dominates the discourse of Romans 4 (Rom 4:3, 4, 5, 6, 8, 9, 10, 11, 22, 23, 24), becoming a trope contextually synonymous with δικαιόω by which Paul expounds his understanding of justification.

(*elogisthē auto eis dikaiosynēn*) serves as a synonymous expression for "to be justified" (*edikaiōthē*). But when Paul explicates the content of "being reckoned righteous" (*logizetai dikaiosynēn*), he does so by recourse to a psalm of David:

> Blessed are those whose *iniquities are forgiven*,
>   and whose *sins are covered*;
> blessed is the man whose *sin the Lord*
>   *will not reckon* [*ou mē logisētai*]. (Rom 4:7-8; Ps 32:1-2 [LXX 31:1-2])

Thus, from the psalm, the substance of being reckoned righteousness is described first positively as having iniquities forgiven and sins covered and then, by antonymic wordplay (repeating *logizomai*), it is *not* having one's sin "reckoned" against him.[45]

But, not surprisingly, the NPP finds this motif less obvious and certainly less central. This works-faith antithesis, which is the hallmark and bulwark of the TPP exegesis of Pauline soteriology, accords with the chief emphases of the NPP only with some considerable awkwardness. Most problematically, it would seem to call into question the claim that Paul's polemic with regard to "works of the law" and "works" (typically regarded as shorthand for "works of the law" in the NPP) consists in the practical barrier of Jewish cultural particularism. But if, in fact, the fault with "works of the law" is that they bid for merit before God, making righteousness a wage of obligation rather than a gift of grace, the NPP is at risk of having labored in vain. Of course, it can hardly be the case that Romans 4:4-8 has caught the NPP by surprise, and alternative accounts are readily available, but it is hard to avoid the impression that, if the NPP ever grasps at straws, it is here.[46] Even if, as

---

[45]Wright initially agrees with this analysis in his Romans commentary. Commenting on Romans 4:6-8, "Paul can assume that 'reckoning righteousness apart from works' and 'not reckoning sin against someone' *are equivalents*" (Wright, "Letter to the Romans," 10:493, emphasis added). Lest, however, mere forgiveness of sins abstracted from the covenant setting be presumed as a more proper definition of *justification*, Wright is quick to add, "The covenant, we must always remind ourselves, was there to deal with sin; when God forgives sin, or reckons someone within the covenant, these are functionally equivalent. They draw attention to different aspects of the same event" (ibid.). But we should at least notice in this case that forgiveness is the more direct explication of justification by Paul himself. Covenant membership must be inferred, and perhaps quite rightly.

[46]Dunn is concerned that "there is a danger therefore that expositions of Paul's theology of justification will focus too heavily on these verses without sufficient regard for the movement of his thought in them . . . for the reader, as for Paul, the picture offered in v 4 possesses relatively

I see it, the TPP exegesis of Romans 4:1-8 is incomplete, the strength of the TPP position is not easily dismissed.

But, having given the TPP an extended and sympathetic hearing, it must be noted that there are motifs running throughout this passage that the TPP seems not so much to overlook as to accord insufficient weight. By any careful reading, the text is suffused with an underlying dynamic of the Jew-Gentile salvation-historical relationship that is at least as fundamental—arguably more fundamental—to the argument as the universal divine-human question.[47] Of course, the two are not mutually exclusive, but reading centuries distant from the originating crisis there is a danger of transforming the substance of the discourse subtly so as to address a different set of concerns. It may then be useful also to highlight those features of the text—

---

little significance in and of itself" (Dunn, *Romans*, 1:204). Dunn's translation ("the reward is not reckoned as a favor but as a debt," *Romans,* 1:195) is notably unhelpful. As a translation of μισθός, "reward" is acceptable in certain contexts, but (1) the English *reward* will frequently connote more gratuity than is intrinsic to the term, which indicates merely a positive or negative requital (BDAG, s.v. μισθός [2], p. 653) and (2) in this context, it is obvious that ὁ μισθός is the "pay" or "wage" earned, and thus "owed," to the one who has worked. The English *reward* is a strange—indeed, in context an entirely misleading—way to describe such a phenomenon. It is fair to wonder if there is something more to this idiosyncartic translation than an attempt at freshness or to be free of certain well-worn tracks.

Along complementary lines, Wright now argues that μίσθος in Romans 4:4 alludes to the "great reward" promised to Abraham in Genesis 15:1 (ὁ μισθός σου πολὺς ἔσται σφόδρα [LXX]) and that, indeed, it is this word that triggers the tangential metaphor of work and wages. He maintains that the relative proximity of this promise to Genesis 15:6 (NRSV: "[Abraham] believed the LORD, and the LORD reckoned it to him as righteousness"; Rom 4:2 and passim) suggests that there is more to this figure than the "side-metaphor . . . which by coincidence happens to overlap with one way of expounding an 'old perspective' view of justification" (Wright, *P&FG,* 2:850; cf. the more detailed treatment in idem, *Pauline Perspectives: Essays on Paul, 1978–2013* [Minneapolis: Fortress, 2013], 584-89). Wright concludes that, though a preoccupation of later Christian discourse, the question of merit over against gift was "certainly not Paul's primary concern." It remains to be seen if this argument will prove persuasive to others (note the critical evaluation of David Shaw, "Romans 4 and the Justification of Abraham in Light of Perspectives New and Newer," *Themelios* 40, no. 1 [2015]: 50-62). At the very least, one might have hoped for a stronger echo than a single rather common and flexible word that is used quite differently in the two contexts. For another account of the passage defending an NPP exegesis, see Michael Cranford, "Abraham in Romans 4: The Father of All Who Believe," *NTS* 41, no. 1 (1995): 71-88.

[47] A useful diagnostic of the sea change in Pauline scholarship is to inquire of the role of Romans 9–11 with respect to the overall argument of the letter. In contrast to earlier generations of Romans scholarship that tended to see it as a sort of excursus, NPP scholars are uniform in regarding it as central, if not the center, of the letter's argument. See, e.g., N. T. Wright, "Christ, the Law and the People of God: The Problem of Romans 9–11," in *The Climax of the Covenant: Christ and the Law in Pauline Theology* (Edinburgh: T&T Clark, 1991), 231-57; and Dunn, *Romans,* 2:519-21. The "excursus" approach is now rare if not altogether abandoned by scholars of all stripes, although the view that in Romans 9–11 Paul meets an interlocutor's hypothetical objection comes close to the same sort of analysis.

largely set aside in the TPP account given above—that highlight the pervasiveness of the Jew-Gentile dynamic. The Jew-Gentile condition is not merely a "red thread" running through an otherwise divine-human diagnosis and prescription; it is rather more of a heavy rope braided of the following strands.

1. While it is a commonplace to say that the climax to Paul's argument in Romans 3:9-20 serves to indict the whole of sinful humanity, Paul himself concludes that indictment with a curiously particularistic flair: he specifies that "whatever the law says, it speaks to *those who are under* [Greek, *en*] *the law*" (Rom 3:19 NRSV; cf. 2:12; 7:1, 23). Yes, this is in order that "*every mouth* may be stopped, and the *whole world* may be held accountable to God" (Rom 3:19), but according to Romans 3:19, the indictment of Romans 3:10-18 remains directed especially toward Israel, presumably in an a fortiori relationship to the "world." This means that, like the argument that preceded it in Romans 1:18–3:8, the concluding coup de grace indictment, although including all of humanity, does so not by obliterating ethnic or salvation-historical distinctions but by encompassing them.

2. Arguably—though this is much disputed—the "works of the law" of Romans 3:20, impotent to justify, are those Jewish practices of particularity that distinguish faithful Jews from surrounding peoples.[48] Whether or not "works of the law" are to be construed so narrowly, it remains the case that Paul highlights the impotence of the law to save (by works of the law "no human being will be justified in his sight") while also consigning the law to its more modest and negative function of illuminating sin ("for through the law comes consciousness of sin," NAB). There can be little doubt that in the broad scope of Pauline theology there is a critique of the law—which is not quite a critique of the *law*—located in an anthropological deficit, that is, in the general human inability to obey God (e.g., Rom 7:7-25; 8:7-8). But, however true that might be, there is no indication that this is Paul's argument at this point.[49] For now, Paul is content to say that the law, though

---

[48]Naturally, Dunn, *Romans*, 1:153-55; and Wright, "Letter to the Romans," 10:460-61.
[49]Contra Gathercole, *Where Is Boasting?*, 222-24. While it is true that this implication (and much more) certainly follows from Paul's use of σάρξ elsewhere, Gathercole overlooks the idiomatic character of the phrase, πᾶσα σάρξ, found over sixty times in the LXX (frequently from כָּל־בָּשָׂר, kāl-bāśār), with another nine in the New Testament (Rom 3:20 excepted). It seems nearly impossible that Paul has smuggled his theological anthropology into a phrase that is a

a dimension of Israel's salvation-historical privilege, is nonetheless not the answer for a disobedient Israel, as, indeed, he has been saying throughout the preceding (see esp. Rom 2:17-29). Thus, the argument here, even with its universal dimensions, remains substantially descriptive of the plight of Israel as revealed by the law. Again, this is not to deny that this passage depicts a universal dilemma but rather to claim that it does so with an a fortiori particularity: if this is the plight of Israel, despite all of her patent advantages (Rom 3:1-9), how much more are the Gentiles impugned?

3. In Romans 3:22-23, Paul "interrupts" his dense soteriological brief with an apparent reference to ethnicity, which could almost seem a distracting tangent according to some interpretations of the passage: "For there is *no distinction*, since *all* [i.e., both Jew and Gentile] have sinned and fall short of the glory of God."[50] This is no tangent at all but, rather, central to Paul's entire argument. The shared Jew *and* Gentile dilemma, however differently it might manifest itself, calls for a solution equally to be shared by Jew and Gentile.

4. Romans 3:27 introduces the question of "boasting." And although also a matter of considerable debate, it seems antecedently probable in light of the argument in Romans 2 that repeatedly marginalizes Jewish self-confidence (esp. Rom 2:1-5, 17-29), that this not a general human boasting before God but a particular Jewish covenantal self-assuredness that is now "excluded."[51] This is not to say that Paul considered Jews characteristically guilty of "works righteousness" and is here censuring that pursuit and a supposed haughtiness in its wake. Rather, nothing could have been more natural to the Jews faithful to the covenant than that they should glory in

---

commonplace biblical idiom for "all of humanity." On the matter of compromised human agency as central to Paul's argument, see not only Gathercole but now also Preston M. Sprinkle, *Paul and Judaism Revisited: A Study of Divine and Human Agency in Salvation* (Downers Grove, IL: InterVarsity Press, 2013), esp. 125-44. I simply doubt that Paul's language betrays this concern at this point in the argument.

[50]In and of itself, that "all have sinned" could simply be a statement of a universal plight (as it is frequently taken), but the introduction, "for there is not distinction" (οὐ γάρ ἐστιν διαστολή), surely intends an ethnic dimension, all the more when the entire context of the argument is given its due (e.g., Rom 1:16; 2:9-10, 17, 28-29; 3:1-2, 9, 29).

[51]In putting it this way, I do not repeat Bultmann's more notorious and extreme version:

"Boasting (in the Law)" is the *fundamental attitude of the Jew, the essence of his sin* (Rom. 2:17, 23 . . .), and the radical giving up of boasting is faith's attitude. Thus, Paul can say of Abraham, who was rightwised not by his works but by his faith, that he has no "boast" ([Rom] 4:2). Righteousness, then, cannot be won by human effort, nor does any human accomplishment establish a claim to it; it is a sheer gift. (Bultmann, *Theology of the New Testament*, 1:281, emphasis added)

divine election, which would be precisely the opposite of autosoterism, much less "sin" (as Bultmann would have it), even if some of the presenting symptoms might share a superficial resemblance.[52] In any case, the mention and exclusion of "boasting" here points to the fact that Paul has never taken his eyes off the Jewish dilemma and the characteristic bent of his beloved kinsmen, now observed through the lens of the gospel.

5. In Romans 3:28-30, Paul's confirms that "a person is justified by faith apart from works of the law" by the *ad absurdum* rhetorical question and its answer: "Or is God the God of Jews only? Is he not the God of Gentiles also? Yes, of Gentiles also, since God is one; and he will justify the circumcised on the ground of faith and the uncircumcised through that same faith" (NRSV). It could not be any clearer that the alienation of Jew and Gentile from one another, on the one hand, and their reconciliation together, on the other, continue to be central themes for Paul, arguably *the* center of this discourse. Were law to remain an exclusive means of covenantal inclusion, the covenant itself would remain exclusive to a people rather than the embrace of Jew and Gentile together into the Abrahamic family. Thus, Romans 3:29-30 (one God making one people of two) forms an essential partnership with Romans 3:22-23: Jew and Gentile sharing a singular dilemma (the argumentative burden of the labyrinthine Rom 1:18–3:20) and finding in "a righteousness apart from the law" (*dikaiosynē chōris nomou*, Rom 3:21) by means of faith a common solution, in which together they form the one people of the one God (the particular burden of Rom 3:21–4:25).

6. Romans 4:1, a text beset with ambiguities and textual uncertainties,[53] may well bear witness directly to the same Jew and Gentile division, now as

---

[52]For a more nuanced view, with which I generally concur, at least as it concerns the import of "boasting," see Gathercole, *Where Is Boasting?*

[53]The manuscript tradition shows three primary forms (leaving aside the less consequential variants of τὸν προπάτορα [τὸν πατέρα, τὸν πατέρας (sic)]; for full data see the apparatuses of NA[28] and UBS[4]).

1. Τί οὖν ἐροῦμεν εὑρηκέναι Ἀβραὰμ τὸν προπάτορα ἡμῶν κατὰ σάρκα; This is the reading adopted by NA[28] and UBS[4] (א*, A, C*, 81, 365, 1506, sa, bo?; Or[lem]; with πατέρα, א[1], C[3], D, F, G, Ψ, 629, pc latt).

2. Τί οὖν ἐροῦμεν Ἀβραὰμ τὸν πατέρα ἡμῶν εὑρηκέναι κατὰ σάρκα; (K, P, 33, 88, 61:4, Byz al).

3. Τί οὖν ἐροῦμεν Ἀβραὰμ τὸν προπάτορα ἡμῶν κατὰ σάρκα; (B, 6, 1739) This is the reading accepted by Wescott-Hort and is followed by the RSV and NJB and noted in the NRSV and ESV text notes.

Not only the external evidence but also intrinsic probability support reading 1 (so also Metzger, *TCGNT*, 450). But, as often, the confused textual tradition points to the ambiguity (in this case grammatical) of the text.

it is restored in the Messiah Jesus. It is customary to translate the verse more or less this way: "What then can we say that Abraham found, our ancestor according to the flesh?" (NAB). This then is an introduction to a discourse concerning Abraham, who is assumed to *be* "our forefather according to the flesh" and who discovered that righteousness was credited to him on the ground of faith (Gen 15:6). But a persuasive case can be made that the text should be understood differently: "What then shall we say? That we find Abraham to be our forefather according to the flesh [i.e., our forefather according to natural descent]?" (my translation, but cf., alone among contemporary English translations, CEB).[54] The traditional translation assumes that the question is simply introductory, preparing as a thematic announcement for a discussion of the ground of Abraham's righteousness.[55] The alternative translation understands the verse as a two-part rhetorical question, clearly expecting a negative answer,[56] not merely a transition but a thesis in question form: "No, as we will see, Abraham is our forefather on grounds other than

---

[54]Here I am following and continue to be persuaded by the general argument of Richard B. Hays, "'Have We Found Abraham to Be Our Forefather According to the Flesh?' A Reconsideration of Rom 4:1," *NovT* 27 (1985): 76-98; repr. in idem, *The Conversion of the Imagination: Paul as Interpreter of Israel's Scripture* (Grand Rapids: Eerdmans, 2005), 61-84.

[55]Despite minor variations, the traditional translations of the verse share four assumptions, all of which can be questioned: (1) It understands the Greek to comprise a single rhetorical question ("What shall we say that Abraham found . . .") rather than two ("What then shall we say? That Abraham is found to be our ancestor according to the flesh?") (2) It requires that a content marker ("that") be supplied for ἐροῦμεν: "What shall we say [*that*] Abraham found . . ." (3) It takes Abraham to be the subject of the infinitive εὑρηκέναι: "Abraham found" (or "gained" or "discovered"). (4) It assumes that Abraham *is in fact* "our forefather according to the flesh" rather than doubting it.

[56]With Romans 4:1 clearly constructed analogously to other passages utilizing the transitional τί [οὖν] ἐροῦμεν;

> Romans 3:5 But if our unrighteousness serves to show the righteousness of God, *what shall we say?* That God is unrighteous to inflict wrath on us? (I speak in a human way.)
>
> Romans 6:1-2 *What shall we say then?* Are we to continue in sin that grace may abound? By no means!
>
> Romans 7:7 *What then shall we say?* That the law is sin? By no means!
>
> Romans 8:31 *What then shall we say* to these things? If God is for us, who can be against us?
>
> Romans 9:14 *What shall we say then?* Is there injustice on God's part? By no means!
>
> Romans 9:30 *What shall we say then?* That Gentiles who did not pursue righteousness have attained it, that is, a righteousness that is by faith.

The pattern is suggestive, to be sure, though not as decisive as Hays supposes. Notably Romans 6:1, 7:7 and 9:14 all confirm the negative answer to the proposed question with the unambiguous μὴ γένοιτο, and even Romans 3:5 has the parenthetical "I speak in a human way" (κατὰ ἄνθρωπον λέγω). The remaining occurrences, Romans 8:31 and 9:30, do not follow with a false premise. Thus, Romans 4:1 stands without a direct parallel, such that these parallels can only be suggestive, not finally probative.

natural descent." Abraham is the forefather of Jew and Gentile alike not as a matter of natural descent ("according to the flesh") but by virtue of a shared righteousness by faith. In other words, Romans 4:1 continues directly on the theme of "no distinction" (Rom 3:23) and the one God being God of Jew and Gentiles alike (Rom 3:29-30), both of whom are made righteous on the ground of faith rather than natural descent.

7. If that is the force of Romans 4:1, then the argument that follows—essentially a detailed exploration of Genesis 15:6, "Abraham believed God, and it was reckoned to him as righteousness"(NRSV)—functions differently than the TPP has assumed. At the very least, what follows Romans 4:1 must be seen as an argument for how it is, in fact, that Abraham is the forefather of all his "seed" (*sperma*, Rom 4:13, 15, 18) inclusive of Jews and Gentiles alike. This makes the transition from the "righteous by faith" motif of Romans 4:1-8 to the inclusion of the "uncircumcised" in Romans 4:9-18 no transition at all but rather a continuation of the original theme announced in Romans 4:1.[57]

This passing survey of certain exegetical cruxes demonstrates not that the TPP exegesis is mistaken but that it is characteristically incomplete. In other words, this passage, which is so easily read as a straightforward universal soteriology in which God's grace provides redemption for ungodly persons by faith apart from works, by a NPP reading becomes an extended discussion of the inclusion of Gentiles into the family of Abraham. This should come as no surprise to the attentive reader of Romans 1:16–3:20, in which the Jew-Gentile dynamic is found throughout, from the articulation of the thesis of the letter (Rom 1:16-17) to the shared culpability of Jew and Gentile that is described in considerable detail in what follows. And, while no recent Romans scholarship in the TPP vein has overlooked all these signs of the Jew-Gentile dynamic, it could be argued that, hurrying to expound Paul's abiding soteriology, TPP scholarship has minimized the very dimensions of the text that the NPP, perhaps to the point of overcorrection, maximizes. In fact, there is perhaps no passage in the Pauline corpus that is so cooperative with *both* paradigms.

---

[57]Here I concur with the primary contours of Hays's argument that Romans 4 as a whole is an argument for the inclusion of uncircumcised Gentiles as full and equal members of the covenant, after the pattern of Abraham and according to the promise given him. However, I part company—and decisively—on the function of Romans 4:2-8, with respect to which I'm convinced the TPP has the better part. That both are reckoned as righteous apart from "work," apart from a moral contribution in conformity with the law but instead by faith, is precisely what allows both equally and on the same terms to be the seed of Abraham.

We might say that the TPP reads Romans 1–4 as though it were Ephesians 2:1-10 while NPP renders the same chapters rather more like they were Ephesians 2:11-22 or, perhaps even more accurately, another version of the substance of Galatians 3:6-29. But, as I am suggesting, herein lies the problem.

I am arguing that the state of the question in Pauline scholarship on Romans betrays diverse understandings of Paul's theology in this letter precisely because Romans marks the developmental crux of Paul's soteriology. The reason that Pauline scholarship divides in its reading of Romans is that ultimately Romans marks a transition in Paul's own soteriology, or at least in its expression, in which characteristic elements of the NPP and TPP coexist, while neither overrules the other. To put it oversimplistically, the besetting fault of the NPP is to read Romans too closely to (its reading of) Galatians, and the prevailing fault of the TPP is to read it too closely to, say, (its reading of) Ephesians, when the letter is not quite the same as either but marks a theological transition between the two, sharing and combining elements of both.

2.3 EPHESIANS 2:1-22

Though a longer text than either of the preceding, my treatment of Ephesians 2 will of necessity be briefer. Because Ephesians is not regarded by a majority of contemporary New Testament scholars as authentically Pauline,[58] it has yet to play a significant role in the NPP debate. But this is unfortunate, for, regardless of authenticity and for all the putative differences, it stands in continuity with Paul's undisputed letters, not least in Ephesians 2, where the contested leitmotifs of the TPP and NPP are again found in near collocation. As Wright has noted, Ephesians 2:1-10 is a sort of locus classicus of the TPP and Ephesians 2:11-22 a demonstration of the ever-present NPP thesis that the unity of Jew and Gentile—the driving concern of Paul's earliest letters— remains a living concern even in this later (if not deutero-) Pauline letter.[59]

---

[58]Though as Harold Hoehner has shown, Raymond E. Brown's estimate that 80 percent of New Testament scholars regard it as inauthentic is an underestimation of the regard for its authenticity (Hoehner, *Ephesians: An Exegetical Commentary* [Grand Rapids: Baker Academic, 2002], 7-20). I set aside for later the question of whether Ephesians is an authentically Pauline letter along with the other introductory questions. I regard it so, as I will argue below, but for now it is sufficient for it to be regarded as part of the Pauline tradition—indeed, famously by C. H. Dodd as the "crown of Paulinism" ("Ephesians," in *The Abingdon Bible Commentary*, ed. F. C. Eiselen, E. Lewis and D. G. Downey [New York: Abingdon, 1929], 1224-25).

[59]N. T. Wright, *Justification: God's Plan and Paul's Vision* (Downers Grove, IL: IVP Academic, 2009), 168 (UK ed., 144).

The dominating theme of Ephesians 2:1-10 is "grace" (Eph 2:5, 7, 8) and its synonyms ("rich in mercy," "great love with which he loved us" in Eph 2:4 NRSV, "kindness" in Eph 2:7), which, over against "works," ground a salvation (Eph 2:9) to be appropriated by "faith" (Eph 2:5, 8). That salvation is all of grace is demonstrated by the sobering account of human sin in Ephesians 2:1-3: the Gentile converts were once dead as a result of trespasses and sins,[60] which were their characteristic manner of life in a helpless complicity with the present eon of the world and subjection to the oppressing diabolical powers. Indeed, *everyone* was once subject to "passions of the flesh" and executing the "desires of the flesh and their impulses,"[61] with the result that they were "by nature" altogether "children of wrath."[62] Nonetheless, God, of his wealth of mercy and great love, meets the dead-in-transgression children of wrath in this hopeless estate and in Christ not only raises them to life but also seats them with him in the "heavenly places." That this is of grace and not of human deserving is evident from the repetition of the theme, "by grace you are saved" (Eph 2:5, 8), and from the twofold denial, "this is *not* of yourselves, but the gift of God" and "*not* a result of works, so no one may boast." Although not entirely unique to Ephesians, it is probably not too much to say that this paean to the gratuity of salvation is unparalleled in the New Testament both in its clarity and its effusion. Even the balancing conclusion of Ephesians 2:10 that properly returns "good works" to the scenario does so with an emphasis on those who, being "created in Christ Jesus," are *God's* "handiwork," whose good works are already a matter of *God's* prior preparation.[63] Thus, it is God who is (re-)creating the vessels and preparing the works that the new creations are to walk in.

---

[60]The frequent refrain of Reformed soteriology that "being dead" here indicates a powerlessness to respond to God apart from an efficacious calling and regeneration may be theologically defensible or even necessary, but is not derivable from the text itself—where death, in any case, is the *result*, in both Ephesians 2:1 and 2:5, of trespasses and sins, not their cause.

[61]In the context, the διάνοια can only be understood pejoratively, as a "carnal mind," thus the translation "impulses" (so NAB).

[62]Clearly in the context τέκνα ὀργῆς is to be construed as a Semitic genitive, in this case pointing less to the characteristics of the "children" than to their destiny.

[63]The emphasis on God's initiative is indicated in the placing of αὐτοῦ in conspicuous first position ("it is *his* handiwork we are"). Likewise that it is *God* who is the explicit subject of προητοίμασεν is more than a grammatical disambiguation (i.e., that *God* and not *Christ* is the subject of the verb), but rather also highlights God's sovereign enabling in the performance of "good works."

Meanwhile, Ephesians 2:11-22 returns to the scene of the trespass, but now with a salvation-historical view. From the wrath due sins and trespasses of Ephesians 2:1-10, Paul now turns to the alienation of Gentiles from the commonwealth and covenants of Israel. While it is true that the Gentile plight included estrangement from God ("having no hope and without God in the world," Eph 2:12 NRSV), primary attention is given to Gentile alienation from the covenant and its consequent privileges: "without Christ [perhaps better, "a messiah"], being aliens from the commonwealth of Israel, and strangers to the covenants of promise" (Eph 2:12 NRSV). The issue here is not, as in Ephesians 2:1-4, sin against the God who judges but exclusion from the people belonging to the God who promises. And it is no less than by means of the cross that this at once historic, social and religious hostility is abolished: Gentiles being "brought near *by the blood of Christ*" (Eph 2:13), Christ having "broken down *in his flesh* the dividing wall of hostility" (Eph 2:14), and "reconcil[ing] us both to God in one body *through the cross*, thereby killing the hostility" (Eph 2:16 ESV).[64] Thus, "atonement" in Ephesians 2:11-22 is directed explicitly to the uniting into "one new person" the formerly estranged and hostile entities of Jew and Gentile. The reconciliation of these two peoples into one must be thought of not as a mere afterthought but as a central element of the gospel as Paul understands it. And, again, this is one of the hallmark contributions to our understanding of Paul that, if not owed to, is especially emphasized by the NPP.

Yet, if there is a certain convenience in thinking of Ephesians 2:1-10 as the "old perspective" epitomized and Ephesians 2:11-22 as the "new," the distinction, upon closer examination, is not quite that straightforward. Although it is generally true that Ephesians 2:1-10 concerns the "vertical" and Ephesians 2:11-22 the "horizontal,"[65] the former having to do with soteriology and the latter ecclesiology, the distinction does not hold absolutely. There are signs already in Ephesians 2:1-10 that Jew-Gentile distinction is factoring

---

[64]Here for sake of convenience I use the ESV, but, as the diversity in translations (even versification) indicates, the grammar of Ephesians 2:14-16 is difficult. Nonetheless, the point being made does not depend upon a certain grammatical construal. For helpful surveys of the options, see ad loc. Hoehner, *Ephesians*; and William J. Larkin, *Ephesians: A Handbook on the Greek Text*, Baylor Handbook on the Greek New Testament (Waco, TX: Baylor University Press, 2009).

[65]As, for example, demonstrated with respect to the συν- compounds by Thielman, which in Ephesians 2:1-10 show solidarity with Christ in resurrection and exaltation and, in Ephesians 2:11-22, common citizenship of Gentiles with Jews (Frank Thielman, *Ephesians*, BECNT [Grand Rapids: Baker Academic, 2010], 149).

into the account, and Ephesians 2:11-22 has also ultimately to do not only with the reconciliation of Jew and Gentile to each other but also with the reconciliation of both together to God (Eph 2:16-18). It is probable that the alternation between the first and second person in Ephesians 2:1-3 is ethnic in force, the first person "we/us" referring to Jews with regard to their covenantal status and the second person "you" (always plural) referring to Gentiles from that Jewish vantage point.

- The "you" who "were dead in your transgressions and sins" of Ephesians 2:1-2 refers almost surely to Gentiles (rather than merely the readers as such), described in terms of their characteristic vices. This is confirmed by the parallelism of the salvation-historical reprise beginning in Ephesians 2:11 (*dio*, "therefore"), where the "you" is shown explicitly by apposition to be "Gentiles in the flesh."[66]

---

[66]And it should also be noted that the second person of Ephesians 2:1 as a designation for Gentiles is not unanticipated in what preceded. Although there is no consensus on this matter, it is plausible that already in Ephesians 1:12-14, Paul is signaling a distinction between "first" generation Jewish Christians (of whom he and his colleagues are representative) and "second" generation Gentile Christians (of whom the recipients of this letter are representative):

so that we [first-generation Jewish believers] who were the first to hope in Christ might be to the praise of his glory. In him you [second-generation Gentile believers] also, when you heard the word of truth, the gospel of your salvation, and believed in him, were sealed with the promised Holy Spirit, who is the guarantee of our [both together] inheritance until we acquire possession of it, to the praise of his glory. (Eph 1:12-14 ESV)

I am not arguing for a wooden "we" = Jews, "you" = Gentiles distinction but rather that, *when qualified*, the pronoun distinction intends more than an epistolary author-addressee distinction—although, of course it is not less than that—and along ethnic lines. In this case, much depends on the much-discussed sense of τοὺς προηλπικότας (= "those having first hoped"). The rare word προελπίζω (a hapax legomenon in the Greek Bible) is susceptible to two possible interpretations: (1) to hope first, in some comparative sense, i.e., *before* others or (2) to hope in advance, i.e., in anticipation. Both meanings make rather good sense in the context. But decisive in favor of the temporal "before" meaning is the "*also* you" (καὶ ὑμεῖς) that defines the hearing and believing, primarily Gentile, community (cf. Eph 1:15; Col 1:4).

The chief argument against the ethnic-distinction interpretation is weighty: that the supposed alternation between Jews (first person) and Gentiles (second person) seems impossible to carry through the text with complete consistency. Quite so. It seems highly improbable, for example, that the first-person references preceding Ephesians 1:12 (repeatedly in Eph 1:3-11) intend to exclude the Gentile readers, nor should we think that the "inheritance" of Ephesians 1:14 is for Jewish believers alone. I am arguing rather that (1) unqualifed first-person references are inclusive of author and addressee by default; (2) that second-person references are always referring to the letter's addressees, the implied readership understood as decidedly Gentile; and (3) that the entire purpose of the distinction is not to assign some set of blessings (or transgressions) to one group and a different set to another but rather to demonstrate that Jews and Gentiles together share alike in the same plight and even more a common blessing—the former "by nature" (Eph 2:3); the latter by a gratuitous and unanticipated adoption.

- The "we all" of Ephesians 2:3 then includes, somewhat surprisingly, the solidarity of Jewish Christians also as those who "once lived in the passions of our flesh, following the desires of body and mind," being "by nature children of wrath, like the rest." That the inclusion of Jewish Christians was Paul's intent in Ephesians 2:3 is indicated by (1) the adverbial *kai* ("in which we *also* all once lived . . ."), (2) the grammatically redundant, thus emphatic, pronoun *hēmeis* ("in which *we* [ourselves] also all once lived"), (3) the reinforcement of the inclusive "all" (*pantes*) ("in which we also *all* once lived"), and (4) above all, the concluding reference to "as also *the rest* [of non-Jewish humankind]" (*hōs kai hoi loipoi*).

Understandably, it is regarded as problematic for the view so far advanced that following Ephesians 2:3 the text turns exclusively to the first person through Ephesians 2:7, save for the interjection of Ephesians 2:5: "by grace you are saved" (cf. Eph 2:8). But this is to apply the pronoun distinction woodenly, and, in fact, to miss the larger dynamic of the passage. Paul's inclusion of the "we" (i.e., Jews) in Ephesians 2:3 should be taken as a rhetorical sympathy, as a kind of humble admission that, over against stock Jewish polemics to the contrary,[67] sin and its oppression are not the unique malady of Gentiles. Thus, the Gentile-including "you also" of Ephesians 1:13 is a generous inclusion, while the Jewish-implicating "we also" is humble concession. If there is an ethnicity-defiant human solidarity as it concerns sin, as it concerns redemption there can be no meaningful lingering distinction between Jew and Gentile, who are now together joined to Christ and thus to one another. In redemption there is no longer a "you," only an "us."[68] There is thus a studied, reflective (not to say contrived) identification of Jew with Gentile in sin, and a reflexive solidarity between the formerly estranged in salvation. The logic here is remarkably similar in compressed form to that which Paul works out at length in Romans. That

---

[67] As, e.g., Romans 1:18-32 at first glance, with its roots in the wisdom tradition (e.g., Wis 13–15). Cf. Douglas A. Campbell, *The Deliverance of God: An Apocalyptic Rereading of Justification in Paul* (Grand Rapids: Eerdmans, 2009), 359-62.

[68] It is unfortunate in this regard that, in an effort to preserve readability, certain translations (RSV following the italicized words of the KJV and ASV) presage the "made alive" of Ephesians 2:5 already in Ephesians 2:1. The effect is not only to ruin the suspense, as it were, but also to dull the ethnic edge of Ephesians 2:1-2, Gentiles described (not unlike Eph 2:11-12) as a dead and hopeless people.

Gentiles are "sinners" is patent, needing no argument, merely revulsive illustration (Eph 2:1-2; cf. Rom 1:18-32). That Jews alike are sinners is the less obvious claim, but no less true for that (Eph 2:3; cf. Rom 2:1–3:18). That a single means of redemption avails for both, they being equally in need of grace, is Paul's satisfaction of a dilemma both soteriological and social (Eph 2:5-10; Rom 3:21–4:25). So, while we find it convenient and even clever to label Ephesians 2:1-10 as "old perspective" in anticipation of Ephesians 2:11-22 as a "new perspective" counterpart, it is an oversimplification to put it that way.

If we turn then to Ephesians 2:11-22, while it is clear that the presenting dilemma is the alienation of the Gentiles from the covenant community, there is more at stake than the human reconciliation of those communities to each other in Christ. Ultimately, the effect of the cross is "reconcile them both in one body *to God*" (Eph 2:16). It is thus again not quite the case that Ephesians 2:1-10 is "vertical" while Ephesians 2:11-22 is "horizontal." Nor is it really possible from the text of Ephesians itself to assign a temporal or logical priority to either the reconciliation of persons to God or of peoples to each other, other than to say that neither captures Paul's emphasis, which is rather for the reconciliation of a people—indeed a new person (*hena kainon anthrōpon*), "a new humanity" (NRSV), one body—to God. Therefore, this decidedly "horizontal" passage is not absent its own important "vertical" dimension; rather, that vertical dimension is its climax and linchpin of the whole.[69]

Having demonstrated the inseparability of the "old" and "new" perspectives in Ephesians 2, we cannot leave the text behind without noting also its witness to the "works of the law" debate. Of course, the phrase itself is not found here, or indeed outside of Galatians and Romans. Nonetheless, Ephesians 2 bears upon the question, though not in an unambiguous, singular direction. Ephesians 2:9 excludes "works" from making any contribution to salvation—though, to be sure, "good works" are shown immediately to be requisite of God's new "handiwork" (Eph 2:10). Here there is no ground for assuming that by "works" Paul really means something more specific like "works *of the law*." It is more likely that he refers simply to righteous human actions in general—acts of piety, justice, charity and so on. Unlike the

---

[69]Cf. Thielman, *Ephesians*, 174.

impression (probably inadvertent) left by some Christian preaching zealous for a gospel of grace uncompromised by human achievement, clearly Paul is zealous for such behavior (cf. Tit 2:14). He simply insists, salvation being entirely a matter of grace, that such "works," however noble and desirable, can make no material contribution to it. Although the "good works" in which God's workmanship is to "walk" are the unmistakable counterpart to the "transgressions and sins" in which we formerly "walked" (Eph 2:2), they are not the means of that salvation but rather its fruit and the evidence of its efficacy. To put it plainly, in itself, Ephesians 2:5-10 makes a rather decisive case for the TPP.[70]

But once again it is not so simple, for Ephesians 2:14-16, on its own terms, reprises strains of the NPP. It is in some sense the *law* itself that counts as the enmity needing to be abolished. Paul's treatment of the law in Ephesians 2:15 is compressed and difficult, susceptible to multiple interpretations. From the vantage point of the NPP, it is notable that this text draws attention to the social function of the law, indeed, its *divisive, excluding* function that separates Jew from Gentile, the law being even the site of hostility.[71] This accords closely with, and to some degree bolsters, Dunn's controversial understanding of "works of the law," an argument he advanced, however, only with respect to the undisputed letters. The law's "commandments" and "decrees" are here described not as that which is impossible to obey or which imprisons those aspiring to obedience in a vicious cycle of failure (although neither can these be excluded) but as that way of life that distinguishes, separates and breeds contempt between peoples.[72]

---

[70]Andrew T. Lincoln, "Ephesians 2:8-10: A Summary of Paul's Gospel?," *CBQ* 45, no. 4 (1983): 617-30.

[71]Assuming, although it is grammatically disputable, that (1) τὴν ἔχθραν ("the enmity/hostility," Eph 2:14) is the direct object of καταργήσας ("setting aside," "disabling," Eph 2:15) and (2) in apposition to τὸν νόμον. Thus, "by disabling the hostility, namely the law . . ."

[72]It is not obvious in Ephesians 2:14-15 precisely what it is about the law that makes it a "hostility," but, as suggested above, it would seem almost certain that it is its exclusive and particularist character, effecting a religio-cultural divide, a contempt from outsiders and self-assuredness from insiders. See, e.g., the discussion in Andrew T. Lincoln, *Ephesians*, WBC 42 (Dallas: Word, 1990), 141-42. Thielman, defending the intrinsic goodness of the law (cf. Rom 7:12-14), is inclined toward a more anthropological explanation, attributing the law's divisiveness not to the law itself but to its "sinful use," "the hostile purposes to which human sinfulness had often put the Mosaic law's good, but temporary, commands about separating from the Gentiles." Again, "this toxic mixture of the law and human sinfulness . . . probably led Paul to speak of the law here in [Eph] 2:15 in negative terms" (Thielman, *Ephesians*, 170). It is not hard to see here a harmonization of

If we are keeping score between a TPP and NPP reading of Ephesians 2, the conclusion can only be that keeping score is pointless. The text is sufficiently multidimensional that it cooperates with both the TPP and NPP and equally frustrates narrow or extreme versions of both. For good reason, the TPP reads it as a clear statement of salvation by grace through faith apart from works, and the NPP sees (or would see, to the extent Ephesians were counted as a Pauline witness) the abiding themes of two peoples once divided, now reconciled within the covenant and the divisive effect of the law now overcome in God's reconciling purpose. It is the regrettable effect of polarizing debates that one should have to choose between interpretations that are intrinsically compatible and only at odds because of the discriminating and polemical habits of interpreters.

The burden of this chapter has been to demonstrate by example that what is true with regard to Ephesians 2 applies more broadly. The TPP and NPP readings of Paul become *exclusive* paradigms for reading Paul only by the willfulness of their proponents and at some unfortunate loss to the fullness of the texts' witness. Neither position is adequate in itself because both are "true" accounts of Paul, becoming false only to the extent that they become exclusive accounts of Paul. Against such tendencies, I have argued that these bifurcating, sometimes polemical, interpretive habits have impoverished, obscured or even held hostage our understanding of the fullness of the Pauline vision. Accordingly, it can be asked whether we can be delivered from the impasse with its false and unnecessary disjunctions. Might the answer be in a "*post*–new perspective on Paul"?

Ephesians 2:14-16 especially with Romans 7, and while the attempt to explicate and defend Paul's theological coherence is only to be welcomed, there is nothing in Ephesians 2 that actually encourages such a line of argument. One might well ask, if "the law of commandments in decrees" did not actually function divisively itself, why should Paul announce its nullification rather than condemn sinful or divisive appropriations?

GETTING POST THE
NEW PERSPECTIVE?

W e are all now post–new perspective interpreters of Paul. Whether one incorporates the insights of the NPP wholesale or stands opposed in adamant refutation, the NPP now influences virtually all scholarly conversation about Paul, not that it is the only game in town.[1] Indeed, even those

---

[1] The chief contending alternative is, of course, the so-called apocalyptic interpretation of Paul. Because the language of apocalyptic can apply to so many varied phenomena—literary genre(s), eschatological expectations, communities that produce literary genres or hold eschatological expectations, and so on—it is not always obvious what proponents of an apocalyptic Paul are referring to. As it is intended by chief proponents (e.g., J. Louis Martyn, Beverly Gaventa, Martinus de Boer, Doug Campbell, Doug Harink, Susan Eastman), we can perhaps isolate two irreducible features: (1) Minimally, the apocalyptic interpretation of Paul will show that Jesus as Messiah renders Paul substantially discontinuous with his Jewish past and also defies explanation by means of the surrounding philosophical and religious influences (as in the "history of religions school"). This naturally puts the apocalyptic in some tension with accounts of Paul that stress a narrative continuity for Paul within a storied Judaism. (2) That Jesus is rather more of an irruptive invasion than a merely paradoxical fulfillment of the Jewish story casts Christian soteriology fundamentally as an assault upon malevolent forces (e.g., hypostasized sin and death, τὰ στοιχεῖα) rather than as a mere remediation of human failure (i.e., sins and transgressions). For accessible statements of the position, see J. Louis Martyn, "The Apocalyptic Gospel in Galatians," *Int* 54, no. 3 (2000): 246-66; idem, *Galatians: A New Translation with Introduction and Commentary*, AB 33A (New York: Doubleday, 1998), 95-105; and Martinus C. de Boer, "Paul and Jewish Apocalyptic Eschatology," in *Apocalyptic and the New Testament: Essays in Honor of J. Louis Martyn*, ed. Joel Marcus and Marion L. Soards, JSNTSup 24 (Sheffield: JSOT Press, 1989), 169-90; summarized in idem, *Galatians: A Commentary*, NTL (Louisville, KY: Westminster John Knox, 2011), 31-35. For the position diversely worked out, see now the collections of essays in Beverly Roberts Gaventa, ed., *Apocalyptic Paul: Cosmos and Anthropos in Romans 5–8* (Waco, TX: Baylor University Press, 2013); and Ben C. Blackwell, John K. Goodrich and Jason Maston, eds., *Paul and the Apocalyptic Imagination* (Minneapolis: Fortress, 2016). For an extensive survey, albeit pointedly critical, see now N. T. Wright, *Paul and His Recent Interpreters: Some Contemporary Debates* (Minneapolis: Fortress, 2015), 135-218.

It is notable that several recent surveys of Pauline scholarship make but passing reference to the NPP and the complex of related issues. See, e.g., David E. Aune, ed., *The Blackwell Companion*

who have been most resolute in their rejection of the NPP find it worthy of contention, and many measured "opponents" find in it salutary corrections of a Paul too abstracted from Judaism and from his own exigencies. Even if some of the influence of the NPP can be chalked up to the rhetorical etiquette of well-behaved scholars, the appreciations for the gains are now appropriately widespread and substantially integrated into the scholarly discourse around Paul.[2] Although some might wish otherwise, there is no substantial evidence that the NPP is a passing scholarly fad. Widespread recantations are not on offer, even if leading advocates have shown themselves open to various adjustments born of interaction with critics and allies. This revolution in New Testament studies appears to have staying power.[3]

Nonetheless, now that this movement of scholarship approaches forty years since the publication of Sanders's *Paul and Palestinian Judaism* and a full half century since the appearance of Krister Stendahl's seminal essays, it is natural to ask what comes next. The NPP continues to exert its considerable influence, but doubters and detractors are not few and their concerns are not trivial. Have we then settled for a stalemate, a permanent "parting of the ways"? Or is there a post–new perspective scholarship that drives toward some new synthesis? The initial answer appears to be that it is too soon to say, that post-NPP scholarship is diverse, save perhaps a general endorsement of the broadest contours of Sanders's thesis, naturally with various

---

to the New Testament (Malden, MA: Wiley-Blackwell, 2010); and Oda Wischmeyer, ed., *Paul: Life, Setting, Work, Letters*, trans. Helen S. Heron (New York: T&T Clark, 2012). It is probably fair to say that the NPP attracts the attention especially of the English-speaking world, those invested theologically and practically in matters soteriological (e.g., Reformed, evangelicals and traditionally minded Lutherans) and those for whom the soteriology of the New Testament runs as direct a course from the New Testament to contemporary formulations as possible.

[2]Note as a case in point that there is no representative of the NPP among a recent collection of introductory essays on Paul: Michael F. Bird, ed., *Four Views on the Apostle Paul* (Grand Rapids: Zondervan, 2012). But within that volume, the NPP frequently drives and always informs the discussion nonetheless. Doug Campbell is said to represent a *post*–new perspective; Luke Johnson, though representing a "Catholic" perspective, makes ample use of NPP insights; Tom Schreiner is well known as a critic of the NPP; and Mark Nanos, offering a Jewish approach, finds frequent fault with the NPP in its failure to take its reappraisal of Judaism far enough.

[3]Although the standard account—this included—credits the NPP primarily to Sanders, Dunn and Wright (with perhaps a tip of the hat to the prescience of Krister Stendahl), New Testament scholars in broad sympathy with this revolution comprise a much longer list, including, among others, such influential representatives as Richard Hays, Bruce Longenecker, Terence Donaldson, Frank Matera, Scot McKnight, Katherine Grieb, John Gager, Lloyd Gaston, Kathy Ehrensperger, Michael Thompson, Kent Yinger and Don Garlington. Even this incomplete list demonstrates that these scholars of shared sympathies constitute anything but a monolith.

qualifications.[4] Beyond that minimalist consensus, accounts of Paul's theology, his soteriology in particular, still range dramatically.

3.1 DESTROYING THE DIVIDING WALL OF HOSTILITY?

It is perhaps not sufficiently noted that a significant element of this debate
is sociological, which is not to say absent exegetical basis and rigor but that
the reception of NPP scholarship and themes is not detached from ecclesial
affiliations, informal coalitions of the like-minded and even generational
tendencies. The NPP has had two distinguishable, though not entirely distinct, receptions: a longer scholarly reception among academics and specialists and another more recent popular reception in the church and among
clergy, students and theologically inclined laypersons. The story line of the
first reception is a provocative rebuke (Sanders), succeeded by a lengthy,
often polemical but characteristically technical, conversation, yielding over
time to increasing moderation. I don't suggest that there is now a settled
equanimity, much less agreement, only that the more unyielding articulations of the NPP have moderated and that even the strongest critics concede
the more patent corrections offered by the NPP.

The first half of that story within the guild was already substantially
played out before the NPP became a matter of interest and then controversy
among North American evangelicals in particular.[5] Wright especially,

---

[4]By post-NPP scholarship, I employ the following as qualifying criteria: (1) work that self-adver-
tises as "post-" or "beyond" NPP; (2) work aiming to mediate or even synthesize formerly disparate positions; and (3) work that, whether or not it self-describes as "post-," clearly launches
from NPP premises, perhaps not to reenact former battles but in order to make new proposals.
In what follows, I have limited the discussion to major figures and book-length offerings. Other
contributions might justly be cited: e.g., Brendan Byrne, "Interpreting Romans Theologically in
a Post-'New Perspective' Perspective," HTR 94, no. 3 (2001): 227-41; and idem, "Interpreting
Romans: The New Perspective and Beyond," Int 58, no. 3 (2004): 241-52. Worthy of particular
notice is Ben C. Blackwell's published dissertation, a keen engagement with Pauline soteriology
with the aid of patristic interpretation: Christosis: Pauline Soteriology in Light of Deification in
Irenaeus and Cyril of Alexandria, WUNT 2.314 (Tübingen: Mohr Siebeck, 2011).

[5]As a barometer on North American evangelicalism, Christianity Today magazine has revisited
this debate over several decades: Daniel G. Reid, "The Misunderstood Apostle," Christianity
Today, July 16, 1990, 25-27; John Ortberg, "Why Jesus' Disciples Wouldn't Wash Their Hands,"
Christianity Today, August 15, 1994, 26; Simon J. Gathercole, "What Did Paul Really Mean? 'New
Perspective' Scholars Argue That We Need, Well, a New Perspective on Justification by Faith,"
Christianity Today, August 1, 2007, 22-28; Trevin Wax, "The Justification Debate: A Primer,"
Christianity Today, June 1, 2009, 34-37; and Jason Byassee, "Surprised by N. T. Wright," Christi-
anity Today, April 1, 2014, 36.

because of his influence in North American evangelicalism and his gifts for popularizing and public speaking, is the face of the NPP for a significant stream of followers and detractors, many of whom are not substantially conversant with the earlier academic thrust and parry. Because North American evangelicalism is a large, diverse, formidable and sometimes wary entity, the NPP would become the occasion for a variety of public arguments. The most notorious was initiated by John Piper's broadside contra Wright, which was matched by Wright's response in kind.[6] It is hard not to conclude that the two largely talked past each other and that the result was a more pronounced polarization that left partisans, extraordinarily on *both* sides, more confident of their position (or in their hero, perhaps we should say).[7] There are any number of other skirmishes, including, for example, the intramural controversy among conservative North American Presbyterians in which, remarkably, Wright would become an unwitting participant in the "Federal Vision" (a.k.a. "Auburn Avenue Theology") dispute.[8] The good news in all of this is the recent evidence of synthetic and moderating perspectives that have the potential to advance our shared understanding and not just a certain partisan position. In some cases, the moderation comes from the key figures themselves, with whom we now begin in a survey of recent "post–new perspective" scholarship.

3.1.1 Dunn and Wright. If there is a post-NPP scholarship, it would seem fair to begin with the architects of the original and to see what sort of remodeling they find coherent with their original vision. Neither Dunn nor Wright has stood still, sometimes later "backfilling" an earlier claim with more data

---

[6]John Piper, *The Future of Justification: A Response to N. T. Wright* (Wheaton, IL: Crossway, 2008); and N. T. Wright, *Justification: God's Plan and Paul's Vision* (Downers Grove, IL: IVP Academic, 2009).

[7]My evidence is anecdotal, but not insignificant. I was surprised frequently to learn that "Piper put the new perspective to rest" and to hear that "Piper exposed Wright for the false teacher he is" while also that "Wright sure put Piper in his place" and "I guess that debate is finally over [in Wright's favor]." Especially disheartening is that I never heard a response to either book that surprised me, given what I knew of the reader's theological and social affiliations. Add to this those honest readers who confessed after reading both books that they were not confident that they even knew what the issues were.

[8]Although this debate is obscure to the point of near inscrutability for any of us not inhabiting the theological tradition and social context. For an affirmation, see Steven Wilkins and Duane Garner, eds., *The Federal Vision* (Monroe, LA: Athanasius Press, 2014); for a critique, see Guy Prentiss Waters, *Federal Vision and Covenant Theology: A Comparative Analysis* (Phillipsburg, NJ: P&R, 2006).

or marshaling a more refined argument, sometimes even correcting an earlier view (or improving its articulation) after considering the claims of various critics. James Dunn's itinerary through the NPP is readily available in the collection of essays *The New Perspective on Paul*, which is introduced by a candid autobiographical account of his work up to that point.[9] In it, we learn what a careful observer might have noticed otherwise: without ever abandoning the original paradigm articulated in the 1982 Rylands lecture, Dunn has been qualifying and nuancing his positions with care, especially his central original claim that "works of the law" worked as veritable technical terminology for the distinguishing "covenantal boundary markers."

If we might describe Dunn's itinerary as one of increasing refinement, and with it a certain moderation, Wright's contribution more clearly transcends the label "new perspective," especially now with the publication of *Paul and the Faithfulness of God*. Not only for reason of its imposing length, Wright's recent work defies easy summary, chiefly because Wright leaves a much larger footprint with his more multidimensional, if fulsome, exposition of Paul, such that he is justified in regarding the "new perspective" label as no longer satisfactory.[10] Wright's account of Paul, like the larger project in which it participates,[11] draws Paul, with Jesus and the early Christian movement, on a large canvas of story, symbol and praxis in which the same are drawn as characters in Israel's story of vocation, stalled in exile, yet alive with variegated hopes. Here Wright reprises—and, it should be said, considerably reinforces—the account first articulated in *The New Testament and the People of God*, but now augmenting the account of Second Temple Judaism with a substantial account of the Greco-Roman context to supplement, especially the deeply enmeshed interplay of the religious with the political.[12] The political implications of Paul's gospel, a theme adumbrated

---

[9]James D. G. Dunn, "The New Perspective: Whence, What and Whither?," in *NPerP*, 1-97.

[10]So, e.g., "the broad and now unhelpful label of 'new perspective'"; "the low-grade either/or that has been taking place between 'old' and 'new' perspectives"; and so on. N. T. Wright, *P&FG*, 2:925n426; 2:1038, respectively.

[11]The Christian Origins and the Question of God, now with four installments in five volumes: N. T. Wright, *The New Testament and the People of God* (Minneapolis: Fortress, 1992); idem, *Jesus and the Victory of God* (Minneapolis: Fortress, 1996); idem, *The Resurrection of the Son of God* (Minneapolis: Fortress, 2003); and now idem, *P&FG*, 2 vols. (Minneapolis: Fortress, 2013).

[12]To my reading, Wright's frequent claim that Israel's self-understanding is as a people still in exile is considerably strengthened in this more recent work (*P&FG*, 1:75-197).

in earlier work, especially *Paul in Fresh Perspective*, is now substantially expanded in this latest work. The same can be said of Wright's account of Paul's Christology, which is substantially in accord with others espousing an "early high Christology," such as Larry Hurtado and, even more directly, Richard Bauckham.[13] Likewise, in following Richard Hays's subjective-genitive rendering of *pistis Christou*,[14] Wright develops its theological implications in some detail, showing the "faithfulness of Christ" to be a messianic remediation of both Adam's and Israel's lapse; the faithfulness of God is embodied in the faithful messianic son, an obedient covenant reprise. We could go on detailing Wright's expansive work, but labeling position by position by name-dropping scholarly genealogy hardly does the synthesis, much less the details, any justice.

For our present purposes, we can make two salient observations: (1) On the whole, it would be fairer to say that Wright's views have expanded more than that they have moderated. While in Dunn we see frequent indications of gentle and partial disavowal without abandoning the original claim, with Wright there is a decided, and I think welcome, move in *P&FG* toward a "both . . . and . . ." on virtually every issue where such a thing is possible. The soteriological dilemma is both personal *and* cosmic.[15] Justification is "forensic" (inasmuch as it carries out a lawcourt metaphor) *and* participationist (in Jewish incorporative rather than Greco-Roman mystical categories).[16] Paul's frame of reference is both "apocalyptic" *and* "salvation-historical," each having its proper meaning only with respect to the integrative motif of covenant.[17] But it should also be noted that Wright's "both

---

[13]Larry W. Hurtado, *Lord Jesus Christ: Devotion to Jesus in Earliest Christianity* (Grand Rapids: Eerdmans, 2003); and Richard Bauckham, *Jesus and the God of Israel: God Crucified and Other Studies on the New Testament's Christology of Divine Identity* (Grand Rapids: Eerdmans, 2008).
[14]Richard B. Hays, *The Faith of Jesus Christ: The Narrative Substructure of Galatians 3:1–4:11*, 2nd ed., Biblical Resource Series (Grand Rapids: Eerdmans, 2001).
[15]E.g., Wright, *P&FG*, 2:756.
[16]E.g., ibid., 2:925-1032; see esp. 2:990, 2:1011-12; 2:1024-25; 2:1263-64; 2:1513 and passim.
[17]E.g., ibid., 2:1512-13. When Wright allows there is a sense in which Paul is properly "apocalyptic," he emphatically does *not* mean to affirm the "apocalyptic school" descended from Ernst Käsemann and theologically from Karl Barth (e.g., J. Louis Martyn, Doug Campbell, Martinus de Boer, Doug Harink, Beverly Gaventa and Susan Eastman), whose radically irruptive view of the divine intervention is entirely at odds with Wright's understanding of the fulfillment of Israel's narrative in Jesus Christ. Indeed, Wright borders on the defensive and caustic in his rebuff of the apocalyptic school throughout *P&FG*. I leave it to others to determine who "started it."

... and ..." is vigorous and, in its own way, sharply polemical.[18] (2) Although Wright's account of Paul expands in important ways far beyond the parameters of the NPP, he does not fundamentally back down from the characteristic claims outlined earlier. If the pre-Damascus Paul is described in much more vivid and political terms, he is still not entirely unlike the Paul whom Stendahl introduced to us. And if Wright is rarely impressed by Sanders's efforts in Pauline theology, Sanders's soteriology of Second Temple Judaism is largely taken for granted in its main contours, even if Sanders's account comes off as dryly propositional in juxtaposition to Wright's more warmblooded, storied rendering. Likewise, Wright follows—while inevitably expanding on—Dunn with regard to "works of the law" and its entailments, even while they are miles apart on Christology, with signs of that gap closing.[19] The simple point is that Wright might well be a "fresh perspective" Pauline scholar, but he remains essentially a "new perspective" scholar, even if his interests far exceed the narrow concerns that spawned and then preoccupied the NPP and its critics.

Perhaps the most disappointing feature of Wright's work from the vantage point of this project is his little interest in the development of Pauline thought and categories from letter to letter and through Paul's career. Rather, Wright treats the whole Pauline corpus as a kind of single source whence can be drawn materials for his theologically constructive project. Not even the immediate circumstances of individual letters, to say nothing of trajectories between them, are of much interest to Wright. Galatians can explicate Romans as much as the other way around; Ephesians might lend a hand with 2 Corinthians and vice versa; and so on. While this is much to be preferred to the atomizing alternative, in which each letter's peculiarities are traced as incoherence, Wright's facility in drawing from the whole in the service of his overarching narrative might be an exercise of control, a will to narrate, that obscures important distinctions, not only unwittingly homogenizing the diversity of Paul's thought but also prizing the interpreter's considerable

---

[18]See the review of John M. G. Barclay, "Paul and the Faithfulness of God," *SJT* 68, no. 2 (2015): 235-43.

[19]Dunn's Christology, being Adamic and originally eschewing preexistence and incarnation, is notoriously "low," especially compared to Wright and his counterparts. But see now James D. G. Dunn, *Did the First Christians Worship Jesus? The New Testament Evidence* (Louisville, KY: Westminster John Knox, 2010).

synthetic and rhetorical skill to such an extent that Paul's own development is set to the side.

3.1.2 Francis Watson. Another figure who can be numbered among the "post-NPP" vanguard, though ambiguously, is Francis Watson. Watson must be regarded as one of the more intriguing figures in the NPP debate, not only because he is one of the most wide-ranging and creative scholars of our generation but also because seemingly he has positioned himself at different times on both "sides" of the issues. Watson's first major study, originally published in 1986, *Paul, Judaism, and the Gentiles*, with its sociological account of the relationship of Jews to Gentiles in the primitive Pauline communities, would seem to have advanced several major tenets of the NPP.[20] Watson argued that Paul's writings evince a pragmatic agenda, to underwrite and justify the separation of Christ-following Gentiles from the synagogue. In many respects the book is almost stereotypical in its advocacy for this new way of reading Paul, including frequent aspersions cast upon Luther's theological interpretation.[21] Yet fifteen years subsequent to its publication, Watson would come out with a rather strongly worded critique of the NPP by means of an unpublished paper delivered at the British New Testament Society in 2001, which naturally elicited significant interest.[22]

But then, perhaps surprisingly, having apparently departed from the NPP, Watson would nonetheless revise and republish his *Paul, Judaism, and the Gentiles* in 2007 with a new subtitle, *Beyond the New Perspective*. The revision marks Watson's further development on the questions raised by the NPP and also seeks to demonstrate that the original work was never quite lockstep with the NPP in any case.[23] In the important introductory essay to the second edition, Watson maintains that his original work differed from

---

[20]Francis Watson, *Paul, Judaism, and the Gentiles: A Sociological Approach*, SNSTMS 56 (Cambridge: Cambridge University Press, 1986), subsequently revised and expanded as *Paul, Judaism, and the Gentiles: Beyond the New Perspective*, 2nd ed. (Grand Rapids: Eerdmans, 2007). Subsequent references are to this later edition.

[21]Watson, *Paul, Judaism, and the Gentiles: Beyond the New Perspective*, e.g., 27-40, although subsequently cf. 346-50.

[22]Francis Watson, "Not the New Perspective," paper presented at the British New Testament Conference, Manchester, September 2001.

[23]To appreciate how Francis Watson distinguishes his positions in *Paul, Judaism and the Gentiles* from the NPP, note esp. the new introduction (pp. 1-26), new conclusion (pp. 344-50) and appendix on theological interpretation ("Christ, Law, and Freedom: A Plea for the *Sensus Literalis*," 351-69) of the second edition.

characteristic emphases of the NPP with respect to four divergences: (1) presumably in distinction from Sanders, Watson's appeal to "covenantal nomism" highlights the particularity of a polemic against "works of the law" rather than participating in a larger argument about the gratuity of the Jewish religion; (2) Watson avers that divine agency played a more fundamental role in Paul's "pattern of religion" than in the Judaism he opposes; (3) although "works of the law" do function as a definition of the distinctive Jewish way of life, the phrase does not (contra Dunn) carry with it the more particular notion of "boundary markers" such as circumcison, food laws or sabbath;[24] and (4) Paul advocates a sectarian separation between Judaism and the emerging Christian community rather than an inclusive understanding of the one people of God as encompassing Jews and Gentiles. It must be said that these are fine distinctions, which even when given full weight do not so much set Watson's original work over against the NPP as nuance the contribution as it is situated with respect to the major voices.

I do not think, in fact, that *Paul, Judaism, and the Gentiles* is as "beyond" as Watson does, but that, in fact, the real *beyond* is to be found in *Paul and the Hermeneutics of Faith*.[25] Here Watson argues that Paul's exigencies are insufficient to account for his theological views, that they are rooted in and driven by his fresh reading and appropriation of the Jewish Scriptures. Thus, the key texts upon which Paul's arguments turn are not, as so often supposed, ad hoc proof texts to which Paul appeals, back against the wall, justifying his innovation with whatever he can get his hands on. Rather, refracted through the Christ event, these texts don't justify but rather *generate* Paul's theological stances. Paul is, above all else, a reader of the Jewish Scriptures, and he has arrived at his positions not haphazardly but by reckoning with the text, especially the Pentateuch, as a whole, including making sense of promises, obligations and curses in a coherent whole and in light of the Christ event.

I confess that it is harder for me than for Watson to find the coherence between this thesis and the argument of *Paul, Judaism, and the Gentiles*, but

---

[24]Note that Dunn's adjustment of his original position on "works of the law" postdates Watson's first edition of *Paul, Judaism, and the Gentiles*.
[25]Francis Watson, *Paul and the Hermeneutics of Faith* (London: T&T Clark, 2004); on his relationship to the NPP, note esp. 29n61.

it is an intrinsically appealing position, brilliantly articulated, that cuts against the grain of much Pauline scholarship on Paul's use of Scripture. Thus, in Watson's scholarship, we can trace a movement from the exigent Paul to the exegete Paul. The former makes do creatively in the warp and woof of primitive Christ-affiliated Jewish communities while the latter finds his mooring in the reconciliation of biblical texts to each other on this side of the Christ event. And, if not obviously the case with *Paul, Judaism and the Gentiles*, surely with *Paul and the Hermeneutics of Faith*, by offering a theologian Paul who is more than a counterpunching pragmatist, Watson takes us quite *beyond* the NPP, even if not in the book so subtitled.

3.1.3 Douglas Campbell. Though ultimately an outspoken critic of the NPP, Doug Campbell's critique stands far apart from most who protest Sanders's revised understanding of Judaism or defend certain details of the standard readings of Paul.[26] Campbell, by contrast, is entirely sympathetic with Sanders's account—if hardly in entire agreement with it—treating it as foundational for his overall project, and is deeply animated by the specter of Christian anti-Judaism.[27] It is clear that for Campbell, the NPP continues to be mired in categories for reading Paul inherited from the Reformation, never mind its bold claims to the contrary. The NPP is still stuck in its own version of what Campbell dubs "Justification theory," which is his moniker for what he regards as the deeply flawed, yet dominant, default reading of

---

[26]Our primary interest here is with Douglas A. Campbell, *The Deliverance of God: An Apocalyptic Rereading of Justification in Paul* (Grand Rapids: Eerdmans, 2009). The book is written not only in conversation with the NPP (note esp. pp. 167-218, 440-59) but with an extraordinarily vast breadth of biblical, theological and historical scholarship as well. Campbell takes up the "post-NPP" label in his contribution to Michael F. Bird's edited volume (Douglas A. Campbell, "Christ and the Church in Paul: A 'Post–New Perspective' Account," in *Four Views on the Apostle Paul*, ed. Michael F. Bird [Grand Rapids: Zondervan, 2012], 113-43).

[27]In Campbell's words, "I am post–new perspective because, on the one hand, I maintain with the new perspective that the Jewish question is a critical one. I agree, further, that certain ways of reading Paul cannot answer this question responsibly; various accounts of Paul's gospel lock the apostle's theology into an indefensible account of Judaism with awful political consequences" (D. A. Campbell, "Christ and the Church in Paul," 114-15). He is "utterly unpersuaded by the various apologetic attempts to deflect or roll back this concern" (noting, e.g., Carson, O'Brien and Seifrid, *JVN:CSTJ*). Likewise, because it only acclimates Paul to his Jewish context but insufficiently addresses the "Jewish question," Campbell does not consider the NPP entirely sufficient, even if much to be preferred to the TPP. Thus, Campbell's "'post' in the title 'post–new perspective' is therefore an emphatic one" (ibid., 116).

Paul's soteriology.[28] Since he takes nearly 100 pages to describe it and another 350 to critique it, a brief summary will have to do.[29]

"Justification theory" is a reading of Paul that begins with the existence of a retributive God. This God is knowable as are his requirements for human beings, being deducible from the created world and by means of moral intuition (per a traditional Christian reading of Rom 1:18-32). Thus, human beings know themselves to be accountable and culpable before this God's bar of retributive justice. God's disclosure of particular requirements by means of (Jewish) law does not bring hope to culpable humanity; rather, it induces greater despair. Since they find themselves unable to maintain a perfect observance of that law—which, according to "Justification theory," is what the law requires—they are driven to despair. That is, unless, as with Jews contemporary with Paul—indeed even Paul himself once—they are given over to the folly of presuming themselves righteous. But God provides a solution for the human dilemma in the death of a sinless Christ who bears the punishment due sinners, who are granted by faith Christ's innocence and righteousness, being thus qualified for a favorable judgment and eternal life.

It would be unfair to say that this account is entirely unfamiliar—it would match fairly closely, for example, summaries of "the gospel" used in certain evangelical contexts, which have in turn exercised an extraordinary theological

---

[28]I retain scare quotes for the term "Justification theory" in order to reinforce not only that this is Campbell's phrase but that its conception and description are entirely his as well and that both the concept and his description are idiosyncratic and problematic. Although several reveiwers have commented on the idiosyncrasy of his account of "Justification theory," see esp. R. Barry Matlock, "Zeal for Paul but Not According to Knowledge: Douglas Campbell's War on 'Justification Theory,'" *JSNT* 34, no. 2 (2011): 115-49; and more briefly, my review, Garwood P. Anderson, "Wrestling a Strawman: Doug Campbell's *The Deliverance of God*," *The Living Church*, March 9, 2014, 23-25.

Campbell has chosen this nomenclature so as to avoid the misleadingness of the label "Lutheran" (e.g., lampooned in Stephen Westerholm, *Perspectives Old and New on Paul: The "Lutheran" Paul and His Critics* [Grand Rapids: Eerdmans, 2004], who relishes that not only Luther but also Augustine, Aquinas, Calvin, Wesley and virtually the whole Western theological tradition are "Lutheran" by the broad-brush definitions of the NPP). But the choice is infelicitous, for, whatever one makes of Campbell's "Justification theory," it remains the case that it is a particular account *of* justification, and every interpreter of Paul needs to give some account of justification, as indeed, does Campbell. But it is hard for Campbell then to avoid a sort of sneering dismissal of justification altogether (perhaps unintentional), which is only exacerbated by his sometime use of *Justification* absolutely (capitalized) as shorthand for *his* account of "Justification theory."

[29]Of necessity, this is an abbreviation even of D. A. Campbell's summary account (*Deliverance of God*, 28-29).

influence on evangelical churches and culture.[30] But Campbell is not successful in attributing this program to notable theologians or biblical scholars. Quite rightly, he notes that the overlap of his "Justification theory" with Luther's soteriology is imperfect, nor is "Justification theory" descriptive of Calvin or even his nearer-in-time heirs. It turns out, in fact, that historical and scholarly proponents of "Justification theory" are actually hard to adduce, though this does not weaken Campbell's zeal to eradicate the scourge.

By virtue of its magnitude (approaching 1,200 pages, including 240 pages of small-type endnotes), its breathtaking learnedness and breadth, and its sheer take-no-prisoners audacity, *The Deliverance of God* has occasioned a firestorm of response, ranging from dubious to harshly negative.[31] The argument of the book—so impressive, if not always convincing, in its details—is substantially flawed at the macrolevel. Despite Campbell's protestations to the contrary, his "Justification theory" foil is an elaborate straw man.[32] His own failure to adduce bona fide scholarly representatives of the entire system of thought exposes and subverts the argumentative function of the foil. One thinks, for example, of certain leading contemporary proponents

---

[30]It is telling and problematic that among Campbell's best exemplars for his "Justification theory" are the Billy Graham Association and Campus Crusade for Christ. Less persuasive in the same context is the attribution of "Justification theory" to Rudolf Bultmann (ibid., 289-96).

[31]D. A. Campbell's *Deliverance of God* was the occasion for a review panel at the 2009 meetings of the SBL. The *Journal for the Study of the New Testament* devoted an entire issue to it (34, no. 2 [2011]) with major review articles and a surrejoinder by Campbell (Grant Macaskill, "Review Article: The Deliverance of God," *JSNT* 34, no. 2 [2011]: 150-61; Matlock, "Zeal for Paul but Not According to Knowledge"; and Douglas A. Campbell, "An Attempt to Be Understood: A Response to the Concerns of Matlock and Macaskill with *The Deliverance of God*," *JSNT* 34, no. 2 [2011]: 162-208). Besides the latter essay, Campbell has summarized or defended his position multiple times: Douglas A. Campbell, "Beyond Justification in Paul: The Thesis of the Deliverance of God," *SJT* 65, no. 1 (2012): 90-104; and idem, "An Apocalyptic Rereading of 'Justification' in Paul: Or, an Overview of the Argument of Douglas Campbell's *The Deliverance of God*—by Douglas Campbell," *ExpTim* 123, no. 8 (2012): 382-93. Additionally, note the more extensive review essays of Douglas J. Moo, review of *The Deliverance of God: An Apocalyptic Rereading of Justification in Paul*, by Douglas A. Campbell, *JETS* 53, no. 1 (2010): 143-50; Bruce Clark, review of *The Deliverance of God: An Apocalyptic Rereading of Justification in Paul*, by Douglas A. Campbell, *Tyndale Bulletin* 64, no. 1 (2013): 55-88; and Francis Watson, review of *The Deliverance of God: An Apocalyptic Rereading of Justification in Paul*, by Douglas A. Campbell, *Early Christianity* 1, no. 1 (2010): 179-85. Finally, Campbell's program is the subject of a dedicated volume of response essays: Chris Tilling, ed., *Beyond Old and New Perpectives on Paul: Reflections on the Work of Douglas Campbell* (Eugene, OR: Cascade, 2014).

[32]Quite rightly, Campbell understands the fatality of the straw-man charge for his argument (*Deliverance of God*, 11-13, esp. n. 3).

of the "Lutheran" approach, Stephen Westerholm, Doug Moo and Mark Seifrid, among them—all of whom have published extensively on the matters at hand. Yet anyone familiar with the work of these would find strikingly little resemblance to the "Justification theory" that Campbell describes. Westerholm argues that Augustine, Luther, Calvin and Wesley all held a view of justification, which, differences in detail and expression notwithstanding, would be called, and dismissed as, "Lutheran" by critics of the traditional view, yet it is hard to find Campbell's "Justification theory" articulated by any of them. Seifrid would come under fire among some Reformed compatriots for disavowing imputed righteousness;[33] he rejects emphatically a rationalist and voluntarist account of faith; he advocates a nuanced definition for the "righteousness of God" rather distinct from a characteristic Lutheran approach; and his understanding of *pistis Christou* could make Karl Barth blush.[34] Likewise, Moo, though committed (some might say staunchly) to readings of Romans and Galatians that are in continuity with the Reformation, takes great care to situate Paul's arguments in their historical and religious contexts—as Jewish pastoral polemics, not Christian systematic theology. One might note Moo's treatment of Romans 7, to cite but one example, which clearly demonstrates more affinities with Wright than with, say, Luther.[35] But if Westerholm, Seifrid and Moo are not representatives of "Justification theory," one must ask who is, or, more pointedly, are there really any?

Campbell's own argument is a creative dismantling of Romans such that Romans 1–4 substantially represent Paul's impersonation of an interlocutor other than himself, arguing for a position contrary to his own. This way Romans 1–4 on the whole constitutes a foil for Romans 5–8, which is a kind of rebuttal of the opening gambit of Romans 1–4. This is, to be sure, a highly imaginative reading of Romans.[36] It imagines, among other things, that,

---

[33]Mark A. Seifrid, *Christ, Our Righteousness: Paul's Theology of Justification*, NSBT 9 (Downers Grove, IL: InterVarsity Press, 2000), 171-77.

[34]Mark A. Seifrid, "Faith of Christ," in Bird and Sprinkle, *FJC*, 129-46, on which see below.

[35]Douglas J. Moo, *Epistle to the Romans*, NICNT (Grand Rapids: Eerdmans, 1996), 432-70.

[36]It should be noted that, although a surprising hypothesis, Campbell's interlocutor of Romans 1–4 is not unanticipated, being the combining and creative development of two strands of recent Pauline research: (1) the reading of Romans as diatribe that makes use of impersonation as rhetorical trope (e.g., Stanley K. Stowers, *A Rereading of Romans: Justice, Jews, and Gentiles* [New Haven, CT: Yale University Press, 1994], esp. 126-75; Thomas H. Tobin, *Paul's Rhetoric in Its Contexts: The Argument of Romans* [Peabody, MA: Hendrickson, 2004]; and Christopher Bryan, *A Preface to Romans: Notes on the Epistle in Its Literary and Cultural Setting* [New York:

aided by a lector's nonverbals, the earliest hearers of Romans would not have fallen into the error of all subsequent readers before Campbell in assuming that the early chapters of the letter are Paul meaning what he seems to be saying (even while not always agreeing what that was). Campbell's reading also expects his readers to exercise their imagination in conjuring a blustery first-century Christian Jew who uncannily anticipates the positions of twentieth-century evangelical populist naifs. Where Campbell lacks imagination is in failing even to attempt a reading of Romans in which the "juridical" opening gambit might be found preparatory for and coherent with the apocalyptic, transformative denouement in Romans 5–8. It is hard to avoid the impression that Campbell, out of distaste for what some have made of some of Paul, makes a challenging text into an impossible one.

As post-NPP scholarship, it is unlikely that Campbell's extraordinary piece of work will have staying power with respect to his exegesis, which seems to have convinced few. As a heuristic for the state of Pauline scholarship on the other side of the NPP, the book serves a useful function, revealing a confused state of affairs born of agonistic and disjunctive scholarly habits, of which Campbell is not only among the latest but perhaps the best example.

3.1.4 Michael Gorman. Michael Gorman has emerged as a recently prolific and adept theological interpreter of Paul, authoring scholarly, introductory and popularizing works.[37] Gorman figures into the NPP debates as a non-combatant.[38] His primary contribution consists neither in advancing nor rebutting NPP premises but rather in a compelling theological-ethical synthesis of Pauline leitmotifs, while demonstrating considerable sympathy for certain recent trends in Pauline scholarship, including, but not limited to, the NPP.

Oxford University Press, 2000]) and (2) the identification of Paul's Galatians opponents as purveyors of a forensic "gospel" that Paul *opposes* (Martyn, *Galatians*, 117-27; and de Boer, *Galatians*, 50-61).

[37] Michael J. Gorman, *Cruciformity: Paul's Narrative Spirituality of the Cross* (Grand Rapids: Eerdmans, 2001); idem, *Apostle of the Crucified Lord: A Theological Introduction to Paul and His Letters* (Grand Rapids: Eerdmans, 2004); idem, *Reading Paul*, Cascade Companions (Eugene, OR: Cascade, 2008); idem, *Inhabiting the Cruciform God: Kenosis, Justification, and Theosis in Paul's Narrative Soteriology* (Grand Rapids: Eerdmans, 2009); and idem, *Becoming the Gospel: Paul, Participation, and Mission* (Grand Rapids: Eerdmans, 2015). Of particular interest for our purposes are the more scholarly works, *Cruciformity* and *Inhabiting the Cruciform God*, with the introductory and survey books as useful background.

[38] E.g., Gorman, *Apostle of the Crucified Lord*, 20-21.

That Gorman shares certain basic sympathies with the NPP while retaining certain criticisms is indicated by his treatment of key terms in the
Pauline corpus. Gorman is particularly averse to what he regards as false
disjunctions in Pauline scholarship—for example, pitting a participationist
view of justification against the forensic, or the horizontal against the vertical, or even "faith" against "works." Although "justification" has a forensic
dimension, it is best understood as "the establishment or restoration of right
covenantal relations—**fidelity** to God and **love** for neighbor—with the
certain **hope** of acquittal/vindication on the day of judgment."[39] This approach to justification is characteristic of Gorman's treatment of numerous
issues. One notes echoes of Sanders and Wright in the emphasis on covenant
but also an intentional correction of certain NPP formulations by insisting
on justification's simultaneous both vertical and horizontal dimensions and
the inclusion of the forensic dimension in the language of "acquittal."[40]
Gorman will play up certain motifs more than others; he has, for example,
not much to say about atonement and acquittal, but it is there. Meanwhile,
he has refreshingly much to say about the community-forming and "theopolitical" dimensions of Paul's gospel, which have peacemaking and inclu-
sivity among its distinguishing marks. It is not hard to discern an effort to
recalibrate an excessively juridical and vertical soteriology by balancing
those dimensions with the gospel's personal and communal transformative
power and its political and ethical ends.

Although it is his briefest contribution, *Reading Paul* articulates Gorman's understanding of Paul's gospel in one, grammar-defying, admittedly
playful, sentence.

> Paul preached, and then explained in various pastoral, community-forming
> letters, a narrative, apocalyptic, theopolitical gospel in continuity with the
> story of Israel and in distinction to the imperial gospel of Rome (and anal-
> ogous powers) that was centered on God's crucified and exalted Messiah Jesus,
> whose incarnation, life, and death by crucifixion were validated and vindi-
> cated by God in his resurrection and exaltation as Lord, which inaugurated

---

[39]Gorman, *Inhabiting the Cruciform God*, 53, italics removed; boldface retained. Cf. Gorman,
Apostle of the Crucified Lord, 138, 201.
[40]See, e.g., the multiple affirmations with as many qualifications (note esp. the footnotes) in his
discussion of justification in Gorman, *Inhabiting the Cruciform God*, 52-57.

the new age or new creation in which all members of this diverse but consistently covenantally dysfunctional human race who respond in self-abandoning and self-committing faith thereby participate in Christ's death and resurrection and are (1) justified, or restored to right covenant relations with God and with others; (2) incorporated into a particular manifestation of Christ, the Lord's body on earth, the church, which is an alternative community to the status-quo human communities committed to and governed by Caesar (and analogous rulers) and by values contrary to the gospel; and (3) infused both individually and corporately by the Spirit of God's Son so that they may lead "bifocal" lives, focused both back on Christ's first coming and ahead to his second, consisting of Christlike, cruciform (cross-shaped) (1) faith and (2) hope toward God and (3) love toward both neighbors and enemies (a love marked by peaceableness and inclusion), in joyful anticipation of (1) the return of Christ, (2) the resurrection of the dead to eternal life, and (3) the renewal of the entire creation.[41]

The short book is an exposition of that thesis (or is it theses?). Absent is any polemic for or against the NPP, but its several leading themes are on full display, albeit with moderating twists here and there.

Gorman ventures into new territory in *Inhabiting the Cruciform God*, though building on his first major Pauline work, *Cruciformity*. He argues that Paul's master narrative, most directly articulated in the Philippians Christ hymn but everywhere present throughout Paul's writings,[42] describes the self-emptying "kenosis" of Christ as constituent and revelatory of the divine character. This pattern expresses itself not only as essentially descriptive of God but also as the pattern for those who are in Christ, who thus, in taking up the pattern of Christ, come to bear the image of God himself. Somewhat provocatively, Gorman calls this "theosis," though it should be said that, apart from the word itself, there is no real pretense of replicating the Orthodox doctrine bearing the same name.[43] Still, Gorman's account

---

[41]Gorman, *Reading Paul*, 8.

[42]Gorman's case for this "master narrative" is convincingly made in *Cruciformity*, esp. 175-201.

[43]Whether Gorman's use of *theosis* is proper is a question better left to others; see, e.g., the appropriate caution of Grant Macaskill, *Union with Christ in the New Testament* (Oxford: Oxford University Press, 2014), 75-76. For my part, I find it less distracting to read Gorman's book as though by *theosis* he simply intends *imitatio Christi*, which, though a more rhetorically modest claim, is already a more robust notion of participation than is customary in some Protestant soteriologies.

shows the sort of wholesome fruit that the NPP can bear when the discussion moves beyond the familiar contested ground.

3.1.5 Michael Bird. Until the publication of John Barclay's new work, I had saved Michael Bird for last, for I find a particular kinship with his approach, especially in his care to make rapprochement between divided factions, showing that the differences are less severe than frequently supposed. To my mind, Bird's monograph, *The Saving Righteousness of God*,[44] is a substantial step forward toward a post-new perspective, which seeks to appropriate the gains of NPP scholarship while shoring up possible weaknesses or curbing excesses. While it is true that Bird's Reformed credentials and commitments frequently peek through his deliberations, sometimes unhelpfully, this should count as more of a distraction than as an invalidation for the overall project.[45] Nonetheless, if sometimes intrusive, Bird puts his Calvinist bona fides toward good use rhetorically, pointing the way forward by drawing out the commonalities and complementarities between the NPP and traditionally Protestant readings of Paul. Scot McKnight echoes my own sentiment when he says of Bird's 2007 collection of essays that it "deserves a 'Nobel peace prize in Theology.'"[46]

Bird's collection of essays evinces a "both/and" approach to the questions at hand—that is, wherever Bird finds complementarity feasible. On balance, however, it is evident that Bird's assessment of the NPP inclines toward the negative.[47] He is far from persuaded by Sanders's account of Judaism,

---

[44]Michael F. Bird, *The Saving Righteousness of God: Studies on Paul, Justification and the New Perspective*, Paternoster Biblical Monographs (Eugene, OR: Wipf & Stock, 2007). The book consists largely of previously published essays, revised for the book, along with a few new pieces, and deserves a wide readership.

[45]For example, it is surprising to read that Sanders's use of the word *election* can be "misleading" because it is "not used by him with the same meaning it is [*sic*] has in systematic theology" (Bird, *Saving Righteousness*, 94). But, of course this is to put things backwards (and depends entirely upon *which* systematic theology). If *election* would become a category of individual soteriology in some Christian theology linked inseperably to categories of providence and decree, surely this is a development (proper or improper) extended from its biblical use as a corporate and covenantal category. Likewise, Bird will frequently appeal to Paul's critique of dependence on "works of the law" as flawed because such would be "synergistic," thus regarding as patent that synergism is an errant category of Christian soteriology. If sometimes intrusive in the descriptive sections of the book, Bird's Reformed credentials become rhetorically useful, coming to the fore in his peacemaking efforts, especially in his defense of N. T. Wright at the conclusion of *Saving Righteousness*, against a backlash of North American anxiety and animus (ibid., 183-93).

[46]Back cover of Bird, *Saving Righteousness*. Cf. the similar sentiments in Dunn's endorsement.

[47]As is especially evident in the essay "When the Dust Finally Settles: Beyond the New Perspective,"

believing that Sanders and others have underplayed the de facto meritocratic function of Torah observance. Even if the covenant is a matter of
unconditional election, that "staying in" depends on Torah obedience would
naturally lead to a soteriology in which "works" assumes a meritorious
function, and Bird sees some evidence that this had become the case in
certain strands of Judaism. Likewise, he rejects Dunn's earliest account of
Paul's use of "works of the law," unpersuaded that the phrase bears the technical sense attributed to it by Dunn, as covenant boundary markers. According to Bird, the extrabiblical evidence simply does not bear this out, nor
do the Pauline arguments require it.[48] "Generally speaking[,] works of the
Torah are just as much *ethical* as they are *ethnic.*"[49] Even here, after an extensive argument rejecting Dunn's position, in characteristic fashion, Bird
concludes that Paul's polemic against works of the law "strikes at both the
ethnocentric and the synergistic nature of any 'works' that are placed before
God as the basis of salvation."[50]

On the other hand, in what must be counted as the signal contribution
of the volume, Bird demonstrates convincingly that the forensic character
of justification and participation in (or union with) Christ are not mutually
exclusive but interdependent categories.[51] A century of Pauline scholarship
has become muddled under an implicit assumption that a choice was needed
between forensic justification and union with Christ (or Schweitzer's "Christ
mysticism" or Sanders's "participatory eschatology"). To the contrary, Bird
shows that justification is fundamentally, although not exclusively, forensic
by means of incorporation into Christ. Far from mutually exclusive, the forensic depends upon the incorporative.[52] Thus, taking on the Reformed

---

ibid., 88-112. Bird offers six major and three minor objections to the NPP and then highlights
five salutary contributions.

[48]Bird essentially critiques Dunn's original position, rather than his later refinements, so his
refutation proves not especially different from Dunn's own modification.

[49]Bird, *Saving Righteousness*, 98-99.

[50]Ibid., 99.

[51]Ibid., 60-87. Originally published as "Incorporated Righteousness," *JETS* 47, no. 2 (2004): 253-75.

[52]The fact that Bird's argument marks something of a breakthrough rather than the articulation
of a common intuition is quite probably owed not only to long-standing and deeply lodged
forensic metaphorical paradigms but perhaps also to the modest berth given to sacramental
conceptions of salvation in evangelical communities. Even Bird is excessively wary of an
understanding of baptism too realistic or sacramental: "The believer passes through the
eschatological judgment by virtue of their association with Christ in his death and is co-
quickened into the eschatological life through his resurrection. The union is *symbolized*

shibboleth of imputed righteousness, Bird shows that the Pauline notion is more aptly described as an "incorporated righteousness." Similarly, Bird seeks to show that justification is not to be conceived either as a forensic status (characteristically Reformed) or as covenant membership (characteristic of the NPP) but, again, that the two conceptions are mutually dependent.[53] Since these are all themes to be taken up below in greater detail, more in-depth engagement and dialogue await. For now, it is sufficient to notice that the overall character of Bird's work points in a helpful direction, both rhetorically and substantially. Although working within an evangelical, Reformed framework, Bird manages to incorporate as much of the NPP as his Reformed soteriology can bear and even allows for his reading of Paul to push back against certain shibboleths.

3.1.6 John Barclay. Among a series of extraordinary major works on the apostle Paul in recent years, it may turn out that John Barclay's *Paul and the Gift* will prove to be the most influential.[54] With enviable breadth and clarity, Barclay returns to durable Pauline cruxes through the lens of grace or gift. In doing so, Barclay shows that most of what we thought we knew about grace in Paul (and Second Temple Judaism) is actually assumed and that, rightly understood, the vantage point of divine gift breaks open several persistent anomalies that have bedeviled Pauline scholarship. Barclay frames his study of grace in an anthropological account of "gift" contemporary with Paul, thus first de-theologizing "grace" in order to properly re-theologize it. To speak of "grace" or *charis* in its ancient setting is to enter a world of favor and favors, benefaction and expected reciprocity: "'Gift' denotes the sphere of *voluntary, personal relations, characterized by goodwill in the giving of benefit or favor, and eliciting some form of reciprocal return that is both voluntary and necessary for the continuation of the relationship*."[55] Following

---

through baptism *but the conduit is, as always for Paul, through faith*" (*Saving Righteousness*, 56, emphasis added).
[53]Bird's proposed rapprochement between the NPP and Reformed soteriology by means of union with Christ bears significant influence on Kevin Vanhoozer's similar proposal, "Wrighting the Wrongs of the Reformation? The State of the Union with Christ in St. Paul and Protestant Soteriology," in *Jesus, Paul, and the People of God: A Theological Dialogue with N. T. Wright*, ed. Nicholas Perrin and Richard B. Hays (Downers Grove, IL: IVP Academic, 2011), 235-59.
[54]John M. G. Barclay, *Paul and the Gift* (Grand Rapids: Eerdmans, 2015).
[55]Ibid., 575, emphasis orginal.

especially the influential study of anthropologist Marcel Mauss,[56] Barclay argues that our reading of gift language in Paul and cognate literatures, to say nothing of Christian theology, perpetuates unnecessary ambiguity for failing to understand how gift "works" in its ancient setting. The assumption, for example, that gifts are nonreciprocal by definition is shown to be a modern anomaly rather than constitutive of the definition of gift. Thus, "pure gift" and "sheer grace" and so on are descriptors not nearly as self-evident as their use in common parlance would imply.[57] Barclay disentangles the presumptions by arguing that at the root of the confusion are differing conceptions of the "perfections" of grace, that is, the variety of ways "grace" or "gift" might be most fully itself. But these "perfections" of grace are not singular, as the adjectives "sheer," "pure" and "unconditioned" might lead us to think; rather, grace can be most fully gracious in a wide variety of ways. Barclay elucidates six:

(i) *superabundance*: the supreme scale, lavishness or permanence of the gift;

(ii) *singularity*: the attitude of the giver as marked solely and purely by benevolence;

(iii) *priority*: the timing of the gift before the recipient's initiative;

(iv) *incongruity*: the distribution of the gift without regard to the worth of the recipient;

(v) *efficacy*: the impact of the gift accomplishes that for which it was designed, whether engendering gratitude and fealty or enabling response;

(vi) *non-circularity*: the escape of the gift from an ongoing cycle of reciprocity.[58]

By means of this finely tuned taxonomy, Barclay demonstrates that "grace" is thus polyvalent: "*To perfect one facet of gift-giving does not imply the perfection of any or all of the others.*"[59] Thus, to speak facilely of grace as "sheer

---

[56]Marcel Mauss, "Essai sur le Don: Forme et raison de l'échange dans le sociétés archaïques," in *Sociologie et anthropologie* (Paris: Presses Universitaires de France, 1950), 145-279. For Barclay's treatment, see *Paul and the Gift*, 12-24.

[57]It might be noted that Barclay's anthropological account of grace, though apparently independent, was already anticipated in briefer, suggestive accounts of grace by David deSilva, *Honor, Patronage, Kinship and Purity: Unlocking New Testament Culture* (Downers Grove, IL: InterVarsity Press, 2000); and idem, *New Testament Themes* (St. Louis: Chalice, 2001).

[58]Barclay, *Paul and the Gift*, 185-86, summarizing pp. 66-78.

[59]Ibid., 75, emphasis original.

gratuity" or "unconditional gift" or "unmerited favor" without further qualification is to speak imprecisely, at best, and presumptuously and misleadingly,
at worst. The entailments of gift with respect to it various perfections are not
singular, nor can it be presupposed which perfections are being invoked
without carefully attending to the discourses in which grace is embedded.

Barclay proves the utility of the taxonomy first by a representative survey
of the Christian reception history of grace in Paul's letters (e.g., Marcion,
Augustine, Luther, Calvin, Barth and representative NT scholars, Bultmann,
Käsemann, Martyn and E. P. Sanders) and then in greater detail by applying
the same taxonomy to a wide representation of Second Temple corpora,
preparing to study Paul. The remainder of the work is a close reading of key
texts from Galatians and Romans (a second volume is projected) showing
how gift functions in these letters, especially the ways in which Paul both
assumes and subverts the dominant social script of gift as congruous, confirming the worth of the recipient rather than, as for Paul, creating it. The
trove of insights that follow deserves a more detailed exposition, but a few
highlights must suffice. This understanding of grace as unconditioned (incongruous, unmerited) is plausibly distinguished from grace as unconditional (requiring or expecting no response). There can be an incongruous
relationship between gift and recipient, but this is not incompatible with an
implied reciprocity, the expectation of a fitting response to the gift. The same
can be said for priority and efficacy; that grace is prior does not in itself
require that it be efficacious, though of course it could be. Barclay demonstrates that neither in Christian theology nor in antecedent Second Temple
Judaism is grace a "package deal" with all its possible perfections manifested
jointly. The tendency of otherwise shrewd interpreters to make just this assumption has beset the interpretation of Paul, especially, with far-reaching
consequences for Christian theology.

As it bears upon the NPP, Barclay's voice is not readily cataloged as "post-
NPP" in the sense that the NPP especially preoccupies him; it doesn't. At the
same time, his project has far-reaching implications for the matters at hand.
Barclay sharpens the now commonplace critique of E. P. Sanders that his
treatment of Second Temple Judaism is too indebted analytically to Christian
categories, which subtly obfuscate and falsify. Barclay shows that, when
Sanders claims that Judaism was a religion of grace, his analysis is afflicted

by a confusion and conflation of two rather different perfections of gift. The explicit perfection to which Sanders constantly appeals is the *priority* of grace, that, in making covenant with Israel, God's election of a people is itself a gift prior, upon which all the rest is premised. In itself, this is uncontroversial, but incisively Barclay observes that Sanders repeatedly confuses the perfection of the *priority* of grace with its *incongruity*. Sanders treats the latter as though it is a concomitant of the former, but as Barclay (and others before him) have shown, this is hardly the singular testimony of Second Temple reflection. Numerous witnesses describe the congruity of divine grace with the worthiness of the recipients.[60]

As it bears on the interpretation of Paul, Barclay's work exposes the fact that disciplined reflection on grace in Paul that is not question begging, either with regard to lexicography or theology, is a surprising lacuna, especially given the intense debates surrounding soteriological matters. Not only does Barclay make a sizable downpayment toward this end, but his work is likely to reshape the conversation. As it concerns the cruxes of the NPP and TPP, he takes an independent tack recognizable to both but differentiated so as to comply with neither. While Barclay upholds the priority and, especially, the incongruity of grace for Paul, the TPP's signature claim that grace stands over against "works" does not withstand his analysis. Again, the unconditioned gift is not necessarily unconditional.[61] A divinely enabled obedience, far from antithetical to grace, is its expected return, and this is a dimension of the grace script that Paul does not rewrite, even with all his investment in the incongruity of gift. But if Barclay does not draw a grace-works antithesis with the same shape of the TPP, neither does he follow the NPP by accounting for Paul's critique of nomism on the grounds of ethnic particularity or implicit nationalism. Rather, Barclay casts Paul's appeal to grace as radically incongruous, as a wholesale reconstitution of identity exclusively in relation to the Christ event rather than with respect to ascribed or acquired

---

[60]On grace in Second Temple Judaism, see ibid., 194-328; on Sanders in particular, ibid., esp. 151-58, 318-21.

[61]It is essential to note that Barclay's frequent use of these terms follows a technical distinction that he makes clear but will not be obvious when engaged secondhand: *unconditioned* means unmerited, undeserved, not requiring that prior conditions have been met; *unconditional* means without expectation of return, nonreciprocating, with no strings attached. The former he describes as "incongruous" and the latter as "non-circularity."

worth, whatever its source. This is neither so much a claim that works are insufficient to save (say, given sinfulness or human incapacity) nor a worry that ethnic exclusivity confounds the Gentile mission and the unity of God's people. Nor is Barclay arguing for a middle position. Although he may not put it quite in these terms, Barclay is arguing that the TPP largely misunderstands grace while insisting on its centrality, and that the NPP underestimates its centrality and radicality with respect to the fuller Pauline vision, substituting a valid exigence in the place of a more primary theo-logic.

Barclay does not fashion himself a post-NPP scholar, but by transcending the protracted debates from a different vantage point, he points to a way forward that breaks open stalemated polarities without trying to forge an uneasy alliance. This study should and will gather a wide scholarly readership, but is also accessible enough to reach a large audience. At the same time, there is subtlety to the application of his analytic to Paul that may not be easily grasped or popularized. It is one of the strengths of the NPP and a significant contributor to its staying power that it was so amenable to a "not . . . but rather . . ." rhetorical construct. It remains to be seen if Barclay's contribution will contend for the imagination of students of Paul in the same way that Wright has, but it will be an enormous step forward if it should. Meanwhile, I have quibbles—chiefly that Barclay, while making space for development in Paul,[62] does not fill that space as much as he might have—which I shall save for my (much briefer) treatment of grace in chapter six (6.2 below).

3.1.7 A post-new perspective? If we were to look for a theme among these various post-NPP scholars, it is, Campbell excepted, a movement toward rapprochement. The stronger, more provocative articulations of the NPP from Stendahl, Dunn, (early) Watson and Wright have in their own way all been qualified, clarified or substantially moderated. In some cases this takes the form effectively of a retraction, albeit partial, and in other cases a retrenchment, albeit more refined, but it is safe to say that none of the architects of the NPP have stood pat, and one of the difficulties of engaging the debate is that it is with moving targets—as well it should be.[63] There is a

---

[62]Barclay, *Paul and the Gift*, e.g., 449-55 and passim.
[63]Even Sanders has gone a long way toward recasting his understanding of Paul's theological "method." From *P&PJ* and *PLJP* one is left with the impression of an inconsistent Paul, arguing

discernible trend in the scholarly dialogue toward evenhandedness and, where possible, comprehensiveness, a move toward as much "both/and" as the texts can bear, if not even more.

This moderation and comprehension are to be welcomed, especially when antagonism yields to new syntheses and deeper comprehensiveness. It remains a fair question, however, whether that sort of "both/and" might sometimes be untenable or at least disingenuous. Will it always work to say of positions once at loggerheads that they are actually *both* correct? If many disjunctions are false, surely not all. For example, Bird's effort to heal certain divides is altogether commendable and, in my judgment, generally successful, but it is not always clear that the "both/and" is warranted. For example, his summary of "justification" rings out with this confident comprehensiveness: "In sum, justification is the act whereby God creates a new people, with a new status, in a new covenant, as a foretaste of the new age."[64] That's hard not to like—rhetorically, at any rate—comprehending, as it does, justification in its covenantal, forensic and eschatological dimensions. But it is fair to wonder if by means of this comprehensiveness, justification is not thereby carrying more freight than it ought, at least if all these dimensions are granted status as equally valid descriptors, all alike invoked at every occurrence of the theme. And when in his Pauline introduction Bird goes on nonetheless to rehabilitate "imputation" (at the whimsical threat of "doctrinal police beat[ing] me to death with a copy of Calvin's *Institutes of the Christian Religion*"),[65] one suspects that he is "rebuilding what he tore down" in earlier essays in the face of pressure from some "men from Jean." Thus, the post-NPP scholarship and its reconciling impulse are to be welcomed, but one must at the same time be wary of conciliation that is more rhetorical than actual. In its own extreme and sometimes pugnacious way, Doug Campbell's massive work stands (in good dialectical fashion) as warning against premature resolution and bids a sober assessment of alternatives.

---

in ad hoc fashion from the ultimacy of Jesus as Messiah, but not always coherently. In his more recent essay, "Did Paul's Theology Develop?," in *The Word Leaps the Gap: Essays on Scripture and Theology in Honor of Richard B. Hays*, ed. J. Ross Wagner, C. Kavin Rowe and A. Katherine Grieb (Grand Rapids: Eerdmans, 2008), 325-50, Paul is given considerably more berth as a coherent, but developing thinker.

[64]Bird, *Saving Righteousness*, 4; repeated in idem, *Introducing Paul: The Man, His Mission, and His Message* (Downers Grove, IL: InterVarsity Press, 2008), 96.

[65]Bird, *Introducing Paul*, 96-98.

My own assessment is that nearly everyone is right but not all the time. I don't mean that Pauline scholars are not right about Paul all the time. Of course. I mean that various accounts of Paul's theology tend to be more or less right about a certain season or episode in Paul's career, or with respect to a certain letter within the Pauline corpus. Many accounts of Paul, while appealing properly to individual letters and seeking to draw together a synthesis of the whole, fail to discriminate sufficiently with regard to the vagaries of diverse rhetorical contexts, on the one hand, while also giving little attention to natural developments that transcend the specifics of rhetorical occasion. On the other hand, the NPP, the TPP and the post-NPP alike frequently falter at just such occasions when "either/ors" or "both/ands" are claimed with respect to the whole corpus, irrespective of time, place, context and development. I propose instead a "both/and-but-not-always-at-the-same-time" model—that certain articulations of Paul's gospel are truer of some periods than of others and that to a substantial degree it is the claims made with regard to the whole that force false disjunctions and fund facile conciliations.

3.2 ANTINOMIES OF PAULINE SCHOLARSHIP

Dichotomies have been something of the stock and trade of Pauline scholarship from the past century to the present day. It is, after all, arguably the strongest way to make one's case, or at least the most efficient, to demonstrate that it is both distinguishable from and superior to the alternative, especially when the alternative counts as unquestioned conventional wisdom. When Jesus said, "You have heard that it was said, . . . but I say to you" (see Mt 5), New Testament scholars learn well from our mentor, if not about the kingdom of God, at least about rhetoric. Yet dichotomizing is not always or merely rhetorical. Pressing between options by forcing alternatives has the heuristic function of driving exploration, of reconsidering what was once patent, of reopening a "cold case." Nonetheless, recent Pauline scholarship has found itself victim of various polarizations, forced choices that not only clarify questions but might also overdetermine the results that follow. The NPP experiment and the TPP rejoinder are, as I am arguing, just two recent examples of the phenomenon. If we should get "post" the NPP versus TPP impasse, I suggest that we would do well to explore and learn from a set of durable conflicts in Pauline scholarship to ask whether they are necessary and helpful or otiose and counterproductive.[66]

In what follows, then, I take up a series of famous antinomies generally relevant to, or even constituent of, the NPP/TPP debate. My purpose in doing so is to offer a sampling survey of recent Pauline scholarship while also arguing that the dichotomizing is frequently an unfortunate shortcut. This is not to say that "both/and" construals are always right and even less to claim that the defined poles or alternatives on a given issue are somehow always both right (they are sometimes simply mutually exclusive) but rather to dissuade us from false dilemmas and even more from the reaching of premature conclusions.[67]

---

[66]As one incisive reader of an earlier draft of this manuscript noted, although the NPP and TPP both understand themselves and defend themselves as essentially *historical* readings of Paul, it bears repeating that they are also profoundly *situated* and deeply *interested* readings, in dialogue with Pauline texts against the backdrop of certain historical and cultural givens. More pointedly, for both "schools"—and for the whole stream of Pauline reception—we observe that Paul characteristically enters a cultural moment as an instrument of correction. That is, Paul read "rightly" repairs someone else's faltering soteriology or restores another's obstructed vision. "Rightly" understood, Paul delivers readers from autosoterism or from antinomianism, from sacerdotalism or from individualism, from ethnic alienation or even from the reification of ethnicity, and so on. It is the at once epistemological and rhetorical leverage of such readings that they should think of themselves as "historical" readings, restoring "what St. Paul really said." It should be obvious that this is a conceit, but it may be a useful conceit—that is, the hermeneutical conceit is useful if unaccompanied by epistemological conceit. It remains a useful aspiration to recover, or at least hold oneself accountable to, "what St. Paul really said," but only if the interpreter acknowledges the elusiveness of the goal and the interested nature of such a pursuit and its results. Thus, we might say that the NPP and the TPP (and, no less, the apocalyptic school) are inevitably twice partial: incomplete and interested. Any governing framework—even if that framework is alleged to derive from Paul—is necessarily a partial or incomplete account of the Pauline corpus, privileging certain texts and themes as the sure footing whence one understands the whole, and any such framework for understanding Paul cannot help but be perspectival in its vantage. There is no illusion that the alternative account I offer escapes these partialities, but neither do I apologize for the aspirational conceit of trying to offer a more satisfactory account of the Pauline corpus.

[67]There are two antinomies that I might have addressed below but which I don't. (1) The "conversion versus call" debate is addressed above, and the matter need not be rehearsed again. (2) The antagonism between the "apocalyptic" school (e.g., J. Louis Martyn, Doug Campbell and Doug Harink, among others, descended from Ernst Käsemann and mentored by Karl Barth) and the "salvation-historical" alternative (e.g., N. T. Wright and many others) seems to have spun out of control with both talking past each other in what can hardly be called a "dialogue"— that is, at least to judge from the recent offerings of D. A. Campbell (*Deliverance of God*, 2009) and Wright (*P&FG*, 2013; *Paul and His Recent Interpreters*, 2015). Rather than enter that unproductive fray, I choose to limit my relevant comments to the related question of whether Paul's theological method, to the extent that it can be described, is best characterized as prospective or retrospective.

3.2.1 Paul's method: prospective or retrospective? In the second chapter, we took account of the consensus in Pauline scholarship that the Damascus event is not best viewed as an archetypal religious conversion, although we regarded it as a kind of conversion. We noted, however, that a considerable swath of Pauline scholarship regards the event as a signal catalyst for the whole of Paul's theological vision. We turn now to a closely related question: whether Paul reasoned prospectively, from a problem to its answer, or retrospectively, from an answer to the problem, or, as Sanders famously put it, siding with the latter, from "plight to solution" or "solution to plight."[68] Although this particular language was made famous by Sanders, the bigger question of how Paul arrives at his convictions and what that says about the shape of those convictions has become a point of contention in Pauline scholarship, being, for example, a major plank of Doug Campbell's massive argument.[69]

The logic of plight to solution would seem self-evident: answers normally follow questions and are naturally shaped by them. But logical does not mean obvious or necessary, and in Paul's case there are reasons to believe that the course of Paul's theological career was a movement from one large "solution" to an increasingly well-defined sense of plight: the Damascus Christophany confronted Paul with a "solution," or, as the case may be, an irruptive revelation, that required a thoroughgoing and explicit revision of the implicit dilemma(s). Whether one follows Sanders all the way, it must be the case that Paul had to reason retrospectively from the Damascus encounter—to the messianic identity of Jesus, to his vindication by God, to a thoroughgoing reassessment of the meaning of his crucifixion, to the nature of human sinfulness and so on. It is not hard to imagine, though quite difficult to prove, that other elements of Paul's theology are similarly derived, whether it be Christology, his view of the law, his understanding of the

---

[68]Sanders, *P&PJ*, 474-511. Ralph P. Martin seems to agree when he approves the "suggestion that [Paul's] thinking moves from what God has done to the malaise itself" (Martin, *Reconciliation: A Study of Paul's Theology*, New Foundations Theological Library [Atlanta: John Knox, 1981], 71).

[69]D. A. Campbell, *Deliverance of God*, passim. Campbell finds prospective accounts of Paul's gospel distorting, and, indeed, he uses what he regards as Paul's singularly retrospective theological method as a criterion for judging prospective readings as mistaken. Clearly this prepares the way for his innovative reading of Romans 1-4, where it *must* be the case that the putative prospective argument is a voice other than Paul's. As I will argue, this is fatally Procrustean.

human condition or even the place of Gentiles in the covenant. Thus, the encounter with the exalted Christ is almost surely the answer that launched a dozen new questions, which themselves elicited a dozen new answers. Although the descriptor *apocalyptic* is fraught with a certain degree of ambiguity, those who see Paul in that category are, above all else, making the claim that Paul's theology was not derived from certain first principles or prior questions into which the truth of Jesus the Messiah was fit. Rather, Jesus was a "revelation" (*apokalypsis*), an irruption into and subversion of all prior "plausibility structures." And whatever else we make of this school of Pauline interpretation, this much at least must be granted.[70]

But here it is necessary to make at least two important qualifications. (1) Obviously Paul's Christian convictions were not construed in a vacuum. If his intellectual journey was, as I think, fundamentally from solution to plight, it was in a necessary (re)negotiation with his scriptural inheritance, which provided the story line, figures and categories by which sense could be made of the Jesus story. I do not suggest that Paul's *Christian* theology could have been read from the ground up from the Scriptures alone, but, by the same token, the irruptive event of the Damascus Road and the story of Jesus that it validated could not in itself have guided Paul to any certain destination. At least in this respect, the divide between the apocalyptic and salvation-historical accounts of Paul represents an obviously false alternative. The Damascus Road event would require a rethinking of everything, but it is impossible that Paul could have done so without the sense-making resources of the biblical inheritance, on the one hand, and the theological hermeneutic bequeathed to him in his training, on the other.

(2) A second qualification follows from the first. If we are speaking of the probable shape of Paul's intellectual biography—to which we have decidedly

---

[70]On the apocalyptic "school," see n. 1 of this chapter. Behind that concern there frequently lurks another, larger-scale theological and philosophical antipathy toward "foundationalism," an epistemology that, when it serves Christian theology, expects to start from indubitable first principles or, as may be the case, an infallible deposit of propositional revelation, and reason deductively such that the Christian gospel and its theological entailments are the inevitable destination. Thus, foundationalism privileges deduction and, if not promising, at least pursues rational certainty and is thus epistemologically prospective. The fact that the "foundationalist" theological method has a certain (actual or superficial?) kinship with Cartesian epistemology makes it an easy target in the wake of modernity's various unfulfilled promises. Thus, Karl Barth and his diverse disciples stand as the giant antithesis of this project, and the pervasive influence of Barth is evident in the Pauline apocalyptic school.

limited access—we might think about this one way; if we are thinking of the shape of certain of Paul's written arguments—to which we have rather direct access—we may see the matter differently. While there is good reason to think that Paul's intellectual life followed a largely retrospective course, it does not follow that certain of his arguments could not exhibit a prospective trajectory, a reasoning from some sort of dilemma to its remedy or (for the sake of the argument) from the indubitable facts on the ground to their evident consequences.[71] While we have no evidence of pre-Damascus Paul as a grace-starved sinner seeking atonement, we have plenty of evidence of his self-possessed zeal for the law. But it does not follow from this that Paul could not have come to regard Israel as deficient in righteousness and humanity as helpless under sin with the law being no solution.[72] Again, Paul must have first regarded a "crucified messiah" as a scandal, as an inexplicable datum rather than an answer to anything. But it would be this very scandal that would require the reevaluation of all that he "knew" about himself, about Israel's story and about the condition of the world. It does not seem at all unlikely that, having done so, Paul could choose to retell the story not as an intellectual biography of a man in search of redemption, lost and now found, but as a story of a world lost and found, when it suited his purposes. This does not squeeze the gospel into a prospective, foundationalist mold of the sort that especially worries Campbell; it simply grants Paul the rhetor as much liberty as he needs to make an argument that befits the occasion.

I regard, then, the prospective-retrospective dichotomy as unnecessary and unhelpful. It is surely a keen observation to note that the Christ story would not have been an obvious answer to the Israel story or human story, that it would require a thoroughgoing reinterpretation of both. It does not follow that Paul could not have found it useful to articulate the gospel in prospective terms. If earlier generations of Paul's interpreters were guilty of conforming Paul's conversion to a particular anxiety-meeting-grace construal

---

[71]See the helpful clarifications in N. T. Wright, "Christ, the Law, and 'Pauline Theology,'" in *The Climax of the Covenant: Christ and the Law in Pauline Theology* (Edinburgh: T&T Clark, 1991), 1-17; and idem, "Putting Paul Together Again: Toward a Synthesis of Pauline Theology (1 and 2 Thessalonians, Philippians, and Philemon)," in *Pauline Theology*, vol. 1, *Thessalonians, Philippians, Galatians, Philemon*, ed. Jouette M. Bassler (Minneapolis: Fortress, 1991), 190-94.

[72]Perhaps the most insightful rejoinder to Sanders's plight to solution is Frank Thielman, *From Plight to Solution: A Jewish Framework for Understanding Paul's View of the Law in Galatians and Romans*, NOVTSup 61 (New York: Brill, 1989).

of his gospel, it is important that we not make essentially the same error in a different guise, of using Paul's reconstructed intellectual biography as though it were a determining or constraining template for his gospel.[73]

3.2.2 Paul's theology: coherent or contingent? Here I am borrowing the famous categories of J. Christiaan Beker. Influentially, Beker would offer a defense of the coherence of Paul's theology in the face of the notorious and unwieldy diversity of his extant writings.[74] He would do so neither by an artificial harmonizing nor by means of a facile concession to Paul's incoherence. Instead, Beker argues in detail that Paul's epistolary rhetoric was a negotiation between a *coherent* core of theological convictions generated by the apocalypse of Jesus Christ that remains essentially intact and the *contingent* and diverse expression of those convictions in view of the crises and pastoral exigencies that he encountered. Beker does not so much deny Pauline contradictions as he accounts for them, showing "contradiction" to be a superficial estimation. To one convinced of Paul's utter consistency, Beker's apologia might seem tepid, but in comparison to the almost celebratory exposure of Paul's radical inconsistencies, Beker is soberly steering a cautious course by demonstrating that *coherence* and *contingency* are not alternative accounts of the Pauline corpus but equally valid and complementary descriptions of the same phenomena. For Beker, there is no dichotomy here; he simply uses the dichotomous language to make that point.

If I am borrowing Beker's categories as *he* understands them, then there is no antinomy; we can move on. In fact, Beker's treatment of the question is so imbued with common sense that one might have expected a hiatus in the quest for Pauline aporias. After all, we should only expect under the circumstances—occasional, unsystematic letters capturing just a few moments,[75] spread over a number of years and a wide diversity of circumstance—that a "theology" cobbled out of such material will run into all sorts of problems in holding things together or in filling gaps. That would not

---

[73]To my reading, this category confusion besets D. A. Campbell, *Deliverance of God*, 125-67.

[74]J. Christiaan Beker, *Paul the Apostle: The Triumph of God in Life and Thought* (Philadelphia: Fortress, 1980), summarized in pp. 11-19 and worked out in the following chapters. Note also the valuable update and clarifications in idem, "Recasting Pauline Theology: The Coherence-Contingency Scheme as Interpretive Model," in Bassler, *Pauline Theology*, 1:15-24.

[75]For Beker the task consists of accounting for a seven-letter corpus of undisputed letters (he regards the remainder as deutero-Pauline), and the primary illustration of his position is limited to Galatians and Romans.

make the author of the letters incoherent or a whatever-it-takes opportunist, however. To suppose so is to confuse the accidents of history—that we have these letters and that they are these kinds of writings—with the character and competence of the writer. The fact that Paul's letters individually show every sign of intelligence and are tolerably coherent (some of the alleged "incoherence" is arguably owed more to a fertile mind than a disorganized one) leads us to expect the same of the whole corpus. When that expectation is disappointed, it is only fair to assume that it has much to do with letters as targeted, occasional texts that are constituent of a larger conversation.[76]

But Beker's book did not produce a moratorium on celebrating Pauline inconsistencies. The aporias would still fuel an engine of Pauline studies finding or explaining inconsistencies in Paul's occasional writings, an effort that continues unabated to the present day.[77] Although Heikki Räisänen is the most-often-noted example,[78] he is not alone. Paul's inconsistencies drive finely tuned partition theories,[79] sophisticated rhetorical analyses[80] and hypotheses regarding rhetorical persona within letters.[81] We might say that the aporias we will always have with us, but the broadest strokes of Beker's argument have survived the test of time, even if its wisdom has not been sufficiently heeded.

---

[76]One can only imagine what the tools of New Testament criticism would render in the critical analysis of any modern corpus of occasional pastoral communication (say, emails to associates) that exhibits any contextual sensitivity whatsoever.

[77]See the survey chapter on Drane, Hübner and Räisänen in Westerholm, *Perspectives Old and New*, 164-77, noting that John William Drane's *Paul, Libertine or Legalist? A Study in the Theology of the Major Pauline Epistles* (London: SPCK, 1975), and the original German version of Hans Hübner's *Das Gesetz bei Paulus* (in English: *Law in Paul's Thought: A Contribution to the Development of Pauline Theology*, trans. James C. G. Greig [Edinburgh: T&T Clark, 1984]) preceded Beker's major study.

[78]Frank Thielman, *Paul and the Law: A Contextual Approach* (Downers Grove, IL: InterVarsity Press, 1994).

[79]Most often with respect to 2 Corinthians (the classic position is Günther Bornkamm, *Paul* [Philadelphia: Fortress, 1971], 100-103; cf. Hans Dieter Betz, *2 Corinthians 8 and 9: A Commentary on Two Administrative Letters of the Apostle Paul*, Hermeneia [Philadelphia: Fortress, 1985], but the disjunctions are acknowledged by all scholars) and Philippians, although conviction on behalf of the latter shows signs of receding.

[80]E.g., Tobin, *Paul's Rhetoric*.

[81]So, e.g., the difficulty in holding Paul's claim that "he" is sold under sin as a slave in Romans 7:14 with his freedom from the same in Romans 6:16-18 is used in support of rhetorical impersonation in Romans 7. The same sort of logic, though on a much larger scale, supports Campbell's claim that the soteriology of Romans 1-4, being incompatible with Romans 5-8, is not Paul's but a "teacher" Paul impersonates and lampoons (D. A. Campbell, *Deliverance of God*).

Beker does not so much argue for a pure logical center of Paul's thought as for a set of coordinates that are more or less unwavering, all rooted in Paul's inherited apocalyptic framework as it was modified in the apocalypse of Christ, the saving intervention and revelation of God.[82] From this proceeds the innovation of an eschatological age *already* present though anticipating the *not yet* final consummation, and within this framework the resurrection, cross, salvation and church find their meaning and—more to the point of Beker's argument—a coherence that is not invalidated by the diversity of pastoral appropriations.

Other scholars bent on demonstrating Paul's coherence are in danger of overplaying their hand by appealing to Paul's alleged conceptual center to make their case. It must be said that the sheer proliferation of proposals (justification, apocalyptic, eschatology, cross, participation in Christ, reconciliation, fulfillment, Christology, God [!] and so on) for the "center" of Paul's theology risks mocking the whole enterprise.[83] Each proposal affirms a Pauline theme the importance of which was never in doubt, but coherence does not require a "center." The quest for a center is an interesting thought experiment, but it simply proceeds from the wrong expectation of this corpus of texts, and, to the extent that various proposals offer themselves back to readers not only as conclusions wrought of close reading but also as a hermeneutical lens for future readings, the quest for a center is circular

---

[82]Beker, *Paul the Apostle*, 135-81; subsequently popularized in *Paul's Apocalyptic Gospel: The Coming Triumph of God* (Philadelphia: Fortress, 1982). This is one of the ways in which Beker's "apocalyptic" Paul differs from others of the apocalyptic school: he places greater emphasis upon Paul's already apocalyptic outlook, in relation to which the Christ event warranted a radical "transposition" of his theological outlook but less as an unprepared for irruption. Indeed, Beker does not see Paul's "apocalyptic" outlook in contradistinction to a salvation-historical framework (to the consternation of J. Louis Martyn, "Events in Galatia: Modified Covenantal Nomism Versus God's Invasion of the Cosmos in the Singular Gospel; A Response to J. D. G. Dunn and B. R. Gaventa," in Bassler, *Pauline Theology*, 1:172n27).

[83]The quest is beset with insurmountable methodological problems: How do we adjudicate the question? Should we count occurrences? Track the distribution of occurrences? Favor certain letters as quintessential and others as peripheral (if not inauthentic)? Or should we argue for what is most original to Paul, the insights he seemed to have happened upon first, on the assumption that the others grew organically from them? Or do we isolate and set to the side the inherited traditional materials in Paul's letters—hymns, creeds, doctrinal formulae and so on— as only incidental? Likewise, do we reconstruct a conceptual taxonomy that demonstrates which Pauline themes fund the others and which are inessential? But, in this case, how would we know that our conceptual map has anything to do with Paul's? And, while we're at it, who, after all, is "Paul": a first-century activist-writer or the sum of his extant or attributed writings, or is "he" the aggregated retinue of his influence?

and possibly mischievous.[84] Historically, the real value—I would suggest the *only* value—of discourse contending for a Pauline center is simply to call into question presumptions, sometimes unspoken, as to what the true center is. The rejection of one supposed center in favor of another has the salutary effect of (literally) de-centering the discourse, until we reach something like the present state of affairs. If we are honest, claims for a Pauline center really amount to something more modest than the claim itself: "Notice this prominent theme too often overlooked, and consider the light it sheds on Paul's writings as a whole when it is given its due attention." If we relinquished the hubris of determining a center and took up this more modest alternative, nothing would be lost, and it would be a more honest assessment of the actual accomplishment.

We do not need a Pauline "center" to have Pauline coherence. A certain kind of common sense and patience are sufficient. Complaining of Sanders's and, especially, Räisänen's predilection for finding incoherence in Paul, Dunn speaks sensibly to the matter.

> That Paul's various claims are radically incoherent must rank as a hypothesis of last resort. . . . Basic to good exegesis is respect for the integrity of the text [over against speculative emendations] and, in the case of someone like Paul, respect for his intellectual calibre and theological competence. Such respect includes a constant bearing in mind the possibility or indeed likelihood that the situations confronting Paul were more complex than we can now be aware of, or include important aspects which are now invisible to us.[85]

This is sound advice and of a piece with Beker's program. However, there is a third axis besides *contingence* and *coherence* that neither Beker nor Dunn

---

[84]Perhaps the best refutation of the quest for a Pauline center ironically comes from observing attempts to establish it. And the more sophisticated and circumspect the attempt, the more persuasive the argument against the utility of the construct. I think, for example, of Schreiner's Pauline theology and the nuanced claim that the center of Paul's gospel is "the centrality of God in Christ" (Thomas R. Schreiner, *Paul, Apostle of God's Glory in Christ: A Pauline Theology* [Downers Grove, IL: InterVarsity Press, 2001], 15-36). Schreiner's demonstration that this is an important theme for Paul is persuasive, while also unnecessary; his attempt to demonstrate that it is *the* center is unpersuasive and also unnecessary; and the fact that he organizes his later New Testament theology around essentially the *same* theme gives pause (Thomas R. Schreiner, *New Testament Theology: Magnifying God in Christ* [Grand Rapids: Baker Academic, 2008]).

[85]Dunn, NPerP, 121. Dunn's point bears particular significance given that he is not elsewhere shy to argue for the theological diversity of the New Testament materials: see esp. James D. G. Dunn, *Unity and Diversity in the New Testament: An Inquiry into the Character of Earliest Christianity*, 3rd ed. (London: SCM, 2006).

explores, and indeed Beker rejects, viz., *development*. So while Beker defends Paul's ultimate coherence and accounts for evidence to the contrary as contingency, he is not impressed by developmental hypotheses, or at least not those on offer when writing *Paul the Apostle*.[86] But, in principle, to give wide berth to the historically contingent character of the letters with respect to their context and addressees is but a small step from acknowledging the likelihood that the letters bear witness to another historical contingency, that of the author's own intellectual itinerary. The contingency of the rhetorical occasion and the development of the author's views and linguistic variations for expressing them are not mutually exclusive; giving credence to the one invites consideration of the other. Thus, in Paul we have a reflective activist, who according to his own self-understanding (1 Cor 9:19-23) was facile in adapting to contingencies, but whose flexibility does not stoop to the level of sheer opportunism or conceptual incoherence. I propose instead a coherent Paul but that we dispense with defining coherence in terms of a center, and that the historically contingent texts that are not readily accounted for by means of a center bear witness instead to traceable development.

3.2.3 Justification (1): constitutive or incidental? The quest for a center of Pauline theology may or may not be a quixotic adventure, but, as we have noted, determined efforts have failed to secure anything like a consensus on the matter. Here we are asking a more modest question: How central, basic or constitutive is Paul's theology of justification to his overall project? We do not need for justification by faith to be the "center" of Pauline theology to answer the question affirmatively; we need only to ask if it is central or basic or a matter of more than ad hoc interest.

The modern version of the question dates at least to the nineteenth century, when F. C. Baur would claim, in what we can now see as a rather crude, largely mistaken, anticipation of the more nuanced NPP, that the impetus of Paul's theology of justification was in the defense of a Hellenistic Christianity, distinct from the Palestinian Jewish alternative, and of the

---

[86]See, e.g., Beker, *Paul the Apostle*, 31-35, 39, 94, especially the critique of Drane, *Paul, Libertine or Legalist?*, and Hübner, *Law in Paul's Thought*. Without reprising the details of Drane or Hübner's theses, I follow a similar intuition in accounting for the material (cf. Mark A. Seifrid, *Justification by Faith: The Origin and Development of a Central Pauline Theme*, NovTSup 68 [Leiden: Brill, 1992]), though with regard to the entire Pauline corpus.

former, Paul was the champion.[87] In other words, justification arises as an
apologetic, but its primary impetus is to be found in the fundamental division in primitive Christianity that was the keystone of Baur's hypothesis.
A revision and popularization of this view would come from turn-of-the-
century German scholars, who found justification to be a "polemical doctrine" (a *Kampfeslehre*, William Wrede), which was merely a "subsidiary
crater" to "Christ mysticism" (Albert Schweitzer), which was forged in the
heat of conflict and subsequently disappeared with the abatement of that
crisis in the second century (Adolf Deissmann).[88] Far from the center of
Pauline thought, justification was an ad hoc and polemical counter to the
threat of Judaizing Gentiles. It might be said that the ubiquity of the language in the two theologically magisterial letters of Galatians (8x) and
Romans (17x) easily misleads the reader to think of "justification" as a pervasive Pauline theme, especially given the canonical and programmatic
pride of place of the letter to the Romans in Christian theology generally
and the generative influence of Galatians in the Protestant movement particularly. But, in fact, save for two references in 1 Corinthians (1 Cor 4:4; 6:11)
and a single occurrence in the disputed letter to Titus (Tit 3:7), *all* of Paul's
uses of the verb and the noun are confined to Galatians and Romans.[89] The
great majority of Paul's letters have no explicit reference to "justification,"
including the Thessalonian correspondence, which most regard as the earliest of Paul's writings. In other words, it is hard to make the case that justification by faith is at the center of Paul's thought, or even the essence of his
gospel, when it is found only in three, albeit important, undisputed letters.
That judgment gains further currency when it is noted that *all* such references to justification by faith—to which now Philippians 3:2-11 can be
added as a conceptual, if not a precise verbal, equivalent—are found

---

[87]Baur's historical approach to the New Testament and primitive Christian history has fared
better than his actual hypothesis, which has been substantially criticized and from several
quarters: see, e.g., Horton Harris, *The Tübingen School* (Oxford: Clarendon, 1975); and Martin
Hengel, *Judaism and Hellenism: Studies in Their Encounter in Palestine During the Early
Hellenistic Period*, 2 vols. (Philadelphia: Fortress, 1981).

[88]William Wrede, *Paul* (Eugene, OR: Wipf & Stock, 2001), esp. 122-46; Albert Schweitzer, *The
Mysticism of Paul the Apostle*, trans. William Montgomery (New York: Holt, 1931), 225; and Adolf
Deissmann, *Paul: A Study in Social and Religious History*, trans. William E. Wilson (New York:
Harper, 1957), 271. I owe the Deissmann reference to Martin, *Reconciliation*, 33.

[89]I am leaving aside 1 Timothy 3:16, in which the reference is to Christ's own "justification," typically
understood as his "vindication" rather than directly soteriological with respect to humanity.

exclusively in contexts where the matter of Jew-Gentile relations, the status of uncircumcised Gentiles and the broader corollary of the role of the law are explicitly at stake. This hardly seems a coincidence. Yet this is not to make the alternative claim, that justification by faith is somehow merely incidental to Paul, only to note that it is crucially important in certain contexts and not others. By almost any account, Paul's earliest reference to justification was in the letter to the Galatians, where justification by faith apart from works of the law is embedded in an epistolary rejoinder, presumably to some alternative claim. If this is so, it is unlikely that this later theological refinement belongs to the essence of the Pauline kerygma.[90] The available evidence from Paul's letters is inconclusive, but in itself it does not support the claim that justification by faith is the gospel Paul preached; rather, it is an entailment of that gospel—not a *mere* entailment, but an entailment, nonetheless.

Although I find this line of argument compelling and suggestive as far as it goes, this oft-repeated tack is perhaps too much an overcorrection when its goal is the marginalization of justification by faith. The chief problem with this approach to the question is its superficial appeal to linguistic data, as if the citation of word occurrences were sufficient in itself. When we move from the word counting of concordance searches to the breadth of expressions that capture and extend the substance of justification, we find it to be a more ubiquitous Pauline theme and not limited to a few polemical contexts. While it is precarious to claim that "justification by faith" is the center of Pauline theology, it is equally mistaken to regard it as merely tangential or incidental.

---

[90]Were Galatians to contain evidence that Paul is reminding the readers of something already preached to them, the absence of justification from kerygmatic summaries in Paul's letters (e.g., 1 Cor 15:3-8; Rom 1:2-6) may be telling. The most salient evidence to the contrary comes from outside Paul's letters in Acts 13:38-39. Near the end of Paul's speech to his fellow Jews and to God-fearers (Acts 13:16, 26) in Pisidian Antioch, Paul concludes, "You must know, my brothers, that through him forgiveness of sins is being proclaimed to you, [and] in regard to everything from which you could not be justified under the law of Moses, in him every believer is justified" (Acts 13:38-39 NAB). While most translations translate δικαιόω as "set free," used twice, it is the same word that is elsewhere rendered as "justify"; thus, this can be read as evidence of justification in the Pauline kerygma. However, even if one assumes that the speeches in Acts reflect the historical content of Paul's preaching, it would be hard to demonstrate that it extends to specific terminology, and, in any case, δικαιόω is used somewhat uncharacteristically here compared to undisputed Pauline use ("justified *from*"; ἀπὸ . . . δικαιωθῆναι). The evidence that Paul preached "justification by faith apart from works of the law" in his initial missionary preaching is inconclusive.

In the first place, that the language itself is limited to a few letters that share parallel concerns is an important observation, but we ought not draw the wrong conclusions from that datum. Since the verb "to justify" (*dikaioō*) cannot be artificially separated from the cognate noun "righteousness" (*dikaiosynē*)—or any of the other cognates, for that matter—the database is expanded by definition. We noted already that the terminology shows up in 1 Corinthians but apparently unprovoked by any Jew-Gentile controversy.[91] If 1 Corinthians 1:30 ("who became for us wisdom from God, as well as righteousness, sanctification, and redemption," NAB) fails as a proof text for imputed righteousness, it nevertheless shows "righteousness" to be a soteriological endowment along with "sanctification" and "redemption."[92] Likewise, the nearly universal understanding of 2 Corinthians 5:21 ("in order that we might become the righteousness of God"; *hina hēmeis genōmetha dikaiosynē theou en autō*) is that it describes the human possession of—or more precisely, the human transformation into (*genōmetha*)—God's righteousness. Again, as most would regard it, this is another expression equivalent to justification, though in cognate terms.[93] And, as already noted, it is clear that Philippians

---

[91]It could be argued that 1 Corinthians 4:4 carries something more of a secular or non-eschatological sense: "but I do not thereby *stand acquitted*" (NAB, capturing well the stative force of the perfect tense; emphasis added). Virtually all translations suggest as much by the translation "acquitted." But the context ("the one who judges me is the Lord") demonstrates that it is clearly divine judgment that is at stake, and ultimately in its eschatological dimension, according to 1 Corinthians 4:5. Meanwhile, 1 Corinthians 6:11 is unmistakably soteriological in force.

[92]So, e.g., Gordon D. Fee, *The First Epistle to the Corinthians*, NICNT (Grand Rapids: Eerdmans, 1987), 86; and Anthony C. Thiselton, *The First Epistle to the Corinthians: A Commentary on the Greek Text*, NIGTC (Grand Rapids: Eerdmans, 2000), 193. Thiselton "reject[s] the claim that justification by grace is emphasized by Paul only in the more explicitly 'anti-Jewish' or 'Judaistic' contexts of Romans and Galatians."

By the insertion of an "and" between "wisdom from God" and "righteousness" (καί is a weakly attested, common-sense "improvement" in handful of manuscripts, but surely secondary), most translations of 1 Corinthians 1:30 obscure the appositional relationship between "wisdom from God" and the following three terms (so, e.g., the punctuation of UBS[4] and NA[28]). The NIV (2011) moves in the right direction with "wisdom from God—that is, our righteousness, holiness and redemption," but the apposition is probably not so much epexegetic ("that is," "namely") than these three terms are a sort of stylish afterthought: "wisdom from God—*for that matter*, righteousness, holiness and redemption" (cf. NAB). And the insertion of the possessive "our" (there being no ἡμῶν in the original) goes beyond what can be inferred from the ἡμῖν, which is better understood as a dative of advantage than some sort of possessive (so also Raymond F. Collins, *First Corinthians*, SP 7 [Collegeville, MN: Liturgical Press, 2006], 112).

[93]A notable exception is Wright's novel exegesis of 2 Corinthians 5:21, in which he continues to work out his program of "righteousness of God" as covenant faithfulness. I am aware of four places where Wright engages this passage, which is prima facie uncooperative with his understanding of the "righteousness of God": originally in N. T. Wright, "On Becoming the

3:7-11 stands as the conceptual equivalent to "justification" ("having . . . a righteousness from God based on faith") but without the verb *dikaioō*. Therefore, contrary to the claim that "justification by faith" is a matter of concern only in relationship to a Judaizing controversy, we find rather that among Paul's seven undisputed letters, *only* 1 Thessalonians and Philemon lack a clear reference to the concept,[94] though again, not always expressed

---

Righteousness of God: 2 Corinthians 5:21," in *Pauline Theology*, vol. 2, *1 & 2 Corinthians*, ed. D. M. Hay (Minneapolis: Fortress, 1993), 200-208; very briefly in idem, *WSPRS*, 104-5; more fully and in light of various criticisms, in idem, *Justification*, 158-672, and in idem, *P&FG*, 2:881-85. This text, a locus classicus for the notion of imputed righteousness, is not, according to Wright, any such thing. Rather, if we take δικαιοσύνη θεοῦ as something like "covenant faithfulness," Wright proposes that Paul's apostolic ministry (taking the "we" in an exclusive sense) "embod[ies] . . . God's covenant faithfulness, God's action in reconciling the world to himself" (*Justification*, 163).

> The verse is not an abstract, detached statement of atonement theology (Paul nowhere offers us such a thing); rather, it focuses very specifically on his own strange apostolic ministry. Insofar as this ministry is a thing of shame and dishonor, it is so despite Paul's intention, and the sin-offering is the right means of dealing with such a problem. Insofar as it is the means of the divine covenant faithfulness being held out to the world, it is because, in Christ, Paul has "become" the δικαιοσύνη θεοῦ ("righteousness of God"). (Wright, "On Becoming the Righteousness," 206)

The argument Wright advances for this nonsoteriological reading makes a maximal appeal to the surrounding context in which Paul's paradoxical, strength-in-weakness apostolic ministry is the focus. While exegesis is always the negotiated balancing of the larger context with nearer details, I'm not persuaded that Wright's exegesis has done justice to the logic internal to the saying itself and its more *immediate* context. Two nearly insuperable difficulties render his exegesis improbable: (1) To restrict the referent of the "we" to Paul and his apostolic associates is artificial and unprepared for, implying even that the "becoming-sin" death of Christ is only for the sake of that apostolic circle. More probably the "we" is inclusive of the whole Christian body, with Paul and his associates referenced as exemplars (see esp. the discussion in Gorman, *Inhabiting the Cruciform God*, 246-49, and the literature cited there). (2) It is hard to see how the first clause—God making him who knew no sin to be sin for us—is causally related to the second—in order that (ἵνα) we (apostles) might become the righteousness of God (i.e., embody God's covenant faithfulness in our ministry of gospel proclamation and reconciliation). This reading requires a logical inference from a very specific account of atonement, the making-to-be-sin-of-the-innocent, as the particular basis of a telic clause (ἵνα) in which the apostolic ministry of Paul is described as embodiment of God's covenant faithfulness (cf. A. Katherine Grieb, "'So That in Him We Might Become the Righteousness of God' [2 Cor 5:21]: Some Theological Reflections on the Church Becoming Justice," *Ex Auditu* 22 [2006]: 65, for a similar critique, although Grieb reaches a different conclusion with respect to the ultimate soteriological import of the text, viz., the church embodying the justice of God). If Wright's exegesis is not impossible, his reconstruction of Paul's reasoning is at best a bit opaque. It is hard to avoid the impression that this reading is driven by an unnecessarily narrow, excessively prescriptive account of δικαιοσύνη θεοῦ. For a convincing treatment of 2 Corinthians 5:21 in light of its larger context and recent treatments, see Blackwell, *Christosis*, 226-32.

[94]That a letter as brief, occasional and personal as Philemon would lack justification by faith—or for that matter, much of any soteriology—should not surprise us. The apparent absence in 1 Thessalonians has understandably occasioned more reflection. But whether we count

precisely in such terms but always by means of the *dikai-* cognates. That five of Paul's undisputed seven letters, all of them highly occasional in character, manifest these themes, sometimes admittedly only in faint traces, must be regarded as a decisive counterpoise to the claim that justification is merely incidental to Paul. That does not make it the "center" of Paul's theology, but justification is not so easily marginalized.[95]

If from the undisputed letters we pan out to the whole of the Pauline corpus, the situation complicates and resolves at the same time. It complicates inasmuch as the language of "justification" all but disappears along with other soteriological uses of the *dikai-* group, save for the striking passage in Titus 3:5-7. At the same time, the soteriological vantage of the disputed letters settles rather snugly into a prescribed, almost stereotyped pattern comprising the following elements: divine grace or mercy is prioritized (Eph 2:5, 8; Tit 3:5, 7; 2 Tim 1:9) and works are excluded (Eph 2:9; Tit 3:5; 2 Tim 1:9) because faith, rather than works, is the means of appropriating grace (Eph 1:13; 2:8; 3:12; 1 Tim 1:16; 2 Tim 3:15). Nonetheless, "works," especially, as it were, "good" ones, are incumbent upon the recipient of undeserved mercy.

Paul, or if it be the case, the Paulinist(s), repeatedly and matter-of-factly sketches a nonpolemical soteriology, not as a first line of defense or refutation but as though this were the settled matter. It is not that these letters are absent polemics. If there is little corrective agenda in Ephesians, the centerpiece of Colossians (Col 2:6-23) is nothing but a polemic against a deviant teaching, even if the reconstruction of it is elusive. Likewise, arguably the whole of 1 Timothy is written to forestall the creep of false

---

1 Thessalonians as the earliest letter or subsequent to Galatians (my position), some surely make too much of its silence with regard to justification, while others perhaps try too hard to find what is not there. As an example of the former, see Douglas K. Harink, *Paul Among the Postliberals: Pauline Theology Beyond Christendom and Modernity* (Grand Rapids: Brazos, 2003), 32-38. Although my developmental argument might be well served by a later developing "doctrine" of justification by faith, I do not find this sort of appeal to 1 Thessalonians convincing. The silences of 1 Thessalonians will cooperate with various reconstructions. The obverse of the absence of justification is that Gentiles are assured that Christ, "who died for us" (1 Thess 5:10) will deliver them from the coming wrath (1 Thess 1:10; 5:9) but with no suggestion that they had taken on Torah observance, only that the "believers" (1 Thess 1:7; 2:10, 13) "received the word" (1 Thess 1:6; 2:13). Indeed, it could be surmised that the Judean hostility "hindering us from speaking to the Gentiles so that they may be saved" (1 Thess 2:14-16) had at least something to do with a Torah-free reception of Gentiles into the covenant.
[95]Cf. Seifrid, *Christ, Our Righteousness*, 77-93.

teaching.[96] And, in shorter compass, Titus takes up similar concerns, while 2 Timothy evidences parallel interests, though more prophylactically. Nonetheless, a grace-prioritizing, works-excluding, faith-acquired, wrath-averting salvation is the consistent witness. But it does not appear that in any instance, save for Philippians 3, this soteriology participates in a polemical interest.

In sum, we can neither regard justification by faith the center of Paul's theology nor be confident that it was original to his evangelistic kerygma. At the same time, the claim that justification by faith is peripheral in Paul's theology is contradicted by the evidence, and, indeed, the themes that constitute the substance of justification by faith are as ubiquitous as any theme in the Pauline corpus.

3.2.4 Justification (2): imputation or participation? As is well known, "justification" would become a Christian-theological category that acquired a life of its own, and what has become of the term is not always directly related to its Pauline meaning.[97] This is not to register a complaint born of biblicist purism. That this should happen is inevitable and even laudable in certain respects, given that biblical vocabulary is the church's inherited lexicon and the natural starting point for subsequent theological exploration and refinement. It becomes problematic only when the anachronisms are regarded as patent of Paul, rather than what they are: variations on a theme, sometimes as with the musical variety, where the theme is hard to detect with all the festooning accompaniment. Moreover, this is not a partisan observation, as if retrojecting later theologies onto Paul's words were the notorious tendency of a particular party. While some want to equate justification with the "imputation" of righteousness as its sine qua non, others are intent to describe justification in as transformative terms as possible; both the Protestant- and Catholic-minded alike will naturally want to see their theology in Paul. We might say that Paul's framing of these matters was challenging enough, but the matter has only been complicated by the well-meaning use of his terminology to engage in debates of which the apostle was innocent.

---

[96]Gordon D. Fee, *1 and 2 Timothy, Titus*, UBCS (Grand Rapids: Baker Books, 2011), 7-10.
[97]Alister E. McGrath, *Iustitia Dei: A History of the Christian Doctrine of Justification*, 3rd ed. (Cambridge: Cambridge University Press, 2005).

When, for example, it is claimed that Paul's "doctrine of justification" means that, by faith, sinners have imputed to them the righteousness of Christ, many Christians believe they are hearing the gospel itself, or at least a summary of Paul's doctrine if not even a paraphrase of a verse or two from his letters.[98] But it is not so simple. For our purposes, the question is not quite whether the "imputation of Christ's righteousness" is true, in some sense; it is rather whether this is an accurate or satisfactory account of Paul, in any sense. Noble attempts to claim as much notwithstanding, there are reasons for doubt.[99]

To begin with, Paul nowhere speaks of "the righteousness of *Christ*," although, of course, in a few key places he speaks of Christ's obedience (Rom 5:19; Phil 2:8)—albeit never of his obedience to the *law*—and, especially in Romans, he frequently refers to the "righteousness of *God*" (Rom 1:17; 3:5, 21, 22, 26; 10:3). It follows, then, that if there is such a thing as the imputation of righteousness, it would take some work to demonstrate that Paul means by that an imputation of "the righteousness of *Christ*."[100] As a primary descriptor or organizing metaphor of a *Pauline* account of justification, the Protestant theological construct of Christ's imputed righteousness is problematic, especially the notion of the imputation of *Christ's active righteousness*, that Christ's perfect obedience to the law is credited to believers as a necessary and corollary

---

[98]For a helpful and nuanced theological lineage, see esp. Brian Vickers, *Jesus' Blood and Righteousness: Paul's Theology of Imputation* (Wheaton, IL: Crossway, 2006), 23-69. Vickers includes Luther (with proper qualifications), Melanchthon and Calvin; numerous Protestant confessions of the sixteenth and seventeenth centuries; and John Owen, Jonathan Edwards, Hendrikus Berkhof, Gresham Machen and John Murray. Modern New Testament scholars who give qualified assent include Herman Ridderbos, Leon Morris, George E. Ladd, Thomas Schreiner and Douglas Moo. To these could be added numerous others, including the classic statement of W. G. T. Shedd, who was followed by Charles Hodge (see D. A. Carson, "The Vindication of Imputation: On Fields of Discourse and Semantic Fields," in *Justification: What's at Stake in the Current Debates*, ed. Mark Husbands and Daniel J. Treier [Downers Grove, IL: InterVarsity Press, 2004], 52-53), and, of course, Carson himself, though with substantial qualification.

[99]So, rightly, Wright, *P&FG*, 2:949-51. It is less helpful, however, when Wright suggests alternatively that "the Messsiah's death and resurrection are 'reckoned' or 'imputed'" (ibid., 2:1028), which amounts to a conflation of the participation motif with the λογίζομαι metaphor, changing objects. Among recent attempts to rehabilitate imputation as a Pauline doctrine, see Carson, "Vindication of Imputation," and, especially, Vickers, *Jesus' Blood and Righteousness*.

[100]One of the unwitting achievements of Vickers's thorough study is to subvert its own claims regarding the centrality of the doctrine in Paul, when the study shows just how difficult it is to demonstrate imputation of Christ's righteousness as a *Pauline* notion at all and that it ultimately depends on extratextual inferences of dubious warrant.

blessing to forgiveness in the declaratory act of justification.[101] Indeed, despite its significant Protestant theological pedigree, it is hard to tease out of Paul a meaningful distinction between Christ's *active* obedience (perfect obedience to the law) and *passive* obedience (obedient yielding to the passion of the cross). At best these are theologians' taxonomies which mean to say that Jesus lived righteously and died obediently, but at worst the distinction bifurcates an indivisible whole toward no particularly useful end.[102] Whereas a distinction between the active and passive righteousness of Christ is a fixture in some Protestant evangelical theology, these are categories not just unknown to Paul; it is not really possible to find a basis for them. Perhaps Paul would not have objected to these constructs, but there is no way to know; for Paul, these are alien ways of speaking of the righteousness of Christ.

That leaves us with the question of whether it is right to speak of the imputation of righteousness in *any* respect. The notion has fallen on hard times, not least within evangelical New Testament scholarship, where its use would have once been relatively uncontroversial,[103] and not surprisingly, some defenses of imputed righteousness as a Protestant sine qua non have emerged, sometimes even expressing alarm at the erosion of biblical foundations in evangelical theology.[104] But the controversy surrounding imputation

---

[101]The emphasis on Christ's perfect keeping of the law in the Protestant imputation model is significantly out of proportion with the New Testament picture. Or to put it more precisely, it is an extrapolation from the not insignificant New Testament witness to Christ's sinlessness (e.g., 2 Cor 5:21; Heb 4:15; 7:26; 1 Pet 2:22; 3:18; 1 Jn 3:5). But it is a speculative abstraction to transform Christ's "sinlessness" into a perfection of Torah observance, and it is an inference that finds no basis in Paul.

[102]As is conceded by some defenders of the doctrine, e.g., by Carson, "Vindication of Imputation," 55; Robert Letham, *The Work of Christ* (Downers Grove, IL: InterVarsity Press, 1993), 130-32.

[103]See Robert H. Gundry, "Why I Didn't Endorse 'The Gospel of Jesus Christ: An Evangelical Celebration' . . . Even Though I Wasn't Asked To," *Books & Culture*, January/February 2001, www.booksandculture.com/articles/2001/janfeb/1.6.html; idem, "The Nonimputation of Christ's Righteousness," in Husbands and Treier, *Justification*, 17-45; Don B. Garlington, "Imputation or Union with Christ? A Response to John Piper," in *Studies in the New Perspective on Paul: Essays and Reviews* (Eugene, OR: Wipf & Stock, 2008), 137-96; idem, "Imputation or Union with Christ? A Rejoinder to John Piper," in *Studies in the New Perspective on Paul*, 197-227; Seifrid, *Christ, Our Righteousness*, 171-76; idem, "Luther, Melanchthon and Paul on the Question of Imputation," in Husbands and Treier, *Justification*, 137-52; and Bird, *Saving Righteousness*, 7-8, 61-87. Bird's actual position on the matter is somewhat confusing, given that he seems to endorse somewhat cavalierly in one place (*Introducing Paul*, 96-98) what he seemed to have qualified so carefully in another (Michael F. Bird, "Incorporated Righteousness," in *Saving Righteousness*, 60-87).

[104]In addition to those cited above in n. 98, see, e.g., John Piper, *Counted Righteous in Christ: Should We Abandon the Imputation of Christ's Righteousness?* (Wheaton, IL: Crossway, 2002).

is a tempest in a teapot. If we set aside the dubious notion of the imputation of *Christ's* righteousness, it is clear that God does indeed give a *gift of right-eousness* (*tēs dōreas tēs dikaiosynēs*, Rom 5:17), a *righteousness from God* (*tēn ek theou dikaiosynēn*, Phil 3:9). Indeed, it would seem that New Testament scholars must put in as much overtime to deny that God "imputes" (leaving aside for now whether that is the best word) righteousness in some sense as those who affirm that it is *Christ's active righteousness* that is imputed. And in both cases—both the denial and the affirmation—these claims understate and overreach, respectively, what Paul actually says.

"Imputation," of course, derives from the verb *logizomai* (to "reckon," "credit," "account," "impute") in Romans 4.[105] It enters that discourse from the LXX of Genesis 15:6 (Rom 4:3), where it is said of Abraham that "he believed God and it was reckoned to him for righteousness" (*kai episteusen Abram tō theō kai elogisthē auto eis dikaiosynēn*), and from Psalm 32:2 (LXX 31:2; Rom 4:8), where blessing is pronounced upon "the man whom the Lord imputes no iniquity" (*makarios anēr hou ou logisētai kyrios hamartian*). Thus, as is well known, Romans 4 is responsible for the introduction of imputation language into accounts of Pauline theology and New Testament soteriology.[106] As such, Romans 4 offers essentially two complementary claims directly relevant to the question at hand: (1) That, after the pattern of Abraham, whose faith, preceding circumcision and his obedient offering of Isaac, was credited for righteousness, so too now it is faith "apart from works" (*chōris ergōn*, Rom 4:6 NRSV) that is reckoned for righteousness. (2) That, like the blessed "man" of Psalm 32:2, those who are in Christ enjoy the "non-reckoning" of their iniquities: "Blessed is the one against whom the Lord will not reckon sin" (Rom 4:8 NSRV).

Although there are numerous details that might be disputed, two conclusions follow from Paul's appropriation of these texts: (1) That, from the repetition of the phrase "reckoned [for] righteousness," it is not improper in some general terms to speak of an "imputation" of righteousness. True, in the appropriation of Genesis 15:6 it is technically not "righteousness" but

---

[105]The verb is found not fewer than eleven times in Romans 4 (Rom 4:3, 4, 5, 6, 8, 9, 10, 11, 22, 23, 24), with various grammatical subjects and objects.

[106]While I grant that *imputation* might carry certain particular freight with it in English, given its long specialized theological usage, for our purposes, there should be no intrinsic difference among "reckon," "credit," "count" or "impute" as English glosses of λογίζομαι.

rather faith (*pistis*, Rom 4:5; or the act of believing, *episteusen*) that "is reckoned" or "imputed."[107] God counts believing or faith *as* righteousness. This is not to say that "imputation" is the essence or sine qua non of justification, only that there is a credibly Pauline—which is to say substantially qualified—version of the notion. But clearly Romans 4 gives us no basis to speak of righteousness of Christ, active, passive or otherwise, as though it were Christ's obedience that was being reckoned.[108]

(2) The argument of Romans 4:3-8 makes it fairly clear that the nonreckoning of sin (Rom 4:8)—what we might otherwise call "forgiveness"—is at the very least complementary to the reckoning of faith as righteousness, that the former is the complement of the latter. In fact, there is every reason in this context to understand the nonreckoning of sin (i.e., forgiveness) not as a separable element but as a second, negative, description of "faith being reckoned for righteousness." Faith being "reckoned unto righteousness" is tantamount to iniquities forgiven, sins being covered and the Lord not reckoning sin against the sinner. This reading, over against its more strongly imputation alternative, is confirmed on contextual grounds. The citation of Psalm 32:2 is introduced by transitional argumentative tissue that echoes the very language of Genesis 15:6 while also anticipating the psalm quotation: "So also David pronounces a blessing [*legei ton makarismon*] upon the man to whom *God reckons righteousness apart from works*" (Rom 4:6 RSV). Clearly, then Romans 4:6 introduces Psalm 32:2 as though it is none other than a description of the one who is reckoned righteous by means of faith apart

---

[107]At risk of pedanticism, in Romans 4:3, 22 and 23, the implied subject of the passive ἐλογίσθη is that "Abraham believed," while in Romans 4:5 and 9 the explicit subject is ἡ πίστις. While it is true that grammatically the prepositional phrase εἰς δικαιοσύνην is not technically the object of the passive forms of λογίζομαι in Romans 4:3, 5, 9 and 22, in Romans 4:6, δικαιοσύνην apart from a preposition is the direct object of λογίζεται in the middle voice; and in Romans 4:11, δικαιοσύνην is probably best taken as the subject of the passive infinitive, λογισθῆναι. Therefore, were one disinclined to count "righteousness" as that which is "reckoned" on the basis of the preposition εἰς, the constructions of Romans 4:6 and 11 count against making too much of the distinction.

[108]Vickers (*Jesus' Blood and Righteousness*, 191-216) "solves" the dilemma of a dearth of evidence for the classical Protestant account of imputation—which to his credit he fully acknowledges—by synthesizing the claims of Romans 4 (whence is derived "imputation" vocabulary) with Romans 5:18 (whence is derived Christ's obedience) in relationship to the language of 2 Corinthians 5:21 and other texts. The result is not convincing unless one is already predisposed to the necessity of the construct, as Vickers's "synthesis" (it is not a *Pauline* synthesis, as he calls it) is in the end rather more of a conflation, and of exegeses that are not always persuasive in their own right.

from works. Simply put, another way to describe a person reckoned righteous is as a person who is forgiven.

Some further clarity comes from considering the force of the prepositional phrase *eis dikaiosynēn* ("for righteousness").[109] The translation "reckoned *as* righteousness" (*logizesthai eis dikaiosynēn*, Rom 4:3, 5, 9, 22; so NIV, NRSV, ESV, NAB and most) is serviceable, but, by rendering *eis dikaiosynēn* as "*as* righteousness," this translation obscures the instructive analogy to other instances of the expression in Romans. Leaving Romans 4, it is evident that Paul elsewhere uses *eis dikaiosynēn* as a soteriological expression of eschatological destiny. For example, in Romans 6:16, it is apparent that the contrasting parallel between "sin, *which leads to* death [*hamartias eis thanaton*]" (NRSV) and "obedience, *which leads to* righteousness [*hypakoēs eis dikaiosynēn*]" (NRSV) describes "righteousness" as an eschatological outcome contrasting death. The eschatological or, we might say, telic force of *eis dikaiosynēn* is even clearer in Romans 10:10, where *eis dikaiosynēn* is paralleled with *eis sōterian* as descriptive of eschatological ends: "For one believes with the heart and so is justified [*eis dikaiosynēn*], and one confesses with the mouth and so is saved [*eis sōterian*]" (NRSV). Similarly, in Romans 10:4: "For Christ is the end of the law *so that there may be righteousness* [*eis dikaiosynēn*] for everyone who believes" (NRSV). Here again it is clear that *eis dikaiosynēn* describes an eschatological telos for the one who believes. Indeed, several translations render *eis dikaiosynēn* as a synonym for *dikaiōsis* ("justification"; so RSV, NJB, NAB; cf. TNIV). Therefore, it is not special pleading to say that faith being reckoned *eis dikaiosynēn* is tantamount to saying that faith is counted *as justification* itself, that is, a status that avails before God with respect to eschatological judgment.

---

[109]Both Carson and Vickers make much of the "*x* is reckoned as *y*" analogy, where *x* and *y* are taken to be fundamentally different (Carson, "Vindication of Imputation," 58; and Vickers, *Jesus' Blood and Righteousness*, 76-88). Carson appeals to the Hebrew grammar of ל חשׁב (e.g., Gen 31:15; Num 18:27, 30; Lev 7:18) where, in each case however, the LXX translates the idiom λογίζεσθαι ὡς ("to be reckoned *as*") rather than λογίζεσθαι εἰς ("to be reckoned *for*") as we have in Genesis 15:6 (LXX; so also Rom 4:3, etc.). It could be argued that the Greek idiom is clearly the more relevant for our purposes, and thus that Carson's analogies of use are not quite analogous. It could even be that LXX translators, understanding the "*x* reckoned as *y*" pattern chose λογίζεσθαι ὡς precisely as a disambiguating expression, which would subvert the syntactical basis of Carson and Vickers's claim that "faith" is to be understood as the reckoning of what is intrinsically "not-righteousness" as "righteousness."

Thus, the language of Romans 4:1-12 proves uncooperative for both the (characteristically Catholic) transformative impartation interpretation as well as the (characteristically Reformed) imputation overreading that intends to correct the former. Whatever else we might want to say about the transformative vision of Pauline soteriology in general, there is every reason to understand *dikaiosynē* in this context as a status conferred rather than a moral righteousness imparted or infused. On the other hand, on the same grounds, there is no basis for finding a crediting of Christ's active righteousness, as though Paul had spoken in terms of *logizetai dikaiōmata* ("credit righteous deeds"). No, faith is reckoned as a status of righteousness *coram Deo*, the equivalent of justification, a virtual synonym in this context for the nonreckoning of sin. Those who describe this in terms of an imputation of Christ's (active) righteousness describe the right outcome—a righteous status before God—by means of an unnecessary and speculative mechanism for which the text offers no support. Thus, if by "imputation" we mean faith counting as righteousness, a vindicated status before God, without the textually unwarranted suggestion that this results from some crediting of Christ's active righteousness, then, yes, we can speak of "imputation" as a properly Pauline concept. But it should be understood that this qualified *Pauline* notion of "imputation" is not the classic Protestant notion of the same name but its thoroughgoing chastening.

Meanwhile, an overdue shift is underway in Pauline studies in which the Pauline notion of union with Christ—in its various descriptions, "participation," "incorporation," etc.—is enjoying a resurgence of interest.[110] Hardly a *novum* in Pauline studies, it is not accidental that this development is especially pronounced among scholars oriented toward evangelicalism and its institutions, and I suspect that it counts as a remediation of the narrowly juridical, and sometimes virtually commercial, soteriology that often characterizes the evangelical movement, at least in its popular expressions.[111]

---

[110]Notably, among New Testament exegetes, Bird, *Saving Righteousness*; Macaskill, *Union with Christ*; Constantine R. Campbell, *Paul and Union with Christ: An Exegetical and Theological Study* (Grand Rapids: Eerdmans, 2012); J. R. Daniel Kirk, *Unlocking Romans: Resurrection and the Justification of God* (Grand Rapids: Eerdmans, 2008); and Gorman, *Inhabiting the Cruciform God*.

[111]For a survey of classic studies in the Pauline literature, see esp. C. R. Campbell, *Paul and Union with Christ*, 31-64; and Macaskill, *Union with Christ*, 17-41. It should not be missed that E. P. Sanders's "participationist eschatology" engendered a significant renewal of interest in this theme (*P&PJ*, esp. 543-56).

N. T. Wright, a scholar bearing enormous influence within evangelicalism, has made eschatological participation in Christ and corporate identity along covenantal lines a chief theme of his New Testament theological scholarship.[112] Moreover, the theme is being recovered in Reformed circles, especially by students of Luther and Calvin.[113] Meanwhile, there is afoot among some evangelicals, especially younger generations of a theological bent, a movement toward more historic, ecclesial and sacramental—especially Anglican, Roman Catholic and Orthodox—expressions of the Christian theological tradition. Participatory union with Christ, incorporation into the body of Christ, is as basic to these traditions as an "alien righteousness" is to the Reformation counterparts—so much so that it is no wonder that these traditions so frequently find the other so hard to understand and so easy to caricature. In any case, it is evident that forensic and commercial metaphors that are native and obvious to certain traditions as part of their metaphorical furniture are, for better or worse, not nearly so intuitive in other traditions, where sacramental participation and liturgical anamnesis are the more fundamental mediations of the soteriological reality.

Whatever its sources, this renewed interest in participation in Christ must be regarded as a constructive influence on Pauline scholarship. Not only so, but the recovery from these varied quarters of a more robust and central participationist account of salvation has the potential to restore to greater wholeness truncated pictures of Christian soteriology. In particular, I would join the ranks of several who are now arguing that the forensic dimension of salvation, justification itself, is incomprehensible apart from the believer's participation in Christ.[114]

---

[112]Although, as I argue elsewhere, for all that, the theme bears less upon his construal of justification than one might have expected: see Garwood P. Anderson, "Justification, Paul and Bishop N. T. Wright," in *Justification in Anglican Life and Thought*, ed. Daniel J. Westberg and Jordan Hylden (Eugene, OR: Pickwick, forthcoming).

[113]Carl E. Braaten and Robert W. Jenson, eds., *Union with Christ: The New Finnish Interpretation of Luther* (Grand Rapids: Eerdmans, 1998); Tuomo Mannermaa, *Christ Present in Faith: Luther's View of Justification*, trans. Kirsi Irmeli Stjerna (Minneapolis: Fortress, 2005); J. Todd Billings, *Union with Christ: Reframing Theology and Ministry for the Church* (Grand Rapids: Baker Academic, 2011); and Robert Letham, *Union with Christ: In Scripture, History, and Theology* (Phillipsburg, NJ: P&R, 2011).

[114]And, although it is slightly tangential to my argument, the same might be said for the vexed and contentious matter of atonement: no "theory" of atonement can be found adequate, or even coherent, that is not rooted in a strongly realistic participatory vision of suffering and death *in Christ*. If one finds the so-called penal-substitution theory frequently on the receiving end of

If it were once true that participationist accounts of Pauline soteriology were introduced as the alternative to reigning forensic (especially imputation) accounts, there are now signs that the long-standing impasse is fading into irrelevance. Although it is still not uncommon to see these pitted against each other, supposing that the affirmation of participation amounts to eschewal of imputation by definition,[115] one is hard-pressed to find the logical necessity of this dichotomy. A growing cadre of New Testament scholars is coming to understand the inseparability of a plausible forensic account of justification from a properly participationist one.[116] It is true that some continue to hold more tightly to the imputation paradigm than Paul's texts require or even allow, but it still constitutes a large step forward that New Testament scholars increasingly are coming to understand the centrality of participation in Christ and that "imputation," whatever form it should take, is contingent on and derivable from union with Christ.

Thus, rather than repristinating imputation as a Pauline account of justification, I join Michael Bird in commending "*incorporated* righteousness" as a more coherent alternative.[117] Put simply, the *ek theou* ("from God") righteousness is always an *en Christō* ("in Christ") righteousness. "Being found *in him*" is the preface to and condition for possessing the righteousness that comes from God (Phil 3:9). Likewise, in 2 Corinthians 5:21, "For our sake he made him to be sin who knew no sin, so that we might become the righteousness of God *in him*."[118] It is, according to Romans 6, only by baptism

---

caricature, it is in no small measure the fault of its proponents, who—never mind the more inapt and theologically inadequate metaphors—have understated, or missed altogether, that the New Testament picture of atonement *depends* upon a realistic understanding of participatory union with Christ in his suffering and death, and in his victorious resurrection.

[115]E.g., Daniel G. Powers, *Salvation Through Participation: An Examination of the Notion of the Believers' Corporate Unity with Christ in Early Christian Soteriology*, Contributions to Biblical Exegesis and Theology 29 (Leuven: Peeters, 2001), 234; Garlington, "Imputation or Union with Christ?"; and Gundry, "Nonimputation of Christ's Righteousness."

[116]E.g., Bird, "Incorporated Righteousness"; C. R. Campbell, *Paul and Union with Christ*, 399-401, who regards imputation and union with Christ a "false dichotomy"; Vickers, *Jesus' Blood and Righteousness*, 218, who regards union with Christ as the prerequisite and means of imputation; and Lane G. Tipton, "Union with Christ and Justification," in *Justified in Christ: God's Plan for Us in Justification*, ed. K. Scott Oliphint (Fearn, Scotland: Mentor, 2007), 23-49.

[117]The language is borrowed from, but not unique to, Bird, "Incorporated Righteousness." I part company with Bird only in his ambivalence toward anything approaching Paul's sacramental realism: e.g., "The union [with Christ] is *symbolized* through baptism, but the conduit is, as always for Paul, through faith" ("Incorporated Righteousness," 56, emphasis added). In a work that so effectively eschews false dichotomies, that this one remains is unfortunate.

[118]It must be judged at least surprising, if not telling, that in his four accounts of 2 Corinthians

union with Christ's death and resurrection that God's judgment of sin in
Christ's body of flesh becomes the judgment of our sin and only by baptism
union with his resurrection that his vindication is our vindication. This is how
Paul can say that Christ "was handed over to death for our trespasses and was
raised for our justification" (Rom 4:25 NRSV). Paul didn't coin the clever aph-
orism simply because the balanced phrases so neatly trip off the tongue. Justification depends every bit as much on resurrection as it does atonement
because it depends every bit on union with the vindicated Christ. Likewise, it
can be no accident Paul concludes his tour-de-force argument in Galatians 3
with an appeal to baptism over against circumcision: "For as many of you as
were baptized into Christ have put on Christ, for *in Christ Jesus* you are all
children of God through faith" (Gal 3:26-27). If there is any sense in which
justification is forensic, it is because it is in every sense participatory; God's
judgment is exhausted in Christ's death, and his vindication is fulfilled in his
resurrection so that those united to Christ in faith and baptism stand with
Christ—indeed, *in* Christ—acquitted and vindicated themselves.

There are several felicitous consequences of holding together the forensic
and participatory dimensions of justification, but chiefly it is a more organic
alignment between the gospel (i.e., the saving acts of God in Jesus Christ)
and "redemption applied," the subjective appropriation of salvation. In its
most unfortunate iteration—arguably the most common iteration—
justification enters as an alien forensic metaphor that functions to "deliver"
a verdict to the individual upon the condition of faith. In this guise, a logic
derivable from, yet not intrinsic to, the Christ narrative (a.k.a. "gospel")
distributes the accomplishment of Christ's atonement to the individual
sinner, whose justification and salvation are earned by Christ and delivered
to Christians upon consequence of faith. At its worst, faith becomes like
unto a PIN code withdrawing a transaction of acquittal from a divine fund
of righteousness deposited by Christ's atoning death. In this scenario, resurrection matters for the validation of the atoning sacrifice, but it is not

---

5:21 (see n. 93), Wright never comments substantially on the capstone phrase (at the very end
of the sentence) ἐν αὐτῷ. But the prepositional phrase, "in him," ties it naturally and unmistakably back to 2 Corinthians 5:17-19: "if anyone is *in Christ*"; "who reconciled us to himself
through Christ"; "that is, *in Christ* God was reconciling the world to himself." Thus, "in him"
of 2 Corinthians 5:21 is a further sign that this verse is a description of the reconciling work of
God by means of atonement rather than a setting forward of the apostles as an instantiation of
the covenant faithfulness of God.

intrinsic to a soteriology that is delivered by these foreign vehicles.[119] But with the adherence of justification as participatory *and* forensic—more specifically forensic *by means of* participation—the gospel and its appropriation coinhere. Christ's deliverance over to death is a satisfying verdict pronounced upon human sin, and his deliverance from the grave is our participation in his vindication and our deliverance from death. In Peter Leithart's (soon to be memorable?) language, justification is God's "deliverdict," wherein by union with Christ we are at once acquitted and delivered, participating at once in Christ's death and resurrection, respectively.[120]

3.2.5 Pistis Christou: *objective or subjective?* I have saved for last one more antinomy of recent Pauline scholarship, how the Greek phrase *pistis Christou* is to be understood. The debate has been cast largely in terms of two alternatives: the traditional interpretation, "faith *in* Christ" (usually described as the "objective genitive"), or the ascendant alternative, "faithfulness *of* Christ" (usually described as the "subjective genitive"). Strictly speaking, this crux of recent Pauline interpretation is not part of the NPP "package"—that is, scholars sympathetic to the NPP are not of one mind on the question.[121] Famously, Richard Hays has championed, though not pioneered, the subjective-genitive reading ("faithfulness of Christ") and is joined by many NPP-inclined scholars, N. T. Wright, Michael Gorman and Doug Campbell, among numerous others.[122] And advocates of the subjective-genitive reading also hail in equal measure from the apocalyptic school (e.g., Martyn, de Boer, Campbell), who, if anything, ask this construal

---

[119]This worst-case scenario will be familiar from D. A. Campbell, *Deliverance of God*. Again, I regard Campbell's "Justification theory" as representative of certain popular construals but ultimately unpersuasive as an account of scholarly proposals.

[120]Peter J. Leithart, *Delivered from the Elements of the World: Atonement, Justification, Mission* (Downers Grove, IL: IVP Academic, 2016), esp. 179-214 (anticipated in idem, "Justification as Verdict and Deliverance: A Biblical Perspective," *Pro Ecclesia* 16, no. 1 [2007]: 56-72). I am grateful to InterVarsity Press for galley proofs and indebted not only to Leithart's clever coinage but also to his robust account of justification as both forensic and participatory. Regrettably, my exposure to his larger argument is so late as not to allow a more inclusive and detailed engagement with his work.

[121]See Roy A. Harrisville III, "Πίστις Χριστοῦ and the New Perspective on Paul," *Logia* 19, no. 2 (2010): 19-28.

[122]The most influential work is Hays, *Faith of Jesus Christ* (2nd ed.; originally published in 1983). For Hays's predecessors and for an account of the debate, see Debbie Hunn, "Debating the Faithfulness of Jesus Christ in Twentieth-Century Scholarship," in Bird and Sprinkle, *FJC*, 15-32. Arguably the most influential predecessor to Hays was George Howard, whose 1967 article was the first in a series of publications on the theme ("On the Faith of Christ," *HTR* 60, no. 4 [1967]: 459-65).

of *pistis Christou* to bear even *more* weight than do their NPP counterparts. Meanwhile, James Dunn has been outspoken in support of the more traditional objective-genitive reading ("faith in Christ"). So, although a majority of scholars sympathetic to the NPP seem to favor the subjective genitive, it cannot be described as a defining issue.

The question at hand will be quite familiar to some readers, having become an interpretative crux in Pauline interpretation over the past generation, especially in English-speaking scholarship. For readers not aware of the discussion and especially its grammatical basis, I offer a brief introductory summary.[123] *Pistis Christou* (or its equivalent)[124] is a phrase, occurring eight, perhaps nine, times in the Pauline corpus (Rom 3:22, 26; Gal 2:16 [2x], 20; 3:22; [3:26 in p[46] and other witnesses;] Phil 3:9; Eph 3:12), which can be translated in at least one of two basic ways.

1. Almost all modern English translations render the phrase "faith *in* [Jesus] Christ." The words "Jesus" and/or "Christ," which are in the Greek genitive case, are understood then to be the syntactic object of the faith (i.e., what/whom is believed), thus, the *objective* genitive. This translation will make contextual sense to almost all readers of the English text, and until relatively recently it was treated by virtually all modern English translations as though it were the clear sense of the text.[125]

2. On the other hand, because "Jesus [/] Christ" is in the genitive and not preceded in Greek by a preposition that would mean "in" (e.g., *en, eis,* or

---

[123]Efficient surveys of the grammatical dimensions of the question are available in George E. Howard, "Faith of Christ," *ABD* 2:758-60; and Wallace, *GGBB*, 114-16.

[124]The phrase in question is found in a variety of forms. Following convention, I use *pistis Christou* as shorthand inclusive of the variants: Ἰησοῦ Χριστοῦ (Rom 3:22; Gal 2:16; 3:22); Ἰησοῦ (Rom 3:26); τῇ τοῦ υἱοῦ τοῦ θεοῦ (Gal 2:20); αὐτοῦ (Eph 3:12).

As shorthand for the two predominant views, I will use the gloss "faith in Christ" to refer to the objective-genitive view and "faithfulness of Christ" to refer to the subjective-genitive position, these rather than the grammatical descriptions. This, I hope, saves the reader from the mental gymnastics of remembering which is which. I mention this only because I have learned that it is a source of confusion for students new to the debate and inexperienced with Greek grammatical categories: The words *objective* and *subjective* are strictly grammatical in this context, bearing none of the overtones we might attach to the same words if we were talking about a person's perception of a text, an event or the world. In that regard, the subjective genitive is ironically the more "objective" and the objective genitive the more "subjective"—no wonder students get confused! In this respect, I find M. Seifrid's use of the labels "subjectivist" and "objectivist" unfortunate ("Faith of Christ," 129-46).

[125]Although the KJV translates these texts with "faith *of* [Jesus] Christ" with the exception of Romans 3:26.

pros), it is entirely possible that the sense should be the "faith [or "faithfulness"] of Jesus [/] Christ." In this instance Christ is not the object of the faith that humans are exercising but the one who exercised faith or faithfulness himself. He is the grammatical subject of the verbal notion of "exercising faith"; thus, we call this the *subjective*-genitive interpretation.[126]

The potential ambiguity of the "so immensely versatile and hard-worked" genitive case is well known.[127] In Greek (and by numerous English analogies) we can imagine similar genitive expressions (generally analogous to English expressions with "of") in which the genitive term could function as the grammatical possessor or as the subject or akin to the direct object or, indeed, in any number of other ways. To use a standard pedagogical example, the phrase "love *of* God" could mean (1) love God possesses (God's love), (2) love God exercises or (3) love that a human being has toward God (as, e.g., in the expression "for the love of God!"), or (4) "God" could even be almost like an adjective in relationship to "love." For example, "People are always looking out for themselves, but the love *of God* (i.e., love that is God-like) puts the needs of others first." With this background, we can consider the standard approaches to *pistis Christou* and weigh the merits of each.[128]

3.2.5.1 In favor of the subjective genitive: faithfulness of Christ. (1) All things being equal, the subjective genitive would arguably be a more natural interpretation, grammatically speaking.[129] Were one to refer in Greek to the faith

---

[126]In some ways, to make the rendering of the genitive (objective or subjective) as the key identifying feature of each view obscures what is the more primary question, namely, whose faith it is that is being exercised. In the case of the objective, it is *human pistis* toward Christ and in the subjective, it is *Christ's* own *pistis* that he exercises. So, in fact, there are two intermingled issues: (1) whose faith and (2) how it is grammatically related to "Christ."

[127]C. F. D. Moule, *Idiom Book of New Testament Greek* (Cambridge: Cambridge University Press, 1960), 37.

[128]For a taxonomy of uses of the genitive, it is hard to improve on Wallace, *GGBB*, 72-136.

[129]It is hard to avoid the impression in some instances that the subjective genitive has commended itself on the English gloss "of" as a convenient habit so deeply engrained it prejudices the question. Anecdotally, I've noticed the tendency of students to say that "literally" the phrase means "faith *of* Christ, not faith *in* Christ." That sort of woodenness is expected of students early in their study of Greek, but it persists more subtly among scholars as well. Note this comment on a use of the phrase in Origen from Preston Sprinkle's otherwise excellent article: "Those who are 'outside the πίστις Χριστοῦ' are not simply outside 'the faith in Christ'—*which is awkward*—but outside a certain community of believers who are living to God" (Sprinkle, "Πίστις Χριστοῦ as an Eschatological Event," in Bird and Sprinkle, *FJC*, 181). Sprinkle might have this exactly right, but note his appeal to the alleged awkwardness (emphasis added) of the objective-genitive translation. Clearly he can only be referring to the awkwardness of the English *gloss*, which can hardly count as exegetical evidence.

that a person possesses or exercises, it would be natural to do it by means of *pistis* + personal genitive. Thus, for example, when we hear of the "faith of Abraham" (Rom 4:16; cf. 4:12), a parallel construction, it does not occur to us that this could mean "faith *in* Abraham"; we naturally assume it means the faith which Abraham possessed or practiced. Elsewhere in the New Testament, when a person (or personal pronoun) is in the genitive modifying "faith," it is naturally subjective or simply possessive.[130]

(2) Presumably if Paul had wanted to say the equivalent of "faith *in* Christ," with Christ being the explicit object, he could have expressed it explicitly with a prepositional phrase and not the genitive modifier. *Pistis* with a prepositional phrase specifying the object of faith is by no means an unusual expression,[131] and, were the objective-genitive meaning his intention, it can at least be asked why or toward what end Paul would have chosen a genitive modifier instead of a preposition.

(3) The subjective-genitive view avoids what would otherwise be an almost grating redundancy in certain texts where a soteriological benefit is premised upon *pistis Christou* and yet there is a second near reference to faith or believing (*pistis* or *pisteuō*).[132]

- Romans 3:22: "righteousness of God through *faith in* Jesus Christ for all who *believe* [*eis pantas tous pisteuontas*]"

---

[130]See, e.g., in Paul, Romans 1:8, 12; 3:3; 4:5, 12, 16; 1 Corinthians 2:5; 15:14, 17; 2 Corinthians 10:15; Philippians 2:17; 1 Thessalonians 1:8; 3:2, 5, 10; Philemon 6; in disputed Paul, 2 Thessalonians 1:3; Colossians 1:4; Titus 1:1; and in the remainder of the New Testament, Matthew 9:2, 22, 29; Mark 2:5; 5:34; 10:52; Luke 5:20; 7:50; 8:25, 48; 17:19; 18:42; 22:32; 1 Peter 1:9, 21; 2 Peter 1:5.

[131]Limiting to the substantive, i.e., excluding πιστεύω + preposition: (1) πίστις ἐν: (a) in undisputed Paul: Romans 3:25 (τῷ αὐτοῦ αἵματι); Galatians 3:26 (probably, though the syntax/punctuation is debatable); (b) in disputed Paul: Ephesians 1:15; Colossians 1:4; 1 Timothy 3:13 (possibly); 2 Timothy 3:15. (2) πίστις εἰς: (a) in disputed Paul: Colossians 2:5; (b) in the remainder of the New Testament: Acts 20:21; 24:24; 26:18 (ἐμέ; i.e., God); 1 Peter 1:21 (πιστοὺς εἰς θεόν). (3) πίστις πρός: 1 Thessalonians 1:8 (τὸν θεόν); Philemon 5. (4) πίστις ἐπί: Hebrews 6:1 (θεόν).

Curiously—and to me unconvincingly—Porter and Pitts use this same data (specifically Gal 3:26; Rom 3:25; 1 Tim 3:13; and 2 Tim 3:15) to argue the reverse: that the parallel structure of πίστις as object of preposition further modified by ἐν + dative is an argument *in favor* of the objective genitive (Stanley E. Porter and Andrew E. Pitts, "Πίστις with a Preposition and Genitive Modifier: Lexical, Semantic, and Syntactic Considerations in the πίστις Χριστοῦ Discussion," in Bird and Sprinkle, *FJC*, 33-53).

[132]Matlock identifies this as the "single most frequent exegetical argument against the objective-genitive reading of πίστις Χριστοῦ" and proceeds to argue that the appeal to redundancy is not compelling (R. Barry Matlock, "The Rhetoric of πίστις in Paul: Galatians 2:16, 3:22, Romans 3:22, and Philippians 3:9," *JSNT* 30, no. 2 [2007]: 173-203). I concur with Matlock's argument while proposing that there is a more compelling alternative to the objective genitive.

- Galatians 2:16: "through *faith in* Jesus Christ, even we have *believed in* Christ Jesus [*kai hēmeis eis Christon Iēsoun episteusamen*], in order to be justified by *faith in* Christ"

- Galatians 3:22: "the promise by *faith in* Jesus Christ might be given *to those who believe* [*tois pisteuousin*]"

- Philippians 3:9: "which is through *faith in* Christ, the righteousness from God that *depends on faith* [*epi tē pistei*]"

Although it could be said that the double stress on believing or faith could be nothing more than repetition for emphasis—the equivalent in words of "structural redundancy" in engineering—there is at least some reason for thinking that something more nuanced is happening. *Pistis Christou* can rather be seen almost as the objective ground or basis, the pioneering representative faithfulness of the Messiah for a new humanity, in relation to which reciprocating "faith" is the appropriate and appropriating response. This reading not only eliminates the apparent redundancy but highlights an intrinsic theological balance between the objective basis of salvation and its subjective appropriation.

(4) Moving (cautiously!) from grammar to theology, this observation leads to a closely related fourth observation. The "faithfulness of Christ" construed as a subjective genitive is thus consistent with Paul's understanding of Christ's human and paradigmatic faithfulness and subsequent vindication, elsewhere expressed in terms of humility and obedience. Of course, this is most famously narrated in the Christ hymn of Philippians 2:6-11, wherein, for his self-abasement (*ouch harpagmon hēgēsato to einai isa theō*), his self-emptying (*heauton ekenōsen*), his humility (*etapeinōsen heauton*) and his obedience (*genomenos hypēkoos*), Christ is vindicated by means of exaltation (*auton hyperypsōsen*) and given the name "Lord."[133] The same pattern, though in different language, is also found elsewhere in the Pauline corpus (e.g., 2 Cor 8:9; Rom 15:3) and, indeed, is an attested theme in other New Testament literature (e.g., Heb 5:7-9; 1 Pet 2:21-25; Rev 1:5). What these texts share is a dynamic narratival construal of the Christ event as at once representative, paradigmatic and epochal. On a more expansive

---

[133]The literature on the Philippians Christ hymn is voluminous, but for the unpacking of the passage as a paradigmatic, soteriological narrative, see esp. Gorman, *Cruciformity*.

theological tableau, the subjective genitive is consistent with and participates in the larger narrative structure of the gospel, namely, that Christ is
the second (obedient) Adam (Rom 5:14-21; 1 Cor 15:22) and the new (faithful)
Israel (Gal 3:16, 29).

Thus, the subjective-genitive reading, which starts as a grammatical possibility, might be said to vindicate itself as a compelling theological vision
coherent with Paul's gospel. However attractive this interpretation has
proven to be, it is not unproblematic, and many remain unpersuaded.[134]

3.2.5.2 In favor of the objective genitive: faith in Christ. (1) While it is over-
whelmingly the case that personal genitives modifying *pistis* are elsewhere
essentially subjective or possessive, we might note that "Christ" is not a
garden-variety "personal genitive qualifier." Intrinsically he is a possible
object of faith, whereas, for example, Abraham would at best be an *example*
of faithfulness. All the more so is this the case when we understand *Christos*
as more fundamentally titular than a surname, much less a personal name.
It is both useful but ultimately perilous to advance syntactical arguments
independent of lexis.[135]

(2) The theme of Christ exercising faith or practicing trust would be considerably strengthened were Christ ever the subject of the cognate verb
pisteuō, "to believe" or "to have faith." But Paul never speaks of Jesus exercising faith, overcoming doubt or trusting, even though, to be sure, this
accords with the witness of certain non-Pauline New Testament texts.[136]
Unlike the case with Abraham, *Paul* never speaks of Christ "having faith" or
"trusting."[137] Jesus "acts righteously" (Rom 5:8, *dikaiōma*), is obedient (Rom

---

[134]The discussion of πίστις Χριστοῦ has made various appeals to genitive objects of πιστ- vocabulary
outside of the Pauline corpus (esp. Mk 11:22; Acts 3:16; Jas 2:1; and Rev 14:12), arguing for the
precedent of the objective genitive, on the one hand (cf. Roy A. Harrisville III, "Before ΠΙΣΤΙΣ
ΧΡΙΣΤΟΥ: The Objective Genitive as Good Greek," *NovT* 48 [2006]: 353-58), or casting doubt on
that presumption on the other (see, e.g., Bird and Sprinkle, "IV. The Witness of the Wider New
Testament," *FJC*, 210-74). These data form a sort of wishbone in the larger argument, and I am
not persuaded that they are unambiguous enough to count for or against either position.
[135]See, e.g., Porter and Pitts, "Πίστις with a Preposition and Genitive Modifier"; and R. Barry
Matlock, "Saving Faith: The Rhetoric and Semantics of πίστις in Paul," in Bird and Sprinkle,
FJC, 73-89.
[136]At the same time, it is hard to avoid the impression that the evidence for a "non-docetic," faithful, obedient and even epochally pioneering Jesus amounts to pushing on an open door, on the
one hand, while being of no particular probative value for the construal of *pistis Christou*.
[137]Although see Kenneth Schenck, "2 Corinthians and the πίστις Χριστοῦ Debate," *CBQ* 70, no. 3
(2008): 524-37.

5:19; Phil 2:8) and "knew no sin" (2 Cor 5:21), but he is never described as "believing," "trusting" or even "faithful" (*pistos*).

(3) As for the argument that the objective genitive introduces an intolerable redundancy, the claim is not nearly as decisive as is sometimes thought. While it is true that there is an attractive stylistic and even theological grace to the notion of Christ's faithfulness eliciting human fidelity in response, it remains the case that one person's redundancy is another person's repetition for emphasis. In any case, the aspersions cast on the objective-genitive reading on this ground are at best overstated, if not the imposition of a stylistic bias that lacks any serious controls.[138]

(4) Especially problematic for the subjective-genitive interpretation is the accumulation of strong evidence that the earliest Christian interpreters read the expression as essentially an objective genitive—not only so, but that this reading was apparently uncontroversial and instinctive.[139] The argument here is not that the Fathers can be relied upon as Paul's infallible theological interpreters but that their native linguistic intuitions should be accorded considerable weight, if not regarded as definitive. And, although the point is not always made, the fact that certain church fathers were inclined toward a recapitulative Christology—Irenaeus, of course, chief among them—makes the absence of evidence for the subjective-genitive reading even more telling when Paul's *pistis Christou* would have served so well as a pointer to the new, faithful Adam had the early interpreters so understood the expression.

(5) Finally, although advocates for neither position are innocent at this point, it is hard to avoid the impression that the "faithfulness of Christ" interpreters exercise a singular, reforming zeal in their advocacy of the position and in the harvesting of its considerable theological fruit.[140] This is

[138]For a brief catalog of the characteristic hyperbole on this point, see Matlock, "Saving Faith," 175-76.

[139]Roy A. Harrisville III, "ΠΙΣΤΙΣ ΧΡΙΣΤΟΥ: Witness of the Fathers," *NovT* 36 (1994): 233-41; idem, "Πιστις Χριστου and the New Perspective on Paul"; Ian G. Wallis, *The Faith of Jesus Christ in Early Christian Traditions* (New York: Cambridge University Press, 1995); and Mark W. Elliott, "Πιστις Χριστοῦ in the Church Fathers and Beyond," in Bird and Sprinkle, *FJC*, 277-89.

[140]Here I concur with Matlock's call to step back from the theological freighting of the expression (R. Barry Matlock, "Detheologizing the ΠΙΣΤΙΣ ΧΡΙΣΤΟΥ Debate: Cautionary Remarks from a Lexical Semantic Perspective," *NovT* 42 [2000]: 1-23; see also idem, "'Even the Demons Believe': Paul and πίστις Χριστοῦ," *CBQ* 64, no. 2 [2002]: 300-318, esp. 309-13). It is important to say that not only those advocating the subjective genitive can be guilty of having the theological tail wag the exegetical dog. For a rather extreme, and I think unconvincing, example, see the

evident, for example, not only in the overstatement of the theological consequence that follows from the "faithfulness of Christ" view but also in an
overestimation of the decisiveness of this one expression for the overall
theological construal of Paul.[141] R. B. Matlock is right to note that to some
extent "the debate over πίστις Χριστοῦ is a proxy war" over other related
questions of Pauline interpretation. It is perhaps insufficiently acknowledged by advocates of both the "faithfulness of Christ" and the "faith in
Christ" positions that, whether the *pistis* is that exercised *by* Christ or human
pistis directed *toward* Christ, these same texts become no less explicit in
declaring the exercise of human faith as the means of appropriating justification.[142] By the same token, all the attractive theological features of the
"faithfulness of Christ" are elsewhere attested in the Pauline corpus, so it
cannot be the case that it all rides on the construing of one phrase.

   3.2.5.3 Toward a third option. As many have noted, the exegetical arguments come to something of a stalemate, as plausible arguments can be
adduced on both "sides" of the question, and the debate has become unwieldy and protracted. At least a partial cause of the stalemate is that the
question has been generally construed as though a choice largely between
only two "sides." There is an increasing disquiet, though nothing approaching
a consensus, that perhaps the objective/subjective dichotomy has skewed
the discussion by offering a choice only between two positions when these
are hardly the only possibilities, syntactically speaking.[143] While both the
objective- and subjective-genitive views are theologically coherent, they are
also syntactically problematic with neither bearing the force of necessity,

argument that πίστις Χριστοῦ should be taken as *genitivus auctoris*, that Christ gives the gift of
faith, understood as *fides quae creditur* (Seifrid, "Faith of Christ").
[141]Martyn, *Galatians*; idem, "Apocalyptic Gospel in Galatians," 249-50; Harink, *Paul Among the
Postliberals*, 25-65; and D. A. Campbell, *Deliverance of God*. Barclay notes how indispensable
the subjective genitive is to Martyn's overall reading of Paul (Barclay, *Paul and the Gift*, 149-50,
381-83), and the same can be said no less of Campbell, *Deliverance of God*.
[142]So, rightly, Barclay, *Paul and the Gift*, 380.
[143]Especially helpful in this regard is Sprinkle, "Πίστις Χριστοῦ as an Eschatological Event." Sprinkle surveys a history of alternatives, or a "third view," concluding that for all their differences,
they view πίστις Χριστοῦ as something objective, albeit with variations: the Christ event, the
message of the Christ event or the sphere of salvation the gospel creates. Thus, despite differences in a grammatical construal, these interpreters offer what is tantamount theologically to
a subjective-genitive interpretation. Sprinkle follows suit. More significant for my purposes is
simply the record of interpretations that do not reduce the question to a binary subjective vs.
objective genitive.

perhaps even alternatives overconditioned by English glosses. And although some have proposed the possibility that the phrase is somehow both objective and subjective simultaneously, this is a counsel of despair even if we were perfectly willing to concede the "underdetermined" ambiguity of this and many other genitive expressions.[144]

There remains the possibility that the genitive should be construed neither as objective ("faith *in*") nor subjective ("faithfulness *of*"). I suggest, rather, that the strengths of both views are retained and the liabilities ameliorated if we take the genitive term *Christou* in some more basic defining sense, whether we should describe it as "attributive," "qualitative," or even "Semitic": that is, "faith defined by, oriented toward, or specified with respect to Christ."[145]

Although not decisive in itself, some weight should attach to what is arguably the generative context for the *pistis Christou* formula, its use as counterpoint to *erga nomou* (works of law).

> We know that a person is justified not by the works of the law [*ex ergōn nomou*] but through faith in[/of] Jesus Christ [*dia pisteōs Iēsou Christou*]. And we have come to believe in Christ Jesus, so that we might be justified by faith in[/of] Christ [*ek pisteōs Iēsou Christou*], and not by doing the works of the law [*ex ergōn nomou*], because no one will be justified by the works of the law. (Gal 2:16 NRSV)

The contrast here between two alternative paths to justification—"works of law" and "faith of Christ"—is clear. The two phrases are syntactically parallel, consisting of a preposition expressing something like means (*dia*) or source

---

[144]Even the apparent middle ground of those arguing for a kind of "plenary" genitive—both objective and subjective (e.g., Sam K. Williams, "Again πίστις Χριστοῦ," *CBQ* 49, no. 3 [1987]: 431-47; and MHT, 3:76)—falls prey to the binary while seeking to eschew it. Cf. the comments of Matlock, "Saving Faith," 88.

[145]This use of the genitive is described under a diverse set of roughly synonymous labels: qualitative, adjectival, descriptive, attributive and even "Semitic," although the latter should probably be reserved for uses dependent on or analogous to the Hebrew construct. Under the heading *"quality, definition or description,"* Porter notes that "this may well be considered the essential use of the genitive case" (Stanley E. Porter, *Idioms of the Greek New Testament* [Sheffield: Sheffield Academic Press, 1994], 92). It should also be noted that the proper conditions for an objective genitive are (1) a head noun with verbal force, (2) a verbal force that is transitive (i.e., the cognate noun is transitive in character) and (3) a genitive term that is conceptually suitable as an object of the verbal force (cf. ibid., 94). Notably, πίστις Χριστοῦ satisfies the first condition, but the second only ambiguously, and the third only with extensive qualification.

(*ek*), the contrast of "works" over against "faith," and a genitive modifier, "*nomou*" and "*Christou*," respectively. If, as seems to be the case on any Pauline chronology, this is the earliest extant expression of the *pistis Christou* formula,[146] then perhaps some weight should attach to the parallelism of the terms. Clearly, in the nature of the case, in "works of law," *nomou* can be neither an objective nor subjective genitive.[147] It is rather a generally qualifying or essentially adjectival genitive—works that befit the law or, effectively, works that the law commands. It would be fitting, though not required, that the parallelism of *erga nomou* with *pistis Christou* extend to the implicit force of the genitive terms. If this is so, then the genitives (*Iēsou*) *Christou* in Galatians 2:16 are very naturally taken as neither subjective nor objective but more simply as "defining," "adjectival" or "attributive" genitives, that is, faith which is in some way given further specificity in reference to Jesus Christ. We might say "Christ-faith" or "Christic-faith," though wishing for a more elegant way to put it.[148]

To be sure, this translation is not only artless but also fraught with ambiguity itself. It is not therefore otiose, however. It must be remembered that from within the framework of Paul's Jewish worldview, fidelity to God would be entirely uncontroversial as a soteriological condition, being productive of and manifesting obedience to the law. It is thus not *erga* and *pistis* that make, at first, the controversial antithesis as though faith were intrinsically over against works, but rather *nomos* and *Christos*. Thus, it is essential that Paul specify the distinguishing character of that faith that stands over against "works of law." What distinguishes this *pistis* is that it is qualified by the Messiah, Jesus. It is not fidelity toward God in some general sense, which

---

[146]I find Watson's suggestion that Paul's use of ἐκ πίστεως is dependent on the LXX of Habakkuk 2:4 intriguing but unconvincing (Francis Watson, "By Faith [of Christ]: An Exegetical Dilemma and Its Scriptural Solution," in Bird and Sprinkle, *FJC*, 147-64), not least because its twice appearance in Galatians 2:16 points toward Paul's coinage of the phrase in a contrasting parallel to ἐξ ἔργων νόμου. Cf. Martyn, *Galatians*, 270.

[147]Obviously an objective genitive is impossible for ἔργα νόμου, though some sort of subjective genitive seems at least plausible on first consideration ("the working of the law"). Clearly, howerver, it is strained compared to the more natural qualifying/adjectival genitive ("law-works," "works befitting the law").

[148]The same position, which I had thought was an "original" solution, is suggested as a variant of the objective-genitive view in Barclay, *Paul and the Gift*, 380. Barclay notes that Michael Wolter regards the genitive modifier as effectively the adjective "Christian" (Michael Wolter, *Paulus: Ein Grundriss seiner Theologie* [Neukirchen-Vluyn: Neukirchener Verlag, 2011], 76-78).

would be uncontroversial, but faith qualified by and defined in relationship to Jesus Christ, who is the distinguishing and delimiting criterion for the faith that justifies.

It is then unnecessary to choose between that sort of *pistis* that characterized the saving obedience of Jesus (i.e., akin to the subjective genitive) and *pistis* as the fidelity toward Jesus Christ whose obedience saves (i.e., akin to the objective genitive). This, I suggest, is a proposal for a simpler—dare I say, more elegant?—alternative. On balance, this construal of the genitive is closer to the objective genitive inasmuch as it concerns the exercise of human faith and not specifically the faithfulness of Christ himself, but it is not therefore merely a variant of the objective genitive. Paul's use of the expression serves less to identify the object of faith—although he could have had no objection to that notion given his alternative ways of expressing the same—than it does to *specify* the precise character of that faith and *contrast* it to the alternative, works of the law, just where such a definition and contrast is needed.

This construal also meets objections frequently voiced by advocates of both the objective- and subjective-genitive interpretation. For example, the charge of redundancy against the objective genitive no longer pertains. The genitive, *Christou*, is not redundant but essential as the specification of the sort of fidelity that avails before God for justification. Likewise, the subjective-genitive emphasis on the paradigmatic character of Christ's faithfulness is not lost but retained, but without surrendering the proper emphasis of the objective genitive on Christ as focal for faith that justifies. The attractive theological fruit of the subjective genitive is retained—or at least not effaced—but the branch on which it hangs is not bowed to the ground by the gravity of interpretive enthusiasm.

3.3 CONCLUSION

It would have been hard to predict forty years ago what a proliferation of fascinating Pauline scholarship would lie ahead. Not just the "new perspective" but Paul's social and religious context, his political bearing, his literary praxis, his ethical vision, his engagement with Scripture, these and so much more—not to mention the traditional historical, biographical and critical questions—have unleashed a flood of literature the likes of which not even specialists can manage. If, however, future generations are inclined to separate chaff from wheat—the enduring gains, insights and course corrections—they would be justified in wondering how much of the dichotomizing rancor was actually necessary. To a large extent the antinomies turn out to be ours, not Paul's, and this approach to Pauline research has resulted in a mixed blessing. On the one hand, the vigorous disputes are generative of new questions, new tacks taken on durable questions, resulting in fresh insight, sometimes game-changing. In a very real way this modus is what makes this field exciting. On the other hand, as I have sought to demonstrate above, certain questions have proven themselves to be self-imprisoned in the dominions of the either/or when a both/and was always a possibility, and a "something else" remains explored as a result. I am arguing that the division between the NPP and the TPP is a signal example of this sort of at once fruitful and frustrating discourse. And in what follows I argue for a both/and by means of a "something else."

Establishing the
Pauline Itinerary

W hat follows, in this chapter and the next, is admittedly a dubious prop-
osition—if not doomed to failure, at least quixotic. To begin with, these
chapters are already too long and yet hopelessly brief given the number of
long-contested questions taken up. Readers may find themselves either
drowning in detail or unpersuaded for the lack of it. It would not be an offense to read the immediate following two sections and to regard the remainder of this and the following chapter as extended footnotes, fulfilling
all righteousness, and so to move on rather more quickly to the arguments
of the final three chapters. Nonetheless, if there is to be a developmental
hypothesis, it is necessary (1) to explain what is—and isn't—meant by *development*, (2) to offer a working *chronology* upon which the argument of development is grounded and (3) to delimit, in this case inclusively, the *corpus*
upon which both the chronology and the development are based.[1] (1) and
(2) are the subject matter of this chapter and (3) of the next.

4.1 The Promise and Perils of a
Developmental Hypothesis

The problems attached to positing a developmental hypothesis are legion,
and the wariness of Pauline scholars in this regard is justified.[2] Before we

---

[1] It would make excellent sense for chronology to follow corpus, yet I have followed this plan since
the disputed corpus falls mostly *after* the important and disputed chronological questions.
[2] See, e.g., Robert Jewett, *A Chronology of Paul's Life* (Philadelphia: Fortress, 1979), 75-78. Although
Jewett's particular objection is the degree of uncontrolled subjectivity in using a scheme of

acknowledge and surmount the practical problems inherent in tracing a thinker's alleged development, we must begin with a simple, and I think incontrovertible, premise: *it is impossible that Paul's thought would not have developed.*[3] Leaving aside for now all the formidable questions (e.g., Did it develop substantially or minimally? Do the literary remains provide enough data to reconstruct that development? What does it mean for the theological authority of these texts that there was an alleged "earlier" and "later" Paul?), it remains impossible that Paul's thinking was static for the final fifteen or so years of travel, missionizing and letter writing that constituted the end of his life. Indeed, it is the *static* hypothesis that bears the burden of proof rather than the developmental assumption. Beyond just common sense, common human experience demands as much—none of us stands still. How much more so for Paul, encountering new opportunities, contingents, contingencies and threats at every turn. This is all the more certain when it is noted that Paul saw himself as highly adaptive to circumstance and was routinely criticized by others for being excessively so.

None of this, of course, demonstrates any particular development or even that any is demonstrable, only that it is not a fool's errand to pursue the question. There are, thus, three questions requiring further reflection: (1) Just *how much* development is being posited, and what is its character? (2) Do the extant letters really supply the sort of data needed to reconstruct

---

theological development to establish chronology, his skepticism concerning developmental schemes is a cautionary word that applies more generally. Significant discussions of the prospect of Pauline development include C. H. Dodd, "The Mind of Paul: A Psychological Approach," *BJRL* 17 (1933): 91-105; idem, "The Mind of Paul: Change and Development," *BJRL* 18 (1934): 69-110; Charles Henry Buck and Greer Taylor, *Saint Paul: A Study of the Development of His Thought* (New York: Scribner, 1969); Richard N. Longenecker, "On the Concept of Development in Pauline Thought," in *Perspectives on Evangelical Theology: Papers from the 30th Annual Meeting of the Evangelical Theological Society*, ed. Kenneth S. Kantzer and Stanley N. Gundry (Grand Rapids: Baker Books, 1979), 195-207; and idem, "Is There Development in Paul's Resurrection Thought?," in *Life in the Face of Death: The Resurrection Message of the New Testament*, ed. R. N. Longenecker (Grand Rapids: Eerdmans, 1998), 171-202.
[3]The point is made forcefully and persuasively in E. P. Sanders, "Did Paul's Theology Develop?," in *The Word Leaps the Gap: Essays on Scripture and Theology in Honor of Richard B. Hays*, ed. J. Ross Wagner, C. Kavin Rowe and A. Katherine Grieb (Grand Rapids: Eerdmans, 2008), 325-50; cf. idem, *Paul: The Apostle's Life, Letters, and Thought* (Minneapolis: Fortress, 2015), 710-23. Sanders's essay is strongly corroborative of my own views on the matter of development in Paul though for Sanders the tracing of development does not represent a theological concern that he feels obliged to ameliorate, and Sanders holds to a smaller, seven-letter, corpus and thus holds to a different, more compact, chronology.

that development with any degree of confidence? (3) What are the theological and hermeneutical implications of a developmental hypothesis? To each now in turn.

While I insist that the thesis of Pauline development is valid, it is just as improbable that *most* of that development took place in the latter half of his Christian-mission phase, for which we have a record, as that it *all* happened in the first half, for which we have almost no record and from which no letters.[4] If, with most New Testament scholars, we place Paul's Damascus Road event in the mid-30s and, with some New Testament scholars, his death in the mid-60s, Paul's Christian-mission phase spans roughly three decades. What we know of Paul's career before any of his extant letters is minimal, and for this reason they are sometimes even called the "unknown years." By the reckoning described below we have then roughly a fifteen-year span of mission activity, of which we know very little, directly followed by another roughly fifteen years, about which we know comparatively rather much, even if we could wish it were more. This sketch depends, of course, on a set of critical judgments hardly shared by all. If, for example, we were to regard only the undisputed letters as authentic, 1 Thessalonians (rather than Galatians) as the first extant letter (ca. 51), Philemon and Philippians written from an Ephesian provenance (rather than Rome), and Paul's Roman imprisonment as the final event of his life (ca. 61), a different picture emerges, in which Paul's seven letters are composed from 51 to 56, and represent a span as brief as 20 percent of a twenty-five-year career, rather than my proposed 50 percent of a thirty-year career. While charting this is the business of the second half of this chapter, suffice it to say that the "room" for development is substantially constricted in this set of critical assumptions, and one might have more reason to chafe at the suggestion of substantial

---

[4]It cannot be demonstrated that Paul did not write letters during this period, only that none of the letters we possess is likely to be dated in that time frame (although see now Douglas A. Campbell, *Framing Paul: An Epistolary Biography* [Grand Rapids: Eerdmans, 2014], who dates 1 and 2 Thessalonians from AD 40-42). It remains a matter of speculation why Paul took to letter writing when he did, not least since Acts takes no notice of Paul's letter writing at all. It appears likely that Paul's authoritative letter writing commenced as a consequence of his westward (if near) mission following his investiture in Antioch. We can only speculate, but it may well be that, despite his renown and activity as one who proclaimed the gospel in the mid-30s through mid-40s, Paul's apostolic authority was not sufficiently accepted apart from that imprimatur of the Antioch community.

development in a five-year slice of a twenty-five-year career that itself followed almost two decades of Christian reflection, preaching and teaching.

The point remains even in my proposed scenario that Paul had spent not fewer than fifteen years making sense of his Christian convictions, to himself no less than others, before penning any of our extant letters. I agree, then, with all of those who insist that Paul must have had his "theology" rather substantially worked out before he (or, more likely, an amaneuensis) ever set quill to parchment. On the other hand, many who write know the experience of finding out what they think while they write, and it is not impossible that this happened to Paul on occasion—otherwise latent insights taking form in the process of written expression. Yet it seems antecedently improbable that we have ex nihilo formulations in any of Paul's letters, early or late. It strains credulity to imagine, for example, that Paul had given no thought as to whether the gospel he would proclaim to Gentiles would oblige them to keep Torah. These were, after all, proselytes, and we know that there was long-standing controversy on just that question. No doubt, Paul had an opinion of the matter before his conversion,[5] and no doubt he reflected on the same question, first in crisis and then in relative "leisure," in view of his convictions concerning Jesus as Messiah. It is hard to imagine that the resistance of Jewish-Christian teachers among the Galatian converts confronted Paul with a perspective that he had never previously encountered, though it is entirely possible that there were dimensions to their arguments that Paul had not previously considered. And the same could be said for any number of issues, including the law more generally, Christology, eschatology, the parousia, Israel and so on. To put it plainly, while there is good reason to expect development in Paul's thinking from his first to his last letter, we should not expect that this was a season of radical innovation, about-faces or even necessarily generative creativity. It can be expected that the main contours of Paul's thought, if not every detail or application, were more or less in place. But to circumscribe the scope of Pauline development is not to deny it altogether.

---

[5]So, in great detail, Terence L. Donaldson, *Paul and the Gentiles: Remapping the Apostle's Convictional World* (Minneapolis: Fortress, 1997). Whether or not one follows Donaldson in every particular, his study demonstrates precisely the *kind* of ruminations that would befit Paul's circumstances.

Closely related to the scope of Paul's development is the question of the nature of the development. What actually do we mean by *development* in this context? Put simply, development implies two conditions: *traceable change* that happens *over time*, resulting in a trajectory. Development *is* change, but that change must be of substance and not merely a matter of linguistic variation. To say the same thing differently is not in itself the sort of change that would count as development. It is not enough that vocabulary changes, though a change in vocabulary might indeed point to a variation of substance. Likewise, it follows that the change must occur over time and with some serial sense of direction, lest differences simply be accounted for as rhetorical variations on a theme or, less charitably, contradiction, incoherence or even duplicity. Direction is admittedly a potentially imprecise category, as is the notion of tracing development precarious. One thinks of the shepherd stargazers of old who could turn a dozen stars—seemingly random to the naked, unimaginative eye—into a centaur with a bow and arrow! While it would be hard to demonstrate that, say, two discrete points of data could substantiate a claim for development, were we able to note a pattern more extensive, involving the passage of time, a claim for development becomes more plausible. And something can be said about the nature of that development, especially if there are corroborating or even explanatory historical or rhetorical data.

As I have suggested, if we regard the pre-letter-writing phase of Paul's Christian-theological formation as the formative period, we would not expect grand about-faces in his positions, even if this possibility cannot be excluded.[6] While it is entirely possible that Paul "changed his mind" on this or that issue, the formative momentum of a long season of reflection and mission preceding the extant letters suggests an a priori unlikelihood of seismic shift. Therefore, I concur with E. P. Sanders in supposing that

---

[6]A possible, though disputed, example might be Paul's eschatology, especially as it regards the presumed imminence of parousia and the nature of the resurrection. Did Paul disavow his original expectation to be alive at the parousia (note the first person of 1 Thess 4:13-18) and substitute a personal and immediate resurrection upon death (2 Cor 5:1-10) for his original corporate and historical understanding (Murray J. Harris, "2 Corinthians 5:1-10: Watershed in Paul's Eschatology?," *Tyndale Bulletin* 22 [1971]: 32-57; albeit retracted in idem, *Raised Immortal: Resurrection and Immortality in the New Testament* [Grand Rapids: Eerdmans, 1985])? If there is a candidate for a Pauline change and retraction, this would seem to be one of the more compelling examples.

"development" in Paul need not involve "retraction" as such,[7] especially when rhetorical contingencies are given their full due. We can say at least that the burden of proof rests on the demonstration that a claim in "later" Paul ultimately vitiates a claim in "earlier" Paul. We can expect—and, I will argue, observe—that the general nature of the development is organic: from seed to flower, from particular to general, from seminal insight to its principled outworking, from ad hoc claim to more settled abstraction, from a case in point to its implicature and so forth.

It might be noted in passing that the critical sensibility of conservative scholars who wish to affirm the authenticity of the entire inscribed Pauline canon is frequently handicapped by a theological sensibility that resists the notion of development. Data that critical scholarship finds patent of a different author could sometimes just as well be accounted for as a development of Paul's own thought or means of expression. Thus, although an appeal to development could well be an ally in defending certain critical stances, conservative scholars may find themselves chary of that move on the grounds of its theological implications. To resist development in Paul is not unlike parallel theological instincts to flatten the diversity of the New Testament witness more generally or an overcommitment to theological harmonization of the biblical materials. But diversity of thought and expression is simply a given and to be expected given the irreducibly historical character of the biblical witness. With respect to Paul in particular, our acknowledgement of the diversity of expression and even conceptual development amounts to nothing more or less than the untroubled affirmation of the historical character of the texts and, theologically, a grateful acknowledgment of canon as gift. It is what we should expect. The irony should not escape us that the anxious conservative apologist and the eager skeptical proponent of theories of pseudonymity and partition have one thing in common: they both insist that Paul should be consistent, if not univocal, and they will both do what is necessary to make him so!

But both impulses threaten to falsify Paul, who self-consciously takes his place at the vanguard of a movement that by his own reckoning is pioneering,

---

[7]Sanders, "Did Paul's Theology Develop?" (Cf. idem, *Paul*, 720: "I see the developments we are discussing [participation in Christ by the Spirit] as organic growth. I do not see 'change' of the sort that requires retraction.") It is hard not to see in Sanders's helpful essay a disavowal of certain readings of his primary works on Paul, in which reviewers found him to be asserting a stronger version of Pauline incoherence than Sanders now claims he intended.

epochal and supple by necessity and design. Thus, the significance of Paul's vexing flexibility, his improvisatory theological method, cannot be overstated, even if it is frequently underestimated. This is often on display, but perhaps nowhere more so than, say, in 1 Corinthians 8–10 or Romans 14–15, where Paul can articulate or even advocate for positions that he himself does not hold![8] But here pride of place must go to 1 Corinthians 9:19-23, in which Paul confesses his flexibility, not as a concession as though he had been caught out in some inconsistency but as an expressly articulated modus operandi.[9] Although all Pauline scholars are well aware of this text, one can only marvel when his modern readers treat Paul's elasticity as a "bug" when Paul himself regarded it as a "feature."

But it remains a fair question for the theological reader of Paul whether the notion of development leaves in its wake the difficulty of an unstable and uneven revelation. Theologically, does the later—one presumes "more mature"[10]—trump the earlier conception? What authority does an incipient view of this or that matter hold? Hermeneutically, do certain texts function as normative lenses through which other texts are to be read, and how does that not devolve into a canon-within-a-canon hermeneutic? Fair questions all, but I regard these concerns as largely theoretical rather than actual when we encounter the texts themselves. If by *development* we mean a transformation of views such that the earlier are nullified by the later, then this set of concerns would carry some weight, although I might be quick to add that if that sort of discontinuity characterized the Pauline corpus, we would still

---

[8]Both texts are historically complicated, and they are parallel to each other only at the level of principle. Nonetheless, in 1 Corinthians 8–10 the dangers of eating food sacrificed to idols is not lost on Paul, but he refuses an absolute prohibition, treating it as a matter of freedom constrained by charity. And in Romans 14–15, it is clear that Paul's *convictions* are with the "strong" (Rom 15:1) while his *sympathies* are with the "weak."

[9]One of the incidental corroborations of the general historicity of the portrait of Paul in Acts is the way in which Acts 13–28 reads as though a historical narration of Paul's own self-description in 1 Corinthians 9:19-23.

[10]Although in fact not all advocates of Pauline development have presumed later is "better." For example, J. C. Hurd argued for Paul's "development" from an earlier, more pneumatic and libertine vision to a later nomistic regression brought about by his acquiescence to the Apostolic Decree (Gal 2 = Acts 15), thus throwing the Corinthians into confusion for which 1 Corinthians was the response (J. C. Hurd, *The Origin of I Corinthians* [New York: Seabury, 1965]). Similarly, Paul Jewett argued that Paul backed down from his early egalitarian impulse (regrettably, for Jewett) to accommodate to patriarchalism in his later letters (Paul K. Jewett, *Man as Male and Female: A Study in Sexual Relationships from a Theological Point of View* [Grand Rapids: Eerdmans, 1975]).

be obliged to deal with the texts as they are rather than conforming them to a less troublesome, presupposed mold. But I am not asserting that sort of development. Indeed, the sort of development one can observe in Paul's letters is such that insights and claims of earlier letters remain intact, not effaced by the later developments. It is not that Paul's "early" soteriology is flawed for being early, but rather sufficient to the needs of the moment. Although there is a traceable continuity of thought, development is not independent of the circumstances that call it forth. Flattening Pauline soteriology such that Galatians merely adumbrates Romans or in which Ephesians only restates Galatians is not only problematic on historical and exegetical grounds; it also misidentifies the partiality of each discrete witness as though it were a shortcoming needing supplementation rather than what it is, an apt "word on target," sufficient to the circumstances.[11]

This, then, is the sort of "development" presupposed in the argument that follows. I will argue that alternative accounts of Paul's soteriology contend precisely for inattention to the development of Paul's thinking, preferring a foothold for an itinerary, which I will propose is traceable through the Pauline corpus, especially given the *whole* of that corpus and in what I regard as the most plausible order. While I acknowledge the inevitable perils inherent in advancing a developmental hypothesis, I maintain that in the nuanced tracing of Paul's soteriological development the salient insights of the NPP are retained and its shortcomings remediated.

4.2 STAKING THE ITINERARY

A developmental hypothesis is not possible apart from some foundation that establishes the database, on the one hand, and a chronology, or at least a relative chronology, on the other. The literature on these durable questions is vast, and there can be no hope of settling long-standing controversies in the span of two chapters.[12]

---

[11]"Word on target" is a favorite of Beker, and the notion of a circumstantially fitting application of Paul's core theological vision is central to his account of Paul as basically theologically coherent while rhetorically supple (e.g., J. Christiaan Beker, *Paul the Apostle: The Triumph of God in Life and Thought* [Philadelphia: Fortress, 1980], 12, 24, 352).

[12]In fact, this sort of exercise is apparently something of a trap. More than one New Testament scholar, setting out on a different, more theological errand, has ended up working out an extensive Pauline chronology along the way as a byproduct. E.g., Robert Jewett, *Chronology of Paul's Life*, which was the fruit of his earlier study, *Paul's Anthropological Terms: A Study of Their*

EXCURSUS: METHODOLOGY

Indeed, Pauline scholars dispute not only chronology, but also the method by which it is derived. In the interest of full disclosure, it is only appropriate that I locate my own working hypotheses in relationship to the larger discourse. Three primary coordinates define the methodological divides: (1) The most contested question is what, if any, weight to accord to the historical sequences of Acts. A traditional approach assumes that Acts is sufficiently accurate in such matters that the letters are to be fit into that framework, acknowledging that the fit is not always unproblematic.[13] With variations, numerous Pauline chronographers have followed this path, believing it the most responsible treatment of all the available data. Others, finding the author of Acts neither finally interested or possessing sufficient information to reconstruct Paul's activities with accuracy, regard only Paul's letters—that is, primary rather than secondary evidence—as the appropriate raw material for reconstructing a chronology.[14] A third, middling alternative accepts the priority of Paul's letters but allows for the critical use of Acts, that is, using the narrative material to supplement what cannot be demonstrated from the letters alone while allowing that Acts may fall short in places as a chronological guide to Paul's life.[15]

Two other methodological axes are frequent loci of differences among Paul's chronographers. (2) When sifting the data of Paul's letters, Pauline

---

Use in Conflict Settings (Leiden: Brill, 1971). So also Douglas A. Campbell, whose Framing Paul precedes, follows and informs his The Deliverance of God: An Apocalyptic Rereading of Justification in Paul (Grand Rapids: Eerdmans, 2009).

[13] As a mere sampling: it is unclear how to square the post-conversion visits to Jerusalem with the record of the same in Galatians 1–2; the itineraries presupposed in the Corinthian correspondence are substantially more involved than what is depicted in Acts by itself; 2 Corinthians 11:23 refers to "more frequent imprisonments" (ἐν φυλακαῖς περισσοτέρως; cf. 2 Cor 6:5), but Acts narrates only one, the Philippian imprisonment, prior to his Jerusalem arrest. Those eschewing Acts for chronological reconstruction find the abundance of such material confirms their case. Those favoring Acts as a framework believe that these are the result of the partiality of the data from both sources and that they can finally be harmonized.

[14] The classic statement, followed by many, is John Knox, Chapters in a Life of Paul (New York: Abingdon, 1950) (cf. idem, "On the Pauline Chronology: Buck-Taylor-Hurd Revisited," in The Conversation Continues: Studies in Paul & John in Honor of J. Louis Martyn [Nashville: Abingdon, 1990], 258-74). Knox's position is recently reinvigorated in Gregory Tatum, New Chapters in the Life of Paul: The Relative Chronology of His Career, CBQMS 41 (Washington, DC: Catholic Biblical Association, 2006); Campbell, Framing Paul.

[15] This approach is nicely illustrated and patiently executed in L. C. A. Alexander, "Chronology of Paul," in Dictionary of Paul and His Letters, ed. Gerald F. Hawthorne, Ralph P. Martin and Daniel G. Reid (Downers Grove, IL: InterVarsity Press, 1993), 115-23.

scholars grant varying significance to diverse sorts of epistolary evidence. It is agreed that the incidentals of travelogue, circumstance and personnel function as a chronographer's pay dirt, but scholars divide as to whether theology and its alleged development prove reliable for the reconstruction of chronology.[16] Many are dubious, noting that there are insufficient controls for using the ad hoc material of occasional letters as means of sequencing the writings. (3) Although most who reconstruct Paul's career seek to corroborate NT data with secular historical data, some insist that a datable, absolute sequence of letters is beyond what the data can yield. They are, therefore, left to settle for a *relative* chronology, a sequencing of letters, but without sufficient evidence to assign dates to those letters.[17]

Finding our bearings in the foregoing, it is necessary to briefly confess the primary methodological commitments that underlie the decisions that follow. First, I do not think it is naive to grant a presumption of innocence as it concerns the historical competence of Acts, especially with respect to Paul's travels and missionary activity. I leave it to others with competence far surpassing mine to make the case for the historiographical aspirations of Acts.[18] The decision to grant credence to Acts in the reconstruction of Paul's chronology follows also from a corollary methodological premise, namely, that more data are preferable to fewer, all the more when independent sources can be corroborated. There can be no doubt that privileging primary source data (the letters) is the methodologically purer approach. But to exclude from consideration other ancient, arguably almost contemporary, evidence is a choice to extract more from less—more speculation (albeit educated) from

---

[16]Most scholars are wary of this criterion, finding it too subjective and perhaps too negligent of the rhetorical exigencies of the letters, as if Pauline development is the unilinear product of a man who is only a writer.

[17]This distinguishes the two recent heirs of the Knox, letters-only method. Campbell (*Framing Paul*) takes generous recourse in (certain) datable external events, arriving at an absolute chronology while Tatum (*New Chapters*) argues that only a letter sequence, a relative chronology, is possible.

[18]Among the numerous positive assessments of the historicity of Acts, note especially W. Ward Gasque, *A History of the Criticism of the Acts of the Apostles*, Beiträge zur Geschichte der biblischen Exegese 17 (Tübingen: Mohr, 1975), 136-57; Martin Hengel, *Acts and the History of Earliest Christianity* (Philadelphia: Fortress, 1980); F. F. Bruce, "The Acts of the Apostles: Historical Record or Theological Reconstruction?," *ANRW* II, no. 25.3 (1985): 2569-603; Colin J. Hemer, *The Book of Acts in the Setting of Hellenistic History*, ed. Conrad H. Gempf (Winona Lake, IN: Eisenbrauns, 1990); C. K. Barrett, "The Historicity of Acts," *JTS* 50, no. 2 (1999): 515-34; see now esp. Craig S. Keener, *Acts: An Exegetical Commentary*, 4 vols. (Grand Rapids: Baker Academic, 2012–2015), esp. 1:90-220.

less evidence (albeit pristine). In the nature of the case, all approaches to Paul's chronology engage in some degree of speculation, a certain amount of inevitable gap-filling. Best practice makes critical use of all three available strands: the incidentals gleaned from Paul's letters, the admittedly perspectival narrative of Acts, and the marking and tethering data of secular history, whether historiographic narratives, epigraphy or archeology.

That said, I do not regard Paul's theological development as a reliable guide for reconstructing the order in which the letters were written.[19] Inasmuch as I am making an argument for theological development, this point deserves some emphasis. I do not arrive at the chronology proposed because it serves my particular argument for Paul's developing soteriology.[20] This is an argument *from* a Pauline chronology, not *for* it. Were I constructing a chronology that would most perfectly cooperate with the development I propose, it would take a slightly different shape, but to do so would not only be "cooking the books" but would commit me to chronological decisions of which I am not persuaded.[21]

Thus, students of the NT will immediately recognize that my decisions regarding Pauline chronology and corpus lack novelty while perhaps betraying credulity. In a field of discourse that prizes incredulity and innovation, I am perfectly aware of the vulnerabilities of my stance. These chapters make up the middle of the book for a reason—the ends of the argument are not to determine the chronology and corpus of the Pauline writings.

If the positions advocated below are not necessarily the majority view of critical scholarship, neither are they idiosyncratic, having been given

---

[19]Perhaps the best, that is, most methodologically rigorous, example of this approach is Tatum, *New Chapters in the Life of Paul*. Tatum's study is of immense heuristic value, demonstrating both the fruitfulness and the peril of an approach left to the letters themselves and without even the presumption of their literary integrity.

[20]While it hardly proves the integrity of my approach, the book largely reads after the fashion of its genesis: disquiet about the explanatory capacity of "old" and "new" perspectives, a corresponding dis-ease with the either/or temperament of Pauline studies, an independent conviction regarding the shape of the Pauline corpus and its chronology, the outworking from that chronology of a hunch that various elements of development could thus be traced.

[21]E.g., the Thessalonian correspondence would precede an early Galatians rather than follow it, allowing justification by faith apart from works of the law a later entry into the Pauline discourse. I would prefer an earlier Philippians, perhaps an Ephesus provenance, but I am not persuaded by that position on other grounds.

credible, plausible, in some cases erudite, articulation by leading scholars, especially certain leading historians of primitive Christianity. I acknowledge in advance my debt to and dependence on scholars who have convinced me of their positions with scholarship more original than mine.[22] In some cases I am content to state my position and stand on the shoulders of others. However, I will give more attention to certain questions either when those judgments bear more directly upon the larger argument of this study or when I think the implications of certain data are insufficiently reckoned with. The primary coordinates of my position can be summarized, for now without argument, as follows.

An early Galatians. Persuaded of the South Galatian hypothesis, I regard Galatians as the earliest extant Pauline letter, dating it prior to the event narrated in Acts 15, rather than equating that "Jerusalem Council" as an idealized narrative of the same event Paul describes in Galatians 2:1-10. This will mean that Galatians is dated circa AD 49, being quite probably the earliest New Testament document. This view has numerous advocates, as we will see, even if a majority of New Testament scholars regard 1 Thessalonians as Paul's earliest letter.

Distinguishing Galatians from Romans. More significantly, if, with almost all New Testament scholars, we date Romans circa 56–58, this means that seven to nine years have elapsed between Galatians and Romans. Were we, with some, to date Galatians in the mid-50s, say, from an Ephesian provenance, we might find but a span of only a few years, or even months,

---

[22]In broad contours, my positions on matters of authenticity and chronology follow a significant swath of New Testament scholarship, including Eckhard J. Schnabel, *Early Christian Mission: Paul and the Early Church* (Downers Grove, IL: InterVarsity Press, 2004), 983-1292, although I am unpersuaded that Paul engaged in the mission to Spain (pp. 1271-83); F. F. Bruce, *Paul, Apostle of the Heart Set Free* (Grand Rapids: Eerdmans, 1977); Ben Witherington III, *The Paul Quest: The Renewed Search for the Jew of Tarsus* (Downers Grove, IL: IVP Academic, 1998), 304-31; Paul Barnett, *Paul: Missionary of Jesus*, After Jesus 2 (Grand Rapids: Eerdmans, 2008), although Barnett maintains an Ephesian provenance for Philemon, Colossians and Ephesians, which he regards as authentic; Michael J. Gorman, *Apostle of the Crucified Lord: A Theological Introduction to Paul and His Letters* (Grand Rapids: Eerdmans, 2004), although Gorman's support for an early Galatians is only apparent, and he is more dubious of the authenticity of certain disputed letters. I stand in broad agreement with James Dunn regarding Pauline chronology, differing only in that (1) I argue for an earlier date for Galatians (though he also supports the South Galatian destination) and that (2) I regard Colossians (of which he is uncertain) as well as Ephesians and the Pastoral Epistles (all of which he rejects) as authentic. Dunn, *Beginning from Jerusalem*, Christianity in the Making 2 (Grand Rapids: Eerdmans, 2009), 497-521.

between Galatians and Romans. This is an attractive hypothesis, given the apparent overlap of language and themes, but I will show instead that the kinship between Galatians and Romans is more incidental than actual and that the tendency of scholars to read them as a common witness to shared matters of concern is too simplistic (see section 8.1.1 below). In fact, the TPP and NPP are, by my estimation, guilty of opposite versions of the same error in this regard: the TPP tends to read Galatians as an adumbration of Romans and the NPP to read Romans as an extension and elaboration of Galatians.[23] Both tendencies, I contend, are consequential and mistaken.

Between Galatians and Romans. Both less controversial and, for my argument, less consequential, I locate the other undisputed letters in relationship to Galatians and Romans, though I must leave aside a set of introductory issues that do not bear upon my argument.[24] Given my position on an early Galatians, the Thessalonian and the Corinthian correspondences fall between Galatians and Romans, and in that order. I do not, however, date Philippians or Philemon (or Colossians and Ephesians) to this period as some do, being persuaded in both cases that the Roman imprisonment, rather than a possible but otherwise unattested Ephesian incarceration, is the more likely provenance. Therefore, I do not regard Romans as Paul's final letter—not his theological "last word and testament"—both because it is postdated by Philippians and Philemon and because, as I will argue, Colossians and Ephesians are of Pauline origin, dating with Philemon and originating from the Roman imprisonment. Although this view has a strong pedigree, it is now a minority position, even if like-minded scholars are not hard to find.

After Romans. *The Roman provenance of Philippians.* While a case can be made for assigning Philippians to an otherwise unattested imprisonment

---

[23]Note J. Louis Martyn, "Romans as One of the Earliest Interpretations of Galatians," in *Theological Issues in the Letters of Paul* (Nashville: Abingdon, 1997), 37-45.

[24]The authenticity of 2 Thessalonians, which I accept, has no particular bearing on my argument; likewise, if 2 Thessalonians is authentic, the original order of 1 and 2 Thessalonians is immaterial with respect to my argument. Whether 2 Corinthians was originally the same, single letter that we know is much disputed. I remain agnostic on the matter. For defense of the unity of 2 Corinthians, see Ben Witherington III, *Conflict and Community in Corinth: A Socio-Rhetorical Commentary on 1 and 2 Corinthians* (Grand Rapids: Eerdmans, 1995); Frederick J. Long, *Ancient Rhetoric and Paul's Apology: The Compositional Unity of 2 Corinthians*, SNSTMS 131 (Cambridge: Cambridge University Press, 2004); and Murray J. Harris, *The Second Epistle to the Corinthians: A Commentary on the Greek Text*, NIGTC (Grand Rapids: Eerdmans, 2005). My primary appeal falls within 2 Corinthians 1–7, about which, save for certain possible interpolations within, there is relatively less controversy.

that precedes the Roman incarceration (usually Ephesus), I continue to think that internal clues point to composition of Philippians in Rome.

The authenticity of Colossians and "Ephesians" and, with Philemon, their Roman provenance. The Pauline origin of Colossians and, even more, Ephesians remains a minority view in New Testament scholarship, but the authenticity of either or even both is gaining adherents. Arguing especially from their internal testimony of interrelationship, especially with Philemon, I posit the authenticity of these letters and tentatively locate their provenance, with Philippians, in Rome.

The authenticity of the Pastoral Epistles. More controversially, I'm persuaded that Paul survived his Roman imprisonment and turned his attention east, rather than west to Spain, during which time he could have, and I think did, write the letter to Titus and the two letters to Timothy.

Thus, I am working with a thirteen-letter corpus and a Pauline soteriology that stretches from AD 49 to the mid-60s—indeed, as I will argue, with a soteriology that itself *stretches*. By way of comparison, some studies of the development of Pauline soteriology are limited to seven letters while having primary interest in but two (Galatians and Romans), and these may be separated by a span of mere months. Of course, there is no virtue in exploring more letters or dating them over a longer span of time if it is a matter of naive credulity, wishful thinking or even a kind of obligation, any more than it is noble to limit the Pauline corpus in docile obedience to the reigning critical orthodoxy. I'm well aware that the acceptance of a thirteen-letter Pauline canon will be enough to invalidate the whole enterprise in the minds of some, but I'm persuaded that excessive trepidation on this matter has precluded New Testament scholars from seeing a possibly larger picture. And, not incidentally, certain evidence that has suggested the un-Pauline character of the disputed letters is susceptible to a different account, namely, that conceptual and verbal differences mark transitions in Paul's own conception and expression of his soteriology.

4.3 CHRONOLOGY: LOCATING PAUL'S LETTERS

4.3.1 Paul before the letters. The "unknown years" are so called for a reason. We have only a few hints of what might have occupied Paul from the period following his conversion to his "first missionary journey," and from these few data we are left to surmise. That gap has been filled by valiant and impressive efforts of reconstruction, but even these remain educated surmises.[25] For our purposes, it is sufficient merely to affirm the consensus of contemporary New Testament scholarship that Paul's Damascus call seems to have resulted rather immediately in his active missionizing in the eastern Roman Empire. That is to say that Paul is already deeply experienced in articulating and defending his reconfigured convictions and surely already adept in reflecting upon and appealing to his scriptural heritage toward that end. As indicated above, the degree to which this is so counts against the likelihood of radical shifts in Paul's basic convictions, though by no means obviates development altogether. New challenges, new opponents and new counter-arguments are sure to have arisen during the years that followed this first phase of mission. And it is impossible to estimate how the response of Paul's fellow Jews to his new message—spanning acceptance to persecution—would motivate his reflection on salvation-history in process. For example, the notorious difference in the emotional tone between 1 Thessalonians 2:14-16 and Romans 9:1-5 has inspired interpolation theories regarding the former, but it is rather more likely that Jewish rejection and hostility that was initially regarded as an offending affront became, with the aid of further experience and reflection, a matter of deep sorrow. This is not a change in Paul's "theology" but a variation of disposition, quite probably betraying a personal maturation from understandable antipathy to wistful grief. Nonetheless, for our purposes, we can safely affirm that Paul was already a "theologian" before he wrote his first (extant) letter, and yet the new opportunities and challenges of the late-40s, 50s and 60s inspired still more reflection, new insights, even reconsiderations, though doubtfully any full about-faces.

4.3.2 Locating Galatians. Locating does double duty in this heading. The matter at hand is both geographical—where is "Galatia" and who were the "Galatians"?—and temporal—when in Paul's career and among Paul's letters is Galatians to be dated? And the two questions are inextricably related. All

---

[25]The most important accounts remain Rainer Riesner, *Paul's Early Period: Chronology, Mission Strategy, Theology*, trans. Doug Stott (Grand Rapids: Eerdmans, 1998); helpfully summarized in idem, "Pauline Chronology," in *The Blackwell Companion to Paul*, ed. Stephen Westerholm (Malden, MA: Wiley-Blackwell, 2011), 9-29; Martin Hengel and Anna Maria Schwemer, *Paul Between Damascus and Antioch: The Unknown Years* (Louisville, KY: Westminster John Knox, 1997); and Schnabel, *Early Christian Mission*, 1031-72.

modern students of Paul's letters will know that there is a protracted discussion about the destination, the original readership, of Paul's letter "to the
churches of Galatia." The alternatives have been dubbed the so-called South
and North Galatian hypotheses. According to the South hypothesis, the
"Galatians" (Gal 3:1) are understood as the inhabitants of a political province,
the area that Paul had traversed in mission, according to Acts 13–14, planting
churches.[26] According to the North hypothesis, the recipients of the letter
are not defined by the province of Galatia but are rather an ethnic group,
originally immigrants from Gaul to the north and west of provincial Galatia.[27] Although the North Galatian hypothesis has been the majority view
within critical scholarship for some time (especially in Germany and North
America), there are signs that the weight of evidence may be moving opinion
toward the South Galatia destination.[28]

The details of this protracted debate cannot be reprised here; it will be
necessary to defer to the extensive arguments of others.[29] In any case, the

---

[26]Representative proponents of the South Galatian (provincial) destination include most
famously William Mitchell Ramsay, *St. Paul the Traveller and the Roman Citizen* (New York:
Putnam's Sons; London: Hodder & Stoughton, 1909); Ernest DeWitt Burton, *A Critical and
Exegetical Commentary on the Epistle to the Galatians*, ICC (Edinburgh: T&T Clark, 1921), xxi-
liii; F. F. Bruce, *The Epistle to the Galatians: A Commentary on the Greek Text*, NIGTC (Grand
Rapids: Eerdmans, 1982), 3-18; James D. G. Dunn, *A Commentary on the Epistle to the Galatians*,
BNTC (Peabody, MA: Hendrickson, 1993), 5-8; Richard N. Longenecker, *Galatians*, WBC 41
(Dallas: Word, 1990), xli-lxxii; Ben Witherington III, *Grace in Galatia: A Commentary on St.
Paul's Letter to the Galatians* (Grand Rapids: Eerdmans, 1998), 2-20; and now Douglas J. Moo,
Galatians, BECNT (Grand Rapids: Baker Academic, 2013), 1-18.

[27]Influential supporters of the North Galatian (territory) destination include J. B. Lightfoot, *Saint
Paul's Epistle to the Galatians: A Revised Text with Introduction, Notes and Dissertations*, 10th
ed. (London: Macmillan, 1890), 1-56; J. Louis Martyn, *Galatians: A New Translation with
Introduction and Commentary*, AB 33A (New York: Doubleday, 1998), 15-17; and Hans Dieter
Betz, *Galatians: A Commentary on Paul's Letter to the Churches in Galatia*, Hermeneia
(Philadelphia: Fortress, 1979), 1-5; cf. Hans Dieter Betz, "Galatians," *ABD* 2:872-75. Although it
is less well known, an impressive argument can be found in Jerome Murphy-O'Connor, "Mission
in Galatia, Macedonia, and Achaia Before the Jerusalem Conference," in *Keys to Galatians:
Collected Essays* (Collegeville, MN: Liturgical Press, 2012), 1-36, a revised and expanded version
of "Pauline Missions Before the Jerusalem Conference," *Revue biblique* 89, no. 1 (1982): 71-91.

[28]In addition to the general works of commentators cited above, see the work of historians: Hemer,
The Book of Acts in the Setting of Hellenistic History, 277-307; Stephen Mitchell, "Galatia," *ABD* 2:870-
72; Cilliers Breytenbach, *Paulus und Barnabas in der Provinz Galatien: Studien zu Apostelgeschichte
13f.; 16,6; 18,23 und den Adressaten des Galaterbriefes* (Leiden: Brill, 1996); and Schnabel, *Early
Christian Mission*. Although Mitchell overstates the case to say that Ramsay's study "should have
long ago put the matter [of the South Galatian destination] beyond dispute" ("Galatia," *ABD* 2:871),
it appears that historical research is slowly vindicating this assessment.

[29]In addition to what follows, chief arguments that incline me to the South Galatian hypothesis
are as follows: (1) It is not convincing grammatically or geographically that Acts 16:6 and 18:23

South Galatian destination does not secure any particular date, although it makes possible a date following the first missionary journey of Acts 13–14 and even preceding the council recorded in Acts 15. In some respects, though they are interrelated, the question of date is both more consequential and more complicated than the matter of destination. The question turns substantially on whether the Jerusalem encounter recounted by Paul in Galatians 2:1-10 should be equated with that which is narrated in Acts 15:6-29. Although, on balance I am inclined to think that they are not the same event and that Galatians 2 describes an earlier, more private conference, it should be admitted that this judgment is susceptible to the charge of apologetic motives in defense of the historical veracity of Acts. Thus, in fairness, we must sit loosely with respect to certain oft-rehearsed arguments, which carry less probative value than is sometimes attributed to them by advocates of an early Galatians.

(1) On balance, were it possible to show the narrative of Acts consistent with the report of Paul's letters, we should prefer that reconstruction to the alternatives, but we cannot make the defense of the sequential historicity of Acts a primary motive in historical reconstruction. Therefore, the famine

---

describe a mission in the (ethnic) territory of Galatia; rather these are in fact references to the "Phrygian region of [provincial] Galatia" (Acts 16:6, my translation) and "the [provincial] Galatian region and [Asian] Phrygia" (Acts 18:23, my translation; on which, see Schnabel, *Early Christian Mission*, 1131-34, 1199; and Hemer, *Book of Acts*, 277-89). (2) Claims to the contrary notwithstanding, that Paul could refer to the provincial readers as "Galatians" (Gal 3:1) is both well attested and makes considerably better sense unless we are to assume the anomaly of an ethnically homogenous collection of churches in North "Galatia" (on which, see esp. Hemer, *Book of Acts*, 299-305; cf. Mitchell, who regards it as a deliberate, ethnically tinged, slight ["Galatia," *ABD* 2:871]). (3) The apparently immediate influence of the Judean Jews (Gal 1:6; 2:12) and the immediate relevance of the Cephas Antioch incident (Gal 2:11-14) are both more plausible given the southern and eastern location of the province of Galatia and Antioch for the letter's provenance (Mark D. Nanos, "Galatians," in *The Blackwell Companion to the New Testament*, ed. David E. Aune [Malden, MA: Wiley-Blackwell, 2010], 456-57). (4) The two temporal markers in the letter are corroborative of an early, South Galatian destination. That the Galatians are "so quickly [ταχέως] deserting" (Gal 1:6) casts Galatians a hurried reply, as would be the case if the Torah party had intervened with some immediate success and news reached Paul on his return to Antioch. More significantly, although it often cited as evidence of more than one visit to the churches in question, τὸ πρότερον (Gal 4:13) is a comparative in form only; idiomatically it refers to what happens "before" or "originally" but without a sense of contrast. Nowhere in the LXX or New Testament does it denote a "first" as opposed to a "second" or later event. Thus, here Paul is simply explaining that his ailment was the reason he came to them, as we might say, "in the first place." (5) The most conclusive evidence is the presence and absence of various persons in the letter and in the various events it recounts (on which, see below and R. N. Longenecker, *Galatians*, lxx-lxxiii).

visit of Acts 11:27-30 may well be the meeting otherwise described in Galatians 2:1-10 (note esp. 2:10), but conforming the post-conversion Jerusalem visits of Galatians to those described in Acts can, at best, serve only as a secondary criterion for dating. We simply do not know enough about the historical intent of the author of Luke-Acts to know that the chronological freedom exercised in the first volume was decisively chastened in the second. (2) While it is true that in matters of detail there is considerable difference between the Galatians 2 and Acts 15 accounts (private versus public, personnel involved, precipitating motivation, etc.), this is a precarious argument, given that there is considerable motivation for the narrator of Acts to present a meeting between Paul and the Jerusalem leaders as a felicitous model of consensus-building rapprochement and as a public settlement of the otherwise divisive issue. This is not to cast aspersions on the historicity of Acts per se (although it may seem so) but to acknowledge the rhetorical value of such an account, should a more private and tentative historical meeting be narrated as a more public and victorious settlement. (3) Therefore, neither can too much be made of the absence of the Apostolic Decree (Acts 15:19-20, 28-29) from Galatians. It is often asserted on behalf of a pre-Jerusalem Council date for Galatians that an appeal to the decision of the Jerusalem Council would have been the coup de grâce for Paul's argument. But this assumes that the Jerusalem Council was as straightforward and definitive as Acts depicts, on the one hand, and that Paul would have wanted to yield to the judgment of the Jerusalem meeting and authorities, on the other. It could in fact be claimed instead that the "handshake" agreement of Galatians 2:6-10 was nothing other than the Apostolic Decree but in its more modest original form, designating spheres of authority but not making provision for the social intercourse of Jews and Gentiles. Cephas's later misstep would then show him less in a cowardly violation of the Jerusalem accord than having failed to appreciate its logic as radically as Paul would have.

I am inclined to be less skeptical with regard to Acts 15 and tentatively affirm the traditional arguments favoring a distinction between Galatians 2:1-10 and Acts 15, the informal Galatians 2 meeting preceding the later council. But it must be admitted that, in the nature of the case, the probative value of individual arguments for these conclusions remains modest so that certainty eludes us. Even so, the preponderance of evidence still points toward an early date for a letter sent to churches of the province of Galatia, preceding the Jerusalem Council. Tipping the scales in this regard is the incidental evidence of the named participants, which deserves to bear more weight than it usually does.[30] We must begin with Barnabas, whose presence and depiction in Galatians is worthy of closer scrutiny as the sort of detail that is especially revealing for being incidental.[31] The depiction of Barnabas in Paul's letters is corroborated by Acts. He features prominently in Acts, first as Paul's disarming and reconciling senior partner and then as his missionary colleague until their eventual falling out over John Mark,[32] after which he disappears from the narrative and nearly from the letters as well.[33] Since Barnabas is said to be present for both the "famine relief" visit (Acts 11:27-30) and the Jerusalem Council (Acts 15:6-29), his presence among the Jerusalem "pillars" in Galatians 2:1-10 is inconclusive in itself. It is naturally tempting to see the falling out of Paul and Barnabas as not so much precipitated by their difference over John Mark, as Acts 15:36-41 depicts it, but as the result of Barnabas's devastating backpedaling at Syrian Antioch (Gal 2:13). Although these need not be mutually exclusive motives for the breakup, it is at least possible that Acts has chosen the less damning alternative, depicting Barnabas as solicitous rather than erratic. Even if this were the case, and the "real" reason for the Paul and Barnabas breakup was the latter's failure in Antioch, this still points in the direction of an early date for the letter. The Antioch incident (Gal 2:11-14) is the conclusion to the Galatians *narratio*, and it is thus the proximate precipitating motivation for the writing of the letter. Barnabas would be well known to the South Galatians, and this recent double-cross in Antioch—thus the incredulous "*even* Barnabas" (*kai*

---

[30]Here I am concurring esp. with R. N. Longenecker, *Galatians*, lxx-lxxiii, although I would regard this as primary data whereas Longenecker sees it as secondary or corroborating.

[31]In addition to Longenecker, see Richard Bauckham, "Barnabas in Galatians," *JSNT* 1, no. 2 (1979): 61-70.

[32]As frequently noted, his name precedes that of "Saul" prior to the first missionary journey (Acts 11:30; 12:25; 13:1, 2, 7), after which "Saul" becomes "Paul" and the name order is frequently reversed (Acts 13:43, 46, 50; 15:2, 22, 35; although cf. Acts 14:12, 14; 15:12, 25).

[33]The reference to Barnabas in 1 Corinthians 9:6 does not require that he is any longer in the regular or recent company of Paul; in fact, the immediately preceding reference to "the other apostles and the brothers of the Lord and Cephas" (1 Cor 9:5) suggests otherwise. The chronological significance of his "reappearance" in Colossians 4:10 depends on the questions of authorship, provenance and dating.

Barnabas; Gal 2:13)—required an immediate response. Whereas it is rather hard to imagine how the actions some time ago of a Barnabas unknown to north Galatians in a city rather far away would matter much, if at all, the recent betrayal of the provincial Galatians' father in the faith, their connection to Jerusalem, in the patron city of Antioch, would have been of great consequence and require Paul's immediate response.

On balance, the references to Barnabas point not only to an early dating but also to a date preceding the Jerusalem Council, that is, if we can assume that the Acts 15 account bears even a remote resemblance to the historical event. It would have been remarkable that Barnabas should abandon immediately the very agreement that was designed precisely with those concessions that would make ongoing Jew-Gentile commensality possible rather than seek to implement the modest strictures of the decree.[34] The same, only more so, could be said with respect to Peter, an architect of the agreement, whose intimidation by "certain men from James" would be almost impossible to explain on the other side of an agreement he had worked out with James himself. The behaviors of both Peter and Barnabas are much more readily explained if Paul's mission worked under the aegis of an implicit and informal approval of the Jerusalem leaders that was known among them but that did not yet carry full assent in Jerusalem.[35] Were that so, it cannot be surprising if the full social implications were grasped differently and unevenly; all parties could have implicitly agreed to a Torah-free Gentile conversion without all understanding that Jew-Gentile commensality followed as a consequence. That variance of understanding becomes much more difficult to sustain after the Jerusalem Council—again, assuming that we can accord the Acts 15 account at least a modest degree of historicity.

There is, second, the complete absence of Timothy from the letter, which is extraordinary upon a later dating. Timothy makes an appearance in every

---

[34]The probable authenticity of the Apostolic Decree is supported by the very particularity of its prohibitions (Acts 15:19-20, 28-29). The original form of the text addresses Jewish scruples and thus lacks a broader moral application, later rectified by scribes seeking to broaden or contemporize the text's relevance (on the textual question, see Metzger, *TCGNT*, 379-84).

[35]Witherington suggests plausibly that the event of Galatians 2:11-14 corresponds to Acts 15:1-2. Ben Witherington III, *The Acts of the Apostles: A Socio-Rhetorical Commentary* (Grand Rapids: Eerdmans, 1998), 444n36.

undisputed Pauline letter, save for this (and Ephesians and Titus among the disputed), and is indeed prominent in almost every one, as Paul's coauthor six times and frequently as his travel companion and most trusted deputy.[36] It is almost impossible that he should not have been mentioned either in connection with the founding of the Galatian churches or with respect to recent events if we were to date Galatians to a Corinthian or, as is more common, an Ephesian provenance. This is a datum not sufficiently reckoned with by advocates of the North Galatian hypothesis. But that no sign of Timothy is found in this letter supports both the provincial destination and the early date of Galatians and, indirectly, the historicity of the account of Acts, in which Timothy joins Paul's entourage in Lystra only after the Jerusalem Council (Acts 16:1-3). Likewise, although he is not as ubiquitous a character as Timothy, the same can be said with respect to the absence of Silvanus in Galatians. We first meet him in Acts as a delegate from Jerusalem sent to Antioch with Paul and Barnabas (Acts 15:22, 27), but he makes no appearance in the Jerusalem meeting of Galatians 2:1-10. Of course, following the fallout between Paul and Barnabas, he becomes Paul's traveling companion, with the soon addition of Timothy, for the second missionary journey. He is listed as a coauthor of 1 and 2 Thessalonians and referred to in 2 Corinthians as though belonging to an inner circle with Paul and Timothy (2 Cor 1:19). Were Galatians to be dated any time later than 1 Thessalonians, his absence from the letter, like Timothy's, is telling.

The roles of Titus and Cephas are less probative since we have less evidence for their early history with Paul than we have for Barnabas and Timothy; Acts does not mention Titus at all, much less when he joined Paul's missionary enterprise, and, of course, Peter fades from sight in Acts after the Jerusalem Council. We can know from Galatians that Titus was a Gentile (Gal 2:3) and that he served as a kind of test case in Paul's Jerusalem deliberations, not being compelled to be circumcised.[37] Longenecker is probably correct to regard this a strange happening if it were in the context of a formal gathering dedicated to deliberating the matter of Gentile circumcision at a

---

[36]As Paul's coauthor: 1 Thessalonians 1:1; 2 Thessalonians 1:1; 2 Corinthians 1:1; Philippians 1:1; Philemon 1; Colossians 1:1; as his traveling companion and deputy: 1 Thessalonians 3:2, 6; 1 Corinthians 4:17; 16:10; 2 Corinthians 1:19; Philippians 2:19.

[37]Whether he was personally acquainted with the Galatian churches is unknown, but that Paul tells them that he was a "Greek" (Gal 2:3) suggests otherwise.

principial level (i.e., the Jerusalem Council). And I would add that it would
be a strange recollection on Paul's part to report the outcome of such deliberations as though Titus's case and a division of labor between Peter and
Paul constituted the whole outcome of the meeting. On the other hand, as
a description of a rather more informal gathering, the appeal to Titus as an
emerging precedent makes perfect sense.

Although certainty on this matter will forever elude us, on balance, the
South Galatian hypothesis is to be preferred on several grounds, and following from it, an early date, circa AD 49, which would make Galatians the
earliest extant letter of the Pauline corpus.

4.3.3 From Galatians to Romans. For our purposes, we need not spend
a great deal of time on these matters. Although an early date for Galatians
might be a minority view, I am not aware of any New Testament scholar who
locates the Thessalonian and Corinthian correspondences *after* Romans,
save for the possibility of a pseudonymous 2 Thessalonians. If Galatians is
the earliest letter, then the correspondence to the new churches in these two
cities clearly falls in between. It is true that questions abound as it concerns
the order, integrity and, as it concerns 2 Thessalonians, authenticity of these
letters. It is possible, despite their traditional names, that 2 Thessalonians is
not only authentic but *precedes* rather than follows 1 Thessalonians,[38] although this remains a minority position and has no particular bearing on
our argument. Likewise, the story of Paul's correspondence with the Corinthians is one of the more interesting adventures in historical reconstruction.[39] It is certain that he wrote a letter to the Corinthians that preceded our
1 Corinthians, because he refers to it in 1 Corinthians 5:9 ("I wrote to you in
my letter," NRSV), in order to clarify what he had meant over against their
apparent misunderstanding of the earlier instruction. Likewise, it is almost
certain that he had written at least one letter *between* 1 and 2 Corinthians,
the so-called tearful letter, which, according to 2 Corinthians 2:1-4, he dispatched in lieu of another "painful visit" (NRSV). Given Paul's description of

---

[38] According to W. G. Kümmel, the claim goes back at least to Hugo Grotius (1641). Werner Georg
Kümmel and Paul Feine, *Introduction to the New Testament*, rev. ed. (Nashville: Abingdon, 1975),
263. Perhaps the best recent argument on its behalf is from Charles A. Wanamaker, *The Epistles
to the Thessalonians: A Commentary on the Greek Text*, NIGTC (Grand Rapids: Eerdmans, 1990).
[39] One could scarcely improve on the careful and detailed reconstruction of M. J. Harris, *Second
Epistle to the Corinthians*, 101-5.

the letter and its purpose, it seems unlikely that this letter is what we call 1 Corinthians, and, although it is slightly more possible that it is what we now call 2 Corinthians 10–13, subsequently appended to an originally briefer letter, this too seems unlikely. This "tearful letter" is, therefore, probably at least the third correspondence from Paul to the Corinthians, followed by 2 Corinthians, or at least some part of it, including at least 1 Corinthians 1–7. If the New Testament contains a composite letter, 2 Corinthians is surely the best candidate.[40] In any case, although questions of chronology and literary integrity abound, there is not much doubt that the Thessalonian correspondence (whatever it includes) preceded the Corinthian correspondence (whatever its precise components). Despite the complicated questions surrounding the composition of, especially, 2 Corinthians, there is little doubt about the general, relative chronology, and, save for 2 Thessalonians and an awkward excerpt in 2 Corinthians (6:14–7:1), the authenticity of this material is not seriously doubted.

I will have more to say about the composition of Romans in a later chapter (see section 8.1 below). For now, it is sufficient to say that there is perhaps as much agreement on the relative date of Romans as any Pauline letter, with the possible exception of 1 Thessalonians. The internal indications show it to have been written before Paul had ever visited the city and immediately before his imminent and anxious journey to Jerusalem with the collection for the saints (Rom 15:25-31). In light of this, Romans must almost certainly be the final reference to the Jerusalem Collection (cf. 1 Cor 16:1-4; 2 Cor 8–9) and thus the final letter written before that journey commenced. The internal data of the letter (Rom 16:1-2, 23) are corroborated by Acts 20:1-3, placing Paul in Corinth for three months before setting out to Jerusalem. A majority of Pauline scholarship dates the letter from AD 55 to 58, depending on other chronological considerations, and all scholars understand it as the conclusion to an eventful season of mission

---

[40]On which, see the standard critical introductions and commentaries: Helmut Koester, *Introduction to the New Testament: Literature and History*, vol. 2, 2nd ed. (New York: de Gruyter, 1995); Kümmel and Feine, *Introduction to the New Testament*; Raymond E. Brown, *An Introduction to the New Testament*, ABRL (New York: Doubleday, 1997); Hans Dieter Betz, *2 Corinthians 8 and 9: A Commentary on Two Administrative Letters of the Apostle Paul*, Hermeneia (Philadelphia: Fortress, 1985), 1-36; and Margaret E. Thrall, *A Critical and Exegetical Commentary on the Second Epistle to the Corinthians*, ICC (Edinburgh: T&T Clark, 1994), 1:3-49. For defenses of the integrity of 2 Corinthians, see n. 24 above.

in Macedonia (e.g., Thessalonica, Philippi), Achaia (e.g., Corinth) and Asia (e.g., Ephesus, Troas).[41]

4.3.4 Locating Philippians. That Philippians is written from an imprisonment is clear (Phil 1:7, 13, 17), but the dating of the letter depends on which of several possible imprisonments is presupposed. Traditionally, dating at least to the Marcionite prologue and leaving traces in the manuscript tradition, Paul's Roman imprisonment (Acts 28:16) is understood or assumed to be the site of composition, and this continues to be the majority view,[42] though not without dissent.[43] Several data corroborate that traditional surmise: (1) Paul refers to a *praetorium* (Phil 1:13; frequently translated "praetorian guard") who have come to understand the purpose of his chains, and he extends greetings from Christian members of "Caesar's household," that is, members of the imperial administration (Phil 4:22 RSV). Whatever is meant by praetorium here, it is evident that it is a body of *people*, the "whole" of which (*holō tō praitōriō*) having come to understand that Paul's loyalty to Christ is the reason for his chains. That the "whole praetorium" refers to a company of people rather than to a building or even an

---

[41]D. A. Campbell (*Framing Paul*, 187-88) revives the position of John Knox and followers (Knox, *Chapters in a Life of Paul* [New York: Abingdon-Cokesbury, 1950]) with a date of AD 52.

[42]For a classic statement, see J. B. Lightfoot, *Saint Paul's Epistle to the Philippians: A Revised Text with Introduction, Notes and Dissertations*, 8th ed. (London: Macmillan, 1885), 1-45, 99-104. Among recent Philippians commentators, the Roman provenance is favored by F. F. Bruce (*Philippians*, UBCS [Grand Rapids: Baker Books, 1989]), Peter T. O'Brien (*The Epistle to the Philippians: A Commentary on the Greek Text*, NIGTC [Grand Rapids: Eerdmans, 1991]), Gordon D. Fee (*Paul's Letter to the Philippians*, NICNT [Grand Rapids: Eerdmans, 1995]), Markus N. A. Bockmuehl (*The Epistle to the Philippians*, BNTC 11 [Peabody, MA: Hendrickson, 1998), Moisés Silva (*Philippians*, BECNT [Grand Rapids: Baker Academic, 2005]), and Ben Witherington III, *Paul's Letter to the Philippians: A Socio-Rhetorical Commentary* (Grand Rapids: Eerdmans, 2011). Pauline biographers preferring a Roman provenance include Bruce, *Paul, Apostle of the Heart Set Free*, 389-91; Dunn, *Beginning from Jerusalem*, 1011-20; and Udo Schnelle, *Apostle Paul: His Life and Theology* (Grand Rapids: Baker Academic, 2005), 366-69. Perhaps the most authoritative argument for the Roman provenance of Philippians is now to be found in Hans Dieter Betz, *Der Apostel Paulus in Rom*, Julius-Wellhausen-Vorlesung 4 (Berlin: de Gruyter, 2013). I owe this last reference to Michael Cover.

[43]Gerald Hawthorne prefers a Caesarean provenance (Gerald F. Hawthorne and Ralph P. Martin, *Philippians*, rev. ed., WBC 43 [Nashville: Nelson, 2004], xxxix-li), although few have followed his lead. A compelling argument for Ephesus is found in Frank Thielman, "Ephesus and the Literary Setting of Philippians," in *New Testament Greek and Exegesis: Essays in Honor of Gerald Hawthorne*, ed. Amy M. Donaldson and Timothy B. Sailors (Grand Rapids: Eerdmans, 2003), 205-23; cf. idem, *Philippians*, NIVAC (Grand Rapids: Zondervan, 1995); and John H. P. Reumann, *Philippians: A New Translation with Introduction and Commentary*, Anchor Bible 33B (New Haven, CT: Yale University Press, 2008), 13-17, although adopting a three-letter partition theory.

administrative center and who exist as a subset of a larger body is confirmed by Paul's expression "and to the rest" (*kai tois lopois*). In fact, "Caesar's household" would be an apt description of that whole body, within which a praetorium is an identifiable subbody. As Lightfoot demonstrated well over a century ago, although nowhere is *praetorium* used to refer to the imperial residence on the Palatine, it is used frequently of a detachment of persons rather than a building, but only in Rome, where it refers by metonymy to the "imperial guard." Thus, in Philippians 1:13, Paul deftly reinterprets his otherwise odious circumstance as a divine stratagem for penetrating the imperial administration—a delicious irony that would not have been lost on the proud Roman colonists in Philippi.

(2) Besides that primary consideration, a few circumstantial details also support a Roman provenance. In Philippians 1:19-26, Paul describes his circumstance as an impending matter of life and death and implicitly an imminent trial.[44] This would seem unbearably melodramatic were Paul, a Roman citizen with the right to exercise an appeal to Caesar (which, indeed, he exercised), incarcerated in Caesarea Maritima or Ephesus or, for that matter, Corinth. Second, it is arguably the occasion, not to say purpose, of the letter for Paul to express his gratitude for the Philippians' financial support, a theme that begins and ends the letter (Phil 1:5; 4:10-19). The Philippians' gift would make perfect sense as contribution toward Paul's maintenance during his house imprisonment.[45] Indeed, it would be hard to know what else it might have been for were Paul in a more "institutional," less independent, setting. Meanwhile, the letters that can be assigned to an Ephesian provenance or dated within that time period (ca. 53–55; 1 Corinthians, 2 Corinthians; cf. Romans, after the fact) have a clear interest in Paul's collection for the Jerusalem poor, of which there is no hint in Philippians, even though the Philippians were presumably at least *among* the Macedonians whom Paul regarded as the models of generosity for that project (2 Cor 8:1-5; cf. 1 Cor 16:5). Third, although we only have

---

[44]Paul's trial is alluded to and transposed eschatologically in Philippians 1:19 by virtue of his allusion to Job 13:16 (LXX): "this will turn out for my salvation" (τοῦτό μοι ἀποβήσεται εἰς σωτηρίαν). Paul, like Job, anticipates his vindication (σωτηρία) before God, of which his temporal trial will prove to be the prefigurement.

[45]On this, see Brian Rapske, *The Book of Acts and Paul in Roman Custody*, The Book of Acts in Its First Century Setting 3 (Grand Rapids: Eerdmans, 1994), 228-35.

hints of the local circumstances in which Paul writes, there is evidence of dissension that taints even the evangelistic motivations of "some" whose proclamation of Christ betrays underlying "envy," "rivalry" and "partisanship" (*phthonos, eris, eritheia*, Phil 1:15, 17). Paul does not care to describe the source of this bitterness—his purpose being to exult in the law of unintended consequence—but, given that the rivalry is presumably with Paul himself, it may well be a version of the Christian message having taken on a more Jewish, more superficially "authentic" and more scrupulous character than that for which Paul advocated. This party would therefore be preaching Christ to gather adherents to its particular vision of messianic faith, but instead of Paul being "troubled" (*thlipsis*, Phil 1:17), he would find the fact that Christ was preached a reason for rejoicing.[46] This scenario—is there a more plausible one?—would accord with the internal tensions Paul had addressed just a few years earlier in his letter to Rome (esp. Rom 14–15, but passim).

The Roman imprisonment has against it one substantial, though not insuperable, objection, which is also the driving force behind a hypothesized Ephesian imprisonment as the letter's provenance: the distance of Rome from Philippi.[47] The letter presupposes several communications requiring a sequence of itineraries thought to be unrealistic. As though a demonstration of the New Testament guild's penchant for woodenness, sometimes even five journeys are posited: (a) the Philippians must learn that Paul (though not necessarily *from* Paul) is in Rome (or on his way); (b) they dispatch Ephaphroditus with their gift (Phil 2:25; 4:18); (c) they learn that Epaphroditus has fallen ill; (d) a messenger from Philippi is dispatched to Rome and informs Epaphroditus of their concern for him in his illness (Phil

---

[46]This is Paul's reason for the passive, Χριστὸς καταγγέλλεται: Paul wishes to draw attention only to the results and not give notice of the actors. It can fairly be assumed that Paul was biting his lower, while keeping a stiff upper, lip!

[47]Although Acts narrates only three incarcerations (Acts 16, a brief and eventful one in Philippi; Acts 24, a two-year incarceration in Caesarea Maritima; Acts 28, Rome), already in 2 Corinthians 11:21-23, well before the Caesarean and Roman imprisonments, Paul can "boast" of his "far more imprisonments" (cf. 1 Cor 6:5; Rom 16:7). Of these we know nothing more—how many? where? when? (1 Clement 5:6 refers without elaboration to "seven times bearing chains." While this does not seem an improbable claim, there is no way to assess the historical pedigree.)—although an allusion in 1 Corinthians 15:32 that Paul "fought with wild animals" suggests, even if the phrase should not be taken literally, that Paul endured a hardship in Ephesus that might well have included an incarceration.

2:26); (e) Epaphroditus, restored to health, returns to the Philippians, as most suppose, bearing the letter (Phil 2:25, 28). But these supposed five journeys, Rome-to-Philippi or vice versa, are easily reducible to only one that is necessary within the timespan of Paul's Roman imprisonment.[48] Of course, (e) only *follows* the composition of the letter and does not presuppose it, and (d) is otiose. Surely Epaphroditus could infer his friends' concern apart from a messenger, and Paul's purpose in Philippians 2:25-28 has nothing to do with specifying who knew what but rather to rejoice that all parties were spared grief and to commend Epaphroditus as a model of selfless faithfulness. As for (a), it is entirely conceivable that the Philippians learned of Paul's appeal to Caesar prior to his arrival, and then there is no reason that they could not have dispatched Epaphroditus proactively with their gift per (b), perhaps, given Paul's misadventures, even preceding his entourage. This leaves only (c) as a *necessary* journey to have taken place between the beginning of Paul's imprisonment and the dispatch of Philippians. And although a long distance indeed, there is not a substantial enough basis to overturn the Roman hypothesis with all its corroborating support in favor of an otherwise unattested—not to say unlikely—Ephesian imprisonment. I date Philippians then toward the latter part of Paul's Roman imprisonment—perhaps AD 61–62—four to six years following the composition of Romans and, as I will argue, within the same time frame as Philemon, Colossians and Ephesians.

4.3.5 Life after Rome? More letters from Rome? With one further question we begin a transition to the following chapter, in which we consider the case for the authenticity of various disputed letters. In fact, we are jumping into an argument, if not circular, in which at least the parts are mutually dependent. The question is whether Paul survived the Roman imprisonment, described briefly in Acts 28 and the possible site of the composition of as many as four "Captivity Epistles." New Testament scholars are

---

[48]In what follows, I assume a picture of a highly mobile early Christian movement, not least of a merchant class who doubled business with mission, such as is presented in Michael B. Thompson, "The Holy Internet: Communication Between Churches in the First Christian Generation," in *The Gospels for All Christians: Rethinking the Gospel Audiences*, ed. Richard J. Bauckham (Grand Rapids: Eerdmans, 1998), 49-70; and Brian M. Rapske, "Acts, Travel and Shipwreck," in *The Book of Acts in Its Graeco-Roman Setting*, ed. David W. J. Gill and Conrad H. Gempf, The Book of Acts in Its First Century Setting 2 (Grand Rapids: Eerdmans, 1994), 1-47.

split on the question. Put simply, if Paul didn't survive the Roman imprisonment, then the letters written to Timothy and Titus, called "Pastoral," are
almost certainly not authentically Pauline, and while the supposition of a
"second career" makes the authorship of these letters possible, it hardly secures it. Should we be honest, all sides would admit we labor with a paucity
of data and every argument depends on inference and reads silence. The
chief reason for doubting Paul's survival of his Roman imprisonment is the
impression left in Acts by Paul's words of foreboding, especially to the pres-
byters on Miletus: that he does not know what will befall him in Jerusalem
(Acts 20:22); that he does not value his life as such, save that he might finish
the course appointed by Christ (Acts 20:24); and, above all, that he "know[s]
that none of you, among whom I have gone about proclaiming the kingdom,
will ever see my face again" (Acts 20:25 NRSV), this last sentiment causing
the Ephesians the greatest sorrow (Acts 20:38). If the author of Acts knew
that Paul had survived the events in Jerusalem and then Rome, then the
pathos of this encounter is at least a bit curious. Many read it as Luke's own
tip of the hand to Paul's future.[49] But this is slender and ambiguous evidence
on which to reach such a conclusion. Whether we hear any more of Paul
after Rome depends on the ambiguous evidence of the Pastoral Epistles—or
what we make of it—and, even more remotely, uncertain testimony from the
apostolic fathers.

Admitting that there is no certain evidence for the outcome of Paul's
Roman trial, we may well be on safer ground to consider Paul's expectations
as they are expressed in the Captivity Epistles (undisputed Philippians and
Philemon; disputed Colossians and Ephesians). While Paul does describe
his circumstance in Philippians in life-and-death terms ("whether by life or
by death"), he ultimately expresses a hope bordering on confidence that he

---

[49]At risk of going too far afield, perhaps we should not attribute too much tipping of the hand to
the character Paul in the Acts narrative. As a preacher, he is, by the nomenclature of narrative
criticism, a "reliable character," but when it comes to his decision making and discernment, he
is a man realistically, if heroically, drawn. We are not inclined either to affirm or to reject his
judgment in parting ways with Barnabas over John Mark; we merely understand it. His demand
for an apology from the Philippian magistrates (Acts 16:35-38) bears the marks of petulance.
And, when, for example, Paul says in response to the prophet Agabus's warning that "I am ready
... to die in Jerusalem" (Acts 21:13 NRSV), the narrative disconfirms that outcome, admiring Paul
more for his courage than his prescience.

will survive and come to see the Philippians (Phil 1:25-27; 2:24).[50] We turn, then, to the disputed letters, which presuppose certain possible end-of-life scenarios, while also possibly providing data for their reconstruction.

---

[50]That Paul did not turn his attention to Spain, as planned according to Romans, is hardly a substantial argument against a Roman provenance for Philippians. Under the conditions in which he found his way to Rome, it would only be natural for Paul to turn his attention toward the east both for the comfort of the familiar and in order to turn his attention to the pastoral needs of these congregations. The evidence that Paul actually engaged in a Spanish mission is late, unreliable and probably the result of a pious surmise that Paul fulfilled his intentions. I address the question of Paul's mission to Spain below (section 5.4).

RECONSIDERING THE
DISPUTED LETTERS

Arguments over the authenticity of New Testament texts are not everyone's preferred form of entertainment—or so my students frequently remind me. And they, many being of a generally Catholic mindset, are quite happy to trust the wisdom of the church in receiving her constitutive texts, not to mention that it is less work for them. I, on the other hand, get paid to worry about such things, and they pay reasonably good money to watch me worry. Under normal circumstances, there is not much to worry about. The presumed authenticity of New Testament letters, though a decisive factor in their canonical reception, is no longer so. Proof of inauthenticity, were it possible, would no more render a text noncanonical than would the discovery of an indisputably authentic text, were such a thing possible, add a new member, untimely born, to the canon.[1] But our interest here is not to justify the canon or to defend the Bible from scurrilous accusation but to ask questions about Paul as a theologian, and to do so we must establish our sources. My claim is that the minimalist database typically invoked on both sides of the NPP debate has skewed the conversation. While it makes good procedural sense to conduct an investigation sharing common ground, we shouldn't underestimate the unintended consequences of dismissing certain texts as irrelevant to questions upon which they bear rather directly. It is highly doubtful that in brief compass I will succeed in persuading those

---

[1]Contra Stanley E. Porter, "Pauline Authorship and the Pastoral Epistles: Implications for Canon," *BBR* 5 (1995): 105-23.

convinced of the pseudonymity of some or all of the disputed letters, though I would be content even to sow some seeds of doubt. This has all been done by others in greater detail and bringing greater expertise to the technical matters, and I refer and depend on such works going forward. In any case, even readers skeptical of the authenticity of some or all of the disputed letters can benefit from the thought experiment of reading the disputed letters "as if" from Paul.

First, a word about the shape of the authenticity debates, which will both clear ground and save some repetition. These arguments tend to follow a prescribed course, predictable enough that it is not hard to replicate letter by letter, only plugging in a different set of details for the variables. The seven undisputed letters form a database that is collated into a prototype of the authentic Paul, sometimes with the *Hauptbriefe* of Romans, 1 and 2 Corinthians, and Galatians forming a sort of inner circle. The disputed letter is then subject to an analysis, usually according to three categories, and sometimes a fourth: (1) linguistic, showing that its style and vocabulary differ from the undisputed counterparts; (2) conceptual, showing a theological variance with the undisputed letters; (3) circumstantial, showing that the life-setting of the letter reflects conditions that are improbable given what can be known of Paul's life and circumstances. And in some cases, (4) the ambivalence of reception and use of the letter especially by the early church, that is, its place (or absence) among early copies and difficulties with respect to its canonization, can cast doubt on a writing's authenticity.

While not all these claims are equally weighted or persuasive in every case, defenders of authenticity can be too facile in their dismissal of this sort of evidence. Yes, the variations in vocabulary are sometimes not as statistically significant as the proponents assume, but it remains a curiosity whenever "Paul" substitutes a new alternative expression for a perfectly serviceable word or phrase well precedented in the undisputed writings. Likewise, although Bible translations of necessity obscure this, tending toward homogenization of style in the interest of readability, no reader of Koine can fail to just *feel* that, say, Ephesians is quite a different thing from its canonical neighbor, Galatians. Neither the attempts to define and quantify the difference nor the rejoining refutations completely erase the Koine reader's perception of inhabiting a subtly different literary milieu. This is all to say that those dubious of authenticity are not imagining things. We may wish to account for those same observations differently or weigh the data in an alternative fashion, but the questions don't thereby go away.

The defenders of authenticity also tend to follow a common pattern of reply, typically in the form of a divide-and-neutralize maneuver, rebutting each claim one by one. It can sometimes be shown, for example, that statistically speaking, the variations of vocabulary are not as anomalous as supposed, indeed, that the statistical variation between a disputed letter and the undisputed corpus is no more pronounced than between an undisputed letter, once extracted, from that same corpus. As for theological differences, it can often be shown that what looks to be a case of *departure* might just as well be a continuity in the *development* of a notion already evident in seed form in the undisputed letters.[2] As for style, it is customary to note that different circumstances elicit different rhetorical styles and, especially of late, de rigueur to leave wide berth for the influence of an amanuensis in the composition of the letter itself, although one might wonder why this phenomenon attaches especially to later, disputed letters and less, if at all, to earlier, undisputed letters, where we frequently find evidence of the amanuensis or even coauthors in the text itself.[3] The force of the counterpoise regarding linguistic, conceptual and circumstantial evidence is that the arguments against authenticity are not as decisive as often supposed. The arguments against authenticity having been rendered inconclusive, the argument will typically appeal, to the extent that they are available, to those positive evidences for the authenticity of the letter in question: for example, Paul's self-reference, the sometimes abundance of personal references and greetings, circumstantial evidence of varying sorts, and the normally uniform belief of

---

[2]Although it remains curious that the defenders of the authenticity of Paul's letters don't more frequently capitalize on this possibility and explore a more robust theory of development.

[3]Romans 16:22; 1 Corinthians 16:21; Galatians 6:11; Philemon 19; cf. Colossians 4:18; 2 Thessalonians 3:17. For a representative appeal to the amanuensis, see D. A. Carson and Douglas J. Moo, *An Introduction to the New Testament*, 2nd ed. (Grand Rapids: Zondervan, 2005), 334-37; and Luke Timothy Johnson, *The Writings of the New Testament: An Interpretation*, 3rd ed. (Minneapolis: Fortress, 2010), 527. Though not a new argument, this tendency is given a refreshed appeal by E. Randolph Richards, *Paul and First-Century Letter Writing: Secretaries, Composition, and Collection* (Downers Grove, IL: InterVarsity Press, 2004); cf. idem, *The Secretary in the Letters of Paul*, WUNT 42 (Tübingen: Mohr, 1991). For a pointed rebuttal, see esp. Bart D. Ehrman, *Forgery and Counterforgery: The Use of Literary Deceit in Early Christian Polemics* (New York: Oxford University Press, 2013), 218-22.

the early church on the matter. It is good form to disclaim certainty about the matter while concluding that the traditional view of authorship remains a responsible, if not even more persuasive, rendering of the data.[4]

One particular argument, although perhaps a bit well worn, still represents a hurdle for advocates of pseudonymity, and it is not clear that it has been sufficiently answered. Any account of stylistic and, especially, theological discontinuities between a disputed letter and the undisputed has to live with an anomaly, namely, that the pseudonymist succeeded to some extent in offering a replication of the authentic while at the same time failing repeatedly to replicate with consistency. If, as the argument goes, an author had a characteristic way of saying something, presumably the pseudonymist knows this, or else it is hard to explain those cases in which the language has been simulated. Thus, in any theory of authorship, equally in need of explanation as the apparent discontinuities are the continuities of style and content with the undisputed letters.[5] But then it can only be wondered why more consistency is not found, why more care was not employed. The obvious answer is a lack of skill or care. And yet in certain respects the pseudonymists are credited with an extraordinary degree of cleverness, especially when, for example, they are said to exploit verisimilitudes so as to pawn off their literary efforts as historically realistic.[6]

This general observation carries more weight when the possibly pseudonymous letters attributed to Paul (2 Thessalonians, Colossians, Ephesians, 1-2 Timothy, Titus) are compared to the patently pseudepigraphical letters (e.g., 3 Corinthians, Epistle to the Laodiceans, Epistles of Paul and Seneca).[7]

---

[4]Understandably, conservative scholars are generally loath to concede that disclaiming Pauline authorship would, in some settings, amount to a violation of fealty to biblical inerrantism. Not all inerrantists will think this is the case, but it is rare indeed to find an inerrancy-professing New Testament scholar who disclaims the inscribed (and characteristically also the attributed) authorship of a New Testament text. Demonstration of traditional authorship then becomes an obligation with theological motivations. In my judgment, critical scholarship is justified in looking askance at the objectivity of such scholarship, but it does not follow that apologetically motivated arguments, if suspicious, are necessarily weak or lacking evidentiary merit.

[5]Luke Timothy Johnson, *The First and Second Letters to Timothy: A New Translation with Introduction and Commentary*, AB 35A (New York: Doubleday, 2001), 81-82.

[6]See, e.g., Ehrman, *Forgery and Counterforgery*, 122-23, who cites Norbert Brox, "Zu den persönlichen Notizen der Pastoralbriefe," in *Pseudepigraphie in der heidnischen und jüdisch-christlichen Antike* (Darmstadt: Wissenschaftliche Buchgesellschaft, 1977), 272-94; cf. Lewis R. Donelson, *Pseudepigraphy and Ethical Argument in the Pastoral Epistles* (Tübingen: Mohr, 1986).

[7]We know of the Letter to the Alexandrians only through a reference in the Muratorian Fragment,

The standard critical procedure is to establish a Pauline template from, usually seven, undisputed letters, against which the disputed letters can be compared. The method, though imperfect—not least for the obvious question begging and also for employing a database too small to be of statistical significance—is still not unreasonable as a heuristic. But it only follows that the opposite procedure should also apply: the characteristics of undisputed pseudepigrapha can also be used as a complementary template to demonstrate characteristics of this kind of literature from its most indubitable exemplars. What we find is that the kind of deft verisimilitude characteristic of the *possibly* pseudonymous is notably absent from the *certainly* pseudepigraphical. For example, with respect to the Epistle to the Laodiceans, the terse judgment of M. R. James still stands: "It is not easy to imagine a more feebly constructed cento of Pauline phrases."[8] The text consists of a pastiche of phrases from the Pauline corpus, especially Philippians 1–2 and to a lesser extent Galatians, concluded by a transparent attempt to replicate Colossians 4:16 in reverse (Ep. Lao. 20). The case is similar with 3 Corinthians, dating earlier than the Epistle to the Laodiceans. Although it evinces more original material—antiheretical in character—the patent phrasal borrowings from canonical Paul are easily discerned.[9] What we *don't* see is the very kind of material that vexes the analysis of the canonical disputed Paulines: concepts that are recognizably, if not exclusively, Pauline but cast in idioms that are otherwise uncharacteristic of Paul. It is this combination of fidelity and freedom that presents itself as a testimony on behalf of Pauline authenticity, admittedly ambiguous. Yet it is beyond question that these canonical disputed letters have considerably more in common with the undisputed than with the pseudepigraphical. It may be that the simplest theory is still to be preferred, that Paul's own theological vision is the red thread that explains both the realistic continuity as well as the variability of thought and language.

---

and the Letter to the Laodiceans referred to there seems almost certainly to be a different letter from the extant letter by the same name, which has no relationship to Marcionism.

[8]M. R. James, *The Apocryphal New Testament* (Oxford: Clarendon, 1924), 479.

[9]The correspondence of Paul and Seneca (Epistles of Paul and Seneca) is so sufficiently late, obviously secondary and imaginary, it is hard to see any way in which it quite bears upon this question. The author's interest is in the imagined relationship, but he shows no interest in replicating a believable Paul by drawing from or reprising Pauline language or ideas.

The debates concerning the authorship of the disputed Pauline letters have carried on apace now for almost two centuries and, in some cases, by means of arguments of extraordinary technical merit. At the same time, there does not appear on offer any sort of new evidence or any new argument that might break the stalemate, even if scholarly trends vacillate. We have no equivalent in ancient philology of game-changing DNA evidence in modern criminology standing ready to revolutionize the field.[10] In what follows, I choose not to reprise readily available arguments in toto. My goal is more modest: I will prefer to focus on those matters of evidence that are sometimes overlooked or undervalued that corroborate the authenticity of the disputed letters in the hope that the files be left open or "cold cases" reopened with respect to certain "assured results of biblical criticism."

5.1 A CASE FOR COLOSSIANS

Of the texts surveyed in this section, Colossians must count as the most probably authentic of the five letters.[11] Without minimizing the linguistic and theological arguments against Pauline authorship, it must be admitted that the circumstantial evidence in favor of Pauline authorship is considerable. The chief observation is the almost entire overlap of persons and circumstance between Colossians and its undisputed counterpart, Philemon. Indeed, this positive evidence for the shared authorship and dispatch of Colossians is so strong, it is no wonder that those rejecting the Pauline authorship of Colossians give such slight and sometimes glancing attention to the matter and, as I see it, unconvincing explanations of the phenomena. It will be useful to set out the data in summary form, beginning with a parallel setting of the personal references in the two letters. See table 5.1, in which I have boldfaced the names shared by both letters and italicized those unique to each.

---

[10]The best bet might have been stylometrics, but there are reasons for doubting the absolute probity of such methods. See now the insightful discussion in Douglas A. Campbell, *Framing Paul: An Epistolary Biography* (Grand Rapids: Eerdmans, 2014), esp. 210-16, and regarding Colossians particularly, 286-92.

[11]It being largely incidental to my argument, I do not take up the question of the authenticity of 2 Thessalonians.

Table 5.1. Comparison of Philemon and Colossians

Philemon	Colossians
Paul, a prisoner of Christ Jesus, and **Timothy** our brother, To **Philemon** our dear friend and co-worker, to *Apphia* our sister, to **Archippus** our fellow soldier, and to the church in your house: (Philem 1-2 NRSV) . . . For this reason, though I am bold enough in Christ to command you to do your duty, yet I would rather appeal to you on the basis of love—and I, Paul, do this as an old man, and now also as a prisoner of Christ Jesus. I am appealing to you for my child, **Onesimus**, whose father I have become during my imprisonment. Formerly he was useless to you, but now he is indeed useful both to you and to me. I am sending him, that is, my own heart, back to you. (Philem 8-12 NRSV) . . . **Epaphras**, my fellow prisoner in Christ Jesus, sends greetings to you, and so do **Mark, Aristarchus, Demas**, and **Luke**, my fellow workers. (Philem 23-24 NRSV)	Paul, an apostle of Christ Jesus by the will of God, and **Timothy** our brother, To the saints and faithful brothers and sisters in Christ in Colossae: Grace to you and peace from God our Father. (Col 1:1-2 NRSV) . . . *Tychicus* will tell you all the news about me; he is a beloved brother, a faithful minister, and a fellow servant in the Lord. I have sent him to you for this very purpose, so that you may know how we are and that he may encourage your hearts; he is coming with **Onesimus**, the faithful and beloved brother, who is one of you. They will tell you about everything here. **Aristarchus** my fellow prisoner greets you, as does **Mark** the cousin of Barnabas, concerning whom you have received instructions—if he comes to you, welcome him. And *Jesus who is called Justus* greets you. These are the only ones of the circumcision among my co-workers for the kingdom of God, and they have been a comfort to me. **Epaphras**, who is one of you, a servant of Christ Jesus, greets you. He is always wrestling in his prayers on your behalf, so that you may stand mature and fully assured in everything that God wills. For I testify for him that he has worked hard for you and for those in Laodicea and in Hierapolis. **Luke**, the beloved physician, and **Demas** greet you. Give my greetings to the brothers and sisters in Laodicea, and to *Nympha* and the church in her house. And when this letter has been read among you, have it read also in the church of the Laodiceans; and see that you read also the letter from Laodicea. And say to **Archippus**, "See that you complete the task that you have received in the Lord." (Col 4:7-17 NRSV)

In summary, we note the following:

- In both letters the writer is imprisoned (Philem 9-10, 13; Col 4:3, 10, 18).

- In both letters, Timothy, "our brother," is named as a coauthor/cosender (Philem 1; Col 1:1).

- Those on behalf of whom Paul sends greetings include an overlap of five named persons between the letters—Epaphras, Mark, Aristarchus, Luke and Demas (Col 4:10-14; Philem 23-24)—although there is considerably more detail about each in Colossians than in Philemon (save for Demas), and the order is not the same.

- Archippus is an addressee at the beginning of Philemon, along with Philemon and Apphia (Philem 2), while singled out for a particular charge at the end of Colossians (4:17).

- Onesimus is returning to Colossae in both letters (Philem 10; Col 4:9), while the fact that he does so with Tychicus is mentioned only in Colossians (4:7-9). The circumstances of his return, the subject matter of Philemon, are not mentioned in Colossians.

- There are certain persons unique to each letter: (1) Philemon and Apphia, in the letter bearing the former's name (Philem 2). (2) In Colossians greetings are sent uniquely only from "Jesus called Justus" (Col 4:11), and (3) only in Colossians is Tychicus is named (Col 4:7), presumably as the bearer of the letter. (4) Additionally, a greeting is conveyed to Nympha, presumably of Laodicea, and the host of a house church there (Col 4:17).

There can be no question that, if pseudonymous, Colossians has deliberately chosen to present itself as a letter dispatched with the letter to Philemon, Apphia and Archippus or, more probably, now to recast Philemon as a companion to the longer letter. Thus, there can be no serious question in this case of an innocent or nondeceptive act of pseudonymity; the pseudonymist wants to leave the illusion of an authentic letter located in a specific circumstance from the life of Paul and addressed to a particular community.[12] If this is so, the pseudonymist should be given full credit for a rather deft piece of work, in fact much more deft—and much riskier—than is usually noted. By attaching the fortunes of his forgery to the letter to Philemon, the alleged pseudonymist takes a kind of a gamble. It is not that he wishes for his letter to sound *like* Philemon; he wants it to be regarded as permanently attached *to* Philemon, and, therefore, presumably his letter will enjoy the fate of this, the briefest extant Pauline letter.

---

[12]It is fundamental to the thesis of Bart Ehrman's recent scholarly study to show that pseudonymity was a *deceptive* rather than innocent practice in early Christianity: Ehrman, *Forgery and Counterforgery*; anticipated in his earlier, popular work, idem, *Forged: Writing in the Name of God—Why the Bible's Authors Are Not Who We Think They Are* (New York: HarperCollins, 2011).

We might say two things about this alleged course of action. First, it is at least surprising that the pseudonymist should choose a letter this brief, this undistinguished and this occasional to forge his entry into a broad circulation. Was it the only orthonymous Pauline letter on hand? How and why Philemon managed to find a place in the Pauline collection and to be canonized is a matter of some debate and even possibly the source of a legend, but though it was apparently always regarded as authentic Paul, it was never considered constituent of the "essential Paul."[13] If this literary back door were the pseudonymist's chosen vessel for bearing his more substantial work, we should regard him as clever indeed.

Second, it is unprecedented, indeed unique in the New Testament, for a putatively pseudonymous Christian letter to have attached itself to another letter in this way, that is, obliquely by means of circumstantial insinuation. Possible analogies only illustrate the difference. While 2 Thessalonians shares the same coauthors and salutation as 1 Thessalonians—there is nothing oblique if this is imitation—there are no comparable personal allusions or familiar narrations that a pseudonymist might have used to attach that letter to its (presumed) predecessor.[14] Outside of the Pauline corpus, while it is true that 2 Peter describes itself as the "second" letter written to the same putative audience, the author does not seek to make any other incidental references that would connect his letter to 1 Peter—no mention of the geographical constituency of 1 Peter 1:1, no reference to Silvanus (cf. 1 Pet 5:12) or Mark (cf. 1 Pet 5:13), no greetings from his church (= "elect lady") in Rome (= "Babylon") (cf. 1 Pet 5:13). Perhaps the singular other example of a disputed letter attaching to another in this manner—that is, by

---

[13]Note, e.g., that Philemon is not included in the codex of p46, and it remains unknown what factors motivated its canonical inclusion, beyond the assumption that it was an authentic letter. The "possible legend" is the frequently told story of a certain Onesimus, who was the bishop of Ephesus at the turn of the second century (Ign., *Eph.* 1.3; 6.2). Thus, as the story goes, the letter became a permanent memory of the humble and scandalous beginnings of a new creation in Christ made good, a story so good, if it is not true, it should be.

[14]Of course if 2 Thessalonians preceded 1 Thessalonians, this is a moot example, but this continues to be the minority view. On the priority of 2 Thessalonians, see Charles A. Wanamaker, *The Epistles to the Thessalonians: A Commentary on the Greek Text*, NIGTC (Grand Rapids: Eerdmans, 1990); on the debates more generally, see Karl P. Donfried and Johannes Beutler, *The Thessalonians Debate: Methodological Discord or Methodological Synthesis?* (Grand Rapids: Eerdmans, 2000). In any case, were 2 Thessalonians deliberately patterned after 1 Thessalonians, as some have suggested, it is not an example analogous to the alleged use of circumstantial material from Philemon in Colossians.

means of circumstantial happenstance—is Ephesians, which, by a closely parallel reference to Tychicus (Eph 6:21-22; cf. Col 4:7-9), might be seeking to attach itself to Colossians. But if this were so, one can only wonder why the author of Ephesians did not go further. Why not a reference to Timothy in Ephesians again as a coauthor? Why no mention of Paul's fellow prisoner, Aristarchus, or the other "fellow workers" who attended to him in his imprisonment (cf. Col 4:10-14)?[15]

There is too much that the pseudonymity theory leaves unaccounted for in the alleged expansions in the personal references of Colossians and patent differences between the two. Epaphras, who, in Philemon, is merely Paul's fellow prisoner and the first to send greetings, has been transformed into the pioneering evangelist and founder of the church in Colossae (Col 1:7). But why, unless the pseudonymist knew this to be the case, would he venture such a claim?[16] And why should a pseudonymist make Aristarchus Paul's "fellow prisoner" in Colossians when it was Epaphras in Philemon? Should we take this to be a mistake? Or is it not more likely that it is more germane to the whole congregation that Epaphras, the "apostle" to Colossae, be noted for his indefatigable work and concern for the churches of the Lycus Valley? And what did the pseudonymist hope to gain by fabricating a "Jesus (also known as Justus)" (*Iēsous ho legomenos Ioustos*),[17] rather than, say, another more well-known Pauline associate, like Mark or Luke? Or for that matter, why bother with Laodicea and "especially Nympha and the church in her house" (Col 4:15)? In all these instances, the pseudonymist exposes himself unnecessarily to charges of fabrication and falsification. Of course, the obvious answer—the conveniently unfalsifiable hypothesis—is that he was

---

[15]It should be noted that *only* Onesimus and Epaphras are identified with the church in Colossae; thus there is no reason a pseudonymist could not have appealed to other persons allegedly with Paul in his imprisonment both to give a ring of verisimilitude and to further secure the attachment of Ephesians to Colossians, if that were the purpose of the mention of Tychicus.

[16]As suggested, though without any account of the motivation, by Ehrman, *Forgery and Counterforgery*, 190n46.

[17]Lohse's ingenious but nearly impossible conjecture following Zahn is that Philemon 23 may have read Ἐπαφρᾶς ὁ συναιχμάλωτός μου ἐν Χριστῷ Ἰησοῦς, with the nominative Ἰησοῦς (rather than the dative Ἰησοῦ). This would then be the source for the reference to "Jesus who is called Justus" in Colossians 4:11 (Eduard Lohse, *Colossians and Philemon*, trans. William R. Poehlmann, Hermeneia [Philadelphia: Fortress, 1971], 207n16; cf. 176n54). Besides it being unattested and all but grammatically impossible (one wonders if Lohse would have also conjectured a καί preceding the article or between Χριστῷ and Ἰησοῦς), the exact phrase ἐν Χριστῷ Ἰησοῦ is ubiquitous in the Pauline writings, both undisputed (29x) and disputed (17x).

good at what he did, and all the little personal touches, the scattered bits of just tolerable inconsistency, the gratuitous fabrications and the stroke of genius to attach the parasitic forgery to this most unsuspected host, these are evidence of just how good he was—so good at all the incidentals, so clever to cover his tracks, if not especially skilled in emulating the apostle's style and replicating his theology. To this whole line of argument, it can be said that it is certainly not impossible, but it is not only conservative apologists who have their moments of hoping against hope.

The failure of proponents of psuedonymity to give a plausible account of the circumstantial relationship to Philemon, the most concrete evidence, weighs heavily against such theories, even if the weight of that evidence is not often given its due,[18] and even when it is acknowledged, the explanations are frequently superficial and unpersuasive.[19]

---

[18]Note, e.g., the treatment, or lack thereof, in the published version of his Harvard dissertation: Mark C. Kiley, *Colossians as Pseudepigraphy*, Biblical Seminar 4 (Sheffield: JSOT Press, 1986), 83-84. While noting briefly the overlap of personal references between the letters, this is simply cited in passing as evidence that Philemon, along with Philippians, formed a literary template for Colossians. Kiley feels no compulsion to account for the craft of the pseudonymist's use of the circumstantial material from Philemon or the choice to attach Colossians circumstantially to the minor letter (cf. similarly Raymond F. Collins, *Letters That Paul Did Not Write: The Epistle to the Hebrews and the Pauline Pseudepigrapha*, Good News Studies 28 [Wilmington, DE: Glazier, 1988], 184-86).

[19]Lohse finds the circumstantial corroboration between Philemon and Colossians clear evidence of a pseudonymist's attempt at verisimilitude. But Lohse offers little serious reflection on the numerous incidental differences between the texts and gives no account for why the disciple of Paul would choose the letter to Philemon as his prototype. He does, however, advance several suggestions that have an air of desperation about them. (1) He asks, for example, why, on the assumption of Colossians' authenticity, Philemon makes no reference to the dangerous "philosophy" with which Colossians is consumed (Lohse, *Colossians and Philemon*, 176n57). But, of course, on the premise of a simultaneous dispatch, the answer would be precisely because Colossians addresses it. One might just as well ask why Colossians doesn't have more to say about the situation regarding Onesimus or, for that matter, why Philemon is absent a Christ hymn. (2) Lohse's further claim that the authentic Philemon must precede the pseudonymous Colossians on the grounds of "the approved rule that the shorter text should be considered the older text" (ibid.) can be set aside as a spurious application of a text-critical generalization (hardly an "approved rule"), having no relevance to this sort of question. (3) Lohse's synoptic display of the parallels between Philemon and Colossians (ibid., 175-76), while useful, obscures the variation of order of those named in Philemon and Colossians, implying a more direct literary relationship between the two than is in fact the case. (4) Lohse will also claim that "greetings serve to prove that his writing is an apostolic message; at the same time, they serve to recommend to the communities the men explicitly named as faithful ministers and helpers of the Apostle," concluding in his footnote that "consequently, the list of greetings and the news notes cannot be used as a proof of the epistle's Pauline authorship" (ibid., 177 and n. 59). It is hard to see how the use of personal references could both insinuate the authenticity of the pseudepigraphon while also actually commending the named but, as it turns out, occasionally

The circumstantial case for the authenticity of Colossians is strong indeed, but the language and theology of Colossians remain a barrier, the insuperable barrier for many scholars to accept Colossians as authentically Pauline.[20] And likewise, the argument for pseudonymity on the ground of style, it must be conceded, is strong indeed—stronger than proponents of its authenticity might wish to admit. Even if arguments against Pauline authorship sometimes fail to take sufficient account of those numerous commonalities of style and theology that conform to Paul's undisputed letters,[21] it is not merely scholars looking for trouble or wishing to upset the confidence of biblicists who find the Greek of Colossians at some considerable variance from what we read in undisputed Paul.[22] What the reader of the Greek text intuits seems to be confirmed by stylometric analysis. The sentences are characteristically longer than in the acknowledged Pauline letters, often extended by means of multiple circumstantial participles and especially a marked proliferation of relative clauses; infinitives are altogether rare, and conjunctions of all kinds are also comparatively rare. Even more obvious to the naked eye is the prolixity of style, with frequent piling of genitives, frequent prepositional modifiers and various pleonasms. It is more florid than its undisputed counterparts though, in this regard, not to the degree that is found in Ephesians.

There are various ways to account for the differences of style, some more plausible than others, but none that is unproblematic. That the author addresses what he regards to be a particular false theological outlook (the so-called

---

fictitious persons. This is all the more improbable if, per Lohse, Colossians is dated to a later post-Pauline generation.

[20]For a recent negative assessment, see Ehrman, *Forgery and Counterforgery*, 171-81. The definitive detailed treatment of the stylistic issues in Colossians remains Walter Bujard, *Stilanalytische Untersuchungen zum Kolosserbrief als Beitrag zur Methodik von Sprachvergleichen* (Göttingen: Vandenhoeck & Ruprecht, 1973); see also Kiley, *Colossians as Pseudepigraphy*.

[21]Cf. Lohse, *Colossians and Philemon*, 84-91; Peter T. O'Brien, *Colossians, Philemon*, WBC 44 (Waco, TX: Word, 1982), xlii, xliv-l; and Kümmel and Feine, *Introduction*, 341-42.

[22]See, e.g., Dunn's comment on the matter:

First, having studied the text with the care necessary for a commentary of this scope . . . I have to confirm the strong likelihood that the letter comes from a hand other than Paul's. This is not a mechanical judgment, based merely on vocabulary counts, sentence construction, and the like, but, as with all evaluations of literary style, is dependent also on the subjective appreciation of manner and mode of expression. The fact is that at point after point in the letter the commentator is confronted with features characteristic of flow of thought and rhetorical technique that are consistently and markedly different from those of the undisputed Paulines. (Dunn, *Colossians and Philemon*, 35)

Colossian heresy) would naturally introduce certain expressions peculiar to this text. And, as seems probable in this case, the author also makes use of certain preexisting traditions (e.g., Col 1:15-20; 2:13-15; 3:18–4:1), which also could have implications for an analysis of the style of the letter, especially when that is cast in statistical terms.[23] But these considerations take us just so far. The differences between Colossians and the undisputed letters remain, and these observations do not cover the spread between this letter and the undisputed counterparts. There are at least three ways to account for the real differences of style.

1. For many, pseudonymity is still the best account of the evidence. But, as we have seen, that speculation stumbles, perhaps even as to fall, in light of the quantity and character of circumstantial evidence. Prima facie, an alternative account that gives a credible account of Colossians' relationship to Philemon will be preferred.

To the rescue, it would seem, is the hypothesis that in some sense the letter is a deputized composition, nonetheless with Paul still being responsible for the letter written and dispatched in his lifetime and from his location. Thus the *writer* could be none other than Timothy (Col 1:1) with Paul remaining in some sense the *author*.[24] This attractive hypothesis is as credible as the secretary theory in general, but as it regards Timothy, stumbles, though perhaps not so as to fall, on the evidence of undisputed Pauline letters in which Paul names cosenders (including Timothy at least three times) who seem to have no evident influence on the style of the letters in which they are named (1 Thess 1:1; 1 Cor 1:1; 2 Cor 1:1; Phil 1:1; cf. 2 Thess 1:1).[25]

2. Finally, it might be claimed that Colossians showcases Paul's adaptive rhetorical skills as he adjusts his style and rhetoric to the audience and

---

[23]Although the use of traditional material is granted by virtually all scholars, few have been willing to go as far as George E. Cannon, *The Use of Traditional Materials in Colossians* (Macon, GA: Mercer University Press, 1983). Cannon finds over 50 percent of Colossians to be composed of traditional materials, which, in turn, would substantially neutralize claims against Pauline authorship on the ground of style.

[24]This is the position of several scholars who are frequently categorized with a pseudonymity position: e.g., Dunn, *Colossians and Philemon*, 38; and Lohse, *Colossians and Philemon*, 90-91, although more tentatively.

[25]Cf. n. 3 above.

occasion, taking on an Asiatic style for his Asia Minor recipients.[26] For all its attractiveness and simplicity, this essentially traditional account of authorship has for its only shortcoming that it is unfalsifiable.

Discriminating between these alternatives is not easy, nor are they altogether mutually exclusive. The best solution gives pride of place to Colossians' circumstantial ties to Philemon and finds deceptive pseudonymity an unlikely hypothesis in the case of this letter. The alleged theological differences are readily explicable by means of Paul's address of an aberrant teaching and by means of various intuitive Pauline developments. Whether the stylistic differences are due to an amanuensis or to Paul's rhetorical adaptability is impossible to know, but the stylistic variations among Paul's undisputed letters alone give credence to the possibility that he has adapted his style to the conventions and expectations of his audience, especially given that the Asiatic style is otherwise attested in Greek literature. In sum, the phenomena counted against Colossians' authenticity, although not insignificant, are at best ambiguous, susceptible to various more plausible explanations and not nearly as weighty as the cumulative improbabilities that are required of pseudonymity. We cannot know that Paul was the author of Colossians, but it is not mere wishful thinking to regard the letter as authentic.

5.2 A Case for "Ephesians"

If I have expended too much energy on the authorship of Colossians, it is because the fate of Ephesians is not unrelated. If Colossians is not Pauline, then it is all but impossible that Ephesians could be. Whatever features of Colossians incline scholars to see it as un-Pauline, those same features are only further exaggerated in Ephesians, especially matters of style and theology, to which can be added, unlike any other Pauline letter, an entirely undefined historical exigency. Although on occasion a scholar will regard Colossians as dependent on Ephesians, a considerable majority of those who regard Ephesians as pseudonymous understand it rather as the dependent letter. It is, as many note, rather much like Colossians in style and theologically, only more so and without any of the former's specificity of occasion and without its polemical bent. The nearly exact verbal and formal parallels

---

[26]Ben Witherington III, *The Letters to Philemon, the Colossians, and the Ephesians: A Socio-Rhetorical Commentary on the Captivity Epistles* (Grand Rapids: Eerdmans, 2007), 4-20, 100-103.

between the two letters only confirm that they stand in some kind of genetic literary relationship while, at the same time, the express differences suggest to many the work of a different hand.[27]

There is a less skeptical hypothesis that has the further advantage of being less convoluted than direct literary borrowing: Paul himself "wrote" (or possibly authorized the same amanuensis to write) both letters, and they were dispatched simultaneously via Tychicus (Col 4:7; Eph 6:21). This is the nearly universally held position of all who hold to the authenticity of Ephesians: that Colossians is authentic and that the two letters were dispatched together (with Philemon). Not only the literary differences but also the considerable similarities are accounted for under this hypothesis, and the role of Tychicus is given the most straightforward explanation. Of course, it can be argued that this is precisely what the pseudonymist hoped we would think.

The proposal suffers from two shortcomings: (1) If overcoming the stylistic and theological anomalies of Colossians is difficult, those of Ephesians are only more so. (2) A considerable swath of New Testament scholarship doubts Ephesus as the destination (or sole destination) of this letter, for textual and contextual reasons, preferring instead a circular hypothesis. I propose instead that the letter we call "Ephesians" was written by Paul or under his direct aegis but was dispatched to Laodicea, possibly with other Lycus Valley or East Asia locations in sight. Thus, with certain important qualifications, we should understand it as the letter referred to in Colossians 4:16. This is not a novel proposal, even though it has not always received the consideration that it deserves.[28] The destination of "Ephesians" is much discussed and complicated by uncertain textual evidence, but the significance

---

[27]For a helpful tabulation of the shared and unique material, see Andrew T. Lincoln, *Ephesians*, WBC 42 (Dallas: Word, 1990), xlix; cf. Rudolf Schnackenburg, *Ephesians: A Commentary* (Edinburgh: T&T Clark, 1991), 30-34; and John Muddiman, *A Commentary on the Epistle to the Ephesians* (London: Continuum, 2001), 7-11.

[28]Earlier advocates for the position include Adolf Harnack, "Die Adresse des Epheserbriefs des Paulus," *Sitzungsberichte der Königlich Preussischen Akademie der Wissenschaften* 37 (1910): 696-709; Benjamin Willard Robinson, "An Ephesian Imprisonment of Paul," *JBL* 29, no. 2 (1910): 181-89; and Shirley Jackson Case, "To Whom Was 'Ephesians' Written?," *Biblical World* 38, no. 5 (1911): 315-20. More recently, John Muddiman (*Commentary on the Epistle to the Ephesians*) regards a Laodicean destination as the first edition of the letter that, under post-Pauline editing, became "Ephesians," with the building of a "homiletical superstructure" on the original "Laodiceans." For a more recent case for a Laodicean destination and the authenticity of the letter, see now D. A. Campbell, *Framing Paul*, 307-38, 387-91.

of the question extends beyond itself, having far-reaching implications for authorship as well.

EXCURSUS: THE DESTINATION OF "EPHESIANS"

For starters, we will defer the vexed question of the text of Ephesians 1:1 (on which, see below) and instead acknowledge that to affirm Pauline authorship of Ephesians *and* a destination of Ephesus is to climb uphill into the wind. The strikingly impersonal and general quality of the letter makes it all but impossible both that Paul could have written this letter and that it was sent in the first instance to the Ephesians.[29] According to Acts, Paul's sojourn in Ephesus was at least "for two years" (Acts 19:10),[30] making it the longest urban missionary outpost for which we have testimony and requiring that Paul have had an intimate familiarity with the churches and Christians around the city. Yet in the letter called "Ephesians," the author can speak of these Christians coming to faith in the very same terms as he did the Colossians, whom, we know explicitly, he had never met (Col 2:1): "*ever since I heard* about your faith in the Lord Jesus and your love for all God's people" (Eph 1:15; cf. Col 1:9: "*from the day we heard*, we have not ceased to pray for you"). It seems nearly impossible that the founding apostle for the church in Ephesus could refer to the foundation of that church in faith and love as though it were news he had received through a third party and as one

---

[29]The problem is well acknowledged by scholars affirming the authenticity of "in Ephesus" in Ephesians 1:1, who note (1) that the vast majority of manuscript evidence contains the destination, (2) the absence of any destination is grammatically problematic and (3) there is, save for Marcion, a nearly uniform tradition in the early Christian centuries that associated the text with Ephesus (so, e.g., with variations, Frank Thielman, *Ephesians*, BECNT [Grand Rapids: Baker Academic, 2010], 11-17; Clinton E. Arnold, *Ephesians*, ZECNT 10 [Grand Rapids: Zondervan, 2010], 23-29; and Harold W. Hoehner, *Ephesians: An Exegetical Commentary* [Grand Rapids: Baker Academic, 2002], 78-80). It remains to explain the impersonal character of the letter, written as though the author is personally unacquainted with the recipients. The characteristic rejoinders are unpersuasive: that Paul is writing especially to more recent converts, subsequent to the founding of the church, or that Paul, Ephesus being a large city, would have only secondhand knowledge of the factions of the church and only in general terms. Such explanations falter given that Ephesians casts Paul's relationship (Eph 1:15; 3:2; 4:21) in terms so similar to Colossians and that it is improbable that such a majestic apostolic pastoral communication should be designated for only some subset of the Ephesian Christians.

[30]This time frame described in Acts 19:10 is the period in which he lectured in the Hall of Tyrannus (τοῦτο δὲ ἐγένετο ἐπὶ ἔτη δύο); presumably the three months in the synagogue that preceded (Acts 19:8) are to be added on to these two years for a stay in Ephesus of at least two years and three months.

wishing to show his deep and *long-standing* interest nonetheless.[31] Along the
same lines, Paul implies that the recipients' knowledge of him is a matter of
reputation rather than firsthand acquaintance: "assuming that you have
heard of the stewardship of God's grace that was given to me for you" (Eph
3:2 RSV).[32] Indeed, taken by themselves, these expressions of distant and
unacquainted solidarity support the notion that Ephesians was simply
modeled after Colossians and, were one to insist on an Ephesian destination
for the letter, all but confirms both pseudonymity and literary dependence.

Moreover, the letter betrays no knowledge of any peculiar circumstances among the recipients, distinguishing it, in that regard, from every
other Pauline letter, including even Romans and Colossians (assuming the
authenticity of the latter), churches Paul had never met but of which he
nonetheless had sufficient knowledge to write targeted pastoral letters. The
letter also lacks any personal touches in the form of greetings or reminiscence, again distinguishing it from every other writing of the Pauline
corpus, undisputed and disputed. It stretches credulity that, were this from
Paul, a letter to Ephesus would be altogether less personal than his letter
to the Colossians (to say nothing of Romans), again, with whom he had
no personal acquaintance.

The single personal reference in the letter is Tychicus (Eph 6:21-22), who
is described in terms virtually identical to that of Colossians (Col 4:7-8 RSV):
"Now that you also may know how I am and what I am doing, Tychicus the
beloved brother and faithful minister in the Lord will tell you everything. I
have sent him to you for this very purpose, that you may know how we are,
and that he may encourage your hearts."[33] It would seem on the face of it

---

[31]The participle, ἀκούσας, could be taken as either temporal ("ever since"; NIV, CEB) or causal
("because"; RSV, ESV, effectively NRSV). The logic of the διὰ τοῦτο ("on account of this"; "for this
reason") presumably inclines certain translators toward the causal construal of the participle;
not only does this result in an awkward redundancy ("for this reason, because I also heard . . ."),
but also it probably overreads the logical force of the simple resumptive, διὰ τοῦτο. Paul's likely
simple point is that his prayer for the recipients is long-standing. This conforms to the similar
emphasis of Colossians 1:9, "from the day we heard, we have not ceased to pray for you."
[32]The contingency for rhetorical effect of this parenthetical comment (εἴ γε ἠκούσατε) is hard to
convey. See, e.g., CEB: "You've heard, of course, about the responsibility to distribute God's grace,
which God gave to me for you, right?" A possible counterpart to this tentative "getting acquainted"
rhetoric may also be found in Ephesians 4:21 RSV: "assuming that you have heard about him and
were taught in him" (εἴ γε . . . ἠκούσατε). If so, this is secondary evidence that Paul is uncertain
of what the recipients know of him and reluctant to overstate what is true of them.
[33]The degree of direct overlap of wording is striking and points either to (1) direct borrowing by a

that there are only two possibilities here: Ephesians 6:21-22 is a direct replication of Colossians 4:7-8, obviously the work of a later imitator, or Ephesians and Colossians are produced by the same hand and were written and dispatched together, borne by Tychicus to their various destinations.

Meanwhile, Colossians itself bears testimony to another letter possessed by (and/or originally intended for?) the church at Laodicea, referred to in Colossians 4:16 (*tēn ek Laodikeias*; hereafter "Laodiceans"). Although it cuts against the grain of most New Testament scholarship, it does not seem probable that this text was lost, which is a too-little-considered dimension of the question of the destination of Ephesians. Of course, we know of letters written by Paul that are not extant (1 Cor 5:9; 2 Cor 2:3-4);[34] however, temporarily leaving aside whether "Ephesians" is actually "Laodiceans," there is good reason to doubt that "Laodiceans" suffered the same fate. As with Colossians, which was directed to be read in the church of Laodicea, "Laodiceans" was to be read in Colossae; that is, both letters (presumably) were copied and put into immediate circulation. It would seem almost certain also that Tychicus himself would have been responsible for the dispatch of the complementary letters in Colossae and Laodicea. Indeed, it may be only a slight exaggeration to understand this early reproduction and sharing of edifying documents between Christian communities as the beginning of the process of canonization.[35] Moreover, as may have been the case with all of Paul's

---

second author, (2) common authorship and simultaneous dispatch, or (3) a variant of (2), a replication of Colossians 4:7-8 in Ephesians 6:21-22 deputized to the amaneuensis. For a helpful analysis of these passages on analogy to the Ignatian correspondence, see E. Randolph Richards, "Silvanus Was Not Peter's Secretary: Theological Bias in Interpreting διὰ Σιλουανοῦ . . . ἔγραψα in 1 Peter 5:12," *JETS* 43, no. 3 (2000): 417-32, esp. 419-22. See the comparison in table 5.2.

Table 5.2. A comparison of Colossians 4:7-8 and Ephesians 6:21-22

Colossians 4:7-8	Ephesians 6:21-22
Τὰ κατ᾽ ἐμὲ πάντα γνωρίσει ὑμῖν Τύχικος	<u>Ἵνα δὲ εἰδῆτε καὶ ὑμεῖς</u> τὰ κατ᾽ ἐμέ, <u>τί πράσσω</u>, πάντα γνωρίσει ὑμῖν Τύχικος
ὁ ἀγαπητὸς ἀδελφὸς καὶ πιστὸς διάκονος <u>καὶ σύνδουλος</u> ἐν κυρίῳ, ὃν ἔπεμψα πρὸς ὑμᾶς εἰς αὐτὸ τοῦτο, ἵνα γνῶτε τὰ περὶ ἡμῶν καὶ παρακαλέσῃ τὰς καρδίας ὑμῶν.	ὁ ἀγαπητὸς ἀδελφὸς καὶ πιστὸς διάκονος ἐν κυρίῳ, ὃν ἔπεμψα πρὸς ὑμᾶς εἰς αὐτὸ τοῦτο, ἵνα γνῶτε τὰ περὶ ἡμῶν καὶ παρακαλέσῃ τὰς καρδίας ὑμῶν.

[34] Assuming with most New Testament scholars that the tearful letter of 2 Corinthians 2:3-4 is neither 1 Corinthians nor a fragment reincorporated back into the Corinthian correspondence (e.g., 2 Cor 10–13).

[35] L. T. Johnson, *Writings of the New Testament*, 527.

letters, it can be expected that he followed ancient epistolary practice and had made for himself a copy of letters before they were dispatched.[36] There are several good reasons, then, to believe then that "Laodiceans" was, like Colossians, "backed up" from the very beginning and that together they were from the beginning deemed to carry a general benefit even for Christians who were not the original recipients. This differentiates "Laodiceans" from the lost letters attested to in the Corinthian correspondence, which, arguably, had no purpose in being shared with other communities and which, for the same reason, Paul himself, if he had retained copies, could have withheld then from any further distribution. Thus, although we have no extant letter of primitive Christian origins from Paul unambiguously addressed to the Laodiceans,[37] it seems highly doubtful that "Laodiceans" of Colossians 4:16 is a lost letter.[38]

Almost certainly related, there is a notorious text-critical puzzle as it concerns the original addressees of Ephesians, namely, that the designation "in Ephesus" (*en Ephesō*), the only internal indication the letter is directed toward Ephesus, is missing from certain of the earliest copies along with other minor variations among the manuscripts, including what are regarded as the three earliest manuscripts of the Greek New Testament ($\mathfrak{p}^{46}$ [of the Chester Beatty collection, 3rd c.], Sinaiaticus [= ℵ, 4th c.], and Vaticanus [= B, 4th c.]).[39] It is highly improbable, however, that the original form of the letter

---

[36]Richards, *Paul and First-Century Letter Writing*, 156-70. This is consistent with David Trobisch's argument that Paul himself was responsible for the collection of his corpus (Trobisch, *Paul's Letter Collection: Tracing the Origins* [Minneapolis: Fortress, 1994]).

[37]Setting aside the apocryphal Epistle to the Laodiceans of uncertain provenance and date (Wilhelm Schneemelcher suggests second to fourth century in *New Testament Apocrypha*, vol. 2, *Writings Relating to the Apostles: Apocalypses and Related Subjects*, trans. Robert McL. Wilson, rev. ed. [Louisville, KY: Westminster John Knox, 1992], 42-45).

[38]So also, J. B. Lightfoot, *Saint Paul's Epistle to the Philippians: A Revised Text with Introduction, Notes and Dissertations*, 8th ed. (London: Macmillan, 1885), 139-40, who regards the letter as "Ephesians." In a footnote, Lightfoot promises to follow up on the destination of Ephesians, which unfortunately was an ambition that went unrealized.

[39]For more detailed treatments of the text-critical question, see esp. J. B. Lightfoot, *Biblical Essays* (New York: Macmillan, 1904), 377-96; Case, "To Whom Was 'Ephesians' Written?"; A. van Roon, *The Authenticity of Ephesians*, NovTSup 39 (Leiden: Brill, 1974), 72-99; Geurt H. van Kooten, *Cosmic Christology in Paul and the Pauline School: Colossians and Ephesians in the Context of Graeco-Roman Cosmology, with a New Synopsis of the Greek Texts*, WUNT 171 (Tübingen: Mohr Siebeck, 2003), 197-201; Thielman, *Ephesians*, 11-17; Arnold, *Ephesians*, 23-29; and D. A. Campbell, *Framing Paul*, 309-13.

The text-critical data of the four extant textforms and a fifth conjecture can be summarized as follows (noting that two extant textforms are lacking ἐν Ἐφέσῳ [1 and 2] and two extant textforms have ἐν Ἐφέσῳ [3 and 4]):

lacked a designation of place. The grammar is at best quite awkward (*tois hagiois [tois] ousin kai pistois en Christō Iēsou*; "to the saints being and [or "also"] faithful in Christ Jesus"). And despite various attempts to rehabilitate by means of English gloss,[40] it is an altogether unlikely Greek expression.[41]

---

1. τοῖς ἁγίοις οὖσιν καὶ πιστοῖς ἐν Χριστῷ Ἰησοῦ (𝔭⁴⁶; cf. D, which also omits τοῖς)

2. τοῖς ἁγίοις τοῖς οὖσι[ν] καὶ πιστοῖς ἐν Χριστῷ Ἰησοῦ (א*, B*, 6 [13th c.], 1739 [10th c.], Origen, Basil [PG 29:612-13]; cf. 𝔭⁴⁶; on traces of this reading also in Latin witnesses, see Lightfoot, *Biblical Essays*, 383-86)

3. τοῖς ἁγίοις τοῖς οὖσιν ἐν Ἐφέσῳ καὶ πιστοῖς ἐν Χριστῷ Ἰησοῦ (B, D [omitting τοῖς], F, G, Ψ, 0278, 33, 104, 365, 630, 1175, 1241, 1505, 1881, 𝔐; Marcus Victorinus, Jerome)

4. τοῖς ἁγίοις πᾶσιν τοῖς οὖσιν ἐν Ἐφέσῳ καὶ πιστοῖς ἐν Χριστῷ Ἰησοῦ (א², A, P, 81, 326, 629, 2464, b, f, vg⁽ᶜˡ⁾·ˢᵗ·ʷʷ, bo)

Additionally, it can be conjectured with some probability (contra Arnold, *Ephesians*, 25) that the textform familiar to Marcion had a Laodicean destination:

5. τοῖς ἁγίοις τοῖς οὖσιν ἐν Λαοδικείᾳ καὶ πιστοῖς ἐν Χριστῷ Ἰησοῦ (via Tertullian [*Marc.* 5.11.12; 5.17.1]; Epiphanius [*Pan.* 42.9.4; 42.11.8; 42.12.3; 42.13.4]; Theodoret of Cyrrhus [*Interpretatio XIV epistolarum sancti Pauli apostoli* 82.625C]). For the Epiphanius and Theodoret references I depend on van Kooten, *Cosmic Christology*, 198n79, where the Greek texts are also given. It should be noted that the Theodoret passage (Τινὲς ὑπέλαβον καὶ Λαοδικέας αὐτὸν γεγραφέναι ["some supposed it to have been written even to Laodicea"]) is significant evidence for a tradition of a Laodicean destination, but that it does not count together with Tertullian and Epiphanius as a third attestation of Marcion's address (contra D. A. Campbell, *Framing Paul*, 309-13).

[40]Ephesians 1:1 RSV: "To the saints who are also faithful"; Goodspeed: "to God's people who are steadfast" (Edgar J. Goodspeed, *The New Testament: An American Translation* [Chicago: University of Chicago Press, 1923], 362); cf. also Peter T. O'Brien, *The Letter to the Ephesians*, PNTC (Grand Rapids: Eerdmans, 1999), 85.

[41]As noted more bluntly in BDF, which, while noting that "the ptcp. ὤν can only be used when there are other adjuncts to the predicate," regards the reading τοῖς ἁγίοις οὖσιν καὶ πιστοῖς as "impossible" (§413[3], p. 213). Similarly, see G. Zuntz, who avers that "τοῖς οὖσιν without an indication of place . . . following makes no sense" (*The Text of the Epistles: A Disquistion upon the Corpus Paulinum* [London: Oxford University Press, 1953], 228n1).

The difficulty of the grammar when the text is absent ἐν Εφέσῳ is characteristically understated by those convinced of its originality on text-critical grounds (e.g., O'Brien, *Letter to the Ephesians*, 86; Lincoln, *Ephesians*, 1-4). This ignores particularly the telling evidence of third- and fourth-century Greek commentators, Origen and Basil the Great (rightly Thielman, *Ephesians*, 12-13), who clearly found the Greek grammar (i.e., οὖσι without ἐν + place name) so difficult that only a theological interpretation of οὖσι could explain it. (On the relevance of Origen and Basil for the textual question in general, see esp. Lightfoot, *Biblical Essays*, 377-80.)

Origen first notes the uniqueness and peculiarity of τοῖς ἁγίοις τοῖς οὖσι without a reference to destination: "In the case of the Ephesians alone we have found the phrase 'to the saints that are'. We ask what the phrase 'who are' can mean, if it is not redundant when added to 'the saints'." He is thus moved to venture that some theological intent lay behind the anomaly: "Consider, then, if not as in Exodus, he who utters the words 'he who is' to Moses speaks his own name (Exod. 3:14), so those who participate in 'the one who is' become those 'who are', called, as it were, from 'not being' into 'being'. For God 'chose the things which are not', Paul himself says, 'that he might abolish the things which are' (1 Cor 1:28-9)" (adapted from Ronald E. Heine, ed., *The Commentaries of Origen and Jerome on St. Paul's Epistle to the Ephesians*, Oxford Early

Moreover, it is syntactically unprecedented in Paul's letters. Wherever one finds the participle *ousin/ousē[i]* in the address of a Pauline epistle, it is *always* followed by *en* + designated city name.[42]

We are left, then, to explain the uniform absence of "in Ephesus" in the earliest textual tradition. Of course, defenders of an Ephesian destination find the ungrammatical variants evidence for the secondary character of those readings.[43] In this case, the *lectio difficilior* canon of textual criticism (that the more difficult form of the text is to be preferred—at best an index and not a rule as such) can be obviated on the ground that certain "difficult" readings are simply too far beyond the pale. We can concur with that judgment without regarding it as decisive in favor of "in Ephesus." To the contrary, the amount of evidence and its varied provenance do not let us set aside this anomaly as though it were a mere transcriptional error replicated.[44]

Christian Studies [Oxford: Oxford University Press, 2002], 80; cf. Lightfoot's more interpretive translation [*Biblical Essays*, 377-78]).

Basil, also bearing witness to the absence of ἐν Ἐφέσῳ, is moved by the same grammatical anomaly to a very similar theological interpretation:

But also, when writing to the Ephesians, as those truly united with "the One who is" [or "Being"; τῷ ὄντι] through complete knowledge, he [Paul] uniquely named them "being" when he said, "to the saints, those 'being' and faithful in Christ Jesus" [ὄντας αὐτοὺς ἰδιαζόντως ὠνόμασεν εἰπών· τοῖς ἁγίοις τοῖς οὖσι καὶ πιστοῖς ἐν Χριστῷ Ἰησοῦ]. For so also those before us passed it down, and we also have found [the same to be so] in the ancient of the copies [ἐν τοῖς παλαιοῖς τῶν ἀντιγράφων]. (my translation)

It is clear, thus, that both Origen and Basil are interpreting texts lacking ἐν Ἐφέσῳ, and that Basil maintains that this is the more ancient form of the text. Jerome, albeit in apparent dependence on Origen, bears witness both to the absence of ἐν Ἐφέσῳ, paraphrasing Origen's interpretation, while also conceding that "others, however, think it has been written straightforwardly not to those 'who are', but 'who are the saints and faithful in Ephesus'" (Heine, *Commentaries of Origen and Jerome*, 80).

[42]Romans 1:7 (τοῖς οὖσιν ἐν Ῥώμῃ); 1 Corinthians 1:2 and 2 Corinthians 1:1 (τῇ ἐκκλησίᾳ τοῦ θεοῦ τῇ οὔσῃ ἐν Κορίνθῳ); Philippians 1:1 (τοῖς οὖσιν ἐν Φιλίπποις); cf. Colossians 1:2 (τοῖς ἐν Κολοσσαῖς ἁγίοις καὶ πιστοῖς ἀδελφοῖς ἐν Χριστῷ). First and Second Thessalonians (τῇ ἐκκλησίᾳ Θεσσαλονικέων), Galatians (ταῖς ἐκκλησίαις τῆς Γαλατίας) and the letters to individuals use different constructions, lacking the participle. Although admittedly a minor datum, the form of the address in Galatians, akin to 1 Thessalonians and contrary to all the other church-addressed letters, is consistent with an early date for the letter.

[43]E.g., Thielman, *Ephesians*, 13; and Arnold, *Ephesians*, 25-26.

[44]It is true that the external evidence for the omission is almost exclusively Alexandrian (p[46], uncorrected ℵ and B, much later minuscules 6 and 1739; although 424 [corrected] is of an ambiguous text type, arguably Byzantine) and that the majority of, albeit *later*, Alexandrian witnesses read ἐν Ἐφέσῳ (e.g., A, 33, 81, 1175, 1881 and 104), but this observation should not be accorded too much weight (contra Thielman, *Ephesians*, 14; and Hoehner, *Ephesians*, 146). While it would be true that greater text-type diversity would much strengthen the case for the destination omission, the very survival into the third and fourth centuries and beyond of *any*

The omission is persistent and widespread enough to appear motivated, even if its very difficulty casts suspicion on its authenticity.

There are, therefore, (1) strong stylistic and circumstantial reasons to attach Colossians and Ephesians to each other as jointly written and dispatched letters (Col 4:7-9, 16; Eph 6:21-22); (2) good reason to doubt, under the circumstances of its reception, that the letter to the Laodiceans would have been lost; (3) even more reason to doubt that Ephesus was ever the original, much less sole, destination of this letter; (4) strong reasons to doubt that the omission of destination is original on the basis both of Pauline usage and the impossibly difficult syntax of the omitted form; and (5) reason to believe that the omission of the destination is a motivated emendation rather than merely a transcriptional error.

It is this last point that deserves further attention, beginning with this observation: the earliest attestation to the destination of this letter is that of Marcion (ca. 140), who believed it to have been written "to the saints who are in Laodicea." Of course, no texts of Marcion survive; what we know of him and his views comes from his opponents, in this case Tertullian. We learn of Marcion's view of the destination of Ephesians from two passages: First obliquely, "I here pass over discussion about another epistle, which we hold to have been written to the Ephesians, but the heretics [to have been written] to the Laodiceans. In it he tells them to remember, that at the time when they were Gentiles they were without Christ, aliens" (Tertullian, *Marc.* 5.11).[45] Then, later, Tertullian more explicitly rejects Marcion's view, albeit without argument:

> We have it on the true tradition of the Church, that this epistle was sent to the Ephesians, not to the Laodiceans. Marcion, however, was very desirous of giving it the new title [i.e., of Laodicea], as if he were extremely accurate in investigating such a point. But of what consequence are the titles, since in writing to a certain church the apostle did in fact write to all? It is certain that, whoever they were to whom he wrote, he declared Him to be God in Christ with whom all things agree which are predicted. (*Marc.* 5:17)

---

texts omitting the destination is the weightier datum. That the earliest witnesses also happen to be Alexandrian should hardly count against the omission, which is all the more remarkable given that p[46], Sinaiaticus and Vaticanus have the superscription ΠΡΟΣ ΕΦΕΣΙΟΥΣ. The fact that Origen and Basil clearly know the text without a destination and problematize it as such adds considerable corroborating weight to omission in the three earliest manuscripts.

[45]The reference to "the heretics" here is, of course, to the Marcionites, and perhaps more specifically to the Marcionite canon prologue.

A few observations are in order. It should first be noted that, according to Tertullian, Marcion is wrong—about everything. He is numbered among the heretics; almost by definition he cannot be right—about anything. Second, it should be noted that Tertullian disparages Marcion for the hubris of supposing "to be extremely accurate in investigating such a point." This suggests that Marcion's view on this matter and its justification—now unfortunately lost—were a matter of some importance to him and that this was a position he "investigated" and for which he presumably had reasons. Over against this, Tertullian has only two rejoinders: (1) that the Ephesian designation is the true tradition of the church[46] and (2) that, in any case, it doesn't matter; the message is universal, that is to say, catholic, so that it is therefore unimportant "whoever they were to whom he wrote." It is not hard to see here that Tertullian is in certain respects on the defensive. Marcion holds a view on a matter that he has investigated and in which he is invested. Tertullian has on his "side" the tradition of the church,[47] which, although he regards it as definitive, is not so much an argument as, in this case, an ad hominem against the notorious heretic who insists on going his own way, not just in matters of theology but now in "biblical criticism." Thus, Marcion's advocacy of the Laodicean destination is for Tertullian of a piece with the more pervasive hubris, and Tertullian's rejoinder treats Marcion's opinion on the matter as akin to heresy, a private opinion against the "true tradition of the Church." It is further interesting to note that, lacking evidence of his own, Tertullian prefers ultimately to prescind by retreating into the irrelevance of titles for a text that is universal in its application: "*whoever they were to whom he wrote.*" In other words, hypothetically, Tertullian could be wrong about this matter, and, in the nature of the case, it simply wouldn't matter. It is fair to wonder if he is hedging his bets. I suggest, then, a straightforward, admittedly undemonstrable, explanation for the absence of any extant manuscript evidence for a Laodicean destination: that textform dropped out of the tradition for the

---

[46]*Ecclesiae quidem veritate epistulam istam ad Ephesios habemus emissam* (Tertullian, *Marc.* 5.17).
[47]There is no reason to think that Tertullian is bluffing here. Substantial early testimony—save for Marcion—corroborates an Ephesian destination (Irenaeus, *Haer.* 5.2.3; 8.1; 14.3; 24.4; Cyprian, *Test.* 7, 8, 11, 13, 41, 70, 72, 117; Origen, *Prin.* 3.5.4.).

simple reason that the archheretic of the early- and mid-second century advocated the view.[48]

A once popular solution that explains both the absence of destination in certain early manuscripts and witnesses but also the wide attestation to Ephesians later and elsewhere is now somewhat in decline—at least in the form in which it is usually offered. According to this hypothesis, Ephesians was intended as a circular letter from the beginning, and the destination omission can be explained by a conjectured gap left to be filled in for each destination city.[49] The problems with this otherwise attractive solution are simply too many. For starters, we have no corroborating evidence that this was ever practiced in the ancient world.[50] W. G. Kümmel's judgment is often noted: "the supposition of a letter with a gap in the prescript for a subsequent insertion of the address is without any parallel in antiquity."[51] It is hard to know what advantage there might have been in leaving a blank in the case of hand-copied documents—the hypothesis smacks of a post-Gutenberg mindset.[52] The only overtly circular letters in the New Testament, 1 Peter (1 Pet 1:1) and Revelation (Rev 2:1–3:20), list all the geographical destinations or, in the case of Galatians, a region. There is probably a patently economic explanation for this: multiple copies of these documents would have been expensive to produce; it would have been much more economical and characteristic for a single document to be borne in person and, should copies

[48]This is not to reprise the surmise of Harnack that Laodicea dropped out of the textual tradition because of the city's notorious reputation, e.g., in Revelation 3:14-22 (Harnack, "Adresse des Epheserbriefs des Paulus"; cf. Case, "To Whom Was 'Ephesians' Written?," 319-20, who accepts Harnack's explanation).

[49]Lightfoot, *Biblical Essays*, 392-93 (following Archbishop James Ussher); Zuntz, *Text of the Epistles*, 228; Nils Alstrup Dahl, *Studies in Ephesians: Introductory Questions, Text- and Edition-Critical Issues, Interpretation of Texts and Themes*, ed. David Hellholm, Vemund Blomkvist and Tord Fornberg, WUNT 131 (Tübingen: Mohr Siebeck, 2000), 62-63; F. F. Bruce, *The Epistles to the Colossians, to Philemon, and to the Ephesians*, NICNT (Grand Rapids: Eerdmans, 1984), 249-50; and Witherington, *Letters to Philemon, the Colossians, and the Ephesians*, 212-13.

[50]A point Bruce concedes (*Epistles to the Colossians, to Philemon, and to the Ephesians*, 250).

[51]Kümmel and Feine, *Introduction*, 355. Zuntz's surmise to the contrary regarding Hellenistic "royal letters" sent to multiple destinations is sometimes cited (e.g., Bruce, Witherington) as though he had provided evidence to the contrary, but in fact (as Kümmel recognizes) Zuntz is only engaging in a supposition that what he alleges happened in the case of Ephesians happened in these letters as well: "The letters collected, in the Epicurean *corpus*, under the heading 'To many' . . . afford another parallel; for who would imagine one copy only to have been dispatched with the vague heading, for example, 'To the friends in Asia'?" (*Text of the Epistles*, 228n1).

[52]Thielman (*Ephesians*, 13) also asks why, on this hypothesis, the preposition ἐν before the city name would not have been copied.

have been made, for them to have been sponsored by the receiving communities. Finally, were this the cause of the textual variants, it is at least
surprising that no other destinations but Ephesus are ever found. Why not
"Laodicea" or "Hieropolis" or some other Asian city in the textual tradition?

There is, however, a version of this hypothesis that is not so rigidly textual
in character, which as a result, carries all its strengths and none of its liabilities. The alleged "gap" was not a blank to be filled in by pen on paper but left
for a courier-lector who would fill the "gap" orally while bearing the same
document from city to city.[53] Here then is a solution to the primary three
dilemmas: (1) the overwhelming early textual evidence, both manuscripts
and patristic testimony, for the absence of en Ephesō; (2) the grammatical
impossibility of the text without a destination reference; (3) the very general,
secondhand character of "Ephesians." While the intentional textual gap hypothesis for a circular letter solves these problems, it leaves us with a different
set of improbabilities, as we have seen. However, if the insertion of destination is oral and not textual, it becomes possible to explain all the evidence.

I conclude thus with this proposal: The letter known as "Ephesians" is the
same letter referred to in Colossians 4:16 and was borne with Colossians and
Philemon by Tychicus. The original form of its address is "to the saints who
are <in place name> and faithful in Christ Jesus," that is, with no place name
written, but rather supplied by the courier-lector (presumably Tychicus) at its
oral delivery to gathered Christians, in which the "letter" would function
rather more as a homily for a gathered community.[54] There is no place name
because it was written as a circular letter for the predominantly Gentile
churches of the Lycus Valley, which would include Laodicea, Colossae and
presumably Hieropolis. Whether the homily was originally intended for
Ephesus at all is harder to determine, though both the original form of the
address and even more the content and tone make it nearly impossible for

---

[53]Witherington offers this hypothesis more tentatively than he might have:

> It is then possible that the name of the particular audience in Ephesians was left blank so
> that the oral deliverer of the discourse could insert the name according to where he was
> sharing the sermon. This is a plausible thesis, but there are no manuscripts that have "in"
> with no location, nor is there any ancient epistolary evidence for such a practice. But this
> document should not be compared to letters, as it really is not one. (Witherington, Letters
> to Philemon, the Colossians, and the Ephesians, 218)

[54]For which Hebrews serves as the most ready analogy, though lacking an epistolary prescript.
On Ephesians as homily, see ibid., 215-24.

Ephesus to have been the sole destination. That the letter would have become associated with Ephesus relatively early (i.e., by the mid- to late-second century) was only natural given the size of that major port city and its prominence as a Christian center, all the more by comparison with the humbler Lycus Valley alternatives, especially since Colossae and Hieropolis had suffered from a massive earthquake. Therefore, I deem Marcion's judgment correct, if perhaps too specific, and the judgment of Tertullian and other Fathers who knew the letter as "to the Ephesians" to be unlikely and anachronistic.

The destination of Ephesians (having left the question of destination, I will dispense with the scare quotes) is an intriguing piece of detective work but not irrelevant to the question of authorship, the question with which this excursus began. Again, if Ephesus is the destination of this letter, then it is almost impossible that it is Pauline. If, however, it is the very letter dispatched to the Laodiceans, then it is not only possibly Pauline, but probably Pauline, that is, as probably Pauline as Colossians itself, which, as I have argued, is as Pauline as Philemon.

As for the matters of style and theology that are thought to set Ephesians apart from the undisputed Pauline letters, making the former the work of a successor to Paul, this can be accounted for substantially as a question of genre. If the "letter" is rather a circular pastoral homily directed especially toward the edification of Gentile converts, then stylistic comparisons to actual Pauline *epistles* are intrinsically problematic. In some degree, all of Paul's church-designated letters have a homiletical cast and function to them, but with Ephesians the circular character of an expressly homiletical writing is of no small consequence. It is only to be expected that a circular homily written for Lycus Valley Christians whom Paul knew only by reputation would be general in character, addressing no particular exigency, appealing to no prior relationship. Moreover, as homily, the dense, baroque style would find a natural origin in the apostle's desire to describe the Christian gospel and its entailments in elevated, mythopoetic language. And that language—quasi-liturgical, as many have suggested—would find a natural home in the early communal worship settings of primitive urban churches, in which the arrival of the apostle Paul's letter may well have served as a celebratory, galvanizing event. In short, once the matter of its destination and the closely related question of its genre are clarified, the authenticity of the letter proves to be entirely plausible.

5.3 LOCATING COLOSSIANS AND EPHESIANS

If the authenticity of Colossians or Ephesians is rejected, it is nearly impossible to locate either the provenance or date for either, other than presumably after Paul's death. But at that point, further specificity is considerably more difficult, being tributary to larger but no less speculative questions about developments in the Christianity of the final generation of the first century, a period for which we have only minimal and uncertain evidence. If, however, the letters are deemed authentic, it is possible to narrow a probable provenance and date more specifically, though no particular setting commends itself as obvious or unproblematic. Classically, the provenance of Colossians and Ephesians (with Philemon) together with Philippians, deemed the Captivity Epistles, is associated with Paul's Roman imprisonment. As with Philippians, the same two alternative imprisonments are proposed—Caesarea (Acts 23–26) and Ephesus, the latter hypothesized, though not improbable for that. In most respects, the arguments for and against a Roman imprisonment each apply to Philemon, Colossians and Ephesians, though in different proportions.

The distance between Rome and the Lycus Valley destinations remains an impediment, yet not as much travel within a constrained time frame is presupposed as in the case of Philippians. The journeys assumed in the letters have minimal bearing on the time frame for the letters. (1) Onesimus must have found his way to Paul's location, although it bears noting that there is no time frame related to Paul's incarceration. He could have already been in the location before Paul's arrival; we can't know. It is often surmised that a fugitive Onesimus would have been much more likely to make his way to nearer by Ephesus than to distant Rome, but others suggest that the massive capital would have been a desirable destination for a runaway slave in search of anonymity.[55] (2) More pertinent is the arrival of Epaphras, whose journey to Paul presumably commenced upon his learning of his circumstances. This is the only journey that bears upon the timing of the

---

[55]Historical support for this frequent supposition is now available in S. R. Llewelyn, ed., *New Documents Illustrating Early Christianity* ([North Ryde], NSW: Ancient History Documentary Research Centre, Macquarie University, 1997), 8:40-42.

letter per se, and both the Roman and possible Ephesian imprisonments are perfectly viable alternatives. (3) The return of Onesimus and Tychicus has no direct bearing on the timing of the letter, requiring only that Paul still be imprisoned upon their departure. (4) On the other hand, Paul's request in Philemon 22 for lodging to be made ready for his arrival seems at least a little surprising coming from Rome, 1,200 miles away, but not implausible from Ephesus, a comparatively modest 120-mile trip. Yet in the context of a personal missive in which a visit to the Colossian Christians remains desirable but uncertain, perhaps the request has a colloquial, almost playful quality—"get my room ready"—marking Paul's hopefulness. In sum, the proximity of Ephesus to the Lycus Valley churches counts significantly in its favor, but there is nothing in the scenarios of the letters that rules out Rome.

Unlike Philippians, none of these texts has strong internal clues for a Roman provenance (e.g., "praetorium" and "Caesar's household"). The closest we have to such clues is that the author enjoys a freedom in receiving and sending guests that accords well with the Roman house-arrest scenario.[56] While it is clear that Paul was imprisoned on several occasions of which we have no record,[57] we know of no imprisonment in which the conditions of length and the freedom to receive colleagues and compose letters are more plausible than in the conditions of the Roman imprisonment.[58]

Some scholars find evidence also in the theology of these letters of a "later" Paul, especially with an allegedly more exalted Christology (Col 1:15-20; 2:9-10; Eph 1:21-22), the mystical or spiritually realized eschatology (Col 2:13; 3:1-3; Eph 2:6), and the universalist and high ecclesiology (Col 1:18-20; Eph 1:22-23; 3:10; 4:4-6). In short, the very material that inclines a majority of scholars to

---

[56]Brian Rapske, *The Book of Acts and Paul in Roman Custody*, The Book of Acts in Its First Century Setting 3 (Grand Rapids: Eerdmans, 1994), 173-89, 313-67.

[57]See chap 4, n. 43 above.

[58]The Caesarean imprisonment compiles too many improbabilities: (1) If the distance of Rome from the Lycus Valley counts against a Roman provenance, the same counts against Caesarea. (2) We know less about Paul's conditions in Caesarea, but on balance it does not seem nearly as conducive to the exercise of administrative leadership and letter writing (see Rapske, *Book of Acts and Paul*, 151-72, who describes that imprisonment as "a lightened form of military custody"). (3) Knowing that he was appealing to Caesar, would Paul have expected an imminent release from this imprisonment? (4) If Paul were to have been released from Caesarea, it would be more probable that his attention would have turned to Spain as forecasted in Romans 15 whereas, from a Roman imprisonment, a turn to the east is more understandable at the conclusion of a five-year, life-and-death ordeal.

doubt the authenticity of the letters as post-Pauline inclines others to see them as a mature or late Paul, and thus to prefer the provenance of the Roman imprisonment as the latest possible setting for Paul to have written the letters. It is acknowledged that this is a precariously circular, question-begging, possibly even specious, sort of argument when the goal is establishing the coordinates of a chronology that is meant to ground arguments tracing development.[59] And even beyond that, one might be skeptical of the inherent subjectivity of any claim that posits one conception as development of another. At the same time, as it regards the provenance of these Captivity Epistles, internal and external evidences are so wanting that an appeal to these considerations cannot be ruled out, even if the results must be regarded as tentative. Therefore, we can say that the very features that incline some scholars to see these letters as late and post-Pauline also count in favor of Colossians and Ephesians, if authentic, being later than their acknowledged counterparts and that the Roman provenance is the singularly attested biographical circumstance that fits the writing of these letters. The provenance of the letters must be regarded as uncertain, but given the limited and disparate clues that we have, the Roman provenance seems the most likely alternative.

5.4 A Case for the Pastoral Epistles

Finally, we come to the question of the Pastoral Epistles (hereafter PE).[60] Fewer scholars regard these letters as authentic than affirm the Pauline origin of Ephesians, or we might say that it is largely the same scholars in both cases, perhaps just not quite as many. The arguments for and against are readily available in the major introductions and commentaries, are well known and will be summarized only briefly, given the wide availability of detailed accounts.[61] The objections against can be summarized as essentially

---

[59]Here again, in this regard D. A. Campbell's recent study (*Framing Paul*, see esp. 13-15) must be regarded as a model of austerity and discipline.

[60]I concede to the protest of scholars against the treatment of critical issues for all three letters as though they were one (so, e.g., L. T. Johnson, *First and Second Letters to Timothy*; and Philip H. Towner, *The Letters to Timothy and Titus*, NICNT [Grand Rapids: Eerdmans, 2006]). Although we reach different conclusions, D. A. Campbell's patience and discipline in this regard is notable (*Framing Paul*, 339-403). At the same time, both because they share considerable affinities with one another and for the sake of the economy of the discussion, I treat them more or less together in what follows, noting distinctions as necessary.

[61]For a representative sampling arguing against Pauline authorship, see the concise and classic argument of Martin Dibelius, *The Pastoral Epistles*, trans. Philip Buttolph, Hermeneia

three, although admittedly with each there are extensive subsets in the details:

Style and theology.[62] As with Colossians and Ephesians, stylistic and even theological differences seem to abound when compared to the undisputed letters, but the problem is compounded in that the idiom of the PE is different yet again from the disputed captivity epistles.[63]

Historical anachronisms. The distinctive plank in the pseudonymity platform with respect to the PE is historical. On the assumption that Paul did not survive his Roman imprisonment, it proves exceedingly difficult to work the biographical details and the circumstances of the recipients presupposed in the PE into Paul's life.[64] Moreover, many find church-historical elements in these letters that betray a postapostolic context.

Ambiguous reception. Also distinctive to the PE is the relatively scant, late and more ambiguous reception of these letters in the early Christian tradition.

Attempted rebuttals of the evidence are not hard to find, but this three-stranded cord is not easily broken. If the weight of the first family of arguments—stylistic and theological distinctiveness—relegates Colossians,

---

(Philadelphia: Fortress, 1972), 1-5; Raymond E. Brown, *An Introduction to the New Testament*, ABRL (New York: Doubleday, 1997), 662-70, who, however, is open to 2 Timothy (pp. 673-75); Jerome D. Quinn, "Timothy and Titus, Epistles to," *ABD* 6:560-71; Kümmel and Feine, *Introduction*, 370-84; Bart D. Ehrman, *The New Testament: A Historical Introduction to the Early Christian Writings*, 5th ed. (New York: Oxford University Press, 2012); idem, *Forgery and Counterforgery*, 192-217; and now D. A. Campbell, *Framing Paul*, 339-403.

Representative supporters of Pauline authenticity include L. T. Johnson, *First and Second Letters to Timothy*; idem, *Writings of the New Testament*; Carson and Moo, *Introduction*; William D. Mounce, *Pastoral Epistles*, WBC 46 (Nashville: Nelson, 2000); Towner, *Letters to Timothy and Titus*; and, regarding 2 Timothy, Michael Prior, *Paul the Letter-Writer, and the Second Letter to Timothy*, JSNTSup 23 (Sheffield: JSOT Press, 1989). I. Howard Marshall's "allonymity" proposal runs closely parallel to certain versions of authenticity (I. Howard Marshall and Philip H. Towner, *A Critical and Exegetical Commentary on the Pastoral Epistles*, ICC [Edinburgh: T&T Clark, 1999]; cf. Witherington's argument for Luke's hand in the composition of the Pastoral Epistles: Ben Witherington III, *Letters and Homilies for Hellenized Christians: A Socio-Rhetorical Commentary on Titus, 1-2 Timothy and 1-3 John* [Downers Grove, IL: InterVarsity Press, 2006], 56-62).

[62]Combining matters of "style," essentially linguistic data, with matters of "theology," matters of content, is perhaps no more arbitrary than separating the two, inasmuch as vocabulary and theology are not easily disentangled.

[63]Towner, *Letters to Timothy and Titus*, 24-25.

[64]On which, see Kümmel and Feine, *Introduction*, 375-82.

Ephesians and 2 Thessalonians to pseudonymous origins, how much more so do the further arguments of historical anachronism and ambiguous reception of the PE consign them to a different author, if not a different generation. Having already tested fate by arguing for the authenticity of Colossians and Ephesians, it is tempting to leave well enough alone and yield to the scholarly consensus that regards these letters as deutero-Pauline.[65] But that may be a conclusion too safe or premature—or too respectable?—or at least not required by the evidence, however resilient it might be. Instead, I wish not so much to "defend" the authenticity of these letters as to reconsider data frequently underestimated that, when given its due, problematizes the pseudonymity hypothesis.

5.4.1 Personal and occasional references. The personal and occasional references that saturate especially the conclusion of 2 Timothy and that are scattered throughout 1 Timothy and Titus require a satisfactory explanation. The ready explanation is that such references are nothing other than a pseudonymist's artifice calculated to charge the texts with verisimilitude. This, after all, is what pseudonymists do.[66] Except when they don't. While the lack of this sort of material makes Ephesians suspiciously detached, the abundance thereof shows 2 Timothy patently artificial. Heads I win; tails you lose. What of the fact that 1 Timothy and Titus have comparatively little of such material? At the least, it should be admitted that this is a flexible criterion. The fact that such judgments are employed toward skeptical ends does not exempt them from skeptical evaluation. Skepticism can also be naive or even hopeful in its own way. It cannot be doubted that pseudonymists were capable of the literary artifice even to the detail of personal notes, greetings and reminiscence, of the sort one finds in 2 Timothy. At the same time, that this material *should* be accounted as such requires more than the claim that pseudonymists *could* do such a thing in general. It gives pause that this is a falsifiable hypothesis only if the pseudonymist has shown his hand by errors and that such errors can only be exposed in such contexts where contradicting and indubitable sources are available. Failing that, we

---

[65]So, e.g., Wright, *P&FG*, 1:61, while holding on to the probable authenticity of 2 Timothy.

[66]Ehrman, *Forgery and Counterforgery*, 212 and nn. 34, 35. Cf. Donelson, *Pseudepigraphy and Ethical Argument in the Pastoral Epistles*, 23-42; and Brox, "Zu den persönlichen Notizen der Pastoralbriefe."

devolve into a stalemate: one scholar's marks of authenticity are another's sign of mischief.

In the end, there is no way through this impasse other than to assess the character of such personal references and the plausibility of their pseudonymous creation. In the case of 2 Timothy 4:9-21, for starters, the character of this material cautions against consigning it to pseudonymous deception. The persons mentioned are a curious mixture of those known from Paul's undisputed and disputed letters and Acts, including some of the more famous (at least multiply attested) characters of primitive Christianity and, with them, figures otherwise entirely unattested.[67] Seventeen persons are named in this passage, of which eight are otherwise unknown.[68] Although certain names overlap with other letters and Acts, there is only partial overlap with any particular letter and no parallel sequences, and it would be difficult to demonstrate any lines of literary dependence, even if this is sometimes asserted.[69] Although certain of Paul's companions in Philemon

---

[67]Among the more multiply attested are Titus (2 Cor 2:13; 7:6, 13, 14; 8:6, 16, 23; 12:18; Gal 2:1, 3; cf. Tit 1:4), Prisc[ill]a and Aquila (Acts 18:2, 18, 26; Rom 16:3; 1 Cor 16:19), and Erastus (Acts 19:22; Rom 16:23). Among the known figures, two are otherwise known only from Philemon and Colossians: Demas and Luke (Philem 24; Col 4:14), but the former has now "forsaken" Paul, while Luke is his sole companion. Mark is also known from Philemon (Philem 24) and Colossians (Col 4:10), but, assuming this is meant to be the same Mark as "John Mark" of Acts (Acts 12:12, 25; 15:37, 39), he is an otherwise attested figure. Trophimus is a figure otherwise referenced only in Acts (Acts 20:4; 21:29).

[68]Crescens (2 Tim 4:10), Carpus (2 Tim 4:13), Alexander the metalworker (2 Tim 4:14; assuming, as seems probable, he is not the Alexander of 1 Tim 1:20 or Acts 19:33), the household of Onesiphorus (2 Tim 4:19; cf. 1:16), Eubulus, Pudens, Linus and Claudia (2 Tim 4:21).

[69]Contra D. A. Campbell, *Framing Paul*, 372-74. But Campbell's suspicion that the pseudonymist has used Colossians 4:7-14 as a source for personalia is unconvincing; in fact, his attempt to demonstrate the case serves the present argument rather well. Campbell discerns that there should be a considerable temporal distance between 2 Timothy (were it authentic) and Colossians, which, according to his reconstruction is written from Pisidian Apamea at least a decade earlier. Nonetheless, he considers it plausible that Timothy, Titus, Tychicus and Crescens could still be intimately tied to Paul at this later date in Rome but finds the presence of Luke and Demas in both Apamea and Rome "stretches credulity," although we are not told why (ibid., 373). He also wonders why we would have never heard of Crescens until this point if he were a Galatian. Leaving aside whether there is any good reason to believe that Crescens was a Galatian (was Demas of Thessalonica or Titus any more of Dalmatia than of Crete?), there is at least some irony that the introduction of an otherwise unknown figure arouses the same sort of suspicion as does the reference to previously attested figures. Ultimately, it is the near collocation of these figures in Colossians 4:7-14 and 2 Timothy 4:10-12 that catches Campbell's attention. But, again, the partiality of overlap between the two, the lack of parallel sequencing, the interspersion of new figures and the gratuitous disappointing failure of a coworker (Demas) all point away from literary dependence. There is a simpler explanation: that both Colossians and 2 Timothy were written from Rome, near the end of Paul's career and life, respectively, and thus a partial overlap

and Colossians—Demas, Luke, Mark and Tychicus—are all mentioned here, "missing" are Aristarchus, Epaphras and Jesus Justus. Moreover, the four who make an appearance here are now clearly differentiated. Demas has gone bad: "loving this present age," he has abandoned the prisoner Paul for Thessalonica.[70] Now Luke is Paul's sole companion, and Paul wishes to have Timothy bring Mark to see him. Meanwhile, Paul himself has sent Tychicus to Ephesus. Attempts to read this as evidence of literary dependence are unpersuasive.[71] The ad hoc character of the whole section smacks of spontaneity more than calculation.

Likewise, the character of Paul drawn from this material is complex—rounded and uneven. His pleas evoke pathos—indeed, sympathy—and a kind of admiration for one who has fought to the bitter end (2 Tim 4:7) and for the fact that the end was bitter. Loneliness is apparent. The personal section is bracketed with nearly the same appeal: "Do your best [*spoudason*] to come to me soon" (2 Tim 4:9 RSV). "Do your best [*spoudason*] to come before winter" (2 Tim 4:21 RSV). The pathetic appeal for the cloak left with Carpus on Troas and for the scrolls (*ta biblia*) and "above all the parchments" (2 Tim 4:13 RSV) not only inspires some speculation;[72] it depicts a man gathering but a few prized possessions to himself for his final chapter. These are nice touches, if they are that. But if this picture of the hero of the letter evokes sympathy, he is notably unheroic in other respects. It is impossible to know how literally to take Paul's rescue "from the lion's mouth" (2 Tim 4:17 RSV; cf. 1 Cor 15:32, "wild beasts at Ephesus"), but it is hardly hagiography when Paul confesses that Trophimus was in ill health when he left him behind on Miletus.[73] After all, the Paul of Acts demonstrated extraordinary

---

of key mission personnel would be expected.

[70]It is not clear why Campbell regards not only Demas but also Crescens and Titus as deserters (ibid., 373, 384). Only Demas is said to have "deserted" (ἐγκατέλιπεν) and to "love this present age" (ἀγαπήσας τὸν νῦν αἰῶνα), and grammatically, Κρήσκης εἰς Γαλατίαν and Τίτος εἰς Δαλματίαν are obviously dependent on the verb ἐπορεύθη, which implies nothing about desertion. Thus, whatever the merits of the larger argument, Campbell's attempt to link this (fictional) account of "division and desertion" to the Marcionite crisis is unpersuasive.

[71]Somewhat credulously, Ehrman takes this as evidence of the pseudonymist's dependence on (the presumed pseunonymous) Ephesians 6:21-22 (*Forgery and Counterforgery*, 217), even though, as we have seen, there is no evidence that any early copy of "Ephesians" depicts Tychicus delivering that letter to Ephesus.

[72]On which, see Harry Y. Gamble, *Books and Readers in the Early Church: A History of Early Christian Texts* (New Haven, CT: Yale University Press, 1995).

[73]It is notable that Trophimus is the direct object of a transitive verb, ἀπολείπω. Paul didn't depart

healing powers, not least in Ephesus (Acts 19:11-12), and the same for the Paul of later legend (e.g., Acts of Paul and Thecla, where his intercessions from a distance delivered Thecla from flames). But the Paul of 2 Timothy is human, vulnerable—and while admirably persevering, also testy. Besides his disparagement of Demas, Paul warns against his active antagonist, Alexander, the metalworker who did him "great harm" (*polla kaka*, "many evils"), and wishes the Lord's just requital upon him (2 Tim 4:14-15 RSV). At the same time, he hopes for mercy on those associated Christians who deserted him and failed to come to his aid in his "first defense" (2 Tim 4:16 RSV). Whether offering forgiveness or not, in his final days he remembers and draws attention to those who had done him wrong.

Although we find nothing else like this passage, dense with personal references in PE, such specific allusions are not entirely absent elsewhere. The nearest example is the conclusion to Titus (3:12-15), where we have four personal references: Paul will send Artemas or Tychicus to Crete, perhaps freeing Titus to meet Paul in Nicopolis while he winters there. And Titus is to send Zenas the lawyer and Apollos on their way, perhaps to Paul, though their destination is uncertain. Again, the unselfconscious mixture of well-known (Apollos and Tychicus) and unknown characters (Artemas and Zenas) is notable. Meanwhile, 1 Timothy lacks these kind of concluding personal references altogether, although the letter makes an early reference to Hymenaeus and Alexander, who have shipwrecked their faith, though apparently not irredeemably, since Paul has "handed [them] over to Satan that they may learn not to blaspheme" (1 Tim 1:19-20; cf. 2 Tim 2:17, which censures Philetus along with Hymenaeus). Thus, the evidence from the three letters taken together is intriguing, if inconclusive. If the purpose of the material in 2 Timothy 4:9-21 is to camouflage the pseudepigraphon with pathos and realism (really, what else could it be, if the letter is pseudonymous?), it could be asked why virtually no effort was made toward these ends in the case of 1 Timothy. Even should one argue that 2 Timothy engages in excess so as to supply an end-of-life scenario, why not at least employ the more modest approach of Titus? This could indeed be grounds for distinguishing the authenticity of 2 Timothy from its counterparts, but the

---

from Trophimus but left him in his sickly condition, with the possible implication that he may otherwise have traveled with Paul.

presence and absence of personal material will always be a two-edged sword for the pseudonymity theory. While it is granted that authenticity cannot be demonstrated by these sorts of personal references, both their presence and their relative absence are better accounted for by the assumption of authenticity than any competing explanation.

5.4.2 Second-century evidence, especially ecclesial order. On the whole, the evidence of the second century is thought to count against the authenticity of PE. Notorious in this regard is the rejection of the letters from Marcion's canon, the absence of the PE from late-second-century papyrus $\mathfrak{p}^{46}$, and the late or contested acceptance into the church's canon. The arguments are well rehearsed elsewhere, but not nearly as decisive as sometimes supposed.[74] In particular, the evidence of Marcion's rejection is an interesting datum, but inconclusive, given that we cannot know why he rejected these letters, and it goes without saying that Marcion's failure to count a text as "canonical" cannot imply that he is unaware of the text.[75] Not surprisingly, our source, Tertullian (*Marc.* 5.21), insinuates that Marcion rejects these letters because they have to do with the theme of ecclesiastical discipline, which is at least a plausible surmise.[76] But if Tertullian knows that Marcion did *reject* (*recusaverit*) them, it follows that he must have known them, requiring a dating early enough for their broad dissemination.[77] Likewise, the absence from $\mathfrak{p}^{46}$ must be regarded as ambiguous evidence at best. Indeed, several considerations are enough to safely set this datum aside: (1) the only other Pauline letter to an individual, the indubitably authentic Philemon, is also excluded; (2) Hebrews, of dubitable Pauline origins, to say the least, *is* included; and (3) even with the final seven

---

[74]On the early attestation of the letters, see J. H. Bernard, *The Pastoral Epistles* (Grand Rapids: Baker Books, 1980), xi-xxi; Ceslas Spicq, *Saint Paul: Les Épîtres pastorales* (Paris: Gabalda, 1947), xcv-ci; L. T. Johnson, *First and Second Letters to Timothy*, 20-26, 84-85; Towner, *Letters to Timothy and Titus*, 3-7; and esp. the comprehensive list in Mounce, *Pastoral Epistles*, lxiv-lxix. Both Johnson and Towner regard the possible allusions in Ignatius and the Epistle of Barnabas to be uncertain (L. T. Johnson, *First and Second Letters to Timothy*, 20n16; and Towner, *Letters to Timothy and Titus*, 4n6).

[75]Contra Helmut Koester, *Introduction to the New Testament: Literature and History*, 2nd ed. (New York: de Gruyter, 1995), 2:301, 334.

[76]A more particular reason for Marcion's rejection of the letters might be found in the specific language of 1 Timothy 6:20-21, which, indeed, some scholars count as an argument for a late, anti-Marcionite origin of the letters (see D. A. Campbell, *Framing Paul*, 364-66).

[77]L. T. Johnson, *First and Second Letters to Timothy*, 85.

missing leaves, the codex was never long enough to have included the PE at the end.

Not only are some of the appeals to second-century evidence inconclusive; some even backfire upon closer examination. It is frequently argued that the ecclesial order of the PE reflects the circumstances of the second-century churches, but the evidence actually points in the opposite direction. Although the PE make reference to (the names of) three "offices," the *episkopos* (bishop, overseer; 1 Tim 3:1 [*episkopē*], 2; Tit 1:7), *presbyteros* (presbyter, elder; 1 Tim 5:1, 17, 19; Tit 1:5) and *diakonos* (deacon; 1 Tim 3:8, 12; 4:16), this cannot be confused for the clear threefold office with a monarchical episcopate to which Ignatius (d. AD 107) attests so frequently. Upon closer examination, it is evident that in the PE, *episkopos* and *presbyteros* are two descriptors for the same function, or at least overlapping descriptions of the same persons.[78] This is probable, for example, in Titus 1:5-7, where "elders" are to be appointed in every town (Tit 1:5), whose qualifications are further described under the descriptor "overseer" or "bishop" (*episkopos*, Tit 1:7). The fact that a very similar, though more extensive, list of qualifications is given for the office of the *episkopē* in 1 Timothy 3:1-7 and yet the *presbyteros* is understood to lead or govern the affairs of the church later in the same letter (1 Tim 5:17) is further evidence that the terms are used interchangeably.[79] Acts witnesses to this same pattern when Paul addresses the

---

[78]For the latter position, see now Alistair C. Stewart, *The Original Bishops: Office and Order in the First Christian Communities* (Grand Rapids: Baker Academic, 2014).

[79]This was the consensus of New Testament scholarship until Stewart's recent work; see, e.g., Towner, *Letters to Timothy and Titus*, 241-47; and Raymond E. Brown, "Episkope and Episkopos: The New Testament Evidence," *TS* 41, no. 2 (1980): 322-38. The classic study is J. B. Lightfoot, *The Christian Ministry* (New York: Whittaker, 1878), originally published as idem, *Saint Paul's Epistle to the Philippians: A Revised Text with Introduction, Notes, and Dissertations*, 2nd ed. (London: Macmillan, 1868), 179-267. Stewart argues, to the contrary, that *episkopos* originally designates only the singular leader of a Christian congregation (house church) while *presbyteros* describes those same leaders but in their aggregation as a collective leadership of metropolitan or regional churches. Thus, the same persons may be described by the two terms, but the terms themselves are not synonymous. The transition, then, to a *monepiskopos* (or "monarchical bishop") is not a separation in function of the previous twice-named but singular function but is a natural development from the original singularity of the *episkopos*. It remains to be seen whether Stewart's extensive argument will overturn that consensus. There is no direct bearing on the circumstantial arugment offered here other than that I am describing the transition to the monarchical episcopate in different terms. Of Stewart's thesis I remain open but unpersuaded. I suggest rather that, if a significance attaches to the two descriptors of the same persons, it may simply be that the *presbyteros* refers to the person as such and *episkopē/episkopos* to the office or function of oversight.

Ephesian *presbyteroi* (Acts 20:17) as *episkopoi* (Acts 20:28), clearly describing the same group of people. Far from betraying an early second-century setting, this usage of the key terminology decisively links the PE to the apostolic era and, indeed, to Paul's undisputed writings.[80] Only once, in the address of Philippians 1:1, do the undisputed letters give a hint about ecclesial "offices," but it is "with the *overseers* and *deacons*" (*syn episkopois kai diakonois*). Philippians thus points to a twofold office and the PE to the same, albeit with much more interest in the qualifications of those who serve.

The oft-repeated claim that the undisputed letters depict a fluid, charismatic ministry rooted in Spirit-endowed *charismata*, in contrast to the PE's supposed rigid institutionalism and structured hierarchy is an unhelpful caricature.[81] Although it is frequently seen as an anachronism reflecting the circumstances of the later church, the appointment of *presbyteroi* in Lystra, Iconium and (Pisidian) Antioch upon Paul and Barnabas's return visit may just as well reflect a standard procedure (Acts 14:23). Even among the earliest of Paul's letters, there are already clear indications of identifiable leaders. In what many regard as Paul's earliest (and everyone as *among* his earliest) letter, he enjoins the Thessalonians "to respect those who labor among you, and have charge of you in the Lord and admonish you; esteem them very highly in love because of their work" (1 Thess 5:12-13 NRSV). It should not go without notice that, almost by anyone's chronology, this is written to a *very* recently founded church, that compliance to the request requires that the leaders be distinguished and identifiable,[82] and that the description of the leaders as *proïstamenoi* is the same language used repeatedly in 1 Timothy

---

[80]It might justly be said that Timothy and Titus are depicted in functions not unlike what would become a monarchical episcopate, but the very fact that such a function is unattached to the title *episkopos* marks that ministry as transitional from the apostolate to the episcopate. It is hard to avoid the impression that historians of early Christian ecclesiology find it difficult to resist value judgments, especially as it concerns church order. For those who regard "early Catholicism" (*Frühkatholizismus*) as a declination from something not just earlier but intrinsically healthier and more authentic, hints of an emerging episcopate serve as a sign of the second-century church structure. One detects a similar impulse from the opposite end of the critical spectrum when Mounce effectively quarantines Paul from any hint of an episcopate bearing any resemblance to Ignatius, consistently casting the latter in the most unsympathetic terms possible (Mounce, *Pastoral Epistles*, e.g., 186-92).

[81]So, e.g., Ehrman, *Forgery and Counterforgery*, e.g., 203-5, who finds the charismatic-to-institutionalized narrative patent and uncomplicated.

[82]The verb translated "respect," εἰδέναι (from οἶδα), indicates naturally that they identified and distinguished leaders for the work.

of those holding ecclesial "office" (1 Tim 3:4, 5, 12; 5:17; cf. Rom 12:8). Likewise, in 1 Corinthians, the very letter frequently appealed to for an alleged "charismatic" model of leadership, the "household of Stephanas" is set forward as an example among others ("every colaborer and hard worker") of the sort of persons to whom the Corinthians should subject (*hypotassō*) themselves (1 Cor 16:15-16). And, for that matter, perhaps because it is inconvenient for the "early-catholicism" (*Frühkatholizismus*) narrative of degeneration, the pneumatic dimensions of the PE are too frequently overlooked. It was by "prophetic utterances" (*prophēteia*) that Timothy was either identified or ordained for his role (1 Tim 1:18; 4:14).

While it is true that only Philippians 1:1 describes a twofold office that the later PE simply assume, that datum remains extremely significant, for it is the only circumstance in which Paul makes mention of church order by means of offices, and, as discussed, it coheres precisely with the PE. That the picture of the PE coheres more nearly with the undisputed Paulines, albeit with greater emphasis and specificity, over against the obvious developments in the ecclesial structures of the early second century, positions the PE as a middle term in the development of ecclesiastical structure. The imminent passing of the apostolic generation is itself a sufficient explanation for the increasing codification of offices. Of course, this does not confirm the Pauline authorship of the PE, but this evidence corroborates such a conclusion, while chastening an oft-repeated argument on behalf of pseudonymity.

5.4.3 Life after Rome, but without Spain. The end of Paul's life is shrouded in mystery exacerbated by the scant and uncertain testimony. The Pauline authorship of the PE is frequently assumed impossible on the grounds that the itinerary the letters presuppose cannot be accommodated within the biography of Paul's pre-Roman imprisonment, on the one hand, and because it is held as certain that Paul did not survive that incarceration, on the other. The confidence with which especially the latter is asserted is a bit surprising given the sparse data available to us. If we exclude the PE as any kind of evidence, pseudonymous or otherwise, it remains the case that no ancient source confirms that scenario, and several imply his survival of a "first" Roman imprisonment.[83] Furthermore, if Philippians is dated to the

---

[83]The most important bit of evidence, 1 Clement 5:1-7, is unfortunately ambiguous, accommodating a variety of scenarios (see the discussions of F. F. Bruce, *Paul, Apostle of the Heart Set Free* [Grand

Roman imprisonment, on balance there are indications of optimism that he expects his soon release (Phil 1:25-26; 2:24, although 1:27; 2:17); and Philemon witnesses to the same confidence without qualification (Philem 22). An argument against authenticity that depends on Paul not surviving his "first" Roman imprisonment depends too much on an uncertainty, if not an unlikelihood.

Although it could be counted as something like an argument from silence, on closer examination, the fact that the PE give no hint of a Spanish mission must surely count against the pseudonymity theory. *Every* postapostolic source that comments on the end of Paul's life places his martyrdom in the period of the Neronian persecution, and every source that ventures a surmise implies or states that he fulfilled his intention of a mission to Spain (Rom 15:24, 28).[84] But the PE have no hint of a mission to Spain. It could be expected that a pseudonymist who had set Paul's biography to rhetorical use might have made the most not only of the first chapter (cf. 1 Tim 1:11-16) but also of the last, extrapolating a victorious Spanish mission from the clues provided by Romans, as was the custom of Paul's earliest hagiographers. It might have been regarded as something of an embarrassment that Paul's crowning achievement was left unaccomplished, and this may well be the motivation for the consistent but muted second-century testimony that Paul had in fact fulfilled his promise. Yet, the evidence of Philippians, Philemon (if a Roman provenance is allowed), Colossians and the PE (if authentic) is that, with the unanticipated circumstances of his Roman sojourn, Paul had turned his attention entirely eastward. Paul had always been at once a pioneering missioner and a problem-solving pastor, and it appears that the

---

Rapids: Eerdmans, 1977], 446-48; and Jerome Murphy-O'Connor, *Paul: A Critical Life* [Oxford: Oxford University Press, 1997], 361), especially his much-disputed reference to the "farthest limits of the west" (τὸ τέρμα τῆς δύσεως; 1 Clem. 5:7). On balance, it seems a loose allusion to a Spanish mission; that Clement is writing from Rome makes Rome an unlikely referent.

The evidence of Acts is especially inconclusive. While it is true that had the author known of Paul's acquittal and release, it appears strange to us that he did not record it, it is also true that Paul's martyrdom could have served his literary purposes equally well (cf. Stephen, James of Zebedee). Nothing can be inferred from the ending of Acts. Likewise, Paul's disregard for his life (Acts 20:24-25) and the anticipatory sorrow of the Ephesian elders (Acts 20:38) are simply too ambiguous to count as evidence for an early Roman martyrdom.

[84]The sources are three: (1) depending of course on how it is read, 1 Clement 5:5-7 implies it; (2) the apocryphal Acts of Peter assumes Paul's mission to Spain (lines 1-3, 40); and (3) the Muratorian Fragment references a journey to Spain explicitly (line 39).

latter impulse may quite understandably have overtaken the former on the other side of his near-death experience. In any case, it must be regarded as incidentally significant that the author(s) of the PE attempted neither to retrace Paul's earlier itineraries so as to create a historically familiar scenario nor to exploit the heroic potential of a Spanish mission as a fitting tribute to the author. That no hint of this is found should be counted as evidence for the historicity and, thus indirectly, the authenticity of the letters.

There can be no final verdict as it concerns the PE. Second Timothy is making an authenticity "comeback" of sorts, and arguments on behalf of the three letters as akin to a corpus, or at least an interrelated set, continue to prove compelling.[85] Admittedly, the arguments that distinguish 2 Timothy from its counterparts in defense of its authenticity alone are not meant to combine with those arguing for the commonality of the three, but, on balance, these letters clearly have more in common with each other than any one of them shares with an undisputed letter.

5.5 What If "Disputed" Is Really "Deutero-"?

In the nature of the case, the preceding arguments concerning chronology and, especially, authenticity will fall short of convincing some, perhaps even many, readers. In the realm of critical New Testament scholarship, I am filing a minority report—or maybe this is an "innocence project." On the other hand, some readers needed no convincing, especially those under the influence of conservative evangelical scholarship, which frequently follows the contours outlined in this chapter, if not always for the same reasons.[86] It remains to ask what becomes of the larger argument if the foregoing is found unpersuasive. To what extent does the overall argument depend on the authenticity of the disputed letters or, for that matter, the proposed chronology of the undisputed? While much could be said, three points will suffice.

At the very least, if deutero-Pauline, these letters are, almost by definition, later than the authentic counterparts. Thus, they still mark a trajectory of some kind though now, of course, not Paul's per se but that of the Pauline

---

[85]So, recently, Ehrman, *Forgery and Counterforgery*, 191-201, using 2 Timothy as the middle term.
[86]Although I make certain of the arguments differently, the positions argued here are largely consistent with two of the more influential conservative, evangelical New Testament introductions: Donald Guthrie, *New Testament Introduction*, 4th ed. (Downers Grove, IL: InterVarsity Press, 1990); and Carson and Moo, *Introduction*.

tradition. There is still, then, a question of development, but it is, to be fair, a rather different phenomenon than the development of a single figure within the course of his own life. On the premise of a restricted, authentic Pauline corpus (whether it be seven or ten letters), we should then say that the earliest interpretive performances of the "historical Paul" discern a certain soteriology in the apostle's writings and that there is a marked similarity in their appropriation of the authentic Paul. This is a datum of no small significance.

It is tempting at this juncture to appeal to a "canonical Paul" as a noncontroversial and even theologically elegant way to elide the impasse of historical criticism. In all candor, I have even tried to talk myself into this expedient but without success; it would save one from so many worries. Of course, to the extent that these texts are the privileged and constitutive texts of the faith of the Christian church, their actual historical authorship is not immediately relevant with respect to their canonical authority. And, to be sure, there is a proper sense in which one could construct an "implied author," a text-connoted author, from the Pauline corpus and leave well enough alone. By some accounts of pseudonymity—those that regard it as an honest fiction—it could be argued that this is exactly the *right* way to read the Pauline corpus.[87] It may indeed be a right way, but to advert to this strategy *for the purposes of this study* is essentially to change conversations midsentence.[88] It is to give a reception-historical, ecclesial answer to a conversation that had been about a historical figure, his writings, his thought. And once the move to the Pauline tradition is made, it becomes increasingly arbitrary to privilege the writings that belong to the Christian canon, irrespective of authorship or, for that matter, to set aside Hebrews, respective of authorship. The only way forward, if we are to have *this* conversation and with these colleagues, is to continue down the historical-critical road (recently) more traveled.

---

[87]The canonical Paul gains significant momentum from Brevard S. Childs, *The Church's Guide for Reading Paul: The Canonical Shaping of the Pauline Corpus* (Grand Rapids: Eerdmans, 2008).

[88]Although I am entirely sympathetic, I do not find C. R. Campbell's appeal to a canonical Paul convincing (Constantine R. Campbell, *Paul and Union with Christ: An Exegetical and Theological Study* [Grand Rapids: Eerdmans, 2012], 27-28), especially for a study that is located in the linguistic particularities of the Pauline corpus. It simply smacks too much of expediency to prescind from the question of authenticity when the arguments of the study depend upon lexical and grammatical choices of what is treated as a single voice.

At the same time, even on the condition of pseudonymity, there remains something important to be said about the contribution of deutero-Pauline epistles to the question at hand. By almost every account, whether regarded as forgery or innocent homage, these letters intend to carry on the Pauline tradition, to be its reapplication to new challenges and circumstances, perhaps even to say what the apostle would have were he in a circumstance to do so. This general intent seems beyond question in the elaborate auto-biographical material found as a standard feature of these letters.[89] Yet this also means that these letters cannot be facilely set aside on the presumption of their pseudonymity, as so often happens. Any truly *historical* account of Paul's theology would need to reckon seriously with *Pauline* theology in full compass, if nothing else than as an element of its reception-history or its *Wirkungsgeschichte*.[90] It must therefore be a matter of greatest consequence to ascertain how Paul's most immediate and loyal successors understood him. Demonstration of pseudonymity does not set texts aside as automatically irrelevant for the project of Pauline theology; rather, it reassigns them as a different sort of data to a related task, effectively becoming the earliest, albeit accidental, commentary on the undisputed Pauline epistles. It is not inconsequential how, say, Ephesians works out a Pauline soteriology or Colossians eschatology or the PE ecclesiology or church order.

The relevance of this observation for our purposes should be fairly obvious. At least one index on the direction of Paul's soteriology, if it is not later Paul himself, must be the earliest tradents of the Pauline tradition. We are not therefore required to identify *their* meaning as Paul's, but we are obliged to inquire how and why they might have understood Paul in a particular way. And while it has been the stock and trade of historical criticism to distinguish the authentic Paul from his successors, the genuine from the derived, the claim that the pseudonymous theological vision is derivative has not

---

[89]E.g., Ephesians 3:1-21; Colossians 1:24–2:5; 1 Timothy 1:11-16; 2 Timothy, passim.

[90]Reception-history and *Wirkungsgeschichte* (effective-history) are overlapping topics of considerable interest in recent biblical studies, especially with respect to the burgeoning movement of "theological interpretation," in which, following Hans-Georg Gadamer (*Truth and Method* [New York: Seabury Press, 1975]), the text's reception and effective conditioning of readers is considered a necessary dimension of a text's interperetation. See, e.g., Michael Lieb, Emma Mason, Jonathan Roberts and Christopher Rowland, eds., *The Oxford Handbook of the Reception History of the Bible*, Oxford Handbooks in Religion and Theology (Oxford: Oxford University Press, 2011).

been taken seriously enough. If, indeed, we are to regard it as *derivative* and not merely later or secondary, the theological particulars function not merely as the data harnessed for historical-critical judgments but in some arguable continuity with its inspiration. This effectively subverts—or at least substantially qualifies—the claim that such material can be simply counted as "un-Pauline" in some simplistic way and dispensed of in the pursuit of "Pauline theology." Rather, the burden of proof is shifted to the assumption that his followers have left an authentic Paul behind in pursuing their new agendas irrespective of the apostle's own trajectory. This is not to ignore, or even less to disclaim, apparent breaches between authentic and deutero-Paul (or early and late, as the case may be) but simply to be held accountable to consider and explore organic trajectories when they might present themselves. Thus, although an extended, but still too brief, case has been made for the authenticity of certain letters, the argument that follows does not strictly require assent to those judgments to retain its integrity.

In what follows, I will appeal to, indeed assume, the corpus and chronology here argued, not because I consider it to have been established in the foregoing, but as a matter of expedience going forward. I will not track developmental trajectories of competing views regarding authenticity or chronology, even though it could be interesting to do so, nor continue to argue the matters of critical introduction. It would simply prove too unwieldy. I am persuaded, having reached the critical positions that I've articulated in this chapter independent of any "developmental hypothesis," that the trajectories that derive from the foregoing function as a secondary corroboration, acknowledging the inherent precariousness of such arguments. The purpose of these exercises in biblical criticism was never that they be ends to themselves, but that these would be prolegomena for the actual constructive argument, to which we now turn.

Table 5.3. Timeline of Paul's life

Event	Probable Date	Acts	Epistles
Birth	AD 5–10	Acts 7:58, a "young man"	Phil 3:5; Philem 24, "an old man"
Study under Gamaliel	15–20	Acts 22:3	
Conversion/Call	33	Acts 9:1-22	Gal 1:15-16

Ministry in Damascus and Arabia	33–35		Gal 1:17
Escape from Damascus; first visit to Jerusalem	35	Acts 9:23-30	2 Cor 11:32-33; Gal 1:18-19
In Syria and Cilicia	35–45	cf. Acts 9:30; 11:25	Gal 1:21
Ministry in Antioch	45–46	Acts 11:25-26	
Second Jerusalem visit ("famine relief")	46	Acts 11:27-30	[Gal 2:1-10]
First missionary journey (Cyprus and Galatia)	47–48	Acts 13:1–14:26	
Stay in Antioch (incident with Peter) *Galatians* (if S. Galatia hypothesis)	48–49	Acts 14:27-28	Gal 2:11-14
Jerusalem Council	49	Acts 15:1-29	[Gal 2:1-10]
Second missionary journey (until Corinth)	49–51	Acts 15:40–17:34	
Stay in Corinth *1 & 2 Thessalonians*	51–52	Acts 18:1-18	1 Cor 2:1-5
Third Jerusalem visit and departure for third missionary journey	52	Acts 18:18-23	
Stay in Ephesus *1 & 2 Corinthians* [Galatians if N. Galatia hypothesis]	52–55	Acts 19:1–20:1	1 Cor 16:8
Macedonia and Greece; winter in Corinth *Romans*	56–57	Acts 20:2-3	1 Cor 16:5; Rom 16:1
Final Jerusalem visit	Spring 57	Acts 21:7	Rom 15:25-32
Imprisonment in Caesarea	57–59	Acts 23:23–26:32	
Voyage to Rome	59–60	Acts 27:1–28:14a	
Under house arrest in Rome *Colossians-Philemon, Ephesians, Philippians*	60–62	Acts 28:16, 30-31	
Further travels (Asia Minor? Macedonia? visit to Spain?) *Pastoral Epistles*	62–65?		
Death of Paul in Rome	65–67?		

Markers of the Itinerary 1

Works and Grace

W e turn now to the constructive proposal the preceding has been inviting and for which it has been preparing. I have demonstrated that the impasse and sometimes polarization of NPP and TPP construals of Paul's soteriology are the result of a view of Paul too narrowly focused. The NPP has restored to us the dynamics of the earliest Gentile mission through the lens of the Galatian crisis of ethnic cultural distinction and has interpreted that letter in a particular way, carrying those insights throughout the Pauline corpus (or that corpus limited to the letters deemed authentic). The TPP that engages the NPP responsibly acknowledges the NPP's insights but finds swaths of Pauline testimony unaccounted for, especially that having to do with the gratuity of salvation over against human accomplishment.

Both "parties" share three tendencies: (1) whether as a matter of critical conviction or guild expediency, to engage these questions largely, if not exclusively, through the undisputed letters; (2) to read Paul (however the corpus is delimited) essentially synchronically, that is, with his letters proving to be mutually informing, but without significant attention to their chronology and life settings;[1] and (3) to read that whole, whether consciously or unconsciously, through a lens by which the dynamics of one letter (or one part of a letter) or one motif has an implicitly controlling influence over the reading of the rest. Admittedly, I've painted with a broad brush—numerous exceptions could be noted—but as a sketch of the prevailing approaches, I

---

[1]The best example is perhaps N. T. Wright, *P&FG*, who proves so deft in doing so that one scarcely notices how controlling Wright's own synthesis becomes in the course of its frequent repetition.

don't believe the picture is inaccurate. These are the scholarly tendencies that, in this and the following chapters, I will push against by tracing trajectories of Pauline use and thought with the critical judgments of the preceding chapters in play. I propose that a set of overlapping and corroborating patterns of usage point to a traceable development of Pauline soteriology from its earliest ad hoc, exigent expression to its later principled articulation.

6.1 From "Works of the Law" to "Works"

Perhaps the clearest path into the argument that follows will be to observe Paul's use of "works" language for the pattern it reveals when traced across his corpus. As is well known, the original insights of the NPP were forged substantially with respect to the phrase "works of the law" (*erga nomou*), especially, of course, in Galatians, where it is found six times (Gal 2:16 [3x]; 3:2, 5, 10) and where the phrase and correlates play a critical role in the central argument of the letter. Besides Galatians, the phrase is found only twice in Romans (3:20, 28) and then never again in the remainder of the Pauline corpus.[2] Moreover, in Galatians Paul speaks *only* of "works of the law" and never of "works," that is, within the context of soteriological argument.[3] He uses both expressions in Romans, but with a preponderance of references to "works" alone, and following Romans he only refers to "works" absolutely and never again "works of the law" in any context. Beginning with Romans, and for the first time in Paul's corpus, "works" are repeatedly disclaimed as the ground of eschatological righteousness, a theme carried through the Captivity Epistles and reasserted emphatically in two passages from the PE. Meanwhile, emerging in the Captivity Epistles and ubiquitous in the PE is the favorable commendation of "*good* works" (*agatha* or *kala erga*, on which, see below, section 8.2.3). Paul's use of "works" and "works of the law" can be seen in table 6.1 below.[4]

---

[2] For now, I leave aside Romans 2:15, "the [sg.] *work* of the law," although that text is not insignificant for our larger discussion.

[3] Paul does, of course, speak of the "*works* of the flesh" in Galatians 5:19 and "each person test[ing] his own work" in Galatians 6:4. Admittedly, the use of "works" in Galatians 5:19 probably has a polemical edge, being set against the "fruit [sg.] of the Spirit" in Galatians 5:22, so perhaps in some general way there is some wry diminution of "works." Nonetheless, there is no disparagement or disavowal of "works" as a means of justification such as one finds with the six references to "works of the law."

[4] Another relevant category, examined later, is the commendation of "good works" (see table 8.2).

ɔrks" in Paul

	Galatians	Thessalonian and Corinthian Correspondences	Romans	Captivity Epistles	Pastoral Epistles
"works of the law" disclaimed for justification/ salvation	6x: Gal 2:16 [3x]; 3:2, 5, 10		2x: Rom 3:20, 28 [cf. 2:15]		
"works" disclaimed for justification/ salvation			6x: Rom 3:27; 4:2, 6; 9:12, 32; 11:6 (cf. 9:11)	1x: Eph 2:9	2x: Tit 3:5; 2 Tim 1:9
"works" as basis of judgment		1x: 2 Cor 11:15 (cf. 5:10)	3x: Rom 2:6, 7, 15	1x: Col 1:21	1x: 2 Tim 4:14

I propose that this pattern of use, from "works of the law" to the un-qualified "works," reflects a pattern of development in Paul's conception of the matters at hand, from a soteriology originally grounded in the dilemma of Gentile inclusion to a more formal rejection of human attainment as the antithesis of grace. In this development, Romans marks the overlap of these concerns, neither of which can be subsumed under the other. Although it points in this direction, merely tracking the occurrence of terms cannot demonstrate these claims; their use and force must be ascertained in their argumentative contexts. It particular, it will be necessary to show that Paul's use of "works" is not, contra the NPP, shorthand for "works of the law" and that, contra most TPP interpreters, "works of the law" is not a synecdoche for "works" more generally.[5] Both positions are mistaken in choosing one expression to determine the other, but to make the case it will be necessary to survey usage, according to my chronology, beginning with Galatians.

6.1.1 "Works of the Law" in Galatians. For our purposes, enough has been said about the "works of the law" (*erga nomou*) debate by way of introduction above.[6] In short, *with respect to Galatians,* I accept the substantially chastened

---

[5]"Synecdoche" is Moo's helpful way of describing the Reformers' (and his) understanding of "works of the law" in relationship to "works" (Douglas J. Moo, *Galatians,* BECNT [Grand Rapids: Baker Academic, 2013], 176).

[6]Going forward, I will frequently use the transliteration of the Greek, *erga nomou,* not to be effete but as a reminder that we are considering a specific phrase that has an idiomatic cast—and it spares the reader of endless quotation marks. When taken as an idiom, I conjugate it with singular verbs; otherwise I conjugate *erga* as plural.

version of Dunn's claims: that *erga nomou* is not *in Galatians* a generalized denunciation of autosoterism but the correction of a definition of covenant membership on the terms of ethnic and cultural particularity.[7] This is not a claim that "works of law" functions as a technical term for a limited subset of Jewish boundary markers—circumcision, kosher laws and calendrical observance. Rather, *erga nomou* refers more generally to the practices that the law expects and requires. The evidence does not support a narrower referent than this, but it does not follow that the genitive modifier *nomou* is merely incidental to Paul's sense.[8] This is a particularly defined and enacted righteousness, a way of life, a *halakah* specifically consisting of Torah observance. Thus, if they are not to be taken as a narrow reference to "boundary markers," neither is Paul's *erga nomou* a general description of good behavior only incidentally cast in Jewish idiom. As Dunn has often noted, in contexts of religious self-definition and debates over validity of conversion, references to *erga nomou* are bound to connote especially those practices that distinguish the practitioners from their non-observant neighbors as well as what will differentiate the would-be proselyte's new life from his or her former one.

This is borne out in a closer examination of Paul's uses of the phrase in Galatians and, as we will see, in Romans as well. However, confusion has frustrated the debate over "works of the law," a confusion around three ways one can construe the "meaning" of the phrase: (1) with respect to the proper *referent* of the phrase, (2) the *connotations* and *associations* of the phrase in specific argumentative contexts, and (3) the bearing of Paul's argument against *erga nomou* on the meaning of the phrase. Thus, regarding (1),

---

[7]This debate suffers from confusion when Paul's opponents or the position he opposes is described with the language of "exclusivity" and "ethnocentrism" (i.e., apart from proper definitions). Unfortunately, the confusion is perpetuated by both NPP adherents and critics, leading to subtle distortions and easy caricature. It is not the exclusivity of the covenant that concerns Paul's opponents but rather its integrity. Presumably, properly proseltyzed and converted Gentiles are perfectly welcome to confess allegiance to the one true God and to adhere to the Jewish way of life. If the evidence does not support an actively missionizing Judaism (this is debated), presumably proper proselytes were received with joy and open arms. The question is, of course, what counted as *proper*. But to describe the more rigorous position as *exclusivist* is a mischaracterization, and to say that it is fundamentally *ethnic* in character is correct only if by *ethnic* we are adhering to a strictly religio-cultural definition of the term, irrespective of racial descent.

[8]This is an instance where attempting to (over)specify the force of the genitive νόμου to a syntactical grid of "uses of the genitive" proves unfruitful. It is, broadly speaking, qualitative or attributive in force: "works that the law requires," "works in keeping with the law" or even "Torah observance."

following Dunn's lead, a narrow social definition of the phrase is now largely and rightly abandoned,[9] yielding instead to (2), the phrase having a natural, but not semantically formal, association with socially distinguishing Jewish practices. But, as critics of the NPP are quick to point out, Paul's actual *argument* against "works of the law," and the law more generally, takes up a larger set of concerns than that *erga nomou* imposes social impediment between Jew and Gentile, or even between observant and non-observant Gentiles. That Paul's argument, (3), engages much more than the socially divisive dimensions of *erga nomou* should not be mistaken as indifference to this concern but rather be seen as a sign of the argument's rhetorical complexity. It does not follow that an argument more multidimensional than the presenting symptom makes the originating crisis a matter of no concern. Thus, Paul is addressing precisely the sociological function of the law, devastatingly illustrated by the divisive behavior of Cephas and Barnabas (Gal 2:11-14), but he does so with a rhetorical onslaught that almost amounts to a theological overload. This is Paul's characteristic approach to such matters: a rejoinder much more theological and multidimensional than the presenting symptom would seem to require.[10] Yet it is a mistake to confuse the rejoinder with the exigence that called it forth, such that Paul's answer is mirror read for an equal and opposite crisis that eventuated it.[11] This is not the way Paul's theologically overloaded arguments work. Rather, characteristically—if we can generalize with respect to such a diverse set of rhetorical strategies—Paul teases out theological implications that run deeper than the exigence that calls forth his rebuttal. So also here. Paul's extended argument against *erga nomou* includes at least the following elements, most of which extend well beyond the crisis of which the Cephas incident was the presenting symptom:[12]

---

[9]See, e.g., Frank Matera, who indicates that his view has changed since the publication of his Galatians commentary in 1992 (Frank J. Matera, *God's Saving Grace: A Pauline Theology* [Grand Rapids: Eerdmans, 2012], 105n26).

[10]This theological "overloading" is evident throughout the Pauline corpus but in sharper relief in a letter like 1 Corinthians, where the "presenting symptoms" are more clearly isolated (e.g., with the περὶ δε formula in apparent response to the Corinthians' letter: 1 Cor 7:1, 25; 8:1; 12:1; 16:1, 12).

[11]John Barclay's article continues to serve as a helpful chastening of mirror reading run amok but without dismissing a natural and necessary tool: John M. G. Barclay, "Mirror-Reading a Polemical Letter: Galatians as a Test Case," *JSNT* 10, no. 31 (1987): 73-93.

[12]For other, more detailed and competing rehearsals of Paul's argument, see, e.g., Frank Thielman, *Paul and the Law: A Contextual Approach* (Downers Grove, IL: InterVarsity Press, 1994), 123-35;

1. He argues that, even for Jews such as himself and Cephas, *erga nomou*, in and of themselves, are impotent to justify: "We ourselves are Jews by birth and not Gentile sinners; yet we know that a person is justified not by the works of the law except through faith in Jesus Christ" (Gal 2:15-16, my translation).[13] Paul's premise, which ought to be shared by his believing kinsman, is that, even for us who are obliged to *erga nomou* "by nature" (*physei*), they are impotent for justification. The implicitly a fortiori argument implies that, this being the case for Jews such as Cephas and Paul, how much more otiose are *erga nomou* for Gentiles, who have no intrinsic obligation. Why this is so remains to be seen, but this is the essential first move.

2. Paul notes that an instatement of *erga nomou* for Gentile converts reerects the very barrier that the gospel of Christ had destroyed. Although, along with the rest of Galatians 2:15-21, the meaning of Galatians 2:17-18 is not undisputed, a compelling contextual case can be made that the "things abolished" or "dismantled" (*ha katelysa*) of Galatians 2:18 are the very social barriers imposed by the "works of the law."[14] Virtually all interpreters are agreed that, in some general sense, it is the law that Paul regards as the "things dismantled" and that he refuses to "build up again" (*palin oikodomō*), lest in doing so he become, ironically, a "transgressor." But there are good

---

Moo, *Galatians*, 21-31; Wright, *P&FG*, 2:861-79; and J. Louis Martyn, *Galatians: A New Translation with Introduction and Commentary*, AB 33A (New York: Doubleday, 1998), 294-96, 301-6 and passim.

[13]Even apart from the πίστις Χριστοῦ debate, which I'm leaving aside here having addressed it above (section 3.2.5), this text has elicited considerable debate in the aftermath of the NPP, and I cannot even survey that discussion. I can only make the following observations: (1) By joining himself to Cephas as "we who are Jews by nature" (ἡμεῖς φύσει Ἰουδαῖοι), Paul is setting the stage for an a fortiori argument: "If this applies to *us*, how much more to Gentiles?" (2) The use of the emphatic first-person plural in Galatians 2:15 ("we," ἡμεῖς) and its resumption in Galatians 2:16 with the ascensive adverbial καί ("*even* we"; καὶ ἡμεῖς) assume that Cephas agrees with him or should. Thus, he begins this argument on what should be common ground among Christ-believing Jews. (3) Although much debated, the phrase "not by works of the law but through faith of Jesus Christ" is better taken as "not by works of the law *except* [ἐὰν μή] through faith in Jesus Christ" (Dunn, "The New Perspective on Paul," 212-13; idem, *A Commentary on the Epistle to the Galatians*, BNTC [Peabody, MA: Hendrickson, 1993], 137). This is the normal force of ἐὰν μή (elsewhere always so in Paul when used idiomatically; Rom 10:15; 1 Cor 9:16; 14:6, 9; 15:36; 2 Thess 2:3; 2 Tim 2:5), and theological considerations should not overrule the natural force of the idiom. While it is true that the context—both the immediate and the larger argument—supports an adversative meaning, the exceptive meaning is perfectly sensible and rhetorically the more subtle option.

[14]So, e.g., Dunn, *Galatians*, 142-43; Frank J. Matera, *Galatians*, SP (Collegeville, MN: Liturgical Press, 1992), 95; and Moo, *Galatians*, 166 (albeit more cautiously).

reasons to believe that Paul has in mind the law, not just in general but with respect to its more specific discriminating social function.[15] In the first place, there is the immediate context of the Cephas Antioch incident over table fellowship, which continues to be not only the instigation but arguably even the occasion of Paul's summarized rebuttal captured in Galatians 2:15-21.[16] Moreover, it is a trope of sociologically sectarian Judaism that the law functions as an erected protective barrier for the faithful over against transgressing, idolatrous neighbors.[17] Paul is capitalizing on that image and leveraging the irony that the *real* transgression would be to reerect what had been destroyed, the *erga nomou*. If reinstated as constituent of the gospel, the *erga nomou* threaten to destroy what the gospel had formed, a humanity restored into one family, the progeny of Abraham according to faith rather than *erga nomou*. Rich with irony, Paul is essentially saying, "Transgression? If you want to see transgression, it is not that I extend the covenant to non-observant Gentiles; the real transgression would be if we went backward and rebuilt the wall between us that Christ leveled."

3. Harking back to the Gentile Galatians' initial "Christian" experience, Paul argues that *erga nomou* had no role in the Galatians' palpable encounter of the Spirit (Gal 3:1-6). Although this is frequently considered an argument "from experience"—and in some respects it is—more importantly, with the allusion to the new age of the Spirit (e.g., Joel 2:28-32; Ezek 11:16-20; 36:24-27; 39:28-29), it is an implicitly biblical and theological argument, pointing the way forward to the following extended salvation-historical argument. That being so, the gift of the Spirit being the sign of the new age of the Messiah and the renewal of the covenant, it follows that *erga nomou* cannot be regarded as essential to life in the covenant, neither to its membership nor to its blessings. This recall of the palpable ministry of the Spirit in mighty works

---

[15]If so, Galatians 2:17-18 is a more implicit and ambiguous precursor to the explicit claim of Ephesians 2:14-16.

[16]It is probably best to see Galatians 2:15-21 neither as straightforward continuation of the scene narration begun in Galatians 2:11-14 nor as a new "chapter" in the letter's argument but rather as a free dramatization of Paul's censure of Cephas in Antioch put to use toward this letter's rhetorical ends, a dramatization functioning at once as the conclusion of the *narratio* and the statement of the *propositio*.

[17]Perhaps the most famous example is from the Letter of Aristeas 139, 142. See John M. G. Barclay, *Jews in the Mediterranean Diaspora: From Alexander to Trajan (323 BCE–117 CE)*, Hellenistic Culture and Society (Edinburgh: T&T Clark, 1996).

(*dynameis*) functions for Paul as indisputable evidence that it ˅ of faith" not "works of law" that initiated these Gentile believers into the realm of the Spirit, which is to say the new covenant.

4. The dominant and most textured argument in the whole letter is a multipronged, scriptural and salvation-historical argument (Gal 3:6–4:20). The scope of my treatment does not allow a thorough rehearsal of each dimension, but the argument turns substantially on the temporal and salvation-historical priority of God's covenant making with Abraham over against Moses and the giving of the law. The promise made to Abraham is prior in time and consequently superior in precedence to the giving of the law on Sinai. *It*, and not the Mosaic law, is the covenant (*diathēkē*) God made with Israel, the law being but a mere codicil to the covenant, 430 years after the fact (Gal 3:15, 17). Because Abraham met that covenant with faith (Gen 15) and both God's covenant making and Abraham's faithful reception preceded not only the giving of the Mosaic law but even the commandment to observe the sign of circumcision (Gen 17), the covenant, Paul can argue, has always been a matter of promise received by faith rather than a work performed in obedience (e.g., Gal 3:5). Reinforcing this claim, Paul can make two subtle but profound rhetorical moves: (a) He effectively substitutes the term "promise" (*epangelia*) as though a virtual synonym for "covenant" (Gal 3:14-21; esp. 3:17), a usage not presaged in the Genesis narrative but polemically useful here.[18] The effective substitution of "promise" for "covenant" functions then as a freighted recharacterization of the covenant with Abraham *as* a promise, a unilateral promise made by God. In the nature of the case, whereas a covenant can be "kept,"[19] not only by the one who makes it but also by the recipients in faithful response, a promise can be kept only by the initiating party but can only be believed by the recipient. A promise cannot be obeyed; it can only be received and trusted. Thus, in recasting covenant as promise, Paul leaves room only for faith as the appropriate response. That

---

[18] By describing the Spirit as the "promise" (Gal 3:14; assuming with most that τὴν ἐπαγγελίαν τοῦ πνεύματος should be taken as an epexegetic genitive: "the promise *which is* the Spirit"), Paul shows that the powerful endowment of the Spirit is epochal in character. The experience of the Spirit thus functions as a kind of middle term by which covenant membership becomes understood as promise-fulfillment.

[19] E.g., Genesis 17:9-10 (!); Exodus 19:5; Deuteronomy 33:9; 1 Kings 11:11; Psalms 78:10; 103:18; 132:12; Jeremiah 34:18; Ezekiel 17:14.

Abraham was "reckoned righteous"—effectively justified—by his faith in the promise is thus paradigmatic of the covenant promise from its origination. (b) Paul succeeds in deftly recharacterizing circumcision as a "work of the *law*," as a Mosaic stipulation, when, in fact, though it is that (Lev 12:3), it was first and more fundamentally a sign of the covenant made with Abraham.[20] As a matter of textual interpretation of the Pentateuch, the move is breathtaking—one might even say suspicious—though with respect to popular Jewish consciousness, there is ample evidence that circumcision was understood as part and parcel of Torah observance.[21]

5. Finally, it bears some emphasis that the denouement of the argument is gathering as one "seed" (the descendants of Abraham; Gal 3:29) into the one "seed" (Christ; Gal 3:16, 19). Along with his allegorization of Hagar and Sarah (Gal 4:21-31), Paul's appeal to the singular *sperma* in Galatians 3:16 is frequently thought of as a special pleading, desperate expedient. It is evident that all the Genesis texts invoked (Gen 12:7; 13:15; 15:8; 17:8-10; 22:17-18; 24:7; etc.) are using "seed" as a collective singular for the full sum of Abraham's many descendants rather than as a reference to any particular person. But the judgment of Paul's special pleading is premature and superficial given the context of the larger argument. By twice identifying the seed, first as the Messiah (Gal 3:16, 19) and later as Abraham's "descendents" (still singular *sperma*), Paul is showing that Christ is the new incorporative term in a redefinition of the covenant people, Abraham's "seed" narrowing to One in whom all who believe (Gal 3:26), which is to say those who are baptized into Christ (Gal 3:27) are incorporated into the one Seed so as together to become Abraham's seed.[22]

---

[20]One only has to scan the circumcision vocabulary casually to note that it is profoundly Abrahamic and only incidentally Mosaic. Note, e.g., eighteen Pentateuchal references precede the Sinai narrative (10x in Gen 17 alone), and only one reference occurs in Leviticus (Lev 12:3). The references in Deuteronomy 10:16 and 30:6 are already metaphorical (i.e., circumcision of the heart).

[21]Circumcision is routinely associated with taking on the "law" itself: e.g., Josephus, *Jewish Antiquities* 13.9.1 §§257-258; 13.11.3 §§318-319; 20.2.4 §§38-41; *Jewish War* 2.17.10 §454; Philo, *On the Migration of Abraham* 92-93; John 7:23; Acts 15:5.

[22]N. T. Wright is at his very best in the treatment of this theme: *The Climax of the Covenant: Christ and the Law in Pauline Theology* (Edinburgh: T&T Clark, 1991), 157-74; idem, *P&FG*, 2:868-79; and idem, "Messiahship in Galatians?," in *Galatians and Christian Theology: Justification, the Gospel, and Ethics in Paul's Letter*, ed. M. W. Elliott, Scott J. Hafemann, N. T. Wright and John Frederick (Grand Rapids: Baker Academic, 2014). Cf. Francis Watson, *Paul and the Hermeneutics of Faith* (London: T&T Clark, 2004), 193-201.

We can thus summarize Paul's Galatians refutation of *erga nomou* as follows: (1) Torah observance is impotent apart from faith in Christ; (2) insistence upon *erga nomou* reerects a Messiah-eliminated barrier to covenant membership for Gentiles; (3) the new era of the Spirit had already dawned on the Galatian Gentiles apart from *erga nomou*; (4) the *erga nomou* (even circumcision) were predated by a unilateral covenant promise, with respect to which the later addition of Torah obedience is a nonconstitutive addendum; and (5) the Abrahamic promise is fulfilled in his Seed, in whom, by faith and baptism, Abraham's seed are incorporated, though apart from *erga nomou*.

Moving on from that admittedly cursory summary, it remains to give an even briefer account of the argument against *erga nomou* in the final two chapters of Galatians. It is generally understood that Galatians 5 and 6 turn substantially to the ethical implications of Paul's allegiance transfer from Torah to Christ. It is unclear whether Paul is arguing constructively or essentially defensively, answering the charge, explicit or anticipated, that his diminishment of the law can only devolve into an antinominan moral chaos; there appear to be elements of both. After all, numbered among the law's many blessings—expressed so many times in so many ways—would be not only that it marked inclusion into the covenant family but also that it guards that people from the vice and folly so ruinous of their Gentile neighbors. What would become of a people untethered from the law and unsocialized by its precepts? But Paul is unimpressed by the moral-chaos worry, and, in fact, if he is on the defense in his reply, apparently he would agree that also in rhetoric "the best defense is a good offense." Paul argues that, far from a moral panacea, the law—at its best!—functioned as a moral ceiling, that there is a capacity for human goodness that the law neither elicits nor empowers. It is, of course, not an innate human capacity for goodness; it expressly requires the Spirit's decisive intervention. Nonetheless, Paul's claims aggregate to this startling conclusion: the Spirit and "law of *Christ*" (Gal 6:2) are not only sufficient for moral guidance but are actually *superior* to the Torah for moral transformation. Thus, "the whole law is fulfilled" in the practice of love of neighbor (Gal 5:14 rsv; Lev 19:18). And, again, those who "walk by the Spirit will assuredly not gratify the desire of the flesh" (Gal 5:16).[23]

---

[23]The curious rsv and nrsv translation of the emphatic negation οὐ μὴ τελέσητε as though a prohibitive subjunctive ("do not gratify the desires of the flesh") amounts to a regrettable

Even more astonishingly, "if you are under the direction of the Spirit, you are not under the law" (Gal 5:18).[24] More wryly, after enumerating the fruit of the Spirit—a litany of virtues and dispositions, not concrete behaviors as such—Paul adds, "Against such things, there is no law" (Gal 5:23). The prohibitions of "law" are rendered at best redundant and unnecessary in the face of the transcending virtues worked by the Spirit's transformation. Finally, it is by the bearing of one another's burdens that his readers will fulfill the "law of Christ" (Gal 6:1). Even granting that we cannot know with certainty precisely what Paul intended by "law of Christ"—if, indeed, Paul meant something *precise* by the phrase—it is clear that there is no attempt in Galatians at rehabilitating the law, in speaking of its ongoing usefulness for moral guidance, in affirming it in some dimensions while qualifying it in others.[25] No, Paul's understanding of the law in Galatians is not that it is a necessary evil to dispense with it on soteriological grounds or that in the Spirit and the "law of Christ" we can almost fill the yawning gap. To the contrary, the law comprises walls and ceilings. Walls that once protected the covenant people from encroaching contamination now exclude persons made holy in the messianic family. And what might have been a floor, a common moral foundation, is shown by Paul, at its best, to be a moral ceiling too low, "too small a thing," for new-covenant saints bearing the fruit of the Spirit. Thus, Paul would not recognize the facile Christian caricature of his position, that the law is too hard, but would contend instead that humanity *kata sarka* is too weak. Nor would Paul join in the protest that the law asks too much but would insist instead that it actually asks too little and that the Spirit supplies so much more.

I have saved for last the most disputed dimension of Paul's argument in Galatians: the claim that Paul opposes *erga nomou* because the law demands a perfect obedience of which no person is capable, leaving human beings—

---

moralizing that obscures Paul's point. So, e.g., John M. G. Barclay, *Obeying the Truth: A Study of Paul's Ethics in Galatians*, Studies of the New Testament and Its World (Edinburgh: T&T Clark, 1988), 111, noting BDF, §365.

[24]"Under the direction of" is my translation of ἄγεσθε (cf. "guided," NAB).

[25]Of course, various Christian traditions have done so and, if with varied results, nonetheless for all kinds of good reasons. Still we needn't hold Galatians hostage as an unwilling witness on behalf of the "third use of the Law" or in defense of a distinction between the so-called civil, ceremonial and moral dimensions of the law. Whatever one makes of these hermeneutical moves, it is kicking against the goads to find an ally in Galatians.

Jew or Gentile—helpless to achieve their justification if this perfect standard is the measure. This, of course, is a bulwark of the TPP reading of Paul, and it is the dimension of that reading of Paul's argument most vigorously confronted by the NPP.[26] There are several places in the letter where Paul might be making this claim, at least obliquely. When Paul says that "everyone who receives circumcision is obligated to do the whole law" (Gal 5:3), there may be an implication that it cannot be done; this is why it would be such a precarious thing to choose circumcision. Or when Paul complains that "even the circumcised do not themselves obey the law" (Gal 6:13), he may be implying that it is unkeepable. But, in fact, these texts do not require the thesis of an impossible-to-achieve perfect obedience to the law. And many, emboldened especially by Sanders, have been quick to point out that it is a strange reading of the law in Judaism that understands it to require perfect obedience.

But the crux text for this reading of Galatians as an argument against *erga nomou* is Galatians 3:10-14 understood a particular way, here outlined.

Galatians 3:10 declares that (a) those "depending on works of the law" (*ex ergōn nomou*)[27] are "under a curse." This is so (b) because (*gar*) Deuteronomy 27:26 says, "Cursed is everyone who does not observe and obey all the things written in the book of the law." This is but to repeat the words of the text; the question is the nature of these claims. Perhaps without exception, TPP scholars understand an unstated, implied minor premise that completes the logic of these two clauses: "no one succeeds in keeping all that the law requires." A conclusion, it is argued, that is implied—perhaps even necessitated—by the collocation of these two clauses.

---

[26] Articulating the TPP position, see, e.g., Hans Hübner, *Law in Paul's Thought: A Contribution to the Development of Pauline Theology*, trans. James C. G. Greig (Edinburgh: T&T Clark, 1984), 15-20; Thomas R. Schreiner, *The Law and Its Fulfillment: A Pauline Theology of Law* (Grand Rapids: Baker Academic, 1993), 44-65; Thielman, *Paul and the Law*, 124-30; A. Andrew Das, *Paul, the Law, and the Covenant* (Peabody, MA: Hendrickson, 2001), 145-70; Moo, *Galatians*, 21-31; and Moisés Silva, "Faith Versus Works of Law in Galatians," in Carson, O'Brien and Siefrid, *JVN:PP*, 2:217-48. Among various NPP rebuttals, note esp. James D. G. Dunn, "Works of the Law and the Curse of the Law (Galatians 3.10-14)," in *NPerP*, 137-56; and N. T. Wright, "Curse and Covenant: Galatians 3.10-14," in Wright, *Climax of the Covenant*, 137-56.

[27] While translating the preposition ἐκ as "depend on" (NAB) or "rely on" (NRSV, ESV, NIV) perhaps conveys the sense adequately, it runs the risk of overspecifying, bringing to mind assumptions about the nature of that dependence or reliance as self-achievement. But, of course, there are other ways that "works of the law" *could* be relied on, such as identity definition.

This train of thought is then further verified by the claim of Galatians 3:11 (here translated to retain the Greek word order): "that by the law no one is justified before God is obvious." It is "obvious" because (*hoti*), as Habakkuk 2:4 says, "The one who is righteous by faith will live." Thus, as the argument goes, that no one is justified by the law is substantiated by Habakkuk 2:4, because it is rather *by faith* (*ek pisteōs*) that one can be called "righteous" (= justified) and granted eschatological life.[28]

The reason the law cannot justify is that it is "not based on faith" (*ouk estin ek pisteōs*). Rather, citing Leviticus 18:5, Paul avers that "the one who does them [= the statutes commanded in the law] will live [eschatologically] by them." The TPP exegesis invariably stresses the evident contrast between faith (*pistis*) and "doing" (*ho poiēsas*), the difference between passive reception and the active accomplishment, respectively, with stress on the statutes of the law (i.e., "them," *auta*), the doing of which are both necessary and the means (*en autois*) of "life."

The whole contrastive picture of Galatians 3:10-12, so understood, is given its grounding in an account of the atonement that picks up on the original statement of the plight described as "curse" in Galatians 3:13: "Christ redeemed us from the curse of the law, becoming a curse for us." Again, the logic is that the law brings a "curse" to those who are "of the works of the law" (Gal 3:10), because they do not keep the law— the implied minor premise is never far from sight in this interpretation. But the curse that the law invokes upon the disobedient is ameliorated in the crucifixion of Jesus, construed as a tree hanging:

---

[28] As with its even more programmatic use in Romans 1:17, there is a dense set of issues (even apart from the form of the *Vorlage* of Hab 2:4), which can only be outlined here: (1) The identity of ὁ δίκαιος (the righteous one): (a) most take this to be a reference to a righteous person (in context one "justified") in general terms, though some see (b) ὁ δίκαιος as a reference to Jesus Christ as the one uniquely righteous by means of his faithfulness—thus, following the subjective-genitive interperetation of πίστις Χριστοῦ. (2) The sense of ζήσεται: Does it refer to (a) eschatological life (i.e., shall live *eternally*) or (b) a manner of life (i.e., shall conduct one's life)? (3) Thus, ἐκ πίστεως could modify either (a) ὁ δίκαιος (the one who is righteous by means of faith) or (b) ζήσεται (shall live by faith). I am persuaded of option (a) in each case: "The one who is righteous on the ground of faith will live (eschatologically)." If this is a reinterpretation of the original sense of Habakkuk 2:4, as it almost certainly is, it is an appeal to theological premises that transcend the originating circumstances of Habakkuk's composition but that are not antithetical to its vision. See especially the extraordinary treatment of F. Watson, *Paul and the Hermeneutics of Faith*, 127-63.

"Cursed be everyone who hangs on a tree" (Deut 21:23). In a manner Paul does not explain directly, but presumably implying some manner of vicariousness or substitution, Christ himself becoming "cursed" serves as a "for-us-curse" (*hyper hēmōn katara*), rendering us liberated from the curse of the law.

Although recently much disputed, this line of interpretation is satisfactorily coherent—indeed, easier to trace than many of its alternatives—perhaps for its familiarity, but perhaps not. In any case, that familiarity should not be confused for the "plain sense" of the text; this interpretation is not without its own intrinsic difficulties. Two problems immediately emerge: (1) In the first place, it depends heavily on the *unstated*, arguably implied, minor premise of Galatians 3:10 that no one is able to keep the law unfailingly. It is frequently claimed that this silence can hardly bear the weight foisted upon it by the traditional interpretation and that it is not the only or even preferable way to fill the space between. And the presumption of an implied minor premise is made all the more problematic to the extent that it presupposes perfect obedience to the law was the contemporary Jewish expectation, a supposition not easily demonstrated.[29] As many have noted, this interpretation thus puts Paul in the position of having either misunderstood or mischaracterized his own ancestral religion.[30] (2) There

---

[29]While it does not prove especially difficult to find texts in the Second Temple era that seem, even rather clearly, to require perfect obedience to the law, the Jewish materials that stress strict obedience to the law do not offer TPP interpreters the necessary corresponding soteriological anxiety necessary to read Galatians 3:10-14 as they suppose it ought to be read. See, e.g., the evidence marshaled in Das, *Paul, the Law, and the Covenant*; idem, "Paul and Works of Obedience in Second Temple Judaism: Romans 4:4-5 as a 'New Perspective' Case Study," *CBQ* 71, no. 4 (2009): 795-812. A consistent flaw in arguments that seek to generalize from these data is the failure to appreciate the rhetorical motive—one is tempted even to say form—of appeals for perfect and comprehensive obedience to the law. What else would one expect from an exhortation to obedience but an appeal to "all that is written in the law," "not turning from the left or right," reference to "every command" and so on? These tropes should be understood as rhetorical, as calling for an uncompromised, comprehensive obedience. But if the purpose was to assign an absolute soteriological *requirement*, we should expect also what in fact we find missing, namely, corroborating evidence of an extraordinarily high anxiety, indeed despair, should but one transgression forfeit eschatological inheritance. But this corroborating evidence is not found. Thus, high ideals and rhetorically high expectations should not be confused with an actual *expectation* of perfect performance as a strict requirement, in which case, if it were both necessary and possible, means of atonement and restitution would be unnecessary.
[30]Richard B. Hays, "The Letter to the Galatians," in *NIB*, 11:257 ("a ridiculous caricature of Judaism"); cf. Barclay, *Obeying*, 235-42.

is nothing in this interpretation, centering as it does on the dilemma of human incapacity, that obviously follows from the preparation of Galatians 3:7-9 or prepares for the conclusion in Galatians 3:14. On both sides of the argument of Galatians 3:10-13, however understood, is the matter of the inclusion of Gentiles into the family of Abraham, described with no small emphasis:

> So, you see [ginōskete ara], those who believe are **the descendants of Abraham**. And the scripture, foreseeing that **God would justify the Gentiles** by faith, declared the gospel beforehand to Abraham, saying, "**All the Gentiles shall be blessed in you.**" For this reason, those who believe **are blessed with Abraham** who believed. (Gal 3:7-9 NRSV)

> In order that [hina] in Christ Jesus **the blessing of Abraham might come to the Gentiles**, so that [hina] we might receive the promise of the Spirit through faith. (Gal 3:14 NRSV)

Unless we are to regard Galatians 3:10-13 as something of a digression[31]—surely a counsel of despair—or even more impossibly, the membership of Abraham's family as but an incidental concern in Galatians 3 (cf. Gal 3:8, 16, 18, 29), a satisfactory exegesis of Galatians 3:10-13 will have to account for the relationship of the material surrounding it, arguably the larger concern that is somehow served by this dense argument contained within. This is the intuition followed by NPP interpreters, seeking to read Galatians 3:10-13 as integral to Galatians 3:7-9 and 14, and it is a characteristic shortcoming of TPP interpretation of the passage that this dimension of the argument factors so little in the exegesis of Galatians 3:10-13.[32] These are substantial objections to the TPP reading of Galatians 3:10-14, especially the second, but I maintain that they call for a substantial chastening of the traditional interpretation not its rejection.

The criticism of the omitted minor premise is appropriate but wrongly aimed. Virtually every reading of Galatians 3:10-11 depends on an implied minor premise; the question is not whether Paul argues in such a way but of the content of the implied premise.[33] Numerous studies have demonstrated

---

[31]Galatians 3:10 is connected to what precedes by γάρ: "for all who rely on the works of the law."
[32]E.g., Moo, *Galatians*, 214-16.
[33]So, e.g., Wright and other NPP interpreters require that Israel's present exile constitutes the

that the omitted but implied minor premise is not at all an unusual form for the enthymeme; indeed, arguably the enthymeme *is* a "truncated syllogism" by definition.[34] All the more so is this to be expected in an argumentative context as compressed, allusive and inferential as what we find in Galatians 3:10-13. It remains, however, to note that the substance of the minor premise normally presumed ("no one is able to keep the law") is not the only possible way to infer the logic. There is a characteristic inconsistency in the articulation and defense of the TPP understanding of this argument, such that frequently interpreters wish to "excuse" the omitted minor premise by appealing to the informality of Paul's argument while at the same time arriving at a formal and categorical syllogism, which, not incidentally, may smuggle more theology into the text than is necessary. In the typical TPP construal, Paul is claiming that all human beings are under a curse and are constitutionally incapable of keeping the law perfectly. Irrespective of the truth of such a claim, this way of construing the matter is excessively categorical and, I would add, imposes a particular reading of Romans intrusively into the Galatians discourse. But for Paul's dissuasive against works of the law to "work," he needn't appeal to a (Christian!) theologoumen of human incapacity or depravity; even less necessary to his argument is the presupposition that the Jewish law requires perfect obedience, such that a single failure renders a person irretrievably lost in guilt. Critics of the TPP exegesis are correct to intuit that such notions enter *this* discourse as foreign bodies of presumption.

All that is required for Paul's argument and all that is here implied by way of the inferable minor premise is that, judging from Israel's scripturally narrated track record and observations of human behavior more generally, the path to blessing by means of obedience to the law is fraught with peril. Paul's point is neither quite that the law *requires* perfect obedience (though it certainly *asks* for it) nor that fallen human beings are naturally in themselves incapable of perfect righteousness (which is not to be doubted), but that to

---

curse, reading Deuteronomy 27:26 in its original context. Thus, by this interpretation, the reader is also asked to supply a minor premise: "present Israel is under a curse (i.e., exile) for having not kept the law." This is no less an inference than that made by the TPP interpreters, though it bears less weight rhetorically in the interpreter's argument, on the one hand, and, on the other, its advocates will think it is freighted with less theological presupposition.

[34]On the enthymeme in general, see David E. Aune, *WDNTLR*, 150-57, and the studies cited there. On the omission of the minor premises in Galatians 3:10-11, see Thomas R. Schreiner, *Galatians*, ZECNT (Grand Rapids: Zondervan, 2010), 205, and the studies cited there.

choose *that* path to achieve righteousness before God is not just theoretically perilous but empirically problematic. Thus, filling the logical space between Deuteronomy 27:26 and Habakkuk 2:4 is a rather more modest claim: "people—that is, especially Israel—don't keep the law," with no more theological substructure required or superstructure implied. Whether they could or can keep the law is a different question, Paul just knows that they haven't, and his readers would have to concede the same. As Richard Hays summarizes Paul's argument, "If you [Galatians] affiliate yourself with those who place their hope in obeying the Law (i.e., the Missionaries), you are joining a losing team."[35] This casts the Galatian Gentiles' decision to take on circumcision in a new light; this act of "obedience" would obligate them to the whole law (Gal 3:10-11; 5:3), and here Paul shows that ironically the law itself testifies against such a course of action.[36] Whether or not Paul believed, or would come to believe, that the law required perfect obedience or that human beings were fundamentally incapable of obeying it, it does not follow that all of that is implied here. The argument does not require it; readers need not infer it. Thus, the TPP interpretation of the text is not mistaken for inferring an implied minor premise in the enthymeme of Galatians 3:10-11, but the interpretation can be faulted for overloading and overspecifying its content, perhaps also for smuggling theological presuppositions, a reader's unnecessary inference becoming Paul's certain contention.

If this chastened version of that interpretation is accepted, it becomes evident that the force of this argument to the Galatian Gentiles is ultimately a fortiori, and, when so understood, the argument of Galatians 3:10-13 is properly reintegrated into its immediate context. If the attempted law-observant path toward righteousness has proven problematic (if not disastrous) for Israel, then how much more ill-advised would it be for Gentiles, being under no such obligation intrinsically to take upon themselves an obligation even Israel has been unable to satisfy (cf. Gal 5:3; 6:13)? This is neither a claim about the "sinfulness" of individual Jews nor an expansive generalization about human incapacity but a common-sense appeal to the

---

[35]Hays, "Letter to the Galatians," 11:259.

[36]This interpretation is given further support if we read ὅσοι in Galatians 3:10 an emphasis on its implicitly contingent sense: "an element of 'uncertainty' or 'potentiality' regarding the membership" of the group (Moo, *Galatians*, 201-2, following Christopher D. Stanley, "'Under a Curse': A Fresh Reading of Galatians 3:10-14," *NTS* 36, no. 4 [1990]: 498).

facts on the ground.[37] Paul, persuaded by reflection on the biblical narrative and observation of the current state of affairs, can only conclude that the blessings that should be Israel's are not forthcoming. Meanwhile, another set of facts on the ground remembered in Galatians 3:1-6, the Gentiles' receipt of the Spirit, conspires with Galatians 3:10-13 toward a powerful dissuasive.

Understood this way, the argument of Galatians 3:10-13 does not become the digression that the TPP interpretation essentially makes it to be. Rather than human incapacity and sinfulness and the law's strict, exceptionless requirement taking center stage, this qualified, implicitly a fortiori, account understands Galatians 3:10-13 as a continuation of the argument of Galatians 3:7-9. The question at hand does not become, out of the blue, the theoretical question of whether the law can be sufficiently kept; rather, the question is how ill-advised and disastrous it would be for Gentiles to take a path fraught with failure, testified against by the law itself, when a law-free alternative, which the law itself commends, has presented itself in the atonement wrought by Jesus. In short, although one *might* by extrapolation find the seeds of it here, Paul's argument is not the argument against meritorious achievement and its inevitable failure that the TPP makes it to be. It is rather that the "works of the law," which threaten to divide the one covenant people of God, are a path that has led to curse, whereas faith yields righteousness and blessing, after the pattern of Abraham (Gen 15:6).

If we were to characterize Paul's account of "works" in Galatians, with due caution, we can say that his complaint is actually not with "works" per se. Galatians is absent a polemic against autosoterism, against "works righteousness" as such. Indeed, Paul's primary complaint with *erga nomou* in Galatians is not with "works" but with "law." Paul finds multiple faults with the law in Galatians and several ironies, but they are chiefly salvation-historical. The law is but a codicil to the *diathēkē* (will/covenant) God made

---

[37]That this is so finds support in the sort of argument Paul makes in Romans 2:17-24. There can be no question that this sweeping indictment can hardly be a condemnation of all individual Jews (or Jewish teachers). Paul cannot mean that those who condemn stealing or adultery are to a person thieves or adulterers, only that the proper moral views and their advocacy have not proven to be a safeguard from moral failure and hypocrisy. Especially illustrative is Romans 2:22: "You that abhor idols, do you rob temples?" It is not necessary to imagine that temple robbing was the besetting sin of a large number of Jews! For a plausible background to that charge, see Douglas A. Campbell, *The Deliverance of God: An Apocalyptic Rereading of Justification in Paul* (Grand Rapids: Eerdmans, 2009), 561-62, 1086n95.

with Abraham. The law—late on the scene by over four centuries—has no part in the promise made to Abraham, and that promise, already extended to Gentiles, is now renewed, the law being no condition for the seed of Abraham. While arguably there are seeds in Galatians that carry the DNA of a soteriology later fleshed out in Romans and beyond, it is premature to find it already here.

6.1.2 "Works" in the Thessalonian and Corinthian correspondence. As already noted, references to *erga nomou* are limited to Galatians and Romans, and in the Thessalonian and Corinthian correspondence there are seemingly no examples of "works" ("of the law" or otherwise) set over against faith or grace or mentioned in any soteriologically polemical context.[38] In fact, there are notable passages in which, far from antithetical, *pistis* and *ergon* enjoy a necessary and perfect compatibility; "work" evidently—and evidentially—follows from faith. Thus, in a stylized appeal to the Pauline triad of Christian virtue—faith, hope and love—Paul treats "work," "labor" and "steadfastness" as natural corollaries to the abstract virtues of faith, love and hope, respectively (1 Thess 1:3), presumably as their concretized demonstration or fruit.[39] Likewise, in 2 Thessalonians 1:11, we find the same expression, "work of faith," and in 2 Thessalonians 2:17 "good work" is commended with "good speech" (*panti ergō kai logō agathō*).[40] A majority of references to *ergon* ("work") in the Thessalonian and Corinthian correspondence refer nonpolemically and with approbation to the work of Christian ministry or other commendable behavior.[41]

A sign that the language of "work(s)" is not saddled with polemical concern is the unselfconscious manner in which Paul describes fitting deeds

---

[38]Characteristically, Paul's polemic is reserved for the plural "works," and in these texts the plural is found only once (2 Cor 11:15), where it refers to the deeds that will condemn the pseudoapostles.

[39]This presumes that the genitives, πίστεως, ἀγάπης and ἐλπίδος, are to be taken essentially as source or authorial genitives (e.g., Charles A. Wanamaker, *The Epistles to the Thessalonians: A Commentary on the Greek Text*, NIGTC [Grand Rapids: Eerdmans, 1990], 74-76; and Gordon D. Fee, *The First and Second Letters to the Thessalonians*, NICNT [Grand Rapids: Eerdmans, 2009], 23-26), but it is at least possible that they be read as merely descriptive or adjectival (i.e., faithful work, charitable labor, hopeful endurance).

[40]Assuming that ἀγαθῷ modifies both ἔργῳ and λόγῳ.

[41]References to ἔργον as the work of ministry include 1 Thessalonians 5:13; 1 Corinthians 3:13-15 (4x); 9:1; 15:58 (perhaps); 16:10; and otherwise commendable behavior, 2 Corinthians 9:8; 10:1. Although the "builder's work" will be brought to light in the eschatological "day" (1 Cor 3:13-15) and its quality is tested in the fire of judgment, the builder's eschatological standing is not ultimately determined by it; he will be saved, but only as one escaping fire (1 Cor 3:15).

as a matter of judgment in the Corinthian correspondence. In 2 Corinthians 5:10, eschatological requital is according to "deeds done in the body, whether good or evil" (*ta dia tou sōmatos pros ha epraxen, eite agathon eite phaulon*). How this judgment according to behavior relates to Pauline soteriology more generally—for example, to atonement, faith and baptism—is not worked out. The working assumption seems to be that deeds are the self-evidently appropriate criteria for eschatological judgment; Paul has no reason to suggest otherwise, even if this (with Rom 2:6-16 especially) has left interpreters puzzled who have sought to think Paul's thoughts after him. Not dissimilar in force is the polemical warning of 2 Corinthians 11:5 that "the end [of the pseudoapostles] will be according to their deeds" (*to telos estai kata ta erga autōn*). While some of Paul's interpreters will find a patent contradiction in judgment *according to* works over against justification by faith *apart from* works, others will exert much ingenuity to synthesize the seemingly disparate claims.[42] Meanwhile, Paul himself offers no indication that he has wrought an inconsistency.

However understood, the works-faith antithesis, which figures so importantly in Galatians and Romans and in various disputed letters, does not play any particular role in the Thessalonian or Corinthian correspondences. It is a matter of some speculation as to why this might be the case, but the most probable answer is simply that the question of Gentile standing in the people of God was not a central matter of concern in these letters, nor was it a matter of dispute. It is true, of course, that the condition of faith is everywhere presupposed,[43] but there is no reason that faith should be set over against "works" or obedience or even the law where the matter of Gentile inclusion is not central. This corroborates the working hypothesis that Paul's polemic against "works" was first a polemic against *erga nomou* before it would become generalized into a soteriological principle, for which Romans provides the clearest evidence.

---

[42]See, e.g., Kent L. Yinger, *Paul, Judaism, and Judgment According to Deeds*, SNSTMS 105 (Cambridge: Cambridge University Press, 1999); and Chris VanLandingham, *Judgment and Justification in Early Judaism and the Apostle Paul* (Peabody, MA: Hendrickson, 2006); the question is surveyed in Alan P. Stanley and Robert Wilkin, eds., *Four Views on the Role of Works at the Final Judgment*, Counterpoints: Bible and Theology (Grand Rapids: Zondervan, 2013).

[43]The Gentile converts are simply called "those who believe / believers" (οἱ πιστεύοντες, 1 Cor 1:21; 1 Thess 1:7; 2:10, 13; 2 Thess 1:10; cf. Rom 4:11; Gal 3:22).

6.1.3 Works of the law and works in Romans. The letter to the Romans is unique in the Pauline corpus for having a polemic against both *erga nomou* and "works" in near proximity. As observed above, the relevant use of the terminology falls into three categories:[44]

> The phrase *erga nomou* is found two times, Romans 3:20 and 28; and the singular "work of the law" in Romans 2:15 (though it is frequently translated rather freely: "what the law requires," RSV, NRSV; "the demands of the law," NAB; "requirements of the law," NIV).

> Six times "works" (always plural) are described in polemical terms: as that which will not justify (Rom 3:27; 4:2, 6; 9:32; cf. *ergazomai* in Rom 4:4, 5) and as that which does not ground election (Rom 9:12; 11:6).

> Notoriously in Romans 2, Paul describes "works" as the basis by which human beings are judged (Rom 2:6, 7, 15; cf. 2:10: "to everyone who does the good [*panti tō ergazomenō to agathon*]") and, to the consternation of many of his theological readers, apparently not always unto condemnation.

For our purposes, the presenting question is twofold: (1) What is the relationship of the categories (a) "works" and (b) "works of the law": are they functionally synonymous, differentiated or in some part-to-whole relationship? (2) Given the polemical claims of (a) and (b), what do we make of the apparently contradicting evidence of (c)? That is, given that *erga nomou* and "works" are consistently repudiated as impotent for justification, how do we make sense of Paul's apparent claims to the contrary in Romans 2?

Against both NPP and the TPP, I will argue that the two expressions are not interchangeable. Against the typical NPP exegesis, I will argue that "works" does not function as shorthand for *erga nomou* but rather marks a move toward a soteriological generalizing. Against characteristic TPP exegesis, I will argue that *erga nomou* is not simply a synonym for "works" in some general sense; rather, the two occurrences (Rom 3:20, 28; cf. 2:15) have a distinctive function in the argument of Romans, retaining a particularly Jewish application as was the case in Galatians. We begin with this latter thesis.

---

[44]The uses of ἔργον in Romans 13:3; 14:20; 15:18 are not directly relevant for the argument.

The NPP is correct to intuit that *erga nomou* is not simply interchangeable with generic "works" in Romans 3:20: "For 'no human being will be justified in his sight' by deeds prescribed the law [lit. "works of the law"], for through the law comes the knowledge of sin" (NRSV). It is customary to take Romans 3:20 as the summary statement of a general claim, mounted by way of a catena of Old Testament citations in Romans 3:9-18, to the effect that all humanity, Jew and Gentile alike, is irremediably guilty in its sin, "under the power of sin" (Rom 3:9). The litany that follows, drawn especially from the Psalter, proves the point, preparing for the universalizing conclusion of Romans 3:20. I propose, however, that this is a mistaken reading, too eager for a certain theological conclusion to be drawn and insufficiently attentive to the specific claims of the text. It falters particularly at Romans 3:19 NRSV, when Paul confirms that "we know that whatever the law says, it speaks to those who are under the law, so that every mouth may be silenced, and the whole world may be held accountable to God" (NRSV). It is nearly impossible to take "those under the law" (lit. "in the law"; *en tō nomō*) as anything but a description of Jews. We need not conclude that Romans 3:9 presents a straightforwardly inclusive reference to Jew and Greek alike and that Romans 3:10-18 is an indictment against humanity in general. Rather, Romans 3:9 is Paul's denial that, as it regards sin, Jews are any better off than Gentiles: "No, not at all; for we have already charged that all, both Jews and Greeks, are under the power of sin" (NRSV). There is no burden of proof to be borne in the claim that Gentiles are "under sin"; it is patent to Paul's Jewish worldview. The salient, more startling, claim is that the same is true of Jews, those "entrusted with the oracles of God" (Rom 3:2 NRSV), to whom belong all the privileges and responsibilities of election (Rom 9:4-5; cf. 2:19-20). If *they* are under sin, then, a fortiori, the whole world is under sin.[45]

Therefore, Paul's claim that *erga nomou* is impotent for justification in Romans 3:20 is a more focused claim than is sometimes thought. It is widely

---

[45]Romans 3:10-18 is a further confirmation that we are on the right track in finding a specific indictment of Jews rather than a general indictment of humanity in Romans 3:9-20. All the texts cited in the catena are, in their original contexts, referring to Jews deemed unfaithful and treacherous. Paul's rhetorical reappropriation does not so much apply the texts to Jew and Gentile alike—although he would not deny it—but confront the presumption that covenant membership was invariably attended by righteous behavior. Numbering his Jewish subjects among the wicked of the Psalter is thus of a piece with his presumption-shattering argument in Romans 2:17-29.

understood that Paul appropriates Psalm 143:2 (LXX 142:2) for his clinching conclusion in Romans 3:20.[46] While it is not possible to know the precise wording of Paul's source text, it is apparent that he has emended it for the sake of his argument.[47]

Psalm 142:2b	because no living person will be justified before you (LXX, my translation)		
Romans 3:20	because by works of the law all flesh will not be justified before him (my translation)		
Psalm 142:2b	hoti	ou dikaiōthēsetai	enōpion sou pas zōn
Romans 3:20	dioti ex ergōn nomou	ou dikaiōthēsetai pasa sarx	enōpion autou

Clearly *erga nomou* plays a critical role in the summation of this leg of the argument but, contrary to most TPP exegesis, not to declare that humanity is incapable of keeping the law but rather to demonstrate that Israel's unique privilege in possessing the law functions to reveal rather than to ameliorate sin. Ironically, Israel is worse off for what makes it best off, the possession of the "oracles of God" (Rom 3:9). If this is so for Israel, the circumstances for Gentiles can only be worse (allowing for the possible exception of Rom 2:6-15). There would, thus, need to be a way not only for Gentiles but even for Jews to be made righteous, a way that does not depend on a law that the Gentiles do not have and that Israel cannot keep. And this is precisely "at just the right time" what Romans 3:21-31 provides. This does not make Romans 3:19-20 in itself a claim about the impossibility of works to merit salvation. *Even though that will indeed become a part of Paul's argument*, it is not the point here.

The next, and only other, occurrence of *erga nomou* in Romans is in 3:28: "For we hold that a man is justified by faith apart from works of law." If there is any question that *erga nomou* in Romans 3:20 refers to Judaism in its particularity and uniqueness of privilege rather than general human incapacity for obedience, there can be little doubt of the force of the claim here. Immediately following in Romans 3:29-30, Paul asks the *ad absurdum* rhetorical questions: "Or is God the God of the Jews only? Is he not the God of

---

[46]Not only the strong verbal overlap but also the fact that he does the same in a similar context in Galatians 2:16 confirms the allusion here.

[47]For useful background, see Mark A. Seifrid, "Romans," in *Commentary on the New Testament Use of the Old Testament*, ed. G. K. Beale and D. A. Carson (Grand Rapids: Baker Academic, 2007), 614-18.

the Gentiles also? Yes, of the Gentiles also, since God is one; and he will justify the circumcised on the ground of their faith and the uncircumcised through their faith." The logic is clear from the juxtaposition of Romans 3:28 to 3:29: if justification were by means of "works of the law," it would follow that the one God was the God of the Jews only. Perhaps there is no text in all of Paul's letters that confirms certain premises of the NPP any more clearly than this one. The fault with *erga nomou* in this instance is that possession of the law is a privilege peculiar to Israel, but the one God cannot be partial in such a way as to exclude Gentiles from the sphere of salvation. Thus, Paul deduces it must be the case that justification can only be according to faith for both the circumcised and uncircumcised, that there can only be one and the same ground for all. If Paul believes—as I think he does—that works run afoul of grace, this is not his argument here. That it will soon become the heart of his argument does not make it his point here. As with Galatians, "works of the law" are not flawed in the first instance because they are "works" but because they are "of the law."

So far, what I've offered amounts to a defense of the NPP reading of *erga nomou* as the phrase is used in Galatians and Romans, at least its self-chastened version. But I part company with NPP as it concerns Paul's use of "works" (*erga*). Paul's polemical use of "works," beginning in Romans and then throughout the remainder of his full corpus, cannot be taken as shorthand for *erga nomou* any more than "works" should be taken as simply interchangeable with "*good* works." While it can be argued that Paul's polemic against "works" as the ground of justification or a basis for boasting has affinities with or roots in his polemic against "works of the law," it is better to see it as a theological development or extension related to, but not identical with, the original polemic concerning *erga nomou*.

In addition to the two references to *erga nomou* in Romans, Paul refers to "work/s" (*ergon/erga*) thirteen times in Romans, toward various ends.[48] Our concern will be limited to the soteriologically polemical references of Romans 3–4 and 9–11, in which Paul emphatically disclaims that "works" ground or contribute to justification or salvation, here listed both for convenience and for their cumulative effect:

---

[48] Romans 2:6, 7, 15; 3:27; 4:2, 6; 9:12, 32; 11:6; 13:3, 12; 14:20; 15:18. Of these, we are leaving aside Romans 13:3, 12; 14:20; 15:18 as not directly bearing on matters soteriological.

Then what becomes of boasting? It is excluded. By what law? By that of **works** [(*nomos*) *tōn ergōn*]? No, but by the law of faith. (Rom 3:27 NRSV)

For if Abraham was justified by **works** [*ex ergōn*], he has something to boast about, but not before God. (Rom 4:2 NRSV)

So also David speaks of the blessedness of those to whom God reckons righteousness apart from **works** [*chōris ergōn*]. (Rom 4:6 NRSV)

Even before [Esau and Jacob] had been born or had done anything good or bad (so that God's purpose of election might continue, not because of **works** [*ouk ex ergōn*] but because of his call), she was told, "The elder shall serve the younger." (Rom 9:11-12)

Why not? Because they did not strive for it on the basis of faith [*ek pisteōs*], but as if it were based on **works** [*all' hōs ex ergōn*]. (Rom 9:32 NRSV)

But if it is by grace, it is no longer on the basis of **works** [*ex ergōn*], otherwise grace would no longer be grace. (Rom 11:6 NRSV)

While it is not impossible with some imagination to read "works" as the equivalent to *erga nomou* in certain of these texts,[49] it strains *all* the texts to do so, while proving impossible in the case of *some* of them. We begin with Romans 3:27. The elliptical form of Paul's expression combined with his possibly didactically playful use of "law" make this text difficult with respect to the details. We begin by noting that the best case for equating this unqualified use of "works" with "works of the law" is that, immediately following, Romans 3:28 uses the whole phrase to state the conclusion: "For we hold that a man is justified by faith apart from *works of law*" (RSV). It may be, then, that "works" in Romans 3:27 should be read as shorthand for "works of the law." That argument stumbles, however, when it is noted that Romans 3:27 introduces a play on "works of the law," reversing the (implied)

---

[49]See, e.g., Dunn and Wright on Romans 4:2. "The ἐξ ἔργων should not be taken as a more generalized statement than ἐξ ἔργων νόμου, as the parallel with [Romans] 3:20 and the similar usage in [Romans] 3:27-28 clearly indicate" (James D. G. Dunn, *Romans*, WBC 38 [Dallas: Word, 1988], 1:200). "Paul's main argument is that 'works' (i.e., of Torah) were not the reason for Abraham's justification. . . . If Abraham's covenant membership was indeed defined in terms of 'works of Torah' ([Romans 4:]2*a*), then he and his family would be able to sustain an ethnic boast, and so ([Romans 4:]1) any Gentiles wishing to belong to this family would then have to consider thmselves ethnic Jews—would, in other words, need to become proselytes, with the males among them becoming circumcised" (N. T. Wright, "The Letter to the Romans: Introduction, Commentary and Reflections," in *NIB*, 10:490).

head noun and the genitive qualifier: "law of works." Although there is considerable debate here whether *nomos* refers to the Mosaic law or by wordplay to a kind of "principle," it remains the case that neither the *"principle* of works" nor the "law viewed as a matter of works" is equivalent to *erga nomou* taken as a quasi-technical term.

We turn next at greater length to Romans 4:2-6, something of a fortress for the TPP and an insufficiently acknowledged stumbling block to the NPP. When Paul says, "if Abraham was justified by works, he has something to boast about, but not before God" (Rom 4:2 NRSV), it remains at least possible that Paul rebuts an anachronistic line of Jewish tradition that credits Abraham with Torah observance, such that the "works" here could have that narrower referent. One could argue that, akin to the logic of Galatians 3, this is precisely Paul's salvation-historical point, that Abraham could not have been justified by such not-yet-existent "works of Torah." And, had Paul developed his argument so as to exploit the obvious anachronism and refute it, there might be some basis for taking "works" as though Paul actually means *erga nomou* in this passage as well. But, as it is, everything *in the immediate context* points in a different direction.[50] Paul's "proof" (*gar*) that Abraham was not justified by "works" proceeds first in Romans 4:3 from Scripture, in the appeal to Genesis 15:6: "Abraham believed God, and it was reckoned to him as righteousness" (NRSV).[51] This text, juxtaposed with the

---

[50]Michael Cranford insists that "the 'works' in view here should not be lifted out of context and imbued with significance arising from the theological concerns of the Reformation." To be sure. But it simply won't do to implicate the Reformation in the creation of a works-grace antithesis when it is already part of the immediate grammar of Paul's own argument (however understood). Meanwhile, it is not the case that "the works in view are *clearly* those which are of the law ([Romans] 3.20, 28) and which function *primarily* to designate who is and who is not a Jew ([Romans] 3.22, 29-30)" (Cranford, "Abraham in Romans 4: The Father of All Who Believe," *NTS* 41, no. 1 [1996]: 7, emphasis added). And surely it is special pleading to say, "The fact that the clarifying expression 'of the law' does not occur in [Romans] 4.2-5 should not be used as a license to define 'works' as a general principle depicting man's effort to merit salvation by his good deeds when indication of such a principle has not been expressed" (ibid.). The fact that Cranford appeals to the "specialized vocabulary 'works of the law'" to make a claim about "works" betrays four misjudgments at once: (1) that "works of the law" *is* a "specialized vocabulary"; (2) that its entailment as "specialized vocabulary" is fundamentally, and not indirectly, sociological; (3) that "works" is an obvious ("clearly") shorthand for "works of the law," regardless of its use in context; and (4) that Paul's stress on the gratuity of salvation is counterpoise to an actual claim to the contrary.

[51]Jewish tradition could understand Abraham's "faith" especially in terms of his obedience in yielding Isaac to sacrifice. This is not the direction Paul takes Genesis 15:6, since he is interested in demonstrating that Abraham's faith preceded circumcision (Rom 4:11-12), and thus the Akedah by implication.

disclaimer of Romans 4:2, establishes the raw material of the antithesis that is unpacked in the wage-paying analogy that follows. To the one who *works* (*tō ergazomenō*), wages are counted as what is owed rather than a gift. And to the one who does not work but rather trusts (*tō de mē ergazomenō pisteuonti de*) in the one who justifies the ungodly person, it is that faith which is counted for righteousness.

It is hard to imagine what Paul might have done to make his sense of "works" in Romans 4:2 any clearer than this straightforward, pedestrian analogy. Here "working" is set over against "believing," and "wages" (*misthos*) and "that which is owed" (*kata opheilēma*) over against that which is "according to grace" (*kata charin*). Were righteousness reckoned on the basis of work, it would simply be what had been earned rather than uncondi-tioned gift, but that righteousness is reckoned as pure unconditioned gift is further emphasized not only in that it is reckoned to the undeserving who "does not work but trusts," but even to the ungodly (*asebēs*),[52] whom God

---

[52]Two questions follow with respect to the justification of the ἀσεβής: (1) What is the meaning of ἀσεβής? Although etymologically, the word means something like "irreverent," "irreligious" or "impious" (alpha privative + σεβ-; thus the standard English translation "ungodly"), in use, the term connotes not only impiety but also associated wickedness and immorality (e.g., Rom 5:6; 1 Tim 1:9; 2 Pet 2:5; Jude 4; cf. ἀσεβεία, Rom 1:18), such that it can function frequently in antithetical parallelism with "the righteous" (ca. 100x in the LXX; cf. 1 Tim 1:9; 1 Pet 4:18) and in synonymous parallelism with "sinner" (Ps 1:1, 5; Prov 11:31; Sir 12:6; 1 Pet 4:18). The indictment is a stronger one than etymology alone would have implied. (2) What is the referent of ἀσεβής? Commentators are divided as to whether ἀσεβής here refers to a class of persons by means of a collective singular (the position by omission of several commentators: e.g., C. K. Barrett, *The Epistle to the Romans*, 2nd ed., BNTC [Peabody, MA: Hendrickson, 1991], 84; Douglas J. Moo, *The Epistle to the Romans*, NICNT [Grand Rapids: Eerdmans, 1996], 264; cf. Wright, *P&FG*, 2:1004) or if it is a specific reference to "pagan" Abram (C. E. B. Cranfield, *A Critical and Exegetical Commentary on the Epistle to the Romans*, ICC [Edinburgh: T&T Clark, 1975], 1:222; Brendan Byrne, *Romans*, SP [Collegeville, MN: Liturgical Press, 1996], 149; Thomas R. Schreiner, *Romans*, BECNT [Grand Rapids: Baker Academic, 1998], 212, 217; Robert Jewett, *Romans: A Commentary*, Hermeneia [Minneapolis: Fortress, 2007], 313-14). The strength of the ἀσεβής indictment lexically counts against a specific reference to Abram, unless it is Paul's purpose to cast his helpless dependence on grace in the strongest terms possible, perhaps over against his traditional reputation for exemplary righteousness (so, e.g., Byrne, Schreiner). On balance, it is more likely, given the use of the language elsewhere in Romans (Rom 1:18; 5:6), that it is a generalized reference: justifying the ἀσεβής by faith apart from works is just what God does in the Christ-eon. I suggest then that a gnomic force is implied by present-tense τὸν δικαιοῦντα ("the one who characteristically justifies the ungodly"), and "*his* [αὐτοῦ] faith" is anyone's to whom the condition applies, as the following appeal to Psalm 32 implies. Dunn (*Romans*, 1:205) is right to see Paul articulating a "general principle" here, but rather than "a principle drawn from the particular case of Abraham," it is more likely that Paul understands ἀσεβής as a class to which Abram would have belonged and of which he serves as the prototype illustration.

justifies merely on the condition of faith. Of course, to "justify the *asebēs*" is, under normal circumstances, to be guilty of an injustice, literally, to do a most un-God-ly thing.[53] Paul has indicated that in the *hilastērion* of Christ (Rom 3:25), these are not "normal circumstances"; rather, God shows himself both *dikaios* and the one who declares those of Christ-faith *dikaios* (*dikaiounta*, Rom 3:26). Thus, Stephen Westerholm is right to describe this justification of the *asebēs* as an "extraordinary righteousness,"[54] the sheer gratuity of justification. And not only in Romans 4:4-5, but in Romans 4:6 also, Paul underscores the grace/faith–works antithesis in terms of the blessedness of "the person to whom God reckons righteousness *apart from works*" (*chōris ergōn*; cf. Rom 3:21, *chōris nomou*).

It is easy to appreciate why NPP scholars will want to treat this labor-wages analogy as a kind of one-off digression, as something other than Paul's actual point. If by "works" Paul means what he *seems* to in Romans 4:2, and if he means what he *seems* to in Romans 4:3-6 by way of a polemical critique, for all its other virtues, the NPP edifice becomes unstable. That is, if the referent of "works" is to good behaviors of any kind and not merely covenant-specific, culturally differentiating adherence to the law, and if the criticism of those "works" is not that they would be exclusivist but that they would be meritorious, then Romans 4:2-6 does not serve the NPP argument very well at all. So one is sympathetic to the valiant NPP attempts to minimize, marginalize or otherwise reinterpret this text—sympathetic, but not persuaded by the counsel of despair it requires.[55] NPP interpreters are thus obliged to insist that not too much be made of the digression with respect to works, wages, faith and grace.

Wright reminds us that it is the only time that Paul uses this sort of "metaphor" regarding work and wages and that we should not, therefore, "allow this unique and brief sidelight to become the dominant note, as it has in

---

[53]E.g., Exodus 23:7; Deuteronomy 25:1; Proverbs 17:15; Isaiah 5:23; Sirach 42:2.

[54]Stephen Westerholm, *Perspectives Old and New on Paul: The "Lutheran" Paul and His Critics* (Grand Rapids: Eerdmans, 2004), 273-84.

[55]A close reading of Wright's ("Letter to the Romans," 10:489-93) and Dunn's (*Romans*, 1:203-6) commentaries on the passage is instructive. In both cases, it is not hard to discern a kicking against the goads, on the one hand, and, on the other, a failure to demonstrate the contribution of the analogy to the larger argument. Coming as it does from scholars who give Paul credit for considerable coherence (Dunn) if not for remarkable subtlety (Wright), this marginalizing exegesis of Romans 4:2-6 is all the more marked.

much post-Reformation discussion."[56] In principle, I agree with Wright, but one searches in vain in his treatments of this text for a persuasive account of just how this "side-light" functions in the larger argument.[57] Likewise, Dunn is quite right to say, as we would expect, "The language used here (working, reckoning, reward) should not be taken as a description of the Judaism of Paul's day."[58] And we can even heartily agree that "there is a danger . . . that expositions of Paul's theology of justification will focus too heavily on these verses [Rom 4:4-5] without sufficient regard for the movement of his thought in them."[59] But again, also with Dunn's account we are at a loss to find a compelling function for Paul's labor-wage analogy other than as an apparent digression or distraction from what he actually intended to say.

Sympathetic though I am to the NPP circumnavigation of Romans 4:2-6 in favor of the "larger argument," the various attempts to set aside *this leg* of that argument are not persuasive. At the same time, it is true the *larger* argument in which Romans 4:2-6 participates has indeed to do with membership in Abraham's family of "all who believe" (Rom 4:11). This is the argument of Romans 4:9-11: the blessing of forgiveness of sins belongs not only to the circumcision (*peritomē*) but also to the uncircumcision (*akrobystia*) because righteousness was already reckoned to Abraham on the condition of faith. It follows that it is likewise exclusively by faith that righteousness is reckoned to those who "walk in the tracks" (Rom 4:12) of the faith of their "father," Abraham. With the NPP, I affirm that membership in the Abrahamic family apart from law (Rom 4:13-16) is what is chiefly at stake in this extended discourse. This does not make Romans 4:2-6 incidental or tangential,

---

[56]Wright, "Romans," 10:491. In *P&FG* Wright describes it as a "*side-metaphor* . . . which *by coincidence* happens to overlap with one way of expounding an 'old perspective' view of justification" (*P&FG*, 2:850, emphasis added).

[57]Perhaps Wright's most compelling treatment of Romans 4:1-6 is in *P&FG*, 2:1002-5. Here, Wright argues that the μισθός ("wage") of Romans 4:5 should be associated with μισθός ("reward") of Genesis 15:1, viz., the promise of his innumerable progeny (Gen 15:5). While the use of μισθός in both Genesis 15:1 and Romans 4:5 is initially suggestive, the alleged allusion is unpersuasive. In the first place, it is clear that Paul has shifted into a generalization in Romans 4:4-5 and to the metaphorical field of work and wages. Save for the word μισθός—now obviously used in a different way—there is no conceptual or linguistic link back to Genesis 15:1.

[58]Dunn, *Romans*, 1:204.

[59]Yet one wonders how convincing an account we can expect when Dunn cites H. M. Gale approvingly, "for the reader, as for Paul, the picture offered in [Romans 4:]4 possesses relatively little significance in and of itself" (ibid.; citing Herbert M. Gale, *The Use of Analogy in the Letters of Paul* [Philadelphia: Westminster, 1964], 174).

but rather central to the larger argument in which it is contained. The reason that Abraham is not "our father according to the flesh" (Rom 4:1)[60] is that his spiritual, covenantal patrilineage is not according to physical descent but according to faith. The originating issue here is neither human incapacity nor the encroachment of works on grace but rather the accessibility *to* all and efficacy *for* all of a path that secures justification, the forgiveness of sin (Rom 4:7-8), for both Jew and Gentile, circumcised and uncircumcised, alike. It is this that drives Paul's emphasis on faith as the singular "condition" of justification and grace as its singular enablement, over against "works"— whether "of the law" or any other kind.[61]

Indeed, this is the argument of Romans 1–4 in broad strokes. The whole of humanity—both Jew and Gentile, equally in degree if rather differently in form—is guilty of wickedness, foolish in their hubris and degraded by their transgressions, not only destined for judgment but already experiencing that wrath as the bitter fruit of sin. And to make matters worse, what might have seemed to be the divine solution, the law of Moses with its clear moral precepts, has proven to be the opposite of a solution but is rather an exacerbation of the plight. The law exposes the guilt of all while also nourishing the pride, and thus further guilt, of some, all the while providing no deliverance. Although the law *defines* righteousness it does not *produce* righteousness—in fact it shines a spotlight on unrighteousness, and from the exposing glare of that spotlight it brings shame and condemnation but no ultimate relief.

Therefore, of his mercy and in faithfulness to his covenant people and to his whole creation, God provides the atoning sacrifice of Jesus Christ as a means by which his justice toward human unrighteousness is satisfied. The

---

[60]On the translation and exegesis of this verse, see section 2.2 above. I am following Hays's translation and exegesis of Romans 4:1 (Richard B. Hays, "'Have We Found Abraham to Be Our Forefather According to the Flesh?' A Reconsideration of Romans 4:1," *NovT* 27 [1985]: 76-98), although I do not share wholly his conclusions as to the larger argument of Romans 4. Barclay maintains that Hays's proposal is "fatally flawed" since if προπάτορα were the predicate (rather than subject) of εὑρηκέναι, it would not have the article (John M. G. Barclay, *Paul and the Gift* [Grand Rapids: Eerdmans, 2015], 483n88). But this overlooks the fact that articles and genitive (possessive) personal pronouns "travel" together (τὸν προπάτορα ἡμῶν) so routinely that the absence of the article would be exceptional. There is no necessity to Barclay's suggestion that the article would otherwise make προπάτορα titular.

[61]That faith is treated as the antithesis of works and that faith's reward is said to be κατὰ χάριν should spare readers from the crude notion that faith operates as a straightforward quid pro quo with justification (on which, see Wright, "Romans," 10:491-92).

enmity-expressing, enmity-producing, defiling and deforming sins of the world are judged in the body of his son, Jesus Christ (Rom 3:24-25; 8:3). Thus God, righteous in judgment and faithful in mercy, can declare the ungodly righteous, without becoming un-God-ly himself. Moreover, this is a provision that ends human division. Jew and Gentile share the same plight and now have available to them the same remedy, the same atoning sacrifice, who is the Lord of all, into whom they become incorporate into one new family, the children of Abraham, not according to the flesh but according to the promise.

Thus, we are to understand the unmistakable labor-wage/faith-gift antitheses of Romans 4:2-6 as the adumbration of the sheer gratuity of "access to this grace in which we now stand" (Rom 5:2; *tēn prosagōgēn eschēkamen eis tēn charin tautēn en hē hestēkamen*). A justification that is independent of the performance of "works" and requiring faith instead puts all of Abraham's children, Jew and Gentile, on the same gratuitous footing, after the pattern of their forebear. In the end, we do not need to choose—Paul's argument in Romans does not let us choose—between a justification rooted in accessible gratuity and the reconciliation of a common family of Abraham. The two motifs are inseparable and mutually dependent, neither alone being the exclusive meaning of the text, however much recent interpreters have contended for an exclusive motif. The "works" of Romans 4 point not to the narrow, identity-defining strictures of Torah but to any and all righteous behaviors that would aspire for merit before God.

That this is so is borne out not only by the immediate context of the labor-wage analogy but also is secured by the consistent use of "works" for the remainder of the letter to the Romans. We find three more uses of "works" in soteriologically charged contexts in the remainder of the letter:

> Even before [Esau and Jacob] had been born or had done anything good or bad (so that God's purpose of election might continue, not because of **works** but because of his call) she was told, "The elder shall serve the younger." (Rom 9:11-12)

Here admittedly the reference to "works" falls into a somewhat different category, of election rather than justification per se, and for that reason, we will be cautious not to rest too much weight upon this particular occurrence.[62]

---

[62]Of course, for some, election and justification in Pauline use belong together in an *ordo salutis*

Nonetheless, it is clear in this instance that a reference to "works" can have nothing in particular to do with "works of the law." Indeed, the context defines "works" as "having done something either good or bad" (*mēde praxantōn ti agathon ē phaulon*), which is to describe "works" in a generic fashion rather than as any kind of law keeping, an obvious impossibility for prenatal Esau and Jacob. Although this cannot determine the substance of the following uses, it is at least suggestive. Paul's point here is that God's salvation-historical purposes of election into the promise did not depend on or follow from works of obedience or merit, a point he proves with the *reductio ad absurdum* of Esau and Jacob in the womb of Rebekah.

More controversially, but also more to the point under discussion, Paul explains the irony that Israel has not attained to righteousness, though it sought it, and how Gentiles have, though they have not pursued it (Rom 9:30-32 NRSV):

> What then are we to say? Gentiles, who did not strive for righteousness, have attained it, that is, righteousness through faith; but Israel, who did strive for the righteousness that is based on the law, did not succeed in fulfilling that law. Why not? Because they did not strive for it on the basis of faith [*ek pisteōs*], but as if it were based on works [*all' hōs ex ergōn*].

Like Romans 4:1-6, this text is the site of a fundamental disagreement between TPP and NPP interpreters—another Rorschach blot, as it were. On the whole, the TPP is confident that this is yet another smoking gun, confirming a fundamental, soteriological works-faith, effort-grace antithesis.[63] This is confirmed in particular by Romans 10:3 in which "their righteousness" (*tēn idian dikaiosynēn*) stands for a righteousness Israel sought by performance of works over against "the righteousness that comes from God" (*tēn tou theou dikaiosynēn*) of which they are ignorant and the "righteousness of God" (*tē dikaiosynē tou theou*) to which they do not submit. That these soteriological alternatives are couched in the particular context of the crisis of

---

of Christian salvation (e.g., John Piper, *The Justification of God: An Exegetical and Theological Study of Romans 9:1-23* [Grand Rapids: Baker Book House, 1983]). I am not persuaded that this is a reading sufficiently attuned to the Jewish-theological question that determines the theodicy discourse of Romans 9–11, esp. as introduced in Romans 9:1-5.

[63]Schreiner, *Law and Its Fulfillment*, 104-12; idem, *Romans*, 541-44; Moo, *Epistle to the Romans*, 634-36; and idem, "Israel and the Law in Romans 5–11: Interaction with the New Perspective," in Carson, O'Brien and Seifrid, *JVN:PP*, 210-12.

Israel's unbelief is not lost on most TPP scholars, but they nevertheless understand that this text participates in a larger Pauline soteriological argument. Meanwhile, NPP interpreters are persuaded that the "works" in view are *erga nomou* with respect to their identity-distinguishing function (à la Dunn), and "their own righteousness" refers to ethnic Jewish privilege and especially exclusivity (*idian*) rather than the presumption that righteousness could be achieved of one's own effort.

It must be said for starters that any approach to this text that facilely mistakes Paul's obvious Jewish-covenantal concerns (Rom 9:1-5) for a straightforward reference to Christian-soteriological matters has tilted the axis suspiciously and distortedly. Nonetheless, it is not clear that the "works" referred to in Romans 9:32 are reducible to *erga nomou* in the specialized sense that the NPP requires. The two fundamental contrasts of this paragraph are "faith" (*ek pisteōs*) over against "works" (*ex ergōn*) and "the righteousness of God" (2x) versus "their own righteousness" (*tēn idian dikaiosynēn*). Good-faith attempts to the contrary notwithstanding, *in this context*, it becomes nearly impossible to construe the *dikaiosynē tou theou* as anything other than a righteousness of which God is the source.[64] In this passage, *dikaiosynē* is something Israel *pursued* (*diōkō*) though did not attain (*phthanō*), sought to *establish* but did not submit to; and yet the Gentiles *apprehended* (*katalambanō*) it. Thus, in the metaphorical matrix of this passage, *dikaiosynē* is named as a goal, even a possession, and ultimately a gift. Nor can this "human" *dikaiosynē* be cordoned off from the *dikaiosynē tou theou*, as so frequently happens in the history of that debate. Indeed, it is hard to see how some notion of "God's covenant faithfulness" (Wright) or "salvation-creating power" (Käsemann) or some other construal of the phrase can make any tolerable sense in a context where *dikaiosynē* is being pursued and attained (or not) and where the *dikaiosynē tou theou* is even granted and submitted to as the solution to the dilemma of human unrighteousness. If the *dikaiosynē tou theou* in this context describes a righteousness that is attained or comes into the possession of persons, it is quite improbable

---

[64]Whatever position one reaches with respect to Romans 10:3, it is a just complaint that the translation "the righteousness *that comes from* God" (RSV, NRSV, NAB, NIV [1973], emphasis added; cf. "righteousness of God," ESV, NIV [2011]) prejudices the reading of the text by resolving the ambiguous expression as though it were unmistakably a genitive of source.

that "their own righteousness" should mean Israel's proprietary, Gentile-excluding righteousness. The contrast is more directly drawn between righteousness as a human attainment (albeit by the divinely mandated means of the law) and the righteousness that God supplies.

It then follows from that contrast that the integral and parallel relationship between righteousness as "of God" (*theou*) or their "own" (*idian*) and the alternative means of attaining each, "faith" or "works," be given its full berth. The righteousness that the Gentiles have attained is "a righteousness *from faith*" (*dikaiosynēn de tēn ek pisteōs*, Rom 9:30). Thus, the contrast of faith with works and that of a righteousness *of God* over against "their own" are of a piece. The righteousness of God is apprehended by faith, whereas the failed-because-misbegotten acquisition of "their righteousness" was attempted by means of works. "Works" in Romans 9:30–10:4 surely include "works of the law," properly understood, but *erga* cannot be construed as a simple contraction of "works of the law," even less to its NPP technical appropriation. At risk of question begging, it might be said that had Paul intended the more specific reference to "works of the law," he surely could have specified as much by use of the expression.[65] As it is, there are no clear contextual indicators that Paul intends a narrower or technical referent for "works."

Finally, we turn to the remaining soteriologically relevant reference to "works" in Romans, 11:6, which continues the pattern we have so far observed. "But if it is by grace, it is no longer on the basis of works [*ex ergōn*], otherwise grace would no longer be grace" (NRSV). In this final movement of the Romans 9–11 argument, Paul returns to the broad theme first announced in Romans 9:6 ("not all who are of Israel are Israel"; *ou . . . pantes hoi ex Israēl houtoi Israēl*), which is subsequently illustrated by various Old Testament story lines that demonstrate the remnant principle to be the norm rather than the exception (Rom 9:7-29). That a "part" of Israel has rejected the Messiah is tragic and devastating but not unprecedented and, more importantly, in no way besmirches God's faithfulness. Now in Romans 11, Paul

---

[65]In fact, ἔργων νόμου *is* an attested reading of Romans 9:32. I concur with the text-critical consensus that νόμου is a later addition, conforming to Romans 3:20, 28. See Metzger, *TCGNT*, 462-63, rating the shorter reading a {B}; Dunn, *Romans*, 579, "the shorter text is certainly more likely to be original"; Schreiner, *Romans*, 548-49, "the reading of NA27 is certainly original"; and R. Jewett, *Romans*, 606.

returns to those themes of election and remnant, applying them to the current circumstance. The remnant now consists of Christ-believing Israel along with the grafted branches of Gentiles. This elect remnant is chosen by grace, and, as Paul understands it, the remnant's election by grace excludes that it could be on the basis of works (*ex ergōn*), lest "grace no longer be grace" (*hē charis ouketi ginetai charis*). It is patent for Paul in this stage of his argument that works and grace are antithetical and antithesized in such a way that the "works" here referenced cannot be reduced narrowly to *erga nomou* in their identity-distinguishing function.

Our survey from Galatians to Romans demonstrates a decisive pattern of development in the Pauline use of "works" / "works of the law" that merits close attention. In Galatians we find only a reference to "works of the law," and, as I have argued, in its chastened form, the NPP account of the language is broadly persuasive. Meanwhile, we noted that the language of "works" does not bear a soteriological polemic in the Thessalonian and Corinthian correspondences, and we are reminded that there is not a general intrinsically antithetical relationship between faith and works in Paul. At least in early Paul, this is a theme reserved for those contexts in which the entry of Gentiles into the covenant people is at stake or, as is the case with Romans, the fragile rapprochement of the two ethnic communities is threatened. With Romans, Paul's soteriological transition begins to take its shape, and the transition from *erga nomou* to "works" is a signpost of that transition from the exigent urgency of the crisis in Galatia to the nagging divisions in Rome. The more expansive reflection of Romans documents the beginning transition from the sociological exigency of Galatians to the more expressly soteriological strategem of Romans. From Galatians we learn that *erga nomou* function to exclude Abraham's adopted Gentile children from the family table; in Romans, without any retraction from the salient themes of Galatians, we learn also that "works," if depended upon as though meritorious, stand opposed to God's gracious purpose of electing a single covenant family. I don't suggest that Galatians is absent "soteriology" and even less that the discourse of Romans is abstracted from its own "sociological" crisis. Rather, as we will explore below (see section 8.1), it remains for Romans for the human dilemma to be constructed explicitly as an alienation from God, remediated in a reconciling atonement appropriated by faith.

Over against both NPP and TPP, I reject the presumption that *erga nomou* and "works" are synonymous expressions. My survey demonstrates that "works" is not simply shorthand for *erga nomou* as is required for the arguments of NPP scholars to cohere, not only in Galatians but into Romans and beyond. And while, to be sure, *erga nomou* are by definition a subset of "works," the former is not simply a more specific instantiation of "works," as though a synecdoche for a larger meritorious soteriological principle, as assumed by most TPP-inclined interpreters. Paul's use of the two expressions is not casual; they are not interchangeable. "Works of the law" prevails when Paul's critique concerns especially the law in its cultural particularity and salvation-historical limitations. But the absolute use of "works" is reserved to express, no less polemically, the counterpart of gratuity.

6.1.4 "Works" beyond Romans. In what follows, I can be more brief, because if *erga nomou* and its possible, but I think unlikely, surrogate "works" are matters of controversy in the undisputed Pauline corpus, the same is not true of Paul's use of "works" in the Captivity and Pastoral Epistles. At the same time, what we find in these letters strongly confirms what I have claimed about "works" in Romans, that this language is indicative of Paul's settling soteriology that eschews any role for a meritorious human contribution.

As with the Thessalonian and Corinthian correspondences, *ergon* has only a minimal function in Philippians, all singular, referring to the work of ministry in Philippians 1:22 and 2:30 and the work, however understood, that God began in the Philippians in 1:6 (cf. *ergatēs* in Phil 3:2).[66] This is not the language Paul uses in the soteriological polemic of Philippians 3:2-11. It is clear there that Paul has come to depend on a righteousness "from God" (*ek theou*) that contrasts "my righteousness from the law" (*emēn dikaiosynēn tēn ek nomou*), but he does not use the language of "works" to describe this antithesis, although it is conceptually parallel. Needless to say, "works" is not the only language Paul could have used to express the larger theme.

With regard to vocabulary, what is true of Philippians applies to Colossians. The only plural reference to "works" is the "evil deeds" that express the estrangement and hostility of the unreconciled (Col 1:21). Otherwise, the

---

[66]Paul uses the compounds συνεργός (Phil 2:25; 4:3), ἐνεργέω (Phil 2:13, 2x), ἐνέργεια (Phil 3:21) and κατεργάζομαι (Phil 2:12), but there is no significant contribution in this terminology to the question at hand. We will be considering Philippians 2:12-13 later in the discussion of σωτηρία.

language of "works" is not used, either positively or negatively, in soterio-logical contexts, and, likewise, "law" is absent from the letter altogether. The closest that Colossians comes to such questions in the much controverted Colossians 2:11-12, where in a more compressed and obscure form, Paul[67] subverts the rite of circumcision as the requisite condition of covenant membership (cf. Rom 2:25-29). When Paul says, "In [Christ] you were cir-cumcised with a circumcision made without hands, by putting off the body of flesh in the circumcision of Christ" (Col 2:11), he implies that this "cir-cumcision not done by hand" is somehow related to baptism: "having been buried in baptism" (Col 2:12).[68] But a soteriological works-faith antithesis does not factor into the discourse of Colossians as such; the soteriological emphases of this letter reside more in the metaphorical fields of atonement (Col 1:20-22; 2:14-15), reconciliation (Col 1:20-22), and union with Christ in death, resurrection and exaltation (Col 2:12-13, 19-20; 3:1-3).

It is at last in Ephesians where we see Paul exploiting the works-faith antithesis most explicitly. The key text, of course, is Ephesians 2:8-10: "For by grace you have been saved through faith, and this is not your own doing; it is the gift of God—not the result of works [*ouk ex ergōn*], so that no one may boast. For we are what he has made us, created in Christ Jesus for good works [*epi ergois agathois*], which God prepared beforehand to be our way of life" (NRSV). Already with the interjection of Ephesians 2:5—"by grace you have been saved" (NRSV)—Paul has signaled the emphatic theme of his Ephesians soteriology, that salvation is of grace, which is to say that it is exclusively through faith (*dia pisteōs*), that it is not of human origin (*ouk ex hymōn*), that it is a sheer gift of God, that "works" can make no material contribution, lest someone might take credit for what is of God's doing alone. It would be hard to offer a clearer and more emphatic grace-affirming,

---

[67]With chap. 5 behind us, I will dispense with the scholarly convention of referring to the author of the disputed letters as "the author" or "deutero-Paul" or a scare-quoted "Paul" and simply refer to the inscribed author of the letters.

[68]Grammatically it appears that the relationship between that "spiritual" circumcision and baptism is quite direct (although this is disputed), baptism functioning as the means or appropriation of the "circumcision of Christ." The most natural way to take the aorist participle συνταφέντες of Colossians 2:12 is as coincident with περιετμήθητε of Colossians 2:11 and as a participle of means: "You were circumcised with a circumcision not performed by human hands . . . when you were [or *by being*] buried with him in baptism." This position is strengthened if we take the antecedent of ᾧ to be βαπτισμῷ. Murray J. Harris, *Colossians & Philemon*, Exegetical Guide to the Greek New Testament (Grand Rapids: Eerdmans, 1991), 104.

works-negating statement, and there can be little doubt that for this reason Ephesians 2:8-9 has exerted a controlling influence on the understanding of Paul disproportionate to its dimensions or prominence. It would be a mistake, however, whatever one makes of the question of Pauline authenticity, to regard this text as though an outlier. Rather, in this regard, Ephesians 2:8-9 does not represent a departure from Romans but merely its extension as a concise, settled soteriological trope. All the elements are already found in Romans, albeit scattered about and participating in a more extended and complex discourse. As it concerns the procurement of salvation, grace and works are antithetical (Rom 4:4, 16; 11:5-6), which is why it depends on faith, rather than works (Rom 3:28; 4:4-6). Salvation is an unconditioned gift (Rom 3:24; 5:15-17; cf. 2 Cor 9:15), and therefore boasting is excluded (Rom 3:27; 4:2). I don't say that each of these staples of the Ephesians soteriology is appropriated in Romans toward precisely the same ends, but that every way Paul asserts the gratuity of salvation in Ephesians is expressly adumbrated and already multiply attested in Romans. Ephesians must be seen as the continuation of Romans, just as Romans is shown to be the development of Galatians. What Galatians might suggest, Romans secures and Ephesians treats as settled.

This congealing pattern is further demonstrated and confirmed in the Pastoral Epistles. The most explicit text in this regard is Titus 3:5-7, which is very much of a piece with Ephesians 2:

> Not because of any works of righteousness that we had done, but according to his mercy, he saved us through the water of rebirth and renewal by the Holy Spirit. This Spirit he poured out on us richly through Jesus Christ our Savior, so that, having been justified by his grace, we might become heirs according to the hope of eternal life. (Tit 3:5-7)

The themes of the earlier texts again assume a concise, quasi-confessional form here. Again there is a firm disavowal of "works which we performed in righteousness" (*ouk ex ergōn tōn en dikaiosynē ha epoiēsamen*) and an unreserved attribution of salvation to "his mercy" (*to autou eleos*), where mercy is a near synonym of "grace," with perhaps a greater emphasis on God's pity (cf. Tit 3:4, "goodness and loving kindness") toward the humanity mired in its self-made misery (Tit 3:3). Likewise, justification—this being the only soteriological use of the term subsequent to Romans—is by grace (Tit 3:7, *dikaiōthentes tē ekeinou chariti*), a theme echoing Romans 3:24 quite directly (*dikaioumenoi dōrean tē autou chariti*). For all of its stereotypical features, two details distinguish Titus 3:5-7 from any other Pauline soteriological formula: (1) There is no reference to "faith" or "believing" in the formulation, thus no express works-*faith* contrast, only works-*grace*. As is well known, faith in the PE frequently is used of the "Christian" faith, more a body of beliefs and distinctive way of life (Tit 1:4, 13; 2:2) than personal, existential trust, although this contrast should not be overdrawn (cf. Tit 1:1). (2) Titus 3 presents the coordinate media of salvation— "washing of regeneration" and "renewal of the Holy Spirit"—as instrumental to a salvation void of works and justification by grace.

Titus 3 is not alone in disavowing "works" in the PE. The same theme is found in 2 Timothy 1:9: "who saved us and called us with a holy calling, not according to our works but according to his own purpose and grace" (NRSV). Here again, we find an emphatic contrast between human "works" and divine initiative, described as God's "own resolve and grace, which was given to us in Jesus Christ before time began."

6.2 THE EVOLUTION OF "GRACE"

Consideration of *charis* and the verbal and conceptual cognates in Paul is itself material sufficient for a full-length study, now abundantly satisfied by John Barclay's recent book.[69] The goal in what follows is much more modest: to propose that Paul's appeal to grace develops with a pattern that is roughly parallel to the development of his appeal to "works." As his disavowal of "works" generalized from his initial repudiation of "works of the law," so also—I argue, not accidentally—"grace" comes to the fore as the more explicit antithesis of "works." Thus the "gift"—already an unmerited beneficence,

---

[69]Barclay, *Paul and the Gift*; for the semantic background, see his appendix, "The Lexicon of Gift: Greek, Hebrew, Latin, and English," 575-82. Previews of Barclay's full study can be found in John M. G. Barclay, "Paul, the Gift and the Battle over Gentile Circumcision: Revisiting the Logic of Galatians," *Australian Biblical Review* 58 (2010): 36-56; idem, "Unnerving Grace: Approaching Romans 9–11 from the Wisdom of Solomon," in *Between Gospel and Election: Explorations in the Interpretation of Romans 9–11* (Tübingen: Mohr Siebeck, 2010), 91-109; idem, "Believers and the 'Last Judgment' in Paul: Rethinking Grace and Recompense," in *Eschatologie* (Tübingen: Mohr Siebeck, 2011), 195-208; and idem, "Pure Grace? Paul's Distinctive Jewish Theology of Gift," *Studia Theologica* 68, no. 1 (2014): 4-20. Cf. also Jonathan A. Linebaugh, *God, Grace, and Righteousness in Wisdom of Solomon and Paul's Letter to the Romans: Texts in Conversation*, NovTSup 152 (Leiden: Brill, 2013).

already divine mercy and initiative—becomes the increasingly explicit and resolute antithesis to human performance as Paul's language is traced from Galatians through the Pastoral Epistles.

Before charting Paul's use of *charis* in particular texts, it is first important to clear the ground by noting that *charis* intrinsically spans a broader and a more general semantic range than the particular freighted uses of the term in Christian theological contexts. Whereas unilateral divine initiative, forbearance, mercy, amnesty, forgiveness and so on are all thought of as instantiations of "grace," we will be misled in our reading of New Testament texts should we assume that this constellation, certainly as a whole but even with respect to the parts, always attaches to every use of the term or even that these theological notions are always proper to the term without qualification.[70] This is not simply to invoke the common sense of James Barr's famous "illegitimate totality transfer"[71]—although it is that—but to insist on the exercise of semantic reserve and openness when reading *charis* in Pauline texts. While we negotiate between the extremes whereby *charis* either means "everything it possibly could" or "as little as necessary," methodologically I incline to the latter unless the context demands otherwise. Moreover, we are now aided by Barclay's taxonomy of "perfections" to further elucidate not only semantic content but also conceptual implicature.

We, thus, begin by noting that *charis* as a ubiquitous secular concept refers simply to gift, favor or benefaction in broad and diverse terms.[72] And we notice, second, that the use of the term in the New Testament is preceded by considerable use in the LXX, but where a strong context-independent, religious connotation is comparatively rare, almost unknown.[73] Nor does

---

[70]Similarly Barclay, though in terms of grace's "perfections" (*Paul and the Gift*, 66-78). My approach, which I regard as complementary, is somewhat more lexical, while his is conceptual and obviously anthropological.

[71]James Barr, *The Semantics of Biblical Language* (London: Oxford University Press, 1961), 218.

[72]In addition to LSJ, a useful lexical orientation can be found in Ceslas Spicq, *TLNT*, 3:500-506. Note, e.g., the wide-ranging glosses: "grace, beauty, charm, favor, goodwill, free benevolence, gift, benefit, gratitude" (*TLNT*, 3:500). Also useful for background, although inevitably more theological, is Hans Conzelmann, "χάρις κτλ.," *TDNT*, 9:372-76.

[73]While LEH substantiates the primarily nontheological use in the LXX, even here the anticipated theological content proves irresistible when inexplicably "grace" is chosen as the first gloss and we are told that χάρις is used "often of the Lord's kindness received gratuitously" (Johan Lust, Erik Eynikel and Katrin Hauspie, *A Greek-English Lexicon of the Septuagint*, rev. ed. [Stuttgart: Deutsche Bibelgesellschaft, 2003], s.v. χάρις). While certain references might imply as much (e.g., Gen 6:8), at best the lexicon overstates the evidence. The χάρις that is "found before the

the LXX ever use *charis* in any even remotely soteriological sense: never does it suggest covenant faithfulness; never is it divine initative; never is it tantamount to forgiveness or divine motivation for reconciliation; never is it a divine attribute. These basic and noncontroversial observations are surprising only because of the frequent retrojection of concepts proper to "grace" as a Christian-theological construct onto *charis* in contexts where it is innocent of any such connotations. One notes, for just one example, the treatment of *charis* in the *Theological Dictionary of New Testament Theology*,[74] which includes an extended discussion of *charis* in relationship to *ḥesed* even though, of the seventy-eight uses of *charis* in the LXX, only one of them (Esther 2:9) translates *ḥesed*![75] That the *TDNT* should mislead in this regard is not surprising, but there remains a durability to these sorts of working presumptions. We ought not approach New Testament uses of the term necessarily expecting what we "know" about "grace" to attach to *charis* automatically or as a foregone conclusion. The lexical data in themselves simply do not yield a patent theological construct, an observation made now indelibly in Barclay's recent study. At the same time, it is clear that the New Testament itself is responsible for launching the trajectory by which "grace" becomes the dense and freighted, if flexible, bearer of theological payload.[76]

6.2.1 Grace in Galatia? We begin with Galatians, asking what significance *charis* bears in this letter, especially when it is read as Paul's first use

---

Lord" is most frequently not "received gratuitously"; rather, the Lord's favorable disposition turned toward those worthy for their virtue (Prov 3:3-4), wisdom, humility (Prov 3:34) and innocence (Ps 83:12 LXX). When the Lord "gives" χάρις, frequently it is that he intervenes such that he grants persons a favorable disposition before a social superior before whom that person's cause is in question, but it is not in any sense the Lord's χάρις that is bestowed. Rather, his intervention is such that a human in a position of power might show favor.

[74]W. Zimmerli, "χάρις," *TDNT*, 9:381-87.

[75]But sixty-seven of the seventy-eight LXX occurrences of χάρις are translations of חֵן (*ḥēn*; "grace," "charm," "favor"). Emmanuel Tov and Frank Polak, *The Revised CATSS: Hebrew/Greek Parallel Text* (Jerusalem; Philadelphia, 2005).

[76]Some readers will be aware that Protestant and Catholic readers characteristically hear different nuances in the word *grace*. For Protestants the chief note *grace* sounds is with respect to an unmerited salvation, toward which the Christian makes no contribution—nor could she. *Sola gratia* is thus concordant not only with an unmerited salvation but also with monergism itself, and, indeed, for many Protestant Christians a predestinarian account of faith is merely the logical outworking of a salvation that is by grace alone. For Catholics, grace is inseperable from its sacramental vehicles and intricately woven into a Christian account of metaphysics, whereby grace is the panoply of divine provision that meets and perfects nature, allowing for a fundamentally synergystic soteriology.

of the term and without the aid of the later uses. It is fair to say that most uses of the term are readily described in reference to God's general benevolence and favor expressed in the particularity of the gospel, that is, the Christ event as an irruption into human social structures, both Jewish and Gentile. At the same time, it is not necessary to see in these early uses a self-conscious and vivid contrast between, say, divine initiative (i.e., priority) and human incapacity or divine forgiveness and human wretchedness (i.e., efficacy). However, that divine grace is, in Barclay's terms, incongruous is granted as basic to Paul's conception, although even here we might ask just how much attaches to that notion.

Charis occurs seven times in Galatians (Gal 1:3, 6, 15; 2:9, 21; 5:4; 6:18). For our purposes, we may set to one side the formulaic uses of Galatians 1:3 and 6:18, since there is nothing in the immediate context that informs us of a precise content in either case.[77] We note, second, that two of the five references in Galatians clearly understand *charis* as tantamount to Paul's missionary vocation (Gal 2:9 RSV; "the grace that was given to me"; *tēn charin tēn dotheisan*) or the divine instrumentality in that calling (Gal 1:15 RSV; "[God], the one who had set me apart before I was born, and had called me through his grace"; *ho aphorisas me ek koilias metros mou kai kalesas dia tēs charitos autou*). Grace here is God's beneficence that rescued primitive Christianity's chief antagonist and appointed him apostle to the Gentiles—a "gift" to be sure, but not a gift set over against human effort and achievement. It is not shorthand for divine enablement in light of human incapacity. Or at least we should say that there is nothing in the context of these Galatians passages that requires such notions to be read into the word, even if there

---

[77]Here I part company, at least methodologically, with Barclay, who treats semantic contribution as sufficiently patent that even its formulaic uses condition the reading of the larger letter: "The formula χάρις καὶ εἰρήνη (Gal 1:3) is uniquely Pauline as an epistolary salutation, and it is here *loaded with semantic content* specific to the Christ-story" (Barclay, *Paul and the Gift*, 352-53, emphasis added). It is not so much that I regard this assumption as false as that I regard it as beyond demonstration. The donation of χάρις in such contexts must be left as an open question. If, as seems probable, χάρις in Galatians 1:3 (cf. Rom 1:7; 1 Cor 1:3; 2 Cor 1:2; Eph 1:2; Phil 1:2; Col 1:2; 1 Thess 1:1; 2 Thess 1:2; Philem 3) is a Pauline substitute or at least echo of the more conventional epistolary greeting, χαίρειν (see Terence Y. Mullins, "Greeting as a New Testament Form," *JBL* 87, no. 4 [1968]: 418-26; and Judith Lieu, "'Grace to You and Peace': The Apostolic Greeting," *BJRL* 68, no. 1 [1985]: 161-78), we have further reason to affirm Paul's emphasis on "grace," though no clear sense from this or the grace wish at the conclusion of the letters (cf. Rom 16:20; 1 Cor 16:23; 2 Cor 13:13; Phil 4:23; 1 Thess 5:28; 2 Thess 3:18; Philem 25) to discern its precise content, if, indeed, a precise content is intended.

are clearly other places in the Pauline corpus where this seems to be nearer to the substance of *charis*. Moreover, there is no suggestion in these contexts that grace amounts to forgiveness for the "chief of sinners," wiping the slate clean for the archenemy of the church (Gal 1:13-14). *Charis* here did not forgive Paul; it called him to his vocation (Gal 1:15), "that I might preach him among the Gentiles" (Gal 1:16 RSV), and if it enabled a response, it was to carry out that charge. That this is so is confirmed first in the widely acknowledged fact that Galatians 1:15 is a deliberate echo of prophetic call language (Is 49:1, 5; Jer 1:5). Second, this sense of *charis* is substantiated by the thematically analogous use in Galatians 2:9. Here it is clear from the immediate context that the "grace given to me" (*tēn charin tēn dotheisan moi*) that the Jerusalem "pillars" perceived can be none other than the "gospel of uncircumcision" that had been entrusted to Paul (*pepisteumai to euangelion tēs akrobystias*).[78] Thus, two of our seven uses of *charis* in Galatians are explicit reference to his apostolic commission. These observations in no way subvert the claim that "grace" is incongruous (unconditioned, undeserved) for Paul. Rather, it casts Paul's commission—his responsibility before God to Gentiles—as sheer privilege, divinely authorized and enabled.

Similarly, in Galatians 1:6 we find a reference to *charis* that does not betray an especially focused theological force: "I am astonished that you are so quickly deserting the one who called you in the grace of Christ and are turning to a different gospel" (NRSV). Unlike Galatians 1:15 and 2:9, referencing Paul's commission, it is clear in this instance that the "call" is soteriological; as in Galatians 1:15, grace is the instrumentality (or perhaps sphere) of that calling.[79] Therefore, *charis*, the incongruous favor of God exhibited and enacted in the gospel, is the context and character of his calling of the Galatians to their new identity in Messiah Jesus. Nothing more or less is implied here than that God acted with a focused benevolence in

---

[78]The claim that these are parallel and effectively epexegetic expressions is substantiated in the following observations: (1) With a majority of translations, I take the γάρ clause Galatians 2:8 as parenthetical. (2) Both Galatians 2:7 and 2:9 speak of a direct object "entrusted" and "given," "the gospel of uncircumcision" and "grace," respectively. (3) Both expressions are the content of an aorist participle of perception (ἰδόντες, γνόντες) for which the "pillars" are the implicit subject: they "saw"; they "perceived."

[79]It is not clear whether ἐν χάριτι is best taken in an instrumental ("by means of") or locative ("in the sphere of") sense, nor is it evident that there is any significant difference beyond style between διὰ τῆς χάριτος and ἐν χάριτι. See the discussion in Barclay, *Paul and the Gift*, 354n10.

Christ. There is no suggestion of divine forgiveness (a theme absent from Galatians), nor is there any suggestion that *charis* has undertaken where human effort failed nor that it makes success possible where failure had been inevitable.[80] This use of *charis* neither grants nor implies any necessity to a certain theological anthropology or soteriology.

This leaves us with the remaining two more interesting and controverted references to grace in Galatians: 2:21 and 5:4. Paul's denial, "I do not nullify the grace of God," in Galatians 2:21 (NRSV) is puzzling. The asyndetic clause bears no obvious relationship to Galatians 2:20, nor is it clear in the context why Paul might feel a need to defend himself from nullifying the grace of God at the conclusion of his refutation of "works of the law." The denial seems superfluous. By most readings of the passage, it is not grace that is in danger of being "nullified" but its assumed antithesis, "works of the law." A natural and plausible surmise for mirror-reading New Testament scholarship is that Paul is answering a charge made by his opponents, namely, that by sitting loose with respect to the law Paul was rejecting Israel's divine gift (cf. Rom 3:1-2; 9:4).[81] In the nature of the case, this would be impossible to know, and some could object that it requires the Galatians to infer more than could be expected of them.[82] Nonetheless, the form of Paul's protest is otherwise hard to account for if he responds to nothing, whether an explicit charge of which Paul was aware or an anticipated objection. A plausible refinement of this view is to understand the denial as litotes: "Far from nullifying the *charis* of God, I affirm it."[83] Understood so, the denial could nevertheless function as rejoinder to an an actual or imagined objection, but particular knowledge or presumption of such is unnecessary to the point being made, the affirmation of grace in strong terms by means of the figure of litotes. Then, by means of *reductio ad absurdum*, Paul goes on to explain why, in fact, his position is *charis*-affirming: that justification could not have been through the "grace" of the Torah since then Christ would

---

[80]It is perhaps not insignificant that the "desertion" is "from the *one who called* you in grace" (μετατίθεσθε ἀπὸ τοῦ καλέσαντος ὑμᾶς ἐν χάριτι) (Gal 1:6), not from grace itself. That is to say that the Galatians' turning to "another gospel" is a desertion of the One calling, not necessarily an abandonment of "grace" in preference for human works.

[81]Martyn, *Galatians*, 259; and Richard N. Longenecker, *Galatians*, WBC 41 (Dallas: Word, 1990), 94-95.

[82]Moo, *Galatians*, 172.

[83]On litotes as rhetorical figure, see Aune, *WDNTLR*, 280.

have died for no purpose (Gal 2:21).[84] If grace has come in the form of the cross, then to cling to "works of the law" amounts to a rejection of both the cross and the grace it signifies. If something like this interpretation is correct, then it is clear that this is a use of *charis* void of a strong Christian-theological content, while the substance of the larger claim begins to point toward *charis* not merely as divine benevolence but divine undertaking through Christ in light of human incapacity. Thus, the text as a whole hints at—I suggest, anticipates—a notion of "grace" that will become clearer in Paul's subsequent writings, but *charis* itself does not carry that content here. We might say that *charis* in this context is fully gift but, in Barclay's terms, a gift "unperfected," highlighting neither grace's priority nor its signature Pauline incongruity.

Finally, we consider *charis* in Galatians 5:4, which is arguably the best candidate in the letter for bearing the sort of strong theological content that is frequently assumed on behalf of the other occurrences. "You who want to be justified by the law have cut yourselves off from Christ; you have fallen away from grace" (NRSV). What does it mean to "have fallen away from grace"? It is tempting—and many theologically inclined interpreters yield to the temptation—to understand "falling from grace" as an idiom for abandoning the gift of God's gracious provision in favor of self-effort. After all, those who are cut off and have so fallen are the same who attempt justification by means of the law.[85] But the metaphorical figure of "falling from grace" suggests that *charis* is not here a principle (of reliance upon God rather than self) but rather a sort of sphere, a metaphorical space of divine favor and blessedness. Thus to "fall from grace" is but a different way of speaking of "being severed from Christ"; the two expressions combine to emphasize the disaster of the outcome for those seeking justification by the

---

[84]The sentence amounts to a contrary-to-fact conditional, though not grammatically marked as such.

[85]Presumably the present δικαιοῦσθε is conative in force ("some who are trying to be justified by law"; so BDF, 167, §319; MHT, 3:63; A. T. Robertson, *A Grammar of the Greek New Testament in the Light of Historical Research* [Nashville: Broadman, 1934], 880; and Wallace, *GGBB*, 535), with the presumption that it is a failed endeavor (although cf. Barclay, *Paul and the Gift*, 375n65, who allows that this occurrence could be regarded as a middle voice). On the other hand, the use of the aorist indicative for κατηργήθητε and ἐξεπέσατε confounds expectations to good rhetorical effect. Given the hypothetical character of δικαιοῦσθε and the dissuasive character of the letter in general, the aorist is a jarring prolepsis, stressing the certainty of the undesirable outcome as patent.

law. Yet *charis* is not, therefore, in this context necessarily a principle of divine initiative or solicitude emphasizing the incompatibility of "works" with "grace," of human striving with divine undertaking. This is not to say that these are not true or Pauline notions, only that they do not constitute the substance of this warning to the Galatians, however obvious such ideas are to Christian readers of the text having been conditioned by the whole of the Pauline corpus and a long theological history of grace. As should be evident, contrary to some NPP scholarship, I do not consider these interpreters fundamentally mistaken on these points; I only consider it mistaken to treat these constructs as patent already in Galatians and especially to credit *charis* with this payload upon its every occurrence.[86]

6.2.2 Grace in the Thessalonian and Corinthian correspondences. Our caution with regard to *charis* in Galatians is further confirmed in the letters that intervene between it and Romans. The six references to *charis* in the Thessalonian correspondence are largely formal in character: in the salutations (1 Thess 1:1; 2 Thess 1:2) and the concluding grace-wishes (1 Thess 5:28; 2 Thess 3:18). The two remaining occurrences are found in prayers in 2 Thessalonians (2 Thess 1:12; 2:16). The *"charis* of God and the Lord Jesus Christ" conditions Christian obedience (2 Thess 1:11) so that the Lord Jesus Christ is glorified in a manner befitting the gift (*kata tēn charin*).[87] In 2 Thessalonians 2:16, *charis* is the sphere or means by which the gifts of eternal "consolation" and "good hope" are given. While the substance of *charis* is relatively indistinct and not specifically soteriological, this is not to say that *charis* is empty of content—only that there is no place in this correspondence where it is leveraged for a strong theological content, especially not in service of distinctive soteriological claims.

---

[86]In this sense, while I am persuaded by Barclay's account of grace in Paul, I have parted company with his treatment of χάρις in Galatians, not to say his reading of Galatians more generally. While clearly distancing his reading of grace from the theologically presumptuous tendencies of his predecessors, it does not seem to me that Barclay has been sufficiently restrained by literary context in his understanding of grace in Galatians. So, although it is not the dominant undifferentiated Christian-theological construct that he finds in Galatians, there is an understanding of χάρις that Barclay might be reading into Galatians, even if it is carefully nuanced by means of cultural anthropology. I am, rather, taking up his permission (*Paul and the Gift*, e.g., 449-55) to observe development in Paul and proposing that the incongruity of χάρις becomes increasingly leveraged in the Pauline discourse.
[87]In Barclay's terms, this text would bear witness not only to incongruity but also to the assumed but free reciprocity of response.

Charis is more ubiquitous in the Corinthian correspondence, especially 2 Corinthians, but, while exhibiting a wider range of use in its twenty-eight occurrences (cf. *charisma*, 8x; *charizomai*, 6x)—some in formulae,[88] some richly theological—*charis* is not yet leveraged in characteristic, theologically stereotyped ways. As in Galatians, in a few instances *charis* is closely affiliated with Paul's vocation, as its ground and energy (1 Cor 3:10; 15:10). More frequently, *charis* is used in relationship to the Jerusalem Collection, sometimes describing the gift itself (1 Cor 16:3), sometimes characterizing it as a gracious or generous deed (2 Cor 8:1, 6, 7, 19) or, indeed, the privilege of taking part (2 Cor 8:4). The generosity of the Corinthians is made possible and necessary as an act of reciprocation to God "paid forward" by the generous *charis* of God, which both provides materially and empowers every good work (2 Cor 9:8, 14). But, above all, the Jerusalem offering is *charis* because it displays and participates in the "*charis* of our Lord Jesus Christ, who though he was rich, yet for your sake became poor, so that by his poverty you might become rich" (2 Cor 8:9). The generosity of God's supply and the liberality of his succor are sufficient for material needs and as the provision that sustains in the face of adversity (2 Cor 9:8; 12:9).

These diverse expressions of *charis* are united as manifestations of the generous provision of God, epitomized in Jesus Christ (1 Cor 1:4; 2 Cor 4:15; 8:9; 9:14). But for all of the frequent and diverse appeals to *charis*, these letters are absent again of an appropriation of *charis* that is pointedly soteriological. Grace is never described as though the antidote to sin or as the remediation of guilt. Nor in these letters is grace ever contrasted with "works" or human effort of some kind. Likewise, grace is never contrasted with law as its antithesis. Grace is the express generosity of God, diverse in its manifold expressions. The grace of God is the source of Christian existence and blessing through Jesus Christ; it grounds and motivates Christian charity and energizes apostolic ministrations. But it is never the antithesis

---

[88]Besides its formal uses in the letters' greetings (1 Cor 1:3; 2 Cor 1:2) and concluding grace-wishes (1 Cor 16:23; 2 Cor 13:13), χάρις is used in the sense of "gift," characterized as a gracious deed in relationship to the Jerusalem Collection (1 Cor 16:3; 8x in 2 Cor 8–10; cf. χάρισμα, 2 Cor 1:11) or even as a simple interpersonal kindness (2 Cor 1:15). It is used as an expression of thanksgiving to God in the stereotyped interjection χάρις [δὲ] τῷ θεῷ (1 Cor 15:57; 2 Cor 2:14; 8:16; 9:15; cf. Rom 6:17; 7:25; εὐχαριστέω, 1 Cor 1:4; 10:30). Gratitude is, of course, a fitting, reciprocal response to gift; χάρις rightly received begets χάρις in return.

to something else, never the polemical alternative to human strivings, never the pardon for sins, nor the power to overcome sin itself. Even if its verbal cognate, *charizomai*, is the preferred term for describing human forgiveness (2 Cor 2:7, 10; 12:13), the same term is not used as an expression for God's forgiveness until Colossians (Col 2:13; 3:13) and Ephesians (Eph 4:32), where human forgiveness follows of necessity from divine forgiveness.[89] Perhaps not incidentally, neither does "mercy" (*eleos*) ever make an appearance in the first five of Paul's letters, save for the Jewish-inspired blessing of Galatians 6:16.[90]

It may come as some surprise that our survey of the earliest five Pauline letters (by almost any reckoning) is largely, if not completely, absent of appeals to "grace" that sound the characteristic theological notes of forgiveness, mercy or divine condescension to and remediation of human incapacity. Our Christian theological discourse and our casual and instinctive appeals to "grace" norm our intuition and stereotype our expectations to such a significant degree that it is difficult to let the language make its more modest donations. It is, however, only with Romans that we begin to hear these notes sounded with clarity. We might say that it is in Romans that *charis* becomes grace.

6.2.3 Grace in Romans. Beyond the formal (Rom 1:5; 16:20) and idiomatic (Rom 6:17; 7:25), there remain twenty decidedly theological occurrences of *charis* in Romans.[91] In a manner unprecedented in Paul's earlier letters,[92] *charis/charisma* are appropriated in the *discursive body of the letter* (Rom 1:18–11:36) toward decisively soteriological ends in a manner unprecedented in the earlier letters. In a sense, this is merely to say what everyone already "knows" to be the case, but it will still be instructive to survey the use of *charis* along with its lexical and conceptual cognates to

---

[89]That the use of χαρίζομαι in 2 Corinthians 12:13 is bitingly sardonic does not affect the point. Of course, χαρίζομαι is used in numerous contexts merely to describe the act of free, unconstrained giving (Rom 8:32; 1 Cor 2:12; Gal 3:18; Phil 1:29; 2:9; Philem 22) and not forgiveness as such. Save for the citation of Psalm 32:1 (LXX 31:1) in Romans 4:7, Paul does not use ἀφίημι in the sense of the forgiveness of offense.

[90]Most commentators see an allusion to the nineteenth blessing, the Birkat ha-Shalom, of the Shemoneh 'Esreh (e.g., Hans Dieter Betz, *Galatians: A Commentary on Paul's Letter to the Churches in Galatia*, Hermeneia [Philadelphia: Fortress, 1979], 321-23; Dunn, *Galatians*, 344).

[91]Cf. χάρισμα, 6x; and in Romans 12:6, χάρις is the source of its concretized cognate χάρισμα.

[92]Whether Galatians is early or later, it remains the case that, along with the Thessalonian and Corinthian correspondences, it precedes Romans in virtually every Pauline chronology.

demonstrate just how pronounced the theme is and, more importantly, how unprecedented.

We begin with those occurrences already noted in our survey of "works," emphasizing the sheer gratuity of God's saving favor. As we saw above with respect to Romans 11:5-6, the current remnant of Israel enjoys its status as an elect people by sheer grace: "But if it is by grace, it is no longer on the basis of works, otherwise grace would no longer be grace" (NRSV). As the means of divine election, grace and works are regarded as mutually exclusive; were grace a response to prior worthiness, the intrinsic character of grace would be nullified.[93] The very fact that Paul's claim here rings tautologous to a modern Christian reader is in fact a sign that Paul is venturing into new territory—not so much that he is employing *charis* in an altogether unprecedented manner, but that he is exploring the reaches of *charis* as a gratuity beyond beneficence, granted not to the condign but to the unworthy.[94]

But the texts in Romans that have functioned most paradigmatically for the Christian theological conception of grace are Romans 3–6, especially Romans 5, where we find the densest concentration of grace language, further reinforced by the language of unconditioned "gift" (*dōrea*, Rom 5:15, 17; *dōrēma*, 5:16; *dōrean*, 3:24). In Romans 3:24, Paul affirms that all who have sinned are nonetheless "justified freely by his grace" (*dikaioumenoi dōrean tē chariti*). Here God's *charis* is the instrument by which sinners are justified. Both the adverb (*dōrean*) and the larger context of Romans indicate that

---

[93]We must leave to the side what is entailed in "election" in this context, or for that matter, in Paul more generally. There are at least three possible answers, not necessarily mutually exclusive: (1) The traditional Reformed view understands election as a soteriological category—to be elect is to be saved, which is all of God's doing, perhaps even the direct result of his immutable decretive will. (2) What is elect are not so much *persons* but a covenant *people*, and, while eternal salvation may well be implied (surely it is for those in right covenant standing), it amounts to a category confusion to treat "elect" as synonymous with "saved." (3) Salvation as such is a mistaken correlate for election; it is rather that the elect people are called to a vocation of witness and demonstration. Election speaks of instrumentality rather than eternal destiny as such. My own view runs closest to a combination of (2) and (3), for which, see esp. Cranfield, *Romans*, 2:445-592; N. T. Wright, "Christ, the Law and the People of God: The Problem of Romans 9–11," in *The Climax of the Covenant: Christ and the Law in Pauline Theology* (Edinburgh: T&T Clark, 1991), 231-57; idem, "Romans"; theologically the classic statement is Karl Barth, *Church Dogmatics*, ed. Geoffrey William Bromiley and Thomas F. Torrance (Edinburgh: T&T Clark, 1936), 4:195-233 (ii.2, §34); and, much more accessibly, Lesslie Newbigin, *The Gospel in a Pluralist Society* (Grand Rapids: Eerdmans, 1989), 80-88.

[94]Barclay, *Paul and the Gift*. Cf. Linebaugh, *God, Grace, and Righteousness*.

sinners justified "freely" must certainly mean that they are justified without making a contribution toward that end. Then, again noting texts we surveyed above with reference to "works" in Romans 4:4, *charis* is contrasted explicitly as the opposite of "what is due" (*kata charin alla kata opheilēma*) to the one who works (*tō ergazomenō*). Exploiting the lexical breadth of *misthos*, Paul argues that a "wage" (*misthos*) is an obligation due a worker, but, to the one who does not work, the *misthos* can only be a "reward" granted according to grace.[95] Later in the same chapter, Paul explores further the *intrinsic* nexus between *faith* as means of receiving the promise that is extended according to *grace* (Rom 4:16): "For this reason it depends on faith [*dia touto ek pisteōs*], in order that it might be according to grace [*hina kata charin*]." While the precise rendering of the elliptical clauses could be debated, it is clear by means of the *hina* clause that this further reinforces the earlier antithesis of "works" with "faith" (Rom 3:27, 28; 4:4), only the latter being congruent (*kata*) with *charis*. That same faith-grace nexus is further affirmed in the summative declaration of Romans 5:1-2: "Therefore, having been justified by faith, we have peace with God through our Lord Jesus Christ, through whom also we have access to the grace in which we now stand." Although grammatically (*di' hou*) it is Christ and not justification or faith per se who grants this "access" to grace, in the nature of the case, it is Christ's saving *accomplishment* yielding justification by faith that grounds this "access to grace." Grace is thus depicted at once as an endowment and sphere of blessing, implicitly contrasted to faith's antithesis, "works."

But this theme of the sheer gratuity of grace find its most robust expression in Romans 5:15-21, here cited at length.

> But the free gift [*charisma*] is not like the trespass. For if the many died through the one man's trespass, much more surely have the grace of God [*hē charis tou theou*] and the free gift in the grace [*hē dōrea en chariti*] of the one man, Jesus Christ, abounded for the many. And the free gift [*to dōrēma*] is not like the effect of the one man's sin. For the judgment following one trespass brought condemnation, but the free gift [*to charisma*] following many trespasses brings justification. If, because of the one man's trespass, death exercised dominion through that one, much more surely will those who

---

[95] It is probable that the double meaning of μισθός is in play here: κατὰ ὀφείλημα, a μισθός is a "wage"; κατὰ χάριν, it is a "reward."

receive the abundance of grace [*tēn perisseian tēs charitos*] and the free gift of righteousness [*tēs dōreas tēs dikaiosynēs*] exercise dominion in life through the one man, Jesus Christ.

Therefore just as one man's trespass led to condemnation for all, so one man's act of righteousness leads to justification and life for all. For just as by the one man's disobedience the many were made sinners, so by the one man's obedience the many will be made righteous. But law came in, with the result that the trespass multiplied; but where sin increased, grace abounded all the more [*hypereperisseusen hē charis*], so that, just as sin exercised dominion in death, so grace might also exercise dominion [*hē charis basileusē*] through justification leading to eternal life through Jesus Christ our Lord. (NRSV)

The passage deserves a closer reading than our purposes allow, but this extraordinary concentration of grace language must not be missed. Arguably, it is the constellation of claims found in this and near surrounding passages that function as the de facto canon for the theological reading of grace in Paul. Instincts for reading Paul more generally—forwards and backwards—derive from the strong theological appropriation of "grace" in this text, and, in turn, this understanding of grace characteristically norms the reading of Paul's soteriology more generally.

Grace, in this passage is, first of all a "gift," and Paul accentuates the point with redundancy in Romans 5:15 and reiterates the language with emphasis throughout the pericope: grace comes as both a *charisma* and a *dōrea/dōrēma*, concretized bestowals of the generous mercy of God. While the translation redundancy of "free gift" (e.g., NRSV, RSV, ESV; cf. NIV, "gift") is jarring stylistically and not specifically warranted from Greek, it nevertheless captures the spirit of Paul's pleonastic exuberance. Moreover, as gift, grace clearly functions to remediate transgression; its purpose in this context is restoration and forgiveness. Adam's trespass brings death to many, but, with even greater certainty,[96] the "gift in grace of the one man, Jesus Christ abounded for the many." The "condemnation" (*katakrima*) born of one transgression is overturned in the gift (*charisma*) that effects acquittal despite the many transgressions (Rom 5:16, 18).[97] Grace abounds and reigns

---

[96]While it may be possible to construe πολλῷ μᾶλλον in some quantitative manner ("to how much greater a degree"; e.g., 2 Cor 3:9, 11; Phil 1:23; 2:12), the *qal wāḥômer* language is characteristically logical for Paul in the context of Romans (Rom 5:9, 10, 17; cf. 1 Cor 12:22).

[97]The translation of δικαίωμα in Romans 5:16 as "justification" is defensible, although the

where sin and death had previously triumphed; indeed, death was the instrument of sin's triumph, but grace reigns by means of the justification by which the condemnation of death is overturned in the acquittal-yielding eternal life (Rom 5:18, 21).

The triumph of grace over transgression is given a pointed application in Romans 5:20, where the "sneaking in" (*pareiserchomai*) of the law creates the increase of trespass; "but where sin increased, grace super-abounded [*hypereperisseuō*]." This abounding grace defeats trespass, sin and even the pernicious effect of the law, proving grace utterly invincible—sin's death, death's doom. This in turn directly occasions the antinomian query of Romans 6:1: "What shall we say then? Are we to continue in sin that grace may abound?" If the question represents an interlocutor's twisted logic (so also Rom 6:15; cf. 3:8), it is still a *kind* of logic derived from the triumph of the grace of Romans 5:15-21, especially Romans 5:20.

That grace is the victorious remediation of sin and mercy and forgiveness for sullied and guilty sinners is obvious to nearly all readers of Romans 5. That is, after all, what we have come to know grace to be. What is not obvious is that, along with Romans 3:24, this is, if not the first time in the extant Pauline writings that he appeals to grace in this way (and I think it is), surely the most explicit appropriation of grace in this direction. If the paean to grace of Romans 5:15-21 occasions the logical but errant rhetorical question of Romans 6:1, it is important to note that there is no previous discourse on grace in the Pauline corpus that could have done so. As we have seen, to find this appropriation of *charis* in the earlier Pauline discourse requires a backfilling of what we already "know" about grace drawn from the later Pauline corpus. It requires us to read Paul as loyal disciples of Kittel's *Theological Dictionary of the New Testament* rather than as students of Barr's *Semantics of Biblical Language*. If grace in Romans is quintessentially divine mercy and acquittal of sin, that is not the whole. "Grace" does not *mean* "forgiveness"; we should say rather that *charis entails* forgiveness in certain contexts. Divine mercy and undeserved acquittal of sinners is now in Romans an expression and entailment of grace, but it is not what grace means in itself. We might rather say that these

---

narrower "acquittal" is probably to be preferred given the obvious contrast intended with κατάκριμα (see BDAG, s.v. δικαίωμα [3], 249-50).

expressions are the quintessence of divine grace, since what could be more undeserved than blessing in exchange for iniquity? This still does not make it the *meaning* of grace. Grace, to borrow from Peter, is "manifold" (*poikilos*, 1 Pet 4:10) in its expressions. As we saw above, another equally relevant dimension now manifest in Romans is that grace stands over against human effort. Of course, these two themes, acquittal for sinners and divine initiative meeting human incapacity, are not unrelated, nor do these two notions exhaust the substance of grace in Paul. Indeed, as we saw earlier, both notions are all but absent, or at least left unexploited, in the first five of Paul's letters.

6.2.4 Grace after Romans. The vocabulary of grace—as distinct from the concept—is largely absent from Philippians. Besides the characteristic grace greeting (Phil 1:2) and concluding grace-wish (Phil 4:23), the only remaining reference is to the Philippians as fellow partakers of grace with Paul in the letter's introduction (Phil 1:7), presumably by means of their assistance in Paul's ministry, in his "defense and confirmation of the gospel" (*en tē apologia kai bebaiōsei*), and in his chains (*en te tois desmois mou*). Thus, "grace" here is probably best understood as a synecdochic summary description of the Christian endeavor in general terms, while perhaps also a characterization of Paul's present circumstances as a bestowal of divine favor (cf. *charizomai*, Phil 1:29).[98] But this letter does not leverage grace language in a soteriological direction. Likewise, Colossians is not rich with soteriological appropriations of *charis*. Beside the standard references in the opening and closing (Col 1:2; 4:18), *charis* is used twice in adverbial prepositional phrases (Col 3:16; 4:6), describing human dispositions: gratitude and graciousness, respectively. The single remaining reference is in Colossians 1:6, "from the day you heard and understood the grace of God in truth." Whether "the grace of God" is the direct object of both "heard" and "understood" or only the latter, it remains the case that *tēn charin tou theou* functions as a virtual synonym for the "gospel" (Col 1:5), akin to Philippians 1:7 and in a similar context. One is hesitant to draw too much from these passing references in somewhat formal contexts, but it is at least interesting to note that in these

---

[98] Assuming that μου qualifies συγκοινωνός rather than τῆς χάριτος. Peter T. O'Brien, *The Epistle to the Philippians: A Commentary on the Greek Text*, NIGTC (Grand Rapids: Eerdmans, 1991), 69-70.

letters "grace" can function as substitute and summary of the gospel itself; this was not evident in letters that preceded Romans.

Clearly, however, it is with Ephesians that we return to the theme of grace in full force. Whether we regard Ephesians as a pseudonymist's "crown of Paulinism" or simply later, "mature" Paul, it is notable that virtually every sense and use associated with grace in the earlier corpus can also be found in this relatively brief letter. Grace is closely associated with Paul's apostolic vocation as an endowment of responsibility of which Paul is intrinsically unworthy (Eph 3:2, 7-8). Grace is also closely tied to an undeserved sonship and the forgiveness of transgressions (Eph 1:5-6). As in 1 Corinthians 12 and Romans 12, *grace* is the summary term for the endowments for ministry granted by the exalted Christ (Eph 4:7). And, in a partial parallel with Colossians 4:6, grace is to be the effect on the hearers of Christian speech (Eph 4:29).

It is, however, most clearly in Ephesians 2:5-9 that the soteriological note of grace is sounded most distinctly and emphatically. We learn that the purpose (*hina*) of the making alive, the raising and the seating with Christ is to demonstrate "the surpassing wealth of his grace" to be made known in the coming ages (Eph 2:7). The "demonstration" of grace consists of making the dead-in-transgressions captives to the "prince of the power of the air" not only alive but, with Christ, also exalted beyond any reasonable or deserved status in the heavenly places. That God made those otherwise dead in transgressions alive together with Christ occasions the programmatic exclamation: "It is by grace you are saved!" (Eph 2:5). The same expression (*chariti este sesōsmenoi*) is repeated and expanded in Ephesians 2:8, "For *by grace you are saved* through faith; and this is not from yourselves [*ouk ex hymōn*], it is the gift of God [*theou to dōron*]; it is not from works [*ouk ex ergōn*], so that no one can boast" (Eph 2:8-9). Unmistakably, it is the gift character of salvation that Paul stresses. It is *by grace* and *through faith*, and this whole scenario is itself a gift (*dōron*) from God rather than something of one's own accomplishment.[99] Were it not a gift, were it not of grace and

---

[99]Although it is common to regard "grace" as the antecedent of "*it* is the gift of God," this is a misreading grammatically, whatever we might make of the claim theologically. The neuter τοῦτο in Ephesians 2:8 refers to the whole of the preceding, that "by grace you are saved through faith," and θεοῦ τὸ δῶρον is the antithetical opposition to the object of the preposition, ὑμῶν: "this fact that you are saved by grace through faith is not of your own accomplishment; rather it is from God a gift."

received by faith, were works its basis, there would be ground for boasting. But the unconditioned gift character of salvation excludes that human beings who were dead (Eph 2:1, 5) in their own "works"—trespasses, transgressions, sins—could appeal to anything but the grace of God for their salvation.

Finally, in the Pastoral Epistles, we see scattered glimpses, albeit less concentrated and emphatic, of the same. Of the thirteen occurrences of *charis* in the PE, eight are formal in character, greetings and grace-wishes (1 Tim 1:2; 6:21; 2 Tim 1:2; 4:22; Tit 1:4; 3:15) and the giving of thanks (in lieu of *eucharistō*, 1 Tim 1:12; 2 Tim 1:3). Of the remainder, in Paul's autobiographical confession of 1 Timothy 1:13-14, grace is paired with "mercy" (*eleeō*) as God's undeserved charity to Paul, once "a blasphemer, persecutor, and violent man" (1 Tim 1:13). In a more generalized soteriological summary, Paul names God's "own purpose and grace, given to us in Christ Jesus before the beginning of time" as cause of salvation over against "our works" (2 Tim 1:9). Likewise, in the soteriological summary of Titus 3:5-7, the grace of Jesus Christ is the means by which we are justified, where, as we noted above, we find the express contrast between grace and "deeds done in righteousness" as the ground of salvation. Therefore, in Ephesians and the PE we have in concentrated form the same soteriology of grace that we found spread throughout Romans but unattested in Paul's earlier letters. In Ephesians, grace saves—it saves from a death deserved because of sin (Eph 2:1, 5), from captivity to malevolent powers (Eph 2:2; 1:21) and from depravity of life (Eph 2:3; cf. 4:17; 5:8).

6.3 CONCLUSION

We have traced two patterns in this chapter: With regard to "works," we have noted a decisive pattern by which Paul's earliest exclusive references to *erga nomou* (Galatians) gave way exclusively to "works" in his later writings, with Romans forming a transition from the one to the other. Against the majority views of the NPP and the TPP, I have argued that *erga nomou* and "works" are not interchangeable, against the NPP that "works" is not shorthand for its definition of "works of the law" and against the majority of TPP interpreters that *erga nomou* is not simply a subset of, or synecdoche for, "works." More importantly, neither is Paul's polemic against *erga nomou* identical to that opposing "works." In both Galatians and Romans, *erga nomou* represents a reliance on Jewish privilege that reinforces the barrier that separates Jews from Gentiles, a barrier that union with Christ, the true seed of Abraham, abolishes, creating one people of God. We saw that the failure of *erga nomou* is less that they are "works" but that they are "of law" and thus implicated in the concomitant cultural exclusivity and salvation-historical impermanence of the law. "Works"—whether "of the law" or not—however, fail to justify because dependence upon them stands over against the unconditional gift character of salvation in Christ. This theme—expounded in Romans 4, reiterated in Romans 9–11, implied in Philippians 3, and restated expressly in Ephesians 2, Titus 3 and 2 Timothy 1—becomes and represents Paul's settled soteriology. To oversimplify, the NPP is essentially correct about *erga nomou* but mistaken with respect to "works"; the TPP doth protest too much with regard to *erga nomou* but is essentially correct as it concerns "works." The misjudgments of both camps are opposite and symmetrical.

This pattern with respect to "works of the law" and "works" is corroborated in the corresponding pattern regarding *charis* and its conceptual cognates. Beginning with Romans and in the letters following, grace is opposed to and excludes works and, thus, boasting. Grace is allied with faith as the alternative to human performance. All these notes—of divine favor exclusive of merit, of intrinsic human incapacity, of divine remediation for sin in forgiveness—are sounded emphatically in Romans and thereafter; none is sounded before.

MARKERS OF THE ITINERARY 2

Reenvisioning Salvation

In the previous chapter we surveyed Paul's arguments concerning "works" and "grace," the putative alternative means by which salvation is appropriated. In this chapter we retrace the same itinerary, though now with interest in salvation itself, how it is named, how it is conceived.[1] I will argue that, in continuity with *Paul's* "new perspective" on works and grace, there is a corresponding and corroborating evolving conception of salvation itself, which can be illustrated and summarized by two decisive developments. (1) Paul recedes from the language of "justification" (and cognates), preferring especially the language of "salvation." I will argue that this development marks a transition from a past-forensic (which is to say proleptic eschatological) conception with covenantal implications to an eschatological-transformational conception of the redemptive accomplishment of Christ. (2) "Reconciliation" enters the picture as a new and unprecedented metaphorical field in the soteriological constellation. I will argue that this development supplements the forensic with an expressly relational metaphor focused on the human creation, expanding to the cosmos. Together these linguistic and metaphorical transitions mark a reenvisioning of salvation that transcends, while never forgetting, the inclusion of Gentiles into

---

[1] *Salvation* in this introductory context is not a reference to σωτηρία as such, but rather a cipher for the whole redemptive enterprise in Jesus Christ, σωτηρία being one significant name for and dimension of the larger reality. Likewise, the adjective *redemptive* will be used in a similar fashion, understanding that redemption is itself one of the subsidiary metaphors. When referring to the specific σῴζω/σωτηρία terminology, I will use scare quotes: "salvation."

the covenant, increasingly to stress the reconciliation of all to each other by means of their prior reconciliation to God.

7.1 FROM "JUSTIFICATION" TO "SALVATION"

It is a well known that, despite its eventual prominence in the subsequent soteriological reflection of the church, justification is neither the exclusive nor pervasive vocabulary of the apostle Paul when speaking of redemptive purposes of God in Jesus Christ. It is frequently noted that the language of justification (*dikaioō, dikaiōsis*) and its *dikai-* variants ("reckoned as righteous," "gift of righteousness," "righteousness from God," "acquittal," etc.) attaches almost singularly to contexts where the matter of Jew and Gentile relationship is at stake: that is, in Galatians and Romans, where the Jew-Gentile theme is ubiquitous, and, with cognate expressions, in Philippians 3:2-11, where Paul apparently confronts (or preempts) advocacy of circumcision for Gentile converts. Besides these texts, thick with the language of justification, we find only passing references in 1 Corinthians 6:11 and Titus 3:7, where "justification" is coordinate with, we might even say diluted by, other soteriological language.[2]

---

[2]We can also include 1 Corinthians 4:4, which describes a less directly theological, almost secular, condition of innocence, yet in a context of divine judgment (cf. chap. 3, n. 90). In 1 Corinthians 1:30, δικαιοσύνη is listed with "wisdom," "sanctification" and "redemption" as among the divine bestowals to those who are ἐν Χριστῷ Ἰησοῦ. And, though much debated, it can be argued that 2 Corinthians 5:21 reflects the substance of justification. The use of δικαιόω in 1 Timothy 3:16 refers to the vindication of Jesus in the Spirit (presumably in the resurrection) and is only tangentially related to the larger observation (although note the discussion in Peter J. Leithart, *Delivered from the Elements of the World: Atonement, Justification, Mission* [Downers Grove, IL: IVP Academic, 2016], 183-88).

A more likely soteriological use of δικαιόω is a sometimes overlooked variant in Philippians 3:12, ἤ ἤδη δεδικαίωμαι following ἤδη ἔλαβον (p⁴⁶, D*; F and G, ἤ ἤδη δικαίωμαι; cf. the Latin of Irenaeus and Ambrosiaster). The external attestation is admittedly slender, though hardly inconsiderable; and whereas the omission is easily accounted for (parablepsis, both homoioteleuton and homoioarkton; O'Brien's appeal to paranomasia with διώκω is unconvincing [Peter T. O'Brien, *The Epistle to the Philippians: A Commentary on the Greek Text*, NIGTC (Grand Rapids: Eerdmans, 1991), 418, n. a]), a supposed insertion is harder to account for, save for a decisive theological motivation (cf., e.g., F. F. Bruce, *Philippians*, UBCS [Grand Rapids: Baker, 1989], 122, who notes the parallel in Ignatius, *To the Romans* 5.1; similarly Gordon D. Fee, *Paul's Letter to the Philippians*, NICNT [Grand Rapids: Eerdmans, 1995], 337). Moreover, were scribes theologically motivated, would they not be more likely to have assimilated the text to the claims immediately preceding, esp. Philippians 3:9, in which, with different language, Paul has claimed already to be justified (ἔχων . . . τὴν ἐκ θεοῦ δικαιοσύνην ἐπὶ τῇ πίστει)? In any case, the variant has probably not received the serious consideration it deserves. UBS⁴ makes no reference to it (but see Metzger, *TCGNT*, 547-48), and among recent commentaries, perhaps only Silva gives

The evidence seems to bear out the claim that justification is the language
of choice when at stake is the place of Gentiles in the covenant or the relationship of Jews and Gentiles to each other. As noted earlier, it was this
observation that would lead William Wrede famously to dethrone justification from its long reign as the center of Pauline theology in Protestant
exegesis, consigning it to the status of "polemical doctrine."[3] I have argued
above (chap. 3) that we should not think of justification as merely a polemical doctrine, but there is still something to be said for Wrede's instinct.
As I will argue, (1) the notion of justification proved especially fitting for the
targeted contexts to which Paul applied it, but (2) it would soon coexist with
and eventually give way to other soteriological concepts, (3) which were
conceptually broader in scope but also continuous with justification. Finally,
I will argue that this transition marks a development of Pauline soteriology
that corresponds to his appropriation of "works" and grace surveyed in the
previous chapter.

Given the structure of the following argument, it is necessary to reiterate
that neither exegesis nor biblical theology can be reduced to word counts or
usage statistics. When in what follows I note that certain words are used here
and not there, I introduce a datum; I do not suppose that the datum is self-
interpreting, that its implications are self-evident. It remains to be asked why
particular language is used in particular settings and with that not to
presume that we will always discern an answer. Yet, having invoked Barr's
"illegitimate totality transfer" in the previous chapter, in this chapter I for-
swear the "word-concept fallacy."[4] We should not suppose that Paul can
speak of the concept of justification only by means of *dikai-* roots nor of
salvation only by means of *sōz-/sōtēr-* cognates, and, for that matter,

---

the variant the consideration it deserves, although in the end he regards the external evidence
as decisive against it (Moisés Silva, *Philippians*, BECNT [Grand Rapids: Baker Academic, 2005],
186-87). The effort to impugn the reading as a second-century Western degeneration from Paul's
theology of justification (Metzger et al., Bruce, Fee, Silva) stumbles on the evidence of p[46]. On
balance, we should probably regard the longer reading as authentic and see this text as evidence
for the fundamentally eschatological character of justification (cf. Rom 2:13), further evidence
that Paul's innovation was to assign that reality to persons who were already participant in the
"justification"—the atoning death and vindicating resurrection—of Jesus. It is a matter of some
interest that, for all his emphasis on the past and future aspects of justification, Wright does not
summon this variant to his cause or, to my knowledge, consider it.
[3]William Wrede, *Paul* (Eugene, OR: Wipf & Stock, 2001), esp. 122-46.
[4]See Barr's famous withering critique of Kittel's *TDNT* in James Barr, *The Semantics of Biblical
Language* (London: Oxford University Press, 1961), 206-62.

reconciliation can just as well be described by "peace making" as by *katallassō*. Likewise, as we are frequently reminded, we should not think that words stand for bounded semantic fields that butt up to each other contiguously without overlap; rather, the natural use of words includes synonymy and variation for stylistic effect, or for no reason at all. I state these caveats up front precisely because, while tracking the lexical usage through the (inclusive) Pauline corpus—hard data, as it were—we should not suppose that graphing such data amounts to an argument in itself.

We begin by noting that the soteriological language of Galatians is limited almost exclusively to the metaphorical field of justification. The verb *dikaioō* occurs eight times; additionally, "righteousness" (*dikaiosynē*) in all its four occurrences and "righteous" (*dikaios*) in a single occurrence describe a status of right standing of some kind.[5] Meanwhile, nowhere in Galatians does Paul speak of "salvation"—as an eschatological, present or past reality. Likewise, Galatians makes no mention of "reconciliation" between God and humans. And that humans are subject to judgment because of their sin and guilt is at best faintly hinted at, if not even absent altogether in the discourse of Galatians. This is not to say that this framework is not presupposed, only that it does not factor into the discourse in any significant way. For that matter, Galatians never speaks of forgiveness or remission of sins. Indeed, except that Christ "gave himself for our sin" (Gal 1:4), sin is not presented as the obstacle damning or an enemy enslaving human beings, although Galatians is profoundly interested in the human dilemma as one of enslavement.[6] The wrath of God, so prominent as a dimension of the human dilemma in other Pauline letters,[7] makes no appearance here. Again, given the Jewish and scriptural context of the letter, surely accountability for sin before a judging God must be presupposed as ingredient to the human condition, but the argument of Galatians does not turn on that reality. God's judgment upon sin and "sinners" can be presupposed, but it is never appealed to, even if subsequent interpretation with the aid of a New Testament canon believed

---

[5]For δικαιόω: Galatians 2:16 (3x), 17; 3:8, 11, 24; 5:4; for δικαιοσύνή as a right standing: Galatians 2:21; 3:6 (from Gen 15:6), 21; 5:5; δίκαιος, Galatians 3:11 (from Hab 2:4), where the referent of ὁ δίκαιος is disputed; see below.
[6]Galatians 4:3, 7, 9, 21-31; 5:1; indirectly Galatians 1:4; 2:4; 5:13.
[7]Cf. 1 Thessalonians 1:10; 2:16; 5:9; Romans 1:18; 2:5, 8; 3:5; 4:15; 5:9; 9:22; 12:9; 13:4, 5; Ephesians 2:3; 5:6; Colossians 3:6.

that the letter speaks to these matters rather directly. The singular soteriological metaphor besides justification that Paul appropriates in Galatians is "redemption," and that redemption is from the law and its curse (Gal 3:13; 4:5). Other soteriological metaphors are all but absent from the letter.[8] Galatians is substantially a discourse on justification, although we are indebted to the NPP for breaking open the question of what justification entails, and we should resist the temptation to prejudge that question without standing back and considering the larger picture.

An important dimension of that larger picture is to note not only that Paul's use of the justification metaphor attaches to certain contexts and not others, but also that, following Galatians, *sōzō* and *sōtēria* ("save" and "salvation") are generously distributed throughout the Pauline corpus (save only for Colossians and Philemon), "salvation" eventually becoming the dominant soteriological metaphor while justification recedes from use.[9] In broad terms, there is a general concurrence of "justification" to "salvation" as with "works of the law" to "works." Galatians knows only "justification" and "works of the law," not "salvation" or "works." Yet in Romans, just as "works of the law" and "works" coexist, so also "justification" and "salvation." But after Romans, just as we find only "works" and never "works of the law," so also we find only "salvation" (*sōzō/sōtēria*) and never "justification" (with the sole exception of Tit 3:5). I do not claim yet that there is an obvious significance to these patterns, but the patterns themselves are significant enough to inquire if there might be correlations of some consequence. Is there a way to account for the transition of vocabulary, or, indeed, is there any particular significance to the variations of vocabulary at all?

We begin by asking if there is a reason that justification language adheres particularly to the Jew-Gentile crisis and is almost nonexistent apart from such contexts. I propose that there are at least two reasons that this metaphor suffuses the discourse of Galatians and Romans and remains almost unattested elsewhere.

---

[8]By giving himself for our sins (τοῦ δόντος ἑαυτὸν ὑπὲρ τῶν ἁμαρτιῶν ἡμῶν) Jesus "delivered [ἐξέληται from ἐξαιρέω] us from the present, evil age" (Gal 1:4).
[9]Although it is but a thumbnail picture, we find forty-seven occurrences of σῴζω (29x) and σωτηρία (18x) in the Pauline corpus, distributed as follows, respectively: Galatians (0/0); 1 Thessalonians (1/2); 2 Thessalonians (1/1); 1 Corinthians (9/0); 2 Corinthians (1/4); Romans (8/5); Philippians (0/3); Philemon (0/0); Colossians (0/0); Ephesians (2/0); 1 Timothy (4/0); Titus (1/0); 2 Timothy (2/3).

First, it cannot be insignificant that the LXX texts to which Paul appeals in his arguments in Galatians and Romans are couched in the *dikai-* language of "righteousness" and "justification." These "donor" texts arguably bear the responsibility for the terms of the discourse into which they are embedded and in which they are put to service.

(1) Although Psalm 143:2 [LXX 142:2] is not cited directly but rather alluded to and clearly emended polemically for the sake of his argument in Galatians 2:16 and Romans 3:20, in both cases it introduces the dilemma of nonjustification for the arguments that follow.

Psalm 142:2	for before you every living one will not be justified
Galatians 2:16	for by works of the law all flesh will not be justified
Romans 3:20	for by works of the law all flesh will not be justified before you

Psalm 142:2	*hoti*	*ou dikaiōthēsetai enōpion sou pas zōn*
Galatians 2:16	*hoti ex ergōn nomou*	*ou dikaiōthēsetai pasa sarx*
Romans 3:20	*dioti ex ergōn nomou*	*ou dikaiōthēsetai pasa sarx enōpion autou*

This text thus establishes the soteriological dilemma as the fact that human beings (*pas zōn*, Ps 142:2 → *pasa sarx*, Paul) "will not be justified before" God. The terms of the ensuing solution are thus set in terms of justification "before" God (*enōpion sou / autou*; although Gal 2:16).

(2) In the same way, Paul's appeal to Genesis 15:6, arguably the most load-bearing text in his argument (Gal 3:6; Rom 4:3 and passim), sets "being reckoned righteous" (*elogisthē auto eis dikaiosynēn*) as the direct consequence of faith. This, Paul argues, is the original and scripturally precedented ground of righteousness. For Paul, "reckoned unto righteousness" (*elogisthē eis dikaiosynēn*) from Genesis 15:6 is explicative of "justification," if not even a virtual synonym of *dikaioō*.

(3) And, then, of course, Habakkuk 2:4 (cf. Gal 3:11; Rom 1:17) declares that "the righteous [*ho dikaios*] shall live by ["my," LXX; "his," MT] faith." Paul's use of this text, to say nothing of its original context, is riddled with questions and alternatives—text-critical, grammatical, theological—and this is not the place to sort that out. I simply note that this text also contributes to the "righteous-" (*dikai-*) vocabulary that is so foundational to the arguments of Galatians and Romans. And, if the long tradition of reading the "righteous one" as descriptive of a person who is justified (by faith) is

correct, we have yet one more description of the substance and language of justification derived from an Old Testament text.[10]

Together then, Psalm 143:2, Genesis 15:6 and Habakkuk 2:4 donate the language for the arguments of Galatians and Romans: *dikaioō, logizesthai eis dikaiosynēn*, and *dikaios*, setting the terms of the Pauline side of the debate. As is frequently noted, it is no accident that Genesis 15:6 and Habakkuk 2:4 bear independent witness that believing/faith is the basis of righteousness, establishing a secure causal alliance between the *pist-* and *dikai-* cognates that is central to Paul's entire argument, and from which Paul can deduce that, if it is faith, it cannot be law that brings about righteousness.[11]

Of course, behind this simple observation that Paul's justification language—at least in Galatians and Romans—is owed to the appropriation of donor texts, there lie a host of vexing questions. Did Paul derive his view of justification *from* these texts, or did he "find" these texts, having already arrived at his position such that Scripture functioned as an after-the-fact fortification? Is Paul merely counterpunching with these texts—that is, reading his opponents' texts in a different way—or were they constitutive of his own position, irrespective of his antagonists'? Above all, what role did (1) Paul's conversion, (2) the pragmatic dimensions of the Gentile mission and its opposition, and (3) ongoing reflection on Scripture combine to secure Paul's theology of justification and corollaries? Suffice it to say for our purposes that we should be highly suspect of any reconstruction that grants an exclusive causation to any one of these three factors. Surely, it is the revelation of conversion, the press of exigency and the pattern of Scripture that conspire together to form Paul's mature convictions. The Damascus Road event

---

[10]See J. Louis Martyn, *Galatians: A New Translation with Introduction and Commentary*, AB 33A (New York: Doubleday, 1998), 313-15. Alternatively, a christological reading ("the righteous one" is the Messiah, Christ himself) has gained support in several quarters: Richard B. Hays, "'The Righteous One' as Eschatological Deliverer: A Case Study in Paul's Apocalyptic Hermeneutics," in *Apocalyptic and the New Testament: Essays in Honor of J. Louis Martyn*, ed. Joel Marcus and Marion L. Soards, JSNTSup 24 (Sheffield: Sheffield Academic Press, 1989), 191-215; idem, *The Faith of Jesus Christ: The Narrative Substructure of Galatians 3:1–4:11*, 2nd ed., Biblical Resource Series (Grand Rapids: Eerdmans, 2002), 134-41; idem, "The Letter to the Galatians," in *NIB*, 11:259; and Douglas A. Campbell, *The Deliverance of God: An Apocalyptic Rereading of Justification in Paul* (Grand Rapids: Eerdmans, 2009), 683-84 and passim.

[11]I concur with Martyn (*Galatians*, 297, 300, 308-9, 312) that Genesis 15:6 and Habakkuk 2:4 are, as it were, *Paul's* texts in the argument and that the intervening texts (Gen 12:3; Deut 27:26) are inherited from his opponents and reinterpreted subversively with the aid of these "righteousness by faith" texts.

functioned as an earthquake, shaking Paul's orderly Jewish edifice to its foundations. While reducing that building to rubble, the earthquake did not also happen to rebuild the edifice in itself. It left debris, which is to say a judgment, on the structural adequacy of the former building while at the same time having shaken loose the very same materials, now available for reconstruction. We might say that the exigencies of the Gentile mission are what require the new edifice to be built. But it is the patterns of Scripture, now thoroughly reconsidered, that count as the blueprint of the new structure. It is not that Scripture would (or perhaps even could) establish Paul's vision for the new enterprise independently of the shattering revelation and the consequent insight that Gentiles in Christ are members of the covenant family. But neither does the conversion itself offer the terms by which this must be the case, nor does it supply the urgency in itself for resolving the matter exegetically and theologically apart from the natural opposition uncircumcised Gentiles would have incited. So Paul's theology is conversion/revelation, exigency/opposition and Scripture/theological reasoning working together as impetus, necessity and substance, respectively.

Second, precisely because it is a forensic metaphor—or at least not less than forensic—justification is intrinsically binary and nonprogressive in aspect. Whereas Paul can properly speak of "being saved" in some progressive sense (1 Cor 1:18; 15:2; 2 Cor 2:15; Phil 2:12), not so with justification.[12] Thus, justification is the especially apt metaphor for describing the equality of status that obtains for both Jew and Gentile.[13] While there can be no doubt that, de facto, persons are more and less righteous, Paul's logic of justification argues that, de jure, there is "no distinction," that is, no distinction and no partiality between Jew and Gentile—distinction neither in sin nor

---

[12]We will want to avoid any simplistic appeal to Greek verb tenses, but it could be argued that a progressive aspect is the force of the present tense of δικαιόω (Rom 3:24, 26, 28; 4:5; 8:33; Gal 2:16; 3:8, 11; 5:4). Or at least we could say that if one makes such an appeal from the imperfective tenses of σώζω, it is not impossible with respect to δικαιόω. But it is much more likely that these are simply timeless or even gnomic in force (A. T. Robertson, *A Grammar of the Greek New Testament in the Light of Historical Research* [Nashville: Broadman, 1934], 866; and Wallace, *GGBB*, 523-25), articulating soteriological principle (Rom 3:24, 26, 28; Gal 3:11) or God's characteristic actions (Rom 4:5; 8:33; Gal 3:8); Galatians 5:4 is normally taken as conative.

[13]Cf. E. P. Sanders, *Paul: The Apostle's Life, Letters, and Thought* (Minneapolis: Fortress, 2015), 721-22, for a similar account of the juridical language, although I dissent vigorously from Sanders's suggestion that the juridical and participatory dimensions are intrinsically incommensurable.

in righteousness (Rom 3:22; 10:12; cf. 2:11; 3:29-30).[14] For all that has been
said about justification in Paul and beyond, this rather modest observation
ought to carry more weight than it has, especially in the protracted debates
between advocates of the NPP and TPP. It should bear more weight because
in this simple observation come together the characteristic concerns of both
camps. The NPP is entirely correct to insist that the presenting issue is the
equal standing of Gentiles with Jews in the Abrahamic covenant and a concomitant Jew-Gentile rapprochement. This, by now, should be beyond
debate, and it probably would be had not the NPP so frequently overplayed
its rhetorical hand with denials that justification has to do with "'What must
I do to be saved?' or . . . 'How can I find a gracious God?' or, 'How can I enter
a right relationship with God?'"[15] But, of course, justification *is* also about
having "a right relationship with God"; it is precisely about that, albeit not
exclusively. Nonetheless, the instinct behind the hyperbolic NPP claim is
not without basis: before justification ever became about persons having a
right relationship with God, it was about *peoples*—Gentiles equally with
Jews—having a right relationship with God. And because they enjoy this
right relationship with God, members equally of Abraham's family, they are
yoked irrevocably together in right relationship to each other. If the TPP has
not always understood this or has not emphasized it enough, this is yet one
more reason to be grateful for the correction of the NPP. But the correction
has not come without some collateral damage, and two extended caveats are
in order as a result.

First, the trend in recent Pauline scholarship to minimalize or marginalize the forensic dimension of justification is rightly motivated—delivering
Paul from a soteriology much narrower than that he espouses—but nonetheless it proves unhelpful and is the source of some confusion. Despite the
consensus view that justification is a forensic metaphor, not all concede the
point, or perhaps, more accurately, not everyone understands the meaning
or consequence of the forensic context in the same way, and many are not
willing to limit justification's meaning to the forensic sphere alone. For example, perhaps no one advocates more unrelentingly for the forensic setting

---

[14]Jouette M. Bassler, *Divine Impartiality: Paul and a Theological Axiom* (Chico, CA: Scholars Press, 1982).
[15]N. T. Wright, *Justification: God's Plan and Paul's Vision* (Downers Grove, IL: IVP Academic, 2009), passim. Cf. idem, *Paul: In Fresh Perspective* (Minneapolis: Fortress, 2005), 10.

of justification than Wright; yet, by declaring the "verdict" justification to be "covenant membership" rather than "not guilty"—or perhaps "not guilty" by means of "covenant membership"?—Wright unnecessarily complicates the metaphorical scenario upon which so much of his exegesis is grounded. Likewise, justification as a transformative metaphor—imparted righteousness—has a long history in Roman Catholic theology, being codified at the Council of Trent.[16] Yet the situation today is more complicated, even ironic. Some of the most articulate advocates of justification as transformation hail from Protestant circles.[17] Yet certain leading Roman Catholic exegetes are not persuaded that the metaphor can reach that far.[18]

To be sure, Paul's soteriological vision extends well beyond the forensic aspect, but the available lexical evidence simply does not support the claim that Paul's use of *dikaioō* or the noun *dikaiōsis* denotes something more or other than favorable or vindicating judgment—that is, in Paul, justification as acquittal or pardon before God and a consequent liberation.[19] This is not to preclude in principle the *possibility* that Paul's notion of justification reaches further or extends beyond this more spartan forensic notion, but given the semantic evidence of both secular and Jewish usage, the burden of proof rests decidedly upon the claim that the semantic donation in Paul transcends the established use.[20] The wide general semantic range of *dikaioō*

---

[16]"Session Six: The Decrees on Justification," in *Decrees of the Ecumenical Councils*, ed. Norman P. Tanner (London: Sheed & Ward; Washington, DC: Georgetown University Press, 1990), 2:671-81.

[17]E.g., Michael J. Gorman, *Inhabiting the Cruciform God: Kenosis, Justification, and Theosis in Paul's Narrative Soteriology* (Grand Rapids: Eerdmans, 2009); and David A. deSilva, *Transformation: The Heart of Paul's Gospel*, Snapshots (Bellingham, WA: Lexham Press, 2014).

[18]E.g., Joseph A. Fitzmyer, "Justification by Faith in Pauline Thought: A Catholic View," in *Rereading Paul Together: Protestant and Catholic Perspectives on Justification*, ed. David E. Aune (Grand Rapids: Baker Academic, 2006), 77–94; idem, *Romans: A New Translation with Introduction and Commentary*, AB 33 (New York: Doubleday, 1993), 116-19, though allowing for a secondary transformative meaning; Brendan Byrne, *Romans*, SP (Collegeville, MN: Liturgical Press, 1996), e.g., 57-60; and Frank J. Matera, *God's Saving Grace: A Pauline Theology* (Grand Rapids: Eerdmans, 2012), 103-11.

[19]For the same conclusion, see the considered judgment of John M. G. Barclay, *Paul and the Gift* (Grand Rapids: Eerdmans, 2015), 375-78.

[20]For lexical background, over against particular theological conclusions, see, e.g., BDAG, 249; Spicq, *TLNT*, 1:338-47; *NIDNTTE*, 1:723-41, esp. 725; and K. Kertelge, "δικαιόω," *EDNT*, 1:330-34. Among broadly corroborative lexical studies, note esp. Nigel M. Watson, "Some Observations on the Use of ΔΙΚΑΙΟΩ in the Septuagint," *JBL* 79, no. 3 (1960): 255-66; J. A. Ziesler, *The Meaning of Righteousness in Paul: A Linguistic and Theological Enquiry* (Cambridge: Cambridge University Press, 1972); Stephen Westerholm, *Perspectives Old and New on Paul: The "Lutheran" Paul and His Critics* (Grand Rapids: Eerdmans, 2004), 261-96; Mark A. Seifrid, *Justification by*

is well attested: "do justly," "prove right," "vindicate" or "judge in favor of" and, in formal and informal judicial contexts, effectively "to acquit." But in the LXX, Paul's inherited theological thesaurus, the evidence for justification as a favorable judgment that effectively acquits is especially pronounced and explicit when God is acting as judge.[21] With respect to the New Testament, Kertelge may not overstate the case when he claims, "Every NT use of δικαιόω has a forensic/juridical stamp: 'justification' and 'vindication' result from judgment."[22] In other words, even the metaphorically nonjuridical uses of the language are also implicitly acts of adjudication, and this is all the more so the case in Paul, using this language in eschatological, soteriological contexts with God acting as judge, as is always the case in Paul's usage.[23] Thus, it is not necessary to imagine a full-on judicial metaphor at every use of this language to see it as properly, if sometimes informally, juridical.

Indeed, there are uses in certain contexts that can *only* bear the meaning of a favorable, acquitting judgment and none that cannot—in which notions of covenant membership or an impartation of righteousness are simply too tangential to be directly relevant other than as the imposition, however attractive, of an overarching theological construct. Note, for example, 1 Corinthians 4:4—useful especially because it bridges the pedestrian and technical senses—stating that Paul's clear conscience is not a guarantee of his *innocence*: "but I am not for that reason *acquitted*" (*all' ouk en toutō dedikaiōmai*).[24] Likewise, clearly in Romans 2:13, the justification of the doers of the law consists in a favorable verdict before God (*dikaioi para theō*; cf. Rom 2:5), and in Romans 5, those who are justified by faith are simultaneously transitioned from enmity to peace toward God and reconciliation with God (Rom 5:1, 9-10), with justification being the first, proleptic installment of the ultimate deliverance from God's wrath in Romans 5:9. In Romans 8:33-34, the "God

---

Faith: *The Origin and Development of a Central Pauline Theme*, NovTSup 68 (Leiden: Brill, 1992), 78-135; and idem, "Paul's Use of Righteousness Language Against Its Hellenistic Background," in Carson, O'Brien and Seifrid, *JVN:PP*, 2:39-74.

[21]E.g., Genesis 44:16; Exodus 23:7; Deuteronomy 25:1; Isaiah 43:26; Micah 6:11; Sirach 9:12; 26:29; cf. in the Qumran scrolls 1QS 11:12-15; 1QH 4:34-47.

[22]K. Kertelge, "δικαιόω," *EDNT*, 1:331.

[23]Note, e.g., the frequent "divine passive": Romans 2:13; 3:20, 24, 28; 4:2; 5:1, 9; 6:7; 1 Corinthians 4:4; 6:11; Galatians 2:16, 17; 3:11, 24; 5:4; Titus 3:7. Even more tellingly, all active voice uses of δικαιόω in Paul are with God as the subject: Romans 3:26, 30; 4:5; 8:30, 33; Galatians 3:8.

[24]Cf. chap. 3, n. 90.

who *justifies"* (*theos ho dikaiōn*) is clearly set over against whoever might suppose to *condemn* (*tis ho katakrinōn*). Indeed, elsewhere in Romans, the explicit antithesis to justification is condemnation (Rom 5:16, 18; cf. 8:1; 2 Cor 3:9). Thus, the specific Pauline employ of the term against the backdrop of biblical usage more generally points to justification as a decidedly forensic metaphor with "favorable verdict" or "acquittal" as its most characteristic semantic force.

Is there any sense, then, that justification can be understood as "transformative," or does the firm entrenchment of the language in the forensic semantic field preclude such a reading? There is admittedly much attraction to justification as entailing transformation. If, after all, justification, even forensically understood, depends as such upon participation in Christ, it is already the enactment of co-crucifixion and resurrection.[25] And, as I have suggested already above, if justification is forensic by means of participation, "justification" names God's effective declaration of both acquittal and liberation—a "deliverdict" in Leithart's coinage.[26] Moreover, Paul's use of *dikaioō* seems to require that "justification" bear a liberative sense in certain contexts, especially, for example, in Romans 6:7: "For the one who has died is *justified* from sin [*dedikaiōtai apo tēs hamartias*]." Virtually all translations and many commentators see *dikaioō* as a liberation from sin ("is freed from"), presumably sin as a dominating power, which fits the context quite well.[27] Others, however, still insist that the verb retains its alleged normal sense of forensic acquittal even here (cf. NAB, "has been absolved from sin").[28] In the end, the outcome of the divergent interpretations is not especially pronounced. In both cases it is understood that there is an element of sin's dominion rendered null for the one who has died; the one who has died with Christ has been released from sin's claim. Even if, as I think, the forensic sense remains truer to the metaphorical domain of *dikaioō*, the release from (*apo*) sin's power is an inevitable corollary to deliverance from the juridical

[25]Gorman, *Inhabiting the Cruciform God*, 40-104.
[26]Leithart, *Delivered from the Elements of the World*, esp. 180-88. Cf. chapter 3, section 3.2.4, n. 120 above.
[27]E.g., Douglas J. Moo, *The Epistle to the Romans*, NICNT (Grand Rapids: Eerdmans, 1996), 376-77; Thomas R. Schreiner, *Romans*, BECNT (Grand Rapids: Baker Academic, 1998), 219; James D. G. Dunn, *Romans*, WBC 38 (Dallas: Word, 1988), 1:320-21.
[28]E.g., Fitzmyer, *Romans*, 437; C. E. B. Cranfield, *A Critical and Exegetical Commentary on the Epistle to the Romans*, ICC (Edinburgh: T&T Clark, 1975), 1:310-11; and Byrne, *Romans*, 192.

sentence of sin. At risk of parsing the metaphor too finely, we might say that at least one of sin's "powers" is its right to condemn the culpable, a power now broken in the proven-false accusation of the vindicated Messiah and thus nullified with respect to his members.

I propose, then, that we understand justification as explicitly, that is to say lexically, forensic and, because participant in the victory of resurrection, derivatively liberative. To the extent that acquittal and liberation are consequent of a union with Christ effected in faith and baptism, we can say that the favorable, vindicating judgment of acquittal and freedom is proper to "justification." However earnestly we might wish to insist that Paul's soteriology is also keenly transformational, it is less clear that "transformation" aptly describes Paul's appropriation of "justification." Rather "justification" language names the forensic dimension of the soteriological spoils of Christ's death and resurrection. That forensic language does not exhaust those spoils, nor does it inventory the entire plunder; rather, "justification" names the remediation of human culpability and consequent restoration from alienation.[29] If a multifaceted metaphor, "justification" remains decidedly forensic.

This leads to a necessary secondary clarification: it is a category mistake potentially harboring confusion to regard justification as "covenantal"—depending, that is, on what one means by covenantal. On balance, the recovery of covenant as a conceptual fixture in Paul's theological reckoning can be regarded as one of the more significant developments in Pauline studies of this generation, for which the NPP can be especially thanked.[30]

---

[29]Thus, despite certain other misgivings (see below), I must side with Wright's discipline in resisting the expansion of justification into a forensic *and* transformational metaphor (N. T. Wright, *P&FG*, esp. 2:912-14, 944-66) over against Gorman's criticism of Wright's too narrowly forensic account (Michael J. Gorman, "Wright About Much, but Questions About Justification: A Review of N.T. Wright, *Paul and the Faithfulness of God*," *JSPL* 4, no. 1 [2014]: 27-36, esp. 31-36).

[30]Noting the vigorous dissent of the apocalyptic school of Pauline interpretation with its emphasis on the radical discontinuity of the Pauline theological vision. See, e.g., J. Louis Martyn, "Events in Galatia: Modified Covenantal Nomism Versus God's Invasion of the Cosmos in the Singular Gospel; A Response to J. D. G. Dunn and B. R. Gaventa," in *Pauline Theology*, vol. 1, *Thessalonians, Philippians, Galatians, Philemon*, ed. Jouette M. Bassler (Minneapolis: Fortress, 1994), 171-74; idem, *Galatians*, 343-49.

Covenant, of course, is the core notion for Sanders's understanding of Judaism (*P&PJ*). And, of course, covenant is the ubiquitous theme of all of Wright's work on Paul, and "covenant membership" is the explicit definition of δικαιοσύνη (Wright, *Paul: In Fresh Perspective*, e.g., 32, 113; idem, *Justification*, e.g., 127, 203, 215-16; idem, *P&FG*, e.g., 2:864-65, 949, 965), even Wright's favored translation of the term in various Pauline texts (Wright, *P&FG*, e.g., 1:87, 488, 514; 2:887, 890, 975, 1077, 1163, 1175).

Indeed, the covenant, with varying degrees of emphasis, has become enough of a commonplace in Pauline scholarship that it might even escape scrutiny.[31] It is, after all, a featured argument of both Galatians and Romans that those in Christ become the children of Abraham (esp. Gal 3; Rom 4). And, though *diathēkē* is not a *word* Paul frequently employs, his uses are frequently strategic and telling,[32] and, in any case, we should not regard word counts as the sole measure of thematic importance in the structure of an author's thought.[33] But we must still ask in what sense and on what grounds is it proper to speak of justification as "covenantal." There can be no question that covenant membership and justification stand in a close relationship with each other, indeed, even that justification *entails* covenant membership for Paul—how could it not? But it is mistaken to identify covenant membership as the *meaning* of justification, as though covenant membership is the core notion rather than the implicature of the more basic forensic notion. While the context for Paul's understanding of justification is covenant, and an ultimate consequence of justification is covenant membership, it creates an unhelpful confusion to identify the two notions or to conflate them under the vocabulary of "righteousness" and "justification."[34] Rather, it is truer to Paul's usage to regard justification or the resultant status of righteousness as a middle term: to be "justified," to be declared righteous, is not covenant membership itself or even tantamount to covenant membership; rather, having been acquitted,

---

[31]See the matter-of-fact assertion of the covenantal basis of justification, e.g., in the Pauline introductions of Michael J. Gorman, *Apostle of the Crucified Lord: A Theological Introduction to Paul and His Letters* (Grand Rapids: Eerdmans, 2004), 116-19; and Michael F. Bird, *Introducing Paul: The Man, His Mission, and His Message* (Downers Grove, IL: InterVarsity Press, 2008).

[32]Romans 9:4; 11:27; 1 Corinthians 11:25; 2 Corinthians 3:6, 14; Galatians 3:15, 17; 4:24; Ephesians 2:12.

[33]Note esp. Porter, "The Concept of Covenant in Paul." It would be perhaps fair to say that verbal recurrence is almost certainly indicative of a thematic emphasis but that the reverse does not hold.

[34]See, e.g., the catena of NPP scholars (Wright, Dunn, B. W. Longenecker, T. L. Donaldson, G. W. Hansen) cited "in their own words" in Westerholm, *Perspectives Old and New*, 252-54; cf. the critique in idem, *Justification Reconsidered: Rethinking a Pauline Theme* (Grand Rapids: Eerdmans, 2013), 48-74. To these can be added, e.g., Richard B. Hays, "Justification," *ABD* 3:1131-32: "This declaration [justification] has a quasi-legal dimension, but there is no question here of a legal fiction whereby God juggles his heavenly account books and pretends not to notice human sin. The legal language points rather to the formal inclusion of those who once were 'not my people' in a concrete historical community of the 'sons of the living God' (Rom 9:25-26)." Caricaturing aside, Hays is correct to deny "legal fiction"—the errant outcome of a properly forensic view of justification detached improperly from union with Christ—but it does not follow that justification *consists in* the "formal inclusion . . . into a concrete historical community."

the justified are qualified for covenant membership, which follows necessarily from justification but is not its substance. That is to say that the justified have been granted the proleptic verdict of acquittal that will be the
verdict rendered on behalf of the covenant people, those in Christ who are
participant in Christ's own early-in-time vindication. Covenant membership
coincides with justification not because it *is* justification but because covenant membership is concomitant to "being in Christ" by faith and baptism
and because justification is sharing in Christ's judgment and vindication by
virtue of that union. It is absolutely correct then to correlate justification and
covenant membership; it is a confusion to equate them.

Table 7.1. Distribution of soteriological language in Paul

	Undisputed Letters	Colossians	Ephesians	1 Timothy	Titus	2 Timothy
dikaioō justify (vb)	25x			[1 Tim 3:16][a]	Tit 3:7	
dikaiōsis justification (n)	2x					
sōzō save (vb)	20x		Eph 2:5 Eph 2:8	1 Tim 1:15 1 Tim 2:4 1 Tim 2:15 1 Tim 4:16	Tit 3:5	2 Tim 1:9 2 Tim 4:18
sōtēria salvation (n)	14x		Eph 1:13			2 Tim 2:10 2 Tim 3:15
apolytrōsis redemption (n)	3x	Col 1:7	Eph 1:7 Eph 4:7			
lytroō redeem (vb)					Tit 2:14	
apokatallassō reconcile (vb)	[*katallassō*] 6x	Col 1:20 Col 1:22	Eph 2:16			
charizomai[b] forgive (vb)		Col 2:13 Col 3:13	Eph 4:32			
aphesis forgiveness (n)	[*aphiēmi*] 1x	Col 1:14	Eph 1:7			

[a]Bracketed, since it is *Christ* being "vindicated" in the Spirit.
[b]Limited to the uses in which God or Christ is the subject of the verb (over against Christians forgiving one another; 2 Cor 2:7, 10; 12:13; Eph 4:32; Col 3:13) and in which the verb carries the sense of "forgive" (over against being "graced" by some gift or endowment; Rom 8:32; 1 Cor 2:12; Gal 3:18; Phil 1:29; 2:9; Philem 22).

I have argued that Paul's appeal to "justification" in certain contexts and
not others is accountable to at least two factors: (1) that the language is derivable from the Old Testament texts to which he appeals and by which his
understanding was shaped, and (2) that the binary, nonprogressive character

of the juridical metaphor was especially fitting to the claim of the shared status of Jews and Gentile acquitted before God. Nonetheless, the fact that justification aptly served a particular rhetorical occasion does not lead us to the conclusion that justification is a uniquely covenantal category on the one hand, and, on the other, it does not follow that justification is merely a polemical doctrine of limited utility, a mere counterpoise. As was argued in chapter three above, although the language of justification and cognates is prominent in Galatians, Romans and Philippians 3, the conceptual coordinates are ubiquitous throughout the corpus. What *is* "missing"—missing in especially the disputed (i.e., later) letters—is the forensic metaphor. That "salvation" (now the preferred term) is all of grace, distinguished from works and appropriated by faith, is the singular soteriology of these letters. But, save for Titus 3:7, this is not described as "justification." Ephesians and the Pastoral Epistles speak of "being saved/salvation" (*sōzō/sōtēria*) but not of justification; Ephesians and Colossians of "reconciliation" (*apokatallassō*), "redemption" (*apolytrōsis*; cf. Tit 2:14, *lytroō*) and "forgiveness" (*aphesis, charizomai*) but not "justification." The distribution of soteriological language in Paul is illustrated in table 7.1.

The absence of "justification" vocabulary and its "replacement" by other terminology is, of course, just the sort of evidence that understandably leads many scholars to doubt that we are hearing Paul's own voice in these letters. Perhaps so, but it is not pedantic to wonder why the pseudonymous disciple(s) of Paul would have replicated Paul conceptually but would not have relied on his language to do so. And it may be at least an equally good explanation of that conceptual correlation and linguistic variation that a single author is responsible for all of it. All that having been said, it is hard to sustain either the notion that justification, even broadly defined, forms the unique center of the Pauline theological vision or, at the other extreme, that it is merely polemical or an ad hoc "subsidiary crater." Rather, Paul's soteriology is larger, but not less than, justification and the entailments of justification; its conceptual moorings and corroborating expressions reach further than the specific use of the vocabulary. Likewise, Paul's understanding of justification by necessity conditions and participates in all other loci of the Pauline vision—an inaugurated eschatology, a christological redefinition of Israel, a reestimation of the Torah and the *arrabōn* of the Spirit.

7.2 "Salvation" in Paul

We have accounted for the concentration of the justification metaphor as the exclusive soteriological metaphor in Galatians and as a dominant metaphor in Romans, though in the later mixed with "salvation" and "reconciliation." We now ask similar questions of the more ubiquitous language—Galatians excluded—of "salvation" in Paul. Our survey of "salvation" in Paul proceeds under three claims: (1) Paul uses the language in an exclusively "religious" sense. (2) As such, the language has, contrary to justification, a decidedly temporally future cast. (3) But it is not the case that "salvation" is merely the future counterpart to the past-ness of justification; for Paul, it becomes a global expression that justification never becomes and allows for a progressive aspect.

7.2.1 "Salvation" (sōzō/sōtēria) as exclusively "religious" in Paul.

Although the biblical uses of "salvation" are much more varied, close analysis demonstrates that Paul's use of the language is exclusively theological or "religious."[35] Whereas *sōzō* and *sōtēria* are ultimately rooted in the secular metaphors of deliverance from threat or harm or, positively, a state of well-being,[36] in Paul's use the language is always used to refer to a "religious" or eschatological salvation, a deliverance from judgment or a transcendent

---

[35]To forestall a potential and natural misunderstanding, my use of "religious" (note the scare quotes) is a lexicographical rather than a theological claim, circumscribing the lexical reference of σῴζω/σωτηρία and where "religious" denotes, in broad terms, the human-divine relationship, especially with respect to its eschatological frame. By "religious salvation" I imply neither a segmented sphere of life distinct from the secular or political nor a narrow concern with afterlife. Indeed, to borrow Gorman's useful expression, Paul's gospel and his ultimate soteriological vision are "theopolitical" (Gorman, *Apostle of the Crucified Lord*, 107-9). Here, however, the adjective "religious" more simply confirms that Paul does not use σῴζω/σωτηρία as deliverance from material or physical danger or harm. Or, to use the broad generalizations of BDAG (985-86), σωτηρία refers either to "1. *deliverance, preservation*, w. focus on physical aspect" or "2. *salvation*, w. focus on transcendent aspects." All of Paul's uses, including the verb, belong to the second category, focused on "transcendent aspects."

[36]The philological data are surveyed most completely by W. Foerster and G. Fohrer in *TDNT*, 7:965-1024 (see also C. Brown and J. Schneider, *NIDNTT*, 3:205-22; W. Radl, *EDNT*, 3:319-21; K. H. Schelke, *TDNT*, 3:327-29; Spicq, *TLNT*, 3:344-57; and Nigel Turner, *Christian Words* [Edinburgh: T&T Clark, 1980], 390-98). For nonbiblical usage, cf. LSJ, 1751; and MM, 621-22. The notion of salvation as a biblical theme is treated by Michael Green, *The Meaning of Salvation* (Philadelphia: Westminster, 1965); and Joel B. Green, *Salvation*, Understanding Biblical Themes (St. Louis: Chalice, 2003). Cf. Marvin E. Tate, "The Comprehensive Nature of Salvation in Biblical Perspective," *RevExp* 91, no. 4 (1994): 469-85; and Michael J. Gorman and J. Richard Middleton, "Salvation," in *NIDB*, 5:45-61.

restoration to wholeness.[37] Indeed, of the forty-seven occurrences of the terms in an inclusive Pauline canon (*sōzō*, 29x; *sōtēria*, 18x),[38] there are none that are unambiguously "secular" or nontheological.

While we find perhaps five possible exceptions, none proves to be exceptional upon closer examination. There are two citations from the Old Testament that refer to Israel's salvation (Rom 9:27 from Is 10:22; Rom 10:13 from Joel 2:32). But in the immediate context, "salvation" has been transposed to a characteristically Pauline, eschatological register as is evident from the use of the terminology in the immediate setting (Rom 10:1, 9, 10; 11:26). In 2 Timothy 4:18, *sōzō* is paralleled by *rhyomai*: "The Lord will deliver [*rhysetai*] me from every evil work, and will save [*sōsei*] me unto his heavenly kingdom." The fact that "will save" is parallel with "will deliver" could imply a synonymous conception, but the context actually suggests the opposite. Paul uses *rhyomai* for deliverance *from* (*apo*) temporal danger (the "evil works" of those who oppose Paul) and *sōzō* for a salvation *into* (*eis*) a heavenly kingdom. Thus, the related terms are distinguished from each other rather than used synonymously. In Philippians 1:19, Paul, alluding to Job 13:16, says "this will turn out for my salvation" (*touto moi apobēsetai eis sōtērian*). Although, given the setting of his imprisonment, it is natural to assume that the reference here is to Paul's release from prison (a majority of translations prefer to render *sōtēria* as "deliverance"), not only Pauline usage in general, but also the specific context, carefully considered, point toward Paul's characteristic eschatological/theological meaning for the term. Moreover, the context of the letter itself is an argument against that use of *sōtēria* in Philippians 1:19.[39] Finally, the most ambiguous use of the verb is

---

[37] I am resisting the potentially misleading qualifier of salvation as "spiritual" since Paul's notion of salvation is more comprehensive than a person's "spirit" and more comprehensive in scope than persons, in any case.

[38] σῴζω: Romans 5:9, 10; 8:24; 9:27; 10:9, 13; 11:14, 26; 1 Corinthians 1:18, 21; 3:15; 5:5; 7:16 (2x); 9:22; 10:33; 15:2; 2 Corinthians 2:15; Ephesians 2:5, 8; 1 Thessalonians 2:16; 2 Thessalonians 2:10; 1 Timothy 1:15; 2:4, 15; 4:16; 2 Timothy 1:9; 4:18; Titus 3:5; σωτηρία: Romans 1:16; 10:1, 10; 11:11; 13:11; 2 Corinthians 1:6; 6:2 (2x); 7:10; Ephesians 1:13; Philippians 1:19, 28; 2:12; 1 Thessalonians 5:8, 9; 2 Thessalonians 2:13; 2 Timothy 2:10; 3:15.

[39] The other two uses in Philippians (Phil 1:28; 2:12) are clearly eschatological/theological, and the immediate context further supports this meaning. First, the instruments of Paul's σωτηρία are described as "your prayers" and the "supply of the Spirit of Jesus Christ," which fit a theological meaning of σωτηρία more readily than the notion of deliverance from prison. Second, one is left wondering how "this" (τοῦτο) will "turn out" (ἀποβήσεται) for salvation. If, presumably, Paul's present circumstances are intended as the antecedent of τοῦτο, we are left with the

in 1 Timothy 2:15: "Yet she will be saved [*sōthēsetai*] through childbearing, provided they continue in faith and love and holiness, with modesty" (NRSV). Several proposals are on offer, each having its own difficulties.[40] But the most contextually satisfying suggestion is that the text refers to "*the* childbearing" (*tēs teknogonias*) par excellence, the bearing of Christ by Mary, thus emphasizing the positive, antitypical, redemptive role of "woman" over against Eve's failure, though in a strongly christrocentric manner. In any case, unless we are to assume that this text means something like surviving the

---

nonsequitous formulation that Paul's present circumstances will result in his deliverance from his present circumstances. It is much more plausible that Paul regards his current afflictions as participant in a larger salvific scheme. Finally, the phrase in Philippians 1:19 "this will turn out for my salvation" (τοῦτό μοι ἀποβήσεται εἰς σωτηρίαν), being an unmistakable direct allusion to Job 13:16 (LXX), points in the direction of eschatological salvation. There Job is appealing for a hearing before the face of God, confident that his innocence will result in his vindication. Thus, Job's context is quasi-eschatological and supports the notion that Paul is working along similar lines: a man suffering innocently, confidently expecting God's eschatological vindication. This is now frequently noted, if not always well accounted for, among the commentators, going back at least to J. H. Michael, *The Epistle of Paul to the Philippians*, Moffat New Testament Commentary (Garden City, NY: Doubleday, 1929); the allusion is teased out to good effect in Richard B. Hays, *Echoes of Scripture in the Letters of Paul* (New Haven, CT: Yale University Press, 1989), 21-24.

[40]There are at least three common interpretations of the phrase: (1) Some take "will be saved" as a reference to safety that faithful women will experience in the act of childbearing ("she will be kept safe through [the act of] childbearing"). Although there is some attractiveness to the suggestion that Genesis 3:15 is here alluded to and is its reversal, the interpretation is beset by insuperable difficulties. Besides the obvious problem of exceptions to the promise, this use of σῴζω is uncharacteristic of Paul in general and in the immediate context particularly (1 Tim 1:15; 2:4). Moreover, the interpretation is altogether ill-fitting with the condition (ἐάν) that the women "continue in faith, love, sanctification and modesty." (2) Others have argued that "childbearing" is a metonymy for mothering in general (on analogy to 1 Tim 5:14) and that women will be saved in an eschatological sense by means of tending to their domestic responsibilities, bearing a godly demeanor (J. N. D Kelly, *The Pastoral Epistles* [Peabody, MA: Hendrickson, 1993], 69-70; Gordon D. Fee, *1 and 2 Timothy, Titus*, UBCS [Grand Rapids: Eerdmans, 2009], 74-76; William D. Mounce, *Pastoral Epistles*, WBC 46 [Nashville: Nelson, 2000], 146-48; and Philip H. Towner, *Letters to Timothy and Titus*, NICNT [Grand Rapids: Eerdmans, 2006], 232-36). So as to avoid the bizarre suggestion that motherhood and its duties are themselves a means of salvation, advocates of this position infer that Paul is responding in an ad hoc manner to a devaluing of women's traditional roles in the Ephesian milieu (see, e.g., Bruce W. Winter, *Roman Wives, Roman Widows: The Appearance of New Women and the Pauline Communities* [Grand Rapids: Eerdmans, 2003]). (3) Another option notes that "childbearing" (τεκνογονία) has the article (τῆς τεκνογονίας) and thus points to "*the* childbearing" par excellence, the bearing of Christ by Mary. Thus, despite Eve's deception and culpability in the human plight, "she" (the implied subject of the third-person singular passive verb) as representative of "womankind" will be saved (eschatologically) by "her" (i.e., Mary's) representative redemptive act in the bearing of Christ, provided "they" (i.e., godly women in general) continue in faith, love, sanctification and modesty. See, e.g., George W. Knight, *The Pastoral Epistles: A Commentary on the Greek Text*, NIGTC (Grand Rapids: Eerdmans, 1992), 144-49.

act of childbearing, then we have *no* instances of *sōtēria/sōzō* that are narrowly physical, secular or non-eschatological in the Pauline corpus, including both the undisputed and the disputed letters.

7.2.2 "Salvation" (sōzō/sōtēria) as future. To the extent that the temporal aspect of "salvation" is highlighted, Pauline use most frequently emphasizes the future-eschatological dimension, almost completely to the exclusion of past uses, although with some present and progressive references. Table 7.2 summarizes the distribution of temporally referring uses of the vocabulary.[41]

Table 7.2. Temporal references with "salvation" (*sōzō/sōtēria*)

	Past-referring	Present-referring	Future-referring	Nonspecific, global or atemporal
σωτηρία	[2 Cor 6:2a][a]	2 Cor 6:2b	1 Thess 5:8, 9 Rom 10:10;[b] 13:11 Phil 1:19; 1:28; 2:12 2 Tim 2:10	2 Thess 2:13 2 Cor 1:6; 7:10 Rom 1:16; 10:1; 11:11[c] Eph 1:13 2 Tim 3:15
σώζω	Tit 3:5 (aor) 2 Tim 1:9	1 Cor 1:18, 15:2 (pres) 2 Cor 2:15	1 Cor 3:15 (fut); 5:5[d] Rom 5:9 (fut); 5:10 (fut); 9:27 (fut); 10:9[e] (fut); 10:13 (fut);[f] 11:14,[g] 26 (fut) 1 Tim 2:15 (fut); 4:16 (fut) 2 Tim 4:18 (fut)	1 Thess 2:16 2 Thess 2:10 1 Cor 1:21; 7:16 (2x) (fut); 9:22; 10:33 Rom 8:24 (aor) Eph 2:5, 8 1 Tim 1:15; 2:4

[a] Paul's quote from the LXX of Isaiah 49:8, thus the past reference is predetermined by the citation.
[b] This is regarded as future-referring in light of Romans 10:11: "For the Scripture says, 'Everyone who believes in him will not be put to shame.'"
[c] Although the standard English translations have "salvation *has come*" to the Gentiles (cf. KJV, "*is come*," italicized), the Greek clause is verbless.
[d] The reference to the "day of the Lord" shows this to be a future reference.
[e] This could instead be taken as temporally nonspecific despite the use of the future tense—related to a result without respect to time.
[f] Old Testament/LXX quote, thus Paul's use of the term is somewhat predetermined. If the context of Joel 2:32 is taken into account, there is an eschatological context for the salvation.
[g] Romans 11:14 could be parsed as a future indicative, but it is more likely an aorist subjunctive.

The absence of past-referring "salvation" language is striking. Only twice do we find bona fide past-referring references to "salvation" in the inclusive

---

[41] Table 7.2 lists texts in my proposed chronological, rather than canonical, order; tense is given for verbs in the indicative mood, acknowledging that tense form is suggestive but not decisive for temporality. For example, of the fifteen indicative uses of σώζω (assuming Rom 11:14 is subjunctive), fourteen are in the future tense (Rom 8:24 being the exception), but the future tense can be used with logical rather than temporal force.

Pauline corpus—both in the PE (Tit 3:5; 2 Tim 1:9).[42] In this regard, "salvation" is a mirror opposite to "justification," where we find only one exceptional occurrence of a future reference to justification (Rom 2:13) and a preponderance of "salvation" language that is future-referring.[43] This is borne out in those texts in which "justification" and "salvation" are set in juxtaposition, such as Romans 5:9-10.

> Much more surely then [*pollō oun mallon*], now that we *have been justified* [*dikaiōthentes*] by his blood, *will we be saved* [*sōthēsometha*] through him from the wrath of God. For if while we were enemies, we were reconciled to God through the death of his Son, much more surely [*pollō mallon*], *having been reconciled* [*katallagentes*], *will we be saved* [*sōthēsometha*] by his life. (NRSV)

Here "being saved" is the future counterpart to already "having been justified" by Christ's blood and "having been reconciled" by Christ's death. Those justified will be saved *from* (*apo*) wrath and *by* (*en*) Christ's life. There can be little doubt that, in this context, *sōzō* is used to refer to the eschatological consummation of salvation—deliverance from wrath and full restorative participation in the resurrected life of Christ.

A similar pattern is approximated, though less transparently, in Romans 10:9-11:

> Because if you confess with your lips that Jesus is Lord and believe in your heart that God raised him from the dead, you will be saved [*sōthēsē*]. For one believes with the heart and so is justified, and one confesses with the mouth and so is saved. The scripture says, "No one who believes in him will be put to shame [*kataischynthēsetai*]." (NRSV)

---

[42]Although the aorist participle of 2 Timothy 1:9 is not in itself temporally referring, the context implies a past referent. English Bible readers will be inclined to read Ephesians 2:5 and 8 as though past-time references to "salvation." Although often translated as though past perfect tense, "by grace you *have been saved*" (also Eph 2:5), the force of the periphrastic present ἐστε with the perfect participle describes a temporally present condition with the perfective aspect: "you *are saved*." As befitting the context, Paul's use of the present tense here is gnomic in force. Mistakenly regarding the temporal reference of these Ephesians texts as past, Ehrman finds these references to a past salvation to be evidence for the pseudonymity of the letter. Bart D. Ehrman, *Forgery and Counterforgery: The Use of Literary Deceit in Early Christian Polemics* (New York: Oxford University Press, 2013), 186n69. On the periphrastic generally, see Wallace, *GGBB*, 575; BDF, 179-80.

[43]Galatians 2:16, Romans 3:20 (both allusions to Ps 142:2 LXX) and Romans 3:30 are all future tense forms that are logical in force rather than strictly temporal (although cf. Gal 5:5).

Here again we have a future passive use of *sōzō*. The citation in Romans 10:11 of Isaiah 28:16 as a substantiation of the preceding claims shows "will not be put to shame" to be the conceptual parallel to "will be saved." Being "put to shame" connotes an adverse eschatological resolution, that is, being shown to be in the wrong, and is thus a near antonym to "justification." Of course, the future tense here can also bear a logical force, especially in the context of the conditional protasis (*ean*)—the options are not mutually exclusive— but there remains a decided eschatological-future association.[44] Nothing in the immediate context suggests anything but a broad complementary synonymy between "salvation" and "justification" (or as is the case here, *dikaiosynē*). "Righteousness" here refers to the vindicated status enjoyed by the one "believing with the heart" and "salvation" of the same by the one "confessing with the mouth." If there is any distinction, it could only be that *dikaiosynē* might accentuate a forensic vindication while *sōtēria* a more global notion—but, in any case, perhaps not too much lexicographical ore should be drawn from the poetic parallelism.

The most basic—and arguably earliest—notion of "salvation" in Paul is that it is a deliverance from eschatological wrath.[45] Paul thinks of "salvation" with a decidedly eschatological emphasis and in terms distinct from, while not unrelated to, "justification." Nowhere is this clearer than when Paul declares *sōtēria* "nearer to us now than when we first believed; the night is far gone and the day is near" (Rom 13:11-12). There can be little doubt that, while Paul understands justification as an essentially past event for those in Christ (Rom 5:1, 9), coincident with the dawn of faith itself, he can speak of salvation in complementary terms as "nearer than when we first believed." Clearly, this can only be because he associates "salvation" especially with the parousia, the consummation of all things—judgment and vindication. Thus "the day" is a day of reckoning in which the faithful not only escape judgment but also enjoy the fullness of Christ's vindication. Likewise, the same theme of eschatological vindication is evident in Philippians 1:28, where the Philippians' charitable bond of gospel co-belligerence serves as a foreboding omen (*endeixis*) of their antagonists' destruction but as a harbinger of the

---

[44]The substantiating γάρ clause of Romans 10:10 functions atemporally, principial in force.
[45]1 Thessalonians 5:9; 2 Thessalonians 2:10; 1 Corinthians 3:15; 5:5; Romans 5:9; Philippians 1:28; cf. 1 Thessalonians 1:10.

Philippians' "salvation." The same eschatological note is struck in 2 Corinthians 6:2, but here the inauguration hinted at in Philippians 1:28 is explicit:

> For he says,
>
> "At an acceptable time I have listened to you,
>   and on a day of salvation I have helped you."
>
> See, now is the acceptable time; see, now is the day of salvation! (2 Cor 6:2
> NRSV)

Even certain texts that are not customarily taken in this eschatological sense perhaps should be. Although Philippians 2:12-13 is frequently read as though describing some sort of progressive sanctification ("work out your salvation with fear and trembling"), it is much more likely that it is calling readers to lay hold of their own eschatological vindication. In the first place, various attempts to construe *sōtēria* as something other than eschatological vindication—for example, communal health or wholeness—falter in the face of the evidence both of Paul's usage of "salvation" language and of various near-contextual indicators.[46] And it is specious to claim that, since the imperative *katergazesthe* and the reflexive pronoun *heautōn* are plural, this directive is inherently communal in focus.[47] Furthermore, the consensus of English Bible translations notwithstanding, *katergazomai* never in Paul, nor indeed elsewhere, means anything like "work out the implications of." Rather, *katergazomai* characteristically means to "attain" or "lay hold of something," especially in Paul, and it

---

[46]Among the more improbable interpretations is that of Gerald Hawthorne: "work at achieving [spiritual] health," where σωτηρία is said to mean something like communal "wholeness" (Gerald F. Hawthorne and Ralph P. Martin, *Philippians*, rev. ed., WBC 43 [Nashville, Nelson, 2004], 139-42; influenced by J. H. Michael, "Work Out Your Own Salvation," *Expositor* 12 [1924]: 439-50; idem, *Epistle of Paul to the Philippians*). To Hawthorne's credit, he rightly understands that κατεργάζομαι does not bear the sense of "working out" that is frequently assumed. Fee reaches a similar, unlikely conclusion, while rejecting Hawthorne's merely sociological understanding of σωτηρία: "What Paul is referring to, therefore, is the *present* 'outworking' of their *eschatological salvation* within the *believing community* in Philippi" (Fee, *Paul's Letter to the Philippians*, 235, emphasis original). This, however, requires him, evidently for theological reasons, to construe κατεργάζομαι in an unlikely way (see ibid., 234n20).

[47]So, e.g., Hawthorne and Martin, *Philippians*, 140; and Fee, *Paul's Letter to the Philippians*, 234n21. Any such directives in this sort of a pastoral letter would be plural simply as a matter of form; some other indication is required to understand it as a call to communal rather than simply common action (rightly O'Brien, *Epistle to the Philippians*, 279).

seems that the meaning is resisted here on theological grounds.[48] No other Pauline use is analogous to "working out," nor is there an analogous use in the remainder of the New Testament or LXX or in the secular use of the verb. Resistance to this more lexically straightforward understanding of the text almost certainly arises not only from the ingrained habits of translation but also from an understandable theological anxiety should Paul be exhorting his readers to work for their salvation. Besides the appeal to unlikely definitions for *katergazomai* and *sōtēria,* most exegeses of Philippians 2:12 significantly underestimate the several clear grammatical and conceptual ties to the preceding Christ hymn. The "therefore" (*hōste*) is a strong inferential link to what precedes:[49] the obedience of the Philippians (*hypēkousate*) recalls the obedience of Christ (*hypēkoos*), and the force of the reflexive pronoun *heautōn* ("*your* salvation") makes best sense if it is neither individualizing ("your own" as opposed to another's, in which case we would expect *idiōn*) nor merely possessive (in which case we would expect *hymōn*), but rather the Philippians' salvation as the counterpart to Christ's vindication of Philippians 2:9-11. Christ's exaltation to universal lordship described in Philippians 2:9-11, as the recompense for his suffering obedience, is nothing other than the narration of his vindication, his *sōtēria*. Thus, Paul is urging his readers again to follow the pattern of Christ, who, by his humble obedience, attained his vindication from God. Christians are to follow suit and attain *their sōteria,* vindication by God, by their obedience with fear and trembling.[50]

7.2.3 "Salvation" (sōzō/sōtēria) as global and sometimes progressive. If eschatologically future use of "salvation" is prominent in Paul, it is not exclusively so. We might say, rather, that all "salvation" language in Paul is eschatologically conditioned, either future-referring or teleological in character or,

---

[48]Note how BDAG (p. 531) strains to include Philippians 2:12 under definition (2)—"to cause a state or condition, *bring about, produce, create*"—by appealing to Michael, "Work Out." G. Bertram understands that the verb indicates "to work at and finally accomplish a task," carrying through to its completion (*TDNT,* 3:634-35).

[49]Paul will frequently use ὥστε with imperatives as the concluding hortatory punctuation of a preceding theological discourse (1 Cor 3:21; 4:5; 10:12; 11:33; 14:39; 15:58; Phil 4:1; 1 Thess 4:18).

[50]It follows from this interpretation that the Christ hymn should be read as bookended by the "ethical" material of Philippians 2:1-4 and 2:12-18. This, in turn, is a corroboration of the ethical, *imitatio Christi,* rather than kerygmatic, interpretation of the Christ hymn and its introduction in Philippians 2:5.

most frequently, both. Romans 8:24 provides a good case in point: "For in this hope we were saved [*esōthēmen*]." The expression is intriguing, for the context is thoroughly eschatological ("in hope"), but uncharacteristically Paul speaks of being saved using the aorist tense (cf. Tit 3:5) rather than the future, as might have been expected in Romans. There are reasons to doubt, however, that *esōthēmen* should be taken as strictly past-referring.[51] More probably, the aorist is global or constative in its force. Hope is not so much the condition as it is the defining characteristic of "salvation."[52]

As noted above, many uses are essentially atemporal or global in character (I count twenty of the forty-seven as such; see table 7.2). If we can say that future-referring uses highlight the consummative aspect of "salvation," these more global uses demonstrate that "salvation" language functions for Paul as the generic, default and comprehensive descriptor of God's saving work in Christ. No other soteriological terminology comes anywhere close in frequency of use (see table 7.1), especially when it is noted that "justification" is concentrated almost exclusively in Galatians and Romans. In Pauline vocabulary, *sōzō* and *sōtēria* become the default—we might even say the term of art—for divine redemption in any or all of its several dimensions. As such, it cannot be assumed that the terminology necessarily trades on its metaphorical senses—say, of safety, deliverance or well-being—in specific ways, other than that salvation is a favorable, desirable, salutary end. Rather, "salvation" vocabulary, when otherwise unqualified contextually, evokes the whole multidimensional reality and its various aspects to varying degrees: transference from wrath to divine favor, forgiveness of sin, reconciliation to and peace with God, rescue from the degradations and

---

[51]Certain commentators are right to note that an aorist of σώζω is uncharacteristic in Romans, to say nothing of Paul more generally, and note that the combination of the unexpected aorist and hope points to Paul's underlying inaugurated but not-yet-consummated eschatology (e.g., Dunn, *Romans*, 1:475; Moo, *Epistle to the Romans*, 521-22). Cranfield captures the significance helpfully, noting that "the aorist tense is justified, because the saving action of God has already taken place, but it would be misleading, were it not accompanied by some indication that the final effect of God's action namely, our enjoying salvation, still lies in the future: τῇ . . . ἐλπίδι makes this necessary qualification" (Cranfield, *Romans*, 1:419-20). The same inaugurated eschatology is evident in 2 Corinthians 6:2, confirming the general eschatological orientation of "salvation" for Paul: "Behold, now is the acceptable time; behold, now is the day of salvation."
[52]The dative τῇ ἐλπίδι is more likely a dative of manner (or "modal") than instrumental (so, e.g., Cranfield, *Romans*, 1:419-20; and Dunn, *Romans*, 1:475). The article should perhaps be taken anaphorically ("this hope").

dissipations of sin, restoration of the divine image, and renewal of the cosmos. Any, or even *all*, of that might be evoked in the use of "salvation" language by Paul, though it is probably the case that certain dimensions are implied more directly in some contexts than in others. In any case, "salvation" language for Paul is, if we can generalize, nonspecific and holistic. For example, the exclamations of Ephesians 2:5 and 8, "by grace you are saved," function as global, holistic summaries.

To the characteristic future-referring and atemporal uses of the language (together constituting forty of Paul's forty-seven uses), we do well to consider the remaining few exceptional uses, the present-referring occurrences. A few times, Paul uses present-tense forms seemingly to stress the progressive aspect of salvation: "For the message about the cross is foolishness to those who are perishing, but to us who are being saved [*tois sōzomenois*] it is the power of God" (1 Cor 1:18 NRSV). And again, "For we are the aroma of Christ to God among those who are being saved [*en tois sōzomenois*] and among those who are perishing" (2 Cor 2:15 NRSV). In both instances, the participles describe "those being saved" in a direct contrast to "those perishing" (cf. Phil 1:28). The contrast is rightly taken as a definition of persons with regard to their respective ends (those *on their way to* salvation/perdition),[53] but it is also appropriate to see a progressive sense here. These are in the *process* of being saved and, alternatively, in the *process* of perishing. The eschatological end is determinative of the present, effecting a perceptual and epistemological divide. The same progressive aspect is probably also to be seen in the present tense in 1 Corinthians 15:2: "Through which [the gospel] also you are being saved [*sōzesthe*], if you hold firmly to the message that I proclaimed to you" (NRSV). While it is precarious to overread verb tense, the contrast here is with the perfect "in which . . . you stand [*estēkate*]" and "through which you *also* are being saved" (1 Cor 15:1-2 NRSV).[54] While Paul could have readily used the future tense instead—this, I have argued, was nearly his default—the use of the present tense implies progress in present time toward the eschatological

---

[53]So, e.g., the gloss of Anthony C. Thiselton, *The First Epistle to the Corinthians: A Commentary on the Greek Text*, NIGTC (Grand Rapids: Eerdmans, 2000), 150, 154-55.

[54]The English participle "you are *being* saved" (NRSV, ESV, NAB) is appropriate, lest by its omission ("you are saved") a perfective notion is mistakenly implied instead (RSV, NIV, NASB).

destiny. Here the gospel is depicted as through "the power of God unto salvation" (Rom 1:16) toward that end.

We can summarize Paul's use of "salvation" language as follows: For Paul, "salvation" is never mundane or secular—never health, survival or physical deliverance from harm. It is always theological in context, frequently eschatological and always teleological. "Salvation" is a flexible, adaptable metaphor, put especially to three partially overlapping uses: (1) In its most straightforwardly metaphorical register, "salvation" refers to ultimate deliverance from eschatological wrath and destruction (1 Thess 5:9; Rom 5:9); it is the antithesis of that destruction (1 Cor 1:18; 2 Cor 2:16; Phil 1:28). (2) In a related metaphorical register, "salvation" points more positively to the vocabulary's restorative dimension, a movement from the fallen state of degeneracy to well-being and reintegration. (3) Finally, the same vocabulary can also point with less metaphorical force to "salvation" in a Christian global sense, inclusive of reconciliation to God, restoration to wholeness and teleologically to every dimension of God's redemptive repair in Christ. Gordon Fee is correct, if guilty of understatement, to note that "[sōzō] is probably the most comprehensive word in Paul's vocabulary for God's redemptive event."[55]

All of that said, it remains clear that "salvation" is most assuredly not a forensic metaphor. As we have seen, if in one instance it can be the future counterpart to "justification" (e.g., Rom 5:1-11), in another it can be conceptually inclusive of, while not coextensive with, "justification" (e.g., Rom 1:16; Eph 2:5, 8; Tit 3:5). But "salvation" and "justification" are never synonyms without remainder. Indeed, the lexical point scarcely needs to be made, were it not for the long-standing and unreflective tendency in common theological parlance for "salvation" to be conflated with "justification," as though "salvation" were simply an alternative way of speaking of acquittal coram Deo or of justification standing for the whole of salvation. This sort of conflation fuels a series of unfortunate, perhaps unconscious, moves. To the extent that salvation is equated with justification, there is the risk of skewing an entire soteriology in a narrowly forensic direction, inviting the equally mistaken backlash, that salvation is not forensic at all, not even justification.

---

[55]Gordon D. Fee, *The First Epistle to the Corinthians*, NICNT (Grand Rapids: Eerdmans, 1987), 68n6.

7.3 ENTER "RECONCILIATION"

Perhaps somewhat artificially, though not without purpose, I have left to the side another Pauline soteriological metaphor until this point: reconciliation. Once again, it should be noted that "reconciliation"—neither the specific language (*katallassō, katallagē, apokatallassō*) nor the concept—has no place in the earliest Pauline letters. We do not find it in Galatians or in the Thessalonian correspondence; as a soteriological metaphor, it is also absent from 1 Corinthians (although note its secular use in 1 Cor 7:11). And then, as though without warning, reconciliation becomes the theme of 2 Corinthians 5:14-21; it is central to the argument of Romans 5:1-11; and, in its compounded form (*apokatallassō*) and supplemented by the language of "peace," it is a key metaphor in Ephesians 2 and Colossians 1.[56] Thus, the entry of reconciliation language dramatically marks the chronological center of Paul's corpus or, as some would have it, transcends the late undisputed and certain disputed letters.

7.3.1 Reconciliation in 2 Corinthians. Reconciliation is distinctive in the Pauline soteriological discourse in that it is virtually unprecedented in Paul's Jewish inheritance. Unlike the various metaphors of atonement, justification, redemption and sanctification, reconciliation comes, as it were, out of the blue. The Hebrew Bible is absent a vocabulary, though surely not the concept, of reconciliation.[57] It is apparent that Paul is drawing from a new metaphorical field and that his appeal to reconciliation as an elucidation of the new circumstance in Christ constitutes a kind of innovation from his Jewish vantage point.[58] But how do we account for Paul's unprecedented use of the

---

[56]καταλλάσσω: Romans 5:10 (2x); 11:15; 1 Corinthians 7:11; 2 Corinthians 5:18, 19, 20; καταλλαγή: Romans 5:11; ἀποκαταλλάσσω: Ephesians 2:16; Colossians 1:20, 22. To these references, we can add the conceptual synonyms of having peace with God (Rom 2:10; 5:1; Eph 2:14, 17; possibly Eph 6:15) and making peace (Eph 2:15; Col 1:20).

[57]The LXX use of καταλλάσσω/καταλλαγή is limited to 2 Maccabees 1:5; 5:20; 7:33; 8:29; Isaiah 9:4; Jeremiah 31:39 (MT 48:39) (cf. T. Job 25:3). Of these, only the 2 Maccabees references have to do with the restoration of the divine-human relationship.

[58]On the lexical background of "reconciliation," see esp. the indispensible study of Stanley E. Porter, *Καταλλάσσω in Ancient Greek Literature, with Reference to the Pauline Writings*, Estudios de Filología Neotestamentaria 5 (Cordoba: Ediciones el Almendro, 1994), 13-116; C. Spicq, "καταλλαγή, καταλλάσσω," *TLNT*, 2:262-66 (cf. 1:309-11); H. Merkel, "καταλλάσσω, κτλ.," *EDNT*, 2:261-63; 2:261-63; Seyoon Kim, "2 Cor. 5:11-21 and the Origin of Paul's Concept of 'Reconciliation,'" *NovT* 39, no. 4 (1997): 360-84; and Cilliers Breytenbach, "Salvation of the Reconciled (with a Note on the Background of Paul's Metaphor of Reconciliation)," in *Salvation in the New Testament*, ed. J. G. van der Watt (Leiden: Brill, 2005), 271-86.

reconciliation image?[59] As Cilliers Breytenbach has demonstrated persuasively, the metaphorical domain Paul invokes in 2 Corinthians 5 is political
diplomacy.[60] I add a second dimension to Breytenbach's analysis, namely,
that Paul's express purpose in trafficking in the politico-diplomatic domain
is to offer an apologia for his apostleship. Thus, it is the rhetorical occasion
of 2 Corinthians 5:14-21 that calls for the first occurrence of reconciliation
in the Pauline corpus. While this is surely a soteriologically rich discourse,
in the larger context of 2 Corinthians, it is clear that the soteriological material participates in a larger-scale apologia and exposition of Paul's apostleship.[61] In this passage, Paul depicts himself as an "ambassador" (*presbeuomen*),[62]
as though God were making his appeal (*parakalountos*) through him, Paul
petitioning (*deometha*) on behalf of Christ: "Be reconciled to God!" This
diplomatic political scenario—the language of ambassador, appeal and pe-
tition (*presbeia, parakaleō, deomai*) being of a piece with "reconcile"
(*katallassō*)—is thus a leg of Paul's apostolic defense. Paul positions himself
as a deputized envoy of God, announcing terms of reconciliation between

---

[59]It is true, as I. H. Marshall ("The Meaning of 'Reconciliation,'" in *Unity and Diversity in New
Testament Theology: Essays in Honor of George E. Ladd*, ed. Robert A. Guelich [Grand Rapids:
Eerdmans, 1978], 117-32) and Seyoon Kim ("2 Cor. 5:11-21") note, that there is some
"reconciliation" precedent in Hellenistic Jewish sources (e.g., 2 Macc 1:5; 5:20; 7:33; 8:29; Philo,
Praem. 166; cf. Josephus, *Ant.* 3.315; 6.143), but both the scarcity of use and, even more so, the
diversity of provenance make it unwise to speak even cautiously, as Kim does, of a "Hellenistic
Jewish tradition of reconciliation." Cf. the trenchant comments of Breytenbach, "Salvation of
the Reconciled," 277. Likewise, Porter notes that the religious appropriation of the terminology
only becomes signficant with its uses in 2 Maccabees and then Paul (Porter, Καταλλάσσω *in
Ancient Greek Literature*, 16).
[60]Cilliers Breytenbach, *Versöhnung: Eine Studie zur paulinischen Soteriologie* (Neukirchen-Vluyn:
Neukirchener Verlag, 1989); summarized in idem, "Salvation of the Reconciled," esp. 272-76.
[61]So most 2 Corinthians commentators; e.g., Murray J. Harris, *The Second Epistle to the
Corinthians: A Commentary on the Greek Text*, NIGTC (Grand Rapids: Eerdmans, 2005), 240-41,
who understands the "Major Digression" of 2 Corinthians 2:14-7:4 as "The Apostolic Ministry
Described." Cf. Wright, *P&FG*, 2:879-80.
[62]The force of the first-person plural, here and in the near context, is not easy to determine. The
simplest explanation is that Paul refers to himself in the company of his apostolic associates,
a possiblity that cannot be discounted. But this makes hard going of certain of the claims. For
example, when Paul says, "For if we are out of our minds . . . if we are in our right mind" (εἴτε
γὰρ ἐξέστημεν . . . εἴτε σωφρονοῦμεν), it is probable that he is engaged in a particular self-
defense against accusations that his visionary pneumaticism marks him as unreliable. It is
hard to imagine that this is anything other than a self-defense, even if certain other of his
claims could be extended to the Pauline circle. Thus, it is probably best to read the first-person
plural throughout as stylistic, and only secondarily inclusive of his associates, to the extent
that the estimation of Paul will extend to his circle. See the discussion in Kim, "2 Cor. 5:11-21,"
268-69, n. 32.

once estranged parties. This is not just an imaginative metaphor taking on a life of its own; it is the realistic scenario of the source domain (political diplomacy) mapping on to the target domain (religious salvation).[63] Reconciliation, then, is not just another complementary way to speak of justification or of salvation but a new apologetic strategy for Paul, whose status with the Corinthians seemed always to be tenuous, surrounded as he was by skeptics within and rivals outside the Corinthian assemblies. Reconciliation—that is, the whole politico-diplomatic complex—is another way of speaking of his apostleship and another *unprecedented* account of salvation in fresh, compelling terms, in which the analogy can scarcely be lost, and if followed, Paul self-evidently becomes God's envoy by virtue of his offer of terms of peace (2 Cor 5:20) and his announcement of salvation (2 Cor 6:2).

The scope of my argument does not permit a fuller exposition of this crucial Pauline text, especially as it bears on the question of atonement in Paul. But two observations must suffice for now. In highlighting the rhetorical function of reconciliation in 2 Corinthians 5, I do not suggest that the soteriological dimensions of this passage are secondary or inconsequential, only that they are rhetorically ancillary to Paul's larger objective of validating his apostolic credentials. Second, it is evident that atonement, broadly conceived as the saving death and resurrection of Jesus, functions in this passage in a manner parallel to several passages in Galatians (Gal 2:20-21; 3:12-14) and Romans (Rom 3:24-26; 4:25; 5:6-8, 14-19). The saving death and resurrection of Jesus are the precondition for reconciliation in 2 Corinthians 5 just as they are in Galatians and Romans the precondition of justification. But a direct appeal to justification, as though it were a kind of ground metaphor for which reconciliation is mere festooning, is absent here. True, we have 2 Corinthians 5:21 as a summarization of the atoning ground of reconciliation, and the language "we might become the righteousness of God" (NRSV) perhaps should be taken as the substance of "justification." The point remains that the language that predominates Galatians and Romans is, at best, muted here. This parallel, though not quite interchangeable, relationship between

---

[63]I owe the metaphorical account of Paul's use of reconciliation and its application in 2 Corinthians to the discussion in Breytenbach, "Salvation of the Reconciled," 272-84. Breytenbach builds on the now familiar cognitive linguistic theory of metaphor articulated originally in George Lakoff and Mark Johnson, *Metaphors We Live By* (Chicago: University of Chicago Press, 1980).

the metaphors does not make justification and reconciliation conflatable or collapsible into a single soteriological reality, two different names for the same "thing"; it shows them rather to be structurally analogous.[64]

7.3.2 Reconciliation in Romans. If the none-too-early introduction of reconciliation into the Pauline constellation in 2 Corinthians can be attributed chiefly to Paul's rhetorical ends, the same does not hold in its next occurrences in Romans. We now depart from Breytenbach's metaphorical maximalism. Whereas Breytenbach sees the politico-diplomatic context of reconciliation fully alive in Romans 5, there are reasons to doubt that this is so. In the first place, the metaphorical apparatus that confirms the diplomatic origins of reconciliation in 2 Corinthians is now absent. None of the language that evoked the whole scenario remains: there is no "ambassador," no "entreaty," no "terms of peace," no exhortation to be at peace.[65] The surrounding

---

[64]On the essentially "forensic" character of 2 Corinthians 5:21, see the careful discussion in Ben C. Blackwell, *Christosis: Pauline Soteriology in Light of Deification in Irenaeus and Cyril of Alexandria*, WUNT 2.314 (Tübingen: Mohr Siebeck, 2011), 226-33. Blackwell is quick to emphasize, however, that "becoming the righteousness of God" extends beyond a mere declaration of status but gestures to "new creation" (2 Cor 5:17) and participation (ἐν αὐτῷ) and is thus implicitly tranformational as well.

[65]There is, of course, the famous textual variant in Romans 5:1 in which, if read as ἔχωμεν, becomes a hortatory subjunctive: "let us have peace toward God." The variant is worthy of serious consideration on both external and internal grounds (in its favor see Robert Jewett, *Romans: A Commentary*, Hermeneia [Minneapolis: Fortress, 2007], 345, n. a, 348). External support for the (hortatory) subjunctive, ἔχωμεν, is strong enough (ℵ*, A, B*, C, D, K, L, 33, 81, 630, 1175, 1739*; pm, lat, bo; Marcion [acc. to Tertullian]) to raise significant doubt for the indicative ἔχομεν ("we have peace with God"), which, however, does not lack for attestation (ℵ¹, B², F, G, P, Ψ, 0220^vid, 104, 365, 1241, 1505, 1506, 1739c, 1881, 2464; 1846, pm, vg^mss). And in this case, it would seem that the subjunctive is also the *lectio difficilior*—at least it is regarded so by a considerable majority of New Testament scholars, who elide the weighty canon of external evidence by insisting that it is actually so ill-fitting to the context that the indicative must have been original. Of course, that cuts both ways, and if even tolerable sense can be made of the subjunctive, it should be preferred. And *almost* tolerable sense can be made—perhaps not so much the mild "let us have" or "let us enjoy," but, freely rendered in anticipation of the theme of enmity overcome with love in Romans 5:5, 8, and 10, "let us[, our antagonism having been overcome, now] live in peace with God [i.e., our former adversary]." This is further fitting in light of the prepositional phrase πρὸς τὸν θεόν—let us have peace, we might say, *toward* God. Thus understood, the hortatory subjunctive, far from ill-fitting, is actually thematically appropriate (though one could wonder why it is an introductory rather than concluding notion in a decidedly declarative paragraph). On the other hand, if not thematically impossible, the subjunctive is syntactically problematic in relationship not only to the perfect indicative of ἔχω, ἐσχήκαμεν (*eschēkamen*, "we have access") but especially with the adverbial καί (*kai*, here "also"). It makes little sense to have first-person plural verbs in contrasting moods joined by an adverbial καί, that is, to say that "we have *also* gained access," if there were not already an assurance of something that we "have." Thus, on balance, ἔχομεν ("we have peace with God") is still to be preferred, even if the confidence of the UBS⁴ {A} rating is unwarranted.

props have been struck from the stage, leaving only "reconciliation" behind. And now in juxtaposition to each other, reconciliation is put into an explicating conceptual relationship with justification. At the head of this transitional section, picking up on "justification" in Romans 4:25 and applying it (*oun*), Paul says that "peace with God" (*eirēnē . . . pros theon*) is the result of having (already; cf. *nyn*, Rom 4:9) been justified by faith (Rom 5:1).[66] That peace toward God, a state of reconciliation expressed in different terms, forms a conceptual inclusio with the paragraph's conclusion, Romans 5:10-11, and thus conditions all that intervenes.[67]

Humans who were successively weak, ungodly, sinners and enemies (Rom 5:6, 8, 10) are the undeserving recipients of divine reconciliation at God's own initiative and expense. Clearly Romans 5:9 and 10 stand in a parallel relation to each other, both employing the "how much more" trope (i.e., a fortiori or *qal wāḥômer,* lesser to greater):

How much more	having been justified now by his blood,	shall we be saved by him from the wrath
pollō . . . mallon	*dikaiōthentes nyn en tō haimati autou*	*sōthēsometha di' autou apo tēs orgēs*
if, though being enemies, we were reconciled to God through his death		
how much more,	having been reconciled,	shall we be saved by his life.
pollō mallon	*katallagentes*	*sōthēsometha en tē zōē autou*

"Having been justified" is clearly paralleled to "having been reconciled" by means of aorist passive participles following "how much more" and climaxing in "shall we be saved" (*sōthēsometha*) and a prepositional modifier ("from the wrath"; "by his life"). Thus, "being justified" and "being reconciled" are two ways of speaking, in this case, of a past dimension of God's saving intervention,[68] complemented by its future consummation (i.e., "shall we be saved"). Although sharing a temporally past orientation, again,

---

[66]Assuming with most exegetes that δικαιωθέντες is implicitly causal in force ("since," RSV, ESV, NRSV, NAB, etc.; cf. Wallace, *GGBB*, 662).

[67]Not only do peace (Rom 5:1) and reconciliation (Rom 5:10-11) form the inclusio, but also Paul's reference to "boasting" (often misleadingly translated as "rejoicing") in Romans 5:2 (καυχώμεθα) and 5:11 (καυχώμενοι).

[68]Since commentators so frequently appeal to the aorist participles as defining a "past" dimension of salvation (and sometimes even an alleged "once-for-all" character), it is important to say that the aorist participle does no such thing in itself. Rather only the context shows these to be past referring (rightly Moo, *Epistle to the Romans*, 298n26).

it does not follow that justification and reconciliation are to be collapsed into a single notion.[69] Rather, they represent two complementary pictures, mutually interpretive, from different metaphorical domains—justification, forensic and, now in Romans, reconciliation more fundamentally relational than diplomatic.

The evidence that reconciliation has evolved into a more properly relational metaphor is not far to seek. As noted, none of the diplomatic apparatus that suffuses the 2 Corinthians 5 text is any longer present here; and there is especially no agent or envoy offering terms of peace. God's reconciling of sinners and enemies is unilateral. Even more significantly, Romans 5 presents motive for reconciliation as without any pragmatic basis, owing only to love. His love was "poured out within our hearts through the Holy Spirit" (Rom 5:5); God's pity for the helpless and mercy to the sinner demonstrate his love concretized in Christ's death for us (Rom 5:8). The reconciliation of humans to God is such that it effects a transformation not only of legal standing—as it would be were the accomplishment merely forensic—but also of affections: those reconciled to God now "boast" proudly in the one with whom they formerly were at enmity. Reconciliation, thus, in Romans is not merely an epiphenomenon to justification, nor is it but a coming to terms or making alliance in enlightened self-interest. Humans do not reconcile themselves to God; God reconciles humans to himself, at great cost, for no advantage other than for the satisfaction and demonstration of love.[70] Here reconciliation is a personal and, thus, an indirectly transformative metaphor. It is not, as Sanders maintains, simply another instance of "transfer terminology."[71]

---

[69]Contra Gorman, *Inhabiting the Cruciform God*, 54-55. Even if we chalk this up to some casual imprecision, it is consequential for Gorman's project of demonstrating that justification is "not merely or even primarily juridical or judicial—the image of a divine judge pronouncing pardon or acquittal. That is part, but only part, of the significance of justification."

[70]Porter (*Καταλλάσσω in Ancient Greek Literature*) demonstrates in exhaustive detail the earlier thesis of Marshall ("Meaning of 'Reconciliation'"), that Paul's use of reconciliation is unprecedented in that the aggrieved party (God) takes the initiative in removing the offense so as to make reconciliation. Thus, reconciliation significantly informs any Pauline understanding of atonement (I. Howard Marshall, *Aspects of the Atonement: Cross and Resurrection in the Reconciling of God and Humanity* [London: Paternoster, 2007]; and Simon J. Gathercole, *Defending Substitution: An Essay on Atonement in Paul*, Acadia Studies in Bible and Theology [Grand Rapids: Baker Academic, 2015]).

[71]Sanders, *P&PJ*, 463-72.

Although having been penned a generation ago, Joseph Fitzmyer's re-joinder to Käsemann on the function of "reconciliation" in Romans 5 vis-à-vis "justification" is worth quoting in full.

> There is no doubt that justification and reconciliation are related in Romans 5; but the real question is, what is the nature of that relation? Is reconciliation subordinated to justification [so Käsemann]? In Rom 5:1 Paul says, "Having been justified . . . , we have peace with God." As I read that verse, it suggests that justification takes place in view of something, viz., reconciliation, so that reconciliation does not "sharpen and point up the doctrine of justification" [Käsemann] in Pauline thought. It is rather the other way round. Further involved in this issue is the subtle question of the relation of Romans chaps. 1–4 to Romans chaps. 5–8, and indeed the place of Romans 5 in the whole of chaps. 1–8. No matter how one decides this question, it seems to me to be clear that the climax of chaps. 1–8 is not in chap. 4, for as Paul begins chap. 5 he moves from justification to the manifestation of God's love in Christ and through the Spirit (chap. 8), so that the latter is the climax of it all. If so, justification is only a part of the process and a stage in the development of his theses in Romans chaps. 1–8—and then justification finds a more adequate expression in reconciliation; indeed, "reconciliation" becomes the better way of expressing that process.[72]

Fitzmyer's claim here is suggestive, if overstated and slightly problematic, but I think basically correct. He implies that justification, having done its work in the juridical movement of Romans 1–4, yields to reconciliation as the "more adequate expression," "the better way of expressing that process." Leaving aside the infelicity of collapsing justification and reconciliation as merely alternative ways of describing "that process," the more significant point remains, namely, that justification recedes (without disappearing; cf. Rom 6:7; 8:30, 33) and reconciliation emerges as a rich, interpersonal description of its accomplishment. Thus, in the same way that the "apocalyptic" stage is set in Romans 5:12-21 for the transformational soteriological discourse that follows in Romans 6–8, the relational conditions are described in Romans 5:1-10. I would add only that not only does justification recede in Romans, but what happens in Romans is a sort of microcosm of the phenomena of the larger Pauline corpus.

---

[72]Joseph A. Fitzmyer, "Reconciliation in Pauline Theology," in *To Advance the Gospel: New Testament Studies*, 2nd ed. (Grand Rapids: Eerdmans, 1998), 172-73, ellipsis original.

In apparent independence from Fitzmyer, Martin reaches a similar, though more specific, conclusion: justification yields to reconciliation not because it is "more adequate" in some general sense, but because reconciliation *"is the way Paul formulated his gospel in communicating it to the Gentiles."*[73] As a sort of friendly amendment to Fitzmyer's suggestion, this is an attractive hypothesis, but Martin offers it more as an assertion than an argument. It is not clear that it has sufficient explanatory power to stand as more than an interesting suggestion. The chief attractiveness of the hypothesis lies especially in the salient fact that justification with its *ṣdq* and *dikai-* cognates has deep roots in Jewish covenantal and eschatological soteriology. By contrast, reconciliation enters the Pauline discourse without that same biblical heritage, the application of an essentially "secular" construct to the new circumstance wrought by God through Christ. This observation, almost understated by Martin,[74] constitutes prima facie evidence for why it might be the case that justification recedes and reconciliation ascends.[75] Furthermore, the metaphor of reconciliation has a particular fittingness for an audience that, by Jewish-Christian presupposition, is estranged from God by definition. That Colossians and Ephesians (whatever the original destination of the latter) are apparently directed to Gentile readers might also serve as a corroborating datum.

Yet, on the whole, Martin's thesis fails to convince. To begin with, in his particular version of the hypothesis, the same tradition-critical grounds that allow him to claim the primitivity of the reconciliation tradition (e.g., in the Christ hymn of Col 1:15-20) now subvert this leg of the thesis: "'Reconciliation'

---

[73]Ralph P. Martin, *Reconciliation: A Study of Paul's Theology*, New Foundations Theological Library (Atlanta: John Knox, 1982), 153, emphasis original. Less persuasively, Martin even claims that Paul even "expressed a dissatisfaction with the forensic-cultic idiom [in Rom 3:24-26] that limited soteriology to covenant-renewal for the Jewish nation and [Paul instead] sought to universalize the scope of Christ's saving deed to include Gentiles on the basis of faith, not covenantal nomism." This is not at all persuasive, requiring us to accept the premise that Paul made use of an ill-fitting tradition in Romans 3:24-26 where he is expressly remediating the equally estranged Jews and Gentiles (Rom 3:22-23).

[74]"The terminology [of reconciliation] is not restricted to the Old Testament-Judaic tradition; it has little if any cultic-forensic association; it relates to a universal human need, namely forgiveness and personal relationship; and it can take within its scope both personal and cosmic dimensions" (ibid.).

[75]Although many New Testament scholars would not find an appeal to Acts probative, it is at least worthy of note that the one reference to justification in a primitive Christian sermon is Paul preaching in the synagogue at Pisidian Antioch (Acts 13:38-39).

was already part of the Christian vocabulary before [Paul] adopted it. But in his hands it took on a new meaning."[76] Besides the obvious difficulty of demonstrating such a claim, one wonders how likely it is that the tradition that preexisted Paul "waited" so long to be put to use in the proclamation to Gentiles. Why have we no evidence that this was a favored way to communicate the gospel to Gentile-majority communities in Galatia, Thessalonica and Corinth? Moreover, the presumption that justification was a narrowly Jewish idiom makes it hard to account for why it plays the dominant role it does in the letters to the (exclusively?) Gentile Galatian recipients and the (predominantly?) Gentile Roman recipients. It is too simplistic to assume that arguments that presume Jewish categories or appeal extensively to Scripture point to a Jewish audience. Before an argument makes sense to an audience, it needs to make sense to its author, and there is abundant evidence from the New Testament that primitive Christian literature presumed on the capacity of Gentile readers to navigate what had been terra incognita as though it had become a new homeland. While one can imagine that reconciliation had great appeal or potential appeal to a Gentile audience, there is no reason to suppose—indeed, evidence to the contrary—that justification would have been unintelligible to Gentiles any more than reconciliation would have been incomprehensible to Jews.

There is a more plausible way to account for the receding of justification and the ascent of reconciliation. As I have suggested above, justification suits the controversy of Gentile status before God apart from Torah observance because with biblical precedent Paul can speak of a righteousness reckoned on the ground of faith (Gen 15:6; cf. Gal 3:6; Rom 4:3) prior to circumcision and prior to Sinai. Thus, the path for Gentiles had already been forged, and neither circumcision (Rom 4:9-12) nor Torah compliance (Gal 3:17) had a role. This status appeals not to a relative moral rectitude but to a declaration of acquittal that depends not on Torah observance but on union with Christ, "who was put to death for our trespasses and raised for our justification" (Rom 4:25 RSV). Meanwhile, reconciliation casts this accomplishment of justification in more universal and relational terms.

Before leaving Romans, we are obliged to note the one other occurrence of "reconciliation" in this letter. Writing, at once wistfully and hopefully, of

---

[76]Martin, *Reconciliation*, 154.

his yet unbelieving kinsmen, Paul declares, "For if their rejection is the reconciliation of the world [*katallagē kosmou*], what will their acceptance be but life from the dead!" (Rom 11:15 NRSV). Whether we take this as an inherited tradition or original to Paul, it contributes to the scenario Paul unfolds just the same.[77] Thus, in its context, the reconciliation *of the world* should be understood as the extension of peace especially to Gentiles (though not exclusive of Israel); Israel's present rejection of the gospel makes opportunity for its wider reach (Rom 9:25-26; 11:11-14, 19-20). The counterpart to reconciliation, predicated upon Israel's acceptance, is "life from the dead." The theological pattern here is akin to that of Romans 5:9-10, in which present reconciliation is related to the consummation of salvation as its first installment. Again, reconciliation is the firstfruit of resurrection, and resurrection is metonymy for the new creation. Thus, "reconciliation of the world" harbingers Paul's expansive and eschatological vision, and "reconciliation" accommodates that vision in a manner that "justification" in itself would not.

7.3.3 Reconciliation in Colossians and Ephesians. Reconciliation continues in this same expansive and eschatological direction when we move beyond Romans to Colossians and Ephesians. Several observations will serve to orient us to this phase of Paul's development of the reconciliation metaphor in these letters.

(1) I have already addressed the question of authenticity, but it bears repeating that when these letters are considered in relationship to a possible theological trajectory rather than to a constructed *Hauptbriefe* template, the plausibility of Pauline authenticity increases. If reconciliation is relatively late and supplemental to the soteriology of the undisputed letters (2 Corinthians and Romans), it is reengaged as a primary, if not the primary, soteriological idiom in Colossians and Ephesians. The too frequent claim that reconciliation is a negligible and ancillary theme for Paul is clearly a prejudgment of the question.

---

[77]Käsemann takes "reconciliation of the world" to be a "fixed tradition" (Ernst Käsemann, "Some Thoughts on the Theme 'the Doctrine of Reconciliation in the New Testament,'" in *The Future of Our Religious Past*, ed. James M. Robinson [New York: Harper & Row, 1971], 51). Given what we have observed about the entrance of reconciliation as a later and uniquely Pauline phenomenon, Käsemann's confidence seems unwarranted (cf. Porter, *Καταλλάσσω in Ancient Greek Literature*, 129-30). Fitzmyer ("Reconciliation in Pauline Theology," 172) is correct to point out that, even so, it is no less Pauline for that.

(2) It is essential to note that the language and conceptual framework of reconciliation is considerably more pervasive than merely three occurrences of the verb *apokatallassō* (Col 1:20, 22; Eph 2:16). First, both Colossians and, even more so, Ephesians describe the readers' dire former state in such terms that *only* reconciliation could ameliorate. In both letters, the readers were once "alienated" (*apallotrioō*, Col 1:21; Eph 2:12; cf. 4:18), the Colossians alienated to God, also being "enemies" (cf. Rom 5:10), their "hostility in mind expressed in wicked deeds" (my translation), the "Ephesians" being "alienated from the commonwealth of Israel and strangers to the covenants of promise—having no hope and without God in the world" (Eph 2:12). The Gentile readers were "once far off" (*hoi pote ontes makran*, Eph 2:13), on the "wrong" side of the dividing wall and at enmity with God and his covenant people (Eph 2:14). Not only is the hapless state of the formerly unreconciled described in diverse terms, so also is reconciliation. Beyond the verb *apokatallassō* itself, Paul will speak in both letters of "peace making" (*eirēnopoieō*, Col 1:20; *poiōn eirēnēn*, Eph 2:15); indeed Christ himself "*is* our peace" (Eph 2:14; cf. 2:17), the one who "makes the both one, breaking down the dividing wall . . . creating the two into one new person" (Eph 2:14-15). We might say that both Colossians and, even more, Ephesians exploit the latent narrative of the figure of reconciliation, scripting a narrative from alienation to reunion. Colossians tells that story more briefly, first in terms of the reconciliation of the created order (*ta panta*) to God (Col 1:20) and then humans (Col 1:22). Ephesians tells the story on a larger canvas and in two personal dimensions, reconciliation to God (Eph 2:1-10, 16) effecting a concomitant reunion of Jews and Gentiles into one new people (Eph 2:11-22).

(3) The second observation leads naturally to a third: it is notable that the objects and scope of reconciliation have expanded from the earlier material in 2 Corinthians and Romans. On the one hand, the objects of reconciliation have expanded beyond the human creation, which is all that the earlier reference had in view, to the nonhuman creation, to the *ta panta* ("all things," Col 1:20), which is inclusive of the human creation (so Col 1:22), but also of the whole created order (cf. *ta panta* in Col 1:16-17), explicated as "things visible and things invisible," including the ruling entities or structures described as "thrones, lordships, rulers and authorities."[78] From the vantage

---

[78]Of course, the identity of these terms is disputed, other than that they are not human beings as such.

point of the Christ hymn, there is nothing that falls outside of God's reconciling purview any more than there are created things whose existence is
independent of Jesus Christ.[79] Indeed, in the Christ-hymn depiction, there
is a fundamental symmetry to the order of creation and order of reconciliation as a new creation.

The exceptionless span of reconciliation has suggested a salvific universalism that some find hopeful and others worrying, or at least hard to reconcile to the discriminating soteriological vision elsewhere stated or presupposed in Paul. Three observations disentangle the apparent incoherence: (a)
The inclusion of *ta panta* within the span of reconciliation (Col 1:20) is expressly for including the wholeness of the created order in reconciliation in
symmetry with the *ta panta* of creation (Col 1:16-17). That is to say, although
ta panta is surely inclusive of the human creation, rhetorically that is not its
primary referent—the account of creation in Colossians 1:16-17 does not
even mention human beings. Moreover, as it concerns the sentient creation,
ta panta more naturally emphasizes the transcendent beings or powers expressly named in Colossians 1:16, whatever we might understand them to be.
The *human* creation only comes into the picture implicitly with the mention
of the "the body, the church" in Colossians 1:18 and "the dead" among whom
he is the *prōtotokos* ("firstborn") and preeminent.

(b) It is only with the second use of *apokatallassō*, in Colossians 1:22, that
the object of reconciliation turns to humans, specifically the Colossians,
who had formerly been alienated and hostile. Thus, there is a movement
from the universality and cosmic character of reconciliation in Colossians
1:18-20 to its more particular object in Colossians 1:21-23. Human reconciliation to God participates in a much larger drama than merely the restoration of friendship among the sentient beings, as if the remainder of the

---

[79]Note, e.g., the way Martin appeals on tradition-critical grounds to a personalizing of the
reconciliation tradition inherited in the Christ hymn by way of Pauline redaction: "First, [Paul]
has shown that reconciliation is primarily concerned with the *restoration of personal relationships.*
Granted that Christ restored the universe to its true state under God, Paul goes on [i.e., in Col
1:21-23] to insist that speculative interest is not adequate to match a moral problem" (Martin,
Reconciliation, 121, emphasis original). On this tendency to marginalize the cosmic dimensions
of reconciliation, see esp. David G. Horrell, Cherryl Hunt and Christopher Southgate, eds.,
Greening Paul: Rereading the Apostle in a Time of Ecological Crisis (Waco, TX: Baylor University
Press, 2010), 87-115, esp. the incisive critique (89-96) of the habit of New Testament exegetes to
focus preemptively on the reconciliation of humans alone. Note also the welcome corrective in
Wright, *P&FG*, 2:1504-18.

created order were only a stage for the actual drama. Yet, that being so, the salvific reconciliation of human beings—the already-believing Colossians here functioning as a case in point—is conditional upon their continuance in faith and steadfastness to the gospel (Col 1:23).

(c) Finally, these observations all but require that "reconciliation" might bear upon its various objects differently. Especially if we regard the powers named in Colossians 1:16 inclusive of malevolent forces or institutions (cf. Col 2:15), it becomes necessary to see reconciliation not only as the exercise of redeeming love but also as the final accomplishment of consummating and perfecting sovereignty. The "peace" that God makes is not to be stereotyped superficially, and it includes at once the free surrender of sentient beings to grace and love, the pacification of the recalcitrant, and the restoration of unalloyed goodness to the inanimate creation.

At the same time, as we have seen in Ephesians, the scope of reconciliation not only is animate and inanimate but also includes the restoration of relations between Jew and Gentile, premised on the restoration of each to God through Christ. Thus, we can say that reconciliation in its expression in Colossians and Ephesians is now cosmic in its scope and ethnically universalist, a restoration of earth to heaven and of historically antipathetic peoples to a state of harmony enjoyed in union with Jesus Christ. Although I will take issue with the reductionism of Ernst Käsemann's influential essay on reconciliation, it would be hard to improve upon this description:

> This [cosmic] peace [depicted in Colossians and Ephesians] is thought of as the eschatological state of salvation, not as a psychological attitude, something in which the NT is very rarely interested.[80] In this situation of peace what was formerly separated becomes solidly united, i.e., the heavenly is united with the earthly, just as warring earthly camps are united with one another. Even religious antipathies now become irrelevant, as may be seen in a radical way in the antithesis between Israel and the Gentile world. The world is made peaceful, as under the *pax romana*, in that it is everywhere subjected to its new Lord, Christ, as Cosmocrater.[81]

---

[80]The New Testament might be more interested in psychological peace than Käsemann acknowledges: e.g., Matthew 6:25; Luke 12:22; John 14:27; Philippians 4:6-7; Colossians 3:15; 1 Peter 5:7.
[81]Käsemann, "Some Thoughts," 54.

All of the above prepares for a more tentative fourth observation, reflecting on the possible significance of the compounded form of the verb, *apokatallassō*.[82] It is conventional wisdom that compounded forms in Koine will often mark no particular intensification as compared to their noncompounded alternatives.[83] Prepositional compounding sometimes merely bears witness to a kind of semantic inflation. To wit, in contemporary English, it might be said that something is "extraordinary" when what is meant is that it is "above the mean" or "somewhat unusual." Or in sport or entertainment, those who were once "stars" are now "superstars" so that we now have "superstars" who are not even "all-stars"! An abundance of such examples can be found in the New Testament.[84] In the case of *apokatallassō*, however, we have a verb that, in all of literary Greek, makes its premiere in this form in the three occurrences of these two letters (Col 1:20, 22; Eph 2:16), and there is, thus, good reason to suppose, assuming Pauline authorship, that it is a Pauline coinage.[85] It is tempting to surmise that the compounded form intends not so much an intensification as to evoke a reconciliation that returns something to its original state. Etymologically (and etymology must carry more weight in the case of neologisms and *hapax legomena*), *apo* may well carry the force of "back" (roughly the equivalent of our prefix "re-") in a verbal compound, allowing either the notion of a reconciliation that is a kind of restoration *back* to original state or, more modestly, a reconciliation complete in itself.[86] Thus, it may be that this compounded form of the verb intends

---

[82]I.e., ἀποκαταλλάσσω in Colossians 1:20, 22; and Ephesians 2:16 over against καταλλάσσω/ καταλλαγή in Romans 5:10, 11; 11:15; 1 Corinthians 7:11; 2 Corinthians 5:18, 19, 20. Of course, καταλλάσσω is itself already a compound verb (κατά + ἀλλάσσω), so technically, ἀποκαταλλάσσω is a double compound, a not infrequent occurrence in Koine.

[83]So, e.g., Markus Barth and Helmut Blanke, *Colossians: A New Translation with Introduction and Commentary*, trans. Astrid B. Beck, AB 34B (New York: Doubleday, 1994), 213-14.

[84]On the general phenomenon, see BDF, §116; Herbert Weir Smyth and Gordon M. Messing, *Greek Grammar* (Cambridge: Harvard University Press, 1956), 366-67; and C. F. D. Moule, *Idiom Book of New Testament Greek* (Cambridge: Cambridge University Press, 1960), 87-90.

[85]So, e.g., James D. G. Dunn, *The Epistles to Colossians and Philemon: A Commentary on the Greek Text*, NIGTC (Grand Rapids: Eerdmans, 1996), 102; and Porter, *Καταλλάσσω in Ancient Greek Literature*, 163, following, by F. Buschel, ἀλλάσσω, TDNT 1:258.

[86]MHT, 297-300, esp. (a) 298; cf. Murray J. Harris, *Colossians & Philemon*, Exegetical Guide to the Greek New Testament (Grand Rapids: Eerdmans, 1991), 50, who favors the latter sense. The analogy of other ἀποκατα- double compounded verbs: ἀποκαθαίρω ("cleanse" or "clear away" [back to an original purity?]); ἀποκαταθιστάνω/ἀποκαθίστημι ("restore," "reestablish") and the noun cognate, ἀποκατάστασις (Acts 3:21; "restoration") (on which, see the entries in BDAG, 11-13; LSJ, 200-201; MM, 63).

not just a conciliation or a peace making resulting in a mere coexistence or cessation of hostility, but literally to *"reconcile"* or perhaps *"restore"* or *"reunite."*[87] In one sense, it is unnecessary to leverage this sense on the morphology of a single word; the context of these passages makes the claim in any case. But the compounded form of the verb is fully corroborative of that sense, otherwise substantiated. It is perhaps, then, not special pleading to see that the use of the (double) compound *apokatallassō* as further testimony to the expansive, cosmic scope of reconciliation in Colossians and Ephesians.

In summary of the preceding discussion of reconciliation in its four prominent Pauline occurrences (2 Cor 5; Rom 5; Col 1; Eph 1–2), I propose the following sketch as a thesis: Reconciliation is a metaphor absent from the first four of Paul's letters, not entering until 2 Corinthians 5. As I have argued (following Breytenbach), this introduction of the metaphor into the Pauline corpus is densely saturated in a politico-diplomatic context, and thus serves rhetorically first to authenticate Paul's apostolic credentials as God's ambassador offering divinely wrought terms of peace. To be sure, especially as it is rooted in atonement, this appeal to reconciliation is richly soteriological and complementary to other soteriological descriptions; it remains, however, for the use of reconciliation in Romans 5 for its relationship to justification as its fruit and accomplishment to be clarified and for its implicitly personal and transformative dimensions to become fully evident. While reconciliation by no means effaces justification in Romans, it becomes a more expansive (Fitzmyer: "more adequate") way of describing the saving accomplishment of God in Jesus Christ. It is that expansive comprehensiveness that makes reconciliation the apt and consummative

---

[87]So, e.g., Lightfoot: "The word ἀποκαταλλάσσειν corresponds to ἀπηλλοτριωμένους here and in Ephes. 2:16, implying a restitution to a state from which they had fallen, or which was potentially theirs, or for which they were destined" (J. B. Lightfoot, *Saint Paul's Epistles to the Colossians and to Philemon: A Revised Text with Introductions, Notes, and Dissertations* [New York: Macmillan, 1892], 157-58; cf. Paul Beasley-Murray, "Colossians 1:15-20 : An Early Christian Hymn Celebrating the Lordship of Christ," in *Pauline Studies* [Grand Rapids: Eerdmans, 1980], 169-83). Porter resists this conclusion less for lexical reasons than theological considerations: "It is not clear that when the author talks of reconciling the universe he is referring to reestablishing an old order. He is probably speaking of establishing a new order which in some way rectifies the shortcomings of the old.... Second, the author does not prefix εἰρηνοποιήσας.... The lexical item is apparently used to talk of a new condition of peace, i.e., a making of peace, not restoration of a previously existent one" (Porter, *Καταλλάσσω in Ancient Greek Literature*, 184). This is surely correct—the reconciliation of τὰ πάντα surpasses the original goodness of the created order—but this does not preclude understanding it as not less than its restoration.

metaphor so fitting to the universal and cosmic vision of Colossians and Ephesians, wherein all things, on heaven and earth, are gathered up in Christ, their head (Eph 1:10).

7.3.4 Reconciliation in Pauline scholarship: An oversight? I wish neither to over- nor understate the prominence or significance of the theme of reconciliation in the Pauline corpus. Nonetheless, for a variety of reasons, the characteristic underestimation of the theme has been highly consequential for the trajectory of Pauline studies in general and for the conception of Pauline soteriology in particular. It remains the case that, despite a handful of important studies, reconciliation is the soteriological stepchild of Pauline studies, a condition yet to be rectified. Whereas Ralph Martin's 1980 study proposed reconciliation as the center of Pauline theology,[88] this does not seem to have been taken up in any significant way in the succeeding generations of Pauline scholarship.[89]

There is, in fact, a history of overlooking reconciliation as a central Pauline category, which can be variously explained. In the first place, "justification" and the "righteousness of God" have dominated the theological landscape, quite understandably preoccupying exegetical, theological and ecumenical discourses to the inevitable marginalization of reconciliation. Second, the fact that "reconciliation" spans the undisputed and disputed letters almost certainly contributes to this slight. As a theme in either the disputed or undisputed letters alone, it is not especially prominent, but in view of the whole "Pauline" corpus, it becomes considerably more prominent, indeed, with a greater "span" than that of justification. Finally, there are doubts on tradition-critical grounds just how integral reconciliation is to the Pauline vision.[90]

---

[88]Martin, *Reconciliation*; and idem, "New Testament Theology: A Proposal; the Theme of Reconciliation," *ExpTim* 91, no. 12 (1980): 364-68. Note also the parallel proposal in Stanley E. Porter, "Reconciliation as the Heart of Paul's Missionary Theology," in *Paul as Missionary: Identity, Activity, Theology, and Practice*, ed. Trevor J. Burke and Brian S. Rosner, Library of New Testament Studies 420 (London: T&T Clark, 2011), 169-79, that "the concept of reconciliation provides the basis and the major essential component of [Paul's] missiological theology" (p. 179).
[89]The most notable exception is Breytenbach, *Versöhnung*, but the influence of this work in the English-speaking world has been minimal. And since Breytenbach follows most scholars in excluding Colossians and Ephesians from the Pauline corpus, his conclusions are conditioned accordingly. Similarly overlooked is the indispensible lexical and suggestive theological work in Porter, *Καταλλάσσω in Ancient Greek Literature*.
[90]See, esp. Käsemann's marginalization of reconciliation on tradition-critical grounds ("Some

Beyond this, there has been an especially curious—perhaps even telling—neglect of reconciliation among NPP scholars. Arguably, this general indifference to the theme of reconciliation and corollaries within NPP quarters has proven consequential for the overall shape of the NPP paradigm. To be sure, the NPP understands reconciliation to have its place in Pauline theology as one soteriological metaphor among others, but until quite recently, it has not held a prominent place in NPP accounts of Pauline soteriology. And, in fact, leading NPP scholars are by no means uniform in their regard for its place in Pauline soteriology. Sanders pays scant and passing attention to the theme, relegating it under the rubric of "transfer terminology." Strikingly, he even considers it a "juristic" metaphor and, like Käsemann, subordinates it to justification.[91] Limiting himself to the undisputed letters, Sanders has no interest in its rhetorical function, to say nothing of tracing a trajectory. Rather, he collapses reconciliation into justification and by all appearance gives the metaphor almost no sustained attention.[92]

For his part, Dunn makes more of reconciliation than does Sanders, although it is clearly on the margins of his expansive Pauline oeuvre.[93] With the majority of critical scholars, Dunn regards Colossians and Ephesians as deutero-Pauline (albeit with Colossians written and dispatched under Paul's aegis), so it comes as little surprise that reconciliation does not feature prominently among the set of concerns that have animated his Pauline scholarship. In *The Theology of Paul the Apostle*, in which the argument of

---

Thoughts"). Käsemann regards reconciliation as an inconsequential metaphor that makes no independent or significant contribution to Pauline soteriology. For persuasive rebuttals, see Fitzmyer, "Reconciliation in Pauline Theology" (originally published as "Reconciliation in Pauline Theology," in *No Famine in the Land*, ed. James W. Flanagan and Anita Weisbrod Robinson [Missoula, MT: Scholars Press, 1975], 155-77). Martin not only pushes back on the tradition-critical argument (ibid., 71-79) but also argues in favor of the promise of reconciliation as an integrating motif for NT theology (ibid., 32-47, 201-33).

[91]Sanders, *P&PJ*, 469-70; cf. 465. Sanders's treatment of reconciliation is reminiscent of Bultmann, who maintains that reconciliation is another term that "can be substituted for the term 'righteousness' (or the cognate verb [justify]) as the designation of the new situation which God Himself has opened up to man: 'reconciliation'" (Rudolf Bultmann, *Theology of the New Testament*, trans. Kendrick Grobel [New York: Scribner, 1951], 1:285).

[92]Neither is this lacuna filled in the sequel to *P&PJ*, E. P. Sanders, *Paul, the Law, and the Jewish People* (Philadelphia: Fortress, 1983).

[93]Subject indexes cannot finally be trusted, but one's memory in reading several of Dunn's works on Paul is confirmed by the almost complete absence of "reconciliation" (James D. G. Dunn, *NPerP*; and idem, *Beginning from Jerusalem*, Christianity in the Making 2 [Grand Rapids: Eerdmans, 2009], see 1047n378, 1113).

Romans functions as a kind of theological template for Pauline loci, he gives relatively brief attention to the theme, mostly by means of a workmanlike treatment of 2 Corinthians 5:18-20.[94] His treatment of the theme in Romans 5:10-11, though not extensive, includes a brief but welcome exploration of the relationship between reconciliation and justification. Dunn falls between Sanders's collapsing of the metaphors and Wright's (see below) rigid distinction between them: "We should simply note that in winding up this section of his exposition, Paul sets in clear parallel 'justification' and 'reconciliation' ([Rom] 5:10-11). . . . Salvation denotes a completed process in both verses, where 'justification' and 'reconciliation' serve equally to denote its beginning. Here again the metaphors are complementary and should not be played off against each other."[95] It remains the case, however, that neither here nor in Dunn's Romans commentary does the fact that justification resolves into reconciliation and peace with God influence his working definition of justification itself. To be sure, Dunn understands reconciliation to be among the "blessings of justification,"[96] but this way of conceptualizing the relationship, common as it is, runs the risk of effectively subordinating "peace with God" and reconciliation to the status of a "fringe benefit," when arguably for Paul the telos of justification is precisely to mend the estrangement of humanity from its Creator.

Reconciliation is a theme even more strikingly absent from Wright's earlier work on Paul,[97] although this lacuna is generously rectified in his

---

[94]James D. G. Dunn, *The Theology of Paul the Apostle* (Grand Rapids: Eerdmans, 1998), 228-30.

[95]Ibid., 387-88. Although Dunn thinks that Martin may be in danger of playing the metaphors off against each other (Martin, *Reconciliation*, 153-54), I do not read him that way. Rather, Martin thinks that the images are complementary though not synonymous and that reconciliation is the more apt metaphor for Paul's Gentile audiences. I'm inclined to think that Cranfield describes the relationship with more insight: "Thus Δικαιωθέντες . . . εἰρήνην ἔχομεν . . . is not a mere collocation of two metaphors describing the same fact, nor does it mean that, having been justified, we were subsequently reconciled and now have peace with God; but its force is that the fact that we have been justified means that we have also been reconciled and have peace with God" (Cranfield, *Romans*, 1:258).

[96]Dunn, *Theology of Paul*, 385-89, §14.9.

[97]I am able to find one occurrence each in two early popular books on Paul (N. T. Wright, *What Saint Paul Really Said: Was Paul of Tarsus the Real Founder of Christianity?* [Grand Rapids: Eerdmans, 1997], 115 [citing from Alister E. McGrath, *Iustitia Dei: A History of the Christian Doctrine of Justification*, 1st ed. (Cambridge: Cambridge University Press, 1986)]; and Wright, *Paul: In Fresh Perspective*, 127). Reconciliation assumes only slightly more important place in his reply to John Piper (Wright, *Justification*, 80 [UK ed., 60; again citing McGrath], 161-64 [UK ed., 138-34; with respect to 2 Cor 5:14-21] and esp. 225-26 [UK ed., 198-99], discussed below).

latest magnum, *Paul and the Faithfulness of God*, about which I will have more to say presently.[98] In any case, this recent exception only highlights that, perhaps for understandable reasons, the theme of reconciliation did not play a significant role in the development of Wright's seminal contribution to the NPP. As it concerns the relationship of reconciliation to justification, Wright falls at the other end of the spectrum from Sanders by insisting on a strict distinction between the two. Quite rightly, Wright understands justification and reconciliation as distinguishable, though complementary, ways of speaking of distinct facets of the soteriological whole. But this common-sense distinction is easily overplayed and might carry with it a subtle but consequential distortion. In this regard, the most significant treatment of justification and reconciliation by Wright predating *P&FG* is illustrative.[99] Wright notes that Romans 5:9-10 "is clearly the point at which 'being justified' in [Romans] 5:1 shades over into 'we have peace with God.' Justification, itself the product of God's self-giving love, effects reconciliation between God and humans."[100] Quite so. That said, it is essential for Wright to distinguish between the two notions: "But justification and reconciliation are not the same thing. Paul clearly distinguishes them in [Romans] 5:1."[101] Again, this is right; it is clear that justification operates in a different, legal, metaphorical domain from reconciliation, which is broadly relational. Yet the means by which Wright maintains the distinction is not unproblematic. It requires that he consign each word to a dubiously sturdy and impenetrable metaphorical domain. His move here is worth quoting in full:

> This act of "justification" enables God to deal, as a consequence, with a **different problem, which Paul has not mentioned up to now, namely the *actual relationship* between God and humans.** (Many, seeing correctly that "justification" is a "relational" concept, make a mistake here, sliding

---

Even Wright's superb essay on the Colossians Christ hymn, being preoccupied with Christology, is almost silent with regard to reconciliation (N. T. Wright, "Poetry and Theology in Colossians 1.15-20," in *The Climax of the Covenant: Christ and the Law in Pauline Theology* [Edinburgh: T&T Clark, 1991], 99-119).

[98]I will consider Wright's latest and extensive treatment of reconciliation separately below, arguing that even this fulsome treatment of reconciliation is not as consequential for his overall account of Pauline soteriology as it might have been.

[99]Wright, *Justification*, 224-26 (UK ed., 197-99).

[100]Ibid., 225.

[101]Ibid.

between the law-court and actual inter-personal relationships without real-
izing that the two are different kinds of things.) Formerly they were at enmity;
now they are reconciled. Once again, this is not simply "another metaphor for
the atonement." It is, rather, a further and essentially different point from that
of the lawcourt. In the lawcourt, the point is not that the defendant and the
judge have fallen out and need to re-establish a friendship. Indeed, in some
ways the lawcourt is more obviously fair and unbiased if the defendant and
the judge have no acquaintance before and no friendship afterwards.[102]

One might take issue with this version of the distinction between reconciliation and justification at several levels. (1) As it regards Romans itself, is
it really possible that the "actual relationship between God and humans"
"has not been mentioned up to now" (i.e., Rom 5)?[103] Isn't the whole of
Romans 1:18-32 targeting and describing precisely the "actual relationship
between God and humans" when the suppression of the truth causes humanity to devolve into all manner of depravity and rebellion, even becoming
"God-haters" (theostygeis)?[104] Surely Romans 1–4 is about more than the relationship between God and humans—but not less or other than. The un-
dercurrent of Romans 1–4 is the relationship of Jews and Gentiles to each
other, framed in the economy of salvation history. But this is the under-
current; the fact that human beings are under the judgment of God is the
dominating theme. After all, that is precisely the circumstance that introduces the whole discourse in Romans 1:18 and suffuses the first four chapters.[105] The only way that it could be plausible to make this claim—that only
in Romans 5 is the problem of humanity's relationship to God taken up—is
by means of a too exclusive distinction between justification and reconciliation, consigning the former to a domain too narrow and idiosyncratic. (2)
As it regards metaphors and lexicography, it is untrue to the development of
metaphors to think that in the context of specialized discourse they forever

---

[102]Ibid., 226, italics original, boldface added.

[103]The same claim is reinforced in P&FG by repeatedly stressing that the function of Israel in the
argument, especially in Romans 2, is to demonstrate not Israel's guilt as such but her vocational
failure as a "light to the nations" (Wright, P&FG, 2:837-38).

[104]Assuming with the lexicons (e.g., BDAG, EDNT) that θεοστυγής bears an active (abhorring
God) rather than passive (abhorred by God) sense.

[105]Cf. ὀργή, Romans 2:5, 8; 3:5; 4:15; κατακρίνω, Romans 2:1; κρίνω, Romans 2:12, 16; 3:4, 6; κρίμα,
Romans 2:2, 3; 3:8. It should be noted that Campbell finds the theme of retributive justice so
exaggeratedly pervasive in Romans 1–4 that it motivates his attribution of the theme to a
Teacher, introduced via prosopopoeia (D. A. Campbell, Deliverance of God).

retain their metaphoric source domain with the sort of rigid durability that Wright requires. Rather, if all language is at least broadly metaphorical, certain metaphors are nonetheless also in some process of dying, their evocation declining and their denotation becoming increasingly fixed and particular, all the more in specialized fields of discourse. We must, then, be wary not to assume that metaphors carry perpetually with them their entire original metaphorical domain.[106] (3) Even if we are to claim that "justification" and "reconciliation" are rather more living than dying metaphors in Paul's letters, the direct causal relationship in Romans 5:1 (justification being the basis for peace with God) and the structural parallelism of Romans 5:9-10 point to both a distinction *and* a conceptual overlap. It is clear that, whatever the precise relationship between the two soteriological descriptors, justification is logically the cause or basis for reconciliation (Rom 5:1, 9-10). There is no hint from Paul that these notions could ever be reversed. Rather, justification, while not coextensive with reconciliation, is essential to it, reconciliation of the sort that Paul envisages being otherwise impossible.

Just as Sanders had good reason for collapsing reconciliation into justification as "transfer terminology," Wright has good reason for this rigid distinction. Put bluntly, the more that justification has to do with reconciliation to God, the harder it is to maintain Wright's working definition of justification as covenant membership.[107] Yet if reconciliation is a nearer synonym

---

[106]When, for example, Paul says of Christ in Colossians 1:14, "in whom we have redemption, the forgiveness of sins," both the editors of our critical Greek texts and virtually every translation understand the relationship between "redemption" and "forgiveness of sins" as apposition: redemption *consists in* the forgiveness of sins. This, however, gives the lie to the frequent claim that "redemption" is a full-blooded metaphor evoking slave manumission or, more commonly now, an allusion to Israel's exodus. I don't say it is impossible that this is so, only that when Paul has offered his own near explication of the term by apposition, it seems that the burden of proof is on those who wish to claim that a whole metaphorical domain is being invoked.

[107]Wright is explicit on this point, which he makes repeatedly:

We are forced to conclude, at least in a preliminary way, that "to be justified" here [Gal 2:16] does not mean "to be granted free forgiveness of your sins," "to come into a right relation with God" or some other near-synonym of "to be reckoned 'in the right' before God," but rather, and very specifically, **"to be reckoned by God to be a true member of his family, and hence with the right to share table fellowship."** (Wright, *Justification*, 116, boldface added)

Again:

To put it in formulae: *righteousness, dikaiosynē*, is the status of the covenant member. Its overtones are, of course, taken from the status that the defendant has after the court has found in his or her favour. *Justify, dikaioō*, is what God does when he declares this verdict.

to justification, a structural counterpart albeit from a different metaphorical domain, it becomes more difficult, though admittedly not impossible, to sustain the notion of justification as a covenant membership. But at some point it appears that Wright is compounding unlikelihoods, ill-fitting pieces requiring a certain amount of force finally to lie flat when there may be easier ways to construe the puzzle.

Thus, if we are to account for the NPP's relative indifference to reconciliation, we may point to an accidental collusion of New Testament scholarship and NPP interests. On the one hand, New Testament scholarship has largely subordinated reconciliation such that it is thinkable to write a Pauline theology with only passing reference to the theme—the history of interpretation does not demand that reconciliation be reckoned with. Meanwhile, to the extent that reconciliation describes the fruit of justification (2 Cor 5; Rom 5), it renders problematic the articulation of justification exclusively, or even primarily, in terms of covenant inclusion and the "reconciliation" of Jews and Gentiles each to the other. One might regard the setting aside of reconciliation by the NPP as a convenient, if innocent, oversight. The more prominent that the theme of reconciliation becomes, the harder it presses on the adequacy of a view of justification in which it is equated with covenantal inclusion rather than with acquittal *coram Deo*. But it is hard to see how (especially Wright's) understanding of justification as covenant inclusion really prepares for the Pauline conclusion in Romans that justification had been aimed at peace with God all along.[108] Rather than a "new

---

But the verdict of the court, declaring "this person is in the right" and thus *making them "righteous"* not in the sense of "making them virtuous," infusing them with a moral quality called "righteousness," but in the sense of creating for them the *status* of "having-been-declared-in-the-right," is the implicit metaphor behind Paul's primary subject in this passage, which is **God's action in declaring "you are my children, members of the single Abrahamic family."** *Righteous, dikaios*, is the adjective which is properly predicated of the one in whose favor the court's announcement has been given, and which, within the covenantal, eschatological and Christological train of Paul's thought, **refers to the one who is in good standing within the covenant**, despite his background, moral, ethnic, social and cultural. (ibid., 134-35 italics original, boldface added)

[108]That this is Paul's intent is evident from the resumptive function of "Therefore, having been justified by faith, we have peace with God" (Δικαιωθέντες οὖν ἐκ πίστεως εἰρήνην ἔχομεν πρὸς τὸν θεόν). Beyond serious dispute, Δικαιωθέντες οὖν ἐκ πίστεως recalls and summarizes the discourse of Romans 3:21–4:25, and εἰρήνην ἔχομεν πρὸς τὸν θεὸν clearly looks forward to the following material, in which enmity is overcome by love (Rom 5:5-8) and the justified are also therefore the reconciled (Rom 5:10-11).

issue," peace with God by the overcoming of the causes of enmity is precisely the work of justification. Justification effects the restoration of right relation to God by means of acquittal, establishing peaceful relations where there had been enmity (on the part of sinners) and wrath (on the part of God). An account of justification which diminishes these dimensions, although it be theologically rich and expansive itself, concords awkwardly with Paul's soteriological grammar.

EXCURSUS: RECONCILIATION IN *PAUL* AND THE *FAITHFULNESS OF GOD*

That Wright's treatment of the theme of reconciliation in Paul is so sparse in his earlier Pauline scholarship only to become so prevalent in *P&FG* is a matter worthy of some reflection.[109] Indeed, several have noted that *P&FG* is structured chiastically, and, if so, reconciliation is arguably both the opening gambit and the stirring conclusion to the massive work. Indeed, it is not too much to say that Wright now offers reconciliation as the essence of the Pauline project: "My proposal is that Paul's aims and intentions can be summarized under the word *katallagē*, 'reconciliation.' I mean this at several interlocking levels."[110]

In structuring his work so, Wright begins compellingly with the story of Onesimus and Philemon, their reconciliation each to the other working as a parable for the larger Pauline vision. The conclusion to *P&FG* then quite intentionally stretches far beyond the scope of the details of Pauline texts (never leaving them behind) and beyond the dilemma of the divine-human relationship (though never leaving it behind) to press the Pauline vision of reconciliation into diverse spheres—from ecclesiology to geopolitics, from intractable ethnic strife to stalemated epistemological divides. Whether this is regarded as a jarring overreach or the inspiring fruit of the Pauline vision will probably depend on the reader, but it is not inappropriate that a work

---

[109]See n. 97.
[110]Wright, *P&FG*, 2:1487. Wright notes that the proposal for the centrality of reconciliation for the Pauline vision is anticipated by others, e.g., Martin, *Reconciliation*; Porter, "Reconciliation as the Heart of Paul's Missionary Theology"; Marshall, *Aspects of the Atonement*; and Peter Stuhlmacher, "The Gospel of Reconciliation in Christ—Basic Features and Issues of a Biblical Theology of the New Testament," *HBT* 1, no. 1 (1979): 161-90 (presumably this is Wright's intended reference).

of this magnitude and a mind this fecund should harvest the fruits of a thinker whose own influence far exceeds his modest corpus.

Yet lest reconciliation be seen as merely rhetorical decoration, it is essential to note that it also makes a substantial appearance in the expository section of the book and that this is without precedent in Wright's earlier constructive work.[111] Although the long introductory and concluding chapters focus on the reconciliation of persons, peoples, institutions and even antagonistic ideas, Wright is clear throughout that reconciliation has ultimately to do with the repair of the relationship of humans to God, whence the rest flows.[112] He attends to that theme in most of the expected places, for example in exegeses of Colossians 1:15-20, 2 Corinthians 5:11-6:2, Romans 5:6-21 and Romans 11:13-15.[113] If Wright previously understated this dimension of Paul's soteriology, it is no longer the case; now it is on display in full view.

Nevertheless, I suggest that for all its prominence, it is not clear that reconciliation as a Pauline category actually figures in a substantial way in the overall construal of Pauline *soteriology*. Or to put it a different way, now, for Wright, reconciliation serves as a structuring center for his Pauline project and as the chief means of the appropriation of the Pauline vision but not as the substantive center. I don't so much argue that it should but rather note that it doesn't. Nonetheless, were reconciliation the goal toward which justification stretches and ground from which salvation launches—as arguably Romans 5:1-11 indicates—it would be harder to maintain the more narrowly focused working definition of justification as demonstration of covenant membership that animates and distinguishes Wright's project. That justification "has to do with" covenant membership, rapprochement of Jew and Gentile, and even a matter as concrete and practical as table fellowship is not

[111]Naturally, leaving aside his commentaries: N. T. Wright, *The Epistles of Paul to the Colossians and to Philemon: An Introduction and Commentary*, TNTC (Grand Rapids: Eerdmans, 1986); and idem, "The Letter to the Romans: Introduction, Commentary and Reflections," in *NIB*, 10:393-770.

[112]Already repeatedly in the first chapter (Wright, *P&FG*, 1:16, 20, 22, etc.). "Much of Paul's ministry is about 'reconciliation' between different people and groups. That was what he was doing with Philemon and Onesimus. But all of that is rooted in the ultimate 'reconciliation' which God himself has effected in the death of his son" (ibid., 888).

[113]Wright, *P&FG*, 2:672-76, 879-85, 885-88, 1197-1203, respectively. Although he regards the letters as authentic, the theme of reconciliation and peace making in Colossians (esp. 1:22) and Ephesians (2:14-16) receives relatively scant attention.

to be doubted. The question is *what* justification has to do with these things. I have argued that it cannot be equated with any of them any more than that it is synonymous with reconciliation to God. Rather, justification is the forensic, thus binary, metaphor that shows Jew and Gentile undifferentiated in a shared, proleptic acquittal before God, which in turn shows them to be of equal standing in a shared Abrahamic heritage. Were reconciliation not just more prominent but more central, it follows that the function of justification as the amelioration of human guilt comes to the fore, justification being the means by which reconciliation is accomplished. And, while these themes of human alienation and guilt rectified and relationship restored are by no means absent from *P&FG*—indeed, more prominent than ever—it can be argued that Wright's privileging repristination of the covenant motif drives these themes to the margins of his larger discourse. Thus, in spades Wright restores to us Paul's Jewish matrix, but it is less clear that Paul's innovative "Christian" vision is given full berth.

CONFIRMING THE ITINERARY

$\mathbf{I}$n the preceding chapters, I have set out signposts for the contours of Paul's soteriological itinerary: first, in the identification of inadequacies of interpretive paradigms followed as though mutually exclusive—thus, establishing the need for a new Pauline itinerary; second, in the form of historical-critical judgments charting the coordinates of the historical course; and, third, noting conceptual transitions with respect to works, grace, justification, salvation and reconciliation across an inclusive Pauline corpus.

In this chapter, I will argue that the largely lexical evidence of the immediately preceding chapters is corroborated in a series of observations that confirm the trajectory so far sketched. Paul's soteriological vision resolves in the space from Galatians to Romans and, having done so, bears the fruit of its expansiveness in the letters that follow.

8.1 PAUL'S RESOLVING VISION: FROM GALATIANS TO ROMANS

In Galatians we meet Paul, back against the wall, swinging from his heels, as it were. By Romans we meet the same Paul, reiterating familiar themes, though now moderated, at greater length, and, while yet full of passion, suffused with an underlying equanimity. In what follows, we consider, beyond the obvious differences of circumstance and passage of time, what accounts for these differences, arguing that the difference between the two letters is not merely that of exigence and style, but of substance.

8.1.1 Disentangling false friends: Galatians and Romans distinguished. By advocating for an early date for Galatians, premised on the South Galatian hypothesis and a pre–Jerusalem Council setting, I have argued that there is a seven- to nine-year distance between this, Paul's first letter, and his letter to the Romans. That gap, of course, feeds the expectation of some inevitable theological development between the two letters. It is not the case, however, that a temporal hiatus between these two letters is absolutely necessary to the argument or that it is the most important claim with respect to the origins of the letters and the relationship between them. Rather more significant is that, for all the apparent thematic overlap, which is not to be denied, these letters are occasioned by different circumstances, exhibit different rhetorical styles, are written toward different ends and betray a development in soteriology from the earlier to the later letter, whatever length of time intervened between them. To describe and substantiate these differences is largely independent of, though corroborated by, the chronological claims made above.

The thematic congruence of these two letters has always made them something of a matched set. Traditionally, Romans was understood to be the earlier letter and Galatians its summarizing sequel,[1] a position nowhere defended in the modern era but nonetheless understandable if the dominant canonical order is given even some unconscious weight and the affinities of the letters noted. For the modern view in classic form, one can scarcely improve on J. B. Lightfoot's tracing of commonalities in the service of his hypothesis of a close chronological relationship.[2] Lightfoot understood the Pauline corpus to consist of four phases and that Galatians belonged with the Corinthian correspondence and Romans to the second of the four phases, dating to AD 57-58, with only the Thessalonian correspondence preceding by about five years. Among these letters, both thematically and stylistically, Galatians can be considered "the typical epistle of the group" and on such grounds it can be shown to fall between 2 Corinthians and Romans although, according to Lightfoot, the letter's deeper affinity is clearly with Romans.[3] To illustrate, Galatians shares with Romans the following notable themes, and together they appeal to the same Scriptures:[4]

[1]Gerald L. Bray, ed., *Galatians, Ephesians*, Reformation Commentary on Scripture, New Testament 10 (Downers Grove, IL: InterVarsity Press, 2011), xlii.
[2]J. B. Lightfoot, *Saint Paul's Epistle to the Galatians: A Revised Text with Introduction, Notes and Dissertations*, 10th ed. (London: Macmillan, 1890), 42-56.
[3]Ibid., 43-45.
[4]What follows is not exhaustive; it is inspired esp. by Lightfoot's analysis, although I consolidate,

Striking thematic elements common to both, often in similar language:

- Justification *apart* from works of the law *by means of* faith (Gal 2:16-21; 3:10-14; Rom 3:20–4:8)

- The priority of the Abrahamic covenant, the promise and the shared fatherhood of Abraham for Jew and Gentile alike (Gal 3:6-9, 14-16, 29; Rom 4:1-3, 9-18).

- The temporary and ineffectual character of the law (Gal 3:19-26; Rom 7:1-3; 8:3-4)

- Baptism into Christ Jesus as constitutive of covenant identity (Gal 3:27-29; Rom 6:2-7)

- Adoption as "sons" by means of the Spirit, by whom we cry "Abba, Father" (Gal 4:4-7; Rom 8:14-17)

- The enabling work of the Spirit transcending the would-be discipline of the law, frustrated by the flesh (Gal 5:16-23; Rom 8:2-14)

An extraordinary shared set of Old Testament texts used in argument:

- The dilemma encapsulated in Psalm 143[142]:2 (Gal 2:16; Rom 3:20)

- The decisive appeal to Genesis 15:6 (Gal 3:6; Rom 4:3)

- The allusion to the blessing of nations (Gen 12:3; 18:8) in Abraham and seed (Gal 3:8; cf. Gen 17:5 in Rom 4:17; Gen 15:5 in Rom 4:18)

- The citation and reappropriation of Habakkuk 2:4 (Gal 3:11; Rom 1:17)

- The counterintuitive appeal to Deuteronomy 27:26 (Gal 3:12; Rom 10:5)

- The fulfillment of the law in the command to love neighbor from Leviticus 19:18 (Gal 5:14; Rom 13:8-10)

The accumulation of these extraordinary commonalities would seem almost to speak for itself: whatever we say with respect to their origins, Galatians and Romans are theologically of a piece, and that thesis seems almost beyond serious dispute. I propose, however, that, upon closer examination, this is not a sufficiently nuanced account of the texts.[5]

---

reorganize and translate his observations. Cf. a similar comparative table including all the undisputed letters in Joseph A. Fitzmyer, *Romans: A New Translation with Introduction and Commentary*, AB 33 (New York: Doubleday, 1993), 71-73.
[5]Barclay also notes the tendency of "Anglophone scholarship" to overlook differences between

The chief point of difference is the very different rhetorical circumstance eliciting each of the letters. For Galatians it was the press of Gentiles Judaizing,[6] apparently instigated by Jerusalem "teachers" arguing for the full conversion of Jesus-believing Gentiles, a crisis exacerbated by the recent separatist behaviors of Cephas and Barnabas in Antioch, personally devastating to Paul and threatening the integrity of the Gentile mission. To be sure, every specific detail of this scenario has been debated (who the teachers were, precisely what their position was, what exactly happened in Antioch, etc.), but there can be little doubt that these are the precipitating factors in the writing of the letter. In comparison, there is a bit less consensus as it concerns the originating circumstances and purpose of Romans, and those questions are the subject of an ongoing debate.[7] Even so, the main contours are hardly elusive: Paul writes from Corinth, on the eve of his journey with the collection to Jerusalem, and his purpose includes preparing the way for his eventual visit to Rome—a church he had never visited but in which he had many acquaintances—where he hopes to find allies and support for his envisioned mission to Spain. This much is uncontroversial. The more intriguing question is Paul's presumptive purpose in writing a letter this long and discursive, in which the apparent internal issues disturbing the concord of the Roman Christians do not emerge until almost the end of the letter, Romans 14:1–15:12. Thus, the question is what Paul's theological discourse (Rom 1:16–11:36) and general hortatory material (Rom 12:1–13:14) have to do with the rather more specific communal concerns beginning in Romans 14 and Paul's disclosure of his future plans and the Romans' part in them beginning in the middle of Romans 15. One way

---

Galatians and Romans in the service of a synthetic Pauline theology. John M. G. Barclay, *Paul and the Gift* (Grand Rapids: Eerdmans, 2015), 453n8.

[6]As is now frequently and rightly noted, to "Judaize" (ἰουδαΐζειν, Gal 2:14) is to "live as a Jew," not to "convert *others* to Judaism." Thus, in the context of Paul's Gentile mission, it is the prospective action of the proselytized, not that of the proselytizers, and, despite its common usage, the influence of teacher-missionaries who are advocating circumcision and Torah observance is not properly labeled as "Judaizing." James W. Aageson, "Judaizing," *ABD* 3:1089.

[7]Besides the contributions of the major commentaries, perhaps the most efficient path into the issues is the collection of essays edited by Karl P. Donfried, ed., *The Romans Debate*, rev. ed. (Peabody, MA: Hendrickson, 2005); see also James C. Miller, "The Romans Debate: 1991–2001," *Currents in Research* 9 (2001): 306-49. For recent advocacy of particular hypotheses, see Mark D. Nanos, *The Mystery of Romans: The Jewish Context of Paul's Letter* (Minneapolis: Fortress, 1996); Thomas H. Tobin, *Paul's Rhetoric in Its Contexts: The Argument of Romans* (Peabody, MA: Hendrickson, 2004); and A. Andrew Das, *Solving the Romans Debate* (Minneapolis: Fortress, 2007).

to ask the question is, just how occasional is the letter to the Romans? That is, how much has it to do with either Paul's circumstances or with his knowledge of and concerns for the conditions among the Roman Christians? From that flow the questions of purpose and intended readership, and here scholarly positions diverge.

If we had to choose—we don't—between Paul's circumstances and those of the Roman churches as the chief motivating factor in the writing of the letter, we should prefer the latter. While it is almost certainly the case that the theological exposition of the letter functions to bolster the Romans' prospective support for Paul, and Paul himself reveals that his trip to Jerusalem weighs heavily on his mind (Rom 15:25-26, 30-31), what appears actually to drive the argument of the letter is an underlying tension in Rome, expressly between the "weak" and the "strong" (Rom 14:1–15:12), which is probably more or less a proxy for a tension between Jew and Gentile. The matter of the relationship between Jew and Gentile pervades Romans. It is evident in the thesis of the letter: "For I am not ashamed of the gospel; it is the power of God for salvation to everyone who has faith, *to the Jew first and also to the Greek*" (Rom 1:16 NRSV). The distinction between Jew and Gentile (or "Greek") also drives the opening argumentative gambit of the letter, beginning with the implicit indictment of Gentile humanity (Rom 1:18-32) and then the turn to a judging, presumably Jewish, interlocutor in Romans 2:1,[8] a dialectic that animates the indicting discourse until the relief of Romans 3:21-26 (Rom 2:9-10, 17, 28-29, 3:1, 19). Indeed, binding the plight of Romans 1:18–3:20 to the solution of Romans 3:21 and following is the one God who is both the impartial judge of both Jew and Gentile (Rom 2:11; 3:9, 19, 22-23) and the universal redeemer of Jew and Gentile alike (Rom 3:24, 29-30; 9:24; 10:12; 11:13-24): alike in guilt before God (Rom 3:9), alike in righteousness through faith, alike in forfeited glory (Rom 3:22-23), alike in conformity to the image of his Son (Rom 8:29).

---

[8]It is true that an explicitly Jewish figure does not enter the discourse until Romans 2:17, but, given the characteristic Gentile sin of Romans 1:18-32 (recognizable as a typically Jewish critique of "pagan" idolatry, folly, sin and vice; cf. e.g., Wis 13:1-9; 14:22-31; 4 Macc 1:26-27; 2:15; Sib. Or. 3:594-600) and that the "overachieving" Gentile soon becomes the topic in the back-and-forth argument (Rom 2:9-11), it is probably the best reading of Romans 2:1-11 to see the indictment on a Jewish interlocutor, which then becomes explicit in Romans 2:17-29 (Fitzmyer, *Romans*, 296-97).

The relationship of Jew and Gentile, therefore, clearly suffuses the primary discourse of the letter, and it apparently lies behind the letter's singular attested exigency, the tension between weak and strong. Although not universally accepted, and by some only tentatively, the internal evidence of Romans and corroborating external evidence support the surmise that behind this Roman Christian tension are circumstances surrounding the Claudian expulsion of Jews from Rome and their subsequent return under Nero.[9] The relevant, much-discussed text in Suetonius's *Lives of the Caesars* tells us that to quell a disturbance among Jews in Rome at the instigation of "Chrestus," Claudius had Jews expelled from the city,[10] an event corroborated in Acts 18:2, where Paul is said to have met recent expatriates of Italy, Priscilla and Aquila, on account of Claudius's expulsion of "all Jews." The majority view, save for minor variations, is as follows: (1) the expulsion occurred in AD 49, which is corroborated by the testimony of Acts 18; (2) the person named "Chrestus" is a mispronunciation or misunderstanding of the Greek *Christos*, accommodating it to a well-known Roman name, when in fact the source of the "disturbance" was Christ; (3) the actual disturbance was a contention between Jews *about* Jesus, some having regarded him as messiah and others, presumably the great majority, refusing that claim; and (4) not literally "all" (all but an impossibility) but only the Christ-following Jews were expelled from the city, among them Priscilla and Aquila.

It is then noted that with the accession of Nero, that ban was relaxed, allowing Jewish Christians to return to the city. The tension reflected in Romans is then accountable substantially to a season of more than half a decade when whatever was left of the Christian movement in Rome was entirely Gentile. It is not difficult to imagine, even apart from the testimony of Romans, that there were significant shifts in the ethos of the community as a result or, perhaps, even disparate reactions among those Gentiles remaining.

[9]The literature on the historical question is vast; for representative treatments and relevant bibliography, affirming its relevance for the composition of Romans, see Das, *Solving the Romans Debate*, 149-202; Eckhard J. Schnabel, *Early Christian Mission: Paul and the Early Church* (Downers Grove, IL: InterVarsity Press, 2004), 807-12; Fitzmyer, *Romans*, 31-33; and Willi Marxsen, *Introduction to the New Testament: An Approach to Its Problems* (Oxford: Blackwell, 1968), 95-109.

[10]Claudius "expelled from Rome Jews who were making constant disturbances at the instigation of Chrestus [*Iudaeos impulsore Chresto assidue tumultuantis Roma expulit*]" (Suetonius, *Claud.* 25.4).

The Gentile-Christian community as a whole might have moved away from matters of Jewish identity such as kosher observance, or perhaps some of the Gentile Christians redoubled on such matters as an expression of solidarity or, as often happens, convert zeal. In other words, although it is natural, and perhaps correct, to assume that the "weak" are to be identified as the Jewish-Christian contingent and the "strong" as Gentiles, it is not necessarily so. Paul himself, of course, is a Jew who self-identifies as "strong" (Rom 15:1), and if God-fearers or even proselytes were among those who had become loyal to Christ, there is reason to believe that they might well be among the scrupulous "weak." That having been said, even if there were not a strict ethnic alignment with respect to the "weak" and the "strong," the categories are still ethno-religious at the root and thus entirely of a piece with the Jew-and-Gentile motif running throughout the letter.

Whereas the question of Jew and Gentile in one Christian body is presumably a matter of intrinsic interest to early Christianity and to Paul in particular (Eph 2:11-22; 3:6-10), the conclusion of the body of the letter to the Romans evinces a more acute motivation for addressing the matter. What is evidently *not* the case in Romans is any hint of the sort of Judaizing crisis that exudes from beginning to end in Galatians.[11] There is no sign of it anywhere in the letter and, unless one is inclined to argue backwards from the similarities of Paul's argument, no reason to make such an assumption, but overwhelming reasons not to. The subject matter of Romans is, thus, similar in broadest terms, but the circumstance is not even analogous, much less comparable. Indeed, in Romans, the Gentile addressees seem to be in no danger whatsoever of Judaizing but rather are vulnerable to the converse.[12] Indeed, it is the hubris of Gentiles who—incredibly, from Paul's vantage—imagine themselves somehow unindebted to their Jewish covenantal primogenitors.[13]

---

[11] For advocates of the Romans "Judaizing" hypothesis and an appropriate critique, see Richard N. Longenecker, *Introducing Romans: Critical Issues in Paul's Most Famous Letter* (Grand Rapids: Eerdmans, 2011), 113-17.

[12] My position that Romans is rhetorically directed to a Gentile-Christian audience is bolsterd significantly by Andrew Das's argument to that effect: *Solving the Romans Debate*; now summarized in idem, "The Gentile-Encoded Audience of Romans: The Church Outside the Synagogue," in *Reading Paul's Letter to the Romans*, ed. Jerry L. Sumney (Atlanta: Society of Biblical Literature, 2012), 29-46. The claim is not that Jewish auditors were absent from the reading of the letter in Rome—and in that sense the audience can be described as "mixed"—but that the targeted (Das, "encoded") audience is Gentiles.

[13] Here I part company with J. Louis Martyn, "Romans as One of the Earliest Interpretations of

That this indifference toward Jewish antecedents is the salient presenting symptom for the letter is indicated throughout, first subtly, and then, especially in Romans 11, 14 and 15, explicitly. Paul announces in the thesis of the letter (Rom 1:16-17) that the gospel is the "power of God for salvation to all who believe, to the Jew first and also the Greek" (Rom 1:16). Although "first" (*prōton*) might be taken in a variety of ways, most probably in the context of the larger argument it is an indication of the salvation-historical privilege of Israel's covenant, upon which depends the salvation of the "Greek."[14] While it is true that the phrase "Jew first and also the Greek" (cf. Rom 2:9, 10) is meant to be explicative of the "*all* who believe" (or who are judged, as the case may be), the addition of "first" points beyond a simply inclusive meaning (i.e., "both"; *te*) to the priority of God's covenantal relationship with his elect people. While apparently Paul's missionary strategy was to begin in the synagogue before turning to the agora, here he is not merely rehearsing that pragmatic fact but is describing its theological basis. The same salvation-historical priority pervades the letter: for example, in Paul's litanizing of Israel's responsible privilege (Rom 3:1-2; 9:4-5; 11:26-30), which makes their rejection of the messiah all the more tragic and culpable, while not necessarily final in Paul's estimation.

But the most explicit and extended exposition of this theme is reserved for Romans 9–11, especially the figure of the olive tree in Romans 11:16-24. Not only does the image make explicit the dependence of Gentile Christians on Israel as those "grafted in," but also Paul directly addresses the same for their hubris: "Do not be arrogant toward the broken off branches [= unbelieving Israel]. Before you start boasting, remember it is not you who support

---

Galatians," in *Theological Issues in the Letters of Paul* (Nashville: Abingdon, 1997), 37-45. Martyn supposes that following the mixed results of Galatians, Paul writes a second, lost letter to Galatia and then the letter to Rome largely "to guard that earlier letter from interpretations he considered misleading" (ibid., 40; cf. Hans Hübner, *Law in Paul's Thought: A Contribution to the Development of Pauline Theology*, trans. James C. G. Greig [Edinburgh: T&T Clark, 1984], 60-65; and Tobin, *Paul's Rhetoric*, 98-103 and passim). Thus, Martyn regards Paul himself as the impetus for the corrective dimensions of the letter to the Romans rather than primarily the circumstances in Rome. I am persuaded by the opposite view, especially since the Roman Gentile Christians fall explicitly under Paul's censure for their arrogance.

[14]So, e.g., C. E. B. Cranfield, *A Critical and Exegetical Commentary on the Epistle to the Romans*, ICC (Edinburgh: T&T Clark, 1975), 1:90-91; James D. G. Dunn, *Romans*, WBC 38 (Dallas: Word, 1988), 1:40; and Douglas J. Moo, *The Epistle to the Romans*, NICNT (Grand Rapids: Eerdmans, 1996), 68-69.

the root, but the root that supports you. Then you [sg.] will say, 'Branches were broken off that I might be grafted in.' Sure. For *unbelief* they were broken off, but you stand because of faith. Don't be arrogant, but fear instead! After all, if God did not spare the natural branches, neither will he spare you" (Rom 11:17-21, my paraphrase translation). It would seem that the same tragedy of Israel's unbelief, which grieves Paul so deeply (Rom 9:1-3), is occasion for Gentile smugness.[15] Did they reason from their newfound divine favor that God had set "his people" aside for a new people? Did they suppose that Israel's call was revocable (Rom 11:29), that they enjoyed this status by merit (Rom 11:6), that there was no advantage in being a Jew (Rom 3:1), that the law and its entailments were a mistake rather than of holy institution (Rom 7:7, 12)? The evidence of the letter, to say nothing of the way of all flesh, suggests such a scenario.

It would be no wonder, then, that these smug and sure would have carried on their Christian faith with indifference toward its roots and perhaps even a kind of contempt for the benightedly scrupulous nomists (whatever their ethnicity) still clinging to outmoded—even superstitious?—concerns. This seems to be just what we find in Romans 14–15. Paul's response is clearly as one of the "strong" (Rom 14:14; 15:1) who takes up the cause of the "weak"— including the attribution to them of the purest motives (Rom 14:5-6)—and launches a vigorous upbraiding of the arrogant and thoughtless "enlightened" ones who, not incidentally, he believes are "right." There is, thus, every reason to draw the strongest connection from the stern theological admonition to Gentiles in Romans 11, to the practical reprimand of the "strong" and defense of the "weak" in Romans 14–15. The same attitudes of hubris, autonomy and self-congratulation are the target of both correctives, and that this is not a tangential but a central issue is substantiated by the repeated allusions to Jewish salvation-historical precedence throughout. But of a Judaizing party internal or a proselytizing party external to the community in Rome, there is no certain evidence.

It is true that some have found evidence in Romans 16:17-20 for prospective teachers of a Judaistic bent and thus see the letter, at least in part,

---

[15]It is tempting, though frequently beyond demonstration, to surmise that other elements of Paul's paranaesis may have to do with this smugness. E.g., is the instruction of Romans 12:3 not to think of oneself more highly than one ought but soberly, according to the measure of faith, directed with an eye to Gentile self-satisfaction?

as a corresponding prophylactic to "countermissionaries" (D. A. Campbell).[16] Three considerations count against this hypothesis: (1) The description of those "making dissension and obstacles" as those "not serving the Lord but their own *bellies*" is more likely an indication of an appetitive proclivity rather than a fixation on dietary laws. It is more likely that these are of an emancipated antinomian bent than a scrupulous one. (2) To the extent that the position of these countermissionaries inclines in the direction of the "weak" in Romans 14:1–15:13, Paul's generous sympathy for them would be both counterproductive and out of keeping with the more vigorous opposition that characterizes his counteroffensives against errant teachers. (3) The fact that the letter to the Romans nowhere hints that these teachers are present or on the horizon in the first fifteen chapters counts against their influence as a primary motivator for the letter.[17] In any case, even were this hypothesis adopted, it remains all but impossible, judging from the measured and balanced tone of Romans if it is taken as Paul's response, that the influence of these interlopers is analogous to the proselytizing parties that Paul opposes elsewhere (cf. Galatians; Phil 3:2-11). It remains the case that Paul evinces no concern whatsoever for a Judaizing movement or even temptation among his Gentile readers. The appeal to similar arguments and many of the same biblical texts as Galatians must be accounted on grounds other than a common opponent or a parallel circumstance.

That the circumstances are not parallel is indicated by the rhetoric of the letter compared even superficially to Galatians. The dissimilarity is well known and need not be belabored. The earlier letter shows every sign of being written in crisis and under duress: its sharp edges are notorious (Gal 1:8-9; 3:1; 5:12), the pathos is palpable (Gal 2:11-13; 4:19-20; 6:17) and expected niceties are absent (e.g., the astonishment of Gal 1:6-9 in lieu of a thanksgiving and intercession). This is not to say that Galatians is necessarily hastily written or ill considered, but it does show signs of hyperbole and

---

[16]Douglas A. Campbell, "Determining the Gospel Through Rhetorical Analysis in Paul's Letter to the Roman Christians," in *Gospel in Paul: Studies on Corinthians, Galatians and Romans for Richard N. Longenecker* (Sheffield: Sheffield Academic Press, 1994), 315-36; idem, *The Deliverance of God: An Apocalyptic Rereading of Justification in Paul* (Grand Rapids: Eerdmans, 2009), 495-518; and James C. Miller, *The Obedience of Faith, the Eschatological People of God, and the Purpose of Romans*, SBLDS 62 (Atlanta: Society of Biblical Literature, 2000), esp. 138-50.

[17]For a more detailed and, I think, persuasive critique, see Das, *Solving the Romans Debate*, 42-49.

intemperance. Every scholar who has tried to reckon with Paul's view of the law, for example, finds obvious differences between, say, Galatians 3 with its negative polemic and Romans 7 with its measured estimation of the law, some holding that Paul's later view was a correction of the former. Indeed, the differences between Galatians and Romans are as impressive as the similarities, and it remains a durable challenge for students of Paul how best to account for them both.[18]

There is, I propose, a plausible way to describe the commonalities and differences between the letters on the primary matters of soteriology, and not surprisingly, I believe it can be best described as a development, an expansion and reappropriation of the apologetic insights of Galatians in a programmatic essay that secures a vision for Jew and Gentile, "weak" and "strong," together as one people in Christ.[19] If, as I have suggested, we find the "weak" and "strong" division symptomatic of division between Jewish and Gentile Christians with their conflicting visions of freedom and fidelity, it follows that Paul's chief, though not singular, concern is to demonstrate the shared and equal status of Jew and Gentile in the believing community. Paul's argument toward that end can be summarized by means of a series of argumentative moves to establish the point:[20] (1) establishing the common guilt of Jew and Gentile (Rom 1:18–3:20), (2) establishing the common remediation independent of the law in the atoning death of Jesus (Rom 3:21-26) and (3) establishing faith apart from law observance as the common means by which two peoples are made the children of Abraham, the covenant family of the one God (Rom 3:27–4:25).

8.1.2 Redeploying Scripture: new uses for the same texts. As noted, the substantial overlap of biblical texts marshaled for Paul's arguments in Galatians and Romans is among the most impressive data supporting a close

---

[18]On the notorious dilemma, especially as it concerns the law, see, e.g., John William Drane, *Paul, Libertine or Legalist?: A Study in the Theology of the Major Pauline Epistles* (London: SPCK, 1975); Hübner, *Law in Paul's Thought*; J. Christiaan Beker, *Paul the Apostle: The Triumph of God in Life and Thought* (Philadelphia: Fortress, 1980); Heikki Räisänen, *Paul and the Law*, WUNT 1.29 (Tübingen: Mohr, 1983); and Tobin, *Paul's Rhetoric*.

[19]To this extent, at least, my proposal is consistent with Aune's description of Romans as a *logos protreptikos*. David E. Aune, "Romans as a *Logos Protreptikos*," in *The Romans Debate*, ed. Karl P. Donfried, rev. ed. (Peabody, MA: Hendrickson, 2005), 278-96.

[20]The argument sketched here is akin to that of Simon J. Gathercole, "Romans 1–5 and the 'Weak' and the 'Strong': Pauline Theology, Pastoral Rhetoric, and the Purpose of Romans," *RevExp* 100, no. 1 (2003): 35-51.

literary relationship between the two letters. At the same time, it is easy to underestimate how the texts shared by the arguments of both letters are nonetheless appealed to differently in each. In table 8.1 I display the Old Testament texts appealed to in Galatians, showing where those texts are also used in Romans.[21]

Table 8.1. Old Testament texts cited in Galatians and Romans

Old Testament Text Cited	Galatians	Romans
Psalm 143[142]:2 "by [works of the law] shall no one be justified"	Gal 2:16	Rom 3:20
Genesis 15:6 "Abraham believed God, and it was reckoned to him as righteousness."	Gal 3:6	Rom 4:3, 9, 22
Genesis 12:3 conflated with Genesis 18:18 (cf. Gen 22:18; 26:4; 28:14; Sir 44:21) "In you [Abraham] all nations will be blessed"	Gal 3:8	cf. Gen 17:5 in Rom 4:17; Gen 15:5 in Rom 4:18
Deuteronomy 27:26 "Cursed is everyone who does not remain in everything that is written in the book of the law and do them."	Gal 3:10	
Habakkuk 2:4 "The righteous [one] shall live by faith."	Gal 3:11	Rom 1:17
Leviticus 18:5 "The one who does them shall live by them."	Gal 3:12	Rom 10:5
Deuteronomy 21:23 "Cursed is everyone who is hung upon a tree."	Gal 3:13	
Genesis 17:8[a] (cf. Gen 12:7; 13:15; 15:18; 24:7) "and to your seed [sg.]"	Gal 3:16	cf. Rom 4:13, 16, 18
Leviticus 19:18 "You shall love your neighbor as yourself."	Gal 5:14	Rom 13:9

[a]It is not certain whether Paul is alluding to a specific text, or which one, with the allusion "and to your seed." Genesis 12:7 is the first occurrence of the promise, but it is "to your seed," lacking "and" (cf. Gen 15:18; 22:18). Genesis 13:15 is the first occurrence of the promise in this form (thus favored by Christopher D. Stanley, *Paul and the Language of Scripture: Citation Technique in the Pauline Epistles and Contemporary Literature*, SNTSMS 69 [Cambridge: Cambridge University Press, 1992], 248), but Genesis 17:8, with its emphasis on covenant and frequent reference to σπέρμα (3x in Gen 17:7-8), may be the more specific allusion (J. Louis Martyn, *Galatians: A New Translation with Introduction and Commentary*, AB 33A [New York: Doubleday, 1998], 339; and Douglas J. Moo, *Galatians*, BECNT [Grand Rapids: Baker Academic, 2013], 228-29).

---

[21]For the sake of this discussion, I am leaving out Isaiah 54:1 (Gal 4:27) and Genesis 21:10 (Gal 4:30). The idiosyncratic appeal to these texts is of great interest, and probably evidence of a counterargument on Paul's part against the opponents. The fact that they are not used again in Romans or elsewhere in Paul is corroborative of that suggestion. With the exception of Psalm 143:2, which is an important shared allusion in both Galatians and Romans, I have limited my list to texts that are explicitly cited, rather than merely alluded to or "echoed." It goes without saying that in Romans Paul appeals and alludes to many times over the number of Old Testament texts than he does in Galatians. Since my limited interest is in the treatment of texts found in both letters, I use Galatians as a baseline.

A satisfactory analysis of Paul's use of Scripture in his arguments is a study far beyond the limits of this one, and I will need to make do with only passing observations with regard to a few of the shared texts, specifically to demonstrate the manner in which they are redeployed in the argument of Romans when compared to their use in Galatians.[22] To begin with, it seems to many scholars that at least some of Paul's "appeals" to Scripture in Galatians are most probably determined by the use of the same texts on the part of his opponents. In particular, it seems highly unlikely that Paul would have chosen Deuteronomy 27:26 ("Cursed is everyone who does not remain in everything that is written in the book of the law and do them") for an argument *against* works of the law.[23] Likewise, on the face of it, Leviticus 18:5 ("The one who does them shall live by them") seems ill-suited to an argument *against* obedience to commandments as constitutive of justification.[24] In the nature of the case such suggestions are beyond demonstration and can only be a surmise with a certain explanatory plausibility. Nonetheless, upon any reconstruction of Paul's circumstance in writing the letter to the Galatians, he finds himself substantially on the defensive. Not only are his apostolic credentials in dispute, but also the very suggestion that covenant membership could be admitted apart from Torah observance had to be profoundly counterintuitive. With a little imagination, it is not hard to approximate the opponents' point of view. Might they have argued something like this?

---

[22]Important and divergent representative studies include Richard B. Hays, *Echoes of Scripture in the Letters of Paul* (New Haven, CT: Yale University Press, 1989); Francis Watson, *Paul and the Hermeneutics of Faith* (London: T&T Clark, 2004); and Christopher D. Stanley, *Arguing with Scripture: The Rhetoric of Quotations in the Letters of Paul* (New York: T&T Clark, 2004). For a helpful recent survey of the field, see J. Ross Wagner, "Paul and Scripture," in *The Blackwell Companion to Paul*, ed. Stephen Westerholm (Malden, MA: Wiley-Blackwell, 2011), 154-71. Essential for the preliminary questions of text-form and citation techniques are C. D. Stanley, *Paul and the Language of Scripture*; and G. K. Beale and D. A. Carson, eds., *Commentary on the New Testament Use of the Old Testament* (Grand Rapids: Baker Academic, 2007). On Galatians 3:7-14 specifically, see now the detailed notes in Moo, *Galatians*, 216-23.

[23]Bruce W. Longenecker, *The Triumph of Abraham's God: The Transformation of Identity in Galatians* (Nashville: Abingdon, 1998), 134-36; Richard N. Longenecker, *Galatians*, WBC 41 (Dallas: Word, 1990), 117-18; and Martyn, *Galatians*, 309.

[24]R. N. Longenecker, *Galatians*, 120-21; and Martyn, *Galatians*, 315-16. By the same token, although perhaps less obviously, it may also be that Genesis 12:3 ("In you all nations [= Gentiles] will be blessed") is a text with cachet among Paul's opponents, by which they might well have argued that to circumvent circumcision was to self-exclude from the promise of covenantal blessing (so, e.g., Martyn, *Galatians*, 300-302; B. W. Longenecker, *Triumph of Abraham's God*, 130-34; the implication is noted in R. N. Longenecker, *Galatians*, 115).

Did not God say to Abraham, "This is my covenant, which you shall keep, between me and you and your seed after you: Every male among you shall be circumcised"?[25] And again, the Lord God says, "Any uncircumcised male who is not circumcised in the flesh of his foreskin shall be cut off from his people; he has broken my covenant."[26] Even of Gentiles, the God of Israel says, "Both he that is born in your house and he that is bought with your money, shall be circumcised. So shall my covenant be in your flesh an everlasting covenant."[27] Yet Paul says it is not an everlasting covenant. But the Lord promises only curses to those who do not keep all the words of the law: "Cursed is every man that continues not in all the words of this law to do them."[28] No, the way to life is by keeping the commandments: "So you shall keep all my ordinances, and all my judgments, and do them; which if a man perform, he shall live by them: I am the Lord your God."[29] So, then, should we believe God or man? Moses the prophet or this self-appointed "apostle"? Our Lord or this one who persecuted his followers? Galatians, would you be the seed of Abraham our father?[30] Be circumcised and obey God's commandments!

If the position of Paul's antagonists was anything like this, we see that their argument is hardly idiosyncratic, making Paul's counterpoise all the more a challenge and helping to explain the complexity of his pluriform response. Given the sort of texts to which his opponents might have appealed (of which Deut 27:26 and Lev 18:5 are but a few possibilities), it is evident that Paul needs to neutralize and counter the plausible arguments that contradict his Torah-free gospel. This he does in two ways: (1) he introduces texts that counter (if not contradict) the presumptions of the opponents' argument—Genesis 15:6 and Habakkuk 2:4—believing them to trump the force of the opponents' texts (Deut 27:26; Lev 18:5), and (2) he counterreads the "plain sense" of the opponents' presumptive texts in light of these texts, inferring from them a countertestimony to their putative sense.

Thus, in citing Genesis 15:6 (Gal 3:6), Paul is able to argue the two essential premises on which all of Galatians 3:6-29 will hang: (1) that Abraham's being

---

[25]Genesis 17:10, where the covenant sign of circumcision is instituted.
[26]Genesis 17:14.
[27]Genesis 17:13; this text would seem to apply especially well to the circumstance of Gentiles.
[28]Deuteronomy 27:26.
[29]Leviticus 18:5.
[30]Cf. Galatians 3:7, 29.

reckoned righteous is the result of his "faith/believing" (*episteusen*) in the promise-making God rather than Torah observance and (2) that his being reckoned righteousness by faith preceded his obedience in circumcision (Gen 17), not to mention his obedience in offering Isaac (Gen 22)—all of this 430 years preceding the Mosaic dispensation (Gal 3:17). Because it can bear this much argumentative weight, it is no wonder that Paul appeals to this text as foundational for the Scripture-dense argument that follows. Indeed, precisely because it substantiates these two legs of his argument—and with respect to the covenant progenitor, Abraham—it is hard to overstate the importance of Genesis 15:6 for Paul's overall position. Therefore, Paul can reason from Genesis 15:6 (Gal 3:7, *ginōskete ara hoti*) that it is "those defined by faith" (*hoi ek pisteōs*) who are actually the "descendants of Abraham," so that Paul can deduce in Galatians 3:8 that this gospel was already proclaimed in the promise to Gentiles through Abraham: "In you shall all the Gentiles be blessed" (Gen 12:3; 18:18; Gal 3:8), faith being Abraham's universally heritable trait and the Gentiles being the ultimate telos of the covenant made with Abraham. And this, in turn, allows Paul in Galatians 3:9 to reiterate and expand his claim of Galatians 3:7 as a preliminary conclusion: "So then, those defined by faith [*hoi ek pisteōs*] are blessed with Abraham, the faithful one" (my translation).

Having established the category of "those defined by faith" (*hoi ek pisteōs*), Paul contrasts its alternative in Galatians 3:10, "whoever might be defined by works of the law" (*hosoi . . . ex ergōn nomou eisin*), declaring them under curse. This he substantiates with perhaps his most opaque, or at least among his most controverted, appeals to an Old Testament text in his entire corpus: "Cursed is everyone who does not persevere in all the things written in the book of the law and perform them" (Gal 3:10, my translation). The difficulty is apparent even to the casual reader; it appears that Paul is arguing for precisely the opposite conclusion from that of the Deuteronomy text, which is, in its own context, naturally advocating law observance. Proposed solutions to this conundrum are not wanting. I reviewed the question above, arguing for a modification of the traditional unstated but implied minor premise that humanity is universally cursed for its inability to keep the law perfectly. I argued instead that Israel's history of failure speaks for itself against the provision of Torah observance leading to life, and that Israel's failed experiment in nomism functions as an a fortiori warning to dissuade Gentiles from taking the same path.

Indeed, the impossibility of Torah observance leading to life Paul regards as "obvious" (*dēlon*) since "the person who is righteous by faith shall live."[31] How this is "obvious" was apparently clearer to Paul than it has been to his recent interpreters, who have exerted themselves seeking to recover his precise train of thought. The closest-to-hand solution—more "obvious" to earlier generations of Paul's interpreters than to more recent scholars— is that already "faith" and "works of the law" are contrary principles of justification, that the former avails unto righteousness and the latter ultimately condemns. The structure of the texts cited in juxtaposition points in this direction:

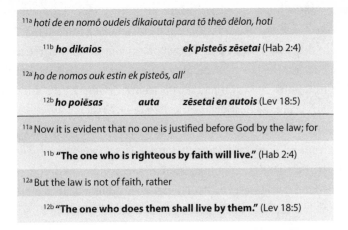

> [11a] *hoti de en nomō oudeis dikaioutai para tō theō dēlon, hoti*
>
> [11b] **ho dikaios**　　　　　　　**ek pisteōs zēsetai** (Hab 2:4)
>
> [12a] *ho de nomos ouk estin ek pisteōs, all'*
>
> [12b] **ho poiēsas**　　**auta**　　**zēsetai en autois** (Lev 18:5)
>
> [11a] Now it is evident that no one is justified before God by the law; for
>
> [11b] **"The one who is righteous by faith will live."** (Hab 2:4)
>
> [12a] But the law is not of faith, rather
>
> [12b] **"The one who does them shall live by them."** (Lev 18:5)

---

[31]There is, of course, an ongoing debate as to the syntax of Habakkuk 2:4 as used by Paul (ὁ δίκαιος ἐκ πίστεως ζήσεται), compounded by the complicated textual history (on which see Joseph A. Fitzmyer, "Habakkuk 2:3-4 and the New Testament," in *To Advance the Gospel: New Testament Studies*, 2nd ed. [Grand Rapids: Eerdmans, 1998], 236-46; and Mark A. Seifrid, "Romans," in Beale and Carson, *Commentary on the New Testament Use of the Old Testament*, 608-11). Here in its Pauline application, it is most probable that we should understand ἐκ πίστεως as modifying ὁ δίκαιος, describing the basis of the righteous person's status, rather than functioning adverbially with ζήσεται, as though describing the manner of life. Besides the fit to the larger argument of this translation, the fact that ζήσεται in Galatians 3:12 (from Lev 18:5) describes eschatological life (or at least covenantal blessing) from God inclines us to take the verb from Habakkuk 2:4 in the same manner in Galatians 3:11 as well. If so, the adverbial rendering of ἐκ πίστεως becomes highly unlikely. While it is true that a redaction to ὁ δὲ ἐκ πίστεως δίκαιος would have made Paul's adjectival rendering unambiguous (Robert Jewett, *Romans: A Commentary*, Hermeneia [Minneapolis: Fortress, 2007], 146, on Rom 1:17), it is impossible to know how constrained Paul might have found himself by the more familiar pattern of the LXX word order.

As it consists of these two neatly parallel verses, the argument here is hardly impenetrable. Habakkuk 2:4 (Gal 3:11b) substantiates the claim that "it is evident that no one is justified before God by the law" (Gal 3:11a): "because [*hoti*] the one who *by faith* is righteous will live." Galatians 3:12 then disclaims that the law's demands originate from faith (Gal 3:12a) by showing that, contrary to the case with faith (*alla*), in the case of the law it is the one who performs its commands (*ho poiēsas auta*) who lives (Gal 3:12b). Thus, by harking back to Genesis 15:6 and reiterating it by way of contrast, Paul declares faith the original and exclusive means of righteousness and nomistic performance, for the sake of this argument, its antithesis.

Paul's second—and, if possible, more dramatic—reappropriation of Deuteronomy 27:26 is to link it to another Deuteronomy curse text: "Cursed is everyone who is hung on a tree" (Deut 21:23; Gal 3:13). Although Pauline scholars are not of one accord with respect to details, it is plain that Paul has thus made this text a witness to Christ's atonement: "Christ redeemed us from the curse of the law by becoming a curse for us" (Gal 3:13 NRSV). This text thus functions as a commentary on Deuteronomy 27:26, showing that the Messiah's accursed death was on behalf of us (*hyper hēmōn*), those who were under the "curse of the law," now redeemed from it by his becoming accursed himself (*Christos hēmas exēgorasen ek tēs kataras tou nomou genomenos*). This substantiates the suggestion made earlier that the curse of Deuteronomy 27:26 is employed by Paul to signal the *failure* of Torah observance as an empirical fact of Israel's history and, thus, to dissuade the Galatians from conversion to nomism.

Finally, Paul makes one more allusion in this dense scriptural argument of Galatians 3:6-18, and it vies with his use of Deuteronomy 27:26 as an appeal that is initially counterintuitive. In Galatians 3:16, Paul notes that the promise to inherit the land was made to Abraham's descendants by means of the collective singular "seed" (Heb *zera'*; Gk *sperma*).[32] As noted above, the highlighting of the singular "seed" prepares for Paul's redefinition of the identity of Abraham's descendants (Gal 3:29) as those now joined to Christ.[33]

---

[32]Probably Genesis 17:8; see n. a in table 8.1 above.
[33]See the helpful discussion in Moisés Silva, "Galatians," in Beale and Carson, *Commentary on the New Testament Use of the Old Testament*, 804-7.

This survey of Paul's appeal to Scripture in Galatians 3:6-18 is surely too brief, begging several questions and prompting others, but it is perhaps sufficient to establish a baseline by which we can observe Paul's appeal (or lack thereof) to the same texts in Romans. The number of shared texts is considerable, yet the differences in Paul's appeal to them should not go unnoticed.[34] The use of these same texts, at least most of them, evinces some considerable reappropriation in the letter to the Romans. To begin with, Deuteronomy 27:26 is not cited in Romans nor in any other Pauline letter (nor in any of the New Testament, for that matter). If there were a suspicion that this was a text favored by his opponents in Galatians and is there subverted by Paul, the fact that the text is used nowhere else corroborates that suspicion. This perhaps also explains why Deuteronomy 21:23 is likewise nowhere repeated in Romans or elsewhere in Paul's corpus. As we have seen, in Galatians 3, the claim that one who is hung on a tree is "cursed" is the counterpart to the foreboding curse pronounced by Deuteronomy 27:26 on any who should fail to observe the law. But as it concerns the atoning effect of Jesus' death, this fecund curse motif is nowhere exploited in the Pauline corpus, suggesting again that Paul's use of Deuteronomy 27:26 derives from the pressure of his opponents.

Meanwhile, another candidate (though less certain in that regard) for an opponent's proof text, Leviticus 18:5, *is* reused in Romans 10:5. Here again, text-critical questions abound,[35] but essentially the textual tradition has witnessed two basic forms with minor variations, here for convenience of comparison set out in relationship to the LXX of Leviticus 18:5 and Galatians 3:12b.

---

[34]Paul does not directly appeal to either Gen 12:3/18:18 ("in you all the Gentiles will be blessed"; Gal 3:8) or Genesis 17:8 ("and to your seed"; Gal 3:16; cf. Gen 12:7; 13:15; 15:18; 24:7) in Romans 4, yet the themes represented in each text are generously reprised in parallel allusions and language in that chapter. E.g., on the blessing to Gentiles through Abraham: "I have made you a father of many nations/Gentiles [πολλῶν ἐθνῶν]" (Rom 4:17; cf. 4:18; Gen 17:5). On the promise fulfilled in Abraham's "seed": "For the promise to Abraham *or to his seed* [ἢ τῷ σπέρματι αὐτου; cf. Gen 18:18; 22:17-18] that he would inherit the world did not come through the law" (Rom 4:13; cf. 4:16). And the two themes of Abraham's "seed" consisting of "Gentiles" come together in Romans 4:18: "that he would become 'the father of many nations/Gentiles' [cf. Gen 17:5], according to what was said, 'So shall your seed be'" (οὕτως ἔσται τὸ σπέρμα σου; Gen 15:5). Thus there is strong continuity between Galatians 3 and Romans 4 on these themes, yet the latter explores the themes in greater detail.

[35]On which, see esp. C. D. Stanley, *Paul and the Language of Scripture*, 126-28; and Preston M. Sprinkle, *Law and Life the Interpretation of Leviticus 18:5 in Early Judaism and in Paul*, WUNT 241 (Tübingen: Mohr Siebeck, 2008), 135-36, 166-67, n. 2.

Leviticus 18:5 LXX	poiēsete auta	ha poiēsas anthrōpos	zēsetai en autois
	You shall do them, such things, should a person do, he shall live by them.		
Galatians 3:12b:		ho poiēsas auta	zēsetai en autois
		"The [one] who does them	shall live by them."
Romans 10:5b (1)	Mōüsēs gar graphei	tēn dikaiosynēn tēn ek nomou hoti	
	For Moses writes	concerning the righteousness based on the law that	
		ho poiēsas auta anthrōpos	zēsetai en autois
		"The person who does them	shall live by them."
Romans 10:5b (2)	Mōüsēs gar graphei hoti		
	For Moses writes that		
		tēn dikaiosynēn tēn ek nomou	
		righteousness based on the law	
		ho poiēsas anthrōpos	zēsetai en autē
		"The person who does . . .	shall live by it [= righteousness]."

The chief text-critical issue is the placement of *hoti* (= "that"), which introduces the quote. In Romans 10:5b (1) it follows *nomou* ("law") such that the
Leviticus 18:5 quote is similar to the LXX and Galatians 3:12. In Romans 10:5b
(2) the *hoti* follows *graphei* ("writes"), thus expanding and freely paraphrasing Leviticus 18:5, with the phrase "the righteousness based on the law"
(*tēn dikaiosynēn tēn ek nomou*) becoming the object "the person who does"
(*ho poiēsas anthrōpos*), and necessary grammatical adjustments following.[36]
Although it has become the minority position, the case for (2) is rather
strong and it is arguably the preferred reading.[37]

---

[36](1) αὐτά is omitted, since τὴν δικαιοσύνην τὴν ἐκ [τοῦ] νόμου is the replacement direct object;
(2) αὐτοῖς becomes αὐτῇ in agreement with δικαιοσύνη. The article (τοῦ) preceding νόμου is
doubtful, but does not bear upon our question.

[37]The reading with ὅτι following γράφει was the preferred reading of the critical editions of the
New Testament until NA[26] (so, e.g., NA[25] and earlier, Tischendorf, Westcott-Hort, ASV, RSV,
NASB; William Sanday and Arthur C. Headlam, *A Critical and Exegetical Commentary on the
Epistle to the Romans*, ICC [Edinburgh: T&T Clark, 1898], 286; Cranfield, *Romans*, 2:520-21; and
Ernst Käsemann, *Commentary on Romans* [Grand Rapids: Eerdmans, 1980], 285). The reading
with ὅτι following νόμου is read by NA[26] and subsequent editions, the UBS (where, by the 4th

The text-critical details of Romans 10:5 notwithstanding, it is evident that Paul has put Leviticus 18:5 to a broadly similar use here as in Galatians 3:12. Paul uses the text to state the law's requirement of "doing" as the condition for "life." Yet, there are signs that the text has transformed in Paul's use from the clever, defensive counterpoise of Galatians 3:12 to an established epitome of a fixed tenet in Romans 10:5. Here Paul has freely integrated the text into his discourse as though it is the law's slogan when it speaks of "law-based righteousness" (tēn dikaiosynēn tēn ek nomou). If we accept the earlier text-critical consensus, it is even clearer this text functions as though a formula for the soteriological path contrary to "the righteousness based on faith" of Romans 10:6 (hē de ek pisteōs dikaiosynē).

A more dramatic repurposing is evident in Paul's use of Habakkuk 2:4 in Romans. As we noted, Paul's use of the Habakkuk text in Galatians 3:11 serves the limited but important role of making explicit the implication of Genesis 15:6, that righteousness is reckoned according to faith rather than

---

ed., the variants do not even warrant notice; cf. Metzger, *TCGNT* [1975], 524-25), and a considerable majority of recent commentators. To be sure, the issues are complex, and the evidence ambiguous, but, on balance, the once-favored reading, (2), is still to be preferred for the following reasons. (i) Although the external evidence weighs slightly in favor of (1) (including 𝔭⁴⁶, ℵ², B, Ψ, 945, D², F, G, Maj), external testimony for (2) is also strong and surprisingly persistent (including ℵ*, A, D*, 33*, 81, 630, 1506, 1739, 1881), especially over against a natural tendency to assimilate to Galatians 3:12 and Leviticus 18:5. (ii) Reading (1) is itself plausibly accounted for as an assimilation at least to Galatians 3:12, if not also Leviticus 18:5. It would be altogether understandable for scribes to have moved the ὅτι so as to "correct" the more paraphrastic rendering of (2), well aware that Leviticus 18:5 makes no reference to ἡ δικαιοσύνη ἡ ἐκ τοῦ νόμου. Thus, reading (2) must be regarded as the *lectio difficilior*, but that Paul could have exercised such freedom is not the least surprising. (iii) Attempts to cast reading (1) as the *lectio difficilior* are not persuasive (e.g., Thomas R. Schreiner, *Romans*, BECNT [Grand Rapids: Baker Academic, 1998], 562-63; Moo, *Romans*, 643n1). The argument that ὅτι was moved to follow γράφει in order to avoid the awkwardness of τὴν δικαιοσύνην κτλ. and the abruptness of ὅτι following νόμου requires the unlikely surmise that scribal intuitions would be such that an awkward, though attested, grammatical phenomenon (i.e., as an accusative of respect) would trump the misquotation of a biblical text. Likewise, the suggestion that the retention in (1) of αὐτά is somehow awkward (and thus probably authentic) for lacking an antecedent is not at all persuasive. The pronoun is, after all, attested in Leviticus 18:5 (including uncials F and M, Aquila and Theodotian and in a quote from Philo; so C. D. Stanley, *Paul and the Language of Scripture*, 126-27), and it is found in Galatians 3:12 without any grammatical antecedent as well. (iv) Most importantly, reading (2) arguably best satisfies "Bengel's maxim" or the Westcott-Hort criterion that "the reading is to be preferred that most fitly explains the existence of the others." Note especially those readings that are grammatically "mixed" in character: e.g., B reads γράφει τὴν δικαιοσύνην τὴν ἐκ νόμου ὅτι ὁ ποιήσας αὐτὰ ἄνθρωπος ζήσεται ἐν αὐτῇ, while D reads γράφει ὅτι τὴν δικαιοσύνην τὴν ἐκ τοῦ νόμου ὁ ποιήσας αὐτὰ ἄνθρωπος ζήσεται ἐν αὐτοῖς. Either reading is, at best, unexpected on the presumption of the originality of (1).

354 PAUL'S NEW PERSPECTIVE

works of the law. And, again as noted, this principle was articulated in tandem with its antithesis, articulated by Leviticus 18:5. Now in Romans, Habakkuk 2:4 plays a decidedly more prominent role; it serves as the scriptural linchpin of the letter's thesis that the gospel "is the power of God for the salvation of everyone who believes" (Rom 1:16 NAB) and that "in it is revealed the righteousness of God from faith to faith; as it is written, '*The one who is righteous by faith will live*'" (Rom 1:17 NAB).[38] The interpretive questions surrounding Habakkuk 2:4 are as diverse and complex as almost any text that Paul employs, for a variety of interrelated reasons: (1) Paul's use of the text, both here and in Galatians 3:11, does not seem on the face of it to accord even by analogical extension to its original meaning. (2) Habakkuk 2:4 is characterized by fluid textual, translation and interpretive traditions. (3) Beyond this, there remain interpretive ambiguities: (a) the identity of the righteous one (is it a person declared righteous, or is it messianic?); (b) the meaning of "faith" (is it "believing" or "faithfulness"?); (c) the possessor of faith/faithfulness (is it the faith of the "righteous one" or the faithfulness of God [as in some LXX manuscripts]?); (d) the syntax of the prepositional phrase (does "by faith" describe how one is righteous or how one lives?); (e) the meaning of "shall live" (describing a manner of life or promising eschatological life?); and (f) the possible relationship of the text to the *pistis Christou* debate.[39]

Obviously, no justice can be done in this context with respect to the details of these questions.[40] Sufficient for our purposes is simply to note again that this text, which served such a modest function in the argument of Galatians as countertestimony to the (probable) opponents' appeal to Deuteronomy 27:26, now functions as the clinching scriptural evidence for the thesis of Paul's magnum opus. As such, it functions to announce and reinforce the central claim of the letter, that the righteousness of God that produces the righteous standing (justification) leading to eschatological life is

---

[38]Besides the NAB, the RSV also takes ἐκ πίστεως as explicitly modifying ὁ δίκαιος, on which, see n. 31 above.

[39]Influenced especially by Richard B. Hays, *The Faith of Jesus Christ: The Narrative Substructure of Galatians 3:1–4:11*, 2nd ed., Biblical Resource Series (Grand Rapids: Eerdmans, 2001), 150-57; cf. the brief treatment in idem, *Echoes of Scripture*, 39-41.

[40]My own understanding of the function of Habakkuk 2:4 in Romans 1:17 is corroborated in F. Watson, *Paul and the Hermeneutics of Faith*, 43-53.

appropriated only by means of faith. This emphasis on faith as the decisive and unique means of being counted righteous animates the whole of Romans, and it is stressed in this thesis statement in multiple ways. Faith conjoins the Jew and Gentile into the *all* who believe (*panti tō pisteouonti*). The gospel itself is all about faith, "faith from first to last" (*ek pisteōs eis pistin*).[41] There is no indication that Paul has found a "new meaning" in the text between its use in Galatians and in Romans, but, by comparison, it is now accorded a prominence and is used as a positive acclamation. Thus, this is less of a reinterpretation than a redeployment, but it signals and participates in the non-apologetic and positive articulation of the gospel that characterizes Romans as a whole.

Finally, we consider Genesis 15:6, the text that launched the scriptural leg of Paul's argument in Galatians 3:6. There we noted that this text functions as Paul's trump card. And, although he does not refer to it verbally in the argument that follows, it is clear that Abraham's being reckoned righteous (1) by faith (cf. Gal 3:7-9, 11-12, 14, 22) and (2) prior to the Mosaic law, and especially prior to the institution of circumcision (Gal 3:15-18, 23-26; 4:1-7), devastates the claims of Paul's opponents. The implication of these two claims is that, faith being the more original means of righteousness, Gentiles have no less claim upon it, unless they should—inexplicably from Paul's perspective—choose to vitiate faith in favor of works of the law. Here again, if Genesis 15:6 functions as something like the thesis of this argument, it remains a counterpoise. The function of Genesis 15:6 is different in the case

---

[41]The phrase ἐκ πίστεως εἰς πίστιν is the inspiration for many theologically tempting interpretations (Cranfield, *Romans*, 1:99): from the faith by which the gospel is preached to the faith with which it is heard (cf. Gal 3:2); from the faithfulness of God to the responding faith of believers (Dunn, *Romans*, 1:43-44; Hays, *Echoes of Scripture*, 41; Wright, "The Letter to the Romans: Introduction, Commentary and Reflections," in *NIB*, 10:425; and Ben Witherington III and Darlene Hyatt, *Paul's Letter to the Romans: A Socio-Rhetorical Commentary* [Grand Rapids: Eerdmans, 2004], 56); or from the πίστις Χριστοῦ to the human response of faith (D. A. Campbell, *Deliverance of God*, 377-80, 618-19). The fault of these interpretations is not that they are theologically untrue; they are all not only true generally but defensible as epitomizations of Romans. It remains more likely, however, that the common idiom ἐκ ... εἰς is simply an expression for "from start to finish" (contra R. Jewett, *Romans*, 143-44, who insists that the prepositions in this idiom always imply movement); but cf. ἐκ θανάτου εἰς θάνατον ... ἐκ ζωῆς εἰς ζωήν (2 Cor 2:16); ἐκ δυνάμεως εἰς δύναμιν (Ps 83:8 LXX); ἐκ τούτου εἰς τοῦτο (Ps 143:13 LXX); and ἐκ κακῶν εἰς κακὰ (Jer 9:2 LXX). Thus, the expression stresses the exclusivity of faith as the means of righteousness (Cranfield, *Romans*, 1:99-100; C. K. Barrett, *The Epistle to the Romans*, 2nd ed., BNTC [Peabody, MA: Hendrickson, 1991], 31-32; and Moo, *Romans*, 77).

of Romans (Rom 4:3), where, if anything it functions rather more as the clinching coup de grâce than as the first salvo. Yet, for all that, Genesis 15:6 determines the succeeding argument in Romans 4 no less than in the case of Galatians 3, yet now its particular phrasing is appealed to and exploited to an unprecedented degree.

In capitalizing on Genesis 15:6 in this way, Paul explores three subsidiary inferences from the text, two anticipated in Galatians, but now expanded, and a third unprecedented in Galatians 3 but now the dominant theme of Romans 4. (1) As with Galatians 3, the text once again emphasizes the exclusivity of faith as the means of righteousness (Rom 4:4-6, 9, 11-14). But beyond anything claimed directly in Galatians 3, Genesis 15:6 becomes the text that disproves that Abraham was "justified by works" (Rom 4:2) in its use in Romans 4:3. In this regard, the substance of Galatians 3:6 is affirmed, but now explicated toward a more comprehensive soteriology where it becomes clear that the exclusivity of faith for righteousness demonstrates that faith is constitutive of grace (Rom 4:16). (2) The appeal to Genesis 15:6 again alludes to the temporal priority of Abraham's pre-circumcision righteousness (Rom 4:9-12), but less is made of that temporal priority (e.g., there is nothing akin to the 430 years of Gal 3:17) and more is made of the universality of Abraham's righteousness-by-faith precedent. In a deliberate irony, Paul declares him the "father of circumcision not only to those of circumcision but to those who walk in the steps of 'the uncircumcision faith' [*tēs en akrobystia pisteōs*] of our father Abraham" (Rom 4:12).[42] (3) Finally, in a manner unprecedented in Galatians, the language of Genesis 15:6 is used to explicate the very nature of justification itself. That faith is "reckoned as righteousness" (*elogisthē eis dikaiosynēn*) is a notion, other than its bare statement by means of Genesis 15:6, unexplored in Galatians, yet that same figure determines the whole of Romans 4. Nine times following Romans 4:3, *logizomai* is repeated in a theological exposition of Genesis 15:6 (Rom 4:4, 5, 6, 9, 10, 11, 22, 23, 24), and the same verb, having been introduced in Romans 4:3 via Genesis 15:6, then suggests another Old Testament text: "Blessed is the one against whom the Lord will not reckon [*ou mē logisētai*] sin" (Rom 4:8; Ps 32:1 LXX). This

---

[42] This understanding of Romans 4:12 substantiates my earlier proposal, following Hays, that Romans 4:1 implies a negative answer to the suggestion that Abraham is "our forefather according to the flesh" (cf. chap. 2 above, nn. 55-57).

is justification for Paul: faith is reckoned as righteousness; sin is not reckoned—which is to say, lawlessness forgiven and sins covered (Rom 4:7). Therefore, as important as Genesis 15:6 is to the argument of Galatians 3:6-29, it assumes an even more prominent role in Romans 4, becoming the clinching, synthesizing text that explains the exclusivity of faith over against "works" (Rom 4:4-6) and "law" (Rom 4:13-16), the priority of faith and promise over against its seal in circumcision (Rom 4:9-12), and the very character of justification as the status of reckoned righteousness and unreckoned sin.

If we were to compare the use of the primary argumentative texts of Galatians 3 with the use, and non-use, of the same in Romans, we might say that the counterpoising and counterintuitive texts and interpretations of Galatians become the constitutive texts of Romans. Where an opponent's argument is no longer in view, neither are the texts used to advocate and refute it any longer necessary (e.g., Deut 27:26; 21:23). Texts that demonstrated that Gentiles were originally and always in the purview of the covenantal promise (Gen 12:3/18:18; 17:8, etc.), though not repeated directly in Romans, suggest a parallel set of similar texts, substantiating the same insight (Gen 15:5; 17:5; Rom 4:16-18). Meanwhile, other texts that anchored a fundamentally defensive argument in Galatians, now in Romans become the bulwark for the settled soteriology by which righteousness is by faith, exclusive of nomistic or any other kind of performance (Hab 2:4; Gen 15:6; Lev 18:5; cf. Rom 1:17; 4:3, 9, 22; 10:5).

8.1.3 Reconfiguring the gospel: the premise of human guilt. It is instructive to explore Paul's own description of the plight, explicit and implicit, for which the Christ event is God's remediating intervention. Or, put more narrowly in the context of Galatians and Romans, what problem does "justification" solve, and is it the same problem in both cases?

It is evident in Galatians that the question of human guilt, which figures so prominently in Romans, remains a theme unarticulated.[43] Rather, when

---

[43]In what follows, I part company with Frank Thielman, *From Plight to Solution: A Jewish Framework for Understanding Paul's View of the Law in Galatians and Romans*, NovTSup 61 (New York: Brill, 1989), esp. 46-86. The difference is not, however, primarily exegetical, where I find myself more often than not in general agreement, naturally with quibbles. Rather, in arguing for the "plight to solution" direction of Paul's soteriology, Thielman is insufficiently concerned for the rhetorical dimensions of Paul's various arguments, being primarily concerned for a

Paul speaks of the human condition in general terms, it is that we are in need of deliverance "from the present evil age" (*tou aiōnos tou enestōtos ponērou*), and this is accomplished by the one who "gave himself for our sins" (*tou dontos heauton hyper tōn hamartiōn hēmōn*; Gal 1:4). Other than that the latter is the purpose of the former, it is not obvious what the more precise relationship between these two dimensions of Christ's redemptive work might be.[44] Indeed, it is hard to see how a purely juridical account of Christ's death (e.g., as a vicarious bearer of punishment) is conceptually related to his act of rescue from the present evil eon. It may be that the precise relationship is elusive because "gave himself for our sins" is a stereotyped confessional tradition that Paul appropriates.[45] In any case, "this present evil age" is but one of several ways of describing present human oppression: while still "children" (*nēpioi*), "we" were enslaved to *ta stoicheia tou kosmou* ("elemental spirits of the world"; Gal 4:3 NRSV), which are "weak" and "beggarly" (Gal 4:9). While *ta stoicheia tou kosmou* remains a contested allusion, the lexical background seems reasonably clear: it is a reference to the basic elements (air, earth, fire, water). How Paul is appropriating the reference is less obvious, but it can be said of these elements that they enslave (Gal 4:3, 8, 9) and, as such, exercise dominion and vie for an allegiance reserved for God alone (Gal 4:8).[46]

It is evident, however, that the primary human dilemma in Galatians is not expressed in the juridical metaphor of guilt and forgiveness but in oppression and enslavement and liberation. No fewer than fifteen times in this

---

theological synthesis. As Thielman demonstrates, it is possible to reconstruct a "plight" from the argument of Galatians. It is another thing to claim that plight-to-solution is the shape of Paul's argument, which it is in Romans and is not in Galatians. A symptom of the shortcoming of Thielman's approach is the vagueness with which the alleged plight in Galatians is articulated.
[44]This is vividly illustrated in the commentaries, where an affirmation of some kind of atoning expiation is affirmed as well as an "apocalyptic" rescue, but commentators themselves are apparently at a loss to describe the relationship, what the former has to do with the latter (R. N. Longenecker, *Galatians*, 7-9; Richard B. Hays, "The Letter to the Galatians," in *NIB*, 11:202-3; and Moo, *Galatians*, 72-73). For his part, Bruce makes a plausible attempt: "Christ's self-oblation not only procures for his people the forgiveness of their past sins; it delivers them from the realm in which sin is irresistible into the realm where he himself is Lord" (F. F. Bruce, *The Epistle to the Galatians: A Commentary on the Greek Text*, NIGTC [Grand Rapids: Eerdmans, 1982], 75).
[45]So, e.g., Martyn, *Galatians*, 88-91.
[46]Martyn argues, plausibly in my view, that the language is determined by the Jerusalem "Teachers," but that Paul, in so using it, transforms their position into his own rhetorical coup—it is in fact the *law* that is the *ta stoicheia* (ibid., 393-406; cf. the useful summary and similar, if more cautious, conclusions of Moo, *Galatians*, 260-63).

letter Paul speaks of enslavement (*doul-* cognates) or imprisonment and another eleven times of freedom or redemption (unto liberation),[47] but never does he speak of forgiveness. The two references to sin in Galatians (only the noun, *hamartia*) are found only in the probable formula of Galatians 1:4 and in Galatians 3:22, in which sin is personified as though a jailer. By contrast, Romans refers forty-eight times to the noun, albeit diversely, and another seven to the verb (*hamartanō*). Only once, and in a non-universal context, does Galatians speak directly of divine judgment ("whoever it is that is confusing you will pay the penalty" [*to krima*; Gal 5:10]), compared to at least sixteen references in Romans to the same.[48] Likewise, Galatians witnesses no reference to the "wrath" of God as the consequence of human sin, whereas the same language is prominent in Romans as the default disposition of God against human wrongdoing, referenced twelve times.[49] In summary, it would be fair to say by way of generalization that the primary soteriological metaphorical domain of Galatians is oppression/slavery over against freedom, whereas in Romans the juridical forms the base, though not exclusive, soteriological domain of the opening gambit of Romans 1–4, crowned in the summary of Romans 5:1-11.[50] Thus, at the most basic metaphorical level, the overlap in other vocabulary and superficial resemblances notwithstanding, Galatians and Romans could scarcely give a more different expression of the human dilemma.[51]

This is borne out in a closer examination of the rhetorical cast of the opening chapters of Romans, where it is Paul's burden to demonstrate that the world of humankind, Jew and Gentile alike, stands under judgment. This is not quite the claim that many assume that Paul has made. Romans 1:18–3:20 is not simply asserting that every single human being has sinned and

---

[47]-δουλ-: Galatians 2:4; 3:28; 4:1, 3, 7, 8, 9, 24, 25; 5:1, 13 (the favorable reference of Gal 1:10 excluded); συγκλείω: Galatians 3:22, 23 (cf. Gal 1:4); φρουρέω: Galatians 3:23 (cf. ὑπὸ παιδαγωγόν, Gal 3:25; ὑπὸ ἐπιτρόπους . . . καὶ οἰκονόμους, Gal 4:2). ἐλευθερ-: Galatians 2:4; 3:28; 4:22, 23, 26, 30, 31; 5:1, 13 (cf. ἐξαγοράζω, Gal 3:13; 4:5).

[48]Romans 2:1, 2, 3, 5, 12, 16; 3:6, 8; 5:16, 18; 8:1, 3, 34; 13:2; 14:10, 23; including only, conservatively, exercises of divine judgment.

[49]Romans 1:18; 2:5, 8; 3:5; 4:15; 5:9; 9:22; 12:19; 13:4, 5.

[50]It is important to note that liberative themes are central to Romans as well (Rom 6:18, 20, 22; 7:3; 8:2, 21), although this note is sounded in full only after the initial forensic exposition of the first five chapters.

[51]In describing the diversity of expression, I am making no suggestion that the letters are somehow in conflict—merely that they describe the human dilemma in different terms.

so stand accountable to God as guilty persons. Although Paul would concur with the point, it is not quite the one he is making. The universal guilt of every human is patent, but Paul's intent is to show by means of dialectic argument that this is a circumstance that applies *equally* to both Jews and Gentiles, and to do so, he must demonstrate that it applies *differently* to Gentiles and Jews. This is what makes Romans 1:18–3:20 so difficult for so many readers: it is a series of rhetorical zigs and zags that would be unnecessary were Paul wanting simply to say that "all persons are guilty." Rather, Paul's exposition is a labyrinthine excursus on Romans 1:18 ("the wrath of God is revealed from heaven," NRSV), showing Jews and Gentiles sharing the same dilemma. But since Jewish rectitude surpassing Gentile vice is assumed, the claim that Jew and Gentile are alike in sin and culpability is counterintuitive and must be demonstrated.

Thus, Paul begins with the rhetorically low-hanging fruit of an implicit Gentile target (Rom 1:18-32), describing humanity's supplanting of the truth of God and the surfeit of misdeeds that follow. However, the one who judges such as these—the description of Romans 1:18-32 invites contempt rather than sympathy—finds that he too is implicated, being guilty of the deeds himself and all the more culpable for casting judgment on others (Rom 2:1-5).[52] While it cannot be demonstrated beyond question that the "O man" of Romans 2:1-5 is a censorious *Jew*, it seems probable that Paul would be happy for his readers to suppose so. That impression is confirmed in Romans 2:6-16 when the argument turns to the impartiality of God (Rom 2:11), "who requites each person according to his deeds" (Rom 2:6). Jew and Greek are judged alike (Rom 2:9-10) according to the evil or good worked, not according to their possession of the law (Rom 2:12-16). Thus, Romans 2:1-5 is sandwiched by the implicit, presumptive Gentile wickedness (Rom 1:18-32) and the prospect—hypothetical or actual—of the Gentile finding eternal life, by perseverance in good work, seeking glory, honor and immortality, internalizing the law's demands though being without it (Rom 2:6-16). Although

---

[52]I choose the masculine and singular pronoun purposely in this instance only because Paul is making use of an undisclosed interlocutor for the sake of his argument: ὦ ἄνθρωπε πᾶς ὁ κρίνων (Rom 2:1; cf. 2:3). The second-person singular is used consistently in Romans 2:1-5 except for the generalization of Romans 2:2. On the use of the interlocutor in the diatribe of Romans, see esp. Stanley K. Stowers, *A Rereading of Romans: Justice, Jews, and Gentiles* (New Haven, CT: Yale University Press, 1994); and Tobin, *Paul's Rhetoric*.

it is beyond the scope of my argument to offer a satisfactory excursus on the set of questions raised by Romans 2:6-16, suffice it to say that the two most common theological maneuvers must both be judged counsels of despair: (1) The standard reading of the TPP is that the prospect of a favorable judgment on the basis of works can only be hypothetical given the universal condemnation of humankind (Rom 3:9-20). (2) Meanwhile, an otherwise diverse set of interpreters (e.g., Bultmann, Cranfield, Wright) hears "written on their hearts" as an echo of the new covenant promise of Jeremiah 31:33 (LXX 38:33). Thus, the "works" resulting in favorable judgment are the Spirit-enabled obedience of Christian Gentiles. Although completely different "solutions" to the *interpreter's* dilemma, neither of these readings offers an interpretation that contributes believably to Paul's actual *argument* rather than as a rehabilitation of his putative theology. But, in fact, the burden of Paul's argument is to de-center assumptions about the intrinsic right-eousness of people groups on religio-ethnic grounds. The unrighteousness of the Gentile (Rom 1:18-32) can no more be assumed than the righteousness of the Jew (Rom 2:17-29); the law-less Gentile is not for that reason lawless any more than the law-possessing Jew is lawful. It is the supreme indictment of Jewish presumption that Paul could say that there are Gentiles attaining to righteousness beyond Jewish performance, but it subverts that entire ar-gument to say that this is but a hypothetical ruse.[53] Thus, Paul has set a

---

[53]Indications that Paul could imagine a "righteous Gentile" beyond the usefulness of such for the sake of his argument include the following: (1) As noted, only an *actual* case in point would supply what is needed for Paul's argument, where by "actual" what is meant is at least "theoretical" but not merely "hypothetical." (2) The description of such a Gentile is complex and appropriately diffident; it describes that character in terms of aspirational disposition ("perseverant in good work, seeking glory, honor, and immortality") rather than, say, in terms of an accumulation of meritorious deeds (note the sg. ἔργου ἀγαθοῦ rather than "good deeds"). (3) That reticence is especially evidenced in the expression "accusing or perhaps excusing" (κατηγορούντων ἢ καὶ ἀπολογουμένων) of Romans 2:15. This would be a singularly inappropriate description of the judgment of "justified" Gentile *Christians*, on the one hand, and, on the other, entirely otiose as a description of a nonexistent hypothetical category. (4) In Romans 2:16, it is said that God's judgment is of the "secret things of men" (τὰ κρυπτὰ τῶν ἀνθρώπων), which is appropriately descriptive of God's omnicient capacity as judge to discern what is knowable to God alone. (5) It is a misreading of Romans 3:10-18 to understand the catena of scriptural testimony regarding human sinfulness as though these texts describe a logician's exceptionless categories. In fact, the texts cited as evidence of human depravity all come from contexts in which exceptions of human righteousness are close at hand (Rom 3:10-12 = Ps 14:1-3, but note Ps 14:5-7; Rom 3:13 = Ps 140:3, but note Ps 140:13; Rom 3:14 = Ps 10:7, but in contrast to the righteous and afflicted poor of Ps 10:1-2, 8-10, 12, 14, 17-18; Rom 3:15-17 = Isa 59:7-8, Judah's present unrighteousness, which the Lord avenges; Rom 3:18 = Ps 36:1, but note Ps 36:10).

rhetorical trap by having offered a typical reproach of Gentile sinfulness as his opening gambit (Rom 1:18-32), by exposing hypocritical judgmentalism as its own sort of unrighteousness (Rom 2:1-5) and by showing certain Gentiles as outdoing their Jewish counterparts in righteousness, against all odds and every Jewish expectation (Rom 2:6-16). This all prepares for the coup de grâce of Romans 2:17-29, an excoriation of Jewish sin that demonstrates that possession of the law only accentuates culpability rather than empowering righteousness. So devastating is Paul's conclusion that his interlocutor must ask in despair whether there is any advantage in being a Jew after all (Rom 3:1). Although Paul answers affirmatively ("much in every way"), while ultimately rejecting any soteriological advantage, he finally returns to the same question from that vantage point. "What then? Are we any better off? No, not at all; for we have already charged that all, both Jews and Greeks, are under [the power of] sin" (Rom 3:9 NRSV).

It is evident, then, (1) that Paul has gone to great lengths to establish the commonality of Jew and Gentile in sin and (2) that, the demonstration of the former being counterintuitive, it required the greater rhetorical exertion. Paul is surely not suggesting that the Jew is more objectively sinful; rather, he asserts that the benefit of election, chiefly the possession of the law and "oracles of God," proves to be no ultimate soteriological advantage. That the Jew, possessing such advantages, finds himself paradoxically at no advantage *coram Deo* demonstrates the law to be soteriologically impotent, and that verdict prepares for the argument of Romans 3:21–4:25. If the law does not save the Jew but only reveals the "knowledge of sin" (Rom 3:20), a soteriological solution will be necessary that elides that law, procuring righteousness by some other means.

We have explored Paul's articulation of the common, if variegated, human dilemma in Romans 1:18–3:20 to demonstrate its singular goal of declaring Gentile and Jew to share alike the dilemma of sin and condemnation, with respect to which the law proves an impotent remediation. As it relates to the development of Paul's soteriology, the significance of

---

Although the position argued here is decidedly in the minority, I contend that it remains the most rhetorically sensitive and plausible of the options. For a similar position, see Klyne R. Snodgrass, "Justification by Grace—to the Doers: An Analysis of the Place of Romans 2 in the Theology of Paul," *NTS* 32, no. 1 (1986): 72-93.

this argumentative move must not be missed. Romans stands apart from all of Paul's earlier writings in describing that human dilemma as the propaedeutic *plight* in preparation for the redemptive *solution*. Paul's purpose in structuring the argument in this way is not merely that there is an apparent logic in a plight preceding solution but that the demonstration of common Jewish and Gentile culpability and just condemnation is necessary in order to demonstrate their commonality in salvation—"to the Jew first, and also to the Greek . . . from faith to faith" (Rom 1:16-17).

Because the stereotyped "gospel" of Christian theology so frequently consists of the reprisal of the human plight ameliorated by divine atoning intervention, divine judgment overcome by forgiveness, and because of the theological centrality of Romans as the articulation of that gospel, it is easy to overlook the fact that this articulation of the "gospel" finds its first expression in this form in Romans.[54] The fact that Romans heads the Pauline canon and summarizes an account of the gospel so efficiently also means that this rendition of the gospel tends to norm the reading of Paul more generally.[55] That humanity stands under God's judgment for sin is no innovation in Paul's thinking; it is part of the conceptual furniture in the letters preceding Romans (Gal 5:10; 1 Thess 1:9-10; 5:9; 2 Thess 1:8-10; 1 Cor 4:4-5; 11:32; 2 Cor 5:10). What distinguishes Romans from these letters is an articulation of the human dilemma in this way as constitutive to the gospel, as part and parcel of the message itself. Preceding this, summaries of the redemptive narrative (e.g., 1 Cor 15:1-7) or summaries of an implicit soteriology (1 Thess 1:9-10) exclude a description of human sinfulness as that for which the saving

---

[54]Describing the plight of humanity apart from Christ is a standard trope of Pauline theologies, thus following Romans as a template to which the other letters are rhetorically conformed (e.g., James D. G. Dunn, *The Theology of Paul the Apostle* [Grand Rapids: Eerdmans, 1998], 79-127; Thomas R. Schreiner, *Paul, Apostle of God's Glory in Christ: A Pauline Theology* [Downers Grove, IL: InterVarsity Press, 2001], 103-50; and Frank J. Matera, *God's Saving Grace: A Pauline Theology* [Grand Rapids: Eerdmans, 2012], 88-102). Not all are as candid as Matera: "Every synthesis is artificial. On the one hand, *themes of Romans tend to dominate the synthesis*, as they do here. On the other, no one letter reflects the entire synthesis since the letters are occasional. My purpose is to present a theology of the Pauline letters. In doing so, I assume that Paul did not forget what he wrote in other letters, nor did those who wrote in his name" (Matera, *God's Saving Grace*, 99n19, emphasis added).

[55]Brevard S. Childs, *The Church's Guide for Reading Paul: The Canonical Shaping of the Pauline Corpus* (Grand Rapids: Eerdmans, 2008).

events of Christ are the repair. The closest we come to such a formulation is in the figure of reconciliation as it is developed in 2 Corinthians 5:14-21. The death of Christ effects a transfer of allegiance from "themselves" to "him who for their sake died and was raised" (2 Cor 5:15); to be "in Christ" is to harbinger the new creation (2 Cor 5:17); but, above all, it is to be reconciled to God (2 Cor 5:18-21). Thus, only in the figure of reconciliation do we have the implicit logic of a breach between humanity and God resultant from sin, repaired by atonement (2 Cor 5:21). Even here, however, it is the *implicit* logic of the gospel as articulated under the figure of reconciliation; it is not the *structure* of Paul's gospel discourse. *That* comes only in Romans and is driven by the rhetorical need to demonstrate that Jew and Gentile share a common plight from which they are delivered by a common solution.

This gospel logic of "humanity apart from Christ" as propaedeutic for God's redemptive intervention, although it was absent prior to Romans, becomes a standard soteriological account following that letter. In Colossians, we learn of a humanity "rescued . . . from the power of darkness and transferred . . . into the kingdom of his beloved Son" (Col 1:13 NRSV); again under the figure of reconciliation, humanity "once estranged [from God] and hostile in mind, doing evil deeds" (Col 1:21 NRSV; cf. 3:6-7), once "dead in your trespasses and the uncircumcision of your flesh" (Col 2:13 NRSV).

But it is in Ephesians that the rhetorical pattern established in Romans is most transparently reproduced, especially in Ephesians 2:1-10. Here we see the pattern now familiar from Romans:

- Humanity is "dead in trespasses and sins," subject to the "prince of the power of the air," following the "sons of disobedience," subject to "passions of our flesh" and the "desires of the body and the mind"—in short, "children of wrath," the lot of all humankind.

- Then in a move structurally akin to Romans 3:21-26, but nowhere else previously attested in the Pauline corpus, Paul turns to the mercy, love, grace and kindness of God, who raises those dead in trespasses and makes them alive together with Christ, even seated in "heavenly realms" with Christ Jesus (Eph 2:4-6).

It is not insignificant that Ephesians is a letter, whether Pauline or deutero-Pauline, functioning as a synopsis of the Pauline vision, and as such this summary of Pauline soteriology demonstrates what had become soterio-logically paradigmatic.

That same, now stereotyped, pattern of sinful estate overcome by God's gracious intervention on behalf of the undeserving is found as the soterio-logical paradigm of the PE as well. Note, for example, the narration of that intervention in Titus 3:3-7:

- Humanity is hopeless in the degradation of its sin: "For we ourselves were once foolish, disobedient, led astray, slaves to various passions and plea-sures, passing our days in malice and envy, despicable, hating one an-other" (Tit 3:3 NRSV).

- God intervening of his kindness apart from human deserving: "But when the goodness and loving kindness of God our Savior appeared, he saved us, not because of any works of righteousness that we had done, but ac-cording to his mercy, through the water of rebirth and renewal by the Holy Spirit. This Spirit he poured out on us richly through Jesus Christ our Savior, so that, having been justified by his grace, we might become heirs according to the hope of eternal life" (Tit 3:4-7 NRSV).

That same ingrained pattern is found in 1 Timothy, as Paul reflects upon the depraved state of humanity (1 Tim 1:9-10) and personalizes it by identi-fying with that depravity as the "foremost of sinners" (1 Tim 1:12-16).

- Like the "lawless and disobedient, for the godless and sinful, for the unholy and profane, for those who kill their father or mother, for mur-derers, fornicators, sodomites, slave traders, liars, perjurers" (1 Tim 1:9-10 NRSV), Paul himself "was once a blasphemer and a persecutor and a vi-olent man" (1 Tim 1:13).

- But he "received mercy" because he had "acted ignorantly in unbelief" (1 Tim 1:13 NRSV). And the "grace of the Lord overflowed for [Paul] with the faith and love that are in Christ Jesus" (1 Tim 1:14).

Thus, the plight and solution of all of humanity is replayed in miniature in Paul himself, the undeserving "chief of sinners," apprehended by grace unto salvation.

No doubt, the foregoing survey can only seem exceedingly elementary: what reader of the Pauline corpus can be unaware of the gospel as "plight and solution," human depravity, and divine intervention? Indeed. I only

point out that this apparently ubiquitous pattern is only apparently ubiquitous. It is the plight of Romans 1:18–3:20 met by the intervention of Romans
3:21–5:11. In this regard, I concur with D. A. Campbell's intuition about the
essential foreignness of the opening gambit of Romans, while arriving at a
completely different account of the phenomenon.[56] While Campbell finds
this juridical, prospective account ultimately un-Pauline (thus, the need to
attribute it to an interlocutor-Teacher), I see it as *constitutively* Pauline,
though not the most *originally* Pauline appeal to justification. In the process,
this argument becomes paradigmatic for subsequent Pauline soteriological
summaries and the plight-to-solution paradigm becomes the normative, if
not quite the exclusive, rhetorical form of the Pauline gospel. This, I propose,
is a development. It is also, not incidentally, the form that the gospel takes
in Paul's final writings. This is his new perspective.

8.2 The Fruit of Resolution: Paul's Second Corpus

Not without reason have scholars (e.g., Godet, Dodd, Bornkamm, Dunn)
found in Romans a working template for Pauline theology, yet it is in the
trajectories that follow Romans that Paul's magnum opus is fully understood,
not as his final word but as a discourse marking transition. In what follows,
then, I trace evidence that the soteriological synthesis that came to resolution in Romans is secured and corroborated in the letters that followed.

8.2.1 Paul, in his own words? Should evidence be sought to confirm that
the hard-won soteriological synthesis first adumbrated obliquely in Galatians (corroborated in the Thessalonian and Corinthian correspondences)
and explicated in much greater detail in Romans has reached a settled equi-
librium, it can be found in three observations: (1) The substance of Paul's
gospel continues to be expressed in the letters that follow, though not in
extended discourses but rather in abbreviated and formalized statements,
largely absent any argument. We noted this phenomenon above in the discussion of the relative centrality of justification (see 3.2.3, "Justification (1):
Constitutive or Incidental"), where we noted that the chief elements of the
Romans 1–5 argument were subsequently reprised in briefer form and, save
for Philippians 3:2-11, without trace of polemic (Col 1:18-23; Eph 2:1-10; Tit

---

[56]D. A. Campbell, *Deliverance of God.*

3:5-7; 2 Tim 1:8-11). There is no evidence that Paul presents these soterio-logical accounts to counter alternatives or specifically to correct errant readers, even though each of these letters is evidently written at least in part to counter or arrest some faulty theology (save perhaps Ephesians, although note Eph 4:14). While errant teaching seems to have plagued Paul from beginning to end of his letter-writing career, there is no evidence that Paul's soteriological summaries are brandished to combat false alternatives. To the contrary, the soteriology of these later letters not only condenses the insights of the earlier letters; it treats what had previously been argued as though now patent. Even in Philippians 3:2-11, where a circumcision party apparently looms, Paul's twofold rejoinder is not so much an argument as a kind of testimony. His impeccable Jewish credentials will withstand the closest scrutiny (Phil 3:2-6); this provides the platform for what he wishes to say, but it is not a substantiating argument. Nor is the following narration of his great reversal in which he declares himself willing to abandon all his "credits" and count them as "debits" for the "surpassing value of knowing Christ my Lord" and "being found in him" with a righteousness that comes "from God based on faith." But even here in this polemical interlude there is no direct *argument* for the inferiority of his prior status nor any case made for the superiority of the current. Paul assumes it. If there is an argument, it is simply Paul's story and the self-evident "surpassing worth" of knowing Christ and being found in union with him.

(2) Not only do the letters following Romans cease to argue soteriology; more remarkably Paul's articulation of that soteriology no longer appeals to Scripture for its demonstration in the letters that follow Romans. Not even Philippians, an undisputed letter that is clearly working within the familiar framework of law, righteousness and faith, makes any gesture to the Abrahamic promise or to the priority of faith or to the tragedy of Israel's story. We can only speculate as to the reasons Paul might have had in appealing much or little to Scripture in a given letter. There is no apparent pattern related, for example, to chronology, audience or authenticity. Setting aside the numerous biblical allusions and use of biblical idioms, the early letters of 1 and 2 Thessalonians have no direct citations from Scripture, but neither does the later letter to the Philippians (or Philemon); the same is true for the disputed letters to the Colossians and Titus, with 1 and 2 Timothy having

only one certain citation each.[57] Interestingly, all the citations in Ephesians come in Ephesians 4–6, typically characterized as the letter's hortatory section, with none in Ephesians 1–3, the "theological" chapters.[58] By comparison, the capital epistles are teeming with biblical citations: Romans has over sixty and many more allusions; Galatians, 1 Corinthians and 2 Corinthians each has a dozen or more.[59]

Yet as it concerns soteriological claims on the other side of Romans, we find not a single appeal to a biblical text—not in Philippians, not in Colossians or Ephesians, nor in the Pastoral Epistles. Why this is so, we cannot say. We can only note that Gentile audiences (cf. Galatians and Romans) or inauthenticity (cf. 1 Thessalonians and Philippians) are explanations subverted by counterexamples. It may simply be that on this side of Romans, as it regarded soteriology, Paul had nothing to prove, just something to proclaim and cause for exultation. It is perhaps not accidental that the theological summaries in the later letters are just as much doxological as they are soteriological. In the letters subsequent to Romans, Paul weighs in on matters soteriological with nonpolemical, doxological summaries and without appealing to biblical evidence to make his case. Indeed, no case is made. Humanity's guilt and enslavement are met by God's gracious intervention, apart from any human contribution or merit—salvation being wholly of grace and its numerous benefits being received by faith.

(3) To this I can add one more observation, which is a kind of restatement of all the foregoing: Paul's soteriology becomes increasingly abstract in its final extant expressions. If we compare the sort of exigent crisis that launches

---

[57]For the sake of convenience, I am using the "Index of Quotations" from UBS[4] as a rough estimate, sufficient for these purposes. It is acknowledged that there are numerous additional allusions in all the letters. To use Philippians for example, it is recognized that Philippians 1:19 alludes directly to Job 13:16 (LXX), that Philippians 2:7 may allude to Isaiah 53:12, that Philippians 2:10-11 almost certainly employs the language of Isaiah 45:23, and so on. The same phenomenon is more or less true for each of Paul's letters, even those lacking direct citations altogether (see Beale and Carson, *Commentary on the New Testament Use of the Old Testament*).

[58]Needless to say, the theological/hortatory distinction is a severe oversimplification in the case of Ephesians; nonetheless, that there is a certain change of character between the first three and final three chapters is widely acknowledged, marked by this transition: "I therefore, the prisoner in the Lord, beg you to lead a life worthy of the calling to which you have been called" (Eph 4:1 NRSV).

[59]Far and away, Romans has the greatest density of biblical citations, almost one for about every one hundred words; Galatians averages a citation for fewer than two hundred words, and 1 and 2 Corinthians and Ephesians each averages a citation roughly every four hundred words.

Paul's soteriological arguments in Galatians, the communal discord that Romans intends to remediate and the suspicion of Paul's apostolic authority that hovers over the Thessalonian and Corinthian correspondences, the post-Romans soteriological discourse is comparatively abstract and detached from evident contingencies. By *abstract*, I do not mean scholastic, merely theoretical, ahistorical or disembodied timeless principles—the kinds of things often meant by biblical scholars when we use "abstract" pejoratively—but rather that the discourse is principial, settled and transcending the sort of circumstances that clearly motivated earlier arguments. By this point, Paul's soteriology is what it has become, not in conflict with or over against alternatives but as the variable expression of what has become a consistent picture. Free of *those* controversies—although never free from controversy—Paul's gospel has settled into forms less driven by contingency and has become the more voluntary rehearsal of a synthesis whence derives the transformation of persons and community.

8.2.2 Jews and Gentiles: from crisis to sign. It is an important observation that the Jew-Gentile question that has animated the NPP and that predominates in Galatians and Romans never disappears from Paul's concern. It is equally important to note that it is not a static concern for Paul and, indeed, that "concern" might not even be the right word. We have already observed that the relation of Jew to Gentile is a multidimensional phenomenon. The differences noted between Galatians and Romans demonstrate that these crises (if the social acrimony in Rome should be called a crisis) can be differentiated, and though Paul's response is tethered to a single theological foundation—God's redemptive accomplishment in Christ—the same is appropriated to each circumstance differently. While Galatians addresses the threat of Gentiles Judaizing under the influence and pressure of Jerusalem teachers, we saw that Romans is troubled by different concerns, on the practical level, a Gentile-Christian indifference toward their covenantal forebears and, theologically, a defense of God's faithfulness, specifically reproached in the Jewish rejection of Jesus as Messiah. To our knowledge, the pressure toward Judaizing, most unmistakable and pronounced in Galatians, probably never abated during Paul's lifetime.[60] This

---

[60]Or, indeed, during the first several Christian centuries (see, e.g., Ignatius, *To the Magnesians* 8.1; 10.4). Those who "Judaize" are finally condemned by the Synod of Laodicea, Canon 29. Of

or related concerns *may* factor into Paul's engagement with the Corinthians; it *could* underlie Colossians obliquely.[61] In any case, the threat of Judaizing remains a concern significant enough that Paul addresses it from his Roman imprisonment (Phil 3:1-11), and a bent toward nomism presumably lies behind the "lawful" use of the law over against "those of the circumcision" in 1 Timothy 1:8-10. Whether intermittent or unabated, nomistic pressure apparently bedevils Paul's entire career.

Nonetheless, beginning with Galatians, Paul's responses are theologically larger than the provoking crises. While there can be little question that Paul is frequently counterpunching and neutralizing the claims, express or implied, of opponents, mirror reading his arguments is sometimes liable to give his challengers too much credit, proliferating parties and exaggerating their theological sophistication.[62] Paul's engagement with the question of the unity of Jews and Gentiles is a case in point. The fact that he addresses the matter does not necessarily mean that behind his address lay a sworn adversary immediately present. For example, in his letter to the Philippians, despite the very strong language, the delay of the warning until Philippians 3:2 suggests that a circumcision party is not the presenting issue for Paul's writing of the letter, nor can it be inferred that there is a contingent of nomistic proselytizers present in Philippi.[63] Meanwhile, Paul is able to leverage

---

course, the precise relationship between Paul's original opponents and the Ebionites is unclear, but the latter attest to the durability of Christian nomism in the primitive church (see D. F. Wright, "Ebionites," *DLNT,* 313-17).

[61]Does nomism lie behind the loyalty of those who are "of Cephas" (1 Cor 1:12)? Even if overplayed in Baur's Tübingen hypothesis, there is probably some element of truth to the claim. Likewise, although it is disputed, it is hard to imagine that a claim to greater Torah fidelity was not at least part of the "super-apostles" presenting portfolio (2 Cor 11:5, 13; 12:11-12; cf. esp. 2 Cor 11:4 with Gal 1:6). And 1 Corinthians 7:18 *may* bear witness to a Judaizing pressure and its opposite: "Was anyone at the time of his call already circumcised? Let him not seek to remove the marks of circumcision. Was anyone at the time of his call uncircumcised? Let him not seek circumcision" (NRSV). On the possible exclusively Jewish character of the Colossians "heresy," see James D. G. Dunn, *The Epistles to Colossians and Philemon: A Commentary on the Greek Text,* NIGTC (Grand Rapids: Eerdmans, 1996).

[62]One thinks, e.g., of treatments of Philippians 3 with a proliferation of no fewer than three or four groups of opponents: a circumcision group (Phil 3:2-11), perfectionists born of overrealized eschatology (Phil 3:12-16), and then antinomians (Phil 3:17-21), sometimes with proto-gnosticism seasoning the mix (see, e.g., the survey in Joseph B. Tyson, "Paul's Opponents at Philippi," *PRS* 3, no. 1 [1976]: 83-96; for characteristic reserve, see Morna D. Hooker, "Philippians: Phantom Opponents and the Real Source of Conflict," in *Fair Play: Diversity and Conflicts in Early Christianity; Essays in Honour of Heikki Räisänen* [Leiden: Brill, 2002], 377-95).

[63]The argument assumes the integrity of Philippians as a single letter. See David E. Garland, "The

what might be only a distant threat toward rhetorical advantage to compose one of his most poetic and pathetic soliloquies to salvation (Phil 3:2-21). This, arguably, is a Pauline pedagogical modus operandi, to exploit occasions of correction as opportunities for exposition. Both historical and theological interpreters of Paul are engaging something equally true to the character of his writings.

This is perhaps what makes Wright's account of Paul so compelling to many while also frustrating to others.[64] Perhaps more than any recent Pauline scholar, Wright understands—one is tempted to say "intuits"—the breadth of the Pauline vision and program and is not content to reduce it to discrete pieces of exigent counterpunching. It is not merely that certain Jewish Christians stopped eating with Gentiles in Antioch. It is that in doing so they denied a common patrilineage according to faith to a single forefather, Abraham, who was himself a first second Adam through whose progeny, Israel, God would remake a broken cosmos in accord with his covenant faithfulness in anticipation of the promise's more ultimate fulfillment in the Second Adam, the Seed, the Messiah, the paradoxical, counterimperial Davidic king, in whom there is neither Jew nor Greek, slave nor free, male or female, but one incorporate people of God proleptic of a world set to rights. *That's* why they need to have mixed dinner parties in Antioch! While not everyone will be convinced that all of that can be teased out of Galatians 2 and 3 or even from the (ten-letter) Pauline corpus as a whole, it is hard not to prefer this sort of narratival, typological grand story to the sometimes cynical reductionism that one can find in some arid, divide-and-conquer, historical-critical accounts. In any case, Wright follows in the steps of his ancient mentor in finding that there are no matters that are merely practical in nature, if "practical" means un-theological.

Paul would thus exploit the theological potential of the relationship of Jew and Gentile with different degrees of urgency and toward a variety of

---

Composition and Unity of Philippians: Some Neglected Literary Factors," *NovT* 27, no. 2 (1985): 141-73; and Duane F. Watson, "A Rhetorical Analysis of Philippians and Its Implications for the Unity Question," *NovT* 30, no. 1 (1988): 57-88.

[64]Though having differences with Wright on any number of details, to the extent that they also honor Paul as an exegete and a theologian and not merely a scrappy operative, Richard Hays (e.g., *The Conversion of the Imagination: Paul as Interpreter of Israel's Scripture* [Grand Rapids: Eerdmans, 2005]) and Francis Watson (e.g., *Paul and the Hermeneutics of Faith*) share this characteristic.

theological ends. What was a crisis requiring immediate intervention in Galatians manifests itself differently through the course of the Pauline corpus, and Paul's reflection on the matter takes on different shades from the beginning to the end of his traceable corpus. The first account of the Judaizing crisis exposed the vulnerability and threatened the viability of the Pauline mission (Gal 2:2). But by Colossians and Ephesians the relationship of Jews to Gentiles is no longer an imposing conundrum but, rather, a crisis averted, at least theologically if not actually. The union of Jew and Gentile in one body functions as a sign of God's larger restorative triumph in Christ (e.g., Col 3:10-11; Eph 2:11-22; 3:4-12). From the perspective of Ephesians and Colossians, the unity of Jew and Gentile into one body is not a crisis to avert but an accomplished reality to celebrate.

We cannot know with any certainty how sanguine and untroubled was the relationship between Jews and Gentiles in local assemblies. The evidence that we do have suggests that it always remained more of an ideal than a reality, that an enduring pax among a united, though ethnically mixed, people proved hard to sustain.[65] According to Paul's letters, conflict, directly or indirectly ethnic in character, bedeviled the churches of Galatia, Corinth, Philippi, Colossae and Rome, and all of Paul's mission outposts were viewed with suspicion by the saints in Jerusalem. The incomplete evidence of the final third of the first century and the first half of the second suggests that a harmonious, Jewish and Gentile mixed church was an exception rather than the norm. And yet, Paul is happy to speak of the shared commonwealth of Jew and Gentile (Eph 2:12-14) and the nondistinction between Jew and Greek as the "new person" being renewed in the image of the Creator (Col 3:10-11). There is reason, then, to doubt that Paul is speaking so much about the empirical conditions of these churches as of the eschatological accomplishment wrought in Christ that energizes his ministry (see esp. Col 1:24–2:3; Eph 3:1-13). It is a truism of Pauline scholarship that the referent of "church" in these later letters has mostly transitioned from local assemblies to the universal

---

[65]Terence L. Donaldson, *Judaism and the Gentiles: Jewish Patterns of Universalism (to 135 CE)* (Waco, TX: Baylor University Press, 2007); James D. G. Dunn, *The Partings of the Ways: Between Christianity and Judaism and Their Significance for the Character of Christianity*, 2nd ed. (London: SCM, 2006); and idem, *Neither Jew nor Greek: A Contested Identity*, Christianity in the Making 3 (Grand Rapids: Eerdmans, 2015).

body of which Christ is head (although Col 4:15-16).[66] And in that "church," there are no longer scruples and squabbles, but "one new person" in Christ. No longer is Paul fighting for the Gentiles' place at the table (literally), as in Galatians. No longer, as in Romans, is he upbraiding smug Gentiles and putting them in their place by reminding them whence their inheritance. No longer is justification apart from works of the law his soteriological refrain. Indeed, I suggest that this is the very reason that Ephesians stands apart from Galatians and Romans as the exception that proves the rule, where justification language is *not* Paul's vehicle for establishing Jew-Gentile rapprochement. All of this is now settled and patent—cause for doxology rather than an argument buttressed by Scripture. "Gentile" is no longer an ethnic-primary designation but a socioreligious category, to which ethnic Gentiles incorporated into Christ *no longer belong.* Thus, Paul must describe them as merely Gentiles "in flesh" (*en sarki*). Having been incorporated into a new socioreligious entity, their primary identity now lies in the "one new person out of two, created in Christ" (Eph 2:14); "Gentile" no longer describes their primary identity. Thus, the ethnically Gentile readers of Ephesians are "no longer to walk as the Gentiles walk" (Eph 4:17). Even though they remain "Gentile in flesh," in terms of basic loyalties and group ethos, they are not "Gentiles" any longer. Nor are Jews who have been incorporated into Christ first Jews, even though it is *their* commonwealth into which the Gentiles have been granted naturalized citizenship. That God in Christ has "created one new person out of two" is a settled fact. Indeed, the accomplishment of one people of God in one faith, one church, one baptism, under one Lord is an object lesson to the malevolent powers (Eph 3:10). Conflict among members does not invalidate the triumph of God in Jesus Christ.

8.2.3 From impotent to "good": works redeemed. It might come as a surprise to some of Paul's readers on this side of the Reformation just what a cheerleader the apostle was on behalf of "works." As charted below, besides the occasional, though hardly incidental, disavowal of works as a means of salvation (Eph 2:9; Tit 3:5; 2 Tim 1:9), the dominant note of the Prison and

---

[66]E.g., Rudolf Schnackenburg, *Ephesians: A Commentary* (Edinburgh: T&T Clark, 1991), 193-94. The attempt to blunt this conclusion by appealing to an eschatological ἐκκλησία or a "heavenly gathering" is unpersuasive (e.g., in Peter T. O'Brien, "The Church as a Heavenly and Eschatological Entity," in *Biblical Interpretation and the Church: Text and Context*, ed. D. A. Carson [Exeter: Paternoster, 1984], 88-119; cf. Peter T. O'Brien, "Church," *DLNT*, 125-26).

Pastoral Epistles is an unabashed commendation of "*good* works" (*agatha* or *kala erga*), an expression found no fewer than eighteen times in these letters, though, at best, weakly attested in the earlier letters.[67] See table 8.2.

Table 8.2. Commendations of "good works"

	Galatians 0x	Thessalonian and Corinthian Correspondences 3x	Romans 2x	Captivity Epistles 3x	Pastoral Epistles 15x
"work" (*ergon*, sg.) affirmed or commended		1 Thess 1:3	Rom 2:7; 13:3		
"good [*kalos*] works"				Phil 1:6	1 Tim 5:10, 25; 6:18; 2:10; Tit 2:7, 14; 3:8, 14
"good [*kalos*] work"					1 Tim 3:1
"good [*agathos*] works"				Eph 2:10	1 Tim 2:10
"every good work" *pan agathon ergon*		2 Thess 2:17; 2 Cor 9:8		Col 1:10	1 Tim 5:10; 2 Tim 2:21; 3:17; Tit 1:16; 3:1

The most obvious explanation for this dramatic difference between the undisputed and disputed letters is again that the latter are inauthentic, that it is patently un-Pauline to commend "works" this profligately.[68] But this flies in the face not only of Paul's occasional restrained appeal to such in the

---

[67]Earlier appeals to this theme are at best tepid, notably all of them singular. In 1 Thessalonians 1:3, Paul commends "your work [ἔργον] of faith and labor of love and steadfastness of hope." However one takes these genitives, clearly the "work," "labor" and "steadfastness" are in some way qualified by the associated virtues, probably as their impetus (an authorial genitive). Thus, work, labor and steadfastness are visible fruit of more primary virtues. In the benedictory wish of 2 Thessalonians 2:17, Paul prays that his readers will be established in "every good work and word" (ἐν παντὶ ἔργῳ καὶ λόγῳ ἀγαθῷ). "Word and deed" is an idiom suggesting comprehension and integrity of speech and action (cf. Lk 24:19; Acts 7:22; Rom 15:18; 2 Cor 10:11; Col 3:17; 1 Jn 3:18), such that no particular emphasis can be drawn to the "work." Second Corinthians 9:8 is thus unique in the earlier Pauline letters in commending "every good work," but even this, in context, should probably be taken to refer not to good deeds in general but to acts of generosity (cf. Phil 1:6) flowing from God's supply of abundance and the resulting self-sufficient satisfaction (αὐτάρκεια). Romans 2:7 speaks of "good work" as a basis for the judgment of Gentiles apart from the law (and apart from Christ?), and Romans 13:3 articulates the abstract generalization that governing powers are predisposed to punish not "good work" but rather evil. Thus, arguably there is no direct precedent for the general commendation of "good works" preceding the Captivity and Pastoral Letters.

[68]So, e.g., Bart D. Ehrman, *Forgery and Counterforgery: The Use of Literary Deceit in Early Christian Polemics* (New York: Oxford University Press, 2013), 185-87; cf. 302.

undisputed letters but also his ubiquitous commendation of obedience, charity, chastity and moral rectitude generally, especially in the hortatory sections of those letters.[69] If Paul insists that "works" do not justify in Romans, he is equally insistent that the "obedience of faith" is the ultimate goal of the Gentile mission (Rom 1:5; 16:26; cf. 15:18; 16:19). Moreover, a lived holiness, a freedom from sin and an unalloyed obedience to God and unfeigned charity toward neighbor are as much the promise of the letter's theological discourse (Rom 6:1–8:27) as of the charge of its paranaetic "afterword" (Rom 12:1–15:12). Moral transformation and performed obedience befitting newness of life (Rom 6:4) are simply part and parcel of the Pauline gospel, not just an awkward appendage.

Therefore, two complementary hypotheses commend themselves as preferable to the pseudonymity explanation. First, as Barclay has now amply demonstrated, there is no fundamental conflict between grace and obedience in Paul. As he frequently reminds us, the unconditioned gift is not unconditional. Thus, a supposed conflict between grace and works is not a sort of "creative tension" but rather a confusion between grace's perfections of incongruity and noncircularity. It would become a tension—creative or not—only because "grace" would come to mean the aggregate of its rhetorically wielded perfections. But, for Paul, grace is incongruous but not for that reason nonreciprocal. Minimally, the gift of Christ evokes grace's cognate counterpart, gratitude.[70] That much is uncontroversial. No less fitting responses to the gift, and no different in kind, include fealty, fidelity, obedience, replication and imitation. "Good works" are merely the overflow and concretization of these relational a prioris.

This, however, does not explain the abrupt profusion of this language in certain Captivity Letters and all the Pastoral Epistles in the face of its almost complete absence in the undisputed letters. Even if we establish that Paul had no allergy to righteous deeds, it could be argued that he has reason to be chary of the language of "works" and "good works" in the press of controversy and is determined to depict a gratuitous salvation. It may be, however, that Paul's enthusiasm for "good works" in his later letters should be treated as the fruit of a theological accomplishment. Having disparaged

---

[69]Galatians 5–6; 1 Thessalonians 4; 1 Corinthians 5–6; Romans 6; 8; 12–15; Philippians 3–4.
[70]As noted above, χάρις can refer to either; see BDAG, s.v. χάρις (3) and (5), 1079-80.

"works" as soteriologically impotent in his earlier letters, having established the sheer gratuity of salvation thereby and now having disentangled "works" from any soteriological accomplishment, Paul has created the space, absent external voices to the contrary, to show "works" to be salutary, fitting and even, in a qualified sense, necessary in the later letters. "Works"—"of the law," "good" or otherwise—are not the condition of grace; they do not avail to justification. But in the settled synthesis accomplished in Romans and confirmed repeatedly in the succeeding letters, Paul has every reason to commend "good works" as befitting a new creation in Christ.

The synthesis can be articulated no more clearly than in the famous juxtaposition of Ephesians 2:8-9 ("not of works lest anyone should boast") and Ephesians 2:10 ("created in Christ Jesus for good works which he prepared in advance that we should walk in them"). This amounts to Paul's entire settled position, stated in as few words as necessary. Grace being incongruous for Paul, "works" will make no contribution to salvation; only receptive trust (*pistis*) will do, not as a work but as a receptive posture yielding all to the gift. At the same time, "good works" proliferate as the overflow of the gift paid forward, in imitation of the generosity of God revealed in the gift of Christ (Eph 5:1). Such works are befitting of the new creation, God's "workmanship," and, indeed, are prepared in advance that we might walk in them.

Similarly, in Titus, good works "adorn [*kosmeō*] the doctrine of God our savior" (Tit 2:10). Rectitude and sobriety not only quell the inevitable defamation wrought of suspicion (*hina*, Tit 2:5, 8, 10) but also commend the Christian ethos as its own winsome apologetic for Christian truth.[71] Indeed it is none other than grace itself that disciplines its objects to "deny ungodliness and worldly passions and to live sober, upright, and godly lives in this world" (Tit 2:11-12). Far from apprehensive of "works," Paul declares that Christ gave himself for the very purpose of redeeming from all iniquity and purifying to himself a "peculiar" people, *zealous for good works* (Tit 2:14). As depicted in the later letters, such "good works" are not merely evidentiary

---

[71]Although written with the *Haustafel* of 1 Peter in mind, Balch's description of the social background of early Christianity as a threat held in suspicion remains very useful for appreciating the Pauline *Haustafeln* and the Pastoral Epistles more generally (see David L. Balch, *Let Wives Be Submissive: The Domestic Code in 1 Peter*, SBLMS 26 [Atlanta: Scholars Press, 1981]). On this passage, see Alan Padgett, "The Pauline Rationale for Submission: Biblical Feminism and the *hina* Clauses of Titus 2:1-10," *EvQ* 59, no. 1 (1987): 39-52.

of something more basic but are integral to gospel itself, just as grace is not the mere forbearance of iniquity but the transforming power animating the new creation. Having overcome the misapprehension of "works" as the creditable merits of self-worthiness, Paul enjoys the unselfconscious freedom to commend "good works" lavishly as the fruit of the very same grace.

8.3 CONCLUSIONS

In the immediately preceding chapters we have surveyed developments in the deployment of Paul's soteriological language: from "works of the law" to "works" more generally, the evolution of grace, the early function of "justification" and Paul's eventual preference for "salvation" and "reconciliation." I have argued that this is driven not merely by the rhetorical exigencies of particular letters but by a larger soteriological development. In this trajectory we note a transition from the crisis provoked by the Gentile mission to an increasingly settled, principial determination that the saving work of Christ is apprehended apart from human performance, received as an incongruous gift.

Here I have argued that there are yet more grounds for understanding Paul's soteriology in developmental terms. Contrary to widespread assumptions, Galatians and Romans are not as similar in circumstance, argument and theology as frequently presumed; Romans is not merely the expansion of a recently written Galatians. Indeed, one evidence normally cited in favor of their close kinship, the use of the same scriptural texts, actually points up differences upon closer examination. In certain cases, Paul's countering interpretations of the opponents' proof texts in Galatians enable him to deploy those same texts constructively to ground his resolving soteriological vision. But perhaps the most consequential transition between Galatians and Romans is the appeal to human guilt before God as the explicit dilemma for which the saving work of Christ is the remediation, producing, in Romans for the first time, the familiar shape of the gospel as "plight to solution." This will remain the shape of the gospel's articulation from Romans through the subsequent letters, and the degree to which this innovation becomes a trope within Paul's resolving soteriology is further evidence of the thoroughgoing character of his soteriological development. That this becomes Paul's "gospel" does not mean that it was always so; it does not require that this have been the original Pauline kerygma; and it certainly is not an interpretive frame for understanding Paul's own conversion nor for stereotyping the existential necessities of those that should follow. But it does become Paul's settled theological position that human guilt and enslavement are universal, that the guilt and bondage are ameliorated in the cross and resurrection of Jesus Christ, and that acquittal and liberation are received apart from deserving works but by incongruous grace in the union of formerly guilty and enslaved humans with the atoning and triumphant Christ. These are claims now made without respect to the ethnic membership of the guilty and enslaved persons, that plight being universal to all. This becomes Paul's gospel. It was not always so, although its seeds were planted already in Paul's conversion, and it was budding already in the letter to the Galatians.

Finally, we observed that early fixtures of Paul's letters, the crisis between Jew and Gentile and the impotence of works for salvation are transmuted in Paul's later letters in light of their earlier resolution. The Jew-Gentile crisis is resolved (if not in fact, in principle), and what had been the greatest threat to Paul's entire project, potentially rendering it void, now becomes a sign of Christ's triumph, a new humanity united to one another in the "new man," Jesus Christ. Likewise, "works," having been disparaged for their impotence to save in the earlier letters, are now, especially in the PE, commended and promoted immoderately and untroubled with the aid of the distinguishing adjective "good." Both the triumph of Jew-Gentile reconciliation and the now surprisingly facile commendation of good works are signs and outworkings of the Pauline soteriology having resolved to his satisfaction with such equanimity (again, in principle if not necessarily in existential fact) that Paul enjoys an unrestrained freedom to pronounce and commend with regard to matters of previous crisis and controversy. That Paul reaches this resolution does not efface the earlier crises and controversies, such that Paul's later resolution should be read backwards into the earlier texts. Nor does Paul's *theological* resolution mean that all is well with regard to the practical realities facing the communities under his influence. We have every reason to suppose that conflict, dissension and misunderstanding continue to abound on the ground, but these do not cancel the clarity of Paul's synthesis, and it is this settled synthesis that becomes the canonical witness to an ever-troubled and frequently confused church of the succeeding generations.

9

CONCLUSIONS

9.1 WHERE WE'VE BEEN

The proposal of this book is that contradictory schools of Pauline interpretation are both right, just not at the same time. The shortcomings of both the TPP and NPP are accounted for in the same way: both schools of interpretation are insufficiently attentive to the manner in which Paul's soteriology has developed from his earliest to later writings. As a result, characteristic readings of particular letters take on a controlling paradigmatic function, becoming the unarticulated basis for reading the others. To the extent that both paradigms work toward a Pauline synthesis, it matters rather much which letters and what set of concerns function so as to define terms and, conversely, what definitions of terms are brought to the letters and whence derived. The thesis of this study is that the new perspective on Paul is Paul's oldest perspective and that the "old" perspective describes what would become (more or less) Paul's settled "new" perspective. The characteristic concerns of the NPP have gone a long way toward illuminating the socioreligious context, especially of Paul's letters to the Galatians and Romans, though not always as convincingly with respect to the latter. Meanwhile, the TPP reads Galatians largely as an early summary of *its* reading of Romans. And because both parties have conducted the dialogue largely within the safe precincts of the undisputed letters (and often presuming a late Galatians), it has proven difficult to gain traction on trajectories in Pauline soteriology compressed in so few letters and in such a short time span.

In a survey of the NPP, I have highlighted four characteristic themes, holding each to be a genuine advancement in our understanding of Paul, but each also subject to qualification. (1) Paul's conversion was not a characteristic conversion from irreligion to religious devotion, nor a change in religions; it was a vocation to bear the good news of the crucified and raised Messiah of Israel especially to the Gentiles, which would require a complete revision of Paul's religious inheritance, but not its rejection. (2) Judaism contemporary with Paul is not best characterized on its own terms as an anxious quest for divine acceptance on the ground of merit. This is as true as a generalization can be, but Sanders's synthesis tends to flatten the diversity of Second Temple Judaism and to idealize it within a framework provided by a post-Pelagian Christianity. (3) It is now undeniable that a prominent function of nomistic observance consisted of social differentiation of Judaism from the cultural encroachment of Hellenism. Dunn is correct to highlight this function of the law repeatedly in numerous discussions of "works of the law," and he is further to be credited with modifying his claim into a less exaggerated form. Nonetheless, it cannot be said that Paul's critique of works of the law can be fully accounted for as a censure of Jewish privilege tending toward nationalism; there is more to it, though not less. Nor can NPP's tendency to regard "works" as a shorthand for "works of the law" be sustained. (4) Finally, the NPP has properly reclaimed the role of covenant as fundamental to all of Paul's theological reflection, effectively chastening widespread individualist assumptions that are unhelpfully superimposed upon Paul. Yet the redefinition of justification as the verdict of covenant membership (à la Dunn and Wright) is not convincing.

To then illustrate the almost-but-not-quite accomplishment of the NPP, I reviewed three crux texts, showing that the NPP illuminates the dynamics of each, while leaving certain features of each text inadequately accounted for. Nor, however, do the texts cooperate fully with the TPP. In all of the above, it is my purpose to commend the NPP unstingily for its many insights while cautioning against certain reductive overcorrections.

Next I have surveyed some recent attempts to move beyond the NPP, chiefly by scholars working from a fundamental, though not uncritical, appreciation for the gains of the new paradigm. There we observe a variety of approaches, from self-correction (Dunn and Wright) to moderating and conciliating efforts (Bird, Gorman) to supplanting paradigms (e.g., Watson, Campbell, Barclay). I suggest that in the several decades of reflection on the issues, no consensus has emerged on the other side of the NPP, though correction, conciliation and new paradigms are all welcome. A path not yet taken up in earnest is the one offered here, the proposal that an alternative explanation for the contending interpretations of Paul is Paul himself, not that he is incoherent but that his soteriology develops and in a trajectory not explicable merely with respect to the vicissitudes of particular rhetorical circumstances. I further argued that the protracted argument between the TPP and NPP evinces a larger pattern in contemporary Pauline studies in which antinomies are invoked toward rhetorical advantage, though sometimes forcing needless choices between alternatives or ignoring third options that might enable a more comprehensive vision. The arguments of the third chapter serve the dual function of disentangling muddles cognate to the NPP while also suggesting that not all of them were quite necessary.

Paul's development requires an itinerary, and I offer one in the fourth and fifth chapters. These chapters are offered as premises scaffolding what follows rather than as weight-bearing conclusions. Several of the positions there sketched reflect widely held views (consensus is too much to ask for), in some cases a "minority consensus" (if we may allow the oxymoron). However, the decision to trace Paul's thought through a thirteen-letter corpus is, if hopelessly traditional, unintentionally brash and novel by the standards of historical-critical orthodoxy, though not without historical-critical basis. At the very least, scholarship interested in "Paul" must give some account of the disputed letters, even if as nothing more than the *Wirkungsgeschichte* of the original vision. But I argue that, far from a misunderstanding of or deviation from Paul's soteriology, these letters corroborate a trajectory already evident in the undisputed letters, so much so that one would be justified in thinking that Paul himself wrote them.

The next three chapters compose the heart of the argument. On the controverted matter of the "works of the law," I part company with the TPP's understanding of the phrase as synecdoche for "works" in general (i.e., as soteriologically deficient human effort), and I depart from the NPP's understanding of "works" as mere shorthand for "works of the law" (i.e., as Judaism's social boundaries). Rather, I argue that the disparagement of "works," used absolutely, marks an abstracting and generalizing development in Paul's soteriology, from a remonstrance against Jewish particularity ("works of the law") to a more settled antithesis between works and grace, lest performance should usurp faith as the medium by which God's saving beneficence is appropriated. This later critique of works can be "found" in an early Galatians only if it is already "known" from a later Romans, but it is not native to Galatians other than in seed form at best, indeed mustard seeds. This account of "works / of the law" is corroborated by the traceable evolution of "grace" through the Pauline corpus. As Barclay has argued, before it was a load-bearing pillar of Christian theology, grace was voluntary beneficence—taking many forms, finding worthy subjects and expecting congruent returns. However, as Paul comes to understand divine grace revealed and enacted in Jesus Christ, it seeks unworthy subjects, though still expecting free but congruent responses, beginning with gratitude and ending in free obedience. Departing from Barclay, I argue that this incongruous grace of God takes its very particular shape as the antithesis of human accomplishment increasingly throughout the span of the Pauline corpus, as *charis* becomes the express Pauline counterpart of *erga*, specifically in Romans and patently thereafter.

From these interlocking, mutually informing patterns, I turned to the language of salvation itself. While not ceding to the claim that justification is merely a "polemical doctrine," I confirmed that its particular function as a binary and broadly forensic status was to demonstrate especially that Gentiles in Christ, no less than God's covenantal heirs by nature, stand acquitted and vindicated in union with Christ, in his death and resurrection, appropriated by faith. If the "soteriology" of Galatians charts the reclamation of the Jew and Gentile Abrahamic family in Abraham's seed, Romans not only restores each to the other into one body, but it does so by showing both (once sinful) parties to have been reconciled to one God by grace. This peace making between once estranged peoples forming a single new people is the fruit of justification, but it is clear, if not in Galatians, in Romans particularly that the peace wrought among peoples depends upon a logically prior peace made with God on shared terms—a peace accomplished in justification. But justification, so prominent to the discourses of Galatians and Romans, gives way to other soteriological idioms when the Jew-Gentile crisis is not the presenting symptom. Thus, Paul prefers the language of *sōzō/sōtēria* in the other letters, and it becomes the dominant, most comprehensive and almost exclusive idiom beginning in Romans and continuing in all the succeeding letters. Likewise, reconciliation is unknown, neither the language nor the concept, in Galatians and Paul's earliest letters until 2 Corinthians and Romans, where, especially in the latter, it is the explicit relational fruit of justification. More expansively, it expresses the unlimited scope of God's redemptive purpose in Christ, including not only restored humans but also spiritual forces and the whole created order. These patterns suggest, on the one hand, that the NPP has laid hold to a sort of original Pauline genius in appreciating how he has leveraged justification toward the reconciliation of peoples into one Abrahamic family. On the other hand, by failing to appreciate the intrinsic relationship of justification to the reconciliation of human beings to God, the NPP has insufficiently accented the vertical aspect of justification.

Finally, we considered a variety of signposts, each pointing differently to the same general phenomenon of the development of Pauline soteriology. I argued that, for all their apparent similarities and continuities, Galatians and Romans are "false friends"—that even beyond the chronological separation for which I argued earlier, they are distinct in terms of rhetorical situation and argumentative form. This is evident already because certain of the same Old Testament texts that featured prominently in the argument of Galatians are redeployed with variation in a differently shaped argument in Romans. But the development of greatest consequence is the reframing of the gospel in Romans such that it features the universality of human guilt as the opening gambit for which Christ's saving acts are the remediation. This evangelical "plight to solution" is a Pauline novum, and only with Romans does this become the explicit and stereotyped shape of the gospel, becoming the gospel trope in the succeeding, later letters. That the gospel was reformulated in such terms is not a change so much as a development, fitting to the rhetorical circumstance of Romans but then also suitable as a gospel summation going forward.

Thus Paul's settled, abstract, increasingly "vertical," transformational and expansive gospel becomes Paul's "new perspective." The "new perspective on Paul" and the "traditional Protestant perspective" were thus both right all along—just not at the same time. On balance, the NPP reads Galatians more adroitly (though I have misgivings) than does the TPP, chiefly because the TPP is too eager for Paul to be already the Christian (Augustinian) theologian he will become. Yet, by allowing Paul to be the Christian theologian he *has* become by the end of his letter-writing career, the TPP yields to a patent soteriological synthesis while the NPP keeps kicking against the goads, often unpersuasively.

Finally, the rapprochement offered here succeeds only under two conditions, to be sketched now briefly: (1) that justification cease to be the center and preoccupation of Pauline theology such that it is made to bear weight for which it is not intended and (2) that union with Christ once and for all take its place as the central and integrative fulcrum of Pauline soteriology in all of its juridical, relational, transformational and ecclesial dimensions.

9.2 Putting Justification in Its Place

The span of Paul's soteriology reaches extensively and intensively well beyond the bounds of justification, which served as its footings. That *justification* would become the controverted and divisive term of Christian soteriology is an accident of Christian history,[1] so raising the stakes that a modest account of justification is now rare.[2] It proves difficult to have a measured engagement with respect to "the article upon which the Church stands or falls." Should one assign a properly modest "forensic" definition to Paul's use of the term, one risks skewing the reception of Paul's soteriology into a truncated, narrowly juridical, mechanical quid pro quo.[3] On the other hand, when justification is conscripted into comprehensive soteriological service, when it carries a load more than it should bear, there can be little wonder that it does it badly and confusions of various kinds follow. But the answer is not to make something different of justification. Justification is like a person with three full-time jobs surrounded on every side by the underemployed. It is a

---

[1]For an argument that there was an early and durable consensus, see Thomas C. Oden, *The Justification Reader*, Classic Christian Readers (Grand Rapids: Eerdmans, 2002).

[2]See, however, Stephen Westerholm, *Justification Reconsidered: Rethinking a Pauline Theme* (Grand Rapids: Eerdmans, 2013).

[3]See Campbell's withering rebuke (Douglas A. Campbell, *Deliverance of God: An Apocalyptic Rereading of Justification in Paul* [Grand Rapids: Eerdmans, 2009], 1-95), which, if not entirely fair, is also not without basis as a description of populist evangelical construals of the "gospel."

metaphor that has borne more weight in Christian discourse than was intended for it in biblical discourse. It is inevitable, even to be celebrated, that biblical words and images will be put to uses beyond those intended in their contexts of origin. It becomes problematic when such uses and meanings are retrojected and made constitutive of the original discourse.[4]

The discourse around justification in Paul can be described with respect to two opposite tendencies. On one side are a variety expositions of justification that seek to show that it is an expansive category for Paul, either that the forensic understanding is reductive or that it is not a forensic notion at all. Thus, J. L. Martyn understands justification as "rectification."[5] Wright (cf. Hays) understands justification as covenant membership that is proleptic of the new creation, the first installment of God setting the world to rights (to use Wright's winsome phrase). Gorman gestures to the Orthodox tradition in naming the fuller meaning of justification "theosis."[6] It must be said that these are not simply attractive ideas, but Pauline ideas. What is less clear is that any of these describes what Paul means by "justification." It will not do to expand the dimensions of justification until it encompasses, or at least gestures to, the whole of Paul's soteriology.

As we saw above, that justification needn't "do all the work" itself is indicated by Paul's language that extends his soteriology beyond justification.

---

[4]I realize that I risk diving into deeper hermeneutical water here than my swimming ability justifies. While not discounting the inevitable and sometimes felicitous function of a text's *Wirkungsgeschichte* for readers, the text's reception remains an extension of the life of the text and, at least theoretically, separable from the text itself, whether or not one regards such a separation favorably and however difficult it might be to execute in practice. I simply regard it as hermeneutical common sense that when meanings attach to words that are patently anachronistic, it confounds the efforts of readers to make proper sense of the text.

[5]J. Louis Martyn, *Galatians: A New Translation with Introduction and Commentary*, AB 33A (New York: Doubleday, 1998), 263-75; originally published in idem, *Theological Issues in the Letters of Paul* (Nashville: Abingdon, 1997), 141-56. Cf. Barclay's disavowal:

> One . . . needs very strong warrant to find here a quite different meaning [than "to declare righteous"], "to rectify," "to set things right" (Martyn), or to "make righteous" (de Boer . . .). . . . One can make good sense of Paul's argument in Galatians without departing from the normal meaning of the verb [δικαιόω]: in the case of a believer, God recognizes as "righteous" a person who has been reconstituted in Christ. That reconstitution is articulated *in other terms* ([Gal] 2:19-20), *not conveyed by the verb* δικαιοῦσθαι. The verb describes the recognition by God of the worth of a person who has already been transformed by participation in Christ. (John M. G. Barclay, *Paul and the Gift* [Grand Rapids: Eerdmans, 2015], 375-76n66, italics added)

[6]Michael J. Gorman, *Inhabiting the Cruciform God: Kenosis, Justification, and Theosis in Paul's Narrative Soteriology* (Grand Rapids: Eerdmans, 2009).

Paul's soteriological vision stretches toward the entire cosmos, with the human creation functioning not only as the special object and crown of re- demption but also as its first fruits in union with Christ, himself the firstfruits of the resurrection (1 Cor 15:20, 23) and firstborn from the dead (Col 1:17). Yet justification, having confirmed the relationship of Jews and Gentiles in a single covenant people, recedes while other language takes over. We noted that Paul's use of *sōzō/sōtēria* especially concentrates on salvation with respect to its eschatological completion and fullness, while also serving as a preferred term to encompass the soteriological whole in all its dimensions. Unlike jus- tification, its connotation is less with respect to a status or a principial achievement but with the accomplishment itself in its entirety, frequently accenting consummation. Likewise, reconciliation language, spanning more Pauline letters than justification, accentuates the relational accomplishment of justification while also explicitly in Colossians and Ephesians extending the redemptive reach to the cosmos, heaven and earth, seen and unseen.[7]

Ultimately, there is almost nothing in the NPP, in the "apocalyptic" variant, in forensic Protestantism or in transformational Catholicism that is untrue to Paul's soteriological vision, that is, considered synthetically as a whole. It is true that Paul's soteriology ultimately has God "setting the world to rights," that the Christ event is God's act of "rectification" and that being "saved" is restoration to the image of God represented par excellence in Jesus Christ. Conceptually, this is exactly right—in the Christ event, God has de- feated evil, broken sin, borne judgment and raised and exalted the firstfruits of the future of the cosmos. The creation languishing in misery and beset with futility will awaken to its glorious future already betokened in Christ. Indeed. But this is not what Paul means by "justification." Even if justifi- cation is essential to this whole picture—and most assuredly it is—this is not what justification itself denotes. Paul has other ways of speaking of these

---

[7] I don't suggest that a "cosmic" salvation is previously unattested in the undisputed letters. Already with the reference to "new creation" (2 Cor 5:17; Gal 6:15; cf. Is 65:17; 66:22), Paul is pointing in that direction. Most explicitly, in Romans 8:18-25 he anticipates the creation, now "groaning in travail," "set free from its bondage of decay" and obtaining "the freedom of the glory of the children of God." Likewise, in 1 Corinthians 15, it is not only redeemed persons who are the object of Christ's saving reign; τὰ πάντα will be subjected to God under the vice-regency of Christ (1 Cor 15:27-28; cf. Eph 1:10, 13; Phil 3:21; Col 1:20). For a recent appropriation of the theme, see David G. Horrell, Cherryl Hunt and Christopher Southgate, eds., *Greening Paul: Rereading the Apostle in a Time of Ecological Crisis* (Waco, TX: Baylor University Press, 2010), esp. 63-146.

realities, among them, salvation, the reconciliation of all things (Col 1:20), liberation unto glorious freedom (Rom 8:21), the summing up or recapitulation of all things (Eph 1:10) and so on.

If the wandering of justification beyond its linguistic habitat is a consequential error, it is not the only misstep. Seeking to fence "justification" within forensic environs, other of Paul's interpreters themselves are complicit in saying true things by using Paul's words differently than he does. The casual use of "sanctification" among TPP interpreters is a signal case in point. It is only natural that, in trying to protect justification from an unwarranted expansion, interpreters would press other terms into service, but the choice of "sanctification" is particularly regrettable. "Sanctification" exempts justification from other responsibilities by becoming its capacious alternative, a catchall for every transforming accomplishment of grace, every kind of growth, any good work. There is irony here. Having labored vigilantly to tamp down any semantic inflation with respect to justification, the same interpreters have frequently given sanctification a life of its own. According to a standard working assumption, "sanctification" is a Pauline description of something like progressive growth in holiness and maturation in faith as a phase following and distinct from juridical justification. But this finds little support and not a little contradiction in Paul's actual use of the language. When "sanctification" works as an overflow reservoir for justification, the way Paul actually uses this language confounds the purpose for which it is being invoked.

Paul's use of "sanctification" vocabulary is, like his use of "justification," more circumscribed than the use of the same language in subsequent Christian discourse.[8] While there are certain uses of "sanctification" that *might* be teased into a progressive growth succeeding justification, there are none that are obviously so. Rather, in Paul's use, "sanctification" is a status or, alternatively, a telos, never a *process* as such, other than that the status and telos implicitly prescribe a conformity in disposition and action. Sanctification as status denotes the consecration of the Christian—or, as the case may be, the church—as God's peculiar possession, designated for

---

[8] By sanctification vocabulary, I mean primarily ἁγι- cognates: ἅγιος, ἁγιασμός, ἁγιωσύνη, ἁγιάζω. It is understood that conceptually there is related language having to do with consecration, on the one hand, and purity, on the other (see, e.g., Louw-Nida, §§53.44-52; 88.24-35).

his sacred purposes.[9] It is not an intrinsically moral or ethical category, although it has far-reaching moral implications. Those consecrated to God's possession and service will naturally, though not inevitably, possess themselves in a manner that befits their (true) identity and that is congruent with those purposes for which God has taken them into his possession. But sanctification is frequently Paul's description of a status *already* premised of those in Christ (1 Cor 1:2; 7:14; 1 Thess 4:7; 2 Thess 2:13).[10] Notably, sometimes it is even coordinate, not to say coterminous, with the status of righteousness wrought in justification (1 Cor 1:30; 6:11). Yet the status of sanctification neither depends on nor even necessarily reflects a moral righteousness. As is often noted, Paul speaks of the Corinthians' sanctification in the most unqualified and profligate terms, and yet their moral rectitude was evidently lacking.

Sanctification as "status"—sometimes described as "positional" or "definitive" sanctification[11]—nonetheless does not account for those texts in which "sanctification" or "holiness" is described less as a "position" and more as a goal, an end currently to be sought but fully realized only eschatologically. Thus, numerous texts use the same language to describe not only what *is* the case but also what *ought* and *will* be the case. Notably, Paul says that *hagiasmos* is the "will of God" for the Thessalonians, and then goes on to define a specific dimension, abstinence from sexual immorality (1 Thess 4:3; cf. 4:4, 7). In his discussion of freedom from sin for those baptized in Christ Jesus, twice Paul describes "holiness" as the goal or outcome (*eis hagiasmon*) for those freed from sin's tyranny (Rom 6:19, 22). And, beyond this, Paul also directly attributes "holiness" or "sanctification" as concomitant with the parousia for those in Christ (1 Thess 5:23; Thess 3:13; possibly Eph 5:26-27). Thus, Paul's notion of sanctification both marks identity and engenders aspiration, but neither of these realities is quite what we should call a "process."

---

[9]Cf. Louw-Nida on ἁγιάζω: "To dedicate to the service of and to loyalty to deity—'to consecrate, consecration, to dedicate to God, dedication'" (Louw-Nida, §53.44).

[10]Additionally, this is the implication of Paul's reference to Christians as οἱ ἅγιοι (Rom 1:7; 8:27; 12:13; 16:2, 15; 1 Cor 1:2; 6:1, 2; 14:33; 16:15; 2 Cor 1:1; 8:4; 13:12; Eph 1:1, 15, 18; 2:19; 3:8, 18; 4:12; 5:3; 6:18; Phil 1:1; 4:22; Col 1:2, 4, 12, 26; 3:12; 1 Tim 5:10; Philem 5, 7; and probably 1 Thess 3:13; 2 Thess 1:10). Paul uses the same designation for the Jerusalem Christians (Rom 15:25, 26, 31; 1 Cor 16:1; 2 Cor 9:1, 12).

[11]David Peterson, *Possessed by God: A New Testament Theology of Sanctification and Holiness*, NSBT 1 (Downers Grove, IL: InterVarsity Press, 1995).

Even if some sort of progress eventuates toward the telos, to speak of that progress as "sanctification" is to use the language in a different manner than Paul employs it.[12] Paul gives no basis for designating the maturing of Christians subsequent to justification as "sanctification," and to privilege that language does not begin to cover the landscape of Paul's various images for transformation—obedience, virtue, love, maturity, sojourn, athletic contest, fruit-bearing, image-bearing, and so on, including "transformation" itself[13]— none of which is proper to the specific notion of "sanctification" per se.[14]

The purpose of this excursus on soteriological language is not merely an appeal for semantic precision. Rather, to the extent that either "justification" or "sanctification" takes up more soteriological real estate than it ought, the breadth and diversity of Paul's soteriological conceptions and the evidence for development are easily crowded out. The unfortunate, contrary twin results are that either too much is expected of Paul's justification or too little is expected of Paul's salvation. Extensively, reaching to the cosmos, and intensively, penetrating the human soul, salvation is an all-compassing and, in its several dimensions, integrated notion in Paul—the making right of what had gone wrong. In the numerous metaphors of transformation of human persons, conformity to the image of Christ harbingers the new creation.

---

[12]The process paradigm is resilient. See, e.g., Stanley E. Porter, "Holiness, Sanctification," *DLNT*, 397-401, who, with most interpreters, understands the choice to be between sanctification as status and process. Cf. BDAG, s.v. ἁγιασμός (p. 10): "The use in a moral sense for *a process or, more often, its result* (the state of being made holy) is peculiar to our lit" (emphasis added); and Eric L. Johnson, "Rewording the Justification/Sanctification Relation with Some Help from Speech Act Theory," *JETS* 54, no. 4 (2011): 767-85.
[13]*Obedience*: Romans 1:5; 6:16-17; 15:18; 16:26; 2 Corinthians 7:15; 9:13; Philippians 2:12. *Virtue*: Romans 13:14; Ephesians 4:24; Colossians 3:10, 12, 14. *Love*: e.g., Romans 12:9-10; 13:8-10; 14:15; 1 Corinthians 13:1-13; 16:14; 2 Corinthians 5:14; Galatians 5:6, 13-14; Ephesians 5:2; Philippians 2:1-2; Colossians 3:14; 1 Thessalonians 4:9-10. *Maturity*: "Growth" (αὐξάνω) in Paul is normally used of the church (e.g., 1 Cor 3:6-7; 2 Cor 9:10; Eph 2:21; Col 2:19), although this does not preclude that members of the body also can be said to "grow" (Eph 4:15) or to reach maturity (Eph 4:13; Col 1:28-29). *Sojourn*: 1 Corinthians 10:1-11 (on analogy to Israel in the wilderness; cf. Phil 2:12-18); Philippians 3:18-21. *Athletic contest*: 1 Corinthians 9:24-27; Philippians 3:12-16; 2 Timothy 2:5; 4:7. *Fruit-bearing*: Galatians 5:19-23; Philippians 1:9-11; Romans 6:21, 22; 7:4; Colossians 1:9-11. *Image-bearing*: Romans 8:29; 1 Corinthians 15:48-49; 2 Corinthians 3:18; Colossians 3:9-10; Ephesians 4:24-25; 2 Corinthians 3:18 describes this as a process, suggested both by the present tense μεταμορφούμεθα, temporally coordinate with the present participle κατοπτριζόμενοι, and in the idiom ἀπὸ δόξης εἰς δόξαν ("from one degree of glory to another," RSV, NRSV, ESV; "with ever-increasing glory," NIV). *Transformation*: Romans 12:2; 2 Corinthians 3:18.
[14]On the theme of moral formation in Paul, see now the major contribution of J. Paul Sampley, *Walking in Love: Moral Progress and Spiritual Growth with the Apostle Paul* (Minneapolis: Fortress, 2016).

Therefore, however foundational a forensic acquittal restoring humans to God might be, it remains a tragic distortion should Paul's gospel be reduced to a forensic declaration or a commercial transaction. Motivating the expansive accounts of justification is the understandable concern that, should a Pauline soteriology turn reductively forensic, we are left with "legal fiction," a contractual, nontransformational, even antinomian "salvation," pardoning sinners without quite saving them.[15] And that concern is validated in certain quarters of reductive evangelicalism or in radical "Lutheranism," popularized in well-meaning gospel tracts or in paeans to grace, so-called. Behind the constrictive rejoinders is the reasonable worry that justification by faith apart from works could be compromised if it comes to mean "being made righteous." And that concern is validated in certain quarters of populist Roman Catholic soteriology, or even in the suggestion that final justification will depend upon the performance of righteousness by those initially justified by faith.[16] As it turns out, only the modesty of a forensic justification preserves the original immodesty of the justification of the ungodly apart from works of the law. And only a modest, stay-in-your-lane account of justification grants a properly wide berth for "salvation," "reconciliation" and the array of expansive and transformational images describing

---

[15]This concern seems to inform and then confound a recent review by David J. Neville: Review of *Justification Reconsidered: Rethinking a Pauline Theme*, by Stephen Westerholm, *Review of Biblical Literature Blog*, April 2015, www.bookreviews.org/pdf/9508_10515.pdf. Neville, preferring an apocalyptic construal of justification, reflects the kind of misapprehensions that frequently attend critiques of a forensic account of justification such as Westerholm's, arguing that a declaration of righteousness can only be a miscarriage of justice. Extraordinarily, Neville can say, "Apparently, in Westerholm's understanding, God nevertheless finds or declares *morally* righteous the self-evidently unrighteous if they believe in Jesus Christ" (Neville, Review, 3, emphasis added; cf. p. 6). Of course, that the justified sinner is "morally righteous" is precisely what Westerholm disavows. Thus, Neville betrays a misapprehension not unlike that of Campbell (*Deliverance of God*). In the interest of disavowing justification as a quid pro quo, an acquittal-for-faith exchange, any notion of union with Christ is elided altogether. But, for Paul, justification is crucially premised on a union by faith and baptism to the vindicated *hilastērion*, such that the believer shares in his sin-absorbing death and vindicating resurrection. The result is not a "moral righteousness"—not directly, in any case—but a rescue from guilt and sin's dominion by means of union with the vindicated and victorious Messiah.

[16]The question of works and final judgment is a topic of renewed interest, at least partly as a result of the NPP. See Kent L. Yinger, *Paul, Judaism, and Judgment According to Deeds*, SNSTMS 105 (Cambridge: Cambridge University Press, 1999); and Chris VanLandingham, *Judgment and Justification in Early Judaism and the Apostle Paul* (Peabody, MA: Hendrickson, 2006); the question is surveyed in Alan P. Stanley and Robert Wilkin, eds., *Four Views on the Role of Works at the Final Judgment*, Counterpoints: Bible and Theology (Grand Rapids: Zondervan, 2013).

the perfecting work of grace. Thus justification, for all its importance, is neither the center of Pauline theology nor the center even of Pauline soteriology; rather it is the forensic dimension of Pauline soteriology that was most well suited to ground the essential claim of common Jewish and Gentile membership in the Abrahamic family. Although rooted in this exigent question, justification nonetheless transcends that historical circumstance, though never to become the center, much less the end or the whole, of Pauline soteriology.

9.3 Participation in Christ: The Red Thread of Pauline Soteriology

The constant in Pauline soteriology, transcending the undisputed and disputed letters, the apologetic and constructive, the exigent and the measured, is that salvation—acquittal and vindication, incorporation and transformation—is wrought in the union of humankind with the crucified and resurrected Christ by faith, effected in sacrament, whereby his atonement and victory are made ours. The revival—in truth, a recovery[17]—of interest in the theme of union with Christ and its variants (e.g., participation, incorporation, identification) is one of the more promising, and potentially consensus-building, developments of recent Pauline and New Testament research. Beyond this growing consensus of the centrality of the theme lie a complex set of questions, including its conceptual backgrounds, various grammatical issues, and the ecclesial and sacramental implications, which have been dealt with in great detail elsewhere. It is unnecessary to reprise the data set out in detail in numerous other studies.[18] It is sufficient for our immediate purposes

---

[17]For the theme worked out historically and in New Testament scholarship, see the survey in Grant Macaskill, *Union with Christ in the New Testament* (Oxford: Oxford University Press, 2014), 17-99; and with regard to Pauline scholarship, Constantine R. Campbell, *Paul and Union with Christ: An Exegetical and Theological Study* (Grand Rapids: Eerdmans, 2012), 31-64.

[18]Richard B. Gaffin, *The Centrality of the Resurrection: A Study in Paul's Soteriology* (Grand Rapids: Baker Books, 1978); Herman N. Ridderbos, *Paul: An Outline of His Theology* (Grand Rapids: Eerdmans, 1975); Douglas A. Campbell, "Beyond Justification in Paul: The Thesis of the Deliverance of God," *SJT* 65, no. 1 (2012): 90-104; J. Todd Billings, *Union with Christ: Reframing Theology and Ministry for the Church* (Grand Rapids: Baker Academic, 2011); Robert Letham, *Union with Christ: In Scripture, History, and Theology* (Phillipsburg, NJ: P&R, 2011); Daniel G. Powers, *Salvation Through Participation: An Examination of the Notion of the Believers' Corporate Unity with Christ in Early Christian Soteriology* (Leuven: Peeters, 2001); Michael F. Bird, "Incorporated Righteousness," *JETS* 47, no. 2 (2004): 253-75; Don B. Garlington, "Imputation or Union with Christ? A Response to John Piper," in *Studies in the New Perspective on Paul:*

to note not only how pervasive the theme is but also how integrally it functions as the working presupposition of Paul's soteriological vision. For Paul, salvation is *through* Christ, because it is *in* Christ. Salvation, in all its manifestations, is shaped by and conformed to the Christ narrative that, when it is told in view of the union of Christ with humanity, we know as the gospel.

There is, for example, no disputing the claim that union with Christ stands in a close relationship with justification. If anything, the conclusion is too tepid.[19] There is no *Pauline* way to conceive of justification apart from union with Christ, even if many systematic and popular construals make surprisingly little of it, preferring a model more implicitly transactional or contractual.[20] But the relationship between justification and union with Christ runs deeper than that handful of texts—prominent though they are—in which justification is explicitly premised on union with Christ.[21] If we do not artificially limit ourselves to lexical collocations, it is evident that union with Christ is even more basic to the structure of Paul's understanding of justification than sometimes supposed. Paul's soteriological appropriation of union with Christ is apparent already in Galatians. Paradigmatically Paul is co-crucified with Christ (Gal 2:19, *Christō synestaurōmai*), such that his subsequent life can be described as "Christ living in me" (Gal 2:20). Even more foundationally, Christ is Abraham's seed (Gal 3:16) into whom Gentiles are incorporated as seed (Gal 3:29), becoming heirs by means of incorporation

---

Essays and Reviews (Eugene, OR: Wipf & Stock, 2008), 137-96; Kevin Vanhoozer, "Wrighting the Wrongs of the Reformation? The State of the Union with Christ in St. Paul and Protestant Soteriology," in *Jesus, Paul, and the People of God: A Theological Dialogue with N. T. Wright*, ed. Nicholas Perrin and Richard B. Hays (Downers Grove, IL: IVP Academic, 2011), 235-59; Lane G. Tipton, "Union with Christ and Justification," in *Justified in Christ: God's Plan for Us in Justification*, ed. K. Scott Oliphint (Fearn, Scotland: Mentor, 2007), 23-49; Macaskill, *Union with Christ*; and Michael J. Thate, Kevin J. Vanhoozer and Constantine R. Campbell, eds., *"In Christ" in Paul: Explorations in Paul's Theology of Union and Participation*, WUNT 384 (Tübingen: Mohr Siebeck, 2014).

[19]So, e.g., Constantine Campbell (*Paul and Union with Christ*, 396): "Justification occurs as an outworking of union with Christ."

[20]See Seifrid's important study, showing Melanchthon's influence on construals of justification subsequent to Luther that diminished union with Christ: Mark A. Seifrid, "Luther, Melanchthon and Paul on the Question of Imputation," in *Justification: What's at Stake in the Current Debates*, ed. Mark Husbands and Daniel J. Treier (Downers Grove, IL: InterVarsity Press, 2004), 137-52.

[21]See C. R. Campbell, *Paul and Union with Christ*, 388-90, who cites Romans 3:24 and Galatians 2:17 (ἐν Χριστῷ) and 2 Corinthians 5:21 and Philippians 3:9 (ἐν αὐτῷ). Contra Campbell, the references to διὰ Χριστοῦ (Gal 2:16; Phil 3:9), though expressing "the instrumentality of Christ" (ibid., 389), are not obviously relevant to the question of union with Christ (cf. ibid., 252-55).

through baptism, being "clothed with Christ" (Gal 3:27). This scheme is structurally basic to the notion of justification and Paul's entire soteriology in all of its expressions and developments. Even though the word "justification" is not found in a verse mentioning a "seed" or "baptism," it is clear that the entire discourse of Galatians 3:6-29 concerns "justification" (Gal 3:11, 24), unpacking the paradigmatic claim that Abraham himself was "justified" by faith (i.e., his faith reckoned as righteousness; Gal 3:6 via Gen 15:6). Just as Abraham's righteousness preceded and excluded the law as its basis (Gal 3:11, 21, 24), so also with his Gentile heirs of the promise (Gal 3:8), who are likewise justified exclusive of the law by being incorporated into the Messiah, Abraham's seed, becoming Abraham's heirs according to the promise (Gal 3:29). This *incorporative* description of justification is basic to all others.[22]

Likewise, consider how multidimensionally the union with Christ theme is appropriated in the soteriology of Romans, especially in Romans 3–8. Following the account of human guilt and enslavement, Romans 3:21-26 describes that remediation in terms including union with Christ, "justified freely by his grace, through the redemption *which is in Christ Jesus* [dia tēs apolytrōseōs tēs en Christō Iēsou]" (Rom 3:24). The prepositional phrase "in Christ Jesus" is patent of a variety of interpretations, and one must be wary of overinterpreting the formula. Nonetheless, plausibly the expression can be taken as the "redemption effected by union with Christ."[23] Although the theme of union with Christ is more muted in Romans 4 by virtue of the dominant language of "reckoning" as determined by Genesis 15:6 (Rom 4:2, etc.), still the interior logic of the chapter is once again incorporationist.[24] Gentiles are incorporated into Abraham's family by faith,

---

[22]It is regrettable that in C. R. Campbell's otherwise nearly exhaustive account of union with Christ in Paul overlooks the seed figure in Galatians 3, incorporation into the Abrahamic people of God by means of union with Christ. Campbell's study would be usefully supplemented by a more robust ecclesiology, a theme largely absent in this volume (although see C. R. Campbell, *Paul and Union with Christ*, 268-89 and 381-83, on the body of Christ).

[23]The article τῆς renders τῆς ἐν Χριστῷ Ἰησοῦ as an attributive prepositional phrase, defining τῆς ἀπολυτρώσεως, i.e., "in-Christ-redemption." While it may be taken as locative (redemption found in Jesus Christ) or instrumental (redemption by means of Jesus Christ), emphasis on Christ union of ἐν Χριστῷ Ἰησοῦ in other occurrences in Romans (Rom 6:11, 23; 8:1, 2, 39) supports the same sense here. Moreover, Χριστὸς Ἰησοῦς may well imply a messianic incorporationist sense (i.e., "in Messiah Jesus": N. T. Wright, "The Letter to the Romans: Introduction, Commentary and Reflections," in *NIB*, 10:471-72; and James D. G. Dunn, *Romans*, WBC 38 [Dallas: Word, 1988], 1:180).

[24]Here Wright provides in ample measure what is lacking in C. R. Campbell (Wright, *P&FG*, 4:966-76 and passim).

and justification—atonement and vindication—results from union with Christ, who "was handed over to death for our trespasses and raised for our justification" (Rom 4:25 NRSV). Although it is not strictly required by the argument of Romans 4, it is clear by means of Romans 5:12-21 and 6:2-10, that the death and resurrection in Romans 4:25 result in justification because of the union wrought between Christ and Abraham's seed (Rom 4:13, 16, 18; cf. Gal 3:16, 29).

More emphatic, though differently configured, is the solidarity of Christ with a new humanity in Romans 5:12-21. Although the precise nature of humanity's solidarity with Adam and then with Christ is a matter of long-standing dispute, minimally the argument requires that actions of one have efficacious consequence for the "all." However that solidarity is understood (representation, identification, incorporation or even quasi-biologically) and whether the solidarities are understood in a parallel fashion, it remains the case that some union exists between the forebear and subjects beyond priority in time or mere example.

But it is finally in Romans 6:1-11 that the notion of union with Christ, elsewhere presupposed and hinted at, is made most explicit, though now in another venue. Here it is supremely in the rite of baptism that Paul says that the Christian dies with Christ and is raised with him in newness of life. Despite occasional protestations to the contrary, Paul's view of baptism is realistic and efficacious. In baptism, the believer is submerged into Christ's death, being "co-buried" (*synestaphēmen*) with him into that death *through* baptism, to be raised with him so to walk in newness of life (Rom 6:3-4): "For if we have been united [*symphytoi*] with him in a death like his, we will certainly be united with him in a resurrection like his" (Rom 6:5 NRSV). The liberation of bondage to sin comes in the co-crucifixion (*synestaurōthē*) of the baptisand with Christ (Rom 6:6). Although there are many expressions of union with Christ in Paul, there is none any more explicit than this one, and baptism is not only a vivid picture of the reality but also the ritual means by which it is effected.[25] The significance of the Romans 6 depiction of union

---

[25]Resistance to the idea that Paul is actually speaking of the ritual act of water baptism as the Christian initiation rite is surprisingly persistent (Dunn, *Romans*, 1:311-12, 327-29, although Dunn's treatment is in other respects quite helpful), and it is hard to avoid the suspicion that the less realistic accounts of baptism in Romans 6 are not impositions of anachronistic theological concerns that, without warrant in Paul, have antithesized "sacraments" with faith.

with Christ is not merely sacramental, as important as that is. It also demonstrates that union with Christ spans the soteriological landscape, for union with Christ roots not only justification (cf. Rom 6:7) but also the transformation of newness of life (Rom 6:4), sanctification (Rom 6:19, 22), lived righteousness (Rom 6:13, 16, 18-20). Union with Christ not only courses through the whole of the Pauline corpus but also joins the members of the soteriological body into a coherent whole.

Romans 7 adds yet another picture of union with Christ by means of the image of marriage. *In union with the crucified body* of Christ, the believer's

---

Remarkably, Campbell argues if "buried with Christ" is metaphorical (as it must be), then baptism also must be metaphorical (C. R. Campbell, *Paul and Union with Christ*, 387). Campbell unwittingly registers his dis-ease with Paul's view of baptism in the succeeding paragraph.

A weakness of the first position [that Rom 6 refers to "baptism" only metaphorically] is that it is difficult to disassociate completely Paul's language of baptism into Christ's death from the specific act of baptism. Paul may not be addressing the physical act of baptism in such contexts [presumably Rom 6 (and *other* references to "baptism"?)], but that does not negate any relationship between the metaphor and the practice. A weakness of the second position [that "baptism is the means through which believers participate with Christ in his death," ibid., 384-85] is that it is unlikely that Paul means to say that it is through the act of baptism that believers are actually united to Christ in his death.

Campbell then closes the loop of his circular reasoning by begging the question.

This goes against the metaphorical context in Romans 6, but it also stands in tension with Paul's clear conviction that believers are united to Christ by *faith*, not by an external *rite*. Furthermore, it does not do justice to Paul's apparently indifferent attitude toward the act of baptism; after all, if union with Christ was understood to be effected by the act of baptism, one would expect it to register more highly among Paul's priorities. (ibid., 385-86, emphasis original)

It is clear to Campbell that Paul has set faith over against the "external rite" of baptism, but one has to wonder where Paul has done this: clearly not in Galatians 3, where the "external rite" of baptism is the coup de grâce of Paul's argument for justification by faith rather than works of the law (Gal 3:27)! Campbell's antithesizing faith and baptism is rooted not in Paul but in an a-sacramental reading of New Testament soteriology by which baptism and the Lord's Supper are mistakenly conflated with works of the law in a patent contradiction of Paul's own view.

As for Paul's alleged indifference toward the act of baptism, this can only come from one passage, 1 Corinthians 1:13-17 (cf. ibid., 335-36), not, e.g., from Romans 6:3-4, 1 Corinthians 12:13, Galatians 3:27, Ephesians 4:5 or Colossians 2:12. In 1 Corinthians, however, it is clear that there is no antipathy toward baptism per se; rather, Paul objects to the false and divisive Corinthian presumption that being baptized by a certain Christian leader had a significance independent of baptism into Christ himself. Paul's imprecise memory (1 Cor 1:16) and his disclaiming that he was sent to baptize (1 Cor 1:17) are, of course, rhetorical flourishes toward the larger point (contra ibid., 336).

In the end, it appears that Campbell wishes that if Paul had meant that the rite of baptism effected union with Christ that he had said so, but more often than in Romans 6:4 (συνετάφημεν οὖν αὐτῷ διὰ τοῦ βαπτίσματος εἰς τὸν θάνατον); Galatians 3:27 (ὅσοι γὰρ εἰς Χριστὸν ἐβαπτίσθητε, Χριστὸν ἐνεδύσασθε); Colossians 2:12 (συνταφέντες αὐτῷ ἐν τῷ βαπτισμῷ); and 1 Corinthians 12:13 (καὶ γὰρ ἐν ἑνὶ πνεύματι ἡμεῖς πάντες εἰς ἓν σῶμα ἐβαπτίσθημεν).

former marriage to the law has been dissolved so that he or she might "belong to another," bearing righteous fruit unto God (Rom 7:4-6). Not only is the image of union marital, but also the full picture is procreative, "fruit" being the righteous "offspring" born of union with Christ. Though a different metaphor of union, here again the unity of Paul's soteriological whole resides in union with Christ. The dissolution and remarriage have everything to do with a new status—indeed, *legal* status—but it is at the same time *relational* status that bears righteous fruit. Although there is taxonomic value in distinguishing, say, a forensic from a transformative dimension of soteriology for lexical purposes, union with Christ resists an artificial dis-integration of the soteric whole.

Finally, in Romans 8, union with Christ resounds in multiple expressions. Those "in Christ Jesus" are now free of condemnation (Rom 8:1). God has condemned sin "in the flesh" of Jesus Christ, thus rendering that judgment exhausted for those who are in Christ (Rom 8:3). Moreover, the vivifying and transforming effects of union with Christ are mediated in the Spirit, through whom the just requirement of the law is fulfilled when allegiance is transferred from the flesh to the Spirit.[26] Indeed, to have the Spirit is to have the Spirit *of Jesus Christ*, which is to belong to Christ (Rom 8:9) and to be indwelt by Christ himself (*Christos en hymin*), who indwells by means of the Spirit (Rom 8:10-11). That mutual indwelling, that belonging irrevocably to Christ, means that God's children in Christ are co-heirs (*synklēronomoi*) of Christ and, provided they are also co-sufferers (*sympaschomen*), they are also co-glorified (*syndoxasthōmen*). All this shared identity and destiny, premised on union with Christ, gains a decidedly triumphant eschatological cast in the verses that follow, wherein those Christ redeemed come to share in his glory and exaltation, who is the "firstborn among many brethren" (Rom 8:29). In Christ, they know a full acquittal (Rom 8:30-34) and safe passage through all earthly harm and hostility to their eschatological home (Rom 8:35-39), enjoying the conformity to the image of the Son, in which the *imago Dei* is fully restored (Rom 8:29).

Space prevents, and the thorough studies of others make unnecessary, a treatment letter by letter of what Galatians and Romans already demonstrate,

---

[26]That Paul speaks of τὸ δικαίωμα τοῦ νόμου being fulfilled "in us who *walk* not according to the flesh but according to the Spirit" implies that it is not only that justice is satisfied in an atonement (Rom 8:3) but also that the actual intent (δικαίωμα) of the law is satisfied in practice in the behaviors (περιπατέω) of lives conditioned by the Spirit.

that union with Christ pervades the Pauline corpus and integrates his soteriological discourse as the presupposition sine qua non. It should also be noted that if linguistic and theological diversity otherwise disturbs the unity of the disputed espistles with the undisputed, it is not so as it concerns the theme of union with Christ. The disputed letters bear no less testimony to this foundational theme, if anything, more. The "in Christ [him/whom]" formula dominates the discourse of Ephesians and Colossians and is prominent in the Pastoral Epistles as well.[27] In Christ are found redemption, forgiveness, election, salvation, reconciliation, peace, grace, vocation and holiness. And while it can be debated as a fine point of grammar to what extent each occurrence is locative or instrumental and so on, the larger and unmistakable point is that all such soteriological blessings not only reside in Christ but also are commuted by means of union with the same. The same dynamic stands behind the proliferation of *syn*- ("co-," "with") compounds in certain of these same letters. Believers die with Christ and so live with him (2 Tim 2:11), and indeed will share in his reign (2 Tim 2:12). In baptism, believers are buried with Christ and also raised with him (Col 2:12); they are made alive together with Christ (Col 2:13; Eph 2:5); they are raised and co-seated with Christ (Col 3:1; Eph 2:6). In Christ, believers are co-constructed into a dwelling for God in the Spirit (Eph 2:22).

This profound concentration of mutually reinforcing language points together in the same direction. Pauline soteriology is not merely a collage of images drawn from diverse metaphorical worlds, metaphors contending for centrality in an agonistic taxonomy. Rather, the very shape of Pauline soteriology as death, resurrection and exaltation to glory is owed to the saving progenitor of a new humanity that, having participated in his fate, shares his destiny—he having become what we were, we becoming what he is. Indeed, we might say that "*in* Christ Jesus" there is neither imputed nor imparted righteousness, neither justification nor sanctification, neither old nor new perspectives, but Christ is all in all.

---

[27]Ephesians 1:1, 3, 4, 7, 9, 10, 12, 13, 20; 2:6, 7, 10, 13, 15, 16, 21, 22; 3:6, 11, 12, 21; 4:21, 32; Colossians 1:2, 4, 14, 16, 17, 28; 2:3, 6, 7, 9, 10, 11, 12, 15; 1 Timothy 1:14; 3:13; 2 Timothy 1:1, 9, 13; 2:1, 10; 3:12, 15. On which, see esp. C. R. Campbell, *Paul and Union with Christ*, 67-199.

BIBLIOGRAPHY

Aageson, James W. "Judaizing." In *ABD*, 3:1089.

Alexander, L. C. A. "Chronology of Paul." In *DPL*, 115-23.

Anderson, Garwood P. "Justification, Paul and Bishop N. T. Wright." In *Justification in Anglican Life and Thought*, ed. Daniel J. Westberg and Jordan Hylden. Eugene, OR: Pickwick, forthcoming.

———. "Wrestling a Strawman: Doug Campbell's *The Deliverance of God*." *The Living Church*, March 9, 2014, 23-25.

Arnold, Clinton E. *Ephesians*. ZECNT 10. Grand Rapids: Zondervan, 2010.

Augustine. *The City of God (De Civitate Dei)*. Edited by Boniface Ramsey. Translated by William S. Babcock. The Works of Saint Augustine: A Translation for the 21st Century. Hyde Park, NY: New City Press, 2012.

Aune, David E., ed. *The Blackwell Companion to the New Testament*. Malden, MA: Wiley-Blackwell, 2010.

———. "Romans as a *Logos Protreptikos*." In *The Romans Debate*, ed. Karl P. Donfried, rev. ed., 278-96. Peabody, MA: Hendrickson, 2005.

———. *The Westminster Dictionary of New Testament and Early Christian Literature and Rhetoric*. Louisville, KY: Westminster John Knox, 2003.

Baird, William. *The History of New Testament Research*. Vol. 3, *From C. H. Dodd to Hans Dieter Betz*. Minneapolis: Fortress, 2013.

Balch, David L. *Let Wives Be Submissive: The Domestic Code in 1 Peter*. SBLMS 26. Atlanta: Scholars Press, 1981.

Barclay, John M. G. "Believers and the 'Last Judgment' in Paul: Rethinking Grace and Recompense." In *Eschatologie*, 195-208. Tübingen: Mohr Siebeck, 2011.

———. *Jews in the Mediterranean Diaspora: From Alexander to Trajan (323 BCE–117 CE)*. Hellenistic Culture and Society. Edinburgh: T&T Clark, 1996.

———. "Mirror-Reading a Polemical Letter: Galatians as a Test Case." *JSNT* 10, no. 31 (1987): 73-93.

———. *Obeying the Truth: A Study of Paul's Ethics in Galatians*. Studies of the New Testament and Its World. Edinburgh: T&T Clark, 1988.

———. "Paul and the Faithfulness of God." *SJT* 68, no. 2 (2015): 235-43.

———. *Paul and the Gift*. Grand Rapids: Eerdmans, 2015.

———. "Paul, the Gift and the Battle over Gentile Circumcision: Revisiting the Logic of Galatians." *Australian Biblical Review* 58 (2010): 36-56.

———. "Pure Grace?: Paul's Distinctive Jewish Theology of Gift." *Studia Theologica* 68, no. 1 (2014): 4-20.

———. "Unnerving Grace: Approaching Romans 9–11 from the Wisdom of Solomon." In *Between Gospel and Election: Explorations in the Interpretation of Romans 9–11*, 91-109. Tübingen: Mohr Siebeck, 2010.

Barnett, Paul. *Paul: Missionary of Jesus*. After Jesus 2. Grand Rapids: Eerdmans, 2008.

———. *The Second Epistle to the Corinthians*. NICNT. Grand Rapids: Eerdmans, 1997.

Barr, James. *The Semantics of Biblical Language*. London: Oxford University Press, 1961.

Barrett, C. K. *The Epistle to the Romans*. 2nd ed. BNTC. Peabody, MA: Hendrickson, 1991.

———. "The Historicity of Acts." *JTS* 50, no. 2 (1999): 515–34.

Barth, Karl. *Church Dogmatics*. Edited by Geoffrey William Bromiley and Thomas F. Torrance. Edinburgh: T&T Clark, 1936.

Barth, Markus, and Helmut Blanke. *Colossians: A New Translation with Introduction and Commentary*. Translated by Astrid B. Beck. AB 34B. New York: Doubleday, 1994.

Bassler, Jouette M. *Divine Impartiality: Paul and a Theological Axiom*. Chico, CA: Scholars Press, 1982.

———, ed. *Pauline Theology*. Vol. 1, *Thessalonians, Philippians, Galatians, Philemon*. Minneapolis: Fortress, 1991.

Bauckham, Richard. "Barnabas in Galatians." *JSNT* 1, no. 2 (1979): 61-70.

———. *Jesus and the God of Israel: God Crucified and Other Studies on the New Testament's Christology of Divine Identity*. Grand Rapids: Eerdmans, 2008.

Beale, G. K., and D. A. Carson, eds. *Commentary on the New Testament Use of the Old Testament*. Grand Rapids: Baker Academic, 2007.

Beasley-Murray, Paul. "Colossians 1:15-20: An Early Christian Hymn Celebrating the Lordship of Christ." In *Pauline Studies*, 169-83. Grand Rapids: Eerdmans, 1980.

Beker, J. Christiaan. *Paul the Apostle: The Triumph of God in Life and Thought.* Philadelphia: Fortress, 1980.

——. *Paul's Apocalyptic Gospel: The Coming Triumph of God.* Philadelphia: Fortress, 1982.

——. "Recasting Pauline Theology: The Coherence-Contingency Scheme as Interpretive Model." In *Pauline Theology.* Vol. 1, *Thessalonians, Philippians, Galatians, Philemon,* ed. Jouette M. Bassler, 15-24. Minneapolis: Fortress, 1991.

Berger, Peter L., and Thomas Luckmann. *The Social Construction of Reality: A Treatise in the Sociology of Knowledge.* New York: Anchor Books, 1989.

Bernard, J. H. *The Pastoral Epistles.* Grand Rapids: Baker Books, 1980.

Betz, Hans Dieter. *2 Corinthians 8 and 9: A Commentary on Two Administrative Letters of the Apostle Paul.* Hermeneia. Philadelphia: Fortress, 1985.

——. *Der Apostel Paulus in Rom.* Julius-Wellhausen-Vorlesung 4. Berlin: de Gruyter, 2013.

——. "Galatians." In *ABD,* 2:872-75.

——. *Galatians: A Commentary on Paul's Letter to the Churches in Galatia.* Hermeneia. Philadelphia: Fortress, 1979.

Billings, J. Todd. *Union with Christ: Reframing Theology and Ministry for the Church.* Grand Rapids: Baker Academic, 2011.

Bird, Michael F., ed. *Four Views on the Apostle Paul.* Grand Rapids: Zondervan, 2012.

——. "Incorporated Righteousness." *JETS* 47, no. 2 (2004): 253-75.

——. "Incorporated Righteousness." In *Saving Righteousness,* 60-87. Paternoster Biblical Monographs. Eugene, OR: Wipf & Stock, 2007.

——. *Introducing Paul: The Man, His Mission, and His Message.* Downers Grove, IL: InterVarsity Press, 2008.

——. *Jesus and the Origins of the Gentile Mission.* Library of New Testament Studies 331. London: T&T Clark, 2006.

——. *The Saving Righteousness of God: Studies on Paul, Justification and the New Perspective.* Paternoster Biblical Monographs. Eugene, OR: Wipf & Stock, 2007.

Bird, Michael F., and Preston M. Sprinkle, eds. *The Faith of Jesus Christ: Exegetical, Biblical, and Theological Studies (FJC).* Peabody, MA: Hendrickson, 2010.

Blackwell, Ben C. *Christosis: Pauline Soteriology in Light of Deification in Irenaeus and Cyril of Alexandria.* WUNT 2.314. Tübingen: Mohr Siebeck, 2011.

Blackwell, Ben C., John K. Goodrich and Jason Maston, eds. *Paul and the Apocalyptic Imagination.* Minneapolis: Fortress, 2016.

Blass, Friedrich, and Albert Debrunner. *A Greek Grammar of the New Testament and Other Early Christian Literature* (BDF). Translated by Robert W. Funk. Chicago: University of Chicago Press, 1961.

Bockmuehl, Markus N. A. *The Epistle to the Philippians*. BNTC 11. Peabody, MA: Hendrickson, 1998.

Boer, Martinus C. de. *Galatians: A Commentary*. NTL. Louisville, KY: Westminster John Knox, 2011.

———. "Paul and Jewish Apocalyptic Eschatology." In *Apocalyptic and the New Testament: Essays in Honor of J. Louis Martyn*, ed. Joel Marcus and Marion L. Soards, 169-90. JSNTSup 24. Sheffield: JSOT Press, 1989.

Bornkamm, Günther. "The Letter to the Romans as Paul's Last Will and Testament." In *The Romans Debate*, ed. Karl P. Donfried, 3rd ed., 16-28. Peabody, MA: Hendrickson, 2005.

———. *Paul*. Philadelphia: Fortress, 1971.

Braaten, Carl E., and Robert W. Jenson, eds. *Union with Christ: The New Finnish Interpretation of Luther*. Grand Rapids: Eerdmans, 1998.

Bray, Gerald L., ed. *Galatians, Ephesians*. Reformation Commentary on Scripture, New Testament 10. Downers Grove, IL: InterVarsity Press, 2011.

Breytenbach, Cilliers. *Paulus und Barnabas in der Provinz Galatien: Studien zu Apostelgeschichte 13f.; 16,6; 18,23 und den Adressaten des Galaterbriefes*. Leiden: Brill, 1996.

———. "Salvation of the Reconciled (with a Note on the Background of Paul's Metaphor of Reconciliation)." In *Salvation in the New Testament*, ed. J. G. Van der Watt, 271-86. Leiden: Brill, 2005.

———. *Versöhnung: Eine Studie zur paulinischen Soteriologie*. Neukirchen-Vluyn: Neukirchener Verlag, 1989.

Brown, Raymond E. "*Episkopē* and *Episkopos*: The New Testament Evidence." *TS* 41, no. 2 (1980): 322-38.

———. *An Introduction to the New Testament*. ABRL. New York: Doubleday, 1997.

Brox, Norbert. "Zu den persönlichen Notizen der Pastoralbriefe." In *Pseudepigraphie in der heidnischen und jüdisch-christlichen Antike*, 272-94. Darmstadt: Wissenschaftliche Buchgesellschaft, 1977.

Bruce, F. F. *The Acts of the Apostles: The Greek Text with Introduction and Commentary*. 3rd ed. Grand Rapids: Eerdmans, 1990.

———. "The Acts of the Apostles: Historical Record or Theological Reconstruction?" *ANRW* II, no. 25.3 (1985): 2569-603.

———. *The Epistle to the Galatians: A Commentary on the Greek Text*. NIGTC. Grand Rapids: Eerdmans, 1982.

———. *The Epistles to the Colossians, to Philemon, and to the Ephesians.* NICNT. Grand Rapids: Eerdmans, 1984.

———. *Paul, Apostle of the Heart Set Free.* Grand Rapids: Eerdmans, 1977.

———. *Philippians.* UBCS. Grand Rapids: Baker Books, 1989.

Bryan, Christopher. *A Preface to Romans: Notes on the Epistle in Its Literary and Cultural Setting.* New York: Oxford University Press, 2000.

Buck, Charles Henry, and Greer Taylor. *Saint Paul: A Study of the Development of His Thought.* New York: Scribner, 1969.

Bujard, Walter. *Stilanalytische Untersuchungen zum Kolosserbrief als Beitrag zur Methodik von Sprachvergleichen.* Göttingen: Vandenhoeck & Ruprecht, 1973.

Bultmann, Rudolf. *Theology of the New Testament.* Translated by Kendrick Grobel. 2 vols. New York: Scribner, 1951.

Burton, Ernest DeWitt. *A Critical and Exegetical Commentary on the Epistle to the Galatians.* ICC. Edinburgh: T&T Clark, 1921.

Byassee, Jason. "Surprised by Wright." *Christianity Today*, April 2014, 36.

Byrne, Brendan. "Interpreting Romans: The New Perspective and Beyond." *Int* 58, no. 3 (2004): 241-52.

———. "Interpreting Romans Theologically in a Post-'New Perspective' Perspective." *HTR* 94, no. 3 (2001): 227-41.

———. *Romans.* SP. Collegeville, MN: Liturgical Press, 1996.

Campbell, Constantine R. *Paul and Union with Christ: An Exegetical and Theological Study.* Grand Rapids: Eerdmans, 2012.

Campbell, Douglas A. "An Apocalyptic Rereading of 'Justification' in Paul: Or, an Overview of the Argument of Douglas Campbell's *The Deliverance of God*—by Douglas Campbell." *ExpTim* 123, no. 8 (2012): 382-93.

———. "An Attempt to Be Understood: A Response to the Concerns of Matlock and Macaskill with *The Deliverance of God*." *JSNT* 34, no. 2 (2011): 162-208.

———. "Beyond Justification in Paul: The Thesis of the Deliverance of God." *SJT* 65, no. 1 (2012): 90-104.

———. "Christ and the Church in Paul: A 'Post-New Perspective' Account." In *Four Views on the Apostle Paul*, ed. Michael F. Bird, 113-43. Grand Rapids: Zondervan, 2012.

———. *The Deliverance of God: An Apocalyptic Rereading of Justification in Paul.* Grand Rapids: Eerdmans, 2009.

———. "Determining the Gospel Through Rhetorical Analysis in Paul's Letter to the Roman Christians." In *Gospel in Paul: Studies on Corinthians, Galatians and Romans for Richard N. Longenecker*, 315-36. Sheffield: Sheffield Academic Press, 1994.

———. *Framing Paul: An Epistolary Biography*. Grand Rapids: Eerdmans, 2014.

Cannon, George E. *The Use of Traditional Materials in Colossians*. Macon, GA: Mercer University Press, 1983.

Carson, D. A. "Atonement in Romans 3:21-26." In *The Glory of the Atonement: Biblical, Historical & Practical Perspectives: Essays in Honor of Roger Nicole*, ed. Charles E. Hill and Frank A. James III, 121-39. Downers Grove, IL: InterVarsity Press, 2004.

———. "Summaries and Conclusions." In Carson, O'Brien and Seifrid, *JVN:CSTJ*, 1:505-48.

———. "The Vindication of Imputation: On Fields of Discourse and Semantic Fields." In *Justification: What's at Stake in the Current Debates*, ed. Mark Husbands and Daniel J. Treier, 46-81. Downers Grove, IL: InterVarsity Press, 2004.

Carson, D. A., and Douglas J. Moo. *An Introduction to the New Testament*. 2nd ed. Grand Rapids: Zondervan, 2005.

Carson, D. A., Peter T. O'Brien and Mark A. Seifrid, eds. *Justification and Variegated Nomism: The Complexities of Second Temple Judaism (JVN:CSTJ)*. Vol. 1 of 2. WUNT 140. Tübingen: Mohr Siebeck; Grand Rapids: Baker Academic, 2001.

———, eds. *Justification and Variegated Nomism: The Paradoxes of Paul (JVN:PP)*. Vol. 2 of 2. WUNT 181. Tübingen: Mohr Siebeck; Grand Rapids: Baker Academic, 2004.

Case, Shirley Jackson. "To Whom Was 'Ephesians' Written?" *Biblical World* 38, no. 5 (1911): 315-20.

Charlesworth, James H., ed. *The Old Testament Pseudepigrapha*. 2 vols. Garden City, NY: Doubleday, 1983.

Chester, Stephen J. *Conversion at Corinth: Perspectives on Conversion in Paul's Theology and the Corinthian Church*. Studies of the New Testament and Its World. London: T&T Clark, 2003.

Childs, Brevard S. *The Church's Guide for Reading Paul: The Canonical Shaping of the Pauline Corpus*. Grand Rapids: Eerdmans, 2008.

Clark, Bruce. Review of *The Deliverance of God: An Apocalyptic Rereading of Justification in Paul*, by Douglas A. Campbell. *Tyndale Bulletin* 64, no. 1 (2013): 55-88.

Collins, Raymond F. *First Corinthians*. SP 7. Collegeville, MN: Liturgical Press, 2006.

———. *Letters That Paul Did Not Write: The Epistle to the Hebrews and the Pauline Pseudepigrapha*. Good News Studies 28. Wilmington, DE: Glazier, 1988.

Conzelmann, Hans. "χάρις κτλ." In *TDNT*, 9:372-76.

Corley, Bruce. "Interpreting Paul's Conversion—Then and Now." In *The Road from Damascus: The Impact of Paul's Conversion on His Life, Thought, and Ministry,* ed. Richard N. Longenecker, 1-17. McMaster New Testament Studies. Grand Rapids: Eerdmans, 1997.

Cranfield, C. E. B. *A Critical and Exegetical Commentary on the Epistle to the Romans.* 2 vols. ICC. Edinburgh: T&T Clark, 1975.

———. "'The Works of the Law' in the Epistle to the Romans." *JSNT* 14, no. 43 (1991): 89-101.

Cranford, Michael. "Abraham in Romans 4: The Father of All Who Believe." *NTS* 41, no. 1 (1995): 71-88.

Dahl, Nils Alstrup. *Studies in Ephesians: Introductory Questions, Text- and Edition-Critical Issues, Interpretation of Texts and Themes.* Edited by David Hellholm, Vemund Blomkvist and Tord Fornberg. WUNT 131. Tübingen: Mohr Siebeck, 2000.

Das, A. Andrew. "The Gentile-Encoded Audience of Romans: The Church Outside the Synagogue." In *Reading Paul's Letter to the Romans,* ed. Jerry L. Sumney, 29-46 Atlanta: Society of Biblical Literature, 2012.

———. "Paul and Works of Obedience in Second Temple Judaism: Romans 4:4-5 as a 'New Perspective' Case Study." *CBQ* 71, no. 4 (2009): 795-812.

———. *Paul, the Law, and the Covenant.* Peabody, MA: Hendrickson, 2001.

———. *Solving the Romans Debate.* Minneapolis: Fortress, 2007.

Davies, W. D. *Paul and Rabbinic Judaism: Some Rabbinic Elements in Pauline Theology.* London: SPCK, 1948.

Deidun, T. J. *New Covenant Morality in Paul.* Analecta Biblica 89. Rome: Biblical Institute Press, 1981.

Deissmann, Adolf. *Paul: A Study in Social and Religious History.* Translated by William E. Wilson. New York: Harper, 1957.

deSilva, David A. *Honor, Patronage, Kinship and Purity: Unlocking New Testament Culture.* Downers Grove, IL: InterVarsity Press, 2000.

———. *New Testament Themes.* St. Louis: Chalice, 2001.

———. *Transformation: The Heart of Paul's Gospel.* Snapshots. Bellingham, WA: Lexham Press, 2014.

Dibelius, Martin. *The Pastoral Epistles.* Translated by Philip Buttolph. Hermeneia. Philadelphia: Fortress, 1972.

Dodd, C. H. "Atonement." In *The Bible and the Greeks.* New York: Harper & Row, 1932.

———. "Ephesians." In *The Abingdon Bible Commentary*, ed. F. C. Eiselen, E. Lewis and D. G. Downey. New York: Abingdon, 1929.

———. "The Mind of Paul: A Psychological Approach." *BJRL* 17 (1933): 91-105.

———. "The Mind of Paul: Change and Development." *BJRL* 18 (1934): 69-110.

Donaldson, Terence L. *Judaism and the Gentiles: Jewish Patterns of Universalism (to 135 CE)*. Waco, TX: Baylor University Press, 2007.

———. *Paul and the Gentiles: Remapping the Apostle's Convictional World*. Minneapolis: Fortress, 1997.

Donelson, Lewis R. *Pseudepigraphy and Ethical Argument in the Pastoral Epistles*. Tübingen: Mohr, 1986.

Donfried, Karl P., ed. *The Romans Debate*. Rev. ed. Peabody, MA: Hendrickson, 2005.

Donfried, Karl P., and Johannes Beutler. *The Thessalonians Debate: Methodological Discord or Methodological Synthesis?* Grand Rapids: Eerdmans, 2000.

Drane, John William. *Paul, Libertine or Legalist? A Study in the Theology of the Major Pauline Epistles*. London: SPCK, 1975.

Dunn, James D. G. "4QMMT and Galatians." *NTS* 43, no. 1 (1997): 147-53.

———. *Beginning from Jerusalem*. Christianity in the Making 2. Grand Rapids: Eerdmans, 2009.

———. *A Commentary on the Epistle to the Galatians*. BNTC. Peabody, MA: Hendrickson, 1993.

———. "Did Paul Have a Covenant Theology? Reflections on Romans 9.4 and 11.27." In *The Concept of the Covenant in the Second Temple Period*, ed. Stanley E. Porter and Jacqueline C. R. de Roo, 287-307. Leiden: Brill, 2003.

———. *Did the First Christians Worship Jesus?: The New Testament Evidence*. Louisville, KY: Westminster John Knox, 2010.

———. *The Epistles to the Colossians and to Philemon: A Commentary on the Greek Text*. NIGTC. Grand Rapids: Eerdmans, 1996.

———. "'A Light to the Gentiles': The Significance of the Damascus Road Christophany for Paul." In *The Glory of Christ in the New Testament*, ed. L. D. Hurst and N. T. Wright, 251-66. Oxford: Clarendon, 1987.

———. *Neither Jew nor Greek: A Contested Identity*. Christianity in the Making 3. Grand Rapids: Eerdmans, 2015.

———. *The New Perspective on Paul*. Rev. ed. Grand Rapids: Eerdmans, 2008.

———. "The New Perspective on Paul." In *The New Perspective on Paul*, rev. ed., 99-120. Grand Rapids: Eerdmans, 2008.

———. "The New Perspective on Paul." *BJRL* 65 (1983): 95-122.

——. "New Perspective View." In *Justification: Five Views*, ed. James K. Beilby and Paul R. Eddy, 176-201. Downers Grove, IL: IVP Academic, 2011.

——. "The New Perspective: Whence, What and Whither?" In *The New Perspective on Paul*, rev. ed., 1-97. Grand Rapids: Eerdmans, 2008.

——. *The Partings of the Ways: Between Christianity and Judaism and Their Significance for the Character of Christianity.* 2nd ed. London: SCM, 2006.

——, ed. *Paul and the Mosaic Law.* WUNT 89. Tübingen: Mohr Siebeck, 1996.

——. "Paul's Conversion—A Light to Twentieth Century Disputes." In *The New Perspective on Paul*, rev. ed., 347-66. Grand Rapids: Eerdmans, 2008.

——. "Paul's Conversion—A Light to Twentieth Century Disputes." In *Evangelium—Schriftauslegung—Kirche*, ed. Jostein Ådna, Scott J. Hafemann and Otfried Hofius, 77-93. Göttingen: Vandenhoeck & Ruprecht, 1997.

——. "Philippians 3.2-14 and the New Perspective on Paul." In *The New Perspective on Paul*, rev. ed., 469-90. Grand Rapids: Eerdmans, 2008.

——. *Romans.* 2 vols. WBC 38. Dallas: Word, 1988.

——. *The Theology of Paul the Apostle.* Grand Rapids: Eerdmans, 1998.

——. *Unity and Diversity in the New Testament: An Inquiry into the Character of Earliest Christianity.* 3rd ed. London: SCM, 2006.

——. "Works of the Law and the Curse of the Law (Galatians 3.10-14)." In *The New Perspective on Paul*, rev. ed., 121-51. Grand Rapids: Eerdmans, 2008.

Ehrman, Bart D. *Forged: Writing in the Name of God—Why the Bible's Authors Are Not Who We Think They Are.* New York: HarperCollins, 2011.

——. *Forgery and Counterforgery: The Use of Literary Deceit in Early Christian Polemics.* New York: Oxford University Press, 2013.

——. *The New Testament: A Historical Introduction to the Early Christian Writings.* 5th ed. New York: Oxford University Press, 2012.

Elliott, Mark Adam. *The Survivors of Israel: A Reconsideration of the Theology of Pre-Christian Judaism.* Grand Rapids: Eerdmans, 2000.

Elliott, Mark W. "Πίστις Χριστοῦ in the Church Fathers and Beyond." In Bird and Sprinkle, *FJC*, 277-89.

Evans, Craig A. "Jesus and the Continuing Exile of Israel." In *Jesus and the Restoration of Israel: A Critical Assessment of N. T. Wright's "Jesus and the Victory of God,"* ed. Carey C. Newman, 77-100. Downers Grove, IL: InterVarsity Press, 1999.

Fee, Gordon D. *1 and 2 Timothy, Titus.* UBCS. Grand Rapids: Baker Books, 2011.

——. *The First and Second Letters to the Thessalonians.* NICNT. Grand Rapids: Eerdmans, 2009.

———. *The First Epistle to the Corinthians*. NICNT. Grand Rapids: Eerdmans, 1987.

———. *Paul's Letter to the Philippians*. NICNT. Grand Rapids: Eerdmans, 1995.

Ferguson, Everett. *Baptism in the Early Church: History, Theology, and Liturgy in the First Five Centuries*. Grand Rapids: Eerdmans, 2009.

Fitzmyer, Joseph A. "Habakkuk 2:3-4 and the New Testament." In *To Advance the Gospel: New Testament Studies*, 2nd ed., 236-46. Grand Rapids: Eerdmans, 1998.

———. "Reconciliation in Pauline Theology." In *To Advance the Gospel: New Testament Studies*, 2nd ed., 162-85. Grand Rapids: Eerdmans, 1998.

———. "Reconciliation in Pauline Theology." In *No Famine in the Land*, ed. James W. Flanagan and Anita Weisbrod Robinson, 155-77. Missoula, MT: Scholars Press, 1975.

———. *Romans: A New Translation with Introduction and Commentary*. AB 33. New York: Doubleday, 1993.

Gadamer, Hans-Georg. *Truth and Method*. New York: Seabury, 1975.

Gaffin, Richard B. *The Centrality of the Resurrection: A Study in Paul's Soteriology*. Grand Rapids: Baker Books, 1978.

Gale, Herbert M. *The Use of Analogy in the Letters of Paul*. Philadelphia: Westminster, 1964.

Gamble, Harry Y. *Books and Readers in the Early Church: A History of Early Christian Texts*. New Haven, CT: Yale University Press, 1995.

Garland, David E. "The Composition and Unity of Philippians: Some Neglected Literary Factors." *NovT* 27, no. 2 (1985): 141-73.

Garlington, Don B. "Imputation or Union with Christ? A Rejoinder to John Piper." In *Studies in the New Perspective on Paul: Essays and Reviews*, 197-227. Eugene, OR: Wipf & Stock, 2008.

———. "Imputation or Union with Christ?: A Response to John Piper." In *Studies in the New Perspective on Paul: Essays and Reviews*, 137-96. Eugene, OR: Wipf & Stock, 2008.

Gasque, W. Ward. *A History of the Criticism of the Acts of the Apostles*. Beiträge zur Geschichte der biblischen Exegese 17. Tübingen: Mohr, 1975.

Gathercole, Simon J. *Defending Substitution: An Essay on Atonement in Paul*. Acadia Studies in Bible and Theology. Grand Rapids: Baker Academic, 2015.

———. "Justified by Faith, Justified by His Blood: The Evidence of Romans 3:21–4:25." In Carson, O'Brien and Seifrid, *JVN:PP*, 2:147-84.

———. "Romans 1–5 and the 'Weak' and the 'Strong': Pauline Theology, Pastoral Rhetoric, and the Purpose of Romans." *RevExp* 100, no. 1 (2003): 35-51.

―――. "What Did Paul Really Mean?: 'New Perspective' Scholars Argue That We Need, Well, a New Perspective on Justification by Faith." *Christianity Today*, August 1, 2007, 22-28.

―――. *Where Is Boasting?: Early Jewish Soteriology and Paul's Response in Romans 1–5*. Grand Rapids: Eerdmans, 2002.

Gaventa, Beverly Roberts, ed. *Apocalyptic Paul: Cosmos and Anthropos in Romans 5–8*. Waco, TX: Baylor University Press, 2013.

Goodman, Martin. *Mission and Conversion: Proselytizing in the Religious History of the Roman Empire*. New York: Clarendon, 1994.

Goodspeed, Edgar J. *The New Testament: An American Translation*. Chicago: University of Chicago Press, 1923.

Gorman, Michael J. *Apostle of the Crucified Lord: A Theological Introduction to Paul and His Letters*. Grand Rapids: Eerdmans, 2004.

―――. *Becoming the Gospel: Paul, Participation, and Mission*. Grand Rapids: Eerdmans, 2015.

―――. *Cruciformity: Paul's Narrative Spirituality of the Cross*. Grand Rapids: Eerdmans, 2001.

―――. *The Death of the Messiah and the Birth of the New Covenant: A (Not So) New Model of the Atonement*. Eugene, OR: Cascade, 2014.

―――. *Inhabiting the Cruciform God: Kenosis, Justification, and Theosis in Paul's Narrative Soteriology*. Grand Rapids: Eerdmans, 2009.

―――. *Reading Paul*. Cascade Companions. Eugene, OR: Cascade, 2008.

―――. "Wright About Much, but Questions About Justification: A Review of N. T. Wright, *Paul and the Faithfulness of God*." *JSPL* 4, no. 1 (2014): 27-36.

Gorman, Michael J., and J. Richard Middleton. "Salvation." In *NIDB*, 5:45-61.

Green, Joel B. *Salvation*. Understanding Biblical Themes. St. Louis: Chalice, 2003.

Green, Michael. *The Meaning of Salvation*. Philadelphia: Westminster, 1965.

Grieb, A. Katherine. "'So That in Him We Might Become the Righteousness of God' (2 Cor 5:21): Some Theological Reflections on the Church Becoming Justice." *Ex Auditu* 22 (2006): 58-80.

Gundry, Robert H. "The Nonimputation of Christ's Righteousness." In *Justification: What's at Stake in the Current Debates*, ed. Mark Husbands and Daniel J. Treier, 17-45. Downers Grove, IL: InterVarsity Press, 2004.

―――. "Why I Didn't Endorse 'The Gospel of Jesus Christ: An Evangelical Celebration' . . . Even Though I Wasn't Asked To." *Books & Culture*, January/February 2001, www.booksandculture.com/articles/2001/janfeb/1.6.html.

Guthrie, Donald. *New Testament Introduction.* 4th ed. Downers Grove, IL: InterVarsity Press, 1990.

Hahn, Scott. *Kinship by Covenant: A Canonical Approach to the Fulfillment of God's Saving Promises.* New Haven, CT: Yale University Press, 2009.

Hall, Robert G. "Circumcision." In *ABD,* 1:1035-42.

Harink, Douglas K. *Paul Among the Postliberals: Pauline Theology Beyond Christendom and Modernity.* Grand Rapids: Brazos, 2003.

Harnack, Adolf. "Die Adresse des Epheserbriefs des Paulus." *Sitzungsberichte der Königlich Preussischen Akademie der Wissenschaften* 37 (1910): 696-709.

Harris, Horton. *The Tübingen School.* Oxford: Clarendon, 1975.

Harris, Murray J. "2 Corinthians 5:1-10: Watershed in Paul's Eschatology?" *Tyndale Bulletin* 22 (1971): 32-57.

———. *Colossians and Philemon.* Exegetical Guide to the Greek New Testament. Grand Rapids: Eerdmans, 1991.

———. *Raised Immortal: Resurrection and Immortality in the New Testament.* Grand Rapids: Eerdmans, 1985.

———. *The Second Epistle to the Corinthians: A Commentary on the Greek Text.* NIGTC. Grand Rapids: Eerdmans, 2005.

Harrisville, Roy A. III. "Before ΠΙΣΤΙΣ ΧΡΙΣΤΟΥ: The Objective Genitive as Good Greek." *NovT* 48 (2006): 353-58.

———. "Πίστις Χριστου and the New Perspective on Paul." *Logia* 19, no. 2 (2010): 19-28.

———. "ΠΙΣΤΙΣ ΧΡΙΣΤΟΥ: Witness of the Fathers." *NovT* 36 (1994): 233-41.

Hawthorne, Gerald F., and Ralph P. Martin. *Philippians.* Rev. ed. WBC 43. Nashville: Nelson, 2004.

Hays, Richard B. *The Conversion of the Imagination: Paul as Interpreter of Israel's Scripture.* Grand Rapids: Eerdmans, 2005.

———. *Echoes of Scripture in the Letters of Paul.* New Haven, CT: Yale University Press, 1989.

———. *The Faith of Jesus Christ: The Narrative Substructure of Galatians 3:1–4:11.* 2nd ed. Biblical Resource Series. Grand Rapids: Eerdmans, 2002.

———. Review of *Galatians: A New Translation with Introduction and Commentary,* by J. Louis Martyn. *JBL* 119, no. 2 (2000): 373-79.

———. "'Have We Found Abraham to Be Our Forefather According to the Flesh?': A Reconsideration of Rom 4:1." *NovT* 27 (1985): 76-98.

———. "Justification." In *ABD,* 3:1131-32.

———. "The Letter to the Galatians." In *NIB,* 11:183-348.

———. "'The Righteous One' as Eschatological Deliverer: A Case Study in Paul's Apocalyptic Hermeneutics." In *Apocalyptic and the New Testament: Essays in Honor of J. Louis Martyn*, ed. Joel Marcus and Marion L. Soards, 191-215. JSNTSup 24. Sheffield: Sheffield Academic Press, 1989.

Heilig, Christopher, J. Thomas Hewitt and Michael F. Bird, eds. *God and the Faithfulness of Paul: A Critical Examination of the Pauline Theology of N. T. Wright*. WUNT 2.413. Tübingen: Mohr Siebeck, 2016.

Hemer, Colin J. *The Book of Acts in the Setting of Hellenistic History*. Edited by Conrad H. Gempf. Winona Lake, IN: Eisenbrauns, 1990.

Hengel, Martin. *Acts and the History of Earliest Christianity*. Philadelphia: Fortress Press, 1980.

———. *Judaism and Hellenism: Studies in Their Encounter in Palestine During the Early Hellenistic Period*. 2 vols. Philadelphia: Fortress, 1981.

Hengel, Martin, and Roland Deines. "E P Sanders' 'Common Judaism,' Jesus, and the Pharisees." *JTS* 46, no. 1 (1995): 1-70.

Hengel, Martin, and Anna Maria Schwemer. *Paul Between Damascus and Antioch: The Unknown Years*. Louisville, KY: Westminster John Knox, 1997.

Hennecke, Edgar, and Wilhelm Schneemelcher, eds. *New Testament Apocrypha*. Vol. 2, *Writings Relating to the Apostles; Apocalypses and Related Subjects*. Translated by R. McL. Wilson. Rev. ed. Louisville, KY: Westminster John Knox, 1992.

Hoehner, Harold W. *Ephesians: An Exegetical Commentary*. Grand Rapids: Baker Academic, 2002.

Hooker, Morna D. "Philippians: Phantom Opponents and the Real Source of Conflict." In *Fair Play: Diversity and Conflicts in Early Christianity; Essays in Honour of Heikki Räisänen*, 377-95. Leiden: Brill, 2002.

Horrell, David G., Cherryl Hunt and Christopher Southgate, eds. *Greening Paul: Rereading the Apostle in a Time of Ecological Crisis*. Waco, TX: Baylor University Press, 2010.

Howard, George E. "Faith of Christ." In *ABD*, 2:758-60.

———. "On the Faith of Christ." *HTR* 60, no. 4 (1967): 459-65.

Hübner, Hans. *Law in Paul's Thought: A Contribution to the Development of Pauline Theology*. Translated by James C. G. Greig. Edinburgh: T&T Clark, 1984.

Hunn, Debbie. "Debating the Faithfulness of Jesus Christ in Twentieth-Century Scholarship." In Bird and Sprinkle, *FJC*, 15-32.

Hurd, J. C. *The Origin of I Corinthians*. New York: Seabury, 1965.

Hurtado, Larry W. *Lord Jesus Christ: Devotion to Jesus in Earliest Christianity*. Grand Rapids: Eerdmans, 2003.

James, M. R. *The Apocryphal New Testament*. Oxford: Clarendon, 1924.

Jerome. *The Commentaries of Origen and Jerome on St. Paul's Epistle to the Ephesians*. Edited by Ronald E. Heine. Oxford: Oxford University Press, 2004.

Jewett, Paul K. *Man as Male and Female: A Study in Sexual Relationships from a Theological Point of View*. Grand Rapids: Eerdmans, 1975.

Jewett, Robert. *A Chronology of Paul's Life*. Philadelphia: Fortress, 1979.

———. *Paul's Anthropological Terms: A Study of Their Use in Conflict Settings*. Leiden: Brill, 1971.

———. *Romans: A Commentary*. Hermeneia. Minneapolis: Fortress, 2007.

Johnson, Eric L. "Rewording the Justification/Sanctification Relation with Some Help from Speech Act Theory." *JETS* 54, no. 4 (2011): 767-85.

Johnson, Luke Timothy. *The First and Second Letters to Timothy: A New Translation with Introduction and Commentary*. AB 35A. New York: Doubleday, 2001.

———. *The Writings of the New Testament: An Interpretation*. 3rd ed. Minneapolis: Fortress, 2010.

Käsemann, Ernst. *Commentary on Romans*. Grand Rapids: Eerdmans, 1980.

———. "Some Thoughts on the Theme 'the Doctrine of Reconciliation in the New Testament.'" In *The Future of Our Religious Past*, ed. James M. Robinson, 49-64. New York: Harper & Row, 1971.

Keener, Craig S. *Acts: An Exegetical Commentary*. 4 vols. Grand Rapids: Baker Academic, 2012–2015.

Kelly, J. N. D. *The Pastoral Epistles*. Peabody, MA: Hendrickson, 1993.

Kiley, Mark C. *Colossians as Pseudepigraphy*. Biblical Seminar 4. Sheffield: JSOT Press, 1986.

Kim, Seyoon. "2 Cor. 5:11-21 and the Origin of Paul's Concept of 'Reconciliation.'" *NovT* 39, no. 4 (1997): 360-84.

———. *The Origin of Paul's Gospel*. WUNT 2.4. Tübingen: Mohr, 1981.

———. *Paul and the New Perspective: Second Thoughts on the Origin of Paul's Gospel*. Grand Rapids: Eerdmans, 2001.

Kirk, J. R. Daniel. *Unlocking Romans: Resurrection and the Justification of God*. Grand Rapids: Eerdmans, 2008.

Knight, George W. *The Pastoral Epistles: A Commentary on the Greek Text*. NIGTC. Grand Rapids: Eerdmans, 1992.

Knox, John. *Chapters in a Life of Paul*. New York: Abingdon-Cokesbury, 1950.

———. "On the Pauline Chronology: Buck-Taylor-Hurd Revisited." In *The*

Conversation Continues: Studies in Paul & John in Honor of J. Louis Martyn, 258-74. Nashville: Abingdon, 1990.

Koester, Helmut. *Introduction to the New Testament: Literature and History*. Vol. 2. 2nd ed. New York: de Gruyter, 1995.

Kooten, Geurt H. van. *Cosmic Christology in Paul and the Pauline School: Colossians and Ephesians in the Context of Graeco-Roman Cosmology, with a New Synopsis of the Greek Texts*. WUNT 171. Tübingen: Mohr Siebeck, 2003.

Kümmel, Werner Georg, and Paul Feine. *Introduction to the New Testament*. Rev. ed. Nashville: Abingdon, 1975.

Lakoff, George, and Mark Johnson. *Metaphors We Live By*. Chicago: University of Chicago Press, 1980.

Larkin, William J. *Ephesians: A Handbook on the Greek Text*. Baylor Handbook on the Greek New Testament. Waco, TX: Baylor University Press, 2009.

Leithart, Peter J. *Delivered from the Elements of the World: Atonement, Justification, Mission*. Downers Grove, IL: IVP Academic, 2016.

Letham, Robert. *Union with Christ: In Scripture, History, and Theology*. Phillipsburg, NJ: P&R, 2011.

———. *The Work of Christ*. Downers Grove, IL: InterVarsity Press, 1993.

Liddell, H. G., R. Scott and H. S. Jones. *A Greek-English Lexicon with 1996 Supplement*. 9th ed. Oxford: Oxford University Press, 1996.

Lieb, Michael, Emma Mason, Jonathan Roberts and Christopher Rowland, eds. *The Oxford Handbook of the Reception History of the Bible*. Oxford Handbooks in Religion and Theology. Oxford: Oxford University Press, 2011.

Lieu, Judith. "'Grace to You and Peace': The Apostolic Greeting." *BJRL* 68, no. 1 (1985): 161-78.

Lightfoot, J. B. *Biblical Essays*. New York: Macmillan, 1904.

———. *The Christian Ministry*. New York: Whittaker, 1878.

———. *Saint Paul's Epistle to the Galatians: A Revised Text with Introduction, Notes, and Dissertations*. 10th ed. London: Macmillan, 1890.

———. *Saint Paul's Epistle to the Philippians: A Revised Text with Introduction, Notes, and Dissertations*. 8th ed. London: Macmillan, 1885.

———. *Saint Paul's Epistles to the Colossians and to Philemon: A Revised Text with Introductions, Notes, and Dissertations*. New York: Macmillan, 1892.

Lincoln, Andrew T. *Ephesians*. WBC 42. Dallas: Word, 1990.

———. "Ephesians 2:8-10: A Summary of Paul's Gospel?" *CBQ* 45, no. 4 (1983): 617-30.

Linebaugh, Jonathan A. *God, Grace, and Righteousness in Wisdom of Solomon and Paul's Letter to the Romans: Texts in Conversation.* NovTSup 152. Leiden: Brill, 2013.

Llewelyn, S. R., ed. *New Documents Illustrating Early Christianity.* Vol. 8. [North Ryde], NSW: Ancient History Documentary Research Centre, Macquarie University, 1997.

Lohse, Eduard. *Colossians and Philemon.* Translated by William R. Poehlmann. Hermeneia. Philadelphia: Fortress, 1971.

Long, Frederick J. *Ancient Rhetoric and Paul's Apology: The Compositional Unity of 2 Corinthians.* SNSTMS 131. Cambridge: Cambridge University Press, 2004.

Longenecker, Bruce W., ed. *Narrative Dynamics in Paul: A Critical Assessment.* Louisville, KY: Westminster John Knox, 2002.

———. *The Triumph of Abraham's God: The Transformation of Identity in Galatians.* Nashville: Abingdon, 1998.

Longenecker, Richard N. *Galatians.* WBC 41. Dallas: Word, 1990.

———. *Introducing Romans: Critical Issues in Paul's Most Famous Letter.* Grand Rapids: Eerdmans, 2011.

———. "Is There Development in Paul's Resurrection Thought." In *Life in the Face of Death: The Resurrection Message of the New Testament,* 171-202. Grand Rapids: Eerdmans, 1998.

———. "On the Concept of Development in Pauline Thought." In *Perspectives on Evangelical Theology: Papers from the 30th Annual Meeting of the Evangelical Theological Society,* ed. Kenneth S. Kantzer and Stanley N. Gundry, 195-207. Grand Rapids: Baker Books, 1979.

———. *Paul, Apostle of Liberty: The Origin and Nature of Paul's Christianity.* Grand Rapids: Baker Books, 1976.

———, ed. *The Road from Damascus: The Impact of Paul's Conversion on His Life, Thought, and Ministry.* McMaster New Testament Studies. Grand Rapids: Eerdmans, 1997.

Lust, Johan, Erik Eynikel and Katrin Hauspie. *A Greek-English Lexicon of the Septuagint.* Rev. ed. Stuttgart: Deutsche Bibelgesellschaft, 2003.

Macaskill, Grant. "Review Article: The Deliverance of God." *JSNT* 34, no. 2 (2011): 150-61.

———. *Union with Christ in the New Testament.* Oxford: Oxford University Press, 2014.

Mannermaa, Tuomo. *Christ Present in Faith: Luther's View of Justification.* Translated by Kirsi Irmeli Stjerna. Minneapolis: Fortress, 2005.

Marshall, I. Howard. *Aspects of the Atonement: Cross and Resurrection in the Reconciling of God and Humanity.* London: Paternoster, 2007.

------. "The Meaning of 'Reconciliation.'" In *Unity and Diversity in New Testament Theology: Essays in Honor of George E. Ladd*, ed. Robert A. Guelich, 117-32. Grand Rapids: Eerdmans, 1978.

Marshall, I. Howard, and Philip H. Towner. *A Critical and Exegetical Commentary on the Pastoral Epistles*. ICC. Edinburgh: T&T Clark, 1999.

Martin, Ralph P. "New Testament Theology: A Proposal; the Theme of Reconciliation." *ExpTim* 91, no. 12 (1980): 364-68.

------. *Reconciliation: A Study of Paul's Theology*. New Foundations Theological Library. Atlanta: John Knox, 1981.

Martyn, J. Louis. "The Apocalyptic Gospel in Galatians." *Int* 54, no. 3 (2000): 246-66.

------. "Events in Galatia: Modified Covenantal Nomism Versus God's Invasion of the Cosmos in the Singular Gospel; A Response to J. D. G. Dunn and B. R. Gaventa." In *Pauline Theology*, vol. 1, *Thessalonians, Philippians, Galatians, Philemon*, ed. Jouette M. Bassler, 160-79. Minneapolis: Fortress, 1991.

------. *Galatians: A New Translation with Introduction and Commentary*. AB 33A. New York: Doubleday, 1998.

------. "Romans as One of the Earliest Interpretations of Galatians." In *Theological Issues in the Letters of Paul*, 37-45. Nashville: Abingdon, 1997.

------. *Theological Issues in the Letters of Paul*. Nashville: Abingdon, 1997.

Marxsen, Willi. *Introduction to the New Testament: An Approach to Its Problems*. Oxford: Blackwell, 1968.

Matera, Frank J. *Galatians*. SP. Collegeville, MN: Liturgical Press, 1992.

------. *God's Saving Grace: A Pauline Theology*. Grand Rapids: Eerdmans, 2012.

Matlock, R. Barry. "Almost Cultural Studies: Reflections on the 'New Perspective' on Paul." In *Biblical Studies/Cultural Studies: The Third Sheffield Colloquium*, ed. J. Cheryl Exum and Stephen D. Moore, 433-59. JSNTSup 266. Sheffield: Sheffield Academic Press, 1998.

------. "Detheologizing the ΠΙΣΤΙΣ ΧΡΙΣΤΟΥ Debate: Cautionary Remarks from a Lexical Semantic Perspective." *NovT* 42 (2000): 1-23.

------. "'Even the Demons Believe': Paul and πίστις Χριστοῦ." *CBQ* 64, no. 2 (2002): 300-318.

------. "The Rhetoric of πίστις in Paul: Galatians 2:16, 3:22, Romans 3:22, and Philippians 3:9." *JSNT* 30, no. 2 (2007): 173-203.

------. "Saving Faith: The Rhetoric and Semantics of πίστις in Paul." In Bird and Sprinkle, *FJC*, 73-89.

———. "Zeal for Paul but Not According to Knowledge: Douglas Campbell's War on 'Justification Theory.'" *JSNT* 34, no. 2 (2011): 115-49.

Mattison, Mark. "The Paul Page," accessed March 25, 2016, www.thepaulpage .com.

Mauss, Marcel. "Essai sur le Don: Forme et raison de l'échange dans le sociétés archaïques." In *Sociologie et anthropologie*, 145-279. Paris: Presses Universitaires de France, 1950.

McGrath, Alister E. *Iustitia Dei: A History of the Christian Doctrine of Justification*. 1st ed. Cambridge: Cambridge University Press, 1986.

———. *Iustitia Dei: A History of the Christian Doctrine of Justification*. 3rd ed. New York: Cambridge University Press, 2005.

McKnight, Scot. *A Light Among the Gentiles: Jewish Missionary Activity in the Second Temple Period*. Minneapolis: Fortress, 1991.

Meek, James A. "The New Perspective on Paul: An Introduction for the Uninitiated." *Concordia Journal* 27, no. 3 (2001): 208-33.

Merkel, H. "καταλλάσσω, κτλ." In *EDNT*, 2:261-63.

Metzger, Bruce M. *A Textual Commentary on the Greek New Testament (TCGNT)*. 2nd ed. Stuttgart: Deutsche Bibelgesell-Schaft; United Bible Societies, 1994.

Michael, J. H. *The Epistle of Paul to the Philippians*. Moffat New Testament Commentary. Garden City, NY: Doubleday, 1929.

———. "Work Out Your Own Salvation." *Expositor* 12 (1924): 439-50.

Miller, James C. *The Obedience of Faith, the Eschatological People of God, and the Purpose of Romans*. SBLDS 62. Atlanta: Society of Biblical Literature, 2000.

———. "The Romans Debate: 1991-2001." *Currents in Research* 9 (2001): 306-49.

Mitchell, Stephen. "Galatia." In *ABD*, 2:870-72.

Montefiore, C. G. *Judaism and St. Paul: Two Essays*. London: Goschen, 1914.

Moo, Douglas J. *The Epistle to the Romans*. NICNT. Grand Rapids: Eerdmans, 1996.

———. *Galatians*. BECNT. Grand Rapids: Baker Academic, 2013.

———. "Israel and the Law in Romans 5-11: Interaction with the New Perspective." In Carson, O'Brien and Seifrid, *JVN:PP*, 2:185-216.

———. Review of *The Deliverance of God: An Apocalyptic Rereading of Justification in Paul*, by Douglas A. Campbell. *JETS* 53, no. 1 (2010): 143-50.

Moore, George Foot. *Judaism in the First Centuries of the Christian Era: The Age of the Tannaim*. 3 vols. Cambridge, MA: Harvard University Press, 1927.

Morris, Leon. *The Apostolic Preaching of the Cross*. London: Tyndale Press, 1955.

Moule, C. F. D. *Idiom Book of New Testament Greek*. Cambridge: Cambridge University Press, 1960.

Moulton, J. H., and W. F. Howard. *A Grammar of New Testament Greek*. Vol. 2, *Accidence and Word-Formation*. Edinburgh: T&T Clark, 1920.

Moulton, J. H., and G. Milligan. *The Vocabulary of the Greek New Testament*. London: Hodder & Stoughton, 1930.

Mounce, William D. *Pastoral Epistles*. WBC 46. Nashville: Nelson, 2000.

Muddiman, John. *A Commentary on the Epistle to the Ephesians*. New York: Continuum, 2001.

Mullins, Terence Y. "Greeting as a New Testament Form." *JBL* 87, no. 4 (1968): 418-26.

Murphy-O'Connor, Jerome. "Missions in Galatia, Macedonia, and Achaia Before the Jerusalem Conference." In *Keys to Galatians: Collected Essays*, 1-36. Collegeville, MN: Liturgical Press, 2012.

———. *Paul: A Critical Life*. Oxford: Oxford University Press, 1997.

———. "Pauline Missions Before the Jerusalem Conference." *Revue Biblique* 89, no. 1 (1982): 71-91.

Murray, John. *The Epistle to the Romans*. NICNT. Grand Rapids: Eerdmans, 1968.

Nanos, Mark D. "Galatians." In *The Blackwell Companion to the New Testament*, ed. David E. Aune, 455-74. Malden, MA: Wiley-Blackwell, 2010.

———. *The Mystery of Romans: The Jewish Context of Paul's Letter*. Minneapolis: Fortress, 1996.

Neill, Stephen, and Tom Wright. *The Interpretation of the New Testament, 1861–1986*. New York: Oxford University Press, 1988.

Neusner, Jacob. *Judaic Law from Jesus to the Mishnah: A Systematic Reply to Professor E. P. Sanders*. South Florida Studies in the History of Judaism 84. Atlanta: Scholars Press, 1993.

Neville, David J. Review of *Justification Reconsidered: Rethinking a Pauline Theme*, by Stephen Westerholm. *Review of Biblical Literature Blog*, April 2015, www.bookreviews.org/pdf/9508_10515.pdf.

Newbigin, Lesslie. *The Gospel in a Pluralist Society*. Grand Rapids: Eerdmans, 1989.

O'Brien, Peter T. "Church." In *DPL*, 123-31.

———. "The Church as a Heavenly and Eschatological Entity." In *Biblical Interpretation and the Church: Text and Context*, ed. D. A. Carson, 88-119. Exeter: Paternoster, 1984.

———. *Colossians, Philemon*. WBC 44. Waco, TX: Word, 1982.

———. *The Epistle to the Philippians: A Commentary on the Greek Text*. NIGTC. Grand Rapids: Eerdmans, 1991.

———. *The Letter to the Ephesians.* PNTC. Grand Rapids: Eerdmans, 1999.

———. "Was Paul Converted?" In Carson, O'Brien and Seifred, *JVN:PP*, 2:361-91.

Oden, Thomas C. *The Justification Reader.* Classic Christian Readers. Grand Rapids: Eerdmans, 2002.

Ortberg, John. "Why Jesus' Disciples Wouldn't Wash Their Hands." *Christianity Today,* August 15, 1994, 26.

Padgett, Alan. "The Pauline Rationale for Submission: Biblical Feminism and the *hina* Clauses of Titus 2:1-10." *EvQ* 59, no. 1 (1987): 39-52.

Pelikan, Jaroslav, Hilton C. Oswald, Helmut T. Lehmann, Christopher Boyd Brown, Benjamin T. G. Mayes and James L. Langebartels, eds. *Luther's Works (LW).* 55 vols. St. Louis, MO: Concordia Publishing House, 1955.

Peterson, David. *Possessed by God: A New Testament Theology of Sanctification and Holiness.* NSBT 1. Downers Grove, IL: InterVarsity Press, 1995.

Piper, John. *Counted Righteous in Christ: Should We Abandon the Imputation of Christ's Righteousness?* Wheaton, IL: Crossway, 2002.

———. *The Future of Justification: A Response to N. T. Wright.* Wheaton, IL: Crossway, 2008.

———. *The Justification of God: An Exegetical and Theological Study of Romans 9:1-23.* Grand Rapids: Baker Book House, 1983.

Porter, Stanley E. "The Concept of Covenant in Paul." In *The Concept of the Covenant in the Second Temple Period,* ed. Stanley E. Porter and Jacqueline C. R. de Roo, 269-85. Leiden: Brill, 2003.

———. "Holiness, Sanctification." In *DPL,* 397-410.

———. *Idioms of the Greek New Testament.* Sheffield: Sheffield Academic Press, 1994.

———. *Καταλλάσσω in Ancient Greek Literature, with Reference to the Pauline Writings.* Estudios de filología neotestamentaria 5. Cordoba: Ediciones el Almendro, 1994.

———. "Pauline Authorship and the Pastoral Epistles: Implications for Canon." *BBR* 5 (1995): 105-23.

———. "Reconciliation as the Heart of Paul's Missionary Theology." In *Paul as Missionary: Identity, Activity, Theology, and Practice,* ed. Trevor J. Burke and Brian S. Rosner, 169-79. Library of New Testament Studies 420. London: T&T Clark, 2011.

Porter, Stanley E., and Andrew E. Pitts. "Πίστις with a Preposition and Genitive Modifier: Lexical, Semantic, and Syntactic Considerations in the πίστις Χριστοῦ Discussion." In Bird and Sprinkle, *FJC,* 33-53.

Powers, Daniel G. *Salvation Through Participation: An Examination of the Notion of the Believers' Corporate Unity with Christ in Early Christian Soteriology.* Leuven: Peeters, 2001.

Prior, Michael. *Paul the Letter-Writer, and the Second Letter to Timothy.* JSNTSup 23. Sheffield: JSOT Press, 1989.

Quinn, Jerome D. "Timothy and Titus, Epistles To." In *ABD,* 6:560-71.

Räisänen, Heikki. *Paul and the Law.* WUNT 29. Tübingen: Mohr, 1983.

Ramsay, William Mitchell. *St. Paul the Traveller and the Roman Citizen.* New York: Putnam's Sons; London: Hodder & Stoughton, 1909.

Rapske, Brian M. "Acts, Travel and Shipwreck." In *The Book of Acts in Its Graeco-Roman Setting,* ed. David W. J. Gill and Conrad H. Gempf, 1-47. Book of Acts in Its First Century Setting 2. Grand Rapids: Eerdmans, 1994.

————. *The Book of Acts and Paul in Roman Custody.* The Book of Acts in Its First Century Setting 3. Grand Rapids: Eerdmans, 1994.

Reid, Daniel G. "The Misunderstood Apostle." *Christianity Today,* July 16, 1990, 25-27.

Reumann, John H. P. *Philippians: A New Translation with Introduction and Commentary.* New Haven, CT: Yale University Press, 2008.

Richards, E. Randolph. *Paul and First-Century Letter Writing: Secretaries, Composition, and Collection.* Downers Grove, IL: InterVarsity Press, 2004.

————. *The Secretary in the Letters of Paul.* WUNT 42. Tübingen: Mohr, 1991.

Ridderbos, Herman N. *Paul: An Outline of His Theology.* Grand Rapids: Eerdmans, 1975.

Riesner, Rainer. "Pauline Chronology." In *The Blackwell Companion to Paul,* ed. Stephen Westerholm, 9-29. Malden, MA: Wiley-Blackwell, 2011.

————. *Paul's Early Period: Chronology, Mission Strategy, Theology.* Translated by Doug Stott. Grand Rapids: Eerdmans, 1998.

Robertson, A. T. *A Grammar of the Greek New Testament in the Light of Historical Research.* Nashville: Broadman, 1934.

Robinson, Benjamin Willard. "An Ephesian Imprisonment of Paul." *JBL* 29, no. 2 (1910): 181-89.

Roon, A. van. *The Authenticity of Ephesians.* NovTSup 39. Leiden: Brill, 1974.

Sampley, J. Paul. *Walking in Love: Moral Progress and Spiritual Growth with the Apostle Paul.* Minneapolis: Fortress, 2016.

Sanday, William, and Arthur C. Headlam. *A Critical and Exegetical Commentary on the Epistle to the Romans.* ICC. Edinburgh: T&T Clark, 1898.

Sanders, E. P. "Did Paul's Theology Develop?" In *The Word Leaps the Gap: Essays on Scripture and Theology in Honor of Richard B. Hays,* ed. J. Ross Wagner, C. Kavin Rowe and A. Katherine Grieb, 325-50. Grand Rapids: Eerdmans, 2008.

————. *Paul and Palestinian Judaism: A Comparison of Patterns of Religion.* Philadelphia: Fortress, 1977.

———. *Paul: The Apostle's Life, Letters, and Thought*. Minneapolis: Fortress, 2015.

———. *Paul, the Law, and the Jewish People*. Philadelphia: Fortress, 1983.

Schenck, Kenneth. "2 Corinthians and the πίστις Χριστοῦ Debate." *CBQ* 70, no. 3 (2008): 524-37.

Schnabel, Eckhard J. *Early Christian Mission: Paul and the Early Church*. 2 vols. Downers Grove, IL: InterVarsity Press, 2004.

Schnackenburg, Rudolf. *Ephesians: A Commentary*. Edinburgh: T&T Clark, 1991.

Schneemelcher, Wilhelm. *New Testament Apocrypha*. Vol. 2, *Writings Relating to the Apostles: Apocalypses and Related Subjects*. Translated by Robert McL. Wilson. Rev. ed. Louisville, KY: Westminster John Knox, 1992.

Schnelle, Udo. *Apostle Paul: His Life and Theology*. Grand Rapids: Baker Academic, 2005.

Schreiner, Thomas R. *Galatians*. ZECNT. Grand Rapids: Zondervan, 2010.

———. *The Law and Its Fulfillment: A Pauline Theology of Law*. Grand Rapids: Baker Academic, 1993.

———. *New Testament Theology: Magnifying God in Christ*. Grand Rapids: Baker Academic, 2008.

———. *Paul, Apostle of God's Glory in Christ: A Pauline Theology*. Downers Grove, IL: InterVarsity Press, 2001.

———. *Romans*. BECNT. Grand Rapids: Baker Academic, 1998.

Schweitzer, Albert. *The Mysticism of Paul the Apostle*. Translated by William Montgomery. New York: Holt, 1931.

Scott, James M. "Exile and the Self-Understanding of Diaspora Jews in the Greco-Roman Period." In *Exile: Old Testament, Jewish, and Christian Conceptions*, ed. James M. Scott, 173-218. Leiden: Brill, 1997.

Segal, Alan F. *Paul the Convert: The Apostolate and Apostasy of Saul the Pharisee*. New Haven, CT: Yale University Press, 1990.

Seifrid, Mark A. *Christ, Our Righteousness: Paul's Theology of Justification*. NSBT 9. Downers Grove, IL: InterVarsity Press, 2000.

———. "The Faith of Christ." In Bird and Sprinkle, *FJC*, 129-46.

———. *Justification by Faith: The Origin and Development of a Central Pauline Theme*. NovTSup 68. Leiden: Brill, 1992.

———. "Luther, Melanchthon and Paul on the Question of Imputation." In *Justification: What's at Stake in the Current Debates*, ed. Mark Husbands and Daniel J. Treier, 137-52. Downers Grove, IL: InterVarsity Press, 2004.

———. "Paul's Use of Righteousness Language Against Its Hellenistic Background." In Carson, O'Brien and Siefrid, *JVN:PP*, 2:39-74.

———. "Romans." In Beale and Carson, *Commentary on the New Testament Use of the Old Testament*, 607-94.

Shaw, David. "Romans 4 and the Justification of Abraham in Light of Perspectives New and Newer." *Themelios* 40, no. 1 (2015): 50-62.

Silva, Moisés. "Faith Versus Works of Law in Galatians." In Carson, O'Brien and Seifrid, *JVN:PP*, 2:217-48.

———. "Galatians." In Beale and Carson, *Commentary on the New Testament Use of the Old Testament*, 278-812.

———. *Philippians.* 2nd ed. BECNT. Grand Rapids: Baker Academic, 2005.

Smyth, Herbert Weir, and Gordon M. Messing. *Greek Grammar.* Cambridge: Harvard University Press, 1956.

Snodgrass, Klyne R. "Justification by Grace—to the Doers: An Analysis of the Place of Romans 2 in the Theology of Paul." *NTS* 32, no. 1 (1986): 72-93.

Spicq, Ceslas. "καταλλαγή, καταλλάσσω." In *Theological Lexicon of the New Testament*, trans. James D. Ernest, 2:262-66. Peabody, MA: Hendrickson, 1994.

———. *Saint Paul: Les Épîtres pastorales.* Paris: Gabalda, 1947.

———. *Theological Lexicon of the New Testament.* Translated by James D. Ernest. 3 vols. Peabody, MA: Hendrickson, 1994.

Sprinkle, Preston M. *Law and Life: The Interpretation of Leviticus 18:5 in Early Judaism and in Paul.* WUNT 241. Tübingen: Mohr Siebeck, 2008.

———. *Paul and Judaism Revisited: A Study of Divine and Human Agency in Salvation.* Downers Grove, IL: InterVarsity Press, 2013.

———. "Πίστις Χριστοῦ as an Eschatological Event." In Bird and Sprinkle, *FJC*, 165-84.

Stanley, Alan P., and Robert Wilkin, eds. *Four Views on the Role of Works at the Final Judgment.* Counterpoints: Bible and Theology. Grand Rapids: Zondervan, 2013.

Stanley, Christopher D. *Arguing with Scripture: The Rhetoric of Quotations in the Letters of Paul.* New York: T&T Clark, 2004.

———. *Paul and the Language of Scripture: Citation Technique in the Pauline Epistles and Contemporary Literature.* SNTSMS 69. New York: Cambridge University Press, 1992.

———. "'Under a Curse': A Fresh Reading of Galatians 3:10-14." *NTS* 36, no. 4 (1990): 481-511.

Stendahl, Krister. "The Apostle Paul and the Introspective Conscience of the West." *HTR* 56 (1963): 199-215.

———. *Paul Among Jews and Gentiles, and Other Essays.* Philadelphia: Fortress, 1976.

Stewart, Alistair C. *The Original Bishops: Office and Order in the First Christian Communities.* Grand Rapids: Baker Academic, 2014.

Stowers, Stanley K. *A Rereading of Romans: Justice, Jews, and Gentiles.* New Haven, CT: Yale University Press, 1994.

Stuhlmacher, Peter. "The Gospel of Reconciliation in Christ—Basic Features and Issues of a Biblical Theology of the New Testament." *HBT* 1, no. 1 (1979): 161-90.

Stuhlmacher, Peter, and Donald A. Hagner. *Revisiting Paul's Doctrine of Justification: A Challenge to the New Perspective.* Downers Grove, IL: InterVarsity Press, 2001.

Tanner, Norman P., ed. *Decrees of the Ecumenical Councils.* 2 vols. London: Sheed & Ward; Washington, DC: Georgetown University Press, 1990.

Tate, Marvin E. "The Comprehensive Nature of Salvation in Biblical Perspective." *RevExp* 91, no. 4 (1994): 469-85.

Tatum, Gregory. *New Chapters in the Life of Paul: The Relative Chronology of His Career.* CBQMS 41. Washington, DC: Catholic Biblical Association, 2006.

Thate, Michael J., Kevin J. Vanhoozer and Constantine R. Campbell, eds. *"In Christ" in Paul: Explorations in Paul's Theology of Union and Participation.* WUNT 384. Tübingen: Mohr Siebeck, 2014.

Thielman, Frank. *Ephesians.* BECNT. Grand Rapids: Baker Academic, 2010.

———. "Ephesus and the Literary Setting of Philippians." In *New Testament Greek and Exegesis: Essays in Honor of Gerald Hawthorne,* ed. Amy M. Donaldson and Timothy B. Sailors, 205-23. Grand Rapids: Eerdmans, 2003.

———. *From Plight to Solution: A Jewish Framework for Understanding Paul's View of the Law in Galatians and Romans.* New York: Brill, 1989.

———. *Paul and the Law: A Contextual Approach.* Downers Grove, IL: InterVarsity Press, 1994.

———. *Philippians.* NIVAC. Grand Rapids: Zondervan, 1995.

Thiselton, Anthony C. *The First Epistle to the Corinthians: A Commentary on the Greek Text.* NIGTC. Grand Rapids: Eerdmans, 2000.

Thompson, Michael B. "The Holy Internet: Communication Between Churches in the First Christian Generation." In *The Gospels for All Christians: Rethinking the Gospel Audiences,* ed. Richard J. Bauckham, 49-70. Grand Rapids: Eerdmans, 1998.

———. *The New Perspective on Paul.* Cambridge: Grove Books, 2002.

Thrall, Margaret E. *A Critical and Exegetical Commentary on the Second Epistle to the Corinthians.* ICC. Edinburgh: T&T Clark, 1994.

Tilling, Chris, ed. *Beyond Old and New Perpectives on Paul: Reflections on the Work of Douglas Campbell.* Eugene, OR: Cascade, 2014.

Tipton, Lane G. "Union with Christ and Justification." In *Justified in Christ: God's Plan for Us in Justification*, ed. K. Scott Oliphint, 23-49. Fearn, Scotland: Mentor, 2007.

Tobin, Thomas H. *Paul's Rhetoric in Its Contexts: The Argument of Romans.* Peabody, MA: Hendrickson, 2004.

Tov, Emmanuel, and Frank Polak. *The Revised CATSS Hebrew/Greek Parallel Text.* Philadelphia: Computer-Assisted Tools for Septuagint Studies Project, University of Pennsylvania, 2004.

Towner, Philip H. *The Letters to Timothy and Titus.* NICNT. Grand Rapids: Eerdmans, 2006.

Trobisch, David. *Paul's Letter Collection: Tracing the Origins.* Minneapolis: Fortress, 1994.

Turner, Nigel. *Christian Words.* Edinburgh: T&T Clark, 1980.

———. *Syntax.* Vol. 3 of *A Grammar of New Testament Greek.* Edinburgh: T&T Clark, 1963.

Tyson, Joseph B. "Paul's Opponents at Philippi." *PRS* 3, no. 1 (1976): 83-96.

Vanhoozer, Kevin J. "Wrighting the Wrongs of the Reformation? The State of the Union with Christ in St. Paul and Protestant Soteriology." In *Jesus, Paul, and the People of God: A Theological Dialogue with N. T. Wright*, ed. Nicholas Perrin and Richard B. Hays, 235-59. Downers Grove, IL: IVP Academic, 2011.

VanLandingham, Chris. *Judgment and Justification in Early Judaism and the Apostle Paul.* Peabody, MA: Hendrickson, 2006.

Vickers, Brian. *Jesus' Blood and Righteousness: Paul's Theology of Imputation.* Wheaton, IL: Crossway, 2006.

Wagner, J. Ross. "Paul and Scripture." In *The Blackwell Companion to Paul*, ed. Stephen Westerholm, 154-71. Malden, MA: Wiley-Blackwell, 2011.

Wallace, Daniel B. *Greek Grammar Beyond the Basics.* Grand Rapids: Zondervan, 1996.

Wallis, Ian G. *The Faith of Jesus Christ in Early Christian Traditions.* New York: Cambridge University Press, 1995.

Wanamaker, Charles A. *The Epistles to the Thessalonians: A Commentary on the Greek Text.* NIGTC. Grand Rapids: Eerdmans, 1990.

Waters, Guy Prentiss. *Federal Vision and Covenant Theology: A Comparative Analysis.* Phillipsburg, NJ: P&R, 2006.

Watson, Duane F. "A Rhetorical Analysis of Philippians and Its Implications for the Unity Question." *NovT* 30, no. 1 (1988): 57-88.

Watson, Francis. "By Faith (of Christ): An Exegetical Dilemma and Its Scriptural Solution." In Bird and Sprinkle, *FJC*, 147-64.

———. "Not the New Perspective," paper presented at the British New Testament Conference, Manchester, September 2001.

———. *Paul and the Hermeneutics of Faith.* London: T&T Clark, 2004.

———. *Paul, Judaism, and the Gentiles: A Sociological Approach.* SNSTMS 56. Cambridge: Cambridge University Press, 1986.

———. *Paul, Judaism, and the Gentiles: Beyond the New Perspective.* 2nd ed. Grand Rapids: Eerdmans, 2007.

———. Review of *The Deliverance of God: An Apocalyptic Rereading of Justification in Paul,* by Douglas A. Campbell. *Early Christianity* 1, no. 1 (2010): 179-85.

Watson, Nigel M. "Some Observations on the Use of ΔΙΚΑΙΟΩ in the Septuagint." *JBL* 79, no. 3 (1960): 255-66.

Wax, Trevin. "The Justification Debate: A Primer." *Christianity Today,* June 1, 2009, 34-37.

Westerholm, Stephen. *Justification Reconsidered: Rethinking a Pauline Theme.* Grand Rapids: Eerdmans, 2013.

———. *Perspectives Old and New on Paul: The "Lutheran" Paul and His Critics.* Grand Rapids: Eerdmans, 2004.

Wilkins, Steve, and Duane Garner, eds. *The Federal Vision.* Monroe, LA: Athanasius Press, 2014.

Williams, Sam K. "Again πίστις Χριστοῦ." *CBQ* 49, no. 3 (1987): 431-47.

Winter, Bruce W. *Roman Wives, Roman Widows: The Appearance of New Women and the Pauline Communities.* Grand Rapids: Eerdmans, 2003.

Wischmeyer, Oda, ed. *Paul: Life, Setting, Work, Letters.* Translated by Helen S. Heron. New York: T&T Clark, 2012.

Witherington, Ben, III. *The Acts of the Apostles: A Socio-Rhetorical Commentary.* Grand Rapids: Eerdmans, 1998.

———. *Conflict and Community in Corinth: A Socio-Rhetorical Commentary on 1 and 2 Corinthians.* Grand Rapids: Eerdmans, 1995.

———. *Grace in Galatia: A Commentary on St. Paul's Letter to the Galatians.* Grand Rapids: Eerdmans, 1998.

———. *Letters and Homilies for Hellenized Christians: A Socio-Rhetorical Commentary on Titus, 1-2 Timothy and 1-3 John.* Downers Grove, IL: InterVarsity Press, 2006.

———. *The Letters to Philemon, the Colossians, and the Ephesians: A Socio-Rhetorical Commentary on the Captivity Epistles.* Grand Rapids: Eerdmans, 2007.

———. *The Paul Quest: The Renewed Search for the Jew of Tarsus.* Downers Grove, IL: IVP Academic, 1998.

———. *Paul's Letter to the Philippians: A Socio-Rhetorical Commentary.* Grand Rapids: Eerdmans, 2011.

———. *Paul's Narrative Thought World: The Tapestry of Tragedy and Triumph.* Louisville, KY: Westminster John Knox, 1994.

Witherington, Ben, III, and Darlene Hyatt. *Paul's Letter to the Romans: A Socio-Rhetorical Commentary.* Grand Rapids: Eerdmans, 2004.

Wolter, Michael. *Paulus: Ein Grundriss seiner Theologie.* Neukirchen-Vluyn: Neukirchener Verlag, 2011.

Wrede, William. *Paul.* Eugene, OR: Wipf & Stock, 2001.

Wright, D. F. "Ebionites." In *DLNT*, 313-17.

Wright, N. T. "4QMMT and Paul: Justification, 'Works,' and Eschatology." In *History and Exegesis: New Testament Essays in Honor of Dr. E. Earle Ellis on His Eightieth Birthday*, ed. S. Aaron Son, 104-32. New York: T&T Clark, 2006.

———. "Christ, the Law, and 'Pauline Theology.'" In *The Climax of the Covenant: Christ and the Law in Pauline Theology*, 1-17. Edinburgh: T&T Clark, 1991.

———. "Christ, the Law and the People of God: The Problem of Romans 9–11." In *The Climax of the Covenant: Christ and the Law in Pauline Theology*, 231-57. Edinburgh: T&T Clark, 1991.

———. *The Climax of the Covenant: Christ and the Law in Pauline Theology.* Edinburgh: T&T Clark, 1991.

———. "Curse and Covenant: Galatians 3.10-14." In *The Climax of the Covenant: Christ and the Law in Pauline Theology*, 137-56. Edinburgh: T&T Clark, 1991.

———. *The Epistles of Paul to the Colossians and to Philemon: An Introduction and Commentary.* TNTC. Grand Rapids: Eerdmans, 1986.

———. *Jesus and the Victory of God.* Christian Origins and the Question of God 2. Minneapolis: Fortress, 1996.

———. *Justification: God's Plan and Paul's Vision.* Downers Grove, IL: IVP Academic, 2009.

———. "The Letter to the Galatians: Exegesis and Theology." In *Between Two Horizons: Spanning New Testament Studies and Systematic Theology*, ed. Joel B. Green and Max Turner, 205-36. Grand Rapids: Eerdmans, 2000.

———. "The Letter to the Romans: Introduction, Commentary and Reflections." In *NIB*, 10:393-770.

———. "Messiahship in Galatians?" In *Galatians and Christian Theology: Justification, the Gospel, and Ethics in Paul's Letter*, ed. M. W. Elliott, Scott J.

Hafemann, N. T. Wright and John Frederick, 3-23. Grand Rapids: Baker Academic, 2014.

———. "New Perspectives on Paul." In *Justification in Perspective: Historical Developments and Contemporary Challenges*, ed. Bruce L. McCormack, 243-77. Grand Rapids: Baker Academic, 2006.

———. *The New Testament and the People of God*. Christian Origins and the Question of God 1. Minneapolis: Fortress, 1992.

———. "On Becoming the Righteousness of God: 2 Corinthians 5:21." In *Pauline Theology*, vol. 2, *1 & 2 Corinthians*, ed. David M. Hay, 200-208. Minneapolis: Fortress, 1993.

———. *Paul and His Recent Interpreters: Some Contemporary Debates*. Minneapolis: Fortress, 2015.

———. *Paul and the Faithfulness of God*. 2 vols. Christian Origins and the Question of God 4. Minneapolis: Fortress, 2013.

———. *Paul: In Fresh Perspective*. Minneapolis: Fortress, 2005.

———. *Pauline Perspectives: Essays on Paul, 1978–2013*. Minneapolis: Fortress, 2013.

———. "Poetry and Theology in Colossians 1.15-20." In *The Climax of the Covenant: Christ and the Law in Pauline Theology*, 99-119. Edinburgh: T&T Clark, 1991.

———. "Putting Paul Together Again: Toward a Synthesis of Pauline Theology (1 and 2 Thessalonians, Philippians, and Philemon)." In *Pauline Theology*, vol. 1, *Thessalonians, Philippians, Galatians, Philemon*, ed. Jouette M. Bassler, 183-211. Minneapolis: Fortress, 1991.

———. *The Resurrection of the Son of God*. Christian Origins and the Question of God 3. Minneapolis: Fortress, 2003.

———. *What Saint Paul Really Said: Was Paul of Tarsus the Real Founder of Christianity?* Grand Rapids: Eerdmans, 1997.

Yinger, Kent L. *The New Perspective on Paul: An Introduction*. Eugene, OR: Cascade, 2011.

———. *Paul, Judaism, and Judgment According to Deeds*. SNSTMS 105. Cambridge: Cambridge University Press, 1999.

Zahl, Paul F. M. "Mistakes of the New Perspective on Paul." *Themelios* 27, no. 1 (2001): 5-11.

Ziesler, J. A. *The Meaning of Righteousness in Paul: A Linguistic and Theological Enquiry*. Cambridge: Cambridge University Press, 1972.

Zuntz, Günther. *The Text of the Epistles: A Disquisition upon the Corpus Paulinum*. London: Oxford University Press, 1953.

Author Index

Subject Index

SCRIPTURE INDEX

435

4:5, *395*
4:7, *279, 296*
4:12, *388*
4:13, *389*
4:14, *367*
4:15, *389*
4:17, *373*
4:21, *197, 198, 397*
4:24, *389*
4:24-25, *389*
4:29, *279*
4:32, *273, 296, 397*
5:1, *376*
5:2, *389*
5:3, *388*
5:6, *285*
5:26-27, *388*
6:15, *309*
6:18, *388*
6:21, *196*
6:21-22, *191, 198, 199,
    203, 214*

Philippians
1, *186*
1:1, *173, 194, 202, 218,
    219, 388*
1:2, *267, 278*
1:5, *177*
1:6, *374*
1:7, *176, 278*
1:9-11, *389*
1:13, *176, 177*
1:15, *178*
1:17, *176, 178*
1:19, *53, 177, 299, 300,
    301, 368*
1:19-26, *177*
1:22, *261*
1:23, *276*
1:25-26, *220*
1:25-27, *181*
1:28, *53, 299, 301, 303,
    304, 307, 308*
1:29, *273, 278, 296*
2:1-2, *389*
2:1-4, *305*
2:2, *261*
2:5, *144, 305*
2:6-11, *145*
2:7, *368*
2:8, *132, 147*
2:9, *273, 296*

2:9-11, *305*
2:10-11, *368*
2:12, *261, 276, 289,
    299, 301, 305, 389*
2:12-13, *261, 304*
2:12-18, *389*
2:13, *261*
2:17, *144*
2:19, *173*
2:24, *181, 220*
2:25, *178, 179, 261*
2:25-28, *179*
2:28, *179*
3, *27, 58, 59, 61, 62,
    63, 66, 67, 131, 281,
    297, 370, 375*
3:1, *59*
3:1-6, *59*
3:1-11, *58, 67, 68, 370*
3:2, *59, 261, 370*
3:2-6, *19, 21, 62, 64,
    68, 367*
3:2-11, *59, 71, 126, 261,
    283, 343, 366, 367,
    370*
3:2-21, *371*
3:3, *61*
3:4-6, *60, 61*
3:5, *224*
3:5-6, *63*
3:6, *20, 66, 67*
3:6-9, *66*
3:7-11, *59, 65, 67, 68*
3:9, *47, 59, 66, 67, 68,
    70, 134, 139, 142,
    144, 145, 283, 392*
3:12, *283*
3:12-16, *370, 389*
3:17-21, *370*
3:18-21, *389*
3:21, *261, 386*
4:1, *305*
4:3, *261*
4:6-7, *321*
4:10-19, *177*
4:18, *178*
4:22, *176, 388*
4:23, *267, 278*

Colossians
1, *309, 323, 327*
1:1, *173, 188, 194*
1:1-2, *188*

1:2, *202, 267, 278, 388,
    397*
1:4, *87, 144, 388, 397*
1:5, *278*
1:6, *278*
1:7, *191, 296*
1:9, *197, 198*
1:9-11, *389*
1:10, *374*
1:12, *388*
1:13, *364*
1:14, *296, 329, 397*
1:15-20, *194, 209, 316,
    323, 332*
1:16, *320, 321, 397*
1:16-17, *319, 320*
1:17, *386, 397*
1:18, *320*
1:18-20, *209, 320*
1:18-23, *366*
1:20, *296, 309, 319,
    320, 322, 386, 387*
1:20-22, *262*
1:21, *228, 261, 319,
    364*
1:21-23, *320*
1:22, *296, 309, 319,
    320, 322*
1:23, *321*
1:24, *223, 372*
1:26, *388*
1:28, *397*
1:28-29, *389*
2:1, *197*
2:3, *397*
2:5, *144*
2:6, *397*
2:6-23, *130*
2:7, *397*
2:9, *397*
2:9-10, *209*
2:10, *397*
2:11, *262, 397*
2:11-12, *36, 39, 262*
2:12, *262, 395, 397*
2:12-13, *262*
2:13, *209, 273, 296,
    364, 397*
2:13-15, *194*
2:14-15, *262*
2:15, *321, 397*
2:19, *389*
2:19-20, *262*

3:1, *397*
3:1-3, *209, 262*
3:6, *285*
3:9-10, *389*
3:10, *389*
3:10-11, *372*
3:12, *388, 389*
3:13, *273, 296*
3:14, *389*
3:15, *18, 321*
3:16, *278*
3:17, *374*
3:18, *194*
4:3, *188*
4:6, *278, 279*
4:7, *189, 196*
4:7-8, *198, 199*
4:7-9, *191, 203*
4:7-14, *213*
4:7-17, *188*
4:9, *189*
4:10, *171, 188, 213*
4:10-14, *189, 191*
4:11, *189, 191*
4:14, *213*
4:15, *191*
4:15-16, *373*
4:16, *186, 196, 199,
    200, 203, 206*
4:17, *189*
4:18, *184, 188, 278*

1 Thessalonians
1:1, *173, 194, 267, 271*
1:3, *244, 374*
1:6, *130*
1:7, *130, 245*
1:8, *144*
1:9-10, *363*
1:10, *130, 285, 303*
2:10, *130, 245*
2:12, *18*
2:13, *130, 245*
2:14-16, *130, 167*
2:16, *285, 299, 301*
3:2, *144, 173*
3:5, *144*
3:6, *173*
3:10, *144*
3:13, *388*
4, *375*
4:3, *388*
4:7, *18, 388*

Finding the Textbook You Need

The IVP Academic Textbook Selector
is an online tool for instantly finding the IVP books
suitable for over 250 courses across 24 disciplines.

www.ivpress.com/academic/